The LIVES of

MARGARET FULLER

Also by John Matteson

EDEN'S OUTCASTS:
THE STORY OF LOUISA MAY ALCOTT
AND HER FATHER

A Biography

The LIVES of MARGARET FULLER

—

John Matteson

W. W. NORTON & COMPANY

NEW YORK LONDON

FRONTISPIECE: On the same day that Fuller sat for what has long been presumed to be the only photographic image of her, daguerreotypist John Plumbe also took this second exposure. It is now published for the first time.

(COURTESY OF KENT BICKNELL)

Copyright © 2012 by John Matteson

All rights reserved
Printed in the United States of America
First Edition

For information about permission to reproduce selections from this book, write to Permissions, W. W. Norton & Company, Inc., 500 Fifth Avenue, New York, NY 10110

For information about special discounts for bulk purchases, please contact W. W. Norton Special Sales at specialsales@wwnorton.com or 800-233-4830

Manufacturing by RR Donnelley, Harrisonburg
Book design by Barbara Bachman
Production manager: Julia Druskin

Library of Congress Cataloging-in-Publication Data

Matteson, John.
The lives of Margaret Fuller : a biography / John Matteson. — 1st ed.
p. cm.
Includes bibliographical references and index.
ISBN 978-0-393-06805-4 (hardcover)
1. Fuller, Margaret, 1810–1850. 2. Women authors, American—
19th century—Biography. 3. Feminists—United States—Biography. I. Title.
PS2506.M38 2012
818'.309—dc23
[B]
2011040432

W. W. Norton & Company, Inc.
500 Fifth Avenue, New York, N.Y. 10110
www.wwnorton.com

W. W. Norton & Company Ltd.
Castle House, 75/76 Wells Street, London W1T 3QT

1 2 3 4 5 6 7 8 9 0

*W*ith deepest appreciation for all they have done to encourage the study of woman in the nineteenth century, this book is gratefully inscribed to Joel Myerson and to the memory of Madeleine B. Stern.

CONTENTS

PROLOGUE

—SAMUEL GRAY WARD

*T*HINK FIRST OF ENDINGS.

Margaret Fuller was, in her time, the best-read woman in America and the one most renowned for her intelligence. She was the leading female figure in the New England movement known as transcendentalism. She edited the first avant-garde intellectual magazine in America. She was the first regular foreign correspondent, male or female, for an American newspaper. As a literary critic, she was rivaled in her era only by Edgar Allan Poe. Three years before the convention that is usually regarded as the beginning of the women's rights movement in the United States, she wrote a groundbreaking book demanding legal equality for women. And yet, if the ordinary person today knows only one thing about Margaret Fuller, that particle of knowledge is likely not to concern any of her achievements, but how her life came to an end.

At the age of only forty, having spent almost three and a half years in Europe as foreign correspondent for the *New-York Tribune*, Fuller sailed back to America to begin a new life with the husband she had met in Rome, Marchese Giovanni Ossoli, and their young son, Angelino. That new life never began. On July 19, 1850, within sight of land, the ship on which the Ossolis were traveling struck a sandbar off the coast of Fire Island, New York, and, in the midst of a fierce and unseasonable hurricane, broke apart and sank. Though most of the people on board managed to reach the shore alive, none of the Ossolis survived. This was how Margaret Fuller became ingrained in our history: not as the sparkling conversationalist enlivening Ralph Waldo Emerson's study or the bookstores of Boston with her wit and erudition; not as the impromptu military nurse giving aid and encouragement to freedom fighters who had fallen in the streets of Rome defending their new republic; not even as the accomplished and dedicated scholar churning out a stunning body of literary criticism and social commentary; but as a forlorn and exhausted figure beside a broken mast, her hands on her knees, clad only in a soaked-through nightgown, soon to feel the wave that would thrust her overboard and into eternity.

Fuller's drowning was a monstrosity of ill fortune. In order for it to happen, it required navigational incompetence, a freak hurricane, and the nearly criminal indifference of at least thirty eyewitnesses. Yet the bizarrely improbable wreck became the defining anecdote of Fuller's life, propelling her almost immediately into the realm of morbid legend. Prematurely silenced, she was—and she remains—the mysterious, presiding ghost of American transcendentalism.

The tragedy of such an early and senseless death resides not only in the death itself. It lies also in the way that the death comes to be perceived as the life's most relevant fact, even as its inevitable outcome. The shattering nature of Fuller's demise threatens to reduce all that preceded it—no matter how unique, affirming, or triumphant—to a mere prologue to the closing catastrophe. The way we view such a death is paradoxical. On the one hand, it is the incongruity of such a death that makes it linger in our minds; we remember it because it is so clearly not the obvious or deserved outcome of the life that preceded it. On the other, because we need for stories to make sense, we find ourselves reacting as if the tragedy *had* to happen, and this bizarre conviction of inevitability transforms the absurd into the inescapable. If we are not careful, the victim's death can easily blight and darken all that he or she did or stood for. We struggle to preserve in our minds how James Dean looked before he climbed into his Porsche on that late September day, the fateful serenity of Martin Luther King as he marched through Memphis, or the boyish smile of Robert Kennedy as he flashed a peace sign and left the ballroom of the Ambassador Hotel. We want to keep such people as they were, full of hope, life, and the thrill of new possibilities. The effort to do so is always futile. Still, it must be attempted, lest we conclude that our own strivings are empty of meaning, since they, too, can be erased in a moment by happenstance and fate. To attempt the biography of a person of energy, resolve, and unfulfilled promise is to engage in a fantasy of rescue and resurrection.[1]

Yet, as even Fuller's first biographers were aware, restoring her to life is a daunting task, because her life was so multifaceted. She lived richly in a myriad of dimensions, leaving deep impressions on those who knew her. Though her health was chronically frail, she embodied a kind of power that defies reduction to the printed page. Moreover, to a degree far greater than any other member of her social and literary circle, Fuller possessed a genius for the reinvention of self. With a tremendous awareness of what she was doing, Fuller lived her life as an ongoing occasion for growth and change.

Fuller biographers must resist the temptation to seize a particular moment in her long development, to espouse the Fuller of that particular moment as *their* Margaret Fuller, and to put aside her other incarnations if they inconveniently complicate the story. Because the very essence of Fuller was her changeability—she referred to herself as a chameleon—no single snapshot can suffice.[2] Some of her protean character was certainly necessitated by her being female in a society that held out few opportunities for women of intellectual vigor and professional ambition. Because she could not afford to wait for ideal circumstances, Fuller became adept at redefining herself to suit the prospects that came her way. "People seem to think," Fuller complained in 1844, "that not more than one phase of character can be shown in one life."[3] Deliberately and intentionally, she proved them wrong, continually willing herself into different roles and reinventions.

Fuller's penchant for shape shifting was a matter not only of situation but also of philosophy. In her late teens and early twenties, Fuller eagerly absorbed the Romantic ideas that she found in the works of Goethe, Novalis, and Schelling, all of whom told her that the world itself was gradually evolving toward a higher plane of consciousness and to a better approximation of perfection. She came to believe that, for an earnest soul, to rise continually toward the celestial was a matter not just of destiny but of quasi-religious duty. She believed that a human life, properly lived, ought constantly to alter itself in its quest for a higher level of self-knowledge. In Goethe's *Faust*, she read the promise of the angels: "For him whose striving never ceases / We can provide redemption," and through her ceaseless striving, Margaret Fuller sought to save herself.[4] She strove to make of herself a fully realized soul, both intellectually complete and all-encompassing in its sympathies. To say that Margaret Fuller's greatest creation was her life may come perilously close to cliché, but it is true.

A person of such ambition almost always encounters great resistance, and to achieve her self-creation, Fuller paid a tremendous price in pain, in poverty, and in ridicule. She also met with resistance in the form of self-doubt; in the limitations of a body that could not always support the incessant activity of her mind; and in the stubbornness of a world that reacted to contain and counterbalance any force that violated its rule of mediocrity. Such a person is always a work in progress, always restless, never final. Emerson, who may have known her better than anyone else, wondered whether Fuller could truly be known, since at every meeting she showed a new and different side of herself. "I see not into you," he complained to her, "& have not arrived at your law."[5] Samuel Ward, whose words begin this work and who also knew Fuller well, thought a biography of her would be impossible. Ward had a point, in large part because he knew that a biography typically moves in a linear fashion, reducing the life of its subject to a single story. Ward doubted that Fuller could be done justice by such a simplification. Although she was a writer, Fuller's essence was life, not writing, and Ward thought that a written account would necessarily omit her vitality, her multiplicity, her soul. The transcendentalists all realized that, as the spirit gives life, the letter kills. Any written description of Fuller's life was destined to die before the ink was dry; it was perhaps impossible to resurrect her in print without killing her all over again.

There was another consequence to Fuller's choice to treat her own metamorphosis as her greatest work. Precisely because her essential creation was her own being, the most precious thing that she produced was tragically ephemeral. Beyond question, Fuller would have loved to write a great and timeless book that would have given her the kind of durability that still attaches to Emerson, Thoreau, Poe, and Hawthorne, all of whom she knew. However, when she drowned, she left behind no adequate representation of the noble work of spirit into which she had fashioned herself. Sadly, too, the only copy of the written work that, had it been published, might have won her a more conventional literary immortality—her unique eyewitness history of the Roman revolution of 1848–49—was lost in the same shipwreck that killed her.

There is, of course, no way to give back to Margaret Fuller what the shipwreck took away. As I prepared to write this book, however, it occurred to me that there might be a way to write her biography that would return to her something more of her life than if I wrote it as a single, linear existence. Although this volume follows Fuller's life more or less chronologically, it invites the reader to observe Fuller's time on earth not as a single life, but as a succession of lives, each one building on those previously lived, each one preserving the markings and conditionings of its predecessors, and each one lived in anticipation of further incarnations. In attempting to recapture the complexity of its subject, this book presents Fuller as a series of identities, each partially encapsulated by the title of its chapter.[6]

This conception of Fuller is admittedly imperfect. Her various identities did not arise in a tidy succession, and they often overlapped. The intended effect is not literal, but metaphorical; by representing Fuller as a series of metamorphic selves, this book hopes to reveal the impossibility of reducing Fuller to a single label. The telling of Fuller's story should be prismatic; if one cannot re-create the unitary light of her existence, one should at least strive to offer up a rainbow.

A final historical challenge presented by a subject who died young is the tendency of the subject's biographers, especially those working near in time to the tragic ending, to hallow and sanctify the memory of the departed. The first light that is turned on such a subject often creates a distorting halo. Such was the case for Fuller. Her first biographers were a trio of her friends: Ralph Waldo Emerson, William Henry Channing, and James Freeman Clarke. If anything, they knew their subject too well. Only two years after her death, the three men who came together to write and edit the *Memoirs of Margaret Fuller Ossoli* worked zealously to preserve and glorify what was best in her, frequently at the expense of objectivity.

Because these biographers had access to innumerable documents that either vanished or were destroyed after they used them, some of their well-meant obfuscations are now permanent. Moreover, because their memoir achieved a broad and unexpected popularity—by some accounts it was briefly the most popular book in America before being pushed aside by *Uncle Tom's Cabin*—their hagiographic portrait became the accepted version of Fuller's life. All of Fuller's subsequent biographers must deal with the limitations of the *Memoirs*, which stands like a great refracting lens between Fuller and the modern scholar. They must also contend with Fuller's understanding of herself, as expressed in her letters and journals, which was liable to be more aspirational than accurate. The modern narration of Fuller's life, then, must act as a counter-narrative, availing itself of the mass of writings that have come down to us from Fuller and her friends, but ready to question their judgments at almost every turn.

A life history of Margaret Fuller fails if it speaks solely of her brilliance, her audacity, and the sincerity and marvelous goodwill with which she took up the burdens of others. Fuller was both gifted and giving, but she could also be arrogant, irritable, and condescending. Although she had no betters when it came to analyzing literary texts, her understanding of the motives of actual people, particularly when those motives were influenced by love or sex, could be badly misinformed. Brimming with goodwill toward men and women, always eager to nudge her friends and neighbors in a better, upward direction, she could be shockingly neglectful of those in direst need of her attention. She was capable of both stoicism and self-pity, of sublime insight and naive self-delusion. She could inspire. She could infuriate. She seldom soothed. There are those in our own time who have unknowingly inherited her passion for knowledge, democracy, and equality between the sexes. As these women and men deserve to know, Margaret Fuller did a great deal more than die young.

The LIVES of

MARGARET FULLER

CHAPTER ONE

PRODIGY

*[H]ow deep the anguish, how deeper still
the want, with which I walked alone in
hours of childish passion, and called for a
Father, often saying the Word a hundred
times till it was stifled by sobs.*

—MARGARET FULLER TO
WILLIAM HENRY CHANNING,
October 28, 1840

*How would the Divinity find everywhere
opportunity to do wonders, if He did not
sometimes try His powers on extraordinary
individuals, at whom we stand astonished and
cannot understand whence they come?*

—JOHANN WOLFGANG VON GOETHE,
IN JOHANN PETER ECKERMANN'S
Conversations with Goethe,
TRANSLATED BY MARGARET FULLER

TIMOTHY FULLER JR., BEING A MAN OF GREAT ENERGY AND GENER-
ally keen perception, saw some aspects of his surroundings with extreme
clarity. As he was only a man, however, there were other facets of life that he
observed less readily. He was apt and attentive when it came to books and
study. His vision was perhaps clearest when he trained his eye on a goal to be

achieved and a prize to be won. He saw with much less acuity, however, when he was called on to examine his own heart or to observe the emotional needs of those nearest him. It would have been unjust to call him a cold man, for a person who lacked passion could never have applied himself so fervidly to perfecting the life of his mind and, as a public figure, to serving the needs of his fellow citizens. Although some whispered that he lacked empathy as a family man, both the volume and the content of his letters to his wife and children argue that this was not the case. Still, there was in Timothy Fuller a curious flaw that kept him from realizing that exacting study, worldly advancement, and devoted public service might not be the only ingredients in human happiness. He denied the gentler requisites of contentment to himself and to the people near him who craved them most, not because he intended any cruelty, for he dispensed the things he valued with generosity. Rather, his lack of warmth arose because he never quite understood that the heart had offices the head could not perform.

With his eldest child, whom her family called Sarah Margaret but whom the world would know as Margaret Fuller, Timothy eagerly shared the wealth of his powerful intellect. Almost alone among the fathers of daughters in his time, he sought to raise her to a level of knowledge and understanding that other men reserved solely for their sons. Nevertheless, as so often happens between fathers and children, he could not share with Sarah Margaret the things she desired most. Out of Timothy Fuller's parental generosity, and also out of his considerable parental failings, grew the most talented and perhaps the most exasperating American woman of her generation.

Wherever prevailing practice or opinion might lead, a Fuller was likely to strike out in the opposite direction. There seems to have been an indefinable element in the family constitution that fostered an appetite, not only for difference but also for disruption and dissent. This reputation for contrariness began with neither Margaret nor her father; it extended backward at least one generation further. Margaret's paternal grandfather, the elder Timothy Fuller, distinguished himself by gaining admission to Harvard, where he studied for the ministry. Once there, he distinguished himself in a more dubious fashion, as on the day when, with no apparent provocation, he hurled bricks and other projectiles through a classroom window while a Hebrew recitation was going on inside.[1] Once graduated, he eventually found a home and a Congregationalist pulpit in the frontier settlement of Princeton, Massachusetts.[2] There, he demonstrated what many would come to recognize as a family trait: a thorough incapacity to recognize when it would be most prudent to keep quiet. In his mid-thirties when the Revolutionary war began, the older Timothy did not join the fight. Age may not have been his only reason for not taking up arms. Indeed, in the town of Princeton, suspicions were rife that the pious reverend harbored pro-British sentiments. When he became a bit too vocal in questioning the patriotic cause, the issue of his loyalties became, in his own words, "a Subject of public Discussion and warm Debate [with] Much Contention & Disorder ensu[ing] in Several Places."[3] In the spring of 1776, despite Fuller's assurances that he entertained no "principles inconsistent with the cause of liberty," his parishioners voted him out of the pulpit.[4] When he tried to flout the congregation's will and continue preaching, he was stopped at the church door by a deputation of the town's most physically imposing men. Persuaded that the force of arms was likely to prevail over the force of argument, the cowed and astonished reverend withdrew from the town.

He did not, however, abandon the ministry. Seeking shelter from the political tempest of the times, he resettled on Martha's Vineyard, in the town of Chilmark, and assumed the leadership of a flock with more Tory inclinations. It was in Chilmark, on July 11, 1778, that the younger Timothy Fuller was born, the fourth child in the family but its first boy.[5] He was eventually to have nine siblings: five sisters and four brothers.[6] Timothy grew up in a generation plagued by the anxious fear that it could never live up to the courage and deeds of its Revolutionary fathers. The fact that Timothy the father had taken no part in the noble cause made Timothy the son all the more anxious, by way of compensation, to prove his own patriotism and sense of duty. The year Timothy Jr. turned twenty-one, 1799, also marked the death of George Washington. Fuller mourned the great man's passing in his journal and wondered how the void left by the general's death could ever be filled. His personal solution to this question was twofold. First, he dedicated himself to a life of public service. Second, he meant to raise a family that, he hoped, might one day surpass the glory of the founding generation.

At his death, Timothy Fuller Sr. was eulogized as "a model for the performance of parental duty."[7] Part of that duty, in his view, meant training his sons to achieve intellectual superiority and, above all, professional success.

He convinced Timothy Jr. at an early age that no young man, particularly one from a family more distinguished for its learning than for its wealth, could expect to win a respected place in the world without working for it, and working hard. Young Timothy would probably have happened upon this awareness on his own. As it was, his father was more than ready to point it out to him. Timothy Jr. was so slight of build that a friend would recall decades later that "the crumbs a bird would pick up would almost suffice him."[8] But like the sparrows who fearlessly contend for such crumbs, Timothy learned quickly that lack of size was no excuse in the competition for worldly prizes.

In an autobiographical sketch written when she was thirty, Margaret Fuller surmised that the vital importance of earthly success was virtually the only lesson the elder Timothy impressed on his namesake. She observed that the great ambition of her grandfather had been to send his sons to college and that, therefore, her father "was taught to think only of preparing himself for Harvard University, and when there, of preparing himself for the profession of Law."[9] If Margaret is to be believed, her father experienced a closely monitored and rather heavily managed upbringing, in which the petty but essential pleasures and freedoms of boyhood were subordinated to a staunch ethic of performance and achievement. It seems that these values powerfully shaped Timothy's later ideas of his own duties as a father.

At Harvard, Timothy Fuller Jr. was a proud young man, eager to succeed and quick to take offense when he felt he had not been given his due. A handful of anecdotes help to paint his portrait. In 1799, while on break from college, Fuller accepted a teaching position in hopes that the sixteen dollars a month he had been promised might defray some of his expenses. On accepting lodgings with a Mr. Furbush, he noted with delight that he was to have a room of his own. In no time at all, however, Fuller found his self-regard unacceptably compromised. The day after his arrival, he fulminated in his journal, "The family I board with are so intolerably dirty, intolerably polite . . . & intolerably intolerable that I anticipate an intolerable winter." After only three days, he found another room to let and left Furbush, whom he derided in his journal as the *commander of the castle*."[10] Fuller's complaint about intolerable politeness is telling; he found good, frank disagreement infinitely preferable to feigned, unctuous displays of manners. Fuller liked to meet people on equal terms; any presumed superiority on the part of an acquaintance was likely to send him into a lather. Offered the chance to give a declamatory oration at the college chapel, Fuller chose as his subject a line from Alexander Pope's *Essay on Man*: "Honor and shame from no condition rise." He exulted in being told afterward that he had never spoken better.[11] Throughout his life, he held firmly to the proposition that one's condition in society mattered little for good or ill; he respected others according to what they could do.

Highly intelligent, but also brash and class conscious, Timothy Fuller was determined to raise his eldest daughter to the highest echelon of New England intellects.

(COURTESY OF FRAN SOTO)

Some of the happiest moments that Fuller recorded in his diary reveal his innate love of competition, particularly competition that involved logic and language. He enjoyed going into Boston to hear debates in the legislature. He also took special pleasure in belonging to a campus group that the members called their Coffee Club. Sometimes meeting in Fuller's room, the Coffee Club dedicated itself to redressing grievances that arose between fellow students. According to Fuller, the group's mock trials were "conducted in such a manner as to be a source of improvement & pleasure." At one session, during which Fuller acted as "attorney in two causes & chief justice in a third," the club did not adjourn until almost one o'clock in the morning.[12]

It was Timothy's misfortune that the Coffee Club was not a sufficient outlet for his love of argument. In his senior year at Harvard, he imprudently helped to lead a student revolt against a newly adopted set of rules for student behavior. Fuller drafted and submitted the student body's petition of protest to the college president, evidently with his habitual bluntness. The college not only rejected the students' petition but also summarily punished Fuller by lowering his class rank by one place. Had Fuller remained silent in the controversy, he would have graduated first in his class.

Disputation came naturally to Timothy Fuller. The gentler arts of living presented more of a problem. Handsome and self-confident, he was attractive to women, and he enjoyed returning their attentions, sometimes by flirting, sometimes more aggressively. He could, however, grow scornful of deeper emotion. One day when he was twenty-one, Fuller wrote in his diary that he had caught a glimpse through a window of a pretty girl named Margaret Rogers "as she sat by Mr. Parkman's parlor fire." Although the sight was inspiring, Fuller felt no impulse to wax poetic. He wrote, "Were I such a milksop as to *love*, I might think [the scene] very precious."[13] In one of his college orations, Fuller warned against falling too easily for the allures of women and denounced "that base passion for the sex" as "the most sordid appetite" of which young men were capable.[14] But he cared little for his own advice. While briefly teaching at a coeducational school called Leicester Academy, he acquired a somewhat scandalous reputation for his forwardness with his female students. In his journal, he boasted of having walked in the moonlight with a Miss Tucker, "a sweet girl, not yet fifteen," and how he "made free with her lips and enjoyed her blushes."[15] Glorying in his rakishness, he detailed his osculatory adventures with a half-dozen girls, vainly noting, "I have . . . perceived myself capable of [a] *plurality* of loves."[16] It is the usual case that young men who profess to love many truly love none; Fuller's petty dalliances with the girls of Leicester Academy were never more than a self-absorbed game.

Young Timothy's ties to his own sex were, perhaps, somewhat noncommittal as well. Fuller had little trouble writing themes and oratories on the greatness of Washington and the moral excellence of Christianity. When he attempted an essay on friendship, however, he found the results "strangely barren."[17] Timothy was no loner; his diaries tell frequently of parties, dinners, and convivial sleigh rides, the latter being an activity he seems especially to have enjoyed. Nevertheless, he tended to be critical in his observations of others. It appears that, at Harvard, he opened himself to only one close, soul-sharing companion, a fellow student named Benjamin Peirce. Peirce once wrote to Fuller that he had been "almost lost in dejection" but had been restored to perfect spirits. "To what must I attribute this sudden change?" Peirce asked. "I owe it to my friend."[18] Yet Peirce could be troubled by the scorn with which Timothy regarded his supposed intellectual inferiors. After Fuller had been "extremely mortified" at having to converse with some unlettered farmers, Peirce cautioned him to remember that "[c]ommon people are not so far sunken as to be void of all ideas of what learning is." Indeed, he added, "people of knowledge may & do sometimes render themselves ridiculous even to the vulgar."[19]

Apart from Peirce, it was to his four brothers—Abraham, Henry, William, and Elisha—that Timothy apparently looked for companionship. With some minor variations, they were kindred spirits. Physically small, they instinctively sought out an alternative form of largeness by achieving academic and professional renown. At their father's urging, all but one of the Fuller brothers took degrees from Harvard, and all five became lawyers. This fact was indicative of a larger cultural shift. In the seventeenth and eighteenth centuries, the most learned men in New England were men of the cloth. In the nineteenth century, more and more of them would be men of the bar.[20] The Fuller brothers became collectively recognized in Boston legal circles as a force not to be taken lightly. Abolitionist and early Fuller biographer Thomas Wentworth Higginson called them "men of great energy, pushing, successful, . . . of great self-esteem."[21]

Taken together, the Fullers seemed to know everything. The zeal with which they published the fact made them hard to take even separately. One day Timothy's brother Abraham called on Higginson's mother and found her darning socks. Unable to bear the ineptitude of her work, Abraham abruptly seized the woman's needle—and proceeded to teach her more about darning than she had dreamed there was to know. She was both grateful for the lesson and stunned by the impudence with which it was given. Contentious, confident, and possessing not "a particle of tact" among them, the brothers were admired more than they were liked.[22]

Strangely for the sons of a minister, the Fuller men were perhaps resented most for their materialism. Surviving accounts denounce brothers Abraham and Henry as men who lived too much in the world. At the age of thirty, Margaret Fuller was to arraign her father for the same failing. She complained that, for Timothy, "[t]o be an honored citizen, and to have a home on earth, were made the great aims of existence. To open the deeper fountains of the soul, to regard life here as the prophetic entrance to immortality, to develop his spirit to perfection,—motives like these had never been suggested to him, either by fellow-beings or by outward circumstances."[23] These inclinations, she felt, made her father an undistinguished, prosaic character. Although his ideas and ambitions made him a good son and brother and a kind neighbor, Margaret claimed that they never inspired her father to imagine a higher existence for himself.

Margaret's observations of her father's character should be accepted only with reservations. Since its publication, the sketch in which she most fully discussed his personality has been termed "an autobiographical romance." In her time, a romance was regarded as a form of writing that, while it had a strict obligation to reveal the truth of the human heart, was expected to do so "under circumstances . . . of the writer's own choosing and creation." It is evident that Margaret made some use of the romanticist's license, as Hawthorne put it, to "mellow the lights and deepen and enrich the shadows of the picture."[24]

It would have been strange if Timothy, the son of a minister, had had as little interest in his spiritual life as his daughter suggests, and, indeed, his journal proves that Margaret considerably overstates her case. He was a regular attendee at church, and his diary often refers to sermons that made impressions on him. When the Fuller family rode in their carriage, Timothy was wont to sing hymns along the way. Often, too, he would offer rides to children whom he saw walking in the same direction and, as they sat beside him, would gladden them by sharing encouraging words and whatever small coins he found in his pockets.[25] Once, after having neglected his diary for some time, Timothy returned to it with a resolve "to make it much better than my former diaries, particularly by admitting less levity, & more moral and religious reflexions."[26] It is evident, however, that Timothy saw his obligation to God in primarily earthly terms. In a journal entry, he made particular note of a sermon he had heard: "We are bought with a price, [and] therefore should glory God in our body & our spirits, which are His. . . . We should employ them alone for his glory [and] God's glory is best promoted by diffusing happiness among his creatures, that being his design in creating them."[27] Fuller felt resonance with the idea that one served God best not through prayer and communion, but by helping others. If his daughter Margaret tried to discover her father's spirituality in mystical effusions of the soul, it is no wonder that she did not find it. His Christianity, like almost every other part of him, expressed itself more in practice than in sentiment.

Yet even to the most driven, practical, and emotionally cautious of persons, love may come. In early 1809, while attending church in Cambridge, Timothy met the woman who, it seemed, stood alone in her power to stir him to a better self. His love for her, their daughter later declared, was "the green spot on which he stood apart from the common-places of a mere bread-winning" life.[28] Her name was Margarett Crane. Gentle and retiring, Margarett found her greatest happiness in growing flowers. One of her sons was later to remember her most clearly "as she stooped over her flower-bed, and toiled long sunny hours over its extensive border." Because she was near-sighted, she would kneel and bend close to her plants. If she discovered some new promise of beauty there, she would turn with a delighted smile and point out the new wonder "with a child-like simplicity."[29]

The elder Margarett's delight in her garden reflects both her spontaneous love of the world around her and her preference for scenes that were free from complexity and conflict. Although the younger Margaret always regarded her mother as "the most disinterestedly generous person . . . I have ever known," Margarett's tremendous kindness was not matched by a powerful will.[30] An essentially passive person, she loved to surround herself with living things even more passive than she was. When she was in true dudgeon over an issue, she was capable of calling Timothy "a ninny," but this was seldom.[31] In her gentleness, she was a helpful balance to the cerebral, contentious Timothy. Whether and how two natures made of such different materials could form a truly sympathetic union is difficult to judge.

Margarett was Timothy's junior by about ten and a half years, and she was not quite out of her teens when the two met. Though her daughter was to remember her as a "young, untaught country girl," Margarett had some experience as a schoolteacher, and, like Timothy, she was descended from Puritan stock.[32] Otherwise, their similarities were not obvious. Margarett was five feet ten inches tall; Timothy was eight or nine inches shorter. Whereas Timothy was brash and ambitious, Margarett was soft spoken and demure. He was stubborn and proud. She was playful and charming. She impressed people, not with the sharpness of her mind and temper, but with the irrepressible cheer of her disposition. Higginson thought she was "one of the sweetest mothers who ever lived."[33]

She was also beautiful. Acquaintances of the Crane family admired her lustrous skin and captivating blue eyes. Undoubtedly enchanted by her appearance, Timothy was also likely enthralled by the pleasure Margarett took in learning, though her formal schooling was only rudimentary. After

Though described as "one of the sweetest mothers who ever lived," Margarett Crane Fuller later had trouble recalling the details of Margaret's early years.
(COURTESY OF FRAN SOTO)

they had been married nine years, she wrote to him, "The first wish of my heart is to make you happy, and the second to cultivate my mind."[34] Her striving for self-improvement succeeded on some fronts better than others. At twenty-nine, Margarett still struggled to master subtraction and multiplication and called her own efforts "perfectly ridiculous."[35] However, she loved to read. She and Timothy enjoyed reading Shakespeare's plays aloud together. Indeed, Timothy came to feel that he needed to have Margarett present to bring his experiences of culture to life. After attending a performance of *Much Ado about Nothing*, he wrote, "The theatre has very few charms for me—especially unless my Margarett is by my side."[36] Their courtship was brief, and its outcome was never much in doubt. On May 28, 1809, after only a few months' acquaintance, Timothy Fuller and Margarett Crane married.

Margaret Fuller was born in this house at 79 Cherry Street in what is now Cambridge, Massachusetts. Unlike the three majestic elms that Fuller's father planted when she was born, the house still stands. (COURTESY OF HOUGHTON LIBRARY, HARVARD UNIVERSITY)

By the following year, the couple had laid the foundations for a happy, bounteous life. In addition to having established a comfortable legal practice, Timothy had also gained a reputation among the leaders of the state Republican Party—the progressive party of Jefferson and Madison that has no ancestral connection to today's GOP. Although the leaders of his party were slaveholding Virginians, Timothy firmly opposed slavery; when Congress debated the Missouri Compromise in 1820, Fuller's speech against the measure was impassioned and important enough that it was published. In 1810, however, Timothy's future career in Washington was only a dream. He and Margarett had settled into a three-story Federal-style house a half-hour's walk from Harvard College, on Cherry Street in the neighborhood known as Cambridgeport. Uncomfortably close to a busy soap works, the house was neither fashionable nor beautiful. "Marshy and imperfectly reclaimed," the area at large compared poorly with the nearby college.[37] But the neighborhood was growing, and Timothy must have considered the property a good investment. On May 23, five days short of her first wedding anniversary, Margarett Crane Fuller gave birth to her first child, whom she and her husband named Sarah Margarett in honor of the baby's grandmother and mother. The terminal "t" of the baby's name was eventually dropped, though her parents habitually referred to her by both her Christian names. This child was almost ten when she insisted on being called simply "Margaret."[38] Timothy marked the day of Sarah Margarett's birth by planting three handsome elm trees in front of the house. As the girl grew up, she regarded these trees and her mother's flower garden as the only things of beauty that adorned the plain and unattractive house.[39]

In her most famous work, *Woman in the Nineteenth Century*, Margaret Fuller described with some sadness the typical reaction a new mother of that time experienced upon learning that her baby was a girl. "Is it a daughter?" Fuller wrote, "There is usually a slight degree of regret, so deeply rooted is the idea of the superiority of man in happiness and dignity." She hastened to add, however, that this disappointment could be more than balanced by worthier emotions. When a mother looked down on her baby girl, Fuller asserted, "she is more and more softened towards it—a deep sympathy—a sentiment of identity with this delicate being takes possession of her; an extreme pity for so much weakness, a more pressing need of prayer stirs her heart."[40] The bond of feeling that Margarett Crane Fuller felt for her new daughter was strong from the beginning. She continually hugged, played with, and slept with her baby. There is no evidence that this tie weakened at all two years and three months later when Sarah Margaret acquired a sister, Julia Adelaide. As far as the somewhat scanty evidence can be pieced together, it suggests that, throughout her infancy, Sarah Margaret combined many of the best traits of both her parents. She had her father's energy and quick capacity for learning, and her mother's cheerful disposition.

By 1813, Timothy had parlayed the goodwill of his political associates into a seat in the Massachusetts state senate, and everything looked bright for the Fuller family. But, as in so many families of the time, the perfect picture was soon scarred by loss. If our lives may be said to begin with our first permanent memories, then Margaret Fuller's life began with a consciousness of death. That awareness came on October 5, 1813, when her little sister, only fourteen months old, died. Remembering the day more than twenty-five years later, Fuller recalled coming home and being met by the nursery maid, her face streaming with tears. The maid led Sarah Margaret by the hand into the room where Julia's body lay. Curiously, Sarah Margaret was neither deeply saddened nor traumatized by this viewing. She was struck, instead, by what she could only call the "beauty of death." Thirty years later, she still believed that the severe sweetness of what she had beheld exceeded the greatest accomplishments of sculpture.[41]

Of a more devastating moment, Fuller retained no direct memory at all. Friends and relatives, however, remembered clearly that, as she stood at her sister's graveside, she sent up a frantic, piercing wail and pleaded with the adults not to put Julia's body in the ground. This story was evidently repeated to her often enough that Fuller had no reason to question its accuracy. As she looked back on it all, she believed that what had repelled her most was the somber, artificial formality of the funeral itself. The black clothes, the stiffness of the procession, and the dour faces of the mourners struck her as false and ugly. She later recalled feeling that her sister's life and death had both been beautiful, but the attempt to encase and deaden everyone's feelings within a bland and ordered ceremony—what she later called "all this sad parade"—was not."[42] Already, Sarah Margaret sensed that instinctive spirituality and formal religiosity could pull powerfully in opposite directions, and she had a sense of the direction she preferred.

That drizzly, darkening October, Sarah Margaret felt a chill of isolation that never completely left her. As an adult, she wrote nostalgically of her lost Julia: "She who would have been the companion of my life was severed from me, and I was left alone. This has made a vast difference in my lot. Her character, if that fair face promised right, would have been soft, graceful and lively; it would have tempered mine to a gentler and more gradual course."[43]

Fuller imagined that Julia would have smoothed the sharp edges of her own personality. She supposed that, in a household dominated by the mind, her younger sister would have helped to nourish and develop her heart. It is extremely unlikely that Julia would have played to perfection the idealized role her sister imagined her fulfilling. And yet, if Fuller was even partly right, a portion of herself was buried in 1813.

After Julia's death, Mrs. Fuller descended into a period of delicate health, which seems not to have ended until her next child was born. During this time, the emotional bond between Sarah Margaret and her mother grew still closer than it had been and arguably closer than it would ever be again. Having lost one child, the elder Margarett became understandably more attentive to the one who remained. She recalled that, in the aftermath of Julia's loss, "the intelligence, rich fancy, buoyant spirits, and extreme activity [of Sarah Margaret] occupied more of my thoughts, and observations, than [in] many subsequent years."[44]

As her mother recollected, Sarah Margaret took some of her greatest pleasures "in reading, in riding with us, [and] in gathering flowers, a love of which seemed to be born with her."[45] As an adult, Margaret, too, remembered going on flower-picking expeditions, many of which took place in the garden behind the family's house. From her back door, she could descend a high flight of steps into a small, quiet oasis of roses, violets, lilies, and fruit trees. As she gathered her handfuls of blooms, she kissed them and pressed them close to her heart with a passion that, it later seemed to her, she never dared to express to any human being. Here the best hours of her childhood were spent. Here she felt at home. But amid the flowers of her mother's garden, Sarah Margaret thought she heard a speechless challenge. "An ambition swelled [in] my heart," she later wrote, "to be as beautiful, as perfect as they." She ruefully added, "I have not kept my vow."[46] It may seem strange that a bower of floral splendor would inspire a little girl with a merciless urge toward perfection. Yet her mother's recollections confirm that Sarah Margaret, even at such an early age, reacted to criticism in a brooding fashion that showed a lack of patience with her own shortcomings. According to Margarett Crane Fuller, her daughter "showed great sensitivity to reproof, not so much in tears shed at the time but silent reserve."[47]

Sarah Margaret's habits of perfectionism and sensitivity were not lessons learned from flowers alone. She had another early, disconnected memory that, although she could not place it precisely in time, remained vivid and powerful into adulthood. She remembered stopping one day on a staircase and asking herself four overwhelming questions: "How came I here? How is it that I seem to be this Margaret Fuller? What does it mean? What shall I do about it?" Between upstairs and down, the bizarre and unaccountable fact of her existence had burst upon her and demanded an explanation. She had none. As her childhood and teens went by, these questions would revisit her again and again like an unbidden ghost. She would be a grown woman before she could effectively respond to them.[48]

Julia's death affected her father almost as profoundly as it did her mother. Though Timothy's health did not give way, he, too, seems to have been made less certain of what he could count on in life. He had regarded Julia as "unusually forward, pretty, & engaging" and had had high expectations for her.[49] Margaret remembered that, after this time of bereavement, all of her father's hopes and feelings became concentrated on her. It may have been that his younger daughter's death drove him to clutch his remaining child tighter to himself. She was the being above all others that he now most dreaded losing. At the same time, he seems to have sought refuge in the state of mind in which he felt most secure. Timothy was happiest when he was either studying or pursuing some coveted honor. In one sense, then, it is not surprising that the relationship into which he drew his surviving daughter was steeped both in academic learning and in a consuming urge toward perfection.

On another level, though, Timothy's conduct was surprising indeed. In early manhood, he had regarded young women chiefly as ornaments and potential conquests. Few would have expected him to raise a daughter who might be admired for her intellect and independence. In fact, he wanted his eldest child to resemble as little as possible the frilly creatures whom he had simultaneously lusted after and disdained. Other well-placed Massachusetts fathers might groom their girls for lives of inoffensive beauty and decorous submission; Timothy's own paternal errors were to end up at the opposite pole.

Whatever his motivations, the task that Timothy set for himself and Sarah Margaret presented a tremendous challenge. "He hoped," Margaret later wrote, "to make me the heir of all he knew, and of as much more as the income of his profession enabled him to give me means of acquiring."[50] Although the details of the first phases of Timothy's educational campaign are sketchy, it is clear that an early mastery of the written word formed one of its cornerstones. In a letter to his wife, written when his beloved pupil was not yet four, he wrote, "My love to the little Sarah Margaret. I love her *if* she is a good girl & learns to read."[51] Considering books written for young children too babyish for her, he quickly plunged her into more sophisticated though still not fully adult material, including Aesop's fables. On New Year's Day 1815, when Margaret was four and a half, he proudly proclaimed that she could read and understand "in a very great degree" the stories in Maria Edgeworth's *Parent's Assistant* and could read tolerably from "any common book."[52] As can be gathered from the fact that her mother ranked reading first among her daughter's early pleasures, Sarah Margaret took to this instruction eagerly. That both her parents "always remarked her superior intelligence" surely encouraged her. In this early period of her mental awakening, she seems to have flourished.[53] At the age of five, her future close friend James Freeman Clarke observed her as a "joyful child, with light, flowing locks and bright face, who led me by the hand down the back-steps of her house into the garden."[54]

The image of five-year-old Margaret, secure in her mother's love and her father's esteem and welcoming a little playmate into her backyard paradise, is irresistibly sweet. Yet there were tiny flaws in this portrait that, although they initially troubled no one, would be painfully felt as time passed. Margaret had little exposure to children her own age. Her brother Richard recalled that their parents "were very careful" in "guard[ing] their children from evil playmates."[55] Yet even benign playmates were few. Her mother noticed that Margaret "had no child to tempt to childish amusements."[56] As Margaret herself recalled, "In the house was neither dog nor bird, nor any graceful animated form of existence. I saw no persons who took my fancy, and real life offered no attraction."[57] The little girl immersed herself in books not only because she loved them, but also because she had no other equally appealing place to go. As wonderful as her world of reading was, she later wished that she had not been given any books until later—that she had lived instead among toys and played in the open air. As it was, Sarah Margaret's "mental activity was greater than her physical," and her mother, to her later regret, failed to recognize "the necessity of constant exercise . . . to give balance to both."[58] Like the fictionalized version of her immature self that Margaret was later to trace in *Woman in the Nineteenth Century*, Sarah Margaret "took her place easily . . . in the world of the mind."[59] There were other worlds in which she was spending far too little of her childhood.

By the time she led little James Clarke into the family's garden, Sarah Margaret's life had already begun to change. The transformation had started on May 14, 1815, when a baby brother joined the Fuller family. Timothy, who was unable to be present at the birth, exulted at the news. He proclaimed his "joy & thankfulness to the Author of all good, which I hope will be confirmed & increased by the character, disposition, & future conduct of the little nameless stranger."[60] The stranger soon acquired the name of Eugene, and his arrival signaled a shift in the family's relationships. Quite naturally, Mrs. Fuller became absorbed in the care of her infant, and Sarah Margaret found herself obliged to depend ever more on Timothy for attention and affection. With redoubled emphasis, she was learning to identify love and acceptance with her intellectual performance.

Timothy might have been expected to diminish his educational ambitions for his five-year-old daughter now that a son had come on the scene. To his great credit, he did not. To the contrary, the lessons became steadily more intense and sophisticated as Sarah Margaret grew older. Although he later came to think somewhat differently, Timothy had not yet dreamed that one could ever have too much instruction, or receive it too early. When she was six, he introduced her simultaneously to English and Latin grammar. The rudiments of Greek followed in due course. By nine, she was reading a compendious list of histories and biographies in English, as well as many of the major works in the Latin canon.[61] The lessons kept up even when Timothy was away; he deputized his younger brother Elisha to continue the unrelenting drill. Even after the first of his four consecutive elections to Congress in 1816 forced him to spend half the year in Washington and manage Sarah Margaret's education only from a distance, Timothy continued to play Prospero to his daughter's Miranda, and the brave new world he showed her consisted of the very best things he knew.

Eventually, Margaret came to identify herself explicitly with the clever but sheltered young woman of Shakespeare's *Tempest*. Later, in both her essay "The Great Lawsuit" and her groundbreaking *Woman in the Nineteenth Century*, she gave the name Miranda to a fictionalized alter ego whose youthful experiences of education closely paralleled her own. Through Miranda, Fuller presents some of the happier aspects of the educational path on which her father placed her. She writes that Miranda's sire "cherished no sentimental reverence for women, but [held] a firm belief in the equality of the sexes." Like Sarah Margaret, Miranda is her father's eldest child "and came to him at an age when he needed a companion." From the earliest moments of his daughter's mental quickening, we are told, Miranda's father treated his child "not as a plaything, but as a living mind." Her "cherished head" was sacred to him, a "temple of immortal intellect." If Miranda's father did not overly indulge her, he refrained from spoiling her out of respect, not coolness of feeling. Under his tutelage, Miranda "was early led to feel herself a child of the spirit" and acquired "a dignified sense of self-dependence" and security. "The world was free to her," Fuller adds, "and she lived freely in it."[62]

Woman in the Nineteenth Century strives to illustrate and praise the tremendous sense of power and purpose that an intelligent, socially egalitarian father can instill in a promising daughter. It presents the relationship between Fuller's imagined Miranda and her father as ideal. Yet the version Fuller gives in the "autobiographical romance" mentioned earlier is as darkly critical as her story of Miranda is laudatory. Somewhere between the sunlight of Miranda's education and the deeper shadows of Fuller's "romance" lies the true nature of Timothy Fuller's tutelage of his daughter.

Fuller's "autobiographical romance" tells a tale of scholarly drudgery, if not outright victimhood. In it, her father looms as an exacting, unfeeling taskmaster. He was, she recollects, "a man of business" in all things, "even in literature." She does concede that the energy and discipline with which he flung himself into the task of educating her had some advantages. At least for a time, he spared her the handicapping experience of "passing through the hands of so many ignorant and weak persons as so many do at preparatory schools." Moreover, Timothy presented his daughter with "a more than ordinarily high standard" of academic performance.[63] Challenged to strive toward perfection in her studies, motivated to win the favor of the most important man in her life, Sarah Margaret applied herself with single-minded determination, and she learned her lessons exceptionally well. At the time, she was in no position to complain. At the age of nine, she wrote to Timothy, "I am possessed of the greatest blessing of life a good and kind father. Oh I can never repay you for all the love you have shown me."[64] Looking back, however, the adult Margaret believed that her father's love had come at an unacceptable price.

If Timothy prized accuracy, he had far less inclination to nurture creativity. His daughter recalled that, trained to seek the perfection of reason and logic, Timothy "had no belief in minds that listen, wait, and receive. He had no conception of the subtle and indirect motions of imagination and feeling." All the habits of his intellect set him squarely against the natural character of his daughter, which was, as she remembered, "fervent . . . disposed to infatuation, and self-forgetfulness."[65] Margaret later observed that her father, while growing up, had somehow lost his "poetical apprehension of the world, free and splendid as it stretches out before the child."[66] Thus lacking in the ability to see the world as a place of unimaginable beauty, perpetually new, Timothy was limited as an instructor. Under his tutelage, fancy gave way to philosophy; dreams yielded to drill. Sarah Margaret came quickly to understand life as an experience of continual struggle and trial. At the age of thirty-six, she was to write, "From infancy I have foreseen that my path must be difficult."[67] Outwardly, Sarah Margaret dutifully conformed. Inwardly, it was a different matter. "My own world," she recalled, "sank deep within, away from the surface of my life. . . . [M]y true life was only the dearer that it was secluded and veiled over by a thick curtain of . . . intellect."[68] Yet the girl was absorbing more of her father's turn of mind than she realized. For the rest of her life, when Margaret reached for her pen, she did so much more confidently as a critic than as a creator.

It has become commonplace to regard Margaret Fuller as a child-genius of truly extraordinary abilities. Certainly, only a very special child could have flourished under, let alone endured, Timothy's relentless regime of study. Yet Timothy's methods were not his alone. He may have had in mind his political hero, Thomas Jefferson, who had also put his daughters through a highly exacting course of study. Fuller biographer Charles Capper sagely notes that several of Timothy's ambitious contemporaries, including the fathers of Frederic Henry Hedge, James Russell Lowell, and Thomas Wentworth Higginson, had their sons reading Latin or French fluently well before they were ten.[69] What made Fuller and Jefferson so unusual in their time was not the ferocity of their educational theories but rather their liberalism; they dared suppose that the rigors of a classical education could be managed by a girl.

Line by line, declension by declension, Sarah Margaret earned her father's grudgingly dispensed pride. As she grew older, though, it was usually the defects, not the excellence of her mind that rose to the surface when she evaluated her own mental powers. Along with the superior attention span and tremendous knowledge she absorbed from her sessions with Timothy, Sarah Margaret also acquired a fierce penchant for self-criticism. The latter trait need not be seen as wholly negative. Rather, her capacity for clear self-assessment, coupled with a sense that no achievement would ever be quite enough, was the perfect antidote to complacency. However, it was also a partial antidote to happiness.

The physical effects of Timothy's teaching were equally long lasting and, Margaret believed, more harmful. His exacting standards, coupled with the chronic lack of rest that Margaret endured, unnaturally stimulated her nerves and kept her feelings "on the stretch" for too long at a time.[70] The toll on her endurance was worsened by the fact that Timothy typically began their lessons only after a long day at his law office, when both he and Margaret were worn out and tempers were likely to flare. Margaret later said that she had never met a man with greater powers of attention than her father. Long into the night, by the flickering light of candles, she did her best to match him.[71] When she did sleep, her rest was fitful and disturbed. Her life began to split into two incongruous halves. By day, she was her father's sunlit "youthful prodigy." By night, she was the helpless prey of "spectral illusions, nightmare and somnambulism."[72] As soon as the lessons were ended and the lights put out, she imagined ugly, colossal faces looming toward her out of the dark. In her dreams, she found herself being trampled by horses or trudging behind the casket in her mother's funeral procession. She recalled with particular vividness a dream she had after a long evening of working her way through Book III of Virgil's *Aeneid*, in which Aeneas pulls the stalks of plants out of the ground, only to discover dark blood oozing up from the earth. In her nightmare, Sarah Margaret found herself

> among trees that dripped with blood, where she walked and walked and could not get out, while the blood became a pool and plashed over her feet, and rose higher and higher, till soon she dreamed it would reach her lips.[73]

Her frightening visions were sometimes so real that they drove her out of bed to walk in her sleep, "moaning all over the house."[74] In her "romance," when she related the worst of her reactions to her father's regimen, Fuller shifted her narration from first to third person, as if to interpose some small but precious distance between herself and her remembered terrors. Hearing of her nightmares, Timothy chided his daughter and told her to set aside such nonsense, never suspecting that he himself was to blame for her agitation. Margaret also averred in later years that her interminable lessons "prevented the harmonious development of my bodily powers and checked my growth, while, later, they induced continual headache, weakness and nervous affections, of all kinds." At the age of thirty, Margaret still suspected that her constitution had been so wasted in these early years that she was destined for "a premature grave."[75]

Fuller's memoir paints a deeply touching picture, and it is impossible to read it without feeling profound sympathy for the little girl wrenched out of childhood and prematurely thrust into a world of geography, Virgil, and Greek grammar. But Fuller's recollections tell only part of the story of her formative years. There is no reason to question, in its larger contours, the traditional view of Timothy Fuller as a nearly obsessed taskmaster where his daughter's education was concerned. However, that overall perception must not be allowed to harden into a reductive caricature. While there can be no doubt that her father made extraordinarily harsh demands on his eldest child, he was far from being an emotionless pedant. Sarah Margaret's younger brother Arthur, who edited many of his sister's works after her death, was horrified to imagine what people would think of his father if they took Margaret's "Romance" to be literally true. Pointing out that Margaret's sketch had been brought to light only after her death and, obviously, without her consent, Arthur claimed that she never would have published it "without such modifications as would have shown our father to have been a most judicious and tender one."[76] Arthur conceded that Timothy had, "to a certain extent," overlooked his daughter's physical health while tasking her mental gifts to the utmost.[77] However, he noted, this error was committed by "all the educators of his time," and Timothy had at least been wise enough to avoid it in the education of his younger children. Arthur was also of the view that Timothy's overstimulation of Sarah Margaret's intellect "would have harmed none but one possessing a mind so precocious and unusual." As time went by, Arthur insisted, Margaret saw her father "more and more [as] a person to be deeply loved and respected."[78]

Is Arthur's exoneration of Timothy to be believed? During the most taxing years of his sister's education, Arthur had not yet been born. In Margaret's and Timothy's mature relationship, he saw no tyranny. As to the more complex story of their earlier relationship, however, he was at best a hearsay witness. In suggesting that it was his sister's sensitive constitution, not their father's harshness, that was most at fault, he comes perilously close to blaming the victim. And yet Arthur knew his father and sister better than any of us can. He also understood from experience what we can see only at a great distance: his culture's assumption—almost universally held before the 1830s—that children could and should be treated as miniature adults.

As has been suggested, one of the reasons Sarah Margaret endured and responded to her father's teaching was that she felt his love, for her and for knowledge, and wished to repay that love. Despite his strictness, Timothy's devotion to his family can hardly be questioned. Until he went to Washington to take his seat in Congress, he and his wife were seldom apart. During their first five years of marriage, Margarett left home only once—to visit her mother—and she stayed away only two days.[79] In March 1813, when Sarah Margaret was almost three, a session of court in Concord obliged her father to spend three nights away from home. Timothy was surprisingly agitated by this seemingly brief absence. He underlined the words "three nights" in his journal and observed that he had "never [been] absent so long at one time before, & not more than 9 or 10 in all since my marriage."[80] He hated to be away from home.

Once Fuller was in Washington, he and his wife began a voluminous correspondence, and it was not uncommon for them to write twice a day. Timothy's letters attest to his larger complexities as a father. In 1817, during Timothy's first year in Congress, another son, William Henry, joined the family, and Timothy's interest in news of his three children was avid. If more than a few days passed without a letter from Margarett, he was sure to send a cajoling letter of his own, demanding a prompt reply. In his letters, a portrait of a devoted husband and a remarkably caring father emerges. Certainly, he was interested in monitoring his daughter's academic progress, and he made sure that Margarett kept him informed regarding the young girl's studies. He kept up a steady stream of assignments, corrections, and advice regarding Sarah Margaret's work. "How does SM improve?" was his incessant, anxious query.[81]

However, it is evident that his concern for her was moral and physical as well as academic. The family preserved one of Margaret's early penmanship exercises, which begins, in very large letters, "Love your enemies. Love your enemies. Love your enemies." The lesson ended with a line that might have served as a motto: "He who would search for truth must dive below."[82] During the opening weeks of his first congressional term, Timothy's letters evince far deeper and more frequent concern about a tooth that his daughter had broken than her efforts at learning.[83] Reports of her condition caused him "great uneasiness," and he wrote to his wife in anxious hopes for "a complete remedy in the easiest & safest manner for my dear girl."[84] Indeed, there is even scattered evidence that he felt Sarah Margaret was reading too much and that her involvement with fictional realms was leading her to forget her affections for real human beings. In one letter, Timothy expressed disappointment that she had not added a line to one of her mother's recent letters. He gently chided, "Sarah Margarett forgot to send her love—I suppose she was bending over some tale of woe or mystery, & so forgot it. I forgive the little girl & expect her recollection will come to her in time."[85]

Timothy was sensitive to the fact that his daughter missed him, and he marked places on his letters that he had touched to his lips, so that Sarah Margaret, now seven, might kiss those spots and feel as if he were with her. When Sarah Margaret heard that a letter from Timothy contained "affectionate notice of her," her eyes would "sparkle with pleasure."[86] When asked how much he loved his father, Eugene replied, "Sixty pounds."[87] Sarah Margaret surely agreed.

Early in his time in Congress, Timothy reported to his wife that he was dreaming more often, and the recurring subject was his wife and "dear children." Fearing that Margarett might suspect him of engaging in a bit of maudlin romanticism, he assured her that he was not exaggerating "This is literally so," he wrote, "& not said to please you."[88] The image of Timothy Fuller, not as an unfeeling martinet, but as a man who wanted the best for his eldest child and sought it unwisely, is not only more accurate but in a sense more tragic: the most lasting wounds he inflicted were those that began with love.

Undeniably, Timothy was deeply proud of Sarah Margaret's academic overachievements. Equally undeniably, Sarah Margaret began to see herself as being cast in the role of the family prodigy. However, it should be emphasized that she enjoyed this role and, at least by the time she was eight, was not being compelled to fill her mind with Latin and Greek grammar entirely against her will. As culture critic Ann Douglas has observed, it became difficult early on to distinguish Timothy's ambitions from Sarah Margaret's own.[89] The month before she turned ten, Timothy admonished her, "To excel in all things should be your constant aim; mediocrity is obscurity."[90] Yet she was not much older when she wrote him, "Be assured that I will do my utmost to acquit myself well. . . . I think of nothing else."[91] Timothy, of course, could not resist showing off his star pupil to the ladies and gentlemen of the Commonwealth who came to dine with their congressman. The reactions of his guests may well have varied, but the response of Ellen Kilshaw, an English visitor of whom much will be said later, may be taken as representative. She wrote:

> I can give [my family and friends] no idea of what my dear Margaret is. She is so surprising for her years, and expresses herself in such appropriate language upon subjects that most of twice her age do not comprehend. I really was astonished when she first conversed with me.[92]

It is a rare child whose head will not be turned by such adulation. Most children, when they discover they have a particular talent that brings them the praise of adults, will dedicate themselves more and more to refining that skill. So, then, with Sarah Margaret. She recalled that, before very long, her heavy course of study ceased to be a burden, and reading became a habit and a passion. To a certain extent, by her middle childhood years, she immersed herself in study because studying was simply what she did.

But there was very likely another reason for Sarah Margaret's continually redoubled efforts at mental self-improvement. It concerned, not the approval of her father, but rather a desire for more recognition from her mother. From the time of the death of her sister Julia in 1813 until the birth of her eldest brother Eugene two years later, Sarah Margaret had been the Fullers' only child. It is clear that, no matter how firmly they insisted on educational opportunities for girls, Timothy and Margarett were delighted to have a boy. To make matters more difficult for Sarah Margaret, Eugene soon exuded an effervescent, prepossessing character. If one may judge from his parents' correspondence, Eugene was almost impossibly cute, winning a generous share of attention and love with charm and personal allure. There was also another layer to the emerging familial relationships: in the Fuller nursery, a subtle reversal of expected gender roles was taking place. From a perspective of adult retrospection, Margaret realized that she had been "the child of masculine energy & Eugene of feminine loveliness."[93] Whereas most people tend to regard gender as distinctly binary, Sarah Margaret's childhood taught her to view gender identity as existing on a fluid spectrum, with subtle differences in shade instead of precise delineations. "Where lies this difference betwixt male and female?" she later asked herself. She then admitted, "I cannot trace it."[94]

During the next decade, Timothy and Margarett added to their family with vigorous regularity. Ellen Kilshaw, born in 1820, was the only break in a torrent of sons: Arthur Buckminster in 1822; Richard Frederick in 1824; James Lloyd in 1826; and, finally, Edward Breck in 1828. These additions to the family—and the constant readjustments they demanded—continually unsettled Sarah Margaret's feelings of acceptance and security.

Predictably, the ever-burgeoning household meant that Margarett had less time to spend with Sarah Margaret than she might have considered ideal. In the early 1850s, soon after the death of her famous daughter, Margarett tried to write a recollection of what her lost offspring had been like during childhood. She found her memories to be embarrassingly sparse. "Why is it," she demanded to know, "that I can recall so little of thy beauteous childhood, my glorified one . . . a being so gifted, so active . . . why is it that I, your mother, so rich in thy affections and ever blessed in thy presence fail in power to weave a wreath to the memory of thy childhood!"[95] Although Margarett was surprised by her incapacity to remember Sarah Margaret as a child, no one who reads her letters to her husband in the late 1810s need share her astonishment.

Even before her quintet of babies in the 1820s, Mrs. Fuller had begun to divert her attention away from Sarah Margaret. Her infatuation with her first two boys, especially Eugene, consigned her eldest child to a lesser position. It is clear from Margarett's letters that, on a purely emotional level, Eugene had an unrivaled place in his mother's heart. In these letters, William Henry is "pleasant as usual"; Eugene is "merry and interesting."[96] Sarah Margaret, by contrast, is chiefly represented as pegging away at her studies. Margarett could seldom resist slipping into her letters some little anecdote of Eugene's charming prattle. Mrs. Fuller always spelled out Eugene's name in full. By contrast, Sarah's name was invariably shortened to "S. M."

Although Margarett freely represented Sarah as hardworking and dutiful, she was not inclined to depict her daughter as unreservedly lovable. Sensing that she was losing her preeminent claim on her parents' affections, Sarah Margaret began to compete with her brothers for attention, deeply grateful when she was noticed with the same cheerful indulgence that was usually reserved for her younger brothers and quietly disappointed when she was treated differently. Her anxiousness can be seen in this passage from one of Margarett Fuller's letters to Timothy:

S.M. wishes me to tell you she loves you and depends upon your writing her, as you promised she inquired very particularly whether you desired me to kiss her *as you did Eugene* and wished me to tell *all* you wrote of her.[97]

In another letter, Mrs. Fuller commented that "S. M. [is] very desirous to have your approbation in every thing she does."[98]

One feels in these letters Sarah Margaret's zeal, almost to the point of desperation, to be recognized and loved. Unable to duplicate Eugene's magnetism, Sarah Margaret quickly learned the trick of winning the attention of her father and his friends by performing marvelous feats of intellect. While her father was in Washington, however, her mother became her only immediate source of parental approval. Margarett was not as impressed as her husband by mental performances. Early in her husband's first congressional term, she somewhat defensively wrote to him of Sarah Margaret, "I never neglect her when I can possibly avoid it."[99] Her wording implies a guilty knowledge that sometimes she could not avoid neglecting her. Arguably, it was not Timothy's physical absence, but Margarett's dwindling ability to relate to her, that was now the more significant emotional gap in Sarah Margaret's life. Mother and daughter became quite close in later years. Still, Margaret the younger could not easily excuse her mother's early inattention. She wrote, "It is not mother's fault that she was ignorant of every physical law . . . but I can't help mourning, sometimes, that my bodily life should have been so destroyed by the ignorance of *both* my parents."[100]

Fuller's own recollections of her childhood, focused as they are on her budding intellectual life, tend to overstate her isolation. Charles Capper avers that young Margaret had "extensive dealings with a wide circle of adults and children" and that the house on Cherry Street welcomed a steady stream of aunts, uncles, cousins, and grandparents. It seems doubtless, too, that Timothy, as a rising politico, entertained assiduously. There were also frequent visits to relatives in Boston, as well as Mrs. Fuller's parents in Canton, whose details no one thought worthy to preserve. "We have company," Mrs. Fuller wrote when Sarah Margaret was eight, "almost every evening."[101] As mentioned, Margaret's uncle took charge of her instruction while her father was away, and Uncles Abraham and Henry looked in regularly.[102] Although Cambridgeport offered few pleasant avenues for walking, Sarah Margaret much enjoyed going for evening strolls on the bridge to Boston and looking at "the river, and the city glittering in the sunset, and the lovely undulating line all round."[103] It was a life not wholly empty of pleasures. Nonetheless, considering the wealth of information available on so much of Fuller's life, one feels that stories of childhood companions, memories of games and frolics, and family anecdotes of playful adventures are strangely and uncomfortably scarce. One wishes there were more with which to challenge Fuller's own assessment that she had "no natural childhood."[104]

Without question, Timothy's firm belief that his daughter was the intellectual and moral equal of any boy laid some of the foundations for his daughter's later desire to be treated on a par with the male intellectuals of her time. Yet it may also have been Sarah Margaret's early realization that, try as she might, she would never be another Eugene in her mother's eyes, that led her to be so critical of society's penchant for setting aside so many of its privileges and prerogatives exclusively for men. She hungered for affection, and neither of her parents gave it to her easily or without conditions. As she grew older, her urge to know was immense, yet it was not as strong as her consuming need to be loved. As Fuller observed in her mid-thirties, "I confess I want indulgence from those I love. . . . [I]t seems to me, it is not that I want blind idolatry, but as a child never finding repose on the bosom of love, I seek it now, childishly perhaps. God knows all about it."[105] It may truly have seemed to her as if an infinite intelligence were needed to fully understand the depth of her want.

Such, then, were the influences that the configuration of her family and the intensity of her education exerted on the developing spirit of Sarah Margaret Fuller. The content of what she was learning, however, mattered no less than the fashion in which she was learning it. Immersed as she was in her father's beloved Latin classics, she was quick to absorb not only the language but also the values of classical antiquity. She thus developed unusual moral opinions for a girl in the consummately Christian New England of the 1810s. In the pages of Virgil and Cicero, she found "an indomitable will . . . self-command, and force of expression."[106] Although her grasp of Greek never advanced beyond the basics, she understood "enough to feel . . . that the law of life in that land was beauty, as in Rome it was stern composure."[107] These beauties and strengths appeared to offer a fuller, more luxuriant life than what she saw in her Bible, and they enticed her.

Sarah Margaret's younger siblings were hardly more disposed toward Christian belief than she was, and the children's lack of religious enthusiasm concerned their mother, who reproached herself and her husband for their "neglect in instructing our children in the principles & practice of our blessed religion."[108] It was not that they did not try; the little Fullers were regularly brought to the Cambridgeport Parish Unitarian Church, where Timothy served on the church council and the parishioners received a weekly infusion of liberal Christianity. Sarah Margaret looked forward to Sundays. For the Fuller family, the Sabbath was a day set apart, a time for more elaborate dinners and finer clothes. The day gave her a rest from the routine of tasks and recitations that filled the remainder of her week, and it also gave her a much-needed chance to play. Church going, however, gave her no pleasure at all. To the contrary, she had a habit of looking around herself with an air of conscious disdain, convinced of her superiority to her fellow worshippers. She wrote later that she "sought everywhere for the Roman or Shakespeare[an] figures, and she was met by shrewd, honest eye, the homely decency, or the smartness of a New England village on Sunday. There was beauty, but I could not see it then; it was not the kind I longed for." She reserved her most withering contempt for a family with five "hard, dry, dwarfed" daughters who sat near to her and who seemed to have nothing in common with the Muses and Graces who danced in her mind. Surely these girls, too, had living spirits and ardent dreams, but in their faces and manners Sarah Margaret could see only the narrow, complacent qualities of "working-day residents in this beautiful planet."[109]

There was an insufficiency in such people, she felt, and it was a quick, though perhaps unjust, step for her to conclude that their beliefs must be insufficient as well. However eloquently its moral truths and calming consolations may have spoken to her, she felt that Christianity answered only a portion of her needs. She was, as yet, too young to find the right words for its perceived inadequacy, but, at the age of twenty-four, she wrote out the sentiments she had been harboring since childhood:

> I well remember what reflections arose in my childish mind from a comparison of the Hebrew history where every moral obliquity is shown out with such naiveté and the Greek history full of sparkling deeds and brilliant sayings and their gods and goddesses, the types of beauty and power with the dazzling veil of flowery language and poetical imagery cast over their vices and failings.[110]

Sarah Margaret desired a faith that would enthrall her entire being—a faith of healthy bodies and curious questing minds that would fulfill her aesthetic as well as her moral cravings. In *Culture and Anarchy*, Matthew Arnold, an English poet and critic born when Margaret Fuller was twelve, observed that western civilization was divided between the two great ideas of Hebraism and Hellenism. Hebraism, according to Arnold, sets its sights on the study and observance of divine law. Its touchstones are self-restraint and strictness of conscience. Hellenism, to the contrary, aspires to a flexibility and openness of mind and spontaneity of consciousness. Fuller never had the chance to read Arnold, yet for much of her life, she would find her allegiances torn between the two models of ideal culture that he postulated. In this first phase of her awareness, Hellenism held a commanding lead.

In his essay, Arnold warned that the modern incarnation of Hellenism, for all its exuberant embrace of life, "had . . . a side of moral weakness and of relaxation or insensibility of the moral fibre." He felt that "this loss of spiritual balance, this exclusive preponderance given to man's perceiving and knowing side" was the great imperfection of Hellenic temperament, and he regarded Puritanism as the necessary Hebraic reaction against the overly voluptuous Hellenistic spirit of the Renaissance.[111] The New England into which Margaret Fuller was born was still nearer in spirit to its Puritan legacy than to the age of romanticism toward which it was gradually moving. Fuller was destined to do as much as anyone to urge New England toward a more

Hellenic concept of the ideal self. Yet she herself partook of the weaknesses that Arnold perceived in the classical Greek character. Along with her clarity and spontaneity of mind came an impulsiveness of emotion; her affections could be mercurial, and her demonstrations of ill temper could be volcanic. Young Sarah Margaret too often stood in need of the law-abiding, dutiful conscience of the Hebraist.

Though she later complained that excessive studying had stunted her growth, Sarah Margaret initially shot up fairly rapidly. Before she was ten and a half, she wrote proudly to her paternal grandmother that she was "a tall girl five feet two inches high." Well before the onset of adolescence, then, she was already approximately as tall as her father. Always desiring to appear significant to others, Sarah Margaret liked the notice that being taller than average brought her way. She invited her grandmother to "multiply my stature with my years and perhaps you may find me grown enough to merit some degree of consideration."[112] At the same time, however, her unusual height presented more than a few problems. For one, along with her inordinately advanced education, it gave adults another reason to expect her to be more emotionally mature than she actually was. When her mother tried to warn her that people would judge her according to her height instead of her age, Margaret complained bitterly to her father: "I do not think this is just, for surely our knowledge does not increase because we are tall."[113]

Somewhat abruptly, not long after writing her lament, Sarah Margaret stopped growing; Emerson was to remember her as being "rather under the middle height."[114] Nevertheless, her early resentment at being judged according to her growth instead of her age may disclose something about how she relished being regarded as a prodigy. Her father was constantly urging her to be exceptional; to deserve his pride and love, she must distinguish herself in all things. She well realized that a ten-year-old girl who could read Virgil was a marvel. A five-foot-two young woman who could read Virgil was less extraordinary. Sarah Margaret had learned the dangerous lesson that most children of exceptional ability soon discover: the cherished status of the wunderkind begins to fade when one ceases to appear young. Paradoxically, then, the brightest of children—those who seem to possess the greatest advantages as they move toward adulthood—perceive an incentive not to grow up, lest they lose the aura of precocity that they believe is their key to acceptance.

This was the first life of Margaret Fuller, a life whose contours she was powerless to choose but which she in some regards readily embraced. Seeking the love of her parents, encouraged by the praise of the adults who made up her world, she conformed to the role of the gifted girl. As she devoured literature and perfected her Latin, the other aspects of her self were shifting out of balance daily. She was becoming more mind than body, more a denizen of the library than a citizen of the world. What her father had given her was, in the abstract, a rich and marvelous preparation, but in a society that had no experience in accommodating female intellectuals, the purpose to which this preparation might be turned was a mystery. In the short term, her early influences and growth would lead her to an adolescence of awkward and painful adjustments. She was to learn that, in the minds of one's less distinguished peers, there is seldom any firm distinction between the exceptional and the abnormal.

CHAPTER TWO

MISFIT

*The things that we love in a young lady are something
very different from [her] understanding. We love in her:
Beauty, youthfulness, playfulness, trustingness . . . but
the understanding is not that which is capable of firing
our hearts and awakening a passion.*

—GOETHE, IN ECKERMANN'S *Conversations with Goethe*

AN ENTHUSIASTIC ELDER SISTER, MARGARET ENJOYED HELPING TO
look after her younger siblings. But she also continued to compete with them
for attention, as when, at the age of ten, she ended a letter to her grandmother: "Pray my dear grandmother if you write to any of your grandchildren write to me[;] you cannot be more beloved by any of them."[1] How deeply
she felt her isolation at the time is uncertain; her later recollections were
rueful. With her mother "in delicate health, and much absorbed in the care
of her younger children," Margaret's overly stimulated mind found no object
on which to vent its pent-up energies. She looked for someone who "took my
fancy," as she put it, but found no one.[2] As a result, the world of books envel-
oped her all the more.

Timothy Fuller maintained no separate room in his house as a library.
Adjoining his bedroom, though, was a large closet filled with books that
attracted Margaret irresistibly. That bedroom looked out on a rich countryside, whose gentle slopes and broad fields gave way at the horizon to a low
range of blue hills. Every winter reacquainted Margaret with "the cruel east
wind of Puritan Boston," and she was soon familiar with the ingrained pes-

simism that prompted New Englanders to regard even a pleasant day as a "weather-breeder."[3] Nevertheless, the part of Margaret that loved to dream of sunnier places adored this enticing vista. Sometimes the thought of what wonders might lie hidden on the other side of the hills moved her to tears.[4] Inevitably, though, the part of her that loved to read called her away from the window, and her real explorations took place on printed pages. [5]

Three authors, more than any others, enchanted her. Years later, she called them "rich and wide . . . racy with experience." In Cervantes, she discovered a "wide wisdom, a discernment piercing the shows and symbols of existence."[6] In the comedies of Molière, she found every laugh accompanied by a new lesson in human folly. But fixed forever in her memory was the cold winter Sunday when, at the age of eight, she first took down a volume whose spine bore the odd name of "Shakspeare." Beside the parlor fire, she opened to *Romeo and Juliet*. An hour or two went by before her father's voice restored her to reality. Seeing his daughter so captivated, he asked her what book she had chosen. Although a confirmed liberal in politics and education, Timothy held fast to tradition regarding the Lord's Day: no novels, no plays. He sent her back to the closet to choose another book. Margaret left the room as she was told but came back empty-handed. Then, unable to sit still without knowing what was to become of the Veronese lovers, she slipped back to the closet and furtively brought out Shakespeare a second time. She turned the pages undisturbed until some guests arrived. An aunt, seeing her niece so deeply distracted, remarked that Margaret had not heard a word addressed to her. In an instant, her deception was exposed. "How—!" Timothy exclaimed in sudden anger, but then, mindful of the company, he said in a more restrained voice, "Give me the book and go directly to bed."[7]

She obeyed, but, as she lay in the darkness, she found that neither her father's anger nor the shame of being banished from the gathering had left their expected sting. Her father came in to reason with her about her defiance, but his words made no impression. She was still in Verona, "where the free flow of life, sudden and graceful dialogue, and . . . the broad lustre of [the poet's] imagination . . . brought home the life I seemed born to live." Her fancies, it seemed to her, "swarmed like bees."[8] Timothy went away "really grieved," shaking his head, figuratively at least, over his daughter's impertinence.[9] As Margaret looked back on it all, it astonished her that two people who were so close could inhabit such distant worlds:

Often since I have seen the same misunderstanding between parent and child,—the parent thrusting the morale, the discipline, of life upon the child, when just engrossed by some game of real importance and great leadings to it. That is only a wooden horse to the father,—the child was careering to distant scenes of conquest and crusade, through a country of elsewhere unimagined beauty. None but poets remember their youth; but the father who does not retain poetical apprehension of the world, free and splendid as it stretches out before the child, who cannot read his natural history, and follow out its intimations with reverence, must be a tyrant in his home, and the purest intentions will not prevent his doing much to cramp him. Each new child is a new Thought, and has bearings and discernings, which the Thoughts older in date know not yet, but must learn.[10]

In Cervantes, Molière, and Shakespeare, Margaret had chosen three authors with an important similarity, one that was clear to her in retrospect. All of them loved and wrote about people, not as perfect archetypes, but as flawed creatures, made all the more precious by their failings. Overflowing with ideas, these authors resisted the impulse to idealize. As Fuller expressed it, "They loved a thorough penetration of the murkiest dens, and most tangled paths of nature; they did not spin from the desires of their own special natures, but reconstructed the world from materials which they collected on every side."[11] The humanism of her early reading supplied her with a kind of intellectual ballast. Years later, her sense of the limits of the human condition would enable her partly to resist the lofty visions of the lighter-than-air transcendentalists.

Nevertheless, the books that Margaret read were more idealistic than she knew, and her favorite fictional characters were subtly spoiling her for the real thing. Although the heroes of Shakespeare had realistic flaws, they carried them with a grandeur that somehow failed to tally with the lesser demeanors of the "lawyers and members of Congress and father's friends" who walked through her front door. At thirty-three, Fuller realized that her supposedly realistic reading had taught her more about how people should be than what they actually were. To a girl "with a head full of Hamlet," her surroundings seemed poor and petty. From an early moment, her New England life seemed to her like an accident. She recalled, "Both from constitution and a premature and excessive culture in the thoughts of Europe . . . I have had slowly to undo or transmute [myself] to live in my own place and with my own people."[12]

It is hardly unusual for a child's physical, mental, and emotional faculties to mature at different rates. Parents are frequently surprised by the apparent lopsidedness of their children's development, though one can generally trust time and patience to even out the process. Yet most of the casual influences that acted on Margaret pressed her further from the norm. Surely the greater part of this misfortune came from Timothy's requirement that the mind be treated as paramount. Yet the absence of a potent counterinfluence was also partly to blame. In comparison to the emotionally unyielding and forcefully intellectual Timothy, Mrs. Fuller was too passive and ineffectual to insist that Margaret's social development keep pace with that of her mind.

Margaret's love of her mother became tinged at its root with resentment for her inadequacies, to the extent that, from an early age, she dreamed repeatedly of her mother's death and burial—a nightmare that always ended with Margaret's waking in tears. These dreams, she later observed, "cast a deep shadow" over her youth, a shadow made all the darker by her sense that the life of dreams was "more real . . . than that of waking hours."[13] Whether Margaret tacitly desired her mother's death or whether the dreams simply dramatized the isolation she already felt within her family is a question for sobering thought.

Thankfully, when she was about seven, Margaret's need for recognition found some momentary relief in an unexpected form. She first saw her temporary liberator in church. On that particular Sunday, her eyes fell upon "a new apparition foreign to that scene." Observing her tasteful dress, her gracefully pliant hair, and her intelligent eyes, Margaret thought that she beheld the sum of European civilization, "a rose-tree from the daintily clipped garden." From the first, her knowledge of this new personage was an "intoxication."[14] Ellen Kilshaw, the daughter of a Liverpool merchant and broker, had come to Massachusetts at the age of twenty-one to visit her married sister, Mrs. John H. Greene, in 1816.[15] She stayed for fourteen months, and, after Margaret's initial sighting of her, she grew warmly acquainted with the Fullers and became a frequent guest, both at their house and at a neighbor's.

After her return to England, the friendship continued by mail on such genial terms that, when Margaret's parents had another daughter in 1820, they named the baby Ellen Kilshaw.

But it was on Margaret that the visitor's impression lasted longest. Apart from some less-than-fruitful efforts to teach her to sing and play the piano, Margaret had learned nothing about art or music. Ellen Kilshaw changed all that. She played the harp and painted in oils. Her "proper speech was dance or song."[16] She carried herself with a gentle, undulating motion that affected Margaret "as the stream does the woods and meadows."[17] Throughout her life, Margaret knew only one way of giving her heart. When she fastened on an object of true affection, she flung her entire being in its direction with a vehemence that astonished some and frightened others. This impulse found its pattern in her early affection for Ellen. She was "a gate of Paradise," "a ruby-red, a perfumed draught," "a star from the east," and "the first angel of [her] life."[18] Given all of Fuller's effusions about the glory that was Ellen Kilshaw, the details she gives regarding their time together are surprisingly sparse. Their friendship seems not so much the sum of days or activities, but a history of the overpowering impressions of sense and emotion that each made on the other. Kilshaw seems to have found Margaret's worshipful attentions flattering; she was, according to the latter, cheered and charmed by "the light cast by the flame through so delicate a vase" as the face of a small admirer.[19] For her part, Kilshaw showed her young friend that one might live for beauty rather than achievement.

Both as a girl and in later years, Margaret was prey to haunting premonitions. One of the first of these struck her while in Kilshaw's company. Ellen had been reading Sir Walter Scott's *Guy Mannering*. One afternoon, when Ellen briefly left her book behind, Margaret picked it up and read from the same page. The scene is of a desolate seacoast where a five-year-old child, Harry Bertram, has just been kidnapped. The corpse of his murdered protector is found, but there is no trace of the boy, and the search party presumes that his body has been washed out to sea. Margaret imagined that she was simultaneously the lonely Margaret and the abandoned Harry, seeking vainly for a friend in dark seaside caverns that slowly filled with water. When Ellen came back for her book, she found Margaret in tears. Margaret laid her head on Ellen's shoulder, "dimly feeling that I must lose her and all . . . that the cold wave must rush over me."[20] The two fears, one of death by water and the other of losing the affection of those she needed most, were already deep in the young girl's spirit.

Eventually Kilshaw traveled back to England, where she was to exert an even stronger influence on another literary girl: her daughter, Charlotte Eliza Lawson Cowan, became a popular British novelist in the 1870s, writing under her married name, Mrs. J. H. Riddell.[21] For many years, Kilshaw exchanged letters with Fuller. Regrettably, the only surviving letter from Margaret to Ellen is one that was never sent. Resisting the stiff formality of letter-writing conventions, Margaret insists on calling her "dear Ellen" and vows not to add the word "Miss" "unless you bid me to do it." Abundantly affectionate, the letter reports two events that Margaret had lately observed, and they both involve spectacles of light. First, it recounts the burning of a rope works in Boston, apparently by laborers who had been thrown out of work by a new mechanized process. Margaret calls the fire "a most awful spectacle" and regrets that she lacks the words to represent the grandeur of the catastrophe. She then tells how, later the same night, as she and her father watched together, that sublime vision of light was transferred to the skies; the aurora borealis, rarely seen in Cambridge's latitude, "shone out in splendor."[22] In her letter, Margaret hoped to share with her friend an Inferno and Paradiso in miniature, the blazing perfidy of the arsonist and the shimmering glory of the heavens. Although clearly interested in impressing her friend—she notes that, though only nine, she is tall enough to be mistaken for thirteen—Margaret writes nothing about her studies. It appears that, in Kilshaw, she had found an adult whom she could please by being something other than a budding genius.

In her letter to Kilshaw, Margaret proclaims, "I, as you well know, am a queen."[23] For years, she could not quite set aside the idea that she was not her parents' child at all, but a European princess secretly entrusted to their care. Timothy was aware of her fancy, and he found it amusing. One day, as Margaret strode beneath the family apple trees with an especially regal air, he was heard to tell her sister, "Incedit regina"—There walks a queen.[24] Nevertheless, the house on Cherry Street seemed far from a palace after Kilshaw's departure. Indeed, Margaret felt its emptiness as never before. Her appetite diminished. Her two most accustomed pleasures, reading and exploring her mother's garden, no longer interested her. Complaining of chronic headaches, she became less attentive to her lessons and spent an unusual amount of time lying in bed or on the floor of her room.[25] Timothy blamed himself for her depression. Accusing himself of keeping his daughter too long at home, merely to please himself, he at long last realized that Margaret needed variety, play, and the company of other girls. Still, he did not slacken his demands with regard to her studies. "To excel in all things," he reminded her, "should be your constant aim; mediocrity is obscurity."[26] At the same time, he began to entertain the idea of supplementing her home schooling by sending her to a local daytime academy.

Surprisingly, Margaret balked at the idea. She sensed that the gap in knowledge between herself and the girls she would encounter might already be too large. When she had tried to meet her peers on any terms other than those of physical play, she had felt thwarted. Her rarified education had made her aloof and condescending. To her, the others seemed childish and dull. The emotion she claimed to have felt on being told she would be sent to school was "disgust."[27] It may have been closer to panic. She resisted, but in vain. In the fall of 1819, Timothy enrolled his daughter in the Cambridge Port Private Grammar School, a boys' college preparatory academy that admitted girls on a part-time basis. Her reputation as a "smart" girl preceded her, and she was quick to make good on it. Among her schoolmates was a boy about nine months her senior named Oliver Wendell Holmes, the future poet and novelist who was also to father the eminent judge. Young Oliver was struck by the new girl's audacity of speech, her stateliness of manner, and the way she behaved "as if she had other thoughts than [ours] and was not of [us]." Still, he was not persuaded that she was any more intelligent than he until the day he happened to look at one of her compositions. It began, "It is a trite remark . . ." His ego was instantly punctured; he had never heard the word "trite."[28] In the space of five words, Margaret had driven him from the field. At the Port School, Margaret continued her instruction in Latin and Greek until it appeared to the family in early 1821 that a still broader academic horizon was required.

For a time, the family quarreled as to where that horizon lay. Her mother sensed that Margaret would profit more from training in the social graces than a further deepening of her scholarship. She wanted to send her to a boarding school in Jamaica Plain dedicated to fostering "elegant accomplishments."[29] The girls there learned to "play country dances and cotillions on the piano forte." They were required to speak French and were fined two pennies if they descended into the forbidden vulgarity of English.[30] Margaret responded with horror to the prospect of such prim surroundings, and she sent a letter to her father in Washington, begging to be rescued. Her words tumbled out in an unpunctuated rush: "I have often pained you but I hope you still love me I should be most happy to be Dr Parks scholar."[31] She was referring to a school across the Charles River, three miles from home, operated by Dr. John Park and called the Boston Lyceum for Young Ladies.

Margaret imagined that the Lyceum was everything she could desire. Since February 1820, a year before she was eligible to enroll, she had set her heart on studying there.[32] She may or may not have heard of Dr. Park's exciting and varied past; a Dartmouth graduate, Park had traveled in 1799 as a ship's surgeon to the West Indies, where he had tried to discover a cure for yellow fever. By 1804, he had quit both medicine and the tropics, returning to New England to found the Federalist newspaper later known as the *Boston Daily Advertiser*. Seven years later, he switched careers again, this time to establish his Lyceum, whose classes met in his well-appointed home at 5 Mount Vernon Street. Margaret was more likely to have known that Park was, like herself, an avid Latin scholar, and she surely knew that his academy was among the most highly regarded in the city, patronized by some of the city's most illustrious Unitarian families. Park's curriculum was notoriously rigorous; he expected his girls to achieve mastery in French, Italian, rhetoric, trigonometry, the natural sciences, and, of course, Latin.[33]

Margaret earnestly pleaded her cause. Park had lately expanded his enrollment, and, if Timothy wrote promptly, he could secure her a place. Studying at the Lyceum would also unite her with one of Timothy's nieces, Susan Williams, who hoped that Margaret would stay with her family so that the two girls might study together. Margaret also played an emotional trump card. Just before bringing up the subject of Park's school, she plaintively asked, "Has your affection [for me] decreased? I fear it has."[34] The inference was hardly subtle. If Timothy really loved Margaret, he would send her to Dr. Park. Whether Timothy was swayed by Park's superior curriculum or by Margaret's blackmail, he sided with her, though the Williamses' offer to house Margaret came to nothing. In April 1821, two and a half months after Timothy made his wishes known, ten-year-old Margaret gladly started walking the daily "rather fatiguing" but "pleasant" six-mile round-trip to Mount Vernon Street.[35]

As an adult, Fuller remembered an unspecified period in her childhood when, as she looked from a window, she could see an eagle chained to the balcony of a museum. Worn down by the insult of captivity, the bird gazed at the world with dull eyes, its plumage soiled and shabby. To Margaret's indignation, the museum patrons could find no better recreation than to poke at it with sticks. Yet, as Fuller recalled, the eagle seemed to bear every degradation with unconquered poise and grandeur. "In its form and attitude," Fuller recollected, "all the king was visible, though sorrowful and dethroned."[36] In her heart, Margaret adopted the eagle as her "monarch-bird," who taught her, no matter how she had been insulted, never to accept humiliation. One did not plead or compromise with one's foes. One held oneself stoically above them. As she grew toward adolescence, Fuller had many occasions to feel like her monarch-bird. Many of them were waiting for her at Dr. Park's academy.

Margaret knew the academy would be rigorous, and she expected to spend almost all her time studying. She was right. Until December, she was evidently too busy with her schoolwork to write a single letter, and her early months under Dr. Park are now a teasing blank. Thankfully, she never had to attempt the trek from Cambridgeport to Park's school during winter. That year, for the first time, Timothy and Margarett decided that they would pass the winter in Washington together without their children. Not even the family's newest addition, Ellen Kilshaw Fuller, born on the seventh of August the previous year, would join them.

In late November, having packed off Margaret's brothers Eugene and William Henry and little Ellen to stay with Margarett's relatives, the couple departed, leaving Margaret to stay in Boston with Timothy's youngest sister Martha, her husband Simeon Whittier, and their children. Margaret was probably willing to accept any arrangement that allowed her to remain at the Lyceum. One may speculate, though, that she felt some inner conflict. She was now denied the pleasure of helping her siblings to grow and learn. While long separations from her father were nothing new and the bonds of understanding that connected her with her mother were less than perfect, her parents' departure likely carried some of the sting of abandonment. The physical surroundings at the Whittiers' were also none of the best. An apparently stingy couple, Martha and Simeon chose not to acquire a proper bed for their long-term guest, and Margaret was consigned to "a little trundle bed about two thirds her length."[37] Furthermore, her aunt and uncle were often too cheap or neglectful to kindle a fire in her room. Thus, Margaret was frequently forced to study in the parlor, and she developed a cough that remained with her for most of the winter.

Yet there were compensations. A far cry from the strictness of Timothy and Margarett, who had supervised Margaret's every move with suffocating scrutiny, Aunt Martha was a woman of decidedly relaxed "domestick regulations."[38] Martha preferred trashy novels to housework and turned a blind eye when her own children neglected their studies and played cards. Under the Whittiers' roof, Margaret's only pressure to excel came from within. With evident relief she wrote to her mother in December that she had not cried once since her parents' departure and was "as happy here as I can be [while] separated from you."[39]

Meanwhile, Dr. Park's Lyceum dovetailed perfectly with Margaret's academic zeal. Park regarded competition as a great spur to learning. He awarded medals for outstanding achievement, and he had a genius for convincing his girls that nothing in their lives mattered more than winning them. Margaret's contentious Fuller blood warmed in the face of such a challenge. Before long, a particular prize transfixed her: the "Eye of Intelligence," an honor reserved for the best scholars in the school. Though the criteria for awarding the Eye are now somewhat obscure, it seems to have been conferred on girls who had won at least twenty-one lesser medals in various subjects. In the waning days of 1821, the coveted Eye had been newly awarded to Susan Channing, a girl three years Margaret's senior who was the niece of the great Unitarian minister William Ellery Channing. On her way to winning the Eye, Susan had amassed seventeen medals in English alone. Margaret, a relative newcomer, had garnered only a paltry three in English and was, overall, a long way from winning an Eye. Still, she would sooner have died than gone on long without one, and she resolved to earn the honor before her parents came back from Washington.

Intent on avoiding a single mistake that would slow the progress toward her goal, Margaret pored over her schoolbooks while her aunt dozed over her novels, her cousins laughed over their cards, and the snows blew down on Boston. Neither her innate gifts nor her copious preparations kept her from feeling anxious as the time of her first examinations drew near. Although she predicted to her father that her tests would "go off with great splendour," she was also grateful that Timothy was not on hand to witness her performance and thereby exacerbate the pressure. "I know what your feelings would be," she wrote. "Mine are sufficient." She felt confident of her languages and expected to do well in history "unless I am frightened quite out of my wits." Geography, however, with its "numberless questions" tormented her.[40] Nine days later, Margaret wrote proudly to her father that "all the dangers and perils of Examination" lay behind her and that she had fared much better than she had expected.[41] This first foray was evidently typical of her efforts at Mr. Park's Lyceum; in due time, the Eye of Intelligence was hers.

Sadly, if her time at the Lyceum was a period of scholastic triumphs, it was also a protracted episode of loneliness and rejection by her peers. Then as now, an uneasy alliance exists between the clever and the rich in elite private schools. To ensure both its prestige and its fiscal health, the institution must attract both populations. Under the right conditions, the two can exist in harmony, but Margaret found no comfort among her more style-conscious classmates. As she herself later confessed, she was not an amiable child.[42] The competitive surroundings at the Lyceum brought out her natural acerbity even more. Tacitly encouraged to compare herself with them, she rapidly conceived a sense of superiority to most of her classmates, and she took little trouble to conceal it. Like many talented children accustomed to impressing adults, Margaret was slow to grasp that such displays win few friends among one's peers.

Unable to assail her academic excellence, the other girls struck at a more vulnerable point: her physical plainness and lack of social sophistication. Fuller was an easy target. Afflicted by nearsightedness, she had already acquired a habitual squint.[43] She also put on weight easily, so that, by thirteen, she was perceived by some as "very corpulent."[44] She spoke with an ungainly New England twang, in which she expatiated on the "náw-véls" she delighted in reading.[45] To make matters still worse, her complexion began to be affected by an "ugly and very painful flush" on her forehead, possibly acne, which mortified even her proud parents.[46] Even those more gently disposed toward her were mildly shocked by her free-thinking opinions. With bemused curiosity, they referred to her as the strangely gifted girl who "had not religion."[47] She found herself subject to furtive whispers about her home life—how she had been systematically overexerted by her father, "who wished to train her like a boy, and that she was paying the penalty . . . in . . .

awkward manners, extravagancies of thought, and a pedantic style of talk."[48] Eager to remain at the school so she could absorb its cerebral benefits, Margaret glossed over the treatment she often received, telling her parents that her companions at school were friendly to her and that she felt they were "all sisters."[49]

That view was not shared by Frederic Henry Hedge, a young man four and a half years Margaret's senior whose family were close friends of the Fullers and who had taken a sympathetic interest in Margaret. Young Henry (he seldom used his first name) knew something about the glories and jealousies that could be earned by an academic prodigy. Before his seventh birthday, he had committed to memory every line of Virgil's *Eclogues* in the original Latin. By ten, he had added much of Homer in the original Greek to his ready repertoire. His father, Levi, a prominent professor of logic and metaphysics at Harvard, had determined that Boston could not adequately educate his son and sent him, at the age of twelve, to study in Göttingen, Germany. Realizing that even so brilliant a boy might not respond well to being packed off alone to a foreign country, the elder Hedge entrusted his son to the care of George Bancroft, the future historian, who was also going off to study in Germany. There were decided limits to Levi's prudence, however; the older, wiser Bancroft was only seventeen. Taking advantage of Bancroft's lax supervision, Henry embarked on a determined campaign of misbehavior and underachievement, which Bancroft reported to Henry's father as "impertinence and unbeschreibliche Faulheit," or unspeakable laziness.[50]

Hedge, however, had more than made up for his poor beginning. Not yet seventeen when he returned to Cambridge in 1822, he immediately entered Harvard as a junior. Almost at once, his attention was attracted by Margaret, whom he both admired for her brains and pitied for her awkwardness. Of her battles at the Lyceum, he later wrote:

The inexperienced country girl was exposed to petty persecutions from the dashing misses of the city, who pleased themselves with giggling criticisms not inaudible, nor meant to be inaudible to their subject, on whatsoever in dress and manner fell short of the city mark. Then it was first revealed to her young heart, and laid up for future reflection, how large a place in woman's world is given to fashion and frivolity.[51]

These attacks doubtlessly made Fuller feel like the monarch-bird at the museum. However, she had not yet learned to follow the eagle's stoical example. Instead, she fought back, retaliating with the weapon that came readiest to hand: her biting wit. Predictably, though, every figurative drop of blood that she drew with her mordant humor scored another mark against her in the minds of her peers. Her isolation deepened, and her resentment grew. As Hedge put it, "A root of bitterness sprung up in her which years of moral cul-

Among the most promising of the young transcendentalists, Frederic Henry Hedge was, for a time, Fuller's closest intellectual friend.

(FREDERICK HENRY HEDGE, ANDOVER-HARVARD THEOLOGICAL LIBRARY, HARVARD DIVINITY SCHOOL, CAMBRIDGE, MASSACHUSETTS)

ture were needed to eradicate."[52] To mask her heaviness, which, according to Hedge, privately disgusted her, Fuller resorted to wearing tightly laced corsets. On one occasion when Margaret was staying with his family, Hedge recalled, the only person on the premises who could lace Fuller to her satisfaction was a stout Irish servant woman, recruited from the kitchen for that purpose. In every possible sense, Fuller was struggling—and failing—to fit in.

In December 1822, twenty months after she began, Margaret Fuller ended her studies at the Lyceum. Despite the accumulated wounds inflicted by her classmates, she took her leave "with much regret." When Park said farewell to Margaret, he told her first that he never engaged in flattery and then added a litany of compliments. "I really do love him," Margaret wrote her father, "for he has a very kind and sweet disposition."[53] Park invited her to visit often, and she thought she might. At the suggestion of her uncles, Margaret asked Timothy by letter whether she might invite some of the girls to the family home in Cambridgeport for a valedictory dance. Timothy sent back his permission, and Margaret set about planning a titanic affair, sending out approximately ninety invitations. Her spirits fell, however, as the responses came in a pathetic trickle. Three days before the party, only nine replies had been received. Margaret tried to reassure herself, assuming that the bulk of her invitees had chosen not to respond until the day of the fête. She sent another letter to her father, denouncing her friends for their rudeness but still confident that they would come.

On January 15, 1823, the grand occasion took place, and with it came some hard lessons. As might have been expected in mid-January on the Charles River, the weather was fierce and forbidding, and "but few" of those invited from Boston ventured the trip.[54] Eager both to reward her guests from the great city for making the journey and to win herself a place in their midst, Margaret made too much of their presence and slighted the girls from her own side of the river, thus bringing down on her shoulders the "indignation of her little world of Cambridge."[55] Margaret's attempt to impress the redoubtable twelve-year-olds of Boston society had failed. Still worse, many of their Cambridge counterparts left the soirée resolving not to speak to their host for some time to come. After the tables were cleared away and the musicians packed up their instruments, the young ladies of Dr. Park's Lyceum retreated to their fashionable, mostly forgettable lives, leaving Margaret scrambling to put the best face on the catastrophe.

Margaret wrote her father that her party had been "exceedingly agreeable" and that she had been very happy with it, but it took her more than two weeks to write this letter, and she included no details.[56] At both her father's and her mother's prompting, she later sent Timothy a further description of the party, a description that, she admitted, "nothing but gratitude could have induced" her to write.[57] But even this account contains little more than an enumeration of the people who attended, and the list is not long. Mindful of the expenditure that had gone into the affair, Margaret more than likely hoped to spare Timothy's feelings—and her own—by not fully confessing the disaster.

The end of her tenure at Mr. Park's did not signal a break in Margaret's studies. Until her parents could decide on a more lasting course, they arranged for her to return to the Port School, where Eugene, now going on eight and quite a "wit" as Margaret put it, was also taking his lessons.[58] Her school work, however, supplied only a fraction of her learning. She had begun reading Adam Smith's *Wealth of Nations*. Eager to finish it and move on to Bacon's *Essays* and William Paley's *Natural Theology*, she set herself a schedule of study that she expected to consume eight hours every day. The strain was too great. Less than a month after leaving the Lyceum, she wrote to her father that her eyes were "extremely weak."[59] Far from reading eight hours a day, she had been unable to look at a book for a week. After the first week in February 1823, Margaret wrote no more surviving letters until December. She may have felt that she had little to write about. The pleasure of studying under Dr. Park was at an end, and her time at the Port School was little more than treading water.

Timothy thought he perceived the causes of his daughter's difficulties, and, like quite a few parents, he was especially aggrieved to realize that her faults were an embryonic version of his own. The impatient youth and the show-offish student that he had once been had returned in feminine form. The social advantages that his station might have conferred on Margaret were evidently being squandered on her; decades later, she recalled, "Indeed, not one of Father's friends ever became mine; in fact I was an odd and unpleasing girl to people generally." Even in the last year of her life, people who had known her as a child were sometimes slow to approach her, fearing, she surmised, that she was "just as odd and disagreeable as ever."[60] As Margaret returned to the Port School, Timothy was anxious lest she repeat the mistakes she had made at Dr. Park's. He firmly admonished her to tone herself down. In her new situation, he advised her, "It would be prudent in you to be a little reserved . . . & by no means display your attainments too soon, lest you should excite observation and incur dislike." As if this counsel were not clear enough, he wrote more bluntly, "[y]ou are now at an age, especially of a size, when great prudence is indispensable, & I hope will by no means be found wanting."[61] Timothy tried to soften the blow by admitting that he, too, sometimes fell short of "perfect prudence." However, in urging his daughter to be more diplomatic, Timothy showed himself to be no diplomat. His message—that overzealous, overfed girls, whatever their intelligence, would be well advised to step to the back row—must have stunned its recipient.

The age of twelve or thirteen is, of course, not too early to experience a crisis in one's social development. As her teen years drew near, Margaret Fuller had experienced social rebuffs so stinging that even her socially indefatigable father, who had routinely pushed her forward, was advising a strategic retreat. Had she chosen to take it, an avenue of escape lay readily at hand. The easy, perhaps even the logical, choice for Margaret was to plunge into the sheltering solitude of her father's library and never resurface. She did, indeed, keep reading, but she was a brave girl, and she had no inclination to withdraw from the cotillions and drawing rooms of Cambridge. Contrary to her father's wishes, she "made up [her] mind to be bright and ugly."[62]

It could have been worse. The Fullers, though never the most popular family in Cambridge, were nonetheless central to its social network. Even in a town where most of the wealthier citizens stood against her father politically, Margaret discovered that quite a few doors would always be open to a congressman's daughter. Moreover, if one may credit the judgment of Oliver Wendell Holmes, it was not too hard for a young woman to shine in the social atmosphere of Cambridge. In 1830, Holmes despaired of finding "a girl in the neighborhood whose blood ever rose above the freezing point." His own romantic researches had turned up "nothing but vinegar-faced old maids and drawing-room sentimentalists."[63] In the face of such pale competition, Margaret kept up a busy round of socializing, dancing and trading ripostes with the young men of Harvard and the children of the town's most formidable families.

A high point came that summer. Timothy, now forty-five, was eager to raise his fortunes beyond those of a mere congressman. He hoped to win the favor of Secretary of State John Quincy Adams, whom he intended to support in the next year's presidential election. Three years earlier Adams had cautioned Fuller that he was disinclined toward anything that savored of "caballing, bargaining [or] place-giving."[64] Still, the men had remained friends and sometimes attended Unitarian services together in Washington.[65] Timothy hoped to garner some sort of patronage, perhaps a diplomatic appointment, if Adams were elected. With a view to helping his cause, Timothy brought his wife and Margaret on a trip to nearby Quincy to visit the secretary's father, former president John Adams. The interview was disappointing. Toothless and losing his hearing, the eighty-seven-year-old was having his portrait painted and preferred not to discuss his son's or Timothy's political fortunes. For Margaret, nevertheless, it was a rare chance to meet an icon of the Revolutionary past.

Closer to home there were murmurings that Miss Fuller was flinging herself into the social whirl a bit too forcefully. Although she was impressing many with the sparkle and erudition of her conversation, she was alienating as many, if not more, with her continuing penchant for aggressive wit and criticism. She had, Hedge recalled, an unfortunate disposition to "quiz"—a word that has now lost two meanings, both of which were, at the time, applicable to Margaret.[66] The first was to peer intently at someone, which Margaret's nearsightedness compelled her to do. The second is to poke fun at someone, and this she seems to have done without mercy. Her ability to devastate a victim with a well-aimed phrase became widely known, and it began to "frighten shy young people from her presence" and to make her "notoriously unpopular."[67] Knowing the harm that an excess of familiarity could do to a young woman's reputation, and perhaps also concerned that his teen-aged loose cannon might cast an unhappy light on the family name, Timothy fretted that Margaret might "cheapen her value by too frequent appearance in company."[68] Almost three years earlier, he had written, "[P]erhaps we may think it best for her to keep more at the domestic hearth a few years yet."[69] He had not yet changed his mind.

Margaret's difficult days in 1823 were made much more bearable when Henry Hedge, who had previously sympathized with her from afar, offered her a closer friendship. He and the thirteen-year-old began to meet frequently in the social circles that embraced the Harvard faculty and their families, and they developed an attachment that was only to strengthen over time. Margaret was impressed by Hedge's knowledge of German literature and philosophy, which was, indeed, already among the most accomplished in the country. By the time Margaret was nineteen, no one enjoyed a loftier place in her intellectual esteem. She was then to write, "I never can feel more perfect enjoyment from any one's conversation. . . . What a pleasure to meet with such a daring yet realizing mind as his!" Hedge's mother did not entirely approve of the friendship, feeling that each confirmed the other's sense of superiority over the rest of the world. Some years later, when Margaret paid a visit to her house, she complained, "Henry and Margaret thought themselves such high geniuses that nobody could get up to or comprehend them."[70]

Henry's interest in Margaret was not romantic. True, he felt that, where her mind was concerned, his friend could have passed for eighteen or twenty. In body, however, she was no more to him than "a blooming girl of a florid complexion and vigorous health." He also later recalled that, although her facial features and expressions "awakened a lively interest that made one desirous of a nearer acquaintance," she had "no pretensions to beauty then, or at any time." Hedge was also put off by Fuller's weight, which he gently called her "tendency to robustness." Still, though he did not think of her as pretty, he considered her far from plain. He could never forget the graceful carriage of her head and neck, her abundant blonde hair, her brilliant smile, and above all "her sparkling, dancing, busy eyes."[71]

It was a face that perpetually moved. Hedge never saw it at rest, and it never gave him time for a steady perusal of its features. He tried to read her face as an index of her character, but he never succeeded. Her morals and sentiments were never on display there. Inevitably, his efforts led him back to the word that hardly anyone could resist when describing Fuller. He later wrote, "You saw evidence of a mighty *force*, but what direction that force would assume—whether it would determine itself to social triumphs, or to triumphs of art,—it was impossible to divine."[72] Hedge called Margaret's face "a face that fascinated, without satisfying."[73] Just what satisfactions he had hoped to find there, he chose not to name.

Their friendship thus remained properly scholarly. Margaret nicknamed him "Germanicus" and grew to rely on him as a source of information on German Romanticism—a topic that grew more and more important to her as time passed. It was from Hedge that she borrowed the bulk of her German books, and it was to him that she turned to discuss that reading. Proudly and independently, she insisted on learning as much German on her own as she could, but when her pronunciation faltered, Hedge was there to set her right.[74] But his technical knowledge of German was not the greatest thing he gave her. Although Hedge was a keen reporter on outward appearances, he was also gifted with the power to see past them. Hedge found enough hints and intuitions in the world at large to realize that external forms were seldom the most important realities. What was true of the cosmos was also true of

Margaret; it was the motivating spirit, not the ungainly outside, that mattered. Some time would pass before he could articulate his perceptions as a philosophy, but the time would come when he would inspire Margaret to see as far and as deeply as he.

Meanwhile, Timothy and Margarett were at wit's end regarding the impressions their daughter made on more superficial minds than Hedge's. Margaret either did not guess or pretended not to notice the awkward figure she was cutting in the drawing rooms of Cambridge. Among the extended Fuller family, however, the prevailing view was that she was making a spectacle of herself.[75] For Timothy, accustomed as he was to asserting control over his family, Margaret's overly gregarious manner was an intolerable defiance. For his wife, Margaret's intransigence was a cause for despair. She complained to Timothy of a social occasion when a friend asked Margaret if she would sing. Not only did she decline, but "nothing could be more repulsive than her manner of refusing." Her manner, Margarett continued, "is often such to pain me excessively and all my arguments seem lost upon her."[76] She appealed to her husband for help. Timothy at first commanded that Margaret must now secure his approval before accepting social invitations. However, now in his last term in Congress, he had weightier things to do than to administer an adolescent girl's social schedule. He was moving toward a decision that, for the first time, would place him firmly at odds with his daughter's desires.

Timothy told Margaret that he might have preferred to continue having her live at home, and there is little reason to doubt that he meant it. Mrs. Fuller had recently survived a battle with breast cancer and had added yet another son, Arthur Buckminster, to a family that now counted five living children. Had Margaret been more docile, she might have been a priceless aid to her recuperating mother. As it was, however, she was more likely a hindrance than a help. Moreover, she had been away from school too long. With this last point, Margaret herself agreed. A Mr. Emerson had lately begun to lead a school in Boston, and Margaret was enthusiastic to attend.[77]

However, this was far from what her parents had in mind. The elder Margarett, who had so often yielded to Timothy on educational questions, no longer held her tongue. She had grown suspicious of the irreverent college boys with whom her daughter preferred to spend her time. Believing that "a young man must possess salamander qualities to pass thro' our University and be *at all* religious," she saw no advantage "in *a moral point of view*" for Margaret to have much contact with students at her age. Mrs. Fuller had also seen enough of her daughter's flouting of feminine propriety to conclude that Margaret's boyish education had been a ghastly mistake. She declared to Timothy, "I am so well convinced that we have *erred* in our system of educating SM. that I intend with your excellent advice [to] reform our method as much as possible."[78]

Timothy weighed every aspect of the decision; he even took into account that, if Margaret walked to school in Boston in warm weather, the exposure might bring back "the eruption on her face, which has given us so much uneasiness." He thought it would be "a painful thing" to have Margaret so far from home for so long.[79] At last, however, he agreed with his wife: their daughter needed to acquire what he termed "a discreet, modest, unassuming deportment" and to submit to some "feminine discipline" and instruction in the fields of "manners, female propriety, & disposition." The foundation in "virtue and religion" that she so glaringly lacked must now be laid.[80] With these goals in mind, Timothy enrolled Margaret in Miss Susan Prescott's Young Ladies' Seminary in the rural town of Groton, Massachusetts, thirty-five miles northwest of Boston.

Miss Prescott's Young Ladies' Seminary was not as flowery and saccharine as it sounded. The school considered itself a place for serious instruction and prided itself on the spirit of friendship and cooperation that it instilled in its young charges. Yet, as Miss Prescott and her small staff were well aware, there would be no college awaiting its graduates, and the curriculum therefore sought to teach only that level of proficiency befitting an upper-class wife. There was French, but no Latin. Chemistry, astronomy, and botany were offered, but only so much as to cultivate a conversational, rather than a professional understanding. The school was ideal for an adolescent girl of ordinary ambitions. Of course, this was the point where Timothy's plan encountered a snag.

As far as her respect for her father—and perhaps her fear of his wrath—permitted, Margaret fought back. In late January, when she answered the letter that had declared his intention, she reiterated her preference "on every account" for Emerson's school. Knowing how much he enjoyed her company, she reminded him that, during a sojourn at Groton, "I must be compelled to give up seeing you at all."[81] She would accept his plan if he wished, she added, but only with the hope that he would not keep her there very long. Timothy remained firm; he argued that placing Margaret in the care of "a judicious country lady, who will be free and faithful in correcting your faults, & in imparting a relish for . . . rural society, may & must contribute immensely to your immediate worth & to your permanent happiness."[82]

Few who engaged Timothy Fuller in a battle of wills ever emerged victorious. In this instance, Margaret also learned that he had the backing of "my very affectionate Aunt Fuller and my excellent uncles," as she sarcastically called them, all of whom wanted to send her to Groton for four years. By mid-April, the die was cast. Margaret assented, though she complained, "How much I regret to leave this charming place, where I am beloved and go to one where I am an entire stranger and where I must behave entirely by rule." As to the extended banishment recommended by Timothy's sister and brothers, she added tartly, "I thank them for their good will, but do not feel myself particularly obliged to them for such testimonials of it. I always hold that those who love me will wish to have me with them."[83]

Nettled by his daughter's whining insolence, Timothy responded with a message that was the verbal correlative of clenched teeth:

> Your reluctance to go "among strangers" cannot too soon be overcome; & the way to overcome it, is not to remain at home, but to go among them and resolve to deserve and obtain the love & esteem of those who have never before known you. With them you have a fair opportunity to begin the world anew, to avoid the mistakes & faults which have deprived you of some esteem among your present acquaintances.[84]

In his letter, at least, Timothy managed to keep his temper. However, he had delivered a clear message. His daughter had, in his view, done herself palpable harm among people whose opinions mattered, so much so that her standing would be better among strangers than among those who knew her well. If she were wise, she would use the present opportunity to redeem herself. Her chances, as well as her father's patience, were wearing thin.

For Mr. and Mrs. Fuller, the choice had been one of rural values over urban, of piety and virtue over scoffing skepticism. To Margaret, now just shy of her fourteenth birthday and eager to test the wider limits of her world, being sent to Miss Prescott's was worse than a demotion. It was a betrayal. Until now, Margaret had been encouraged to consider herself the intellectual peer of the clever young men of Harvard who danced and conversed with her in her father's house. Precipitously, the rules of the game had changed. Instead of academic renown, Timothy now desired for her only the manners and habits of "a good country lady." Had all of the hard lessons in Latin, the late nights, the headaches, and the nightmares been only for this? To all appearances, the father who had taught her to crave and to reach for a paradise of the mind was slamming the gates of that paradise in her face. Still more ironically, the faults with which she was charged—her abrasiveness, her intellectual competitiveness—were flaws that she had absorbed from Timothy himself. Evidently, they were acceptable as ingredients in a congressman, but not in the strangely foreign thing she had been sentenced to become: a young lady. It took the stagecoach six hours to take her to Groton, long enough to brood on the terrible thought that a girl who translated Virgil and loved Shakespeare was still, in the eyes of the world, only a girl after all. By the time the coach had reached its destination, Margaret had resolved not to like Miss Prescott at all.[85]

Yet even she had to admit that Groton was exceedingly beautiful. Its fertile soil amply watered by the Nashua and Squannacook Rivers, the town had a neat and tasteful appearance, and its better houses could justly be called elegant. Groton was an active manufacturing town, producing shoes, chairs, paper, and various other commodities. Then as now, it attracted wealthy would-be residents with the excellence of its educational opportunities. Margaret soon adopted the daily habit of going for walks with some of the other young ladies after tea, a recreation from which she took "a great deal of pleasure."[86] Much to her surprise, she also learned quickly to "love and admire" Miss Prescott and, after a few months, compared her with "gold without alloy."[87] Her spirits were also lightened by the news that, on May 15, just three days after her first term at school began, her mother had safely delivered a fourth brother. She proposed Frank as a name for the as-yet-anonymous infant, with Frederick as a second choice, and hoped the baby would have three names. Her parents partially granted her wishes, christening the boy Richard Frederick Fuller. Timothy, still not having forgiven Margaret for her resistance to his plans for her education, used Richard's birth as an occasion for a gratuitous barb. It could not be pretended, he wrote her, that the baby "has any extraordinary beauty to recommend him . . . as you will very readily believe when I tell you that he is said to resemble his eldest sister."[88]

Initially, Margaret's only great impatience at Groton was with the level of study, which she considered far beneath her. She later recollected, "I was now in the hands of teachers who had not, since they came on the earth, put to themselves one intelligent question as to their business here. . . . They no doubt injured those who accepted the husks they proferred for bread, and believed that exercise of memory was study, and to know what others knew was the object of knowledge."[89] With some obvious hyperbole, she complained to Timothy, "I feel myself rather degraded from Cicero's Oratory to One and two are how many[.] It is rather a change[,] is it not?" Although she wrote that "Miss Prescott knows best" regarding her instruction, she clearly felt otherwise, for, in the very next line, she asked her father to write to Miss Prescott "with regard to the course of my studies."[90] Though hardly enthralled with her situation, she at least mustered the good grace to say, "I am contented here, which I think is as much as could be expected."[91]

It would have been well if, seeing that his daughter had more or less made her peace with Miss Prescott's, Timothy had suspended his criticisms of her for a time and let the episode run its course. He did not. The thought that his experiment in education had failed was galling. The ingratitude of its subject was unbearable. Timothy's letters to Groton persisted in finding ever more minuscule faults in Margaret. Eventually, he descended into unwarranted nastiness. With exquisite fussiness, he objected when her letters neglected to acknowledge receipt of his and when they failed to give an account of her health. He accused her handwriting of "slovenliness." When she asked for news of his political dealings in Washington, he questioned the sincerity of her interest and, dripping with hostility, railed against her supposed frivolity of mind:

> It is difficult to recollect, when in the very act of writing, any thing which you would consider news. For instance you have no inclination to hear that [Treasury Secretary and Presidential candidate William] Crawford has had a shock of the palsy. . . . These things are unimportant to you;—you would prefer hearing of some negotiation or treaty of marriage, to those between nations; & the rivalry of

beaux or beauties would more affect you than the defeat of Mr. Chas. McCarty by the Ashantees in Africa.[92]

It would have been unthinkable for Margaret to reply in kind to her father's incivility. She bore his criticisms quietly until, in a February 1825 letter, she meekly tried to answer his complaints. Assuring him that she extremely regretted ever being unable to fulfill his slightest wish, she pointed out that her letters had, in fact, acknowledged her receipt of his. Just to be sure, she mentioned the dates of six letters she had recently received from him. As to making note of one's health, she reminded him that he himself routinely violated his own rule; she had not had a letter from him all winter that stated whether he was well. She also suggested, with justification, that such reports suggested a babyish, formulaic approach to letter writing. When she came to his accusation of slovenliness, however, her composure wavered. Between the lines, she insinuated that, as her father, he owed her more leniency, and her tone suggests that she had almost despaired of winning his favor:

By the emphasis laid on the word slovenliness I see what you think of my letters. I confess that I do not bestow on you that attention that I do on other correspondents, who will I think be more critical and less kind. . . . Indeed, I cannot make myself interesting to you: to your strictures on my conduct manners &c however valuable to me I can return nothing but thanks; my delineations . . . would not probably interest you, who can contemplate human nature on so much more extensive a scale and under so many diversified forms.[93]

Her last word before closing this letter was "Goodbye." On some emotional level, she seems to have meant it. She did not write another surviving letter to her father for more than five years. As chilling as Timothy's sarcasm and criticism were to his daughter's affections, they may have been preferable to Mrs. Fuller's seeming indifference. From May, when she left for Miss Prescott's, until the end of the year, Margaret did not receive a single letter from her mother. Small wonder, then, that Margaret asked Miss Prescott for the honor of calling herself the schoolmistress's adopted daughter.

The factual record of how Margaret got on with her schoolmates at Miss

Prescott's is lamentably thin. However, there exists a fascinating, if unreliable source. Although she dabbled in the genre here and there, Fuller never thought of herself as a writer of fiction. Nevertheless, when she wrote about herself, she had a persistent urge to fictionalize, preferring to attack the troublesome issues in her life from a standpoint of imaginative romance rather than from the perspective of literal truth. An outstanding example of this tendency concerns her time at Miss Prescott's: an extended sketch, known today as "Mariana." Published in 1844 as part of the mostly nonfictional *Summer on the Lakes*, "Mariana" ostensibly concerns a former boarding-school classmate, the news of whose death Fuller receives while visiting Chicago. However, Fuller herself admitted that the main character was partly autobiographical.[94] A girl of strange impulses and otherworldly inspirations, Mariana was no dead classmate, but rather a living manifestation of Fuller's own personality. Given that such inner visions are as much a part of ourselves as the literal events of our lives, "Mariana" may be accepted for its metaphorical truths. Fuller's fiction reflects the very real discomforts she endured at Miss Prescott's, and it reveals the agitated emotions and unsettled frame of mind that beset her there.

Mariana comes to Fuller's fictionalized boarding school as the daughter of a Spanish-Creole father—an ethnicity that the period's fiction treated as a code for untamed exoticism. Though she initially enthralls her classmates with her love of wild dances and sudden songs, Mariana soon alienates them with her "haughty caprice" and sudden, unexplained vanishings into solitude.[95] Time and again, chafing under "the restraints and narrow routine" of the school, Mariana launches small personal rebellions against authority.[96] It is a pattern of behavior that the other, conformity-loving girls find impossible to understand, and Mariana inspires a host of enemies. The inevitable crisis comes, oddly, in the form of a practical joke. Having put on heavy rouge for a school theatrical, Mariana continues the habit after the play is over. Despising this affectation more heartily than they would reject either "vice or malignity," the other girls respond with one of those youthful conspiracies that blur the line between innocent fun and savage retribution.[97] One day in the school dining hall, Mariana raises her eyes to discover that every girl in the room has caked her cheeks with rouge in mockery of her own attempt at fashion. Seeing that even the teachers and servants are enjoying the prank, Mariana beats down the impulse to dash from the hall and stoically finishes her meal. Later in her room, however, she throws herself on the floor in convulsions and is discovered unconscious.

From this trial, Mariana arises "an altered being," quietly inflamed and morally poisoned by the knowledge that everyone has sided against her.[98] She gives up all her eccentric behaviors and appears to sink into a routine of study and conformity. In fact, she embarks on a subtle campaign of vengeance, imperceptibly playing on the small jealousies and insecurities of her schoolmates and turning them against one another. Mariana remains at this game for four months until a climactic evening when the head of school summons her to stand before the entire school and face charges, "too well-founded, of calumny and falsehood."[99] Seeing no way to shield herself from blame, Mariana throws herself against the iron hearth and beats her head against it until she knocks herself senseless. For several days she lies inert, the victim of a nervous disorder. Again, crisis transforms her. Whereas her first disgrace plunged her into vengeful self-pity, the second opens her eyes to "the baseness of cruelty and falsehood, the loveliness of truth."[100] Buoyed by the sympathy of the lady who has taken charge of her convalescence, Mariana returns to health and humility. She begs and receives the forgiveness of her schoolmates and is soon after summoned home. Fuller writes, "She went thither a wonderfully instructed being, though in ways those who had sent her forth to learn little dreamed of. Never was forgotten the vow of the returning prodigal. . . . A wild fire was tamed in that hour of penitence at the boarding school, such as has oftentimes wrapped court and camp in its destructive glow."[101]

Mariana and the youthful Fuller have many traits in common. Like Fuller, Mariana is given to disturbed sleep and somnambulism. Each girl perplexes potential friends with her strangely passionate energy and then drives them away with her arrogance and pedantry. Although Mariana is "very loving, even infatuated in her own affections," she seems to love only those whom she can dominate.[102] Attempting to rule "like a queen, in the midst of her companions," neither Margaret nor Mariana dreams that love must be gently coaxed rather than commanded and controlled.[103] Another similarity links Fuller with her fiction: the rouge that Mariana applies to her cheeks may have been a refiguring of the angry red blemishes that were Margaret's parents' despair. The scene of mockery in the eating hall may actually have happened—not to ridicule the victim's sense of fashion, but her unsightly skin.

Reading Fuller's papers, one is continually struck by the mental inward-ness with which she lived her life. Thoughts and reactions often matter more to her than events, and the impression that an experience leaves on her is often clearer than the details of the experience itself. So it is with the real-life underpinnings of "Mariana." Whether Margaret was really the victim of a school-wide practical joke; whether she undertook a campaign of dark retali-ation; whether she ever had the kind of self-destructive fits that came over her fictional heroine—no known letter or journal confirms or refutes. What can be said with certainty is that, at the beginning of April 1825, less than a year after she arrived, Margaret's parents whisked her away from Miss Prescott's, never to return. The reasons given were sensible enough. It was clear, for one thing, that Margaret's education had been stagnating. In addition, whatever frictions may have persisted between them, Margarett Crane Fuller missed her elder daughter at home. In the spring of 1825, the Fuller family had five children under the age of ten. The elder Margarett, a gentle woman who was likely overwhelmed by such numerical odds, could have benefited from her daughter's firmness as she struggled to ward off domestic chaos.

In a letter to Miss Prescott, almost five years after the fact, the younger Margaret points to another, unspecified reason for her leaving Groton. Here, in Fuller's own words, is all we know of that cause:

> You need not fear to revive painful recollections. I often think of those sad experiences. True, they agitate me deeply. But it was best so. They have had a most powerful effect on my character. I tremble at what-ever looks like dissimulation. The remembrance of that evening sub-dues every proud, passionate impulse. My beloved supporter in those sorrowful hours, your image shines as fair to my mind's eye as it did in 1825, when I left you with my heart overflowing with gratitude for your singular and judicious tenderness. Can I ever forget that to your treatment in that crisis of youth I owe the true life,—the love of Truth and Honor?[104]

From this fragment, a faint outline can be traced. In some circumstance at least partly reminiscent of Mariana's, Margaret sustained some kind of deep injury to her pride. As in her later fiction, she fought back with some kind of dishonorable "dissimulation" that sowed discord among her schoolmates. A sad, painful interview with the head of the school ensued. Miss Prescott evidently confronted Fuller with her deceptions and powerfully shocked her by showing her the meanness of her conduct. Then, in a fashion for whose tenderness Fuller was enduringly grateful, Miss Prescott impressed on her the importance of honesty and fair dealing. It may be that, after this critical event, Margaret was too ashamed to continue at Miss Prescott's. It is even remotely possible that her offense was so grievous that she was asked to withdraw. The details of the matter remain one of the more tantalizing gaps in Fuller's life story.

When Margaret returned to Cambridge in April 1825, she was outwardly not much different from the plump, blemished, awkward girl who had left her hometown ten and a half months before. Beneath the surface, however, she was subtly but significantly changed. She had learned the lesson that unusually bright children inevitably learn: that the world will not love them simply for being bright. It was not that she had surrendered the tremendous self-regard that struck so many as arrogance; it was not like her to cease to be anything she had already become. But she had discovered the importance of tempering her ingrained loftiness with other values: a knowledge that her gifts could be used for noble or ignoble ends, and a desire to know the difference; a sense that it was better, in the long run, to bear the insults of others than recklessly striking back; and a degree of compassion for people who were less exceptional than she. Although there was not much of the Puritan in Fuller's thinking, she was willing to believe that God chastens the children whom he loves in order to make them more worthy of grace. She later wrote, "I have been a chosen one; the lesson of renunciation was early, fully taught, and the heart of stone quite broken through. The Great Spirit wished to leave me no refuge but itself."[105]

Fuller's failure to find an emotional home among her schoolmates foreshadowed a larger and more important fact of her later existence: the almost inevitable isolation of a spirit that, as it rose toward a higher concept of itself, found time and again that it could only travel alone. The loneliness was heightened by the fact that the striving spirit found itself in a female body. Fuller later observed, "From an early age I have felt that I was not born to the common womanly lot. I knew I should never find a being who could keep the key of my character; that there would be none on whom I could always lean, from whom I could always learn; that I should be a pilgrim and sojourner on the earth, and that the birds and foxes would be surer of a place to lay the[ir] head[s] than I."[106] Another cause of this spiritual separateness came from the prickliness she continued to display long after she ceased being a school-girl. For the remainder of her life, Fuller remained conscious of the "want of delicacy and tenderness" of which she was sometimes guilty. It was a weak-ness against which she continually struggled but could never quite subdue. Uncomfortably aware of this flaw on her own part, she was all the more dis-appointed when she observed it in others. Yet, knowing from her own inner life that someone who was brusque and overly direct could also possess a "heart capable of pure and intelligent love," she tried to forgive lapses in per-sonal diplomacy, forever believing that "we shall all be better, and do better as we grow."[107] Fuller left the school at Groton believing that Miss Prescott's kind but firm chastening had shown her a better way to live. Yet her life had hardly begun.

CHAPTER THREE

"MARGARET GOODCHILD"

*I have learned to believe that nothing,
no! not perfection, is unattainable.*

—MARGARET FULLER TO SUSAN PRESCOTT,
July 11, 1825

THE GREATEST TRANSFORMATIONS OFTEN TAKE PLACE AWAY FROM
the common view. The changes inside an egg or a chrysalis were invisible
until modern science pushed back the limits of our seeing. It seems natural
for human beings in the throes of metamorphosis also to seek the shadows.
In the years from mid-1825 through 1829, Sarah Margaret Fuller became a
woman. In terms of a written record, though, this was to be the darkest
period of her life. Her father, after eight years in Congress, did not stand for
reelection in 1824 and returned home to serve as speaker of the Massachusetts state legislature and to revive his legal practice. Thus, the once-steady
flow of letters to and from Washington evaporated. Fewer than a dozen dated
letters from Margaret to any recipient survive from this period, and only in
1830 did she report that she was beginning to keep a journal "in fearless
sincerity."[1] It would serve as her refuge in a time of "bitter tears, struggles,
and aspirations."[2] However, once this early record had served its private purpose, she burned it, erasing the most vital record of one of her most transformative times.

During these years, the Fuller family added its last two members, each
touched by sorrow. A fifth brother, James Lloyd Fuller, known as Lloyd and
born in 1826, was mentally challenged. A final sibling, Edward Breck Fuller,

"a beautiful child" as Margaret later called him, was born the following year. Because he was born on her eighteenth birthday, Margaret was given the promise that he would be "her child," and she bonded with him closely.[3] Little Edward, however, did not live to see his second winter; he died on September 15, 1829. His illness, of which no diagnosis apparently survives, took several weeks to finish its work. As he slowly weakened, Margaret took care of him for half of every night. Finding that contact soothed him, she carried him in her arms for hours, glad to feel "his gentle weight of helpless purity" against her heart.[4] For years afterward, she could not look at violets without a pang. They reminded her of his large, pleading blue eyes, of how much she had longed to stop his suffering, and of the horrible knowledge that she could not. Yet neither of the births nor Edward's death found its way into Margaret's letters until years later. Most of what we know of her from this time comes through the eyes of others. When, at full maturity, she was ready to announce herself, she would do so in full voice. Now, however, was a time for relative silence; a steady, patient gathering of energies was taking place.

When Fuller left Miss Prescott's shortly before her fifteenth birthday, her formal schooling was almost at an end. Except for a brief return to the Port School, where she received tutoring in Greek, her school days were over. Her education, however, had barely begun. In those times, it was not unusual for boys of fourteen or fifteen to begin their studies at Harvard. This path was, of course, barred to Margaret because of her sex. In her mind, however, there was never much question that her studies would continue, even if there were no institution to give them sanction or structure. Almost immediately after returning to Cambridge from Groton, Margaret embarked on one of the most ambitious odysseys of self-education imaginable—one that would test even her formidable ambition. Now more than ever, reading became the core of her existence.

No longer dependent on her father to direct her, she plunged into her books with far more zeal than system. The month she turned sixteen, she reported to Miss Prescott that she was studying Epictetus, Racine, Milton, and an assortment of Castilian ballads. She immersed herself in the memoirs of European statesmen like Frederick the Great and Cardinal de Retz. Taking a particular interest in romance languages, she devoured the poetry of the great Italians: Dante, Petrarch, Tasso, Alfieri, and others. She basked

in the novels and *Confessions* of Rousseau, and she called Voltaire her "pleasure."[5] Her friend James Freeman Clarke noted that, by nineteen, she was
also familiar with the masterpieces of the Spanish renaissance.[6] Fuller's
absorption in continental literature became so deep that, many years later,
she joked about having "well nigh 'forgotten [her] English'" in her youth.[7]
Nevertheless, she also found time for the novels of Samuel Richardson, Jane
Austen, Benjamin Disraeli, and Edward Bulwer-Lytton, and the poetry of

James Freeman
Clarke made his
pencil sketch of
Fuller when the
two were in their
late teens.
(COURTESY OF
HOUGHTON LIBRARY,
HARVARD
UNIVERSITY)

Wordsworth, Coleridge, Byron, and Shelley. This summary does not attempt
to encompass all the reading of her late teens.[8]

It was probably in her late teens, too, that Fuller first heard the preaching
of the gaunt, narrow-shouldered Ralph Waldo Emerson, who had given up
school teaching and was now a promising Unitarian minister. Though she
seems to have made no note of just what he said, several of his sermons sank
deep into her mind, making landmarks in what she later called her "spiritual
history." From him, she first learned the meaning of "an inward life."[9] In
short order he became in her eyes "that only clergyman of all possible clergy-
men," a status that he continued to hold for her long after he ceased to be a
clergyman in fact, resigning from the ministry in September 1832. For sev-

eral years, Fuller regretted that she could find no convenient way of meeting him. Nevertheless, she continued to "keep his image bright" in her mind.[10]

Fuller's fanatical drive toward self-improvement was spurred by Lydia Maria Francis, a baker's daughter eight years her senior. In 1824, at the age of twenty-two, Francis had published *Hobomok*, a novel about intermarriage between whites and native people in early New England that remains a minor classic. She had followed that book with *The Rebels*, a novel of pre-Revolutionary Boston. A few years were still to pass before she acquired her more famous married name: Lydia Maria Child. The origin of Fuller's acquaintance with Francis is hard to trace.[11] Their friendship was clearly strengthened, however, when each discovered the other's interest in the metaphysics of John Locke and the novels of Madame de Staël. Of all Fuller's reading in this period, Staël's *Corinne* may have sunk deepest into her spirit. Resembling both a priestess of Apollo and a woman "completely natural in the ordinary relationships of life," Corinne is so renowned for her intellect and originality of language that the people of Rome celebrate her with a triumphal parade. She has "such a superior mind, such deep learning . . . that ordinary rules for judging women cannot be applied to her."[12] Eager to discover female models for her future life and finding few, Fuller was doubtless pleased to find one, even in fiction. Also planted in her mind was the supposition that the one city on earth where a bold and brilliant woman like Corinne might flourish just might be Rome.

As with so many of Fuller's early liaisons, her relationship with Francis was principally a friendship of the book, but its bookishness made it no less sincere. Through their shared reading and discussions, Fuller came to admire Francis for her "pleasant and spirited way of thinking" and hailed her as "a natural person,—a most rare thing in this age of cant and pretension."[13] Fuller also could not have failed to be impressed by the confidence and creative energy that had made her friend famous at such an early age. She wrote to Susan Prescott that, thanks to Francis, she felt "the power of industry growing every day, and . . . I have learned to believe that nothing, no! not perfection, is unattainable."[14]

Francis had inspired Fuller to aim at more than mere distinction. Fuller had seen innumerable people who, in her view, possessed genius but wholly lacked the gifts of social grace and "the power of pleasurable excitement." For her part, she resolved to combine both superior intellect and consummate social skill. She was well aware that she had a better start in the first field than in the second. "I am wanting," she admitted, "in that intuitive tact and polish, which nature has bestowed upon some, but which I must acquire." Yet, she bravely added, "all such hindrances may be overcome by an ardent spirit."[15]

Two stories of education are involved here: one pertaining personally to Fuller and the other concerning America at large, for it may be fairly said that the intellects of Fuller and her country came of age at approximately the same time. We must set aside her personal story for a while and consider the philosophical and religious ideas that had seemed self-evident to Timothy Fuller's ancestors but were to become intolerable to his descendants. It made sense for Margaret to focus on Locke, for his was an influence against which she and the rest of American literary culture were to struggle for many years. Locke was one of the intellectual fathers of the American Revolution; in the 1760s and 1770s, as the colonies edged toward revolt, pamphlet after pamphlet cited him on the rights of man and the social contract.[16] With its assertion that a ruler who failed to serve the people's interest had no right to their allegiance, Locke's *Second Treatise on Civil Government* supplied an indispensable foundation for the Declaration of Independence.

But if Locke's politics had dovetailed perfectly with American ideas on the right to revolution, another area of his thought posed more of a problem. Apart from his writings about democracy and individual rights, Locke remains best known for an essay on human understanding which argues that human beings begin life as tabulae rasae and come to possess feelings and ideas only through contact with the world. Human consciousness, he argued, is formed from the outside in, not from the inside out. In Timothy Fuller's generation, most educated Americans would have explained the origins of knowledge by invoking this theory.

Locke's idea of the natural emptiness of human consciousness clashed uncomfortably with the American need to believe in the uniqueness and sanctity of the human soul. Though they would have disagreed on the extent of the family resemblance, most Americans of Timothy Fuller's generation thought of human beings as children of God. What was one to make of that relationship if the Father imparted nothing to the mind of the child, except a passive capacity to receive? This description of the human condition was still less satisfying to Margaret's generation, who wanted to think of human beings as more than empty receptacles to be filled with knowledge. Locke had given Adams and Jefferson the logical and moral impetus to rebel against a crown and an empire. For their grandchildren's generation, however, his denial of the possibility of innate genius and goodness became the new authority against which to revolt.

The philosophical debate in post-Revolutionary New England spilled over into religion. The faith that the Puritans had carried with them to America two centuries earlier had not viewed humanity in a charitable light. Whereas God existed for them in indescribably radiant glory, man was, by comparison, a wretch, depraved by original sin and wholly undeserving of redemption. In the words of Calvinist minister and poet Edward Taylor, even the best of Christians was no more than a "Bag of Botches, Lump of Loathesomeness," capable of being saved from hellfire only by the undeserved mercy of God.[17] While this theology repels most modern minds with its harshness, it once attracted and bound millions with its firmness. In addition, so long as the settlers experienced their surroundings as a wild, inhospitable frontier, the idea of a wrathful, exacting God seemed like a reasonable explanation for the hardships of daily life.

This creed made less and less sense as two powerful influences—the principles of the European Enlightenment and rising financial prosperity—began to thaw the icy theological assumptions of eastern Massachusetts. The Enlightenment asserted that man, instead of being vile and insignificant, was a creature of reason and innate beauty. Prosperity spoke to Bostonians with the even more persuasive logic of wealth. Give the ordinary person delicious food, fine clothes, and handsome furniture, and he will quickly conclude that he deserves them. In the New England countryside, where both the ideas of Voltaire and the blessings of commerce were slower to penetrate, the older Calvinist beliefs maintained their hold. But in the parlors of Beacon Hill and in the classrooms of Harvard, people hungered for a different dispensation, a system of beliefs that affirmed both the possibilities of man's goodness and the gentleness of God's love.

This need was answered by the rise of a milder, more humanistic Christian faith called Unitarianism, the creed to which Timothy Fuller converted at some unascertained time. Unitarians are so called because they emphasize, quite literally, the unity of God. Mainstream Christians assert that God exists simultaneously in three persons: the Father, the Son, and the Holy

Spirit. In their view, God and his son Jesus Christ are equally divine. By arguing that there is no division in the personality of God and that the Father
alone is God, the Unitarians raise a key distinction: the idea that, although
his teachings possessed divine authority, Jesus was not qualitatively different
from any other human being. He was distinct from other people, not because
he possessed a unique, holy essence, but because he developed his human
capacities to an unequalled degree. Theoretically at least, the same potential
existed in everyone.[18]

As Margaret Fuller was passing through girlhood, the most progressive
wing of the Unitarian church was pressing still further. In 1819, the brilliantly eloquent minister William Ellery Channing denied that God could be
cruel and wrathful; he urged his followers to worship God "not because his
will is irresistible, but because his will is the perfection of virtue."[19] It made
no sense to Channing that God would bring people into the world already
maddened by sin, only to damn them later for manifesting the evil traits that
He himself had given them.

Channing instead spoke of God as he would of a kind, patient father who
wants his children to improve, who takes joy in their progress, accepts the
penitent, and punishes the incorrigible. Channing thought the religious
duty of human beings lay not in fearful subservience, but in working to
achieve, through ever-increasing demonstrations of love, piety, and philan-
thropy, "a growing likeness to the Supreme Being."[20] What was moral for
human beings, Channing insisted, must also be moral for God. As people
strove to be kinder and better in God's image, they had, in turn, a right to
expect mercy and justice from Him. As Margaret Fuller read and discussed
Lockean metaphysics with Lydia Francis, the first verbal shots of a new revolution had already been fired.

Yet to some, Unitarianism lacked the awe-inspiring power of Calvinist
teachings. Dreadful as the Puritan God had been, his very dreadfulness had
a sublime majesty, an authentically holy terror. As one believer is said to
have observed, the older teachings "made God so great—SO GREAT!"[21] It
was, in part, the lack of sublimity and excitement in Unitarian worship that
had made Margaret such a disaffected churchgoer. When expressed by a
superb minister like Channing, the paternal forgiveness of the Unitarian God
could move men to tears of gladness. In the hands of a lesser preacher, the
emphasis on reason over revelation could seem, in Emerson's phrase,

"corpse-cold": dry, hyper-rational, and too far removed from the strife and struggles of the listener.[22] If the liberal believers of Boston and Cambridge did not care for agony in their worship, they still craved ecstasy. Revolted by the efforts of Locke "to explain soul out of sense, deducing mind from matter, or tracing the origin of ideas to nerves, vibrations, vibratiuncles," dissatisfied with the well-intentioned blandness of their churches, Fuller and her contemporaries sought deliverance to a new spiritual dimension.[23]

For many of Fuller's male friends, that deliverance began at one of the few places in her hometown where she could not go: Harvard College. Harvard's refusal to admit women did not prevent Fuller from reading as much as, and, in fact, even more than, most of the young men inside its gates. Indeed, her exclusion spared her a great deal of boredom and wasted time. The teaching at the college was notoriously stultifying. It included "no lectures, no unnecessary comments, no flowery illustrations. One ground in one's Latin and mathematics, under a pair of candles, and the next day one ground them out again."[24] Most of the greatest strengths to be acquired in a Harvard classroom—intellectual discipline, exactness of speech, and a powerful foundation in the classics—Fuller had gotten already in her father's study.

There were, however, one man and one institution at Harvard who might have benefited her tremendously. The man was Edward Tyrrel Channing, younger brother of William Ellery Channing and the college's Boylston Professor of Rhetoric and Oratory. Professor Channing guided Emerson, Thoreau, and a crowd of other future luminaries as they sharpened their skills as writers. For sheer knowledge, Fuller may have surpassed every one of Channing's students. Unlike them, however, she never had a mentor to teach her how to spin her knowledge into lucid, melodic prose. With no Channing to comment on her work and shape her style, she was destined always to know more than she could pleasingly communicate.

The great institution that Harvard denied Fuller was its library, which could only be called a marvel. Boasting more than twenty thousand volumes, the library had no equal in America. It was also where the real learning was taking place. There, as Margaret's friend James Freeman Clarke recalled, his classmates put aside their Thucydides and Xenophon and picked up Macaulay. Their real professors of rhetoric, he remembered, were Charles Lamb, Sir Walter Scott, and William Wordsworth.[25] Among the great British romantics, however, there was one above all others who left his imprint on the minds of the Harvard scholars: the ethereal, dream-spinning Samuel Taylor Coleridge.

To anyone who has descended into the swirling realms of fantasy conjured by Coleridge's "Christabel" and "Kubla Khan," it is clear that their author could never have been satisfied with a reality based only on the senses. Coleridge desired another dimension of thought and experience, and he sought it everywhere from writing poetry to acquiring the dependency on laudanum that shattered his health and made a chaos of his career.

The young men of Harvard cared less about Coleridge's poetry than his prose writings on the nature of consciousness. Possessing a mind "habituated *to the Vast*," Coleridge scorned the "rationally educated" intellects around him, to whom the Universe was "but a mass of *little things*."[26] He rejected the Lockean assumption that the senses offered the only true way of knowing the world. Coleridge was attracted instead to the work of the German philosopher Immanuel Kant, who argued that some ideas, like time and space, existed *a priori*, apart from learning or the senses. Kant stated further that the moral law "begins with my invisible self . . . and displays to me a world that has true infinity, but which can only be detected through the understanding, and with which . . . I know myself to be in . . . universal and necessary connection."[27] Against a view of the world grounded entirely in sensation, Kant posited a transcendental reality, capable of being known only by an invisible faculty, seemingly analogous to a soul.

Coleridge became Kant's most influential publicist in the English-speaking world. In his *Aids to Reflection*, Coleridge marked out a distinction between two categories of knowledge: the Understanding, whose grasp was limited to the senses, and the Reason, which he defined as "the Power of Universal and necessary Convictions, the Source and Substance of Truths above Sense." Whereas Kant had stopped short of inferring any religious implications from his bifurcated theory of knowledge, Coleridge took a decisive step beyond. He proclaimed the Reason to be "pre-eminently spiritual" and a product "of the same grace by which we are privileged to say 'Our Father.'"[28] Coleridge had both proclaimed and Christianized Kant's Reason.

For Harvard students who, like Clarke and Hedge, aspired to become Unitarian ministers, Coleridge was deeply formative. Eager for ideas that they could connect with their religious studies, they found Coleridge's Christian focus ideal. Adopting his distinction between understanding and reason, they learned to use logic to systematize their ideas while they sought Truth within their hearts. In 1833, Fuller's friend Hedge published an essay on Coleridge that captured the excitement he and his peers were finding in exploring their interior consciousnesses: "The effect . . . is like being in the company of one who has inhaled an exhilarating gas. We witness the inspiration, and are astounded at the effects, but we can form no conception of the feeling until we ourselves have experienced it." Men like Hedge and Clarke, as well as Emerson, Bronson Alcott, and later Thoreau, who had inhaled the gas, felt as if they had perhaps discovered a path toward a new knowledge, as Hedge put it, of "substance and life, free will and fate, God and eternity."[29] Emerson, upon reading Hedge's essay, pronounced the work a "living leaping Logos."[30] The American transcendental era had begun.

Fuller, however, did not become a devotee of Coleridge, nor did she promptly become a transcendentalist. Although her exclusion from Harvard limited her in some ways—her lack of formal instruction as a writer would be a matter of lifelong regret—it also enabled her to read more broadly and with a greater feeling of adventure than most of her Harvard friends. Even the students there who found a second home in the library tended to be chiefly Anglophilic and Germanophilic in their pursuits. Fuller shared these interests, but she was also engrossed in the masterworks of France, Italy, and Spain. She was far too eclectic to be satisfied with a single line of thought. Moreover, her exclusion from Harvard meant that, unlike Hedge, Clarke, and their brethren, she had no need or impulse to adapt her thought to fit in with Unitarian theology. Her mind was in this sense freer than theirs. At the same time, it lacked the same kind of safe moral center. Whereas their philosophical excursions typically ended with a return to Christ, hers could take her to stranger shores.

For the time being, at any rate, the shape of her mind mattered less to Margaret than the figure she was cutting in Cambridge society. At first, despite the hard lessons she had absorbed at Miss Prescott's, she continued to stumble. One instance suggests the pattern. In 1826, the Fuller family settled into a fine Georgian mansion in an exclusive part of old Cambridge with a captivating view of the Charles River. Timothy remained desirous of securing an ambassadorship with the help of President Adams, in part because he hoped to give his children—and Margaret in particular—a taste of European culture.[31] With this plan in mind, he held a dinner and ball at his newly acquired mansion in the chief executive's honor. The plan failed; the president did not stay for the ball. Though he continued to value Fuller's political opinions and still consulted with him long after the end of his presidency, Adams never offered Timothy a diplomatic post.[32] For Margaret, the evening was a greater disaster. Overweight and squinting, she descended to the party tightly corseted into a poorly cut, pink silk gown. Striving for a memorable effect, she had had her hair "curled all over her head."[33] Her indelicate choice of wardrobe, her absurd coiffure, and her ungainly dancing briefly turned her into a laughingstock among Cambridge gossips.[34]

Where many saw a butt of ridicule, at least one, thankfully, saw a rough diamond. Among the staid and strict Harvard faculty, there was a professor of mathematics and natural philosophy named John Farrar, "a true teacher," as one student called him, "almost the only one in the whole corps of professors."[35] The nervously energetic Farrar had an English-born wife, Eliza Rotch Farrar, whose particular avocation was improving the deportment of young ladies. What Henry Higgins became for Eliza Doolittle, Mrs. Farrar became in short order for Margaret Fuller. Thomas Wentworth Higginson was a friend of the Farrar family. He remembered clearly how Mrs. Farrar set about remodeling Fuller, making her "less abrupt, less self-asserting, more *comme il faut* in ideas, manners, and even costume."[36] In 1837 Mrs. Farrar published *The Young Lady's Friend*, a treatise on manners that touches every subject from the art of conversation to skin care to the proper darning of stockings. Yet if she could righteously inveigh against the wearing of shabby feathers and crushed artificial flowers as "a positive evil," Farrar equally despised the notion that a young woman should aspire only to be pleasingly ornamental.[37] She strongly emphasized that happiness depended not on appearance but on "the faithful performance of duty . . . based upon love to God and love to man." All her advice pointed toward securing "the happiness of virtue [and] the healthfulness of constant, vigorous action, both of body and mind."[38] Farrar not only took Fuller in hand but also issued edicts to the girl's hairdresser and dressmaker. She took Margaret with her on social calls and on short vacations. She also exposed Fuller to young models of sociable charm. Harriet Fay, a striking blonde, became Fuller's paragon in all things hair-related, though Higginson felt that Margaret's imitations fell far short of the ideal.

Another acquaintance made through Farrar was destined to make a more lasting impression. Eliza's New Orleans–born cousin Anna Barker, a girl of consummate breeding and exotic good looks, was then boarding with the Farrars. Three years Margaret's junior, Anna possessed both a nymph-like form and a confiding, harmonious soul, as well as a charm that was simultaneously "sportive and sweet." At the outset, few observed anything remarkable about the relationship between the two girls. One mutual friend, however, did begin to guess the effect of Anna's presence on Margaret. It seemed to William Henry Channing, the somewhat grandiloquent nephew of the great minister, that Margaret wanted "to transfuse [Anna] with her force . . . and to fill her to glowing with her own lyric fire." He felt that Margaret desired "to live in [her new friend's] experience," to act as her guardian angel and "with unfelt ministry to weave bright threads in her web of fate." Channing insisted that the love Fuller felt for her new friend was "sisterly."[39] However, Anna Barker was the kind of girl whose smiles and words could sow potent seeds of feeling in a companion's mind. These traces of emotion might lie relatively dormant for a time, but they could then emerge in the most surprising ways.

Just how far Eliza Farrar succeeded in her campaign to reform Margaret as a social being may be fairly debated. The available sources paint an unclear picture. Certainly, Fuller never before found it so easy to make friends. A trio of girls she had known for years—Elizabeth Randall, Amelia Greenwood, and Almira Penniman—formed the center of her social life, but she was now succeeding in a broader sphere. The other adolescents with whom she mingled were frequently fascinated by both her sparkle and her verbal barbs—as long as they were pointed at someone else. Elizabeth Palmer Peabody, the eldest of the legendary Peabody sisters, was among those taken with the new and improved Margaret. Recalling their first encounter in 1828, she wrote, "I was impressed strongly with her perfect good nature. It seemed to me her eyes overflowed with fun, & this fun was a pure sense of the comic,—inevitable to an intellect sharp as a diamond."[40]

Fuller had also acquired another distinctly appealing trait: the power to take the ordinary hopes and feelings of those she favored and to raise them to a height of poetic beauty and importance. It was said that Fuller "by the conversation of an hour or two, could . . . make an epoch in one's life." After such an encounter with her, one admirer averred, countless friends "came to some clear view of a difficult question, saw our way open before us to a higher plane of life, and were led to some definite resolution or purpose which has had a bearing on all our subsequent career."[41] "She was," in the view of those who flourished under her encouragement, "a balloon of sufficient power to take us all up with her into the serene depth of heaven . . . far above the low details of life."[42] Fuller discovered a gift for seeing in others the power to become the heroes of their own triumphant dramas. This was how Margaret showed love: not through gentle shows of sympathy, but through friendly challenge, the imposition of exacting standards, and exhortations toward excellence. It was not entirely different from the way Timothy had expressed his love for her.

Not all her peers received her favor. By Fuller's own admission, the title of friend "was not given lightly" by her.[43] One acquaintance observed that she required "a sort of personal submission before newcomers could be admitted to a cordial understanding."[44] Though Clarke insisted that she demanded only one thing of her friends—"that they should have some 'extraordinary generous seeking,' that they should not be satisfied with the common routine of life"   she did not always find that her conditions had been met.[45] For those who failed this test, social encounters with her could be chilling. There were many who thought her "dogmatic" and "sneering" and others who complained of her want of graciousness and her tendency to treat them "like a plaything."[46] Even as she praised her companion's humor, Elizabeth Peabody fretted that Margaret seemed to be laughing at her. Clarke admitted, "She seemed, and was to the multitude, a haughty and supercilious person."[47] As long as the mediocre and the worldly outnumbered the exceptional and the spiritually striving, a fondness for Margaret could only be a minority position.

Fuller's competitiveness made it hard for her to meet others on even terms. Her relationships tended to have a superior and inferior partner—and it was Margaret who usually claimed the upper hand. There was also often an inequality in another sense. Eager as she was to plumb the depths of the people she met, Fuller seldom granted the same kind of admission to her own innermost feelings. She was not yet twenty when she observed, "Those who [have] professed to seek my friendship, and whom indeed I have often truly loved, have always learned to content themselves with [an] inequality in the connexion which I have never striven to veil."[48] Beneath her confident, even jaunty exterior lay a sensitivity that few of her friends ever fully recognized. Privately, she wrote, "I blame not those who think the heart cannot bleed because it is so strong, but little they dream what lies concealed beneath the determined courage. Yet mine has been the Spartan sternness, smiling while it hides the wound."[49]

This wound took the form of an intermittent depression that, at its full force, threatened to consume her. After her death, William Henry Channing published fragments of her writing that offered glimpses of the abyss into which Margaret sometimes gazed:

> The heart which hopes and dares is also accessible to terror, and this falls upon it like a thunderbolt. . . . *This* is the dart within the heart, as well as I can tell it:—At moments, the music of the universe, which daily I am upheld by hearing, seems to stop. I fall like a bird when the sun is eclipsed, not looking for such darkness. The sense of my individual law—that lamp of life—flickers. . . . I feel as, when a suffering child, I would go and lie with my face to the ground, to sob away my little life.[50]

These dark moments, Fuller admitted, supplied a motive for the unrelenting zeal with which she drove herself to learn and achieve. The joys of growth and self-discovery were not enough. She wrote, "Remember that only through aspirations, which sometimes make me what is called unreasonable, have I been enabled to vanquish unpropitious circumstances, and save my soul alive."[51] If her refusal to disclose her true self and her implacable drive seemed like "cold doubt [and] selfish arrogance," she accepted the fact and asked only to be forgiven.[52] She kept moving forward because she feared that stopping to observe the wreck of life around her would annihilate her.

If her aspirations saved her soul, however, they also brought a terrible frustration. Even as she increased her intellectual powers, she wondered how, as a woman, she was ever to use them. Without an object, she realized, the triumphs of her intellect were worthless and empty. Her studies, which were her greatest source of pride, were also potentially the cause of a crippling despondency. James Freeman Clarke felt that she actually did at times "despair of all the labor she had taken under the sun." While it may seem clear to us that Fuller was languishing for want of something significant to do, those who observed her at the time thought her melancholy might also vanish if she found someone to love: "She felt keenly . . . the want of a home for her heart. Full of a profound tendency toward life, capable of an ardent love, her affections were thrown back on her heart, to become stagnant, and for a while to grow bitter there."[53]

It is impossible to know just how much of Fuller's social difficulties arose from her being an intellectual young woman at a time when ideas were still seen as a masculine realm. Among friends like Hedge and Clarke who understood her best, Fuller's sex seemed to have been no great obstacle. Her forthrightness and absence of tact would have been somewhat off-putting in any form, male or female. Unfortunately, though, even in our own time, the stigma that can attach to the cleverest person in the room sometimes intensifies if that person happens to be a woman. To imagine that Fuller could conduct herself as she did and never run afoul of gender prejudice is fanciful. To suppose that such biases were alone responsible for her troubles is equally so.

All at once, at nineteen, Fuller found a welcome outlet for all her feelings: a young man who could both share her bitterness and, it seemed, receive her warmest affections. George T. Davis was a distant cousin only four months her senior. For a time, their alliance seemed on its way toward becoming something deeper than friendship. Davis, a member of Harvard's class of 1829, was preparing for a career in law. Among his circle, he was known for his exquisite taste and "his contempt for shows and pretences."[54] Margaret was attracted by his "levity, nay! brilliant vivacity and airy self-possession."[55] He had an intensity reminiscent of her own. She found the lights of his character could be "wintry": while they were generally inspiriting and life-giving, they could also "glare too much upon the tired sense."[56] Davis shared her love of literature, and she wrote him long letters about Byron's *Don Juan* and Richardson's *Clarissa*. However, one of their greatest pleasures seems to have lain in their shared sense of superiority to those around them and the glee with which they verbally dismantled their supposed inferiors. Sarah Clarke, James's sister, was taken aback by the cousins' satirical collaborations. She wrote, "If I had judged only from George and Margaret, I should [have] thought the plan was to pull people to pieces to see what they were made of, and then divert themselves with the fragments. I felt all the time I was with either of them that there was some such design concealed under a manner which was intended to mystify from its very recklessness."[57] Fuller wrote that she and Davis could "communicate more closely with one another than either could with the herd."[58] In the narcissism of early romance, Fuller was delighted to have found someone who, in both his sensitivities and his sarcasm, so resembled herself. She fell in love.

The romance between Fuller and George Davis occurred mostly face-to-face, and only a handful of letters between the two exist. No one seems to question that Margaret loved George, and no one seems to dispute that she was the more assertive party. Nevertheless, her letters to him are only faintly suggestive of her feelings, as, for instance, when she told him, "I shall always be glad to have you come to me when saddened."[59] Indeed, she used her letters more to denigrate sentiment than to proclaim it. Perhaps she feared the intensity of her feelings and was struggling to disguise them, or perhaps the uncertainties of passion were leading her to think more deeply about the role emotion plays in life in general.

For a time, Davis became a sounding board for her religious opinions—a field of discussion where sentiment made her especially uncomfortable. With a tentative double negative and a series of dashes that suggest an agitated mood, she told him that she "d[id] not disbelieve" in the Christian revelation but merely chose to remain ignorant of it for the time being. She cited as her reason a statement that Davis himself had made: "'The philosophers,' you say, 'appealed to the intellect,—Christ to the sympathies'—And these sympathies I do not wish to foster—Shall I quicken the heart to a sense of its wants when I can so ill supply those of the mind?"[60] She told Davis in another letter that he was the only person who could appreciate her true self, that he alone could see her as she truly was.[61] Nevertheless, it was not easy for her to trust her feelings, either for a young man or toward God.

Another letter to Davis discloses the highly relativistic terms on which she was prepared to entertain Christian belief. She did not think such a faith was right for everyone; its value depended on the personality and age of the believer. She conceded that "loving or feeble natures need a positive religion, a visible refuge, a protection." However, she quickly added, "But mine is not such. . . . My affection is strong admiration, not the necessity of giving or receiving assistance or sympathy." When she suffered pain, she did not want to have it soothed so much as she wanted to know and feel it, and thereby to discover its nature and source. Because of this resolve, she continued, "[m]y young life is so singularly barren of illusions." She knew that, as she grew older, her pride and fierceness would erode and she would inevitably "turn from the ardors of Search and Action, to lean on something above." Looking toward that time of dependency filled her with "deepest sadness."[62] The distant prospect of accepting the comforts of the Gospel felt to her like an admission of defeat.

What religious belief, then, did Fuller hold as her teen years neared their end? "I believe," she wrote, "in Eternal Progression. I believe in a God, a Beauty and Perfection to which I am to strive all my life for assimilation." From these two articles of faith, she deduced all the rules by which she meant to live.[63] In Fuller's mythos of perfection, there was no mention of mercy for the weak or forgiveness for the erring. It was perhaps a religion better suited to lions and eagles than to human beings.

Fuller also shared her religious misgivings with her old friend Hedge, who had lately graduated from Harvard Divinity School and had taken a pulpit in West Cambridge. She asked him whether, had he not chosen to become a minister, he would have eschewed Christianity and lived contentedly with what she called "natural religion." Hedge confided that he, too, had once considered Christianity a thing of sympathies rather than ideas. As time passed, however, he had found in his religion "a home for theories cherished before" and for "the most beautifully profound views of life."[64] His answer pleased but did not persuade her.

Meanwhile, as much as Fuller valued Hedge's cultured manner and "daring . . . realizing mind," George Davis remained her closest confidant and beau ideal.[65] He was, as she later expressed it, "the only friend to whom I was all truth and frankness, seeking nothing but equal truth and frankness in return." Perhaps what she loved best about Davis was his contempt for the polite forms and outward shows of goodness. He was, it seemed, determined never to be "like unto [the] Pharisees."[66] Fuller regarded his impatience with mere surfaces a happy omen for the future, a future she expected them to spend together.

No one knows just how George betrayed her trust, but a heartrending letter from Fuller to their mutual friend James Freeman Clarke, written approximately two years later, leaves no doubt as to the effects of that betrayal. Ignoring her evident self-contradiction, she wrote, "I never voluntarily think of him now." She bemoaned George's falsehood and vanity. She deplored the strange distortions of his views. She denounced her own eager selfishness, which had made her think him better than he was. Three times in this letter, she used the same emphatic noun to describe his conduct: "evil."[67]

Davis's rejection may have helped to precipitate the first great emotional crisis of her adulthood. On May 23, 1830, her twentieth birthday, a time when she had not yet learned "the fearful secrets of [her] heart," she felt all at once "a crushing dull despair" that fell on her "like a dreadful weight." She lay down at the foot of a blossoming tree and sobbed. It seemed to her as if God had disdained His work, and she wanted to die. That night, she cried

Of Fuller, James Freeman Clarke wrote, "We never met without my feeling that she was . . . interested in all my thoughts."

(JAMES FREEMAN CLARKE, ANDOVER-HARVARD THEOLOGICAL LIBRARY, HARVARD DIVINITY SCHOOL, CAMBRIDGE, MASSACHUSETTS)

herself to sleep. Then, in a rapturous dream, her eyes were met by a mysterious gaze, "[o]h of such love benign[,] such melting love, such heavenly human love as mothers feel . . . in their virgin hearts." She did not identify the person or spirit that had seemed to gaze on her, and the vision never returned. Still, its recollection soothed her for years to come.[68]

Margaret had not given George Davis her body, for her body she considered no great gift, but she had shared without reserve the things she held much dearer: her ideas, hopes, and dreams. When he spurned them, she was defenseless. Fuller felt he had taught her "to distrust my own heart and lose all faith in my power of knowing others."[69] For good or ill, however, these lessons were imperfectly learned.

Thankfully, her time with Davis brought her one great good. Needing someone to tell that she had lost her capacity to trust, she turned in ironically trusting fashion toward James Freeman Clarke. James, who was just Margaret's age, had stood at the fringes of her life for years. We have already glimpsed him at five, as Margaret led him by the hand into her mother's garden. We have seen him moving intently through the stacks of the Harvard library, seeking out the philosophy and poetry that spoke to him more directly than any living friend. It was Clarke who had noted Margaret's ability to "make an epoch in one's life" and her power to take a friend up in a metaphorical balloon, far above the meanness of life.[70] Now James and Margaret, with each other's help, would rise together.

Clarke had graduated from Harvard alongside Davis in 1829, but he had none of the condescension with which Davis was infected. He seemed incapable of a sneer. A self-confessed dreamer, Clarke had been principally raised by his grandfather, who had seen no need to expose the boy to companions his own age. Just as Fuller complained that she had "had no natural childhood," Clarke reflected in a letter to her that he "never was a boy."[71] From an early age, he had been all observations and sensitivities. He recalled receiving, at the age of five or six, some unspecified "horrible wounds" to his pride that had made him perpetually defensive.[72] Because he was so quiet, few suspected the richer qualities of his mind, and some even thought him dull.

Like Fuller, Clarke had recently experienced heartache. The year 1830, when he and Margaret began exchanging letters, was otherwise a "blank, sad period" for Clarke, whose broken romance had turned his feelings of love to "blackness and ashes."[73] Despite his despair and self-directed anger, Fuller bore him patiently. She listened to his heartsick lament over his lost love, and, when poverty forced him to suspend his studies at Harvard Divinity School, she stepped in to find him a teaching post at her alma mater, the Port School. Clarke found in Fuller what he had never known before: "a full interchange of hearts."[74] For his part, Clarke took Margaret's side against Davis, denouncing him as a "mannerless dog."[75]

When Fuller befriended Clarke, he exulted in having found "a heart joined to an intellect in such just proportion that its fervour should not displease the taste by being ill-directed, nor its wisdom freeze by being too abstract, and she who possessed this nature, desirous of joining it to mine in friendship."[76] Clarke and Fuller had been brought together by both their mutual love of books and their shared need for emotional solace. For a while, they talked of starting a magazine together. It was unclear, though, whether their relationship was to be intellectual or romantic. Certainly, though, at least one of Clarke's relatives thought he knew which way the friendship was leaning. One day James drove Margaret to his grandparents' house for tea. As they drove off, James's grandfather exclaimed, "Poor James! . . . He'll go and marry that woman, and be miserable all the days of his life. Don't you see what a cross mouth she's got? she won't make him happy!" Though another relative tried to persuade him he was mistaken, the elderly man would not be consoled. "Poor James," he repeated. "Poor James."[77]

Such predictions aside, neither James nor Margaret was in any hurry to press the relationship toward marriage. James professed "no taste for the little nicknackeries and conveniences of domestic affection." He added, "It would not make me supremely happy to sit and eat a dinner tête-à-tête of my own raising and my wife's own cooking. . . . I should rather sit and look into her eyes for an hour or so." More to the point, Clarke did not think himself lovable. He was, in his own view, "perpetually labouring to darken and conceal the truths of my character in as many clouds as I can roll myself up in." He admitted that Fuller might find such an enigma "interesting," but he reminded her that interest was different from love.[78]

Fuller, who felt much wiser after breaking up with Davis, now thought she stood above the trivialities of the heart. She observed to James, "Many must love very early or never. The associations of youthful pleasure are necessary in common and unimaginative minds to beautify an attachment. . . . Their love has its birth in dependence and its being in habit." She clearly identified herself instead as "a strong and feeling mind [that] must try many experiments, and the love of its maturity is not the need of sympathy but the joy of admiring." She favored restraining the flow of one's affections until one had "built a fountain of pure and polished marble."[79] She promised James that she would not wrong his generous confidence "by professions and promises, whose folly, indeed, the past has shewn."[80] Nevertheless, for two people who took such trouble to disavow romantic love, they wrote about it a great deal.

A disturbing dream that Fuller narrated to James after they had been exchanging letters for seven months may reveal something about her actual emotions. She found herself in a room with a person whom she loved very much but whose face she could not see. She "urged or tempted" this person to look up a chimney. Then there were two loud noises. The person exclaimed, "God Almighty," in an anguished voice and seemed about to fall back into her arms when she abruptly awoke.[81] The imagery of this dream, in which Fuller lures a lover to peer into a dark, forbidden passage with explosive consequences, cries out for analysis. Did she fear the destructive force that might be released by enticing James into a sexual relationship? What, too, of the fact that, throughout her narration, the second figure in the dream is never identified as male or female? Again and again, in later years, Fuller was to feel powerful attractions to women. Her dream appears to be an early voicing of intense but ambiguous desires.

Few female writers of Fuller's time confronted their sexual urges as frankly as she did. Nevertheless, the most passionate recorded interlude of her young adulthood concerned a realm other than the physical. In people of spirit and sensitivity, moments may come when the soul feels too large for the body to contain it. One feels that one is no longer precisely a person; she or he experiences life not as a stream of thoughts, but as an ecstatic pulse and throb. The mind opens and soars, and all at once one knows oneself as a child of light. There is no accurate name for this tide of emotion. Some feel it and call it a religious conversion. Others may conclude that the feeling is chiefly sexual. Under whatever inadequate label one uses, it is an exhilarating state in which magic does not seem strange and nothing seems impossible but death. A person who has felt it may be subtly and permanently changed, touched by an awareness that he or she has been singled out for something extraordinary, be it salvation or sacrifice, sweet suffering or sweeter joy. Emerson felt this rare pulsation while crossing a bare common through melting snow. Melville's Ishmael discovers it on the masthead of the *Pequod.* Margaret Fuller felt it on Thanksgiving Day in 1831.

She had spent the preceding months under an oppressive cloud, borne down by what she later called "a treble weight . . . of deceived friendship, domestic discontent, and bootless love."[82] She had yearned to face her blue devils in solitude, but "a great burden of family cares" continually required her to make herself available to others. Caught up as well in the demands of Cambridge society, she had been forced to play a role that seemed false and distasteful. As she went through all the socially prescribed motions, she was inwardly absent. She went for long, furiously paced walks through empty, forsaken fields—for hours, if necessary—trying to tire the anguish out of herself. Then, her rage spent, she would return home in what she called "a state of prayer."[83] But the relief was never permanent, and again she took to the fields for another stormy ramble.

She felt no more at home in church now than she had as a child. Even on Thanksgiving Day, Fuller went to church only to avoid displeasing her father. On that chilly December day, seeing others experience a joy that she could not share, Margaret felt more deeply excluded than ever before.[84] "The past," she thought, "was worthless, the future hopeless," and the sermon, the hymns, and the hosannas jarred against her ears. Sunk in "a mood of most childish, child-like sadness," she felt that she had been singled out for exile, that she alone was "the selected Œdipus, the special victim of an iron law."[85]

The benediction was given at last, and all were told to go in peace. She walked away alone as fast as she could. Apparently having come to regard her impulsive retreats as customary, no one followed. No one guessed that her mood was more desperate than before. "Today," Fuller recalled, "all seemed to have reached its height. It seemed as if I could never return to a world in which I had no place,—to the mockery of humanities. I could not act a part, nor seem to live any longer."[86]

The weather, "sad and sallow," was apt for her nihilistic broodings. She felt like the only sentient creature in a barren, blasted world:

> Slow processions of sad clouds were passing over a cold blue sky; the hues of earth were dull and gray, and brown, with sickly struggles of late green here and there; sometimes a moaning gust of wind drove late, reluctant leaves across the path;—there was no life else.[87]

Twice, her feet guided her toward water. She pressed on through the wind until she paused beside a little stream. Merry and full in springtime, it now looked "choked" and "shrunken."[88] No respite here. She continued on her way, taking no notice of time or distance, until she came to a place where a copse of trees surrounded a dark and silent pool. She sat down. No thought entered her mind, and she was one with the cold, dark stillness.

Then everything changed. When Fuller wrote down her recollections of the moment almost a decade later, her sense of astonishment remained fresh, and its effects had not subsided:

> Suddenly the sun shone out with that transparent sweetness, like the last smile of a dying lover, which it will use when it has been unkind all a cold autumn day. And, even then, passed into my thought a beam from its true sun, from its native sphere, which has never since departed from me.[89]

At that moment, the four questions she had first posed to herself as a little girl on a staircase came back to her: "How came I here? How is it that I seem to be this Margaret Fuller? What does it mean? What shall I do about it?" She remembered all the times and ways in which these thoughts had risen up before her. As she later recalled, she saw "how long it must be before the soul can learn to act under these limitations of time and space, and human nature."[90]

Had she been raised in an existential age, Fuller might have experienced this moment as an encounter with the absurd—a tragicomic instant when a spirit believes itself to be infinite but recognizes that it inhabits a world seemingly orchestrated for the purpose of restraint. As it was, her outcome felt more hopeful. Her sense of cosmic imprisonment gave way to a greater, para-doxical, twofold revelation. She saw first that, whatever the impediments to action, the soul "*must* [act] . . . and sow new and immortal plants in the gar-den of God, before it could return again."[91] She felt equally strongly, how-ever, that her feelings of futility and ensnarement existed because she had regarded herself as a self, that is, as a finite subject capable of being fenced in and frustrated. But one need not choose to be defined in this way, and Fuller promptly resolved that she would not:

> I saw there was no self; that selfishness was all folly, and the result of circumstance; that it was only because I thought self real that I suf-fered; that I had only to live in the idea of the all, and all was mine. This truth came to me, and I received it unhesitatingly; so that I was

for that hour taken up into God. In that true ray most of the relations of earth seemed mere films, phenomena.[92]

Fuller had been afforded a glimpse into one of the greatest of spiritual paradoxes: that the discovery and the loss of self may form two sides of the same moment. The transformation through which she passed was not total: she felt later as if she "did but touch then" the possibilities of greater insight, and, nine years later, she still did not think herself "sufficiently purified to be taken back to God." She felt that she had been neither sanctified nor saved in a conventionally religious sense. Her sense of lasting change felt more like insulation than anything else; the old slings and arrows did not wound her as deeply as they previously had. "All the films seemed to drop from my existence," she later told her friend Jane Tuckerman, "and I was sure that I should never starve in this desert world." She was not finished with feeling lonely and misunderstood. However, the pain that these feelings caused her "never went deep after this hour. I had passed the extreme of passionate sorrow; and all check, all failure, all ignorance, have seemed temporary ever since."[93]

In describing her spontaneous shedding of self, Fuller sounded a great deal like Emerson, who wrote in 1836 of his own ecstatic union with the limitless in a passage from *Nature* that ranks as an essential text of transcendentalism:

> Crossing a bare common, in snow puddles, at twilight, under a clouded sky, without having in my thoughts any occurrence of special good fortune, I have enjoyed a perfect exhilaration. I am glad to the brink of fear. . . . Standing on the bare ground,— my head bathed by the blithe air, and uplifted into infinite space,—all mean egotism vanishes. I become a transparent eye-ball; I am nothing; I see all; the currents of the Universal Being circulate through me; I am part or particle of God. The name of the nearest friend sounds then foreign and accidental: to be brothers, to be acquaintances,— master or servant, is then a trifle and a disturbance.[94]

It is essential here to observe the sequence of events. Although Fuller's moment of transcendental discovery took place in 1831, she did not write her interpretation of it until 1840—the same year she first read Emerson's

Nature cover to cover.[95] Fuller's experience of infinitude surely mattered greatly to her when it occurred. However, it was quite likely her contact with Emerson that caused her transformation to flourish into its full significance.

Fuller's description of her transcendental conversion is, of course, no mere repetition of Emerson's. Significantly absent from Emerson's account is the pointed self-questioning that precedes Fuller's revelation. He is buoyed throughout by a confidence that he is nature's child and that there is a secure place for him in the bosom of the world. Fuller evinces no such ease or assurance. Where he has felt ecstatic joy, she has heard the call of a higher responsibility. Her life, though illuminated by her experience, has not been justified. It remained for Fuller to seize control of her newly consecrated existence and to find a way to make it count.

Fuller's afternoon at the pond gave her a renewed sense of purpose. Yet she still required a direction for her freshly galvanized energies. She was still seeking a model after which she might shape her intellect. That model soon came—in the writings and lived example of a man who was arguably the world's greatest living writer: Johann Wolfgang von Goethe. She discovered him through her studies with Clarke, whose friendship was now decidedly more scholarly than romantic. In the early 1830s, and especially in 1831, Clarke was fascinated by the essayist and historian Thomas Carlyle. At that time, most of Carlyle's greatest work—*Sartor Resartus*, *Past and Present*, and *The French Revolution*, for example—remained before him. Still, the fiery Scotsman had already won fame with essays like "Signs of the Times," in which he had roundly denounced the values of the Industrial Revolution and the modern faith in institutions and machinery. Staunchly humanistic, profoundly skeptical of technology, Carlyle accused humankind of having "grown mechanical in head and heart, as well as in hand" and having lost its faith, not only in the nobility of individual endeavor, but also in the greater spirit that, in earlier times, "arose in the mystic deeps of man's soul . . . and flew, like hallowed fire, from heart to heart, till all were purified and illuminated by it."[96] Carlyle urged his readers not to rely on machines or governments but to remember the strength of their own minds and bodies. Arguing that literature was a branch of religion—and the only one that still showed any capacity for growth—Carlyle gave inspiration to people like Clarke and Fuller, who were eager to reform the world with words.

It was reading Carlyle that led Clarke and Fuller to Goethe, whom Carlyle hailed as "neither noble nor plebeian, neither liberal nor servile, nor infidel nor devotee; but the best excellence of *all* these, joined in pure union; a clear and universal *Man*."[97] During his astonishingly active eighty-two years, Goethe made an anatomical discovery, proposed an important botanical hypothesis, published a complex theory of colors, and directed the theater in Weimar for the better part of three decades. He also became one of a tiny handful of writers in history to achieve greatness in drama, poetry, and the novel. Emerson called him "the most powerful of all mental reagents."[98]

The better to absorb Goethe, Fuller taught herself German, sometimes consulting Hedge and Clarke on its finer points. She became Clarke's avid partner in exploring German literature, sharing books and comparing notes on Schiller, Novalis, Tieck, and Richter. From 1831 to 1834, Fuller read almost nothing but German books. Above all, it was Goethe who captivated her. "I am enchanted while I read," she told Clarke. "He comprehends every feeling I ever had so perfectly, expresses it so beautifully. . . . When I shut the book, it seems as if I had lost my personal identity—All my feelings linked with such an immense variety that belong to beings I had thought so different."[99] No one ever accused Fuller of having a small mind. Still, Emerson told a measure of truth when he wrote that, once she took Goethe as her teacher, "the place was filled, nor was there room for any other."[100]

Goethe's formative experiences reminded Fuller of her own. In her longest piece on him, a forty-one-page essay that she published in 1841, she made clear just how much of his early life she saw reflected in her own. She described the poet's father as "a gentlemanly Martinet; dull, sour, well-informed, and of great ambition as to externals. . . . He was always turning [his son's] powerful mind from side to side . . . for the attainment of what are called accomplishments." She then turned to Goethe's mother, whom she saw as "a delightful person in her way; open, genial, playful, full of lively talent, but without earnestness of soul."[101]

Fuller's identification with Goethe's youthful influences and struggles ran deeper still. His early feelings of isolation and the seeming eagerness of others to misperceive him prompted her to write this reflection on the sorrows that can await a brilliant youth:

> The sympathy he seeks flies his touch, the objects of his affection jeer
> at his sublime credulity, his self-reliance is arrogance, his far sight

infatuation, and his ready detection of fallacy fickleness and inconsistency. Such is the youth of genius, before the soul has given that sign of itself which an unbelieving generation cannot controvert.[102]

Fuller could write this analysis with such conviction because she had lived it. If she had disagreed with every word that Goethe ever wrote, she still would have recognized a fellow outsider-prodigy.

In at least three crucial respects, Goethe responded to and confirmed the tenor of Fuller's mind. To begin with, unlike Coleridge and his followers, Goethe had no taste for unifying abstractions. Instead of reaching vainly for a theory that would unite all fields of knowledge, he wanted to understand every distinct phenomenon by its own terms. Like Fuller's, his was an intellect not of the one but of the many. Second, while Goethe notoriously declined to make general pronouncements about the meaning of life, he did, near the end of *Faust*, Part Two, place in the mouths of a chorus of angels the following statement on salvation: "Whoever strives with all his power, we are allowed to save." These words, as philosopher Walter Kaufmann has stated, summarized Goethe's own ethic of existence; he was "imbued with the relentless determination to educate himself and give form to himself."[103] This pivotal idea, that man may save himself not only through faith, hope, and charity, but also through a ceaseless drive toward self-perfection, became an article of faith for many in the Romantic generation. For Fuller, who had already concluded that the highest object of life was perpetual growth, Goethe's ethic of eternal striving was ready-made.

Finally, and perhaps most important, Goethe was, for the time, unusually aware of the obstacles and dead ends that awaited women of genius and ambition. Although his best-known female character, Gretchen in *Faust*, is a kind-hearted yet essentially passive victim, Goethe's slightly less familiar works are peopled with women who speak eloquently against the constraints imposed on their sex. In the verse drama *Iphigenia in Tauris*, the title character wonders whether men alone are entitled to do heroic deeds and demands to know why the world apparently deems only bold, traditionally masculine enterprises worthy of being called "great."[104] Another play, *Torquato Tasso*, bemoans the fact that, whereas men are free to act, women are confined to the spheres of seemliness and morals.[105] As Emerson tells the story, Fuller found in Goethe "her moods met, her topics treated, the liberty of thought she loved."[106] Her own words on the matter reveal an immersion bordering on hero worship. "How often I have thought, if I could see Goethe, and tell him my state of mind, he would support and guide me—he would be able to understand—he would show me how to rule circumstances instead of being ruled by them."[107] Yet in March 1832, at the same time Fuller was discovering his writings, Goethe died. Fuller made plans to translate some of his works and, when she knew enough, to write a full-dress Goethe biography, synthesizing all she had learned about the greatest mind she had ever encountered.

FULLER'S FRIENDSHIP WITH James Clarke continued in placid harmony, perhaps in part because both were wise enough not to alter its foundations. When a separation came, it was not emotional, but physical. Since his retirement from Congress at the beginning of 1825, Timothy Fuller had found his life only intermittently satisfying, and he began to desire a change. As a father, Timothy had mellowed substantially. Instead of drilling his younger children in Latin, he read aloud to them from the Bible. Having learned from his experience with Margaret, he now professed "a poor opinion of involuntary study."[108] Whereas Margaret chiefly recalled her father's criticism, her younger brother Richard recollected his praise.[109] Another brother, Arthur, remembered Timothy as "most judicious and tender."[110] Richard remembered how his father would hand him coins to give the toll-keeper at the bridge from Cambridge to Boston. When, as occurred strangely often, the keeper refused the money, Timothy allowed Richard to pocket the fare. Richard learned only years later that his father had prepaid the fare and that the entire ritual was Timothy's roundabout way of giving Richard an allowance without appearing too generous.[111]

Professionally, Timothy's life was now less illustrious than it had been. Although he had at first moved smoothly from Washington to the speaker's chair in the Massachusetts state legislature, his hopes for an ambassadorship had come to nothing. A campaign for lieutenant governor had also fallen short. Eugene sensed his father's disappointment. One day, standing with Margaret in the family's garden, he said grimly, "Our family star has taken an unfavorable turn; Father had always luck in aid of his efforts till now; now his fortunes begin to decline and we shall never be lucky any more."[112] Fifteen years later, Margaret still thought of this prophecy.

After the excitement of a political career, Timothy found the prospect of returning to a law office only moderately appealing. Nevertheless, he dutifully set up practice on Court Street in Boston, frugally bringing his lunch each day and sharing a few crumbs with a mouse who had been "rendered tame by his bounty."[113] If his admiring son Richard is to be trusted, Fuller practiced his trade with aplomb. As a lawyer, Fuller could earn a respectable five thousand dollars a year, twice the salary of Boston's mayor.[114] Eventually, though, the routine began to feel numbing, and Timothy's staunch practicality gave way to bucolic fantasy.

In April 1833, at fifty-five, Timothy felt he had earned the privilege of living out his productive years according to a long-cherished dream. In imitation of his political idol, Jefferson, Timothy pictured himself as a scholar-farmer, dividing his time between working the land and fulfilling his ambition of writing a history of the United States. He chose as his Monticello an aristocratic-looking farmhouse that lay only a short drive from Groton, the same town where Margaret had once tried the patience of Miss Prescott. The farm that he purchased, which fronted on Pleasant Street, at the beginning of Farmers' Row, was considered one of the handsomest sites in the vicinity.[115] Covering about fifty acres of land, the property could be relied on for a fine yield of corn, pumpkins, beans, and potatoes. The ten acres reserved for pasturage was enough to sustain three cows, a yoke of oxen, and a sturdy horse called Old Charley.[116] Timothy calculated that, with proper maintenance, the farm could be virtually self-sustaining. He also expected the move to benefit his younger sons, who, he feared, were growing soft and languid in the urbane atmosphere of Cambridge. He planned to introduce them to a regime of hard physical labor, regular baths in ice cold water, and, in the winter, barefooted runs through the snow.[117]

The decision was less propitious for Margaret, soon to be twenty-three. It tore her away from ready access to books, from her friends, and, of course, from James Clarke. The move was also indicative of the role that Timothy saw his elder daughter as continuing to fulfill in the world, a position that had much more to do with the interests of the family than with Margaret's own inclinations. He was now in the habit, at least occasionally, of discussing his worldly concerns with her. Margaret, however, paid only polite attention. Her father was fully competent to tend to his affairs, and everything he told her about them was soon forgotten.[118] Again, Timothy and his wife had failed to apprehend both Margaret's promise and the scope of her ambitions. Her friend William Henry Channing observed that her independence "wanted only fit occasion to prove itself heroic."[119] But how, in Groton, might such occasions arise?

Timothy expected his sons to find farm life rugged. He did not expect it to be dangerous. The very day Margaret arrived at her new home, ten-and-a-half-year-old Arthur was struck in the right eye by a large piece of wood, carelessly thrown by a workman. Margaret found the boy burning with fever, the whole side of his face grotesquely swollen. Margaret, who had regarded Arthur as the most promising of her brothers, "greeted [her] new home with a flood of bitter tears."[120] Arthur proved to be a model patient. He submitted bravely to the doctor's sticking plasters, all the while apologizing to his mother for depriving her of her rest. At first, the physician expressed great satisfaction with Arthur's progress. Then, a few days later, the injured eye produced an ominous discharge. Arthur wanted to be taken up and laid down continually, and Margaret was not strong enough to lift him as their mother could. In all other ways, though, she did her utmost to care for her brother, and her mother called her "the best of daughters and sisters." Mrs. Fuller noted ruefully that the workman who caused the accident had never made the slightest inquiry about the boy. As for her, she would have suffered any hardship sooner than speak to the man at all.[121] Although Arthur regained health, his right eye was permanently blinded.

The white house, sitting atop a gradually sloping hill, was tall and spacious. Visitors delighted in its gracefully curving driveway and the stately columns of its handsome veranda, and Timothy took pride in the size and productivity of his apple, pear, and cherry orchards. Robins trilled in the nearby pines. Mrs. Fuller had reason to smile proudly over the beautiful floral borders on either side of the broad walkway, which she carefully tended with her own hands.[122] After Arthur recovered, he and his younger brother Richard took well to the change of scene; Margaret wrote of them "dashing about and enjoying everything to the fullness of animal spirits." Margaret sometimes took part in the fun, playing blindman's buff and forfeits with them until midnight.[123] Even she was to remember Groton as "very beautiful in its way," even if its aspect was "too tamely smiling and sleepy" for her more dramatic taste.[124]

Otherwise, she had little good to say about her father's farm. She could never comprehend how a man who had been so immersed "in the affairs of men could care so much for trees and crops."[125] Margaret disliked the artless townspeople and called her contact with them "profaning."[126] She yearned to have, like Goethe, "always . . . some engrossing object of pursuit." Dejected and suffocated, she was losing "the bright feeling of progression."[127] "The seemingly most pure and noble hopes have been blighted," she moaned, "the seemingly most promising connections broken."[128] Years later she alluded to her father's decision as an "ill-judged exchange" and lamented that it had "violently rent" her and her two eldest brothers "from all their former life and cast [them] on toils for which they were unprepared."[129] The best she could say about the move was to call it an act of "Heaven's discipline," urging an endlessly repeated lesson: "Be humble, patient [and] self-sustaining."[130]

For Eugene and William Henry, clashes with their father became routine and embittering. Approaching their late teens, they demanded more freedom. Timothy became "over anxious," and Margaret foresaw no easy end to their quarrels.[131] Both brothers seized early opportunities to distance themselves from their father by accepting employment, at first around Boston, but then farther afield.[132] The unambitious Eugene, who had scraped through his studies at Harvard, taught school for a term in the nearby town of Stow but then made good his escape, securing a tutoring job in Virginia. William Henry tried to get away by every means he could imagine. He concocted a series of schemes to decamp southward and, in the autumn of 1834, sailed to the West Indies. Margaret's sister, now just entering her teens, had become sufficiently aware of boys to impede her French lessons.[133] Apart from her complaints about being too far from Boston society, Ellen made few contributions to the family records during this time.

Timothy related to his offspring best when they were young and impressionable. At Groton he gravitated toward Arthur and Richard, who, at the ages of eleven and nine, were a receptive audience for his many opinions. Two of his favorite topics were the wonders of literature and the folly of war; Timothy told his sons that Sir Walter Scott would still be read when Napoléon had been all but forgotten. Although he lectured the boys on prudence and economy, holding himself up as a prime example, he also deplored those who, having no higher inclinations, "toil[ed] like the beasts," living only to satisfy their momentary wants.[134] Entertaining romantic visions of farm labor, Arthur and Richard made a bargain with their father: they would do farm work full-time if he would release them for a time from their studies. Timothy required in return that the boys would keep to their contract for a set period of time. All went well at first. Soon, though, Arthur and Richard found that working the land was no vacation. At last, one morning they ran in from the fields and threw themselves at their mother's feet, begging for relief from their chores. Timothy, however, remained firm, and the two gradually accustomed themselves to sweat and blisters.[135]

It was not all drudgery for the boys, however. Not only did Timothy allow them "days of pleasant recreation," but the natural beauty of the area sunk deep into their memories.[136] Richard, in particular, was enchanted by the flowing streams, the waving trees, and the crystal clear mornings that became part of his daily pleasures. For a time, he kept a wild passenger pigeon caged in the attic. Eventually, deciding that the bird's freedom counted more than his own pleasure in keeping it, he opened the window "and saw the liberated bird, as if an arrow shot from my hand, speed far away till he became invisible."[137]

Margaret's own experience of Groton continued to be frightening. She stood by one day as Timothy was giving Arthur and Richard a lesson in weapons safety. He explained that, even though the pistol he was handling was not loaded, he would never point it "at the head of someone, as a boy might do, for bravado. For instance, I shall not point it at your sister Margaret." In so saying, he aimed the "unloaded" gun away from her, pulled the trigger, and, to his horrified surprise, blew a hole through the nearby wall.[138]

One day Richard asked his father whether he was enjoying the change to rural life. Timothy replied that he was sorry only that he had not made the move earlier. However, the move to Groton brought Timothy more regrets than he openly confessed. With his older sons too recalcitrant and his younger sons too small to give more than slight assistance, he was having to work much harder than his pastoral fantasies had ever led him to expect. Though he hired laborers, he could seldom resist encouraging them by his own example. Richard recalled seeing his father loading grain in the violent summer sunshine until perspiration streamed down his face. Exhausted by such efforts, he was often compelled afterward to lie down for hours.[139] Timothy was also having to struggle to turn a profit. Margaret later reflected that her father had become accustomed to a life of "well-earned prosperity." At the farm, where he had expected ease and simplicity, his comfort "was rapidly ebbing from him, and . . . [he] could not reconcile himself to it."[140]

One project that evidently gave Timothy some pleasure was the study he was having built at the end of the garden, in which he proposed to house his papers and to commence his history of America. Another of his pleasures lay in building another structure on his property—a rustic arbor he erected in a space in the woods that he named "Margaret's Grove." It was his gift to his daughter, a place where he hoped she would go and feel contented when her thoughts and feelings cried out for exclusive space. With an offhandedness that she later regretted, Margaret accepted the present by saying, "Where you please, father"—and then never went to the arbor, preferring another space of her own discovery by the side of the nearby river.[141] There, in a little hollow she called "Hazel Grove," she sat among fallen oak leaves, listened to the wind and the songs of birds, and filled her journal with poems and prayers.[142] Despite her general dislike of Groton, there were moments when she felt "so wild and free" and regretted that she had not been "brought up in this solitude."[143] While at the house, she went quietly about her duties, "playing Margaret Goodchild" and crowing to Clarke when her father found no fault with her for an entire month.[144]

For years, Margaret's intellectual interests had been leading her away from her father's, and they now found little to talk about. She began to read American history, in large part because it gave them something to discuss.[145] It was also hard for Margaret to discover common ground with her younger brothers. Lloyd's behavioral problems were persistent and pronounced; without ever precisely defining his mental handicap, Fuller family letters continually refer to him as "poor Lloyd." There seems never to have been the prospect of maintaining an ordinary relationship with him. On the other hand, Margaret craved the companionship and good opinion of Arthur and Richard. Winning their favor was a challenge, if only because she was also expected to tutor them as they prepared for college. It was work she said she did "very thoroughly as far as I go," though her thoroughness was not always appreciated.[146] Richard recalled that Arthur, though naturally gifted, was at this time "very active in the region of fancy, and air castles were more attractive to him than the solid structures of history, mathematics . . . and grammar." Richard, by his own modest recollection, was a boy of "slow as well as obstinate understanding."[147] Neither of the boys regarded study as one of life's great joys, and Margaret agonized over their fidgety habits and lack of progress.

When she introduced the two to Roman history, she tried to use the great men of antiquity as positive examples for them to follow—a stratagem that Richard one day turned neatly on its head. When his sister chided him for his lack of ambition, Richard reminded her that ambition had been Caesar's fatal flaw. Margaret threw up her hands and, as Richard later put it, "left me to my obscure fate." Richard supposed later that his dullness and Arthur's inattention "wounded her sensibilities more . . . than acts of unkindness could have done."[148]

But acts of unkindness were hurtful too. One of the brothers—probably Richard, though the source fails to specify—recollected, "I . . . always viewed her as a being of different nature from myself, to whose altitudes of intellectual life I had no thought of ascending." He thus never dreamed that any insolence on his part could affect her in the least. He learned otherwise one winter's day when Margaret returned after being away and asked him how he had been occupied while she was gone. He was, he remembered, "not frank or warm in my confidence, though I gave no reason for my reserve; and the matter had passed from my mind, when our mother told me that Margaret had shed tears, because I seemed to heed so little her sisterly sympathy." The news astonished him. "Tears from one so learned," he thought, "for the sake of one so inferior!" From that time on, his heart opened to her "as to no earthly friend."[149]

Although Fuller's tutoring and her other "many things to do at home" left her little time for her own amusement, her fascination with Goethe continued.[150] In her secluded grove, she read *Faust* and the *Second Residence in Rome*. She spent much of her spare time translating German texts, choosing *Torquato Tasso* for her most ambitious task. It was a rewarding choice. The play offers an extended reflection on the limited and insecure position accorded to women by society. The drama's leading female character, the Princess Leonora d'Este, is unimpressed by the privileges of her rank, for she knows that her gender consigns her to a realm of politeness and moral rectitude and excludes her from a wider world of action:

> . . . Like a wall, decorum
> Surrounds and guards the frailer sex. Propriety,

Morality, are their defence and fortress,
Their tower of strength; and lawlessness their foe.
And as man loves bold trials of his strength,
So woman, graceful bonds, worn with composure . . .
[Men's] striving is for distant good,
And must be eager to effect its end;
But ours for single, limited possessions,
Which we would firmly grasp, and constant hold.[151]

Goethe's princess laments that her only claim to influence rests upon securing a romantic alliance, a purchase on power that will vanish as her beauty inevitably fades. Until men recognize the lifelong value of a woman's love and trust, the princess concludes, no golden age of women can ever dawn.

While Fuller would have agreed wholeheartedly with the princess's point of view, one senses that she felt a still greater empathy with the play's embattled title character. Everyone agrees that Tasso is brilliant, but, despite the honor he enjoys at court, Tasso is socially ill at ease. His exuberant efforts at friendship meet with bewildering rejection, and his resulting outbursts of temper lead to his being shunned all the more decisively. He misinterprets the princess's admiration of his intellect and concern for his well-being as a display of romantic ardor, and, just when it seems that her kindness will deliver him from his depression and fear, he impulsively embraces her. She recoils in fright, and her astonished brother the duke of Ferrara calls on his chancellor to subdue the impassioned poet. The duke pronounces Tasso mad. The duke is right. Goethe's protagonist is poised on the brink of insanity, and the play charts the devolution of his unraveling mind.

Though Fuller did not share Tasso's paranoia, the story of a brilliant thinker who is unable to produce a satisfactory finished work and whose overly assertive expressions of romantic passion lead to sad misunderstandings must have resonated with her. She may have read a particularly cautionary tale in one of the causes of Tasso's alienation: feeling most at ease in scholarly work, he immerses himself to a dangerous degree in his reading and writing. "I am then best," he argues, "when I at will can give me to my task. The labor which I love can work my cure." In reality, his obsession with words only drives him deeper into himself. The duke warns Tasso that the most terrible chasm into which a man can fall lies within his own heart. But Tasso's impulses toward solitude and inwardness are too insistent: "When I muse not, nor paint poetic visions, life ceases in my soul. Can the poor silkworm pause at his task because he works his death, and from his life is formed the costly thread? His life's last forces eager he bestows, then rests within the shroud his substance shaped."[152]

Fortunately, Fuller had more than visions to sustain her. Her summers took her often to Boston and Cambridge, where she was a frequent guest of her friends the Farrars. She was especially happy when these visits included a rendezvous with Anna Barker, who remained as lovely as always. In August 1834, she and Anna traveled together to Newport, Rhode Island, where their mornings were brightened by long horseback rides along the beach, and their evenings were taken up by quiet moonlit walks. The time with Anna was precious; Fuller wrote, "A delightful harmony reigned between us—we were surprizingly near . . . to each other—and it is a real grief to me that I must live so far from the light of those sweet eyes."[153]

Fuller's visits to Cambridge, however, no longer included James Clarke. Clarke had taken a ministerial position in Louisville, Kentucky, where he hoped to spread the gospel of liberal Unitarianism. Fuller had accepted Clarke's departure "profoundly but calmly." She told him that, two years earlier, when she had first begun to realize "all I must do for myself or be lost," she had never thought she could bear his leaving with composure, and she had despised herself for her dependency on him. Now, however, they both seemed "quite grown up" to her and ready to pursue their separate paths.[154] Although they maintained a lively and steady correspondence throughout Clarke's western sojourn, his physical absence made it all the more likely that their friendship would remain one of words and ideas.

Fuller's grandest excursion of her Groton years came in the summer of 1835. Now twenty-five, she received an invitation from the Farrars to come "with several other delightful persons" on an excursion up the Hudson River, or the "North River," as Fuller called it, for a peaceful week of sightseeing and socializing at Trenton Falls, a popular retreat for the more fortunate classes of New Yorkers and Bostonians. Fuller was able to go only because Timothy was willing to give her the necessary fifty-seven dollars to cover her expenses and spending money, which she had extracted from him with shameless cajolery:

I said I had scarcely a doubt of your consent as you had said several times this winter you should like to have me take a pleasant journey this summer. Oh I cannot describe the positive extacy with which I think of this journey. . . . Oh do sympathize with me—do feel about it as I do. . . . Will you not write to me immediately and say you love me and are very glad I am to be so happy???[155]

Not even Timothy could resist such an onslaught, and consent was given.

Twelve miles or so north of Utica, Trenton Falls remains a picturesque vista. The cold waters of West Canada Creek edge slowly toward a flat bench of coarse, weathered limestone and then turn brilliant white as they plunge down a series of rocky tiers. The gorge through which the waters pass is beautifully rounded, so that the cascading water, at each level of its downward journey, flows in a somewhat different direction. At some points, the water comes down at more than one place, creating a powerful effect of tension, motion, and swirl. Margaret seems to have enjoyed her visit greatly and, after departing, called it a "dear place."[156] Margaret was quick to intimate that water fascinated her, exerting a kind of fatalistic attraction on her emotions. "Perfectly do I comprehend," she wrote in a letter recalling her trip, "what I have heard of gazers on a river-side being tempted to drown themselves by sight of the water, and all those tales of mermaid enchantments which embody this feeling."[157] She also took pleasure in telling her brothers how, on the way back down the Hudson, she saw, of all things, "an elephant with a real howdah on his back and a man dressed like a Hindoo upon him parading the streets."[158] However, neither the glittering mists and raging cataracts of the falls nor the wonders of the elephant were what most attracted Margaret's eye on her journey.

The Farrars had brought with them a young Harvard student who had been boarding with them: seventeen-year-old Samuel Gray Ward. Sam impressed his elders with the brightness of his manner and his talent as a painter. However, unlike other Harvard men in Fuller's acquaintance, Ward had little interest in being an outstanding scholar. He did not need to. The well-heeled son of the American agent of the British bank Baring Brothers, Ward had no fears about his future, and he was also evidently much better looking than likenesses made of him in later life suggest. He believed that every day ought to be "more or less a *jour de fête*."[159] Emerson, who made his acquaintance a few years later, conceived of Sam as being "allied on every side to what is beautiful and inspiring, with noblest purposes in life and with powers to execute [his] thought."[160] Emerson ventured still farther in a letter to Sam; setting aside his usual reserve, he confided to the young artist, "I love you very much."[161]

Fuller, who had met Sam briefly once or twice at the Farrars', was initially less effusive. At first, she did not even like him. However, moonlight and falling water can alter such impressions. By the end of the trip, she was observing that he had been "all kindness throughout," and he was offering to remain with her during a stopover in Newport for as long as she pleased.[162] Just what transpired in between can only be imagined. Ward came away greatly impressed by Margaret's "proud and sensitive nature . . . and unfailing intellectual sympathy."[163] Margaret's recollections were more romantic. Some months later, she wrote to Sam of her delight in going "to that place [at the falls] where the water seemed collecting its energies so quietly, gliding on so stealthily, you could scarcely believe it was firmly resolved to display such vehemence in one more moment of time and rood of space." In the same letter, Margaret had much more to say about water, underlining the passages in which she remarked on its "*winning gentleness*," "*impetuous force*," and "*irresistible subtlety*." Reluctant as one may be to read into these words a coded message of desire, the temptation becomes all but irresistible when Fuller goes on to liken the undulations of a stream "to the heaving of a bosom" and to her expectation that from such a bosom "a heart will leap forth, and I will be able to take it in my hand."[164] A boy seven years her junior had turned her head.

Fuller had much more to enjoy on her journey. The people with whom she traveled were kind to her and "even their defects not uncongenial." Eliza Farrar protected her with thoughtful affection, and in Fuller's growing attachment to Sam she had found "a kind of home."[165] Her journey concluded with a visit to Cambridge, where she had the great fortune to secure an interview with Harriet Martineau. Then Britain's most famous female writer, Martineau was near the midpoint of a two-year tour of the United States, which she would later describe in her book *Society in America*. Martineau was, at that time, the most august personage with whom Fuller had ever conversed, and, to Fuller's great satisfaction, the Englishwoman came away impressed and later lauded her for "her admirable candour, the philosophical way in which she took herself in hand, her genuine heart, [and] her practical insight."[166] Almost fifteen years later, Fuller looked back on her journey to Trenton Falls "as the last period of tranquility in my life."[167]

In mid-September, Fuller returned home, buoyed not only by the memory of her recent travels but also by the prospect of another, grander journey. The Farrars proposed to take an eighteen-month tour of Europe, to begin in the summer of 1836, and they hoped to take Sam, Anna, and Margaret with them. On the same vessel would be Harriet Martineau. The opportunity was almost too wonderful to be believed. Sailing to Europe with her newfound English friend, crisscrossing the continent, perhaps tarrying in Weimar to research her Goethe biography, and doing it all in the company of her two adored beauties, Sam and Anna, was very nearly the most blissful vision of the near future that Fuller could have imagined. But the radiance soon faded as complications intervened.

The first of these she brought upon herself. Hoping to gain some experience as a writer of fiction, Fuller had written a romantic short story called "Lost and Won: A Tale of Modern Days and Good Society." The tale was published in a somewhat saucy literary magazine, the *New England Galaxy*. For the figures in the story's love triangle, Fuller chose as models her former beau, George Davis; his new wife, Harriet Russell; and another mutual friend, Joseph Angier, a somewhat notorious ladies' man who was rumored to have carried on a mildly scandalous flirtation with Harriet before her marriage. Fuller published her story without affixing her name, taking untold satisfaction in the revenge that her anonymous satire would inflict on the unsuspecting Davis. Her pleasure soon turned to panic. Clarke, who had received a copy of the magazine and was in on the joke, could not bear to keep the secret. Ever the social maladroit, he wrote first to George and Harriet, exposing Fuller as the story's author, and then to Fuller herself, boasting of what he had done. Margaret's letter reacting to James's boneheaded indiscretion has not survived; it was likely hot enough to spontaneously combust. The repercussions from the incident may well be a reason why Fuller did not attempt fiction again for years and never tried seriously to establish herself as a novelist.

James scurried about, frantically trying to make amends. Before he could do so, Fuller collapsed. The doctor's diagnosis: typhoid fever. Fuller fell ill on the eighteenth of September. For the next nine days, she lay almost helpless, tormented by a relentless fever and dreadful pain in her head. Everyone in the family expected her to die.[168] Her mother constantly tended to her "like an angel all that time, scarce ever leaving me, night or day." As dark gave way to light and returned to dark again, Margaret contemplated the worst with resignation. "For myself," she later told her journal, "I thought I should surely die; but I was calm and looked to God without fear. When I remembered how much struggle awaited me, if I remained and how improbable it was that any of my cherished plans would bear fruit, I felt willing to go."[169]

One would expect more of a fight from Fuller. It is hard to imagine that someone who had so vigorously prepared herself for the work to come would accept so easy a surrender. And yet, as Fuller reaffirmed to her friend Almira Penniman Barlow four months after the crisis, "You know that I looked upon Death very near, nor at the time should I have grieved to go. I thought there never could come a time when my departure would be easier to myself, or less painful to others. I felt as I thought I should feel at that awful season." Fortunately, Fuller's body was less ready than her mind to give up the fight. Fuller's letter to Barlow continues simply: "It was not to be so, and I returned into life."[170]

During her illness, Timothy had grown perceptibly closer to his daughter. Richard surmised that "the struggle of chaotic elements" in Margaret's character had been too strong for Timothy either to comprehend or to sympathize with. Now, though, as Richard recalled, his father "hung over her couch so tenderly that she learned fully to realize his love."[171] On a late September morning, when it was still not clear that Margaret would survive her fever, Timothy came to her bedside and, after a few moments of conversation, worked himself up to the unaccustomed words he had come to say. "My dear," he began, "I have been thinking of you in the night, and I cannot remember that you have any faults. You have defects of course, as all mortals have, but I do not know that you have a single fault."

Despite its awkward delivery, Timothy's declaration moved Margaret to tears. He had so seldom praised her within her hearing that his words now sounded strange to her, but their very strangeness made them wonderful. His halting words were an "extravagant expression of regard." Even at such a time, he could not say simply that he loved her. As he had so often done, he judged her, but at last the judgment showed favor. Soon after this conversation, Margaret rallied, and by the last Sunday of September, it was evident that she was out of danger. On that morning, Timothy told his wife that he could find "no room for painful thought now that our daughter is restored," and he offered his weekly prayer of thanksgiving with such fervency that everyone was moved.[172] He read to the family from Jonah and the seventy-first psalm: both texts about deliverance and rescue. The next day, Timothy had another cause to celebrate when, at last, he stood in the newly finished study at the end of his garden. Now, finally, he believed he would have the time and space in which to write.

The space stood ready. The time vanished. Timothy had been overseeing the drainage of some low-lying meadows. Evidently, the water was contaminated. On the afternoon of Tuesday the thirtieth, having come back home after inspecting the fields, Timothy abruptly began to vomit and sank to his knees. Rushing to his aid, his children carried him upstairs, laid him on his bed, and sent for a doctor. The diagnosis was swift and accurate: Asiatic cholera. There was no known cure. A person stricken with cholera is a pitiable sight. For a man like Timothy Fuller, so long preoccupied with propriety and self-command, the disease could not have been less congruous. Soon after the vomiting comes uncontrollable diarrhea. The illness is also devastatingly rapid. The Fuller family was powerless to prevent the plunge in their patriarch's blood pressure and his swift descent into shock. Chills and spasms besieged him through the night. As Timothy clung to life into the next day, it became clear that a clergyman, not a doctor, was needed. A minister was called to the house, and his solemn, prayerful tones soon filled the sickroom. In the morning, a lull in Timothy's suffering came. To Richard, it seemed as if his father were preparing himself for the liberation of his spirit.[173] Then it was over. In twenty-five years, Margaret Fuller had done much for her father. Now only one service remained: she closed his eyes. Even ten years after, she did not think she had again performed an act so holy.[174]

CHAPTER FOUR

APOSTLE

All youthful hopes of every kind
I have pushed from my thoughts.

—MARGARET FULLER TO AN
UNKNOWN RECIPIENT, 1836

All this may be very unlovely, but it is I.

—MARGARET FULLER TO
JAMES FREEMAN CLARKE,
April 19, 1836

FULLER BELIEVED THAT, IN CLOSING HER FATHER'S EYELIDS, SHE HAD symbolically hidden "the sad sights of this world from . . . eyes which had begun to weep at them."[1] Her mother's recollection of what Fuller did next sounds a bit too theatrical to have happened just as she remembered. In that sentimental age, however, many such gestures are said to have been made. According to her mother, she brought her siblings together in the presence of her father's body. Prompted perhaps by both reverence and an instant of physical weakness, she sank to her knees. She then "pledged herself to God that if she had ever been ungrateful or unfilial to her father, she would atone for it by fidelity to her brothers [and sister]."[2] Much of her ensuing life was to be shaped by her loyalty to that promise. Helping her siblings, however, would only partly repay the debt she believed she owed her father. Despite her father's awkward benediction less than a week before his death, she knew she had barely begun to realize his hopes for her. Timothy had given his daughter the intellectual training that, if she used it wisely, could lead her to a place among American thinkers that no woman had yet attained. After long years of study, she still stood only at the base of the mountain. Timothy had lived just long enough to tell her that, as a daughter, she had satisfied him. She still had much to do before she could satisfy herself.

It became clear at once that Fuller's obligations to her mother and siblings would hinder her considerably in achieving those satisfactions. Timothy had left no will, and much of his eighteen-thousand-dollar estate was tied up in notes and land. His investments in real estate had been, as Margaret gently put it, "not fortunate."[3] Though not a strong woman, Margarett Crane Fuller vowed to steel herself in the aftermath of Timothy's passing. She wrote to her husband's brother Abraham, who was now in control of the family's finances, that she meant "to be very faithful to the interests of these precious children left to my care by the wisest and best of parents" and "to finish his work upon earth." Her brave words, however, were no defense against the periodic attacks of rheumatism that besieged her. Moreover, the suddenness of Timothy's death had thrown her into a profound melancholy. In this same letter, she added, "I can never hope or expect happiness more upon earth." Formerly dependent on Timothy for advice even in routine matters, she was now bewildered as she found "no wise answers from the silent chamber of death."[4]

Her letters to Abraham during her first months of grief are heartrending, alternately filled with pleas for advice and petitions for money. Yet her brother-in-law was not liberal in dispensing either. By mid-January, he had succeeded in making Margarett feel somewhat embarrassed about her need for guidance. She wrote, "It is perhaps fortunate for you that you are so removed from us, that I cannot see you more frequently to trouble you with questions about our affairs."[5]

Another widow approached her with an offer to buy the house in Groton, and Margarett was forced to choose between the much-needed money and the longings of her heart, which, she wrote, "clings to this little tenement where my husband expended so much thought, labor, and money, and promised himself so many tranquil hours."[6] Sentiment prevailed in the end, and the house remained hers. Her far weightier troubles concerned her children. Along with Margaret, Eugene, who turned twenty-one in May 1836, posed the fewest difficulties. Having graduated from Harvard the year before his father's death, he proposed to remain in Groton for a year or so and study law in the office of a local attorney, and then try his luck either in the South or out West. Of his affectionate temper, Eugene's mother was as confident as ever. As to his capacities "for strenuous exertion, and strict economy," Margarett could only "trust in Heaven."[7]

As for the younger Fuller children, not one failed to contribute to their mother's gray hairs. William Henry was "much sobered" by his father's death.[8] Nevertheless, he had already developed a dangerous love of extravagance. When Uncle Abraham expressed his strong disapproval of William's spending habits, Margarett urged him not to cut William off, fearing that his "prospects in life must be blighted by changing his situation, and becoming a wanderer." William's particular weak spot was a fondness for clothing, which his mother, who was also fond of the ornamental side of life, found it difficult not to indulge. Even as she deplored her son's profligacy, Margarett found herself asking in the same paragraph that he be granted a yearly clothing allowance of $150—almost a third of the annual income of a beginning schoolteacher or fledgling minister. William had, at least, secured temporary employment in a local business, and Margarett hoped he would excite enough "interest in his employers . . . that they will assist by giving him a fair character to begin life with." The most hopeful course she could suggest to Abraham regarding him was, "Let us not despair that he may become an estimable character."[9]

The remaining children were too young to do much to support themselves, although Abraham seemed to think otherwise. Two years after Timothy's death, as the Panic of 1837 was rendering the family's fortunes still more precarious, Arthur, Richard, and Lloyd turned fifteen, thirteen, and eleven, respectively. Their uncle impatiently inquired of their mother why she had not required them to earn their board by working on the farm. Margarett wrestled with her ire as she wrote back, "Will you tell me how this can be? I have very little that [my sons] can do until harvest, that will occupy a week, and then the care of the cattle is all that I have to employ [them]. Would you think in your sober judgement that they could 'earn their board'?" As for any possibility of their finding intellectual employment, Margarett was equally firm. Timothy, who had been so stern a taskmaster with Margaret, had erred in the opposite direction with his sons. Not only were Arthur and Richard both "ignorant of the common branches of knowledge [and] education," but the loss of Arthur's eye had made his particular situation "one of great difficulty." She reminded Abraham, too, of the plight of Lloyd, whose simplicity of mind unfitted him for all but the most elementary tasks and who could not be governed without "a man's control."[10] To Uncle Abraham's opinion that the family's younger daughter, Ellen, just turned seventeen, ought to be keeping a neighborhood school, Margarett responded that almost all the instruction the girl had received had come through sporadic lessons from her older sister and that Ellen was in no way fit to become a schoolmistress.

Without question, Margarett's own solution was more reasonable than her brother-in-law's: Arthur and Richard would receive two years' instruction each to prepare them to find work in a store or some other business. Ellen might reap "a lasting advantage" from only five months of good schooling, and Margarett knew a good master in Stoughton willing to assume the care of Lloyd. But all these plans required money. Shortly after her father's death, the younger Margaret had determined that his estate was sufficient both to maintain his widow and to educate the children decently.[11] Two years later, however, in the suffocating economic atmosphere of 1837, Abraham regarded even Mrs. Fuller's modest plans for her children as unacceptably extravagant. As Margarett pleaded for more help and Abraham flintily denied it, the goodwill between the branches of the Fuller family withered. In April 1838, Margarett wrote to Abraham with resignation, "It seems now as if our family meetings, such as we used to enjoy in bygone days, are dissolved for this life."[12]

The younger Margaret's former life had also been dissolved. If her father had lived to old age, Margaret would have had much less reason ever to become more than what she was at twenty-five: an exceptionally well-read but essentially private person, drawing such quiet satisfactions as would have been offered by her books and her cerebral circle of friends. Her ambitions would likely have taken her not much further than the perfecting of her mind and spirit. Now that it fell largely to her to try to better her family's condition, however, Margaret Fuller could never again be satisfied with mere intellectual transformation and growth. She now had to succeed in the larger world, to take hold of her circumstances and wring a living out of them by whatever talents she could use. She had always accepted that constant change was a criterion for a life well lived. Henceforth, many of her reinventions would come as acts of will, actuated by worldly necessity.

Leading and supporting a family was a business for which she felt little better prepared than those who were depending on her. Although Abraham controlled the purse strings, he evidently wanted little part in settling Timothy's affairs. In the sad autumn of 1835, Margaret found herself trying to sort out her late father's accounts at the same time that she struggled to find meaning in his nonsensical death. Seeing the necessity of giving her family a frank understanding of their situation, she held a series of family councils. The news she delivered at these conferences seldom reassured, and Richard recalled that "helplessness and fear sat there with us. . . . I felt my soul harrowed up at these meetings." In the years following his father's death, Richard acquired a dread of poverty that never left him.[13]

As she tried to comprehend the loss of one father, Fuller's thoughts turned swiftly toward another. As she prepared for new challenges, she inscribed a heartfelt prayer in her journal:

> Grant, oh Father, that neither the joys nor sorrows of this past year shall have visited my heart in vain! Make me wise and strong for the performance of immediate duties. . . . Nothing sustains me now but the thought that God, who saw fit to restore me to life when I was so very willing to leave it . . . must have some good work for me to do.[14]

The work that first confronted her did not suit well with her abilities or with her enjoyment. Like many born academicians, she could sit in a library for hours but could scarcely endure ten minutes in a counting room. Her father had been buried for about a month when she registered her distaste: "I always hated the din of such affairs and hoped to find a lifelong refuge from them in the serene world of literature and the arts."[15] Now that she had no choice, however, she tried to absorb a knowledge of business and estates as best she could, so that she could advise and act decisively when the need arose.

As she well knew, there was a barrier to her doing so that would not be swept aside. If she had been an eldest son, she could have been named the legal guardian of her siblings and the official administrator of the estate. The law, however, granted no such powers to a daughter. Like her mother, she promptly found that she had little influence with Uncle Abraham, who made a show of his power by decreeing that the Fullers would be allowed only one newspaper subscription. Margaret acquiesced. In the same letter, she meekly added, "Pray, my dear Uncle, make things as easy to Mother as you can; the responsibilities and cares of her situation are very great."[16] For a woman of Fuller's native forcefulness, no attitude could have been more repugnant than the submissive, entreating one she was compelled to assume toward her uncle. Yet she found her mother's comfort well worth the sacrifice of her pride.

In dark periods of her life, Fuller knew of only one consoling piece of advice to give herself: "Invite every peaceful thought that shows any willingness to come, and live on courageously as you can for [those] who cherish and the many who will yet need you."[17] On many subjects, Fuller was inexhaustibly garrulous. Where her deepest griefs were concerned, however, it was her habit to say little and keep active. Thus, with stoic determination, she bade farewell to "all youthful hopes of every kind" and drove them from her thoughts. She promised herself, "I will not, if I can help it, lose an hour in castle-building and repining—Too much of that already!" She realized that, heretofore, she had always been "too constantly distracted by childish feelings to acquire any thing properly."[18] From the moment of her father's death, Margaret Fuller's adult life may be said to have begun.

As the Fullers grieved, the Farrars reminded Margaret that their invitation to join them on their trip to Europe was still open. For an aspiring scholar of European literature, this chance was much more than a mere luxury. Far from a "scheme of pleasure," this trip was, in her eyes, an essential "means of needed development," which her health and mind required at that precise moment "as they never could again."[19] There seemed no way for her to get the information she would need for her life of Goethe, no way to give her genius wings, unless she went. Yet how could she go? Although the exact reckoning had not yet been made, it seemed clear that the trip would consume much of her share of her father's estate. Moreover, there seemed no way to ensure her family's comfort unless she stayed.

Torn between her promises to her mother and siblings and her duty to herself, Fuller did not let this dream die easily. Instead of promptly notifying the Farrars that she could not go with them, she delayed for months, clinging to the hope that her family's finances might improve enough for her to take the trip. She marked passages in her New Testament that seemed to offer a solution.[20] She told James Clarke that the choice seemed to her "the crisis of my existence" and that she was "near the parting of the Ways."[21] She prayed that neither rashness nor cowardice would guide her, and she told her eldest brother, who seems not to have fully grasped her desperation, "Oh, dear Eugene, you know not how I fear and tremble to come to a decision. My temporal all seems hanging upon it, and the prospect is most alluring."[22]

In March, she wrote a poem in her journal in which she weighed her options. In the following stanza, the demands of family appeared to be winning:

> *"Not comfortless!" I dry my eyes,*
> *My duties clear before me rise,*
> *"Before thou think'st of taste or pride,*
> *See home-affections satisfied."*[23]

But she had not convinced herself. In April, when she wrote to Eliza Farrar, her refusal was still couched in the conditional, and her anguish was evident: "If I am not to go with you I shall be obliged to tear my heart, by a violent effort, from its present objects and natural desires. But I shall feel the necessity, and will do it if the life-blood flows through the rent."[24]

Then, abruptly, she had no choice at all. Uncle Abraham advised her that her share of Timothy's estate would cover less than half the expenses of her contemplated journey. She could not go. "Heartbroken by sorrow and disappointment," she wrote on her twenty-sixth birthday that a door in her life had been closed forever.[25] But if it was now clear what she could not do, what she could do remained uncertain. Although "so many" had praised her conversational powers, she did not feel enough inner confidence to write a valuable work. Unless she could rally herself soon, only a career in teaching seemed open to her. She would have to fight to avoid coming to a dead end.

During the winter after Timothy's death, Margaret tried to forget her own trials, as always, by reading, but she was also busy doing kindnesses for others. She did her best to prop up her mother, who was still numbed by Timothy's loss. To her mentally unbalanced youngest brother Lloyd, her "chief trouble," she offered both discipline and sympathy.[26] As her two most promising brothers, Richard and Arthur, neared puberty, Margaret supervised them with gentle firmness, though both Richard's mediocrity and Arthur's tendency to dream tested her nerves. She admonished Richard to overcome his dread of Latin grammar and urged Arthur, a fluent talker like herself, to gain equal facility as a writer. At one point she threatened that, if he did not learn to write, "you and I, who have been such good friends, may become as strangers to one another."[27] Fighting a daily, bemused battle against their boyish frivolity and sloth, she kept them on a rather bumpy road that eventually led them both to Harvard.

Her charity only began at home. She noted with particular interest a night she spent by the sickbed of a Groton neighbor, a young girl who not only had contracted tuberculosis but also had been fatally injured in a botched abortion. The ornately delicate language with which Fuller described the girl's condition did not conceal her horror: "It was said she had profaned her maiden state, and that the means she took to evade the consequences of her stain had destroyed her health and placed her on this bed of death." In the room, filled with "poverty, base thoughts, and fragments of destiny," as Fuller cradled the dying girl's head "like a clod that should never have been taken from the valley," compassion vied with judgment. She did not know whether to view the wayward creature as a victim or a felon, but, as she held her, she felt as if she were gazing "into that abyss lowest in humanity of crime for the sake of sensual pleasure," and the moral darkness of the scene seemed overwhelming. Then, in the midst of it all, "a sadness of deepest calm" possessed her. It seemed to Fuller that a star shone above her. "Pale, tearful, still it shone; it was mirrored from the very blackness of the yawning gulf." As Venus shone in the predawn sky, Fuller, both exhausted and exalted by her vigil, made her way home. She unlocked the door, walked alone into the silent room that had been her father's and lay down, awash in "sacredest thoughts." That day, she took no food. She read from the Bible and Wordsworth's *Excursion*, feeling that she now understood the meaning of the life of an ascetic saint. She rejoiced in the barrenness of the winter that lay around her; its pure shroud and judgment-bearing winds would help her discipline herself for the challenges to come.[28]

As on her father's stairs in Cambridgeport, as by the icy pond on Thanksgiving four years earlier, Fuller had again heard a speechless voice, calling her on to a new condition of awareness. It summoned her, among other things, to a renewed self-honesty. She was starting to suspect that some of the weaker points of her character were unlikely ever to change. As she admitted to James Clarke, she not only remained "very destitute of what is commonly *called* modesty," but also saw little point in further efforts either to attain that virtue or to feign its acquisition. "When that blush does not come naturally to my face," she confessed, "I do not drop a veil to make people think it is there. All this may be very unlovely, but it is I."[29] Apart from this show of candor, however, she was not really sure of what to do with her newness. It was in an April 1836 letter to Sam Ward that Fuller wrote her reflections, previously quoted, about the river-gazers whom the sight of water tempts to drown themselves. The image of unstable, flowing water became her metaphor for her lack of resolution. She wrote:

> This morning I felt a short of timidity about standing quite at that point to which the undulatory motions . . . seemed to tend. I felt that, unless I had an arm of flesh and blood to cling to, I should be too much seduced from humanity.[30]

Fuller now wanted neither to drift nor to drown, and she was soon taking on the task of restoring some direction to her life. Although writing her biography of Goethe seemed too huge a task for the present, she wrote a series of perceptive critical articles for the influential *American Monthly Magazine*, treating such topics as modern British poets and the present state of German literature. But her more significant step in the summer of 1836 was toward finding that "arm of flesh and blood" that would give her steadiness and purpose. She did find one, but its possessor invoked reason instead of romance and offered poetry in the place of passion. He was Ralph Waldo Emerson.

Emerson, whom his friends invariably addressed as Waldo, did not publish his breakthrough work *Nature* until September of that year, and he was still little known outside the intellectual and Unitarian communities of Boston. Fuller, however, had already singled him out as a man of rare genius. She had no very precise words for how it felt to be in the audience when he spoke. The best she could do to describe the sensation that came over her when she entered "the atmosphere of his thoughts" was to call it "decided and peculiar."[31] Etiquette forbade her from introducing herself, and, though this was rare for her, she may even have been mildly intimidated by the prospect of meeting him. In any case, circumstances did not immediately supply a chance for an interview, and Fuller was disappointed that Emerson was seemingly the "only clergyman . . . who eludes my acquaintance."[32]

A meeting had been in the works for the better part of two years, thanks to a pair of serviceable go-betweens: Henry Hedge, who had known Emerson since his days at Harvard Divinity School; and her translation of Goethe's *Torquato Tasso*, which was certain to engage Emerson's interest. In late 1834, Margaret gave her *Tasso* to Hedge. At her behest, Hedge later placed the manuscript in Emerson's hands. Fuller herself denied using her translation as a means toward meeting Emerson. She claimed only two reasons for wishing him to see it: first, the pleasure of knowing that a mind that had so impressed

When Ralph Waldo Emerson first met Fuller, he thought, "We shall never get far." They were to forge one of the most complicated literary friendships of the century.

(COURTESY OF
CONCORD FREE
PUBLIC LIBRARY)

her was briefly dwelling on something she had created; and, second, her hopes that he might offer some useful comments and corrections.[33] Nevertheless, *Tasso* breached the castle wall; in January 1835, Emerson told Hedge, who was soon to leave Massachusetts for a pulpit in Bangor, Maine, that he would like to meet the translator.

Surprisingly, Margaret balked. Quite possibly, the shyness that comes with hero worship got the best of her. She told Hedge that she was "flattered" by Emerson's interest, but, instead of jumping at the possibility, she feared that it would "never be." If they were to meet, though, she at least had no fear of a letdown. She added, "I cannot think I should be disappointed in him as I have been in others to whom I had hoped to look up."[34] In August 1835, some six months after Fuller deflected Emerson's request for a meeting and only weeks before the onset of her nearly fatal bout with typhoid, they evidently crossed paths for a moment at a Cambridge party thrown by Eliza Farrar for Harriet Martineau. Nothing came of this first encounter. Fuller briefly noted it in her journal; Emerson could not quite remember its having occurred. It seems that Fuller was still holding back, perhaps consciously checking herself lest one of her characteristic gushes might alienate the minister permanently. She possibly sought the advantage of having *him* acknowledge *her*, not the other way around. In May 1836, in a diffident move to win his notice, she published an elegy on his late brother Charles. However, the poem appeared anonymously, and she could not be certain that Emerson would know it was hers.

Emerson was a widower; indeed, the tragedy of his romantic past was no great secret. In September 1829, at twenty-six, he had married a wealthy girl of eighteen named Ellen Tucker, who, he said, possessed "the purity & confiding religion of an angel."[35] They had married with the terrible knowledge that she had tuberculosis and would not live long. When Ellen died, only sixteen months after their wedding, she left her beloved Waldo the financial security that was to enable his literary career. She had also left a gap in his feelings that was beyond repair. Emerson was so incapable of accepting his loss that a little more than a year after her death, he had had her body disinterred so that he could gaze upon her one more time.[36]

In fact, the man whom Fuller both desired and dreaded meeting had, indeed, been many times marked by grief. His father had died when Waldo was only seven. Two of his younger brothers, Edward and Charles, both of whom everyone had considered more intellectually promising than he, were dead from tuberculosis before Fuller and Emerson met. The frightful disease had not passed him by, either. At twenty-three, he had gone to Florida to strengthen his lungs, and the trip had possibly saved him. Nevertheless, whenever Emerson drew a difficult breath, the moment came as a reminder of dear ones lost. In his writings, Emerson was dismissive of the sadness that had so often touched him, even referring to grief with a kind of disappointment. "There are moods," he wrote years later, "in which we court suffering, in the hope that here, at least, we shall find reality, sharp peaks and edges of truth. But it turns out to be scene-painting and counterfeit. The only thing grief has taught me, is to know how shallow it is."[37] Actually, what grief had taught him was to decrease his willingness to feel.

However, as Fuller mulled the possibility of meeting Emerson, he was moving toward a second marriage. At thirty-one, he had met a tall, slender, retiring woman who, at eight months his senior, had fairly entered a phase of life that, in the 1830s, often amounted to confirmed spinsterhood. Lydia Jackson had heard Emerson as a lecturer and guest preacher in her home town of Plymouth and had felt "so lifted to higher thoughts" that she promptly decided she had been in the presence of "an angelic being."[38] Emerson's response to her was just as powerful. Soon after they were introduced, trusting his pen more than his tongue, he sent a letter asking, "Can I resist the impulse to beseech you to love me?"[39] Rather obviously, he could not. Neither could she. Emerson did impose one curious condition on their relationship. Because New England accents tended to make his new fiancée's name sound like "Liddier," a sound that grated on his poet's ear, he requested that she henceforth be known as "Lidian." She assented. A further proof of Lidian's remarkable willingness to sacrifice her own ego came years later. When her eldest daughter was born, she proposed to Emerson that they name the baby Ellen Tucker Emerson in memory of her husband's first wife. He accepted the suggestion. With smiling affection, Emerson called his second wife "Queenie." She always called him "Mr. Emerson," yet it was surprising to see how much tenderness she could insert into that seeming formality.

In March 1835, when word of the couple's engagement reached Fuller, she responded with a letter to Hedge that displayed an avid interest in Emerson's private life. Although she conceded that Lidian was "every-way calculated to make Mr. Emerson happy," she was at a loss to understand why "men who marry a second time usually select a wife of character and manners entirely unlike their first."[40] Given that Ellen Tucker had been witty, high-spirited, romantic, and beautiful, Margaret's musings hardly reflected charitably on Lidian.[41] A line or so later, Fuller likened Emerson's choice of a second bride to "a similar instance [of] a gentleman in N York [who] married . . . a gentle, fanciful, golden-haired, blue-eyed maid. . . . She died at the age of 19 . . . and here he is engaged to a woman . . . as ugly, as ungraceful, and as simply devoted to duty as possible."[42] Fuller had not literally called Lidian simple, ugly, and graceless, but she had broadly invited a host of unkindly inferences. They were singular observations for a young woman with no evident stake in the happiness of the parties in question, and they foretold, for good or ill, a singular friendship between her and the groom-to-be.

Fuller had much more reason to seek that friendship in the aftermath of her father's death. It is easy enough to suppose that Fuller was hoping to find a strong male figure to compensate for her father's absence. There was now a practical need as well. To support herself and her siblings, Fuller needed to form alliances, and she needed to make the most of them. Emerson's interest in a meeting had also been refreshed; Harriet Martineau had praised Margaret warmly. Thus, after laying the groundwork in what Emerson later called

Emerson modestly referred to his handsome home in Concord as "Bush."
The house became the unofficial headquarters of American transcendentalism.
(COURTESY OF CONCORD FREE PUBLIC LIBRARY)

"a little diplomatizing in billets by the ladies," Margaret set aside her shyness, as well as her preconceptions about Lidian and, on July 21, 1836, made her way to the couple's new home in Concord—a handsome, white, L-shaped house that Emerson humbly referred to as "Bush."[43]

The invitation was for a fortnight, though it is far from clear what reason Lidian would have had for entertaining Fuller for two whole weeks. Emerson had the impression that Fuller had come to visit his wife, and it was with this belief that he emerged from his library to greet her. Fuller beheld an unusually tall, spare man whose arms seemed loosely hung on his narrow, sloping shoulders.[44] In later years, Emerson complained of a bust that Daniel Chester French sculpted of him: "The trouble is that the more it resembles me the worse it looks."[45] Yet there was a handsomeness to his clear, penetrating eyes and his angular Yankee features. When Fuller's brother Richard met Emerson a few years later, he noted the essayist's "demeanor of . . . perfect sincerity and simplicity," as well as his "almost feminine delicacy and refinement."[46] Yet the attraction between the slightly manly woman and the somewhat womanly man was not instantaneous. If he was uncertain about the reasons for her visit, Emerson never forgot the initial impact—"impression" is too gentle a word—of her arrival. Well after her death, he claimed that he still remembered the first half hour of Margaret's conversation. Yet as his memoir of her first moments in his home reveals, he saw her initially not as a fellow scholar, but as a woman:

> She had a face and frame that would indicate fulness and tenacity of life. She was rather under the middle height; her complexion was fair, with strong fair hair. She was then, as always, carefully and becomingly dressed, and of ladylike self-possession.[47]

His remaining observations were not so promising. Her extreme overall plainness and the nasal tone of her voice actually repelled him. So, too, did her distracting habit of incessantly opening and shutting her eyelids—a behavior that Emerson at first regarded as a "trick." He wondered whether he could bear to stay in the same room with her and said to himself, "We shall never get far." He had heard tales of her "dangerous reputation for satire," and his misgivings were now confirmed by her manners, "which expressed an overweening sense of power, and slight esteem of others." He could well understand the judgment often expressed by other men that she "carried too many guns."[48] In all likelihood, though Margaret's aggressiveness on this occasion arose not from a sense of superiority, but from a failure to contain her excitement and a desire to conceal her insecurity. No one knows whether she realized how bad an impression she was making on the man she had hoped above all others to impress. Fortunately, she stuck to her strong suit; she kept talking.

The intensity of the body language in those first moments must have been extraordinary. Nathaniel Hawthorne's son, Julian, later observed that Emerson "had a habit of projecting forward his head, precisely as an eagle on a perch does."[49] Fuller's nearsightedness and the slight curvature of her spine tended likewise to thrust her head forward "in an unfortunate manner."[50] She, too, was likened in her posture to a "bird of prey."[51] The two eagles thus leaned toward each other in anticipation. They had many mutual acquaintances, and Fuller evidently started there, for Emerson initially thought her "too much interested in personal history." Yet, as she unleashed "an incredible variety of anecdotes" about the people she knew, adding "an absurd turn" to all that she mentioned, he began to be taken in by her narrative comedy "in which dramatic justice was done to everybody's foibles."[52]

It was not the kind of conversation he was accustomed to having. His family had always praised the virtues of distance and reserve, and he himself had sought a life of solitude and scholarship. In the amusing gossip into which she drew him, he sensed something that his instincts told him was profane. His most accustomed expression was an urbane half smile; now this unprecedented woman was making him laugh more than he liked. When, at last, her conversation subsided and he retreated to his library, he did so with a sensation in his mind that he obscurely likened to "the crackling of thorns under a pot." Fuller's very determination to make a good debut with Emerson had somehow overbalanced her objective failure to do so. She was, he recalled, "too intent on establishing a good footing between us to omit any art of winning. She . . . challenged frankness by frankness, and did not conceal the good opinion of me she brought with her, nor her wish to please. . . . Of course, it was impossible long to hold out against such urgent assault."[53] Fuller stayed not two weeks, but three.

It did not all go easily. Fuller remained anxious about pleasing her hosts, and her efforts sometimes brought her underfoot. Ensconced in the room across the hall from Emerson's study, she evidently gave in repeatedly to the temptation to disturb him. She had been in residence ten days when her intrusiveness prompted a weary complaint in Waldo's journal: "The wise man has no secrets." She was especially eager to discover his opinion of her—"I know not what you think of me" was her particular complaint—and he wanted neither to swell her vanity with a false answer nor to wound her pride with a true one. With festering impatience, he wrote in his journal what he was too tactful to tell her: "If I, if all your friends should draw your portrait to you—faults & graces, it would mislead you, embarrass you. . . . You must not look in the glass to see how handsome you are but to see if your face is clean."[54] In Fuller's petitions to be judged, Emerson saw only narcissism. He was mistaken. Timothy Fuller's assessment that she had no faults was too little and too late a pronouncement to assure Margaret that she was a satisfactory person. She had not been allowed to drink deeply enough from the fountains of approval, and her thirst was now insatiable.

Lidian, of course, had still more to bear during Margaret's visit. A special sainted corner of heaven may exist for the wives of the transcendental dreamers who strolled through Concord and Boston before the Civil War. The whims of these men, often pursued with seemingly no awareness of the hopes and feelings they were bruising, brought incalculable exasperation to the women who had to endure them. Lidian Emerson, married only ten months and pregnant with her husband's first child, looked on as an unmarried woman, almost eight years her junior, settled under her roof, beguiled her husband with glittering repartee, and was in no rush to leave. Lidian was, however, a Christian woman, and, along with the very best of those who profess that faith, she was preternaturally kind. She saw no ill motive in Fuller's familiarity, and indeed, there was none to see. After Fuller had been in residence for a week, Lidian wrote, "We like her—she likes us." Lidian had come to regard the protracted visit as an "experiment" in whether "three . . . strong & decided" persons could promptly "harmonize."[55] It seemed that they could. After another week had passed, Waldo became rhapsodic. To his brother William, he called her "extraordinary" and observed, "It is always a great refreshment to see a very intelligent person. It is like being set in a large place. You stretch your limbs & dilate to your utmost size."[56]

At last, on August 11, Fuller took her leave. Emerson proffered two going-away presents: an autograph of the late British philosopher Jeremy Bentham that he had acquired in England three years earlier and a copy of his own soon-to-be-published essay, *Nature*. The next day, Waldo's dilation and stretch had only partly subsided; his journal entry praised Margaret's breadth of mind. Still, he maintained a reservation or two regarding her "egotism of place & time & blood." It seemed to him that a truly great intellect should be free from subjectivity. "How rarely," he remarked, "can a female mind be impersonal."[57]

While forging her friendship with the Emersons, Fuller also made the acquaintance of the fair-haired, gentlemanly schoolmaster whom Emerson regarded as a "God-made priest": Bronson Alcott.[58] The self-taught son of an unlettered Connecticut farmer, Alcott had discovered his life's passion in the education of young children, in whose consciousnesses he thought he had found proof of a prior existence.[59] Having absorbed from sundry quarters much of the educational thinking of Jean-Jacques Rousseau and Johann Pestalozzi, he believed that the best qualities of the human mind were innate. He further maintained that, if human beings could escape the contamination of the fallen societies that raised them, they might reclaim their natural station as gods on earth. For Alcott, education worked best when it remained true to its literal meaning; it should be chiefly a "drawing out" of the child's inner sacred nature, not a cramming in of information. Whereas Harvard men like Emerson and Hedge always bore the traces of academic rigidity, the college-deprived Alcott tried to substitute the ecstasies of intuition. Fuller did not entirely trust his method, if method is what it was. Although she had had plenty of unpleasant experience with the kind of memorization and drill that Alcott scorned, she also had intense respect for hard, factual knowledge, and she well knew that one would never draw out a quadratic equation or a Virgilian eclogue from a student's soul. The extent of her initial interest in Alcott's teaching methods may perhaps be reflected in the fact that, after meeting him, she could not recollect his first name.[60]

Very soon, however, she had reason to be more interested. Alcott had lately quarreled with his teaching assistant, Elizabeth Palmer Peabody. A distinguished thinker and scholar in her own right, Peabody had initially observed in Alcott "more genius for education than I ever saw," and her published transcript of lessons that Alcott had given his pupils, *Record of a School*, had received a radiant critical reception.[61] More recently, however, Peabody had come to regard Alcott's teaching methods as excessively autocratic and manipulative. Further concerned by the free-thinking tenor of conversations Alcott was having with the children about the life of Jesus, she had resigned. Although Peabody's sister Sophia, the future Mrs. Nathaniel Hawthorne, had stood in for her on a temporary basis, Alcott needed a new full-time assistant. Though Latin was deemed essential to a respectable curriculum, Alcott had no training in any language, ancient or modern. Fuller, who could offer three languages in addition to Latin, struck Alcott as a superior candidate. Before the month was out, he approached her with a tentative offer.

Fuller, on her side, was not completely eager. She wrote to Alcott that, although his proposal had attracted her more than any other that had been made to her, unspecified family affairs would take a month for her to resolve. Therefore, she could not comfortably begin work until the end of September. Her concerns about her compatibility with the schoolmaster, both person- ally and pedagogically, also made her circumspect. "My acquaintance with your views and character," she wrote, "is not sufficiently thorough to give me a confidence that I could satisfy you." The prospect of working for Alcott struck her initially as nothing more than "an experiment on both sides." Not only did she want to know more about his teaching methods before she made a decision, but also she worried about her ability to accept a secondary role. With more than a hint of pride, she advised him, "I have never yet been sub- ordinate to any one."[62]

The thought of being subordinate was plainly not a welcome one. Fuller remained in her mind the queen of her mother's garden, the prize-winning pupil at Dr. Park's, the young woman who hesitated to make friends until she had proved her superiority. Now, she could bear to shift from a leading to a supportive role only because she could tell herself that it was just an "experi- ment." Yet subordination was soon to become not so much an experiment for Fuller as a frustratingly durable pattern. Aspiring always toward the focal points of her culture, she sought out associations with the most brilliant minds available to her. Yet the irony of these connections is that she would often be remembered as standing on the periphery of *their* stories, not at the center of her own.

For the moment, she left Alcott's offer hanging, but not with an easy conscience. Her family was relying on her for money, and she had not suf- ficiently answered the call. Persuaded that her writing could not supply a steady income, she decided to leave Groton that fall for Boston, where she took a room under the roof of her paternal uncle Henry at 1 Avon Place and made arrangements to rent some rooms next door at number 2. In the latter, she opened a school, which, as she advertised it, would "give instruc- tion to classes of Ladies in German, Italian and French literature."[63] Real- izing that she read and wrote the languages better than she spoke them, she engaged, with Emerson's intervention, a trio of Harvard-educated lin- guists to offer her pupils supplementary sessions in speaking and pronun- ciation. Her classes there met twice a week for twelve weeks, and they moved at a brisk pace; the advanced German class, for instance, covered three plays by Lessing, two by Schiller, and five by Goethe, and other material besides. Fuller enrolled approximately twenty students at her select academy at the rate of fifteen dollars each. It was a respectable beginning, but the overall revenue was not sufficient. At a time when about fifteen hundred dollars a year was needed to finance the basic wants of a family of four, three hundred dollars a quarter could supply only a small amount of relief to Fuller, her mother, and a houseful of siblings. She tried to stretch her income by giving private lessons to five other young women and by reading English history and Shakespeare to a blind boy, but the situation seemed unsustainable.

Still, when Alcott firmed up his offer of employment at the Temple School, so named for its location in Boston's imposing Masonic Temple, Fuller hesitated. The notion of casting one's lot with Alcott would have made anyone a trifle anxious. On the one hand, there was no more famous school in Boston than Alcott's, and some of the most stirring passages in Emerson's *Nature* bore the clear stamp of Alcott's inspiration; he may even have been the "Orphic poet" to whom Emerson alluded in the final chapter. Yet, as she saw with her own eyes, Alcott could be erratic. At a teaching institute in Worcester in late August 1836, which Fuller attended, Alcott had shocked his professional brethren and provoked accusations of blasphemy by announcing his belief that "man is a God on earth."[64] Elizabeth Peabody's sudden defection was another warning signal. Whatever Fuller's thoughts may have been as she weighed the offer, she seems not to have written anyone for advice. In the end, she said yes.

It was a lucky stroke that the first man who had asked her to serve him was not the kind who lorded over others. Alcott, like many liberal reformers, did not wield authority comfortably. If Elizabeth Peabody called him "autocratic," she had in mind his opinions, not his style of management.[65] At a time when corporal punishment was a standard educational tool, Alcott always asked for the pupil's consent before meting out any discipline. On at least one famous occasion, declaring that it was a worse punishment to inflict pain than endure it, he commanded two misbehaving students to apply the ruler to his own knuckles. He also supported the equality of the sexes, although unlike Fuller, who thought women should be free to assert more manliness, he thought men would improve by becoming more feminine. If Fuller had to take on the role of apostle, the temple of Alcott was a better church than most in which to do it.

Physically, the Temple School was the glory of Bostonian elementary education. Light streamed through an immense Gothic window into a room whose four corners were decorated with busts of Plato, Socrates, Shakespeare, and Scott. Bronson had plunged into debt to buy them, not to mention an array of maps, globes, and the finest desks and chairs. For Fuller, it was a place of ceaseless labor, and she had time to write only a small handful of letters while she worked there. None of these discloses much about how it felt to work at the Temple School. As far as daily operations were concerned, Alcott was probably more than happy to leave her to her unsupervised devices. When she began work for him at the beginning of December 1836, he was hard at work editing his discussions with his pupils, whom he had taken to calling his "disciples," regarding the life of Jesus Christ. A first volume of this work, titled *Conversations with Children on the Gospels*, was to come out a few days before Christmas. A second was planned for February. Indeed, Fuller discovered that one of her tasks at the school would be to take over where Peabody had left off as the transcriber of these conversations; she was to be the recording secretary for a planned third volume.

When Alcott did take the time to assess his new assistant's character, his appraisals were glowing. As she and Emerson had done, Fuller and Alcott seemed to grow in each other's presence. Alcott soon concluded that he knew of no one who more greatly promised "to add enduring glory to female literature." He wrote happily of his new second-in-command:

> Miss Fuller seems more inclined to take large and generous views of subjects than any woman of my acquaintance. I think her more liberal than almost any mind among us. She has more of that unspoiled integrity of being, so essential to the apprehension of truth in its unity, than any person of her sex whom I meet; and vastly more intellectual power.[66]

Since Alcott's female acquaintances included the Peabody sisters, Harriet Martineau, and his own wife, Abba, who was no small thinker in her own right, his praise was high indeed. Alcott predicted that Fuller would someday do a good work, though she might have to leave Boston to achieve it. He added, "To her has been given, with the gift of genius, that of prudence."[67]

If Alcott was able to perceive that latter quality in someone else, it was not because he possessed it himself. Even before Fuller began her work with him, Alcott's failure to understand the moral tenor of his time had already seeded the origins of a public uproar. He little realized how few of his contemporaries thought it appropriate to ask six-year-olds to interpret of the word of the Lord, as opposed to telling them exactly what to think about the scriptures. The book that Alcott sent to the press believing that it would cement his reputation as Boston's leading progressive educator was headed for a far different reception.

In the brief calm before the storm, Fuller had her first prolonged exposure to applied transcendentalism, the kinetic, fully formed offspring of the German Romantic influences that had so excited her when she first discovered them alongside Clarke and Hedge in 1832. Unlike them, Alcott had taken the next step to determine whether practice might follow theory; he was trying to show what it might be like to raise children by Romantic principles, training them to look for the metaphoric meanings behind sensory reality, leading them by their highest sentiments toward a view of life that regarded material objects merely as temporary means, not as all-consuming ends. Not only were the intellectual prospects thrilling, but also the surroundings were wonderfully kind. "I . . . loved the children," Margaret told Clarke, adding that Alcott's society "was much to me."[68]

Yet, on a January afternoon, as she dutifully transcribed the schoolmaster's conversation with the children on regeneration, she found herself writing, not with rapture, but with vague unease. That night, she tried to puzzle out the reason. She told her journal, "I wish I could define my distrust of Mr. Alcott's mind. I think constantly he is one-sided without being able to see where the fault lies. There is something in his philosophy which revolts either my common-sense or—my prejudices—I cannot be sure which."[69]

Another ground for objection was financial; as he had also done with Elizabeth Peabody, Alcott found pretexts for deferring the payment of Fuller's salary. Prudently, Fuller had kept on with her language instruction and was thus able to support herself, but the double work schedule was wearing her out.[70] Not only was she holding down multiple instructional positions, but her evenings were often taken up with transcribing her notes on Alcott's classroom conversations. In April, she angrily scribbled, "I earn little or nothing in this miserable school, nor am I [illegible] toward any [illegible] good in it."[71] Still worse, her apprenticeship at the Temple had brought her own scholarly work to a standstill.

In the spring, her objections to Alcott's thinking crystallized. In a document she did not show him until three years later, she privately accused him of a threefold error. First, he had failed to comprehend "the nature of Genius or creative power." One suspects she meant that Alcott grasped only the inspiration essential to creativity; the element of perspiration eluded him. Second, said Fuller, he had misapprehended "the reaction of matter on spirit"—that is, his theories of the psyche failed to recognize the power of the physical world both to shape and to bruise the soul. Finally, lacking both the patience to understand complexity and the playfulness that delights in finding variety within unity, he had tried to impose on life a homogeneity of vision that was simply false.[72] The great failure of Alcott was that, in trying to apply transcendental ideas to practical reality, he had forgotten that it is always theory that must bow to experience, not the other way around. "Thus," as Fuller put it, "the break of your spirit on the crag of the actual makes surf and foam, but leaves no gem behind." To show that there was sympathy behind her criticism, she added, "Yet it is a great wave, Mr. Alcott."[73]

A far greater wave was coming. It hit with all its force when the conservative Boston press laid its hands on *Conversations with Children on the Gospels*. By itself, Alcott's willingness to set the utterances of children alongside those of Saint Matthew stirred serious misgivings among all but the most progressive reviewers of his book. However, in the eyes of popular opinion, he had done far worse. Alcott's classroom discussion of the birth of Jesus had predictably led him into disquisitions on the meanings of "virgin" and "conception," as well as other dodgy subjects. He had addressed the subjects with great delicacy and reverence, but it didn't matter. Before Alcott could respond, his book had been labeled not only blasphemous but also obscene. Rumors circulated that a mob would attack Alcott as he led a conversation with adults at the Temple. Both Emerson and James Freeman Clarke rallied to the schoolmaster's defense, but things began to look desperate when Hedge privately stated his intent to break ranks with his fellow transcendentalists and publish an article in the *Christian Examiner* that would "cut up Mr. Alcott."

Fuller had no pressing reason to defend her employer; not only was she disaffected with his philosophical outlook, but he apparently had yet to pay her a dollar. Nevertheless, she came to his rescue, firing off a letter to Hedge deploring his intentions. Hedge might serve Alcott well by writing "a long, beautiful, wise article showing the elevated aim and at the same time the practical defects of his system." As for cutting up the poor man, however, Fuller protested that "there are plenty of fish in the net created solely for markets &c no need to try your knife on a dolphin like him." Fuller could not believe that her dear, enlightened Germanicus would side with the reactionaries in blotting out "this star of purest ray serene."[74]

Evidently abashed at his own pettiness, Hedge cast aside his plan and, in the end, wrote nothing. Still, Alcott's school had sustained a wound from which it never recovered. His enrollment withered overnight to eleven pupils. He was forced to auction off the fine furnishings he had bought for the classroom and, symbolically, traded his radiant classroom on a top floor of the Temple for a dingy room in its basement. Despite his having failed her financially, Fuller continued to regard Alcott as "a true and noble man, a philanthropist."[75] However, seeing no way to stanch the bleeding at his school, Fuller gave notice and packed away her belongings for a return to Groton. Her foray into teaching in Boston had enriched her in experience only, and she chafed at her failure to convert even that into something original. As she prepared for her journey home she wrote Hedge, "I have learned much and thought little. . . . I faint with desire to think and surely shall, the first oppor[tunit]y, but some outward requisition is ever knocking at the door of my mind and I am as ill placed as regards a chance to think as a haberdasher's prentice or," she added wryly, "the President of Harvard University."[76]

On her way home to Groton, Fuller paid a visit to the Emersons. She looked to Concord as her "Lethe and Eunoi after [a] purgatory of distracting, petty tasks."[77] She was ready to be immersed in beauty, and, although the trees were still bare at the beginning of May, the Massachusetts spring somehow did not disappoint. As Emerson drove her about in his carriage, little birds "revel[led], and carol[led], and wildly [told] their hopes" as a south wind stirred the branches and the pine trees sighed with "soul-like sounds."[78] At Bush, she was greeted by an additional Emerson: the couple's son Waldo had been born the previous October 30. Margaret thought he was beautiful, "a perfect May morning, after regular, grown up winter people."[79] As babies are wont to do, little Waldo drew both his father and Margaret away from their accustomed bookishness and into the pleasure of the moment. Margaret observed, "He comes so *natural*, after Dante and other poems."[80] Fuller was "very happy" while in Concord. After returning to Groton, however, she confessed to feeling a partial emptiness that she could not name. Concord, she told a friend afterward, "was *satisfactory*; nothing is *satisfying* in this wale [*sic*] of tears."[81]

The spring of 1837 was an anxious time for Margaret and for America as well. Beginning in 1832, President Andrew Jackson had taken a series of actions to weaken and destroy the Bank of the United States, a policy that had left the country without any centralized authority regarding its money supply. Decisions later in the president's tenure fatally undermined confidence in paper money. Almost immediately after Jackson left office, the deregulated economy ran aground. At the beginning of April, a wave of business failures struck New York, where, in the two weeks after Easter, more than 125 employers closed their doors. On May 10, the city's banks refused to trade silver and gold for paper currency, and the economy collapsed. The depression was to last five years. "The land," wrote Emerson later that spring, "smells with suicide."[82]

In Groton, Fuller had endured something of a collapse as well. Twenty months after the fact, she found herself still laboring under the shock of her father's death, a blow from which she doubted she would ever wholly recover.[83] Still exhausted by the overwork of the previous winter and the sadness of witnessing the crumbling of Alcott's school, she had had to cut short her visit to Concord and had enjoyed only a few hours since her return home in which she had felt equal to any kind of exertion.[84] Her headaches, she thought, were worthy of a great man. After her "twenty-five weeks of incessant toil" in Boston, almost the only work of which she had been capable, apart from reading, was the translation of some poems by Schiller and Goethe, and these merely served to make her "painfully sensible of my presumption in undertaking what I did."[85] To her deep frustration, she found that Goethe's unrhymed poems were entirely beyond her. Her attempts at Schiller, too, left her "altogether dispirited" and unable to "summon courage to go on."[86] Still, any work that carried the promise of money was welcome to her. "Translations," she wrote Hedge, "are no better . . . than an asylum for the destitute, but that asylum must be provided."[87]

She knew, however, that relief was imminent. Before leaving Alcott's employ, she had already heard from Hiram Fuller, a Providence educator to whom she was not related. Mr. Fuller hoped to bring her to Rhode Island to teach at his progressive Greene Street School. Not only did Mr. Fuller offer her a yearly salary of a thousand dollars, less than two years after Emerson had paid thirty-five hundred dollars for his house and two-acre grounds, but he actually possessed the wherewithal to pay it. Once again, Margaret was forced to strike a balance between scholarly ambition and financial need. She calculated that, since she would no longer have to flesh out her earnings with additional teaching, she would be able to teach at Greene Street in the mornings and set aside her remaining hours for her own long-neglected work. She now had two major projects in view. The first was a translation of a lengthy volume of conversations with Goethe as recorded by his secretary Johann Peter Eckermann. The second was the fairest jewel of her literary ambitions: her long-contemplated Goethe biography. The idea of living in Providence held no charm for her. She was also "still quite unwell." Fears of dying clung to her, and she was not at all sure how the job at Greene Street would affect her health.[88] In the end, though, the prospect of having both time and money proved irresistible. She would give teaching another try.

Although Margaret was later to observe that he was "as unlike as possible to Mr. Alcott," possessing "neither his poetic beauty nor his practical defects," Hiram Fuller admired Alcott so much that he regarded his academy as the spiritual heir of the Temple School.[89] To emphasize the link, he not only invited Fuller to join the faculty but also hoped to persuade Alcott himself to speak at the dedication of the school's new building. Alcott, conscious that his presence was likely to taint any rising enterprise, suggested Emerson instead. Emerson initially thought he was accepting only an invitation to attend. He realized belatedly—and with a mixture of annoyance and surprise—that he was expected to deliver a speech on education. Wishing he had never consented to come, he hastily composed an oration that Mr. Fuller liked well enough to want to publish, though Emerson evidently withheld his permission.

Standing before the overflowing crowd in a Unitarian church, Emerson likely adhered to the mannerisms that frequent attendees of his lectures knew by heart. He would stand, looking down at his manuscript, with his hands folded in front of him, except to turn a page. To emphasize a point, he would clench his right fist, bend the arm upward, and then bring it down with the force of a blow.[90] He chose as his topic the power of education to produce a complete human being.[91] Man in the age of steam and iron, Emerson averred, had become "a money chest . . . the treadle of a factory-wheel . . . an appendage."[92] He hoped that Fuller's school might help to restore men and women to their wholeness by teaching boys and girls "to aspire to be all they can . . . as if we believed in their noble nature."[93] He then cautioned darkly against the great enemy of education, a money-grubbing ethos that called for the training only of "accountants, attornies, [and] engineers," instead of "able, earnest, great-hearted men." If the pursuit of a man should "degenerate into the mere love of money, he dieth daily, he becomes no man but a money machine." He called on Hiram Fuller's faculty to remember "the capital secret of their profession, namely, to convert life into truth."[94]

With these words fresh in her memory, Fuller assumed her task. She lodged at a boardinghouse operated by another teacher's mother. Her room was "not . . . really pleasant," and she had to walk a long distance to find any expanse of greenery. Nevertheless, her fellow roomers seemed neat, kind, and disposed to leave her alone when she wished. She therefore expected to get on well.[95] Again her course offerings demanded a wide breadth of preparation: Latin, composition, elocution, history, natural philosophy, and, eventually, a course on the New Testament. In order to manage her duties efficiently and continue her scholarly work besides, she set herself a bracing daily schedule: up at five and sometimes even half past four, dressed by six and immersed in her own studies until breakfast was served at seven thirty. She went to Greene Street at half past eight, where her teaching absorbed her day until twelve thirty. She took her dinner at the boardinghouse an hour later. Here is how she summarized the remainder of her day: "Lie down till three, then write or study till tea time. After tea walk or make visits till ten—to bed about eleven. So I live very rationally."[96] One may debate the rationality of a schedule that allowed her no more than six hours of sleep a night. Still, she saw the morning hours she spent translating Eckermann's conversations as well worth the sacrifice.

The school to which she traveled each morning was even more splendid in appearance than the Temple School had been. Housed in a Greek Revival edifice with Doric columns, it featured a great hall with white walls and thick orange carpeting—a space suitable for dances, music parties, and evening conversations. Fuller wrote glowingly to her brother Arthur about the room's piano, its handsome urn of drinking water, and its vases of beautiful cut flowers. In good weather, she could expect the girls to bring her bouquets each day. Mr. Fuller made certain that the boys and girls were neatly dressed, and he supplied looking glasses in the dressing rooms, so the children could check their appearance. Fuller taught sixty students, all of whom, she thought, looked "healthy and excessively happy."[97]

In sobering contrast, she found that the intellectual state of her students—a mix of boys and girls in the younger, coeducational classes and a group of older girls—was low in comparison with that of her Boston pupils, a condition she blamed on Providence's embrace of "the hostile element of money getting with but little counterpoise." The facility of language and depth of imagination that Alcott had encouraged were conspicuously absent. For her, the Temple had embodied "a liveliness of mind." At Greene Street, "in many of *these* with well-disposed hearts, [the] mind has been absolutely torpid."[98]

To this torpor, Fuller resolved not to surrender. She would insist on original thought, and she would force her students to be free. In the eyes of her students, she quickly became both an object of admiration and an avatar of continual terror. Fuller was assigned a Latin class whose members were thought ready to begin studying Virgil. Fuller found they were not, and she subjected them to thirty weeks of precise grammatical study. As Fuller pressed them to submit the best work they could do, her sensitivity regressed to an earlier phase; as in her teens, she resorted to satire and sarcasm. One pupil, despite her feeling that it was a great privilege to study with Fuller, lived in dread of her tongue. In a missive home, she wrote, "She is very critical and sometimes cuts us up into bits. When she cuts us all in a lump, it is quite pleasant, for she is quite witty; but woe to one whom she cuts by herself! I do not know what she would say to this letter. I would not have her see it for five dollars!"[99]

When one especially talented but painfully shy student muffed an assignment, Fuller was so merciless that the rest of the class rose to the girl's defense. They wrote out their objections, signed them round-robin style, and delivered them to Fuller.[100] To her great credit, Fuller answered the challenge with humility. She wrote back to her youthful critics:

I often regret that you have not a teacher who has more heart, more health, more energy to spend upon you than I have; for truly I esteem you worthy of much more. . . . But my duties in life are at present so many, and my health so precarious, that I dare not be *generous* lest I should thus be unable to be *just*, dare not indulge my feelings lest I should fail to discharge my duties. [Though] I . . . act by you in so miserly a spirit . . . it is not because I do not value you and even (I use not the word lightly) love you. . . . [Y]ou will do me justice in believing that I generally feel much more regard than I express. . . . Give my love to J. I hope I was not too rough with her this morning.[101]

As Fuller hinted to her scholars, her disagreeableness had a number of causes. She was surely not the only teacher ever to enter a classroom expecting to perform miracles and find her students reluctant or unable to transform as she wished. One student recalled, "She spoke [to us] on what woman could do—said she should like to see a woman everything she might be, in intellect and character."[102] It annoyed Fuller terribly that, when she opened the door to knowledge and opportunity, her young charges were disinclined to walk through. Her health added to her irritation. She had been in Providence only a few weeks when she complained of being tormented by "languor and want of animal spirits."[103] By October, she was "too miserably unwell . . . to make any exertion beyond giving my lessons and reading a little."[104] To her sister, she confessed doubts as to whether she would ever be perfectly well again.[105] Too much of her time seemed wasted on petty annoyances. She complained to Emerson, "I have, maugre my best efforts, been able to do very little" of the scholarly work to which she had looked forward.[106]

Still worse, word came from home that Uncle Abraham was continuing to play the role of hectoring curmudgeon. Margaret received a frantic letter from her mother: Abraham was withholding the money necessary for her brothers and Ellen to proceed with their educations. Unlike his brother Timothy, Abraham had eschewed Harvard, choosing instead to educate himself, and he still had no great regard for fancy schooling. In insulting terms, Abraham had berated his brother's widow for her lack of "good sense" and reminded her that, as the children's legal guardian, he, not she, would decide how the family's modest capital would be spent.[107] Margaret exhorted her tremulous mother to stand firm. "Do not suffer the remarks of that sordid man to give you any uneasiness," she advised. "We pay Abraham and we could as well pay another man who would confine himself to his proper post of managing the money." Whatever the legal state of things, she wrote, Margaret's mother needed to consider herself the guardian of the children and "must not let his vulgar insults make you waver as to giving the children advantages to which they would be well entitled if the property were only a third of what it now is." Margaret showed particular concern for Ellen, who, she was determined, would not pass her teen years without a year of schooling. She would pay her sister's bills, and, failing all else, Ellen could come to Providence, and Fuller would see to her education herself.[108] Ellen did, in fact, join Margaret for most of November and repaid her sister's instruction by taking over the cooking.[109] Fortunately, Margarett and Margaret were at last able to prevail over the parsimonious Abraham. All the Fuller children were allowed to remain in their private schools with the exception of Richard, who, though only thirteen, stayed at home in Groton to manage the farm.[110]

All these concerns aside, though, there was another that gnawed at Fuller more than any other. Trapped in Providence and burdened with a job far beneath her abilities, she saw no means of fulfilling what she had supposed to be her destiny as a thinker and writer. Emerson, after receiving a letter she had sent him complaining about the smallness of her field of action, wrote back in sympathy: "Power and Aim, the two halves of felicity, seldomest meet." The seeming impossibility of finding "work commensurate with [one's] faculty" seemed to him the characteristic malady of the time.[111] Fuller could hardly disagree. True, she was granted membership in the city's premier literary society—the Coliseum Club—but it soon seemed small and petty compared with what she had seen in Cambridge and Boston. Over time, she came to associate Providence generally with "uncongenial pursuits and . . . oppressive intercourse with vulgar minds."[112]

A bright spot was provided during these months by a brisk correspondence with Samuel Gray Ward.[113] Sam had parted company with the Farrars after they sailed together to Europe in the summer of 1836, and had taken a leisurely tour through England, Paris, and Rome on the way to the Swiss Alps, where he rejoined the Farrars in August 1837. Neither Sam nor Margaret had forgotten their time together at Trenton Falls. Sadly, none of their transatlantic correspondence survives, though it is fair to guess that Sam made scant mention of the diversion that was absorbing most of his interest. Anna Barker, the young woman whom Fuller herself had found so attractive in Newport a few years earlier, had traveled separately to Europe but had since rendezvoused with the Farrars. According to Mrs. Farrar, Anna was the kind of beauty for whom prospective landlords lowered their rent and prime tickets for sold-out operas suddenly became available. As Sam and Anna admired the mountains and played together with the Saint Bernard puppy he had purchased, they fell in love.[114] It was an attachment of which Fuller remained blissfully ignorant, at least for the time.

Other escapes were available when she visited Concord and Boston. Her spirits always rose after she spent time with Lidian Emerson. Lidian had intellectual leanings of her own—she was an avid reader of the Swedish idealist Emanuel Swedenborg. Unlike some of her contemporaries, however, she never let ideas stand in the way of charity. In obedience to a verse she read in the Bible, "Give to him that asketh of thee," Lidian dispensed clothes, bedding, and money to the needy of Concord with a ready hand.[115] She also did not hesitate to chastise her husband when she felt his philosophy was taking him too far away from human kindness. She once wrote and presented him with a satire she called "The Transcendental Bible," which advised, among other precepts, "Loathe and shun the sick. They are in bad taste, and may untune us for writing the poem floating through our mind."[116] Waldo took Lidian's jibe as a capital joke. Fuller said of Lidian, "The thought of her holiness is very fragrant to me."[117]

It was still the mind that Fuller cultivated most whenever she came back to Massachusetts. In Cambridge, the previous year, Emerson had met with Hedge and two other Unitarian ministers to form an intellectual society "in the way of protest" against the dry, narrow condition of the American intellect.[118] Soon claiming such members as Alcott, Clarke, and Convers Francis, the symposium had taken to calling itself the "Hedge Club," since it tended to convene whenever Hedge could come down from his pastorate in Bangor. The group became known to posterity, however, as the "Transcendental Club." To Fuller's great satisfaction, the club opened its doors to women, and intellects like Elizabeth Peabody and Sophia Ripley, the wife of transcendentalist minister and club cofounder George Ripley, availed themselves of the privilege. Fuller was there whenever possible. With genial intensity, the members debated religion, education, and American genius. In early September, with a constellation of minds that outshone any college faculty in America, Fuller discussed "The Progress of Society." In their company, she heard Emerson give the great Phi Beta Kappa Society address later known as "The American Scholar."

Fuller wrote no letters that expressed her reaction to Emerson's speech, though one suspects its message to her was a mildly uncomfortable one. The address was a warning to those who deferred utterly to the book, who took their reading as unimpeachable authority instead of living inspiration. Genius lay not in amassing the knowledge of the past, but in using it to construct something new: "Whatever talents may be, if the man create not, the pure efflux of the Deity is not his;—cinders and smoke there may be, but not yet flame."[119] To be sure, Fuller was an active thinker, and no one could accuse her of being unoriginal. And yet, what had she created? What page of her reading had she translated, not merely into another tongue, but into the language of living fire? Despondently, she wrote to her mother, "It is no longer in my power to write and study much. Heaven, I believe, had no will that I should accomplish anything great or beautiful."[120] Emerson complained that his country's thinkers were overly "decent, indolent, complaisant."[121] She had replied by asking him, "Who would be a goody that could be a genius?"[122] But in 1837 the America that lay outside the doors of the Transcendental Club pressed its talented women into the camp of the goodies, and its female geniuses lived with the threat of slow suffocation.

Fuller's association with the Transcendental Club was more personal than philosophical. Too many of her experiences—her ill-fated romance with George Davis, her father's move to Groton, the scandal at the Temple School—had taught her the folly of wishful thinking, and the ethereal optimism of Emerson and Alcott seemed just a bit too easy to her. Perhaps, too, there was something in her identity as a woman that prevented her from embracing their philosophy with an undivided heart. No matter how her mind and soul might aspire, her body would always impose on her a host of social limitations from which her male compatriots had always been free, to say nothing of the chronic headaches and periods of exhaustion that also conspired to keep her mind from pressing forward at top speed. It was hard indeed to espouse the supremacy of the Over-soul when one's body so consistently played the role of betrayer. Then, too, Fuller's romanticism was not the dreamy kind that inspired English poets like Shelley and Coleridge. She remained a disciple of Goethe, who had been not only a poet but also a scientist, a theater director, and a state official. There was, therefore, usually a bit more real-world practicality in Fuller's transcendentalism than in that of her colleagues.

Nevertheless, the transcendentalists offered Fuller what she could have found nowhere else in America. Among no other group were the minds so restlessly alive. Moreover, they valued the soul more than the body. Their regard for the divinity of the mind helped them to look past the nasal-voiced, squinting oddity that others knew as Margaret Fuller and to see her, not as a flawed, mortal woman, but as an aspiring spirit. More simply, they were open-minded, generous men who scorned limitation. In their presence, Fuller could best feel what both her intuition and her reading of German philosophy had convinced her must be true: that eternal aspiration and improvement are the authentic conditions of the spirit.

Yet Fuller also discovered that associating with the members of the Hedge Club had its costs, a fact brought home to her with particular starkness when she invited her dear friend Caroline Sturgis to board with her in Providence. As a friend for Margaret, Caroline was virtually ideal. The daughter of William Sturgis, a sea captain turned merchant whose firm, Bryant and Sturgis, controlled half the trade between the United States and China, Caroline was nine years Margaret's junior and eager to find someone to better fill the role of her emotionally unsteady mother. Caroline had an untamed spirit and an openness to new ideas that somewhat shocked her family. Although Caroline wanted to think new thoughts and break free from convention, she was also introspective and dependent on others to help her choose her directions. Exuberant and malleable, Caroline appealed deeply to Margaret's instincts as a teacher, who saw her as someone she could both liberate and, to a degree, control. Initially keen on the idea of moving in with Margaret, Caroline suddenly balked. It appears that a roadblock had been erected by her father. A man with much to lose if his reputation for prudence were questioned, Captain Sturgis had thought twice about sending his daughter to consort with a woman of such radical associations as Margaret—associations that he dimly connected with the specter of women's rights and a threat to domestic stability. Fuller responded with "strong indignation," and she firmly disavowed having wedded herself to any subversive credo:

As to transcendentalism and the nonsense which is talked by so many about it—I do not know what is meant. For myself I should say that if it is meant that I have an active mind frequently busy with large topics I hope it is so—If it is meant that I am honored by the friendship of such men as Mr. Emerson, Mr. Ripley, or Mr. Alcott, I hope it is so— But if it is meant that I cherish any opinions which interfere with domestic duties, cheerful courage and judgement in the practical affairs of life, I challenge any or all in the little world that knows me to prove such deficiency from any acts of mine since I came to woman's estate.[123]

The dangers of being connected with transcendentalism were revealed again in July 1838, when Emerson addressed the graduating class of Harvard Divinity School. Standing before the eager young ministers-to-be, Emerson had called the doctrines proclaiming the unique divinity of Jesus "a distortion" and had claimed that all human beings possessed the same god-like potential. "That which shows God in me," he had asserted, "fortifies me. That which shows God out of me, makes me a wart and a wen." He argued that the true miracles of life were the blowing clover and the falling rain and that the idea of the miraculous preached in the churches was a monstrosity. "Man," he said, "is the wonderworker."[124] Emerson was not invited back to Harvard for decades. The *Christian Examiner* denounced the address as "repugnant," and Andrews Norton, the most influential voice of conservative Unitarianism, called Emerson's words "a general attack upon the Clergy" and "an insult to religion."[125] At a time when it was still not unheard of for men to be jailed for blasphemy, there were brief whispers that Emerson might be prosecuted. After she visited Emerson in August, when the furor was at its height, Fuller reflected proudly on her friend's ability to "shine out through all this fog. I have fine friends certainly; how dignified they look, while dirt is being thrown at them."[126] But the beauty of Emerson's aura could not dispel entirely the outrage of the mudslinging. First Alcott, now Emerson. Transcendentalism was a philosophy under siege.

Undeterred by the controversies that swirled around her friends, Fuller boldly shared with her students her belief that God intended for the soul "to go on progressing through the ages, and ages of eternity," and "that, in the course of that endless period of time we may even surpass the angels in knowledge, power, and glory."[127] For Fuller herself, a woman devoted to upward transformation, life as a teacher of wealthy girls was literally ungodly. Fuller's students read the signs of her disappointment. Juliet Graves, the sensitive girl whose harsh treatment at Fuller's hands had inspired the round robin, saw it most clearly:

> [T]he better I become acquainted with the infinite capacity of her mind, the more I see of her glorious endowments, I feel that her situation is not that for which she is fitted: it seems to me that she finds not here the sympathy which her spirit craves. The minds around her do not, cannot, sympathize with hers. She cannot exercise her brightest, highest powers, for they cannot be understood. . . . She is obliged to bury, as it were, that which is most congenial to her mind.[128]

One thing Fuller could not bury was her insistence on a better destiny for women. Undeniably, she made an impression. To sit in her classroom was to understand that womanhood need not lead to a domesticated dead end. Despite the obstacles of convention and orthodoxy, a young woman, too, could converse with philosophers and walk among the gods. Mary Allen, one of Fuller's more admiring students, wrote of her classmates, "They do not live to dress and visit, and gossip and get married. They are studious to improve themselves, to do good, to live for their higher natures."[129] None of Fuller's students at Greene Street went on to lasting renown, but this fact hardly reflects on her as a teacher. An instructor's greatest gifts perform their work quietly and invisibly. The inspired teacher leads the willing follower to a rare and celestial state of mind in which knowledge stands revealed as a form of love. Fuller taught with the hope of guiding a few earnest souls to that sacred grove. The fact that the majority of her students became teachers themselves suggests that she succeeded.

Fuller herself did not regard her labors as a success. The physical strain was starting to overpower her. Walking the daily three-mile round-trip between home and school in the summer heat affected her nerves, and she was often obliged "to sit down and cry a long while" at both ends of the journey. She was just dragging herself through the days; never had she felt "so utterly incompetent to do any thing."[130] When the August 1838 recess finally arrived, she returned to Massachusetts in "a state of weak sensitiveness." When she stopped to see the Emersons on her way to Groton, some remark of Lidian's upset her greatly. After Lidian apologized, Fuller graciously blamed her own "evil doing" and expressed the hope that "some time

... of seclusion and repose" under her mother's roof would cure her touchiness. Fuller added that she believed she would leave Providence in December, at the end of the upcoming term. She had reached this decision, she said, "after a noble effort to consult my own health and feelings."[131] Though Fuller's decision to resign her teaching position was plainly a prudent one, it felt to her like an admission of defeat. "I have done and suffered much," she told Lidian, "without obtaining my object, or removing one evil which formerly afflicted me, and I cannot be joyful."[132]

Thankfully, this August recess gave her a different reason to feel glad. Back from his travels in Europe, Sam Ward had returned to Boston after working for several months at the New York mercantile firm of Jonathan Goodhue. The following month, his friendship with Margaret resumed. Referring to Sam's artistic talents, she had taken to calling him "Raffaello." One afternoon, after meeting at the Athenaeum, the two went for a drive together that Fuller recorded with deep satisfaction: "It was one of those soft, gloomy times. . . . Gleams of brassy light succeeded a gently pattering shower, and we sped homeward in the palest starlight. Nature seemed to sympathize with me today. She was not too bright, she was not too wild, and I was with the only person who ever understood me at once in such moods."[133] Sam had come back from Italy armed with hundreds of prints and etchings of the works of the Renaissance masters, as well as a thick portfolio of his own drawings. Together the two examined these leaf by leaf, and Fuller tried to persuade Sam to abandon his fledgling business career for the life of an artist. Emerson noticed that Margaret was watching "the unfolding of [Sam's] powers . . . with the warmest sympathy." Although the two claimed to be principally concerned with the books and studies that they had in common, Emerson surmised that their artistic sympathies, "though sincere, were only veils and occasions to beguile the time, so profound was her interest in the character and fortunes of her friend."[134]

On her way back to Providence, Fuller made a detour to Newport, where she gloried in the natural splendor of the place: "Such cloudless sunsets, with floods of rose and amber light; such overpowering moonlight, such wood walks, such beach walks, and all with proper people." The last perhaps reminded her of the not precisely improper, but certainly boring, people into whose midst she was returning. On September 21, she wrote positively, "I leave Providence in December."[135]

It was a busy autumn. Trying to shore up her finances before the idle winter to come, Fuller gave lessons to four extra students in addition to her regular scholars. She was also balancing a crush of social engagements with her work on Eckermann's *Gespräche mit Goethe*, or *Conversations with Goethe*.[136] While she looked forward to her escape from Greene Street, she was still given to somber reflections. As October winds stirred the dying leaves, she wrote, "I have lived to know that the secret of all things is pain and that Nature travaileth most painfully with her noblest product."[137]

A small part of her was sorry to go. Looking back on her leave-taking, Fuller was later to tell Clarke, "Empty as the world seems at times, it is no easy matter to break the ties which an intelligent being *must* form in the course of a year and a half."[138] However, her ties to Providence were no stronger than those that necessarily arose. The assessment she sent to William Henry Channing was more disparaging. She was leaving Providence, she told him, "with unfeigned delight . . . because I have here been always in a false position and my energies [have] been consequently much repressed. To common observers I seem well placed here, but I know that it is not so, and that I have had more than average difficulties to encounter, some of them insurmountable."[139] She was equally frank to her old friend Almira Barlow: "I have gabbled and simpered and given my mind to the public view these two years back, till there seems no good left in me."[140] Her teaching, she wrote to her brother Richard, had inspired her to "prefer an absolute respite from that occupation."[141] To Channing, she wrote curtly, "I do not wish to teach again at all."[142]

Wisely, Fuller did not share her bitterness with her friends in Providence. When she taught her last English poetry class six days before Christmas in 1838, the tender feelings of the moment inspired her to give an apparently heartfelt farewell. She recalled the difficulty of coming to the school and "finding the scholars so ignorant," and told her students that, though she feared she had wounded many gentle natures, she had done so only to compel them to try harder. She reassured them of her affection for them. She spoke of how the brightest hopes of her life had been blasted and how, having been left without a protector, she had learned to rely solely on her own talents. She recalled how she had placed her trust in the Rock of Ages, which had never failed to console her. She warned her listeners never to place their trust in anything in the material world, for experience had shown her "how vain and unsatisfactory everything is, in this state of continual change and sorrow."[143] Fuller's eyes were moist as she spoke of the blessedness of religion that was the only sure support in a grief-laden world. She remarked that, when she had first come to Greene Street, she had been very ill and had expected to die soon, but that, wishing to do good in the time given her, she had undertaken to instruct them, and she hoped she had been of use to them. Then, after begging their pardon once more for her moments of seeming harshness and injustice and blessing them all, she concluded, "For the last time, my girls . . . you may go."[144] Not one of them moved. All were in tears. After a few moments, Fuller stood and went to each girl, bestowing a kiss and a kind word, and left the room.

CHAPTER FIVE

CONVERSATIONALIST

Think not . . . that thought can save thee
from the grand mistake of sometime
fancying that you love a mortal.

—MARGARET FULLER TO
CAROLINE STURGIS, 1840

I remember you say that forlorn seasons
often turn out the most profitable.
Perhaps I shall find it so.

—MARGARET FULLER TO
RALPH WALDO EMERSON,
December 26, 1839

*I*F FULLER HAD HOPED TO LEAVE HIRAM FULLER'S SCHOOL ON A FIRM
footing by the time she left it, she had failed; after her departure, enrollment
at the Greene Street School declined precipitously. Handicapped both by the
loss of its star teacher and by community hostility to its progressive peda-
gogy, the academy survived Fuller's departure by less than a year. If another
of Fuller's goals had been to earn enough money to save the Groton farm,
here, too, she had fallen short. Unable to satisfy the family's creditors by any
other means, Margarett Crane Fuller had sold the property in late 1838 and
consented to vacate the house by the following April.

As Fuller made her way back to Groton, she enjoyed a stopover in Boston

that "was all tea and dinner parties, and long conversations and pictures."
Though the excitement had its pleasures, she most looked forward to the
chance to retreat into her room at her mother's farmhouse and, amid the
quiet of the winter, restore herself and her surroundings to a state of peace
and order. It took some doing. Her books and papers, having been neglected
for months, lay about her room in disorderly heaps. Fuller required neatness
before she touched a pen, and she was no more willing to dispatch a letter
from a cluttered apartment than to invite a friend to an untidy house.[1] Once
all things were in their proper place, she settled into a comfort she had not
known since the time before her father's death. Resolving to take all her time
for herself, she declined invitations and did not return the short visits of local
friends. In her first two months at home, she ventured out to church only
once. An occasional long walk when the weather permitted and about a half-
dozen sessions of piano playing were the most lavish of her amusements. She
tutored Richard and Ellen twice a week and wrote letters until she was "sick
from fatigue."[2] It had been years since she had been able to spend so long a
time just as she pleased, and she was, for the moment, essentially happy.

She also put some personal matters in better order. One of these involved
James Freeman Clarke, who was still leading a congregation in Louisville,
speaking out against slavery in that slaveholding city and quietly working to
convince the local population to abandon its fondness of fighting duels.[3] In
1837, Clarke had traveled to Meadville, Pennsylvania, to meet with a Dutch-
born philanthropist named Harm Jan Huidekoper. While there, he had fallen
in love with Huidekoper's eldest daughter, Anna. Clarke kept tidings of the
couple's engagement from reaching Fuller for several months. When she
finally received the news, less than two months before Clarke's wedding in
August 1839, it came from a stranger.[4] She was still in the dark when, a few
days after returning to Groton, she wrote to him concerning a conversation
they had had on "a subject which I thought could never lie open between
us." Greatly relieved, she commended Clarke for having taken her unspecified revelations in a way "so manly and noble" that her faith in his character
was wholly restored. She believed that they might yet be much to each other
and hoped she might prove "not unworthy to be a true friend."[5] One may
reasonably guess the reason for Fuller's relief; more than likely, she had
finally and definitively told Clarke that there could be no romantic future
between them. If this was the case, Clarke surely found the task of acting

"manly and noble" was made much easier by the assurance of his undisclosed fiancée. As Fuller looked over the letters that Clarke had sent her over the years, she found allusions to three love affairs "which formed him into manhood," and she wished he had omitted them. Then she scolded herself for feeling jealous. "All that is dead and gone," she wrote. "The pain and passion have passed into Experience."[6]

Having finally placed her relationship with Clarke on an unambiguous footing, Fuller turned to another sensitive personal duty. Her father's papers, evidently untouched since his death, needed organizing. After a week of "fatiguing and melancholy" work, during which she examined more than a thousand letters, Fuller felt she had barely dented the great heaps of paper.[7] Undertaken in the cold, short days of February and with the knowledge that the family was soon to leave the farm her father had loved, it amounted to a second farewell to Timothy, almost as devastating as the first. Yet the task also yielded bittersweet feelings of discovery and resolution. Her father's literary remains had accumulated over forty years. Amid the stacks of journals, Harvard essays, minutes of legislative debates, and letters on every conceivable subject, she saw her father as never before. She wrote, "I know him hourly better and respect him more." She found herself wishing that she could learn to be "so just, so tender, so candid towards men, so devout towards a higher power." She felt not only the tragedy of a life interrupted but also the mournful joy of knowing that he had been well prepared "to meet the fiat which went forth so suddenly."[8] It seemed to her that a "hackneyed moral" might be drawn from the scene, though what it might be she chose not to say.[9] It may have been the strange fact that our flesh, which seems so solid, can vanish so much faster than scratches of ink on paper. It may have been the equally vexing truth that the life we live is never the one we write, but the written life, two-dimensional and never fully true, is the only one that can be preserved. Perhaps Fuller was thinking of a simpler, sadder truth: that we know and love best the people we have lost.

Fuller's other great task of early 1839 was to complete another journey among the literary remains of the dead. In late February, just before tackling her father's papers, she finished her most ambitious literary achievement to date: the translation of Eckermann's *Gespräche mit Goethe*. The genre suited her personally. Fuller worked only occasionally in poetry and fiction, at least as far as publication was concerned. In forms of writing that summoned her personality nearer to the surface, the woman who was so notoriously forward and open in social situations turned perplexingly shy. Believing that every life of value occasionally demanded "the accompaniment of the lyre," she freely wrote poems in private. Yet she created these verses solely as a vent for her overflowing emotions, and she believed that, as soon as they touched the open air of a public forum, their value would shrivel and vanish. "The moment I lay open my heart, and tell the fresh feeling to any one who chooses to hear," she confided to James Clarke as she was finishing her work on Eckermann, "I feel profaned."[10] As a translator, she felt fewer inhibitions. Nevertheless, her translation of Eckermann's *Gespräche* was an intensely personal undertaking. Thinking now that she might never go to Europe, she approached the work of the great man's private secretary as the best window she would ever have into the mind she esteemed above all others.

Eckermann's *Gespräche* is, in fact, anything but a series of dry dialogues. The conversations also describe the dreamy solitude of the poet's garden, the cool air and crimson sofa of his sitting room, and the calamitous burning of the Weimar Court Theater, which Goethe had directed from 1791 to 1817.[11] Even the dexterity with which the poet carved a roast fowl is duly recorded.[12] The book, as Fuller noted in her preface, "paints Goethe to us as he was in the midst of his family, and in his most careless or weary hours."[13] It mattered greatly to Fuller to have the opportunity to present Goethe in so natural a fashion to an American audience, not only so that she might stand vicariously in Eckermann's shoes, but also in order that she might demystify and humanize a man whom Americans had resolutely misunderstood and unthinkingly condemned. With characteristic ginger, she defended the poet in her preface against what she took to be America's four grievances against him: "He is not a Christian; He is not an Idealist; He is not a Democrat; He is not Schiller."[14] For the first three of these objections, Fuller might as easily have written, "He is not an American." And, indeed, part of her objective in translating Eckermann's volume was to help liberate her countrymen from the notion that they could accept and assimilate only those authors who confirmed their existing cultural prejudices.

At the same time, Fuller's preface to Eckermann's *Gespräche* was her own covert apologia, for she, too, was not entirely persuaded that the virtues of Christianity, idealism, and democracy trumped and obviated all others. She began by explaining that, if Goethe was not Christian, he was far from godless. True, his essentially Greek outlook made it impossible for him to embrace the sorrow of the cross or the moral strictures of the Hebraic heavenly Father. Nevertheless, Goethe had his credo: "His God was rather the creative and upholding than the paternal spirit; his religion, that all his powers must be unfolded; his faith, 'that nature could not dispense with Immortality.'"[15] As for Goethe's lack of idealism, Fuller conceded that he thought not so much of what might be as what is. And yet, even as he dealt with the world from a standpoint of realism, Goethe had been "inspired beyond his knowledge and his will."[16] To have departed from realism would have only damaged his exceptional powers of minute and searching observation. She suggested that, if he did not see the world as better than it was, at least he took what was actually there and raised it to its highest brilliance. This was, perhaps, an idealism on its own terms.

Fuller was somewhat more reluctant to defend Goethe's faith in aristocracy. Her own sympathies, she said, lay "with the great onward movement now obvious throughout the civilized world" toward civil liberty and self-rule.[17] Nevertheless, she reflected, the cauldron of liberty had a tendency to boil over, and a social counterweight to the excesses of freedom was forever necessary. Moreover, she hinted that artists and authors, with their superior powers and need for stability and repose, have a natural affinity with aristocratic values. Goethe, she argued, belonged both naturally and socially to the upper orders, and one could hardly expect him not to believe in hierarchy. In thus defending her idol, Fuller found herself embroiled in a debate never likely to be resolved: whether America ought to function as a free marketplace for ideas, where all religions and philosophies are entitled to contend for adherents on equal terms; or whether a nation traditionally idealistic, democratic, and predominantly Christian is obliged to give precedence to those values. For Fuller, as for Emerson, the great sin was limitation. In Goethe's scorn of boundaries, she found a more comfortable home than in the reassuring but confining assumptions of American culture.

Fuller's translation of Eckermann comes to 412 pages. In the conversations that it reports, Goethe addresses almost every conceivable subject, from Byron to geology, from the German theater to French landscape painting. It is not possible to know which of Goethe's countless observations took firmest root in Fuller's mind. However, there was much in the pages she translated that spoke to her situation in life. Frequently prone to ill health, she must surely have taken an interest in Goethe's stoical assertion, "The mind is capable of incredible efforts to sustain the body. I suffer much from pain and oppression, but a strong will keeps me up. The mind need only refuse to indulge the body." An intellectual creature struggling always to understand her passions, she probably found resonance in his observation that children begin as sensualists, pass into idealism when they mature and discover love, and then, when love wavers and the beloved one falls short of perfection, become skeptics before we know it. Fuller's belief in the primary value of self-culture had its echo in Goethe's remark, "One must be something, in order to make something. . . . [H]e who wishes to do any thing great, must be, like the Greeks, so highly cultivated that he will know how to raise up the realities of nature to the height of his own mind." Beyond question, she translated with approval his claim that the true greatness of God lay in His having created the fashioning animal, humankind: "I worship him who has infused into the world such a power of production, that if only the millionth part of it should pass out into life, the world must swarm with creatures to such a degree that war, pestilence, fire, and water cannot prevail against them. That is my God!" Finally, there was much for her to appreciate in his views on immortality. Goethe was fully convinced "that the soul is indestructible, and that its activity will continue through eternity. It is like the sun, which seems to our earthly eyes to set in night, but is in reality gone to diffuse its light elsewhere." Whatever pearls of wisdom she found most precious in Goethe's conversations, she also translated his smiling caveat: "If any one asks me for good advice, I say I will give it, but only on condition that you will promise not to take it."[18]

Although Fuller finished the text of her translation in February, she dated its preface May 23—her twenty-ninth birthday. It requires no stretch of the imagination to suppose that she hoped the book's publication would signal the birth of her literary career. As she prepared to send her manuscript to her publisher, future Brook Farm founder George Ripley, she felt the project had been a useful means of drilling herself in the necessary details of publication.[19] She knew, however, that it was not nearly as perfect a work as she would have wished. She had expected that Eckermann's volume, being a chronicle of conversations, "would be an easy one to translate, as, for a book of table-talk, so much greater liberty would be allowed, and so much less care demanded, than for a classical work, or one of science."[20] In this she had been mistaken. The book's range of topics was immense, and they were addressed with considerable complexity. For the self-taught Fuller, brilliant and determined as she was, Eckermann's conversations had been a formidable challenge. Goethe had advised Eckermann, "Beware . . . of attempting too large a work. That is what injures most our best minds, and prevents fine talents and earnest efforts from accomplishing adequate results."[21] When Fuller translated these words, she might well have felt as if the poet was commenting on her own efforts. A period of ill health had forced Fuller to dictate a sizable portion of her translation, instead of writing it by hand, and these pages dissatisfied her. In addition, topics like Goethe's theory of colors were simply beyond her, and she was compelled to leave them out entirely. She also omitted many other passages, conceding that in doing so, she had laid herself open to criticism. The Englishman John Oxenford, who plagiarized extensively from Fuller's work in preparing his own translation, spoke truly when he observed that her edition's "frequent omissions render[ed] it almost an abridgment."[22] Fuller's text was, in fact, more incomplete than she knew. In 1848, Eckermann published an additional volume of conversations, filling a number of significant gaps in the previously available record, including Goethe's responses to the burning of the Weimar theater and the death of Byron. The newly available material rendered Fuller's work largely obsolete.

Of course, no one could foresee this in 1839, and the response to Fuller's work was generally favorable. Fuller's most important audience, Emerson, lauded her work extensively, calling it "a beneficent action" for which America would long be grateful. He felt that she had "scatter[ed] all the popular nonsense" that had surrounded her subject and had deftly revealed the common sense that Goethe shared with every other majestic poet. He saw in her preface a brilliant proof that she could write about Goethe with decision, intelligence, and "the comfort of good English."[23] Clarke, too, adored Fuller's preface, which he gushingly hailed as "a masterpiece of composition, clear yet cogent, dignified yet playful, with point to attract attention and weighty matter to occupy the thought."[24] Even the finicky Hedge admired Fuller's preface. In later life he championed it as "one of the best criticisms extant of Goethe."[25] In Providence, where Fuller was known, the book sold out promptly.[26] Elsewhere, the response was less resounding, for the *Conversations* brought Fuller no compensation.[27] Still, her efforts had pleased those who could best understand them, and this, perhaps, was victory enough for now. Emerson saw no reason for Fuller not to proceed with her planned biography of the German genius, and he exhorted her to "[s]peed the pen."[28]

No speeding of the pen ensued. Fuller had vowed long ago not to start Goethe's biography until she had mapped out the entire project, and she had never been able to gather all the materials she thought necessary. Moreover, new ideas on the subject had continually dawned on her, so that it had grown ever more difficult to maintain a clear sense of the story she meant to tell.[29] Then, too, there had been the problem of the tremendous versatility of Goethe's mind, which had already posed such a challenge when she translated Eckermann. To write the life of Goethe, one would need to possess the mind of Goethe. Finally, Fuller was loath to proceed without having personally walked the streets and breathed the air of Goethe's world. To write of German culture without ever having visited Germany was to risk unpardonable follies and blunders.

In April, she had told Emerson of her intention to write an experimental chapter of the project, and he had urged her on, declaring that she could "not possibly . . . write a bad book [or even] a dull page, if you only indulge yourself and take up your work somewhat proudly." All Fuller had to do, Emerson thought, was to apply the same perceptiveness and wit that animated her conversation and the journals she had shared with him, and her success would be ensured. Later in the same paragraph, however, he was less sanguine. When he recalled that there were "so many examples of fine wits . . . writing quite characterless & mechanical books," Emerson admitted, "I dare hardly trust the very Muses."[30] Fuller was more attuned to Emerson's doubts than to his exhortations. The experimental chapter seems never to have been written, and Fuller's fondest literary ambition was in danger of going unfulfilled. She felt she would need four or five years to do the task properly. However, she told Emerson late that spring, "I intend to content myself with doing it inadequately rather than risk living so long in the shadow of one mind."[31]

In early spring it was time for Fuller to pack away her books and help with the family's move from Groton. Her mother had chosen an area southwest of Boston called Jamaica Plain. On her way there, Fuller stopped to spend a few days with the Emersons. After her recent "*irksome* though *interesting* duties," it felt good to give herself up to thought in the tangled woodwalks of Concord, where she passed happy hours of meditation. In Emerson's library, she spent many more conversing with the man "whose serene and elevated nature" she appreciated more than ever.[32] Much refreshed, she arrived in Jamaica Plain on April 2.

Since the Fullers' time, Jamaica Plain has been absorbed by the city of Boston and has undergone tremendous change. In 1839, however, the neighborhood was a little Eden. In the weeks that followed the move, Fuller amused herself by gathering wild columbines and resting beside the pretty brooks that flowed past apple trees and willows. Wild geraniums purpled the lanes, the woods seemed paved with violets, and the frequent rains kept the earth as "fresh and delicate as a bride."[33] In mid-May, she was discovering new walks and writing with delight about finding a waterfall and a pond with islands. She attended an exhibit of paintings by Washington Allston and read novels by Balzac and George Sand. Her meanderings made her yearn for a more durable simplicity and for an existence unconstrained by work, obligations, or even human form. In a letter to her friend Elizabeth Hoar, she wrote:

One would fain be no more an artist, or a philosopher, or a lover, or a critic, but a soul ever rushing forth in tides of genial life, or retiring evermore into precious crystals, too pure to be lonely. A life more intense, you say, we pine to have. But we mount the heights of our being, only to look down into darker, colder chasms. It is all one earth, all under one heaven—but the moment—the moment.[34]

The moments were not all heavenly. In June, Fuller and her friend Caroline Sturgis visited the seaside resort town of Nahant. Their friendship had been under a cloud ever since Fuller had accused Cary of "want of affection" when they met in Boston just after Margaret had left Hiram Fuller's school. Although Fuller had dismissed the possibility that her "dear Cary" had ceased to love her and had prophesied that Caroline would not be able "to get free of [her] for some years," Fuller had displayed a possessiveness that her friend could hardly have found welcome.[35] Since then, Fuller had been both invasive and controlling, pestering Cary for more frequent letters, imploring her to "[t]ell me your secret, tell me mine," and making sure that she "always liked [the] right things, and [the] right people."[36]

Despite Fuller's enjoinders and complaints of headache, the trip to Nahant began promisingly enough. On one especially memorable afternoon, clouds of pearl and amber lazily traversed the sky as Fuller lay on a rock low in the water, where she could hear "the twin harmonies of the sucking of the water into the spout and the washing of the surge on the foot of the rock." Caroline, clad in a pale green dress, perched far above, looking to Fuller like an ocean nymph. Throughout their sojourn the sunsets were gorgeous and the moonlight was brilliant.[37] All seemed joyous. It seemed to Fuller as if Caroline might hold as high a place in her life as her beloved Anna Barker.[38] Then, once more, Fuller pushed too hard. "Margaret asked me if I loved her," Caroline recalled, "but I could not at once say yes."[39] Her hesitation evidently provoked a quarrel whose effects, according to Fuller, "no sacred solitary wood walk . . . no hour of moonlight love" could promptly remedy.[40]

In Fuller's era, friends felt free to use much warmer, more romantic words than one often uses in our own time. In both its language and its customs of physical contact, the boundaries of friendship were more fluid. Yet one senses that for Fuller, even in the context of her historic moment, the boundaries were less clear than for many of her acquaintances. She approached friendship as she approached her work and her ideas: with an avid desire to know and feel all that it might offer. She wanted to press her friends until they yielded the very juice of their thoughts and feelings. Mere comradeship was often not enough; she wanted an exultant union of souls. The passion Fuller expressed was not necessarily sexual, but it was intense and hard for others to understand and to reciprocate. After Sturgis balked when Fuller asked her for a declaration of love, their friendship cooled for months.

Fuller's attentions soon found a more absorbing object—one that was largely responsible for her sudden fascinations with flowers and moonlight. She was seeing more and more of Sam Ward. The enchanting boy of eighteen from the trip to Trenton Falls was now an appealing young man of twenty-two. Most of the other young gentlemen to whom Fuller had been attracted, like George Davis and James Clarke, had initially captured her admiration with their displays of philosophical intelligence. Not so with Sam. As Fuller recollected, the two of them "did not begin on the footing of rational good-will and mutual esteem, but of intimacy."[41] From the start, Margaret knew she was "incapable of feeling or being content to inspire an ordinary attachment" with him. She wrote later, "With Spring's fairest flower I poured out my heart to you." Sam, as Fuller later reminded him, responded with "confiding sweetness" and a "natural and prompt expression of attachment."[42] It may have been around this time that, in a somewhat regrettable attempt to show off for her companion, Fuller made her notorious boast, "I now know all the people worth knowing in America, and I find no intellect comparable to my own."[43]

Fuller called Samuel Ward her "Raffaello" and wanted him to love
her "as I deserve to be loved." He could not oblige her.
(COURTESY OF HOUGHTON LIBRARY, HARVARD UNIVERSITY)

In May they walked together through glens and galleries, admiring both nature and art. In a playful comment on their seven-year difference in age, Sam called Margaret "Mother," although his emotions seemed to Margaret to be far from filial.[44] Caught up in the transports of an especially tender moment, he made her a promise, whose details are lost to history, regarding "all that we might be to one another."[45] The sincerity of such a promise tends to fade as the heartbeat slows. Fuller, however, was of mood to regard Ward's effusion as a solemn contract. Her disappointment, when it came, was crushing.

Soon after his obscure promise, with an abruptness that first puzzled Margaret and then angered her, Sam's affections cooled. Instead of inviting her to

Henry Inman painted Anna Barker's portrait when she was seventeen. Anna later inspired Fuller to write, "It is so true that a woman may be in love with a woman and a man with a man."
(COURTESY OF JOAN VON MEHREN)

attend an art exhibit with him, he recommended that she see it alone. He sent her books and pictures, but not as gifts; he wanted only her critical opinion of them. Margaret knew she was being avoided. Confronted with the evidence, Sam pleaded weakly that he was overwhelmed by other engagements, and he implied that she was at fault for distrusting him. Margaret, unappeased, sent a cajoling letter. "What young man of promising character and prosperous fortunes," she desired to know, "has not [an engagement] waiting his every hour?" If Sam were like her, she added, he could find a way to "trample upon such petty impossibilities; if you love me as I deserve to be loved, you cannot dispense with seeing me." As to the matter of distrust, Fuller answered the insinuation with queenly pride: "No, I do not distrust you, so lately as you have spoken the words of friendship. You would not be so irreverent as to dare tamper with a nature like mine, you could not treat so generous a person with levity." She and he had both known for some time that, given the differences in their ages, their interests, and their social positions, nothing but love could bind them together. Resolutely, she declared, "It must not be my love alone that binds us."[46] She vowed to wait while he decided what was truly in his heart. As she waited, she told her friend Jane Tuckerman that she had fallen into "a mood of sadness, nay, of gloom, black as Hades," and that "the sickness of the immortal soul" had come upon her.[47]

Fuller's scoldings did not bring Sam back to her. Instead, they drove him deeper into reticence. At the beginning of September, he at last confirmed what Fuller had suspected; he loved her no more. In the letter Fuller wrote back to him, arraigning him for his fickleness, a clue emerges as to why he had distanced himself from her. Fuller wrote that she would "try to believe that you would not be with me lest I . . . as you have said 'call up the woman in you.'"[48] In this budding romantic attachment, Fuller had evidently tried to assume the dominant position; such was her habit with many of her friends, and Sam's relative youth may have prompted her to assert herself all the more. Sam evidently felt the softer, more submissive elements of his own nature rising in response. The discomfort that this feeling caused him was too powerful to accept. Rather than be Fuller's "woman," he chose to be his own man. Sensing this, Fuller promised Sam in two successive letters that she would "make every allowance," but her offer of accommodation came too late.[49] He withdrew his affections.

Such, at least was Fuller's perception of their falling-out. Yet she did not know the entire story. She seems to have known nothing of what had passed between Sam and Anna Barker in Switzerland. When she lamented that Sam had set aside his artistic ambitions for a career in business, she had no idea that he had done so in hopes of making himself worthy of Anna's hand. Reunited in New Orleans in early 1839, the young lovers had begun their plans for a life together. Sam had returned to New England having promised not to divulge their pact until Anna could join him and become acquainted with his family; he needed to be certain of his father's approval. When Sam saw Margaret again, he may have forgot himself for a brief time, or Margaret may have misread his conduct. Nonetheless, Sam's intention to marry Anna had remained constant. Despite Fuller's bitter insinuations, he kept his secret from her.

Fuller's behavior toward both Caroline Sturgis and Sam Ward in 1839 reveals a peculiar irony in her character. A resolute champion of equality in the realms of education and politics, she was unable to believe in emotional equality. Too frequently, her friendships and romances were founded on ideas of dominance and submission. Her efforts to control Cary's social relations and her faintly minatory assertion that Cary would not be able to get free of her call to mind the tyrannies of an abusive boyfriend. In her letters to Sam, her imperious how-dare-you passages sit incongruously side by side with abject offers of appeasement. Willing to invoke either power or subservience (and sometimes both simultaneously) to preserve an unsteady relationship, Fuller explored every kind of playing field except a level one. The imbalance of power that had defined both her parents' marriage and her relationship with Timothy seemed destined to repeat itself when Fuller reached toward love. The fact that she tried to tip that imbalance in her own direction caused particular problems in an era when the man was expected to dictate the terms of a relationship. A few years later, Fuller was to write, "Oh! it is a curse to woman to love first, or most. In so doing she reverses the natural relations, and her heart can never, never be satisfied with what ensues."[50]

Toward the end of September, Anna Barker arrived in Boston. Around the first of October, in a rather ill-considered move, she came to stay with Fuller, her secret still intact. During Anna's visit, a letter from Caroline Sturgis lay unread on Fuller's desk. Fuller could not think of her troubles with Caroline, "so filled was I, so intoxicated, so uplifted by that eldest and divinest love" that Anna had carried with her.[51] It is almost certain that they shared a bed; there is no question that they did so on other occasions. Such an arrangement was hardly unusual for the time, but for Margaret it was far from emotionally neutral. Barker departed on October sixth, but only after squeezing into her schedule a first meeting with Emerson, who found himself calling her a "very human piece of divinity" and rhapsodizing about the "instinctive elegance" of a being "so lovely, so fortunate & so remote from my own experiences."[52] Fuller, exhausted by the emotional tension, was obliged to take immediately to her bed and was not well enough to get up the next day. With astonishing candor, she confided to Sturgis, "The nights of talks and days of agitation, the tides of feeling which have been poured upon and from my soul have been too much for my strength of body or mind. . . . I cannot tell what I shall think or feel."[53] A deeper agitation was in the offing. Only days later, news circulated in Bostonian social circles that Sam Ward and Anna Barker were engaged. Sam had addressed a phrase to Margaret that she now quoted back to him: "The world has separated us as intimates and may separate us more."[54]

One might well have expected the news that Sam had chosen Fuller's dear friend instead of her to have called forth a torrent of wrath. To the contrary, she outwardly maintained a degree of magnanimity. On a windy, rainy mid-October day, she wrote to Sam that she understood all perfectly. She made no claim on his heart, she told him. To her, his past expressions of affection were like "the flower and fruitage of [a] summer day"; implicitly, she acknowledged that it was natural for them to wither and die. Still, she gently upbraided him for his unmeaning phrases and attentions; her own "entire sincerity in every passage of life" entitled her to reciprocal treatment. Nevertheless, she assured him that they would remain friends and that her knowledge of his nature had become part of her own. Now that what she felt for him was no longer stained with pride or passion, she knew that it was strong enough to endure through eternity. With these words, she gave him her blessing: "Give yourself up to the holy hour and live in the celestial ray that shines on you at present."[55] Even as she kept up a brave front, her private reaction to Sam's announcement was despairing. "Black Friday it has been," she wrote, "and my heart is well nigh wearied out. Shall I never be able to act and live with persons of views as high as my own? . . . Ah, me! what woes within and without; what assaults of folly; what mean distresses; and, oh, what wounds from cherished hands!"[56]

Fuller's most revealing confession of her feelings toward Anna was not intended for public view. It came in her journal of October 1842, two years after Sam and Anna's wedding. To her surprise, she was still not at peace with the fact of their marriage. She marked the anniversary by admitting her confusions in her diary: "I know not yet what to think of this event which dawned so poetically on me. From it the music has not flowed that I expected, nor is my own mind now in harmony with those that seemed so fatally bound to it, yet that heart of love which beat then could not err, only we must grow wiser every day, else the true will become false."[57] Some of the reasons for her unresolved emotions became clear later in the month, when she added a long entry suggesting a possibility that even she was reluctant to confront: that her feelings toward Anna had been even stronger than what she had felt for Sam.

Her reflections were triggered by a large engraving of French cultural patroness Jeanne-Françoise Récamier, whose intimate friendship with the novelist Madame de Staël had often given Fuller cause for thought. The image sent her thoughts beyond the realm of the purely aesthetic:

> It is so true that a woman may be in love with a woman and a man with a man. It is so pleasant to be sure of it because undoubtedly it is the same love that we shall feel when we are angels when we ascend to the only fit place for the Mignon's where
>
> Sie fragen nicht nach Mann und Weib—[58]
>
> It is regulated by the same law as that of love between persons of different sexes, only it is purely intellectual and spiritual, unprofaned by any mixture of lower instincts, undisturbed by any need of consulting temporal interests; its law is the desire of the spirit to realize a whole which makes it seek in another being for what it finds not in itself. Thus the beautiful seeks the strong, and the strong the beautiful, the mute seek the eloquent [and] the butterfly settles always on the dark flower.[59]

Thus far, Fuller had written abstractly. In the following sentences, she was abstract no more:

> Why did Socrates love Alcibiades?—why did Korner love Schneider? How natural is the love of Wallenstein for Max, that of M[m]e. de Staël for de Recamier, mine for Anna Barker. I loved Anna for a time I think with as much passion as I was then strong enough to feel—Her face was always gleaming before me, her voice was echoing in my ear, all poetic thoughts clustered round the dear image. This love was a key which unlocked for me many a treasure which I still possess, it was the carbuncle (emblematic gem) which cast light into many of the darkest caverns of human nature.—She loved me, too, though not so much, because her nature was "less high, less grave, less large, less deep" but she loved more tenderly, less passionately. She loved me,

for I well remember her suffering when she first would feel my faults and knew one part of the exquisite veil rent away, how she wished to stay apart and weep the whole day. Then again that night when she leaned on me and her eyes were such a deep violet blue, so like night, as they never were before, and we both felt such a strange mystic thrill and knew what we had never known before. Now well too can I now account for that desire which I so often had to get away from her and be alone with nature, which displeased her so, for she wished to be with me all the time.[60]

All these thoughts pressed in on Fuller as she gazed at the image of Réca-mier, bare-armed and half-reclining in her boudoir. She had one further thought, but she stopped her pen. She noted only that it had "often come into my mind, but I will not write it down; it is so singular that I have often thought I would never express it in any way; I am sure no human being but myself would understand it."[61]

The dark flowers and caverns of Fuller's journal entry invite a Freudian reading. The thought that she considered inexpressible readily takes a shape in the modern mind that few would hesitate to name. Yet Fuller is at pains to insist that she regards passionate same-sex attraction as a holy impulse, spir-itually consecrated and unprofaned by baser appetites. It is presumptuous to suppose that we know better than Fuller the secret pulsations of her own heart. Yet it is clear that these emotions were tremendously disorienting to Margaret herself. There is this appraisal from Emerson, who, during Fuller's late twenties and early thirties, had a better opportunity to observe her emo-tional framework than anyone else: "Her friendships, as a girl with girls, as a woman with women, were not unmingled with passion, and had passages of romantic sacrifice and of ecstatic fusion, which I have heard with the ear, but could not trust my profane pen to report." He also repeated the observa-tion of an anonymous woman who observed, "Had she been a man, any one of those fine girls of sixteen, who surrounded her . . . would have married her: they were all in love with her, she understood them so well."[62] It may be that Fuller did desire some form of carnal intimacy with Anna Barker, but perhaps what she truly sought was a total awareness of her friend, a knowl-edge not simply of the flesh but through the flesh. Her desire to unite and commune so closely with her female friends may not have been sexual in conventional terms, yet it resembled physical longing closely enough that even Emerson did not trust his pen to delineate the difference.

Fuller's feelings were by no means free from guilt, or at least a knowledge that her emotions could be readily misconstrued. On the same day that she recorded the thoughts inspired by the image of Récamier, she also wrote the following in her journal:

> Oh Father, I see myself all stained unworthy to be translated, yet all my thoughts stretch on to a purer freer state of existence. Let each moment lead me nearer to it. Let the Christ all loving, all renouncing pervade my nature daily more and more. Let the blood of the Lamb wash out the mineral tinge, but let not the intelligent soul forget why it was ever there, and let me not hurry, patience, patience ever.[63]

Fuller's awareness of her "stained" unworthiness and her "mineral tinge" suggests that, no matter how she might insist that her attractions were free from baser impulses, she could not feel them without a nagging consciousness of sin. Thus, her sense of her soul and its likely destination led her to confront a harsh paradox. Her heaven was a place where gender no longer stood in the way of a full range of loving expression. It was a place where one could love with all one's being, regardless of whether the object of one's love had once possessed a male or a female body. And yet, it seemed to her that this heaven might be closed to those who had felt and failed to conquer homoerotic passions on earth. The paradise that her passions led her to imagine and wish for, those same passions might make it impossible for her to enter.

Fortunately, at the same time that she was bruising herself against the barriers she encountered in love and friendship, Fuller was preparing herself for greater success in a direction where the walls had always been easier to climb. She was finding new ways to use her intellect and erudition to inform and inspire others. Some of her own inspiration in this line came from Bronson Alcott, who, since his Temple School debacle, had been giving public conversations as a way to eke out a living. In March 1839, Alcott had described this work to his aged mother:

> I am living rather by *Talking* now, than by School; and shall be able, by and by, I think to live this way entirely. I meet circles of thirty, forty, or

more, persons, for ten or twelve evenings, and hold conversation, on great subjects, with them. . . . Only think of your bashful, silent boy . . . getting bold all at once, and going about to talk, and make talk![64]

Actually, Alcott had not gotten bold "all at once." He had been giving conversations in Boston since 1835. In August 1839, Fuller decided to follow Alcott's model. On the twenty-sixth, she met with Alcott to discuss her plan. The next day, Fuller announced to Sophia Ripley that she had decided to become a conversationalist.

The genre of the conversation differed importantly from the lecture. First, it involved less detailed preparation. The converser announced the topic of the conversation in advance but used no notes. The artistry of the event depended at least on the appearance of spontaneity. Second, the atmosphere was meant to be more intimate than a public oration; a good-sized parlor supplied a better venue than a formal hall. Moreover, though Alcott tended to dominate his discussions more than he would have liked, the ideal conversation was, as the name indicates, participatory. The leader's goal was not only to inform but also to inspire listeners to offer their own reflections on the topic. Finally, the conversation was conceived as a vehicle for social and spiritual reform. Alcott regarded his work as a "Ministry of Talking," calculated to bring participants into sympathetic communion around a shared idea.[65]

Fuller's ambitions in conducting her own series of conversations were generally similar but vitally different in their specifics. Alcott's conversations were open to both men and women. Fuller, to the contrary, chose from the outset to speak only to an assembly of women. In a letter to Sophia Ripley, Fuller offered the incomplete outlines of a manifesto. Her hope, she said, was to supply "a point of union to well-educated and thinking women in a city which, with great pretensions to mental refinement, boasts at present nothing of the kind and where I have heard many of a mature age wish for some such means of stimulus and cheer."[66] She was eager to provide "a place where they could state their doubts and difficulties with hope of gaining aid from the experience or aspirations of others."[67]

It is noteworthy that, in this informal prospectus, Fuller mentioned the need to create a nexus for shared emotional support long before she moved on to her intellectual aspirations for the venture. As she freely admitted, her choice of topics for discussion mattered less than "the experience of each [that] might be brought to bear upon all."[68] Yet she desired much more than to establish a morally supportive sisterhood. At the center of her ambition lay three principles of action:

> To pass in review the departments of thought and knowledge and endeavor to place them in due relation to one another in our minds.
> To systematize thought and give a precision in which our sex are so deficient, chiefly, I think because they have so few inducements to test and classify what they receive.
> To ascertain what pursuits are best suited to us in our time and state of society, and how we may make best use of our means for building up the life of thought upon the life of action."[69]

Without the last of these three objectives, Fuller's plan would have held far less meaning for her. She wanted to lead her circle of well-read women to answer what she referred to as "the great questions" that few women took time to ask themselves until their best years had flown by: "What were we born to do? How shall we do it?"[70] These were, of course, versions of the same questions that the child Margaret had posed for herself that day when she stood on the stairs of her father's house. More than two decades later, she now hoped to infuse her own questions into the best female minds in Boston. She thought the cause a noble one, and if her money held out, she was willing to give the undertaking a large portion of the coming years that she hoped would be her best.

That fall, as she prepared for her first series of conversations, she immersed herself in Plato to tune herself up for the coming challenge. At a party given in late October 1839 by the mesmerist Cornelia Park, Fuller offered a foretaste of what she was to offer. To ease the discomfort caused by her spinal curvature, Fuller brought with her a collapsible stool, on which she perched "like a Sybil" amid Greek roses and oranges. With authority and charm, Fuller discoursed on music and literature. As involved as she evidently was that evening in her conversation, it is possible that she did not think too much afterward about two people she met for the first time at the soirée: Elizabeth Palmer Peabody's younger sister Sophia and her dashing suitor Nathaniel Hawthorne.[71] Sophia came away only moderately impressed. Elizabeth, on the other hand, threw herself into the effort to make Fuller's first season of conversations a success, prevailing on the third Peabody sister, Mary, to donate her apartment at Chauncey Place, southeast of Boston Common, as a venue, and rounding up as many prospective attendees as she could find. For subsequent series, Elizabeth gladly prepared space in her bookstore at 13 West Street, perhaps Boston's foremost venue for progressive thinking.

The conversations began on November 6, 1839. Fuller shrewdly scheduled the series to run on Wednesday mornings, so that the out-of-town attendees could easily stay for Emerson's lecture series titled "The Present Age," being offered on Wednesday evenings at the Masonic Hall. Not surprisingly, the original subscribers were largely drawn from the extensive circle of friends and acquaintances Fuller had been steadily enlarging since her teens. Mary Peabody herself did not attend; the fact that she was away teaching during the day was what had made her rooms available in the first place. But Elizabeth and Sophia were there, as well as Fuller's old mentor Eliza Farrar and her erstwhile partner in Lockean studies, Lydia Maria Child. Caroline Sturgis had sufficiently overcome her quarrels with Fuller to attend. James Freeman Clarke's sister Sarah was also among the faithful, as were childhood friends like Almira Barlow and former students like Jane Tuckerman and William Ellery Channing's daughter Mary. Patrician Boston was present in the person of Eliza Morton Quincy, the wife of former mayor and Harvard president Josiah Quincy. A host of women with philosophical or reform-minded husbands also helped to fill the room. Active roles were taken by Anna Blake Shaw and her sister-in-law Sarah Sturgis Shaw, whose then two-year-old son Robert Gould Shaw would one day give his life commanding the all-black Fifty-Fourth Massachusetts regiment in the Civil War. When she felt well enough, Lidian Emerson would rise before dawn in Concord and be dressed and ready to board the seven o'clock stagecoach to Boston so that she, too, might share in Fuller's conversations.[72] When she arrived, she would have exchanged greetings with Sophia Ripley; Elizabeth Davis Bancroft, the wife of historian George Bancroft; and Lydia Cabot Parker, the wife of the slavery-hating minister Theodore Parker. Also part of the throng was Mary Greeley, "a typical Yankee schoolmistress, crazy for learning," as Fuller called her.[73] Greeley, who rode up from New York to attend, brought home glowing reports of the group's leader to her husband Horace, who was soon to found the *New-York Tribune*. The circle of conversers genuinely interested

Fuller; she called them "devoutly thoughtful" and quietly exulted in her position as a true "teacher and guide."[74]

As a group, the attendees of Fuller's conversations were not spectacularly diverse. As was hardly surprising for the time, the women were all white, and they were uniformly of Protestant origins. They were, moreover, generally from families that, either because of their old, established wealth or because of their connection to Bostonian intellectualism, predisposed their daughters toward an active interest in culture and the consideration of new ideas. It is easy to assume that, whereas she may have intended to use her conversations to broaden the reach of liberal thought, Fuller was, to a considerable degree, preaching to the choir. Yet Fuller ought not entirely be faulted for the fact that her conversations surrounded her with more or less like-minded women and, in many instances, close friends. While it is clear that one of the reasons Fuller undertook her conversations was to earn money, they fulfilled an important psychological need as well. Having so often been rejected in her efforts at romance and having so frequently found that her female friendships were fraught with deep emotional contradictions, Fuller needed an object toward which she might direct both her intellectual and her emotional generosity without fear of the complications that troubled her individual relationships.

The extent to which Fuller drew emotional sustenance from her conversations was revealed on one occasion when the assembled company was much larger than expected and it was disclosed that several attendees either had come from out of town at considerable inconvenience or had, in a few instances, just undergone "extreme experiences of joy and grief." Fuller accepted their presence as "a very great tribute to her. She knew no one came for experiment, but all in earnest love and trust, and was moved by it quite to the heart, which threw an indescribable charm of softness over her brilliancy." There was something about this group that put Fuller uniquely at ease. Part of it, some speculated, came from the all-female composition of her audience. Another influence may have been the general absence of contentiousness among the attendees. Fuller's other intellectual interactions had too often been tinged by a spirit of competition and a need to prove herself. Among these women, however, she felt that "there could be no excitements and gratifications of personal ambitions." Whatever the full range of causes may have been, one observer noted that "Margaret never appears, when I see her, either so brilliant and deep in thought, or so desirous to please or so modest, or so heart-touching, as in this very party."[75]

The rooms in which Fuller gave her conversations became for her a kind of philosopher's Arcadia, where the atmosphere of kindness and cooperation mattered every bit as much to her as the cerebral content of what was said. Her meetings offered not only a platform for ideas, but also a haven within which the bonds of feminine friendship could form and strengthen. Fuller's conversations also marked an important passage in her journey toward intellectual independence. She was no longer implementing someone else's educational vision or translating someone else's words. For the first time Fuller was standing forth entirely in her own right. The conversations enabled her to impart her own message, gaining in certainty and confidence with every session, that women had a new purpose to serve and a higher destiny to fulfill.

At the first meeting of her Arcadia, Fuller had some walls to demolish. The twenty-five or so attendees initially resisted the conversational format. Reinforced by one another's shyness, they all declared that they would not speak a word. Undaunted, Fuller took charge, explaining her intent with such enthusiasm that the women soon agreed it would be "base in the extreme" for them not to do all they could to help the sessions along.[76] Their cooperation secured, Fuller set forth her goal of redressing the errors of feminine education. The great fault that Fuller found with the usual instruction of young women was that, although it gave them a superficial understanding of various studies, it never called on them "to reproduce all that they learn," as young men were routinely expected to do. Leaving tacit the irony that women, whose biological value was largely counted in terms of reproduction, were subjected to sterile, expressly nonreproductive forms of learning, Fuller declared that her conversations had nothing particular to teach. Rather, she proposed, as "the nucleus of conversation," to add rigor and substance to her audience's impressions, "to turn these impressions into thoughts, & to systematise these thoughts."[77] Knowledge was not to be an item for idle display; it was to become a potent tool.

However much she inspired her listeners, Fuller's conversations may have transformed her own thinking just as fundamentally. Fuller is routinely identified as a leading figure of American transcendentalism. Though this categorization may be an acceptable shorthand for describing Fuller's views during a five-year period in her life, it oversimplifies the matter. By far her deepest intellectual identification was with Goethe, whose thought was anything but transcendental. Her most durable contributions to her nation's literature have more to do with literary criticism and social reform than with pursuing the spiritual ideals that captivated Emerson and Alcott. Beyond question, during the years when she edited *The Dial*, Fuller's transcendentalism was thoroughgoing and sincere. Yet after Fuller departed New England in 1844, she promptly dropped her affinity for the Over-soul and was thenceforth transcendental no more. One may persuasively argue that she was initially attracted to transcendentalism for two pragmatic reasons. First, it was the only powerful movement in New England that supplied an outlet for her extraordinary mental energies. Second, transcendental thinkers like Hedge, Alcott, and Emerson were among the few important thinkers of the moment who were willing to see past the façade of gender. True to the transcendental credo that it was the spirit that mattered, not the body or its sex, they were the only ones prepared to accept Fuller at or near her full value. She began as a transcendentalist by convenience and became one by conviction only later. Yet if Fuller's transcendentalism had a birthplace, it was in her conversations from 1839 to 1844.

Transcendental thought is always on the move. It accepts the idea, as Emerson phrased it in his 1844 essay "Experience," that one's outer life is composed of surfaces and that the most agile person is the one who can best skate on them. The entire ethic of Fuller's conversations embodied this restlessness; they depended on a naturalness, a spontaneity, and a quicksilver mobility of thought that might have taken its inspiration from Emerson. Emerson doubtlessly received reports of Fuller's conversations from Lidian, and he also attended the one series of conversations that Fuller gave to a coeducational audience. Thus, Fuller's agility as a converser very likely inspired him in turn. "All good conversation," Emerson wrote in the last year of Fuller's paid conversations, "come[s] from a spontaneity which forgets usages, and makes the moment great. Nature hates calculators; her methods are saltatory and impulsive."[78] It was that spirit of impulse, that capacity of the mind to jump, with which Fuller tried to infuse her conversations, and which she tried to elicit from her participants. She didn't always succeed, partly because her acolytes were too reverential, both regarding her and the ideas they discussed. When she pushed against them, she could not rely on them to push back. Fuller wrote of her fellow conversers, "All are intelligent, five or six have talent. But I am never driven home for ammunition; never put to any expense; never truly called out." She wanted them to "ascend to principles." Too often, they insisted on "clinging to details." Above all, she hoped they would challenge her; one senses that she would even have been grateful if, on occasion, they had debated with her and bested her. Yet, she lamented, "What I have is always enough; . . . I feel how superficially I am treating my subject."[79]

Fuller's early conversation topics were readily transcendentalized. She began with the origins of Greek mythology. Proceeding from the Emersonian idea that all human ideas have a corresponding basis in natural facts, Fuller proposed that the ancient gods were largely conceived in "the Eye of the Greek," who lived outdoors in the genial Mediterranean air and who, being a creature of "all life & energy," personified all he beheld. In creating the gods, he gave personal form to nature, and those deities—Zeus, Apollo, and the rest—became the forms in which instincts, ideas, and facts were delivered into the hands of the poets. Mrs. Quincy, probably the most conservative woman in the room, was quick to detect a whiff of heresy. It vaguely horrified her, she said, to be in a roomful of "*Christians* enjoying *Heathen Greeks*."[80] Instead of taking umbrage at Mrs. Quincy's pious philistinism, Fuller gently replied that Christian cultivation, though deeper and higher than the Greek, was in its infancy, whereas the Greek was in its maturity. She could not bring herself to look upon the expression of a great nation's intellect as a mere series of idle fancies. Rather, Greek myth was an idealization of the universal sentiments of religion and the intellectual gift of a people whose aesthetic and political life had become immortal. She calmly advised Mrs. Quincy to approach these stories with respect and to distrust her contempt of them.

Fuller's reading of Greek mythology, like most other subjects, was inseparable from her belief in the progress of the universe from the base to the celestial. She told her fellow conversationalists that the stories of both Adam and Eve and Cupid and Psyche "represented the human process—Peace & Perfection were to be given up for a season while the Soul went through its human developement [*sic*]—It was at first the victim of temptation by means of its own credulous simplicity & at length it was purified by the sufferings its own errors involved. Psyche's labours were the means of her redemption."[81]

Another excerpt from the 1839–40 conversations shows where Fuller hoped her and the universe's improvements were leading. She said that she could conceive of a human state of being so harmonious with divine order "that there would be no strain upon the soul." She added that her idea of heaven was that we might rise above the "painful sense of the inadequacy of our nature . . . that there would be no above or below . . . but a sense of the fulness of being—a sense so full that there was no room for looking up."[82] She then added a few words that cried forth all her feelings of unfulfillment and existential homelessness. Elizabeth Peabody jotted down the following record:

> Miss Fuller said . . . that in the possibilities of her being was the loss of all imperfection—& [that] the attainment of a divine nature was the faith that reconciled her to this human nature as the pedestal of that divine nature—Only in this view of human nature (as the pedestal of a divine) could she tolerate it at all.[83]

To accept the imperfections of life only on the condition that they are a prelude to the perfection to come is, as every theologian knows, a momentous gamble. As the communicant of no organized religion, depending primarily on her own human efforts to rise above inadequacy and imperfection, Fuller was making a greater gamble still. For years, Fuller had been betting her eternal existence on the hope that the statement by Goethe's angels is the true law of the universe: "Whoever strives with all his power, we are allowed to save." She was intent on letting the wager ride.

Much of the women's deliberations during Fuller's conversations pertained to definitions; they debated the meanings of good, beauty, and truth. Eventually, the search for meaning came around to gender. Fuller asked her audience to discuss "the distinction between feminine & masculine when applied to character & mind."[84] It was Fuller's view from the outset of the argument that no essential difference existed and that so-called masculine and feminine attributes were always a matter of degree. While she admitted some differences on balance—men in her view had more genius and versatility, for instance, whereas women excelled in taste and power of adaptation—she conceded no monopoly on any quality to either sex.

Skeptical as she was of gender categories, Fuller refused to coddle any participant who sought shelter in a sexual stereotype in order to avoid the responsibility of thinking. During her first series of conversations, one of her listeners protested wanly that it was the privilege of her sex to judge solely according to feeling. "I am made so," she whimpered, "and I cannot help it." Fuller fired back, "Yes, but who are *you*? Were you an accomplished human being, were you all that a human being is capable of becoming, you might perhaps have a right to say, 'I like it therefore it is good'—but if you are not all that, your judgment must be partial and unjust if it is guided by your feelings alone."[85]

Of course, when Fuller spoke of women in general, her suppositions began with her assessment of herself. At twenty-nine, she correctly saw herself as a master of adaptation. As a woman, she had come to realize that she would seldom be in a position to create circumstances for herself. She had learned instead to be fantastically resourceful in transforming herself to suit whatever opportunities the male-fashioned world afforded her. Judging herself more severely, Fuller had also accepted that she was more lacking than she would have wished in the quality of genius, which she defined as a spirit of invention, capable of creating new and original beauties. Her power, instead, was in discerning and judging existing beauties. Fuller's critique was, as it pertained to herself, highly accurate. However, she failed to perceive that she was helping to reinforce a concept of genius that was already deeply informed by gender bias. The image of the genius as the lonely hero, bravely striking into unknown aesthetic territory, was powerfully linked to ideas of masculine virtue long before Fuller came to consider it. It was a pity that Fuller was unprepared to suggest that there were movements and forces in a female mind which, though different, might make an equal claim to the mantle of genius. It was unfortunate as well that Fuller denied the capacity of other women to excel where she had not, simply because she assumed herself to be the measure of her sex.

It was a matter of duty, Fuller thought, for a woman not to judge her particular faculties as being either masculine or feminine. Her proper task, instead, was to acknowledge "whatever faculty [she] felt to be moving within [her]," to regard it as "a principle of [her] perfection, & cultivate it accordingly."[86] For those who would fear to cultivate a boy's gentler faculties because they would not help him earn a living or who would neglect a girl's more typically manly talents because developing them might make her discontented, Fuller had a single, withering word: "*impious*."[87] There was, it seems, a kernel of Yankee thrift in Fuller's view; she could not stand to see good material of any sort go to waste. The ultimate economy for her, however, was one of the soul. She told her listeners that, if she had a son, she would prefer seeing her son unthrifty in worldly matters to seeing him unspiritual.

A possibly more challenging question arose, however, concerning the nature of women's sentiments. One of the women wanted to know whether "Brutus' great action could have been performed by a woman."[88] It seems more than likely that she was not referring to the Brutus who assassinated Julius Caesar, but rather Lucius Junius Brutus, who, after discovering that his own sons had plotted against the Roman Republic, ordered their execution. The question, then, was whether a woman could overcome her supposedly innate love of family in the name of a higher political duty. Fuller responded forcefully. She was repelled by the sentimentality that would deny a woman's power to perform a stern duty. No less than a strong man, she gave her listeners to understand, a strong woman could and should refuse to let her personal condition obstruct her perception of what was right. To think otherwise was to sink into a depth of sentimentalism with which she had no patience. Fuller conceded that the best path toward perfection was a solitary one. True, a sympathetic friend might brighten the atmosphere. Yet Fuller's own disappointments in friendship and in love may have been in her mind when she insisted, "Our path can never another's, & we must always walk alone."[89]

Records of all that was said during the six years of Fuller's conversations are sadly incomplete. Also too scarce are adequate descriptions of what Fuller looked and acted like as she led the conversations. Most of the commentaries that exist depict her as "beautifully dressed" and "ladylike & companionable," providing only the dimmest outlines for the imagination.[90] One of those who came closest to giving an adequate portrait was only seventeen when Fuller gave her first conversation and only eighteen when she described her in her journal. Caroline Healey was later to achieve a modicum of fame as a journalist, author, and advocate for women's rights under her married name of Caroline Healey Dall. In the spring of 1841, however, she was just an uncommonly forthright adolescent who had written a few pieces for the *Christian Register*. Healey came to hear Fuller on March 1, 1841, with the expectation that she would depart feeling as if she could never accomplish what Fuller had done. Her actual impression, to her relief, was quite otherwise. She was told afterward that the conversation that day was no fair indicator of Fuller's power, and Healey herself found a certain "want of coherence in her talk and a want of grammar," which she called "a great trial" to her ear.[91] Nevertheless, Healey felt she had never enjoyed an evening so thoroughly.

On a subsequent visit, Healey turned her attention to Fuller's physical demeanor. The objective portion of her description was not flattering. The speaker, Healey recorded, was "lively and sarcastic in general conversation . . . delicately formed with rather sharp feature and light hair." Fuller's head was small and "thrown almost wholly in front of the ears." Her mouth was thin and lacking in grace, and her eyes were small and gray. Yet all the defects of Fuller's features seemed to be balanced by the spirit that animated them. Those small eyes were enlivened by a vivid flash, and her laugh was "almost childlike" in its freshness and sparkle.[92] Healey regarded the series as the high point of her early life.

Before the last session, she took a sum of money that she had "sacrificed many small pleasures" to acquire, and purchased Fuller a bouquet of flowers. She was careful to include as many heliotropes—which Fuller had called her favorite flower—as she could find. To her surprise and disappointment, Fuller received the flowers coldly and without a smile. The memory of the snub remained with Healey for half a century. In hindsight, she wrote of Fuller, "She can discourse, but she cannot converse, at least, she discourses best. To converse, a person must appreciate the minds of others, and so draw them out, and make use of them and send them away proud and happy." Although she had sometimes seen Fuller achieve this feat, Healey concluded, "I do not think Margaret has an uncommon tact at doing this."[93] Around the edges, Fuller was still at times the imperious enfant terrible of Miss Prescott's school.

James Freeman Clarke's sister Sarah was sure that listening to Fuller's conversations had been "the most powerful stimulus, intellectual and moral. It was like the sun shining upon plants and causing buds to open into flowers. This was her gift, and she could no more help exercising it than the sun can help shining. This gift, acting with a powerful understanding and a generous imagination, you can perceive would make an educational force of great power."[94] The more important power, however, was not the one Fuller exercised but the one she gave. It was the power to discover and hone the uniqueness of one's being, regardless of whether that being seemed masculine or feminine to a judging and constricting world, and to develop that being not only for one's greater pleasure but also in fulfillment of a divine command. Fuller carried the message of a new and better world.

During the summer of 1839, while Fuller had been coping with romantic entanglements and laying the groundwork for her conversations, Emerson had been comparatively tranquil. He found that, in the dog days of late July, he could no more write than he could hoe.[95] Summer doldrums notwithstanding, he had been preparing to enter into a fantastically productive era. He had begun work on his lectures on "The Present Age" and had commenced work on essays for a collection that would eventually include pieces like "Self-Reliance" and "Circles." It was not until September came to Concord that his ambitions had moved in yet another direction. He wrote to Fuller that he hoped to move forward with an idea he had been revolving in his mind for years. He wanted a means of putting the critical and creative thought of his transcendental colleagues regularly before the public, in a way that the current Christian magazines and polite literary periodicals would never sanction. He and his friends should have a quarterly journal.

Emerson did not think he had the time or talent to edit the periodical himself. One choice he had in mind was George Ripley, who had just published Fuller's translation of *Conversations with Goethe*. Ripley had also won Emerson's gratitude after the latter had come under attack for his supposedly blasphemous address to Harvard Divinity School. In a series of three public letters, Ripley had not only defended Emerson on the grounds of "mental liberty" but also argued forcefully that Emerson's aim had not been to discredit Christianity but rather to gain a deeper insight into it and to "imbibe more fully its divine spirit."[96] Another leading candidate to edit the proposed magazine, as Emerson advised her on October 16, was Fuller herself.[97]

Four days later, Fuller rode out to Concord together with Alcott to discuss the project at Emerson's house. By early November, it was settled. Ripley, with his practical experience in publishing, would act as business manager. With a lingering hint of skepticism, Emerson wrote to Elizabeth Hoar, "Margaret Fuller is to edit the long-predicted journal—if we die not before the sight." He was really expressing less doubt than impatience. Within weeks, he had already secured a lyric for the first issue from the aspiring poet Henry

David Thoreau and was himself "preparing to rhyme with might and main."[98] He expected everyone else to jump just as fast. When Fuller reminded him of her commitments to her conversations, Emerson argued that she deserved a larger audience than her roomful of women. He expressed dread lest "this flowing river of your speech . . . sweep away so far the fine castle you began to build, whose pinnacle is waited for by the States and the nations."[99] Fuller wanted almost a year to produce the first number; the fretful Waldo thought that sounded like a century. Thus pressed, Fuller thought she might manage an issue by April. Alcott's first contribution to the magazine turned out to be his best. Just as a sundial marked the movements of the sun, he thought, the individual soul was an instrument that registered the greater movements of the universal spirit. In hopes that the new magazine would supply a visible index of the hearts and minds of a new era, he thus proposed a name: *The Dial*.[100]

CHAPTER SIX

ECSTATIC EDITOR

*In my family I have no sister of the heart, and
though my root is the same as that of the other
virgins of our royal house, I bear not the same
blossom, nor can I unite my voice with theirs in
the forest choir.*

> —MARGARET FULLER,
> "THE MAGNOLIA OF LAKE PONTCHARTRAIN,"
> *The Dial*, January 1841

*Through me sweetest harmonies are momently
breathing. Shall they not make me beautiful?*

> —MARGARET FULLER TO RALPH WALDO EMERSON,
> September 29, 1840

*T*O FULLER'S EARS, THE YEAR 1840 HAD A ROUND, PROPITIOUS SOUND
to it. If ever a project like *The Dial* might succeed, the time was ripe.[1] To establish their journal, Emerson, Ripley, and Fuller hoped to gather around them an entire generation of New England's ablest and most adventuresome minds. Not coincidentally, their ideal list of contributors drew heavily on Margaret's dearest friends and early collaborators. Alcott, though his skills as a writer impressed neither Emerson nor Fuller, was ready to offer as much as they would accept. It seemed obvious to them that Hedge, despite his inconvenient domicile in Bangor, would play a central role, and Margaret

could scarcely imagine the journal without a steady stream of material from James Freeman Clarke.[2] She also counted on William Henry Channing, the nephew of the great Unitarian divine William Ellery Channing, to write some pieces for the inaugural edition.[3] Sam Ward, Caroline Sturgis, and Clarke's sister Sarah all eventually contributed. Emerson called the roster of likely participants "the best club that ever made a journal."[4]

It was soon apparent, however, that the club would need quite a bit of convincing if it were actually to come together. On January 1, a day for new beginnings, Fuller sent fervent letters to the three pivotal figures in her plan, urging them to take up their pens at once. To Henry Hedge, she averred that *The Dial* would afford him a perfect opportunity to emerge from his "sentry box" in Maine and to charm "the public ear with such a succession of melodies that all the stones will advance to form a city of refuge for the just." Eager to bring her old ally into the fold on any terms, Fuller told Hedge she would be pleased to receive work of whatever genre, "poems or philosophy or criticism . . . by the yard" from his hand.[5]

To another old friend, she was equally insistent. She acknowledged that James Clarke, who was busy with his own journal, *The Western Messenger*, and expecting his first child, could not easily spare the time to write for *The Dial*. Still, she dangled before him their old dream of joining forces in print, recalling that she had always thought that, if she founded a magazine, it would be with him. She requested that he give her "some vigorous work" and confessed that she did not like the idea of setting sail at all if he were not on board.[6]

Where Hedge and Clarke were concerned, Fuller was drawing on deep friendships of very long standing. The third letter she wrote that day was addressed to a different kind of acquaintance. Fuller had known William Henry Channing since their late teens, but he had only more recently begun to win her greater confidence and appreciation. More socially astute than Clarke, less coolly academic than Hedge, Channing was well disposed to understand Fuller, both in her extraordinary ambition and in her less obvious vulnerability. Regarding him as "one of my kind to whom I can speak a free word," she was learning to prize him as a confidant.[7] Her New Year's missive, however, was avowedly "a business letter." Channing had previously told her that he had pieces "ready written" for *The Dial*'s first issue. Now, she wanted to know "what part you propose to take in the grand symphony" so that she and Emerson might "proceed to tune the instruments."[8]

But Fuller's imagined orchestra soon proved recalcitrant. As Emerson had observed to her in December, "I believe we all feel alike in regard to this Journal; we all wish it to be, but do not wish to be in any way personally responsible for it."[9] Through his sister Sarah, Clarke sent Fuller his best wishes, but he could offer no more than his indefinite intention to write something at some point. Although he would eventually submit some respectable poems, he was never to become the mainstay of the publication that Fuller hoped. Channing's "ready written" work turned out to be less than promised, although he did send the first chapter of a romance, "Ernest the Seeker," for the inaugural issue.

Meanwhile, in Bangor, Henry Hedge faced a moral crisis. He had been among the first to propose a transcendentalist journal, and the idea of such a project would have once been inconceivable without him. Now, however, he wondered seriously whether he should have any part in it at all. No longer the metaphysical young Turk whose 1833 essay on Coleridge had so astonished Emerson, Hedge was now a settled minister with the time-consuming duties of a parish and four children to raise. He had lately had worries about his health and the sufficiency of his income. Still, the urge to contribute was not easy to dismiss.

Now in his mid-thirties, Hedge had cause to weigh his initial promise against his tangible achievements. His superior German education, his stellar record at Harvard, and his Coleridge essay had all portended a radiant future. Yet now he seemed edging toward obscurity. Later in 1840 (ironically enough, in the pages of *The Dial* itself), he was to write, "What can be more tragical, than after long years of weary watching and ceaseless toil, in which all the joy and strength of our days have been wasted in pursuit of some distant good, to find, at last, . . . that the sum total; of our endeavor, with no positive increase has left us *minus* our youth, our faculty, our hope[?]"[10] If *The Dial* succeeded and his writings were at the center of that success, Hedge might again be a cultural force, a pivotal figure in the most exciting public intellectual conversation of his time. But still, he balked, and he did so as a matter of conscience.

Like Emerson and Fuller, Hedge had found great potential in the invisible but powerful movements of the individual soul. Unlike them, he regarded his personal intuitions only as a supplement to his traditional Christian faith. He had never seen in them a substitute for the miracles of the Gospel and the divine love of Christ. Had *The Dial* aspired to proclaim a revitalized, more intellectual Christianity, merging the teachings of Christ and the philosophy of his German heroes into a new perspective on belief, Hedge would doubtless have sought a place on the front line. However, though *The Dial* was far from atheistic, its exuberantly eclectic spirituality assumed no Christian core. Taking a leading role in the journal would mark Hedge as an iconoclast, as one who was willing to set aside the wisdom of the ages for—what, exactly? Hedge wrote to Fuller that connecting himself with *The Dial* would identify him "as an atheist in disguise."[11] He did not wish to be so identified. His days in the transcendental vanguard were over.

Hedge's qualms aside, *The Dial* does not look to modern eyes like the brash experiment that it was in its time. Indeed, the magazine's prospectus, most likely written by Ripley, was intentionally mild-mannered. The magazine's purpose, the public was assured, was simply "to furnish a medium for the freest expression of thought on the questions which interest earnest minds in every community."[12] Disclaiming any fixed agenda, *The Dial* promised to discuss principles, not promote causes; it vowed always to preserve an independent mind.

In a letter to Channing, though, Fuller sounded a more partisan note. Without mentioning *The Dial* by name, she intimated that its constituents had a plain target: the complacent materialism of a money-minded society. She argued that the consistent prosperity enjoyed by Americans since the Revolution had left the nation's nobler faculties undeveloped. The industrial growth of the country had resulted in a "commercial and political fever" that had laid waste to the ethical and spiritual nature of its citizens. Education had become superficial; thought had turned vulgar. Americans cared more for getting a living than learning "to live mentally and morally." In response, a small minority of New Englanders was now on the rise. Disgusted by the meretricious crudeness of commerce, they had become radicals. Revolted by the materialistic premises of rational religion, they had become mystics. Insofar as these rebels demanded the instant creation of Utopia, Fuller disavowed them. Nevertheless, she believed that "every noble scheme, every poetic manifestation, prophesies to man his eventual destiny." Only an enlarged sense of the possible, she thought, could rally Americans out of their gluttonous torpor. "It is on this ground," she concluded, "that I sympathize with what is called the 'Transcendental party,' and that I feel their aim to be the true one."[13]

Yet, as Fuller knew, even transcendental thought did not insulate her from the indignities of sexual politics. She observed, "My position as a woman, and the many private duties which have filled my life, have prevented my thinking deeply on several of the great subjects which these friends have at heart."[14] In other words, Fuller seems to have perceived that true transcendental idealism was a luxury of gender and class, fully available only to men who either did not feel or chose to ignore the press of economic necessity. Fuller's need to mind the practicalities of life, as well as her philosophical allegiance to a distinctly non-transcendental strain of German Romanticism, stood in the way of her becoming a full-blown transcendentalist. Yet Emerson and friends plainly offered the best—perhaps the only—chance for a woman seeking both intellectual employment and a way to free herself and her country from a cultural straitjacket.

In at least one important sense, however, Fuller was not perfectly suited to the tasks of an editor. Her mind functioned by lightning inspirations and leaps of sudden apprehension. Overall, the structure and method, not to mention the physical stamina, demanded by editing did not come easily. She reflexively bridled against what she called "a process so unnatural as the reading of proofs."[15] Thinking herself to be "ignorant and careless in these details," she delegated some of the journal's copyediting to George Ripley, who, she knew, "will be miserable if there is a comma amiss."[16] She wondered to herself, "How can I ever write with this impatience of detail? The first suggestion of a thought delights—to follow it out wearies and weakens me."[17] This impetuosity of mind was becoming peculiarly frustrating for her as a writer. Whereas she had once felt that she possessed too much intellect in relation to her emotions, it now seemed to her that the imbalance had swung drastically in the other direction. She seemed on the edge of despair when she wrote in her journal, "My spirit sinks and my whole heart grieves. . . . I have few thoughts, too much feeling. . . . I feel within myself an immense power, but I cannot bring it out. I stand a barren vine stalk from which no grape will swell, though the richest vine is slumbering in its root." Elsewhere in the same passage, she wrote, "Often, too often do I wish to die."[18]

Fuller's problem was one that often afflicts a romantic spirit: the seeming inability to transform soaring emotion into tangible product. It seems that the surges of feeling that shaped and drove her were beyond the descriptive power of language. She sat down to give form to all that was in her heart and stood up again with a blank or incomprehensible page. She had told her friend Elizabeth Hoar in 1839 that mere eloquence and aestheticism were not enough for her. She desired "no more [to be] an artist, or a philosopher . . . or a critic, but a soul ever rushing forth in tides of genial life, or retiring evermore into precious crystals, too pure to be lonely."[19] Fuller's endless striving against limitation had taken her to a point where she disdained even the limitation of a human body. But the world does not pay one to be merely a soul. A part of her, it seemed, was overpoweringly in touch with the realm of feeling. Another portion of her was brilliantly conversant in the dominion of words. To her chagrin, however, she could not always compel these two facets of herself to talk to each other. The failure could hardly have been from want of desire or discipline; few people ever wanted a literary life as much as Fuller did. What she probably needed most was the last quality that a nervous constitution like hers was likely to acquire: patience.

The first issue of *The Dial* began with a four-page letter from Emerson, hailing the great groundswell of ideas and sentiments that had "led many sincere persons in New England to make new demands on literature" and to cast off the stifling forms and traditions of religion and education that had been "turning us to stone."[20] *The Dial* was a necessary and inevitable rejoinder to a creaking orthodoxy whose greatest horrors were "new views and the dreams of youth."[21] Styling the new magazine as an "antidote to all narrowness," Emerson voiced the editors' wish to print criticism that would "supersed[e], as every new thought does, all foregone thoughts, and mak[e] a new light on the whole world."[22] Seeking above all to "impart life" to their readers and to use *The Dial* to measure "no hours but those of sunshine," Emerson, Ripley, and Fuller placed their pride and joy before the world.[23]

No one in the Western Hemisphere had ever seen anything like the first issue of *The Dial*. It was a fantastic stew of genres and perspectives, united by little more than, for the most part, an earnest wish to speak to the highest propensities of human idealism. From the artistically gifted minister Christopher Cranch came a glittering poem that compared the aurora borealis with the upward strivings of the heart. Theodore Parker, easily the transcendentalists' most intrepid social reformer, pushed politics aside to write an enraptured essay on the omnipresence of God in nature. William Henry Channing's "Ernest the Seeker" celebrated the beauty and charity of the Roman Catholic Church. Sam Ward was represented by a number of sincere but metrically tone-deaf poems. Thoreau had a short poem, "Sympathy," and a well-mannered, scholarly essay on the Roman satirist Persius. Although the tone of the issue was generally cheerful, death was also in its midst. In tribute to his consumption-ravaged family, Emerson persuaded Fuller to include work by both his departed brothers, Edward and Charles. An especially poignant inclusion was a charming poem by Waldo's late first wife. Ellen Tucker Emerson's "Lines" is an innocent meditation on a gentle, happy life, too soon nearing its end. One pensive stanza reads, "The cloud was around me, / I knew not why / Such sweetness crowned me, / While Time shot by."[24]

Among the best contributions was one of Fuller's own: "A Short Essay on Critics." While purporting to classify various types of criticism and to arrive at a definition of the critic's ideal function, Fuller's essay also offers a candid assessment of her own mind; it is the work of a writer who, after years of study and effort, has come to accept that, despite her breadth of mind and poetic temperament, she lacks the innate spark that defines a poet. In her essay, Fuller hails poets as divine. The task of the critic, she suggests, is to translate that divinity for the ears of mundane humanity, completing through analysis what the poet achieves through genius. Unskilled at invention, the critic can still interpret invention; unable to create the beautiful, the critic can help others appreciate beauty. The ideal critic, she argues, "must want nothing of what constitutes the poet, except the power of creating forms and speaking in music." He must be "the younger brother of genius."[25] Fuller consented to her role as a younger sister; if she could not create with genius, she could interpret genius and, in so doing, attempt to awaken fresh thought in others. In her inaugural essay for *The Dial*, Fuller assumed with a glad heart the task of teaching people to love wisely what they had previously loved only well.

The good in *The Dial* far outweighed the bad. However, giving in to Emerson's urging, Fuller made a tactical error. Bronson Alcott's submission for the first issue was a series of fifty obscure aphorisms, assembled under the pompous title "Orphic Sayings." Read patiently, they at times speak movingly about the innate divinity of man. However, Alcott's prose was strangely deft at robbing people of their patience. Though both he and Fuller had their doubts, Emerson prevailed on Fuller to publish the "Sayings." Although none of the issue's other pieces used anything more than an initial to identify the author, Emerson prompted Fuller to print the "Sayings" under

Alcott's full name. Knowing that Alcott was a more persuasive speaker than a writer, he hoped that readers who had heard him speak would hear his voice as they read and would thereby excuse its faults. Emerson miscalculated. Far from winning sympathy for Alcott, including his name only made him the most identifiable target for the magazine's critics. Still worse, Alcott's byline called attention to the journal's weakest spot. *The Dial* demanded thoughtful reading. It was easier to lampoon than to analyze. Consequently, reviewers trained inordinate attention on Alcott and made his work stand for the journal as a whole. One wit in the Boston press wrote a parody of Alcott's effort and called it "Gastric Sayings." Another compared the "Sayings" to "a train of fifteen railroad cars with one passenger."[26]

Such jibes notwithstanding, *The Dial*'s debut was far from ruinous. Some of the reviews were highly encouraging, including a notice from the *New-York Tribune*, edited by the rising newspaperman Horace Greeley, which eventually lauded *The Dial* as "the very best Magazine published in this country."[27] Still, *The Dial* had failed to achieve a truly spectacular launch, and, even before the critical response was known, its creators knew it. Although Emerson said he liked the contents of the journal "better than I feared," Fuller found it "far . . . from that eaglet motion I wanted."[28] She complained to him of a "terrible season of faintness and discouragement," though she refused to live in its somber spirit for a moment.[29] Both she and Emerson resolved that they would do far better with the second number.

Fuller put forth a stalwart effort to make sure that it would be so. Just two weeks after her "season of faintness," and although her violent headaches continually reminded her that she was "in no state for criticism," she was editing "Thoughts on Modern Literature," the essay from Emerson that was to open the second issue, and dunning him for more poems.[30] Between her ongoing public conversations and her editing of *The Dial*, Fuller was doing the most rewarding—and the most mentally and physically taxing—work she had ever done.

It was going to get harder. Fuller and her coeditors were confident that there must be a multitude of thinkers like them who were just waiting for an inspiration like *The Dial* to bring them out of hiding. Once discovered, these readers would give *The Dial* both a solid list of subscribers and a broad field of contributors. Indeed, the editors proclaimed their intention to thrive, not so much on the submissions of "practised writers, as the discourse of the living."[31] However, there were not enough excellent writers in a transcendental vein, practiced or otherwise, to fill *The Dial*, four times a year, with work of the highest quality. Indeed, there seemed to be barely enough readers to cover the magazine's costs. Fuller and Emerson's challenge became steeper still when George Ripley abruptly resigned as managing editor. More interested in the idea of founding a transcendental commune than balancing the books for a journal, he took no part in *The Dial* after its third issue.

It is perhaps a measure of the strain that Fuller began to undergo that, as she pressed on with the highly practical work of editorship, her inner life became progressively dreamy and abstract. Being a member of what she called "the bread-winning tribe who serve the clock" plainly revolted her, and she yearned for an escape.[32] She became more interested in revisiting her own spiritual and mental history; it was during this time that she wrote her recollections of her childhood dreams of rivers of blood, and of her mystical night at the bedside of the deflowered, dying girl in Groton. Her poetic efforts also became more abstract and indicative of inner dividedness. In the debut issue of *The Dial*, she published the first of a series of writings in which she endowed plants with human attributes. In "A Dialogue," a dahlia calls out to the passing sun:

> DAHLIA.
> *My cup already doth with light o'errun.*
> *Descend, fair sun;*
> *I am all crimsoned for the bridal hour,*
> *Come to thy flower.*

> THE SUN.
> *Ah, if I pause, my work will not be done,*
> *On I must run,*
> *The mountains wait.—I love thee, lustrous flower,*
> *But give love to no hour.*[33]

The two parties to the conversation can readily be seen as the two sides of Fuller's character that she was forever laboring to reconcile: the passionate, feminine, potential lover, crimsoned and waiting, but always passed by; and the hurried, work-obsessed striver, passionate in her own way, but with an intellectual ardor that left no time or space for rest or sensuality. In the intellectually fertile year that launched *The Dial*, Fuller was siding with the dahlia. She had her reasons.

To begin with, Fuller had the sense that her circumstances had so greatly changed that she was no longer the person she once was. A meeting with an old congressional colleague of her father's who had known her at fifteen made her conscious of how far she had traveled "since that epoch of pride and fulness." To Fuller, who had always been so conscious of the transformations in her identity, it felt strange to hear someone talk, as she put it, "to my old self." "What a gulf between," she continued. "There is scarce a fibre left of the haughty, passionate, ambitious child he remembered and had loved."[34] Fuller was deeply aware of herself as a creature of change, with a string of half-forgotten identities behind her and numberless others still to come.

In truth, she overestimated the discontinuity. There were, in fact, remnants aplenty of the misfit prodigy in the thirty-year-old Fuller, and her father's friend said repeatedly that he would have known her anywhere. Yet Fuller herself felt she had somehow lost touch with her earlier character. At the same time, Sam Ward and Anna Barker were finally married on October 3, 1840. Fuller attended, even postponing an operation on her brother Arthur's eye so that she might be there. While Fuller had long realized that she had lost Sam and Anna to each other, the knowledge that their love was soon to be solemnized agitated her unexpectedly. It was, on the one hand, an event that "dawned . . . poetically" upon her.[35] At the same time, it marked a heartrending farewell. As for *The Dial*, the hard slog of editing had not only been draining; it had thus far been uncompensated. No hint of the small three-hundred-dollar salary that had been promised her had yet materialized.

Another blow to her stability came that summer when her mother, who had been a steady companion since Margaret returned from Providence, began to make plans to travel in October to New Orleans, where Margaret's brother Eugene had settled with his new wife. The elder Margarett's absence was only temporary; she was to return well before Christmas. Nevertheless, her voyage signaled an ending to her elder daughter. After her mother sailed south, Margaret wrote, "As a family we are finally broken apart now. . . . The last moment was sad."[36] Fuller's daily life was feeling progressively empty. As early as the previous March, she had complained to Channing that her life seemed "but a fragment."[37] By July, she was lamenting, "I cannot make much use of a life which once seemed so full of promise and power."[38] As editor of *The Dial*, she was finally in a position to influence her nation's culture. Financially and romantically, however, she felt blocked and frustrated as never before. As summer turned to autumn, Fuller was desperate for other kinds of stimuli.

Caroline Sturgis was one of the first to notice that something about Margaret was altered. Fuller's letters to the younger woman had always been emotionally honest. Now they began to disclose a surreal quality that even a friend well versed in Fuller's oddities was likely to find peculiar. On September 8, Fuller wrote, "Rivers of life flow, seas surge between me and you. I cannot look back, nor remember how I passed them. I live, I am—*The carbuncle is found*. And at present the mere sight of my talisman is enough. The hour may come when I wish to charm with it but not yet. I have no future, as no past. . . . There can be no 'stern holding back' but all the pure in heart must be seeing God."[39] Less than three weeks later, Margaret sent another perplexing letter: "Of the mighty changes in my spiritual life I do not wish to speak, yet surely you cannot be ignorant of them. . . . All has been revealed, all foreshown yet I know it not. Experiment has given place to certainty, pride to obedience, thought to love, and truth is lost in beauty. 'I am no more below.'" Fuller added that she had no words "to paint . . . the scenery . . . of these great events," but promised that Caroline might soon "perceive all" in her.[40] The following month she reported that, on an evening two weeks after Sam and Anna's wedding, a "sweet harmony" flowed through her "in such full strains that it seemed as if that must be the last of my human life."[41] If Caroline had had access to Fuller's diary, she would have found more evidence of her friend's sudden ascension into the ether. "I grow more and more what they call a mystic," she had written in June. "Nothing interests me except listening for the *secret harmonies of nature*."[42]

Fuller described herself as being in a place of "infinite loveliness" and "infinite holiness," where, "all radiant with faith, and love, and life," she was beginning to become herself.[43] She believed that she had passed into a higher realm. Others found her transformation more worrisome. Emerson fretted over her state of "ecstatic solitude." She was affected by a kind of "restlessness and fever" that he feared might "deceive [her] soul."[44] Channing, with a kind of admiring dismay, later likened her to "a Bacchante, prompt for wild excitement, and fearless to tread by night the mountain forest, with song and dance of delirious mirth"—a pursuit perhaps more appropriate to a maenad than a magazine editor.[45] Fuller was plainly nettled by the failure of her friends to comprehend and rejoice in her newfound spiritual revelation. "Why is it," she demanded, "that the religion of my nature is so much hidden from my peers? why do they question me, who never question them? why persist to regard as a meteor an orb of assured hope? Can no soul know me wholly?"[46] Her quest for a fully sympathetic soul mate led her predictably to Emerson. Less predictably, it proved to be a wrong turn.

Fuller and Emerson's friendship had already moved onto uncertain ground. Beneath their seemingly cordial working relationship, tensions had evidently been brewing for some time. In the fall of 1840, Margaret wrote that, when she had left Waldo in the past, she had often done so "despairing and forlorn," saying to herself, "[T]his light will never understand my fire; this clear eye will never discern the law by which I am filling my circle; this simple force will never interpret my need of manifold being."[47] Yet she managed to keep her frustrations within bounds until August of that year.

On the fourteenth of that month, they suddenly erupted, catching Emerson off guard. After spending the afternoon together visiting Anna Barker, Fuller and Emerson shared a stagecoach as she rode back to her home in Jamaica Plain. No one knows just what provoked Fuller to assail Emerson, accusing him, as he put it, of "inhospitality of soul."[48] She pleaded that both she and their mutual friend Caroline Sturgis would gladly befriend him, but that their current relationship was not friendship at all, but merely "literary gossip." She hotly informed the man who had once been her "only clergyman" that he could count and weigh but was incapable of love. No matter how often they met, they came together as strangers. Speaking also for Caroline, she added that they both felt "wronged in such relation, & do not wish to be catechised & criticised."[49] Emerson sputtered in response that Fuller was asking too much; he could not converse with even the divinest person for more than a week. Margaret would not be mollified. She thought it was no friendship that could be so soon exhausted, and added that Emerson ought to know how to be silent and companionable at the same time. Alluding to their business collaboration on *The Dial*, she condemned their relationship with the most horrible epithet a transcendentalist could hear: it was "commercial."[50]

Sturgis took some of the sting out of Fuller's raillery by telling Emerson that she, at least, was "sure of" him. Sturgis's rejoinder was "delicious" to

Emerson.[51] Still, he had been stunned. He confessed "to all this charge with humility unfeigned."[52] He had, in his own mind, credited himself with a "solid good understanding" of Fuller and, he thought, had finally stood in full admiration of her genius.[53] Now it seemed he knew her not at all. In gentlemanly fashion, he claimed the fault as his own. She was right; the ability to forge a simple friendship, one that did not depend on ideas or books or journals, was beyond him. "Would nothing be so grateful to me," he wrote, "as to melt once for all these icy barriers, & unite with these lovers." Yet his love of solitude and self stood in the way. He added, "But . . . such a one as I must do nothing to court their love which would lose my own." He would have taken great joy if he could "form permanent relations with the three or four wise & beautiful whom I hold so dear."[54]

Emerson was not entirely to blame for his coldness of manner. The losses of his father, first wife, and brothers had all been lessons in the dangers of trying to "form permanent relations." Even the warmth of his feelings toward Lidian were limited by the memory of Ellen Tucker; to give himself wholly to love would both express disloyalty to his lost beloved and expose himself to a further wound. His philosophy and his poetry were the fortress he had built around a scarred and timid heart. He could not now take down its walls, at least not for Margaret Fuller. There was just one for whom his soul stood open: his three-year-old son, Waldo. Emerson adored his bright-eyed boy and took delight in recording his cute and clever sayings in his journal. He found genial humor in the child's innate conservatism when, after his morning bread and milk fell on the floor, the boy declared that "he wanted the same milk & bread that he had at first." Surely, his father predicted, "he will bewail presently that today is not yesterday."[55] But the portals that little Waldo had opened were prone to close only tighter against the fierce accusations of a Cambridge-bred bluestocking.

Nevertheless, in the wake of Fuller's verbal assault, Emerson did make a conscious effort to jettison some of his reserve. Only a few days after their confrontation, he suggested to Fuller that they, along with Alcott, Ripley, Hedge, and some others, might found a college in Concord. "What society shall we not have!" he enthused, "What Sundays shall we not have!"[56] He swore to her, "I shall never go quite back to my old arctic habits—I shall believe that nobleness is loving, & delights in sharing itself."[57]

In the ensuing days, he wrote a series of protestations and appeals. He sent a zealous invitation: "Come & live near me & if you confide in me so far I will engage to be as true a brother to you as blood ever made."[58] With unaccustomed openness, he also proclaimed, "Now I will identify you with the Ideal friend, & live with you on imperial terms. Present, you shall be present only as an angel might be, & absent you shall not be absent from me."[59] There was only one problem with all this effusiveness: every word quoted so far in this paragraph was addressed, not to Fuller, but to the third party to their heated conversation, the twenty-one-year-old Caroline Sturgis. Flattered by his attentions, Caroline responded with equal ardor: "You, my dearest brother, shall be my saint & purify me wholly. . . . If my friend gives me thought more lofty & beautiful than my own, it seems to me that he must for the time, be my God." High-minded as Emerson and Sturgis may have been, it takes some effort to believe that the electricity between them was as exclusively saintly and fraternal as their literal language would imply. In any event, Caroline was willing to shed the mantle of the pious innocent long enough to slip in a rivalrous dig at Fuller: "Where we differ in nature from Margaret & others, is that we unfold from within, while they seek without, & having accumulated much treasure, look for a treasure house that can contain it all."[60] She was, of course, wrong in her supposition that Fuller was inwardly empty and subsisted intellectually merely by filling herself with acquired data from the outside world. Yet the fact that one of her closest friends could profess so little knowledge of her inner richness is an indication of how poorly Fuller sometimes communicated herself.

Had Emerson kept his correspondence with Sturgis between the two of them, all might have been well; however, he had the effrontery to write to Fuller, "I write letters lately to Caroline, with whom I have agreed that we are brother & sister by divine invisible parentage, and she has sent me golden epistles."[61] It was as if he were telling Margaret, "There—you see? I can be warm and intimately friendly; just not with you." Toward Margaret, he remained ambivalent at best. He did admit that the gap in sympathy between them was narrower than it had once been. He noted, "I understand now your language better, I hear my native tongue." Nevertheless, he saw limits to their progress. "Still I see not into you," he confessed, "& have not arrived at your law. Absent from you I am very likely to deny you and say that you lack this & that. The next time we meet you say with emphasis that very word." With finality, he averred, "You & I are not inhabitants of one thought of the Divine Mind, but of two thoughts, that we meet & treat like foreign states, one maritime, one inland, whose trade & laws are essentially unlike." Her mental habits were driven by willfulness; his were of a mode of "pure acquiescence." Two people could only be friends, he thought, if they dwelt in the same truth; thus, his relation with her must, "for the time," be something distinct from friendship. Yet he repeated, with emphasis, the phrase "For the time!"—dangling before her the possibility that patience might finally guide them to an "ultimate unity." Despite all his disclaimers, he still said he was willing to "open all my doors to your sunshine & morning air."[62]

Fuller was not impressed. She wrote back to say that, for some time, the feeling of distance had been even stronger on her side. "I have felt the impossibility of meeting far more than you," she told him, "so much that, if you ever know me well, you will feel that the fact of my abiding with you thus far affords a strong proof that we are to be much to one another." She hastened to deny Emerson's apparent insinuation that she desired some inappropriate control over him. She assured him, "Could I lead the highest angel captive by a look, that look I would not give, unless prompted by true love: I am no usurper. I ask only mine own inheritance."[63]

But, as the remainder of her letter revealed, what Fuller claimed as her inheritance was a grand estate indeed. She wanted him to recognize the purity and ethereal calm into which her nature, which had once been "darting motion, and restless flame," was now resolving. She wanted him to perform for her "the highest office of friendship, by offering me the clue of the labyrinth of my being." She wanted him to appreciate "the fearlessness which shrinks from no truth in myself and others, and trusted me, believing that I knew the path for myself." Fuller was indignant that Emerson should have but had not seen "this stair on which God has been so untiringly leading me to himself."[64] It was wearisome enough simply to read and decipher Fuller's litany of demands. Emerson must have been wondering how any mortal man could satisfy them when he read Fuller's most withering accusation:

> Then indeed, when my soul, in its childish agony of prayer, stretched out its arms to you as a father, did you not see what was meant by this crying for the moon; this sullen rejection of playthings which had become unmeaning?[65]

The core of Margaret's indictment—that Emerson had failed to respond to her cry for a father—confirms what others may already have assumed: that she had sought in the Sage of Concord an idealized substitute for the demanding but oddly beloved sire whom cholera had stolen from her five years earlier. But Fuller's hope for a second father explains only part of her anguish at not being received into Emerson's spiritual bosom. The great remaining cause behind her agitation is revealed in her complaint that Emerson had failed to recognize the stairway that was leading her to God.

Fuller was not the only one of Emerson's disciples to dedicate herself to an inner reality with such earnestness that the sensory world began to be of secondary significance. To one extent or another, Alcott, Thoreau, and the poet Jones Very all ventured down a traceless mystical path. There was something in the philosophical concoction Emerson served his friends that brought their mercurial idealism to the surface and opened their minds to indescribable epiphanies. Yet when his friends attested to these flights of the spirit, Emerson never knew how to respond. The kinds of mental states to which expansive thinkers like Alcott and Fuller were inclined might be compared with the conversion experiences reported by the Puritans of an earlier century; they functioned as an inner confirmation that the soul bore the markings of divinity. The transcendentalist who suddenly felt an instinctive nearness to the ultimate Power was, like the Puritans, anxious to know whether her experience was the real thing. Fuller sought confirmation from the man who, in *Nature*, had literally written the book on transcendental self-discovery. She further hoped that two people who had apparently traveled to the same miraculous shore might embrace each other on a celestial plane that lay beyond the meeting ground of ordinary, earthbound friends. She found instead that, although Emerson offered abundant light, the heat she expected was strangely lacking.

One might also have expected Fuller to remind Emerson that, although the first issue of *The Dial* had been out for several months, she had not been paid. Instead, her letters skirted this issue. Fuller no doubt knew as well as Emerson that the issue had not turned a profit and that demanding a paycheck would have been futile. More to the point, however, worldly compensations were not much on her mind. Her prolonged ecstatic state dominated her thinking. Even in the letters she wrote Emerson dealing with her editing work, she waxed prophetic, announcing that "there will come a purer mode of being even in the world of Form."[66] She told Channing that her health had so greatly failed that she was "little better than an aspiration, which the ages will reward, by empowering me to incessant acts of vigorous beauty."[67] When Sturgis sent her a letter that contained some "recognition" of her beatified state, Fuller pronounced her young friend "ready for the Genesis" and added, "I cannot plunge into myself enough. . . . The life that flows in upon me from so many quarters is too beautiful to be checked. I would not check a single pulsation. It all ought to be;—if caused by any apparition of the Divine in me I could bless myself like the holy Mother. But like her I long to be virgin."[68]

The flow of revelations and prophecies rolled ceaselessly on. Before long, they spilled over into Fuller's writings for *The Dial*. For the journal's third issue, published in January 1841, Fuller authored a short story inspired by a visit from a man whose visionary excesses may even have surpassed her own. Dr. William Eustis, according to Fuller, recorded his rather subjective observations of nature "not like a botanist, but a lover." With what level of earnestness no one can now determine, he told her of a "most romantic" conversation he had had with a magnolia tree on the bank of Lake Pontchartrain.[69] Fuller reworked his fantastic tale into a metaphoric biography of her own spirit.

The nameless stranger who narrates the tale comes upon a sweetly fragrant magnolia tree, which he describes as a "Queen . . . singing to herself in her lonely bower," her presence made all the more affecting by the narrator's familiarity with "sickness and sorrow." It is evidently the stranger's deep affinity for flowers—a trait he shares with Fuller's mother—that enables him to hear the tree as she tells her story of woe and metamorphosis.[70] From the outset, the tree stresses her loneliness, saying, "I stand alone. . . . I have no sister of the heart, and though my root is the same as that of the other virgins of our royal house, I bear not the same blossom, nor can I unite my voice with theirs in the forest choir."[71]

The magnolia, which also appears to understand poetry quoted in Italian, is quick to disclose a past as improbable as its linguistic prowess: it was once an orange tree, with whom, strange to say, the narrator had spoken on an earlier occasion. The magnolia recalls that, when an orange tree, she was never silent or alone and "had a voice for every season. On me the merchant counted, the bride looked to me for her garland, the nobleman for the chief ornament of his princely hall, and the poor man for his wealth."[72] At first pleased and proud to be so useful, the orange tree grows tired of being looked on solely as a dispenser of material gratification to others. Ceaselessly called upon for her beautiful gifts, she comes to realize that her ungrateful despoilers cannot feel sympathy for her precisely because her generosity makes her seem so rich.[73] Killed by a frost, the orange tree is brought before the godlike queen of flowers, who, after counseling her to "take a step inward" and become "no longer a bounteous sovereign [but] a vestal priestess," transforms her into a magnolia, in which form she is to bide her time until a further change refines her into a creature of pure spirit.[74] Withdrawing ever deeper into her inner being, the reincarnated tree has now attained contemplative bliss and feels "the Infinite possess me more and more." The tree bids the stranger farewell, hoping to meet him again "in prayer, in destiny . . . in elemental power."[75] Fuller later wrote that she had written her "Magnolia" story when she "was well and every way at ease."[76] If so, its oddness is even harder to explain.

For all its strangeness, Fuller's magnolia story was, in its way, a personal manifesto, and it had been several years in the making. After her time of unpaid apprenticeship with Alcott, her exhausting stint in Providence, her thankless months at *The Dial*, and her years of sacrificing for her family, Margaret was more than entitled to feel like her fictional orange tree, celebrated and used by all but understood by none. The fantasy of transformation embedded in her story reflects her theory of creation, which maintained that all creatures were gradually shedding their earthly failings on their way to ultimate rebirth as perfected spirits. More than this, Fuller was attempting to proclaim a personal resurrection and evolution. She wanted no longer to be the benevolent martyr, and the alternative she imagined for herself was the life of an inward-gazing, all-renouncing ascetic, interested not so much in benefiting an ungrateful world as in achieving a personal, aphysical Nirvana.

Fuller's most elaborate effort at fiction for *The Dial* was even stranger than her "Magnolia." Appearing in April 1841 in the magazine's fourth issue, "Leila" has withstood determined efforts to plumb its mysteries. The title character—if that is the right noun—apparently begins the piece as a flesh-and-blood woman, though a rather unusual one, whom most men are unable to look at without feelings of pain, befuddlement, and anger because, being "bound in sense, time, and thought," they shrink from beholding "the overflow of the infinite."[77] And overflow Leila does, transcending "sex, age, state, and all the barriers behind which man entrenches himself from assaults of the spirit."[78] In the space of only two pages, Leila becomes, in the eye of the narrator, the sky, the wind, a sunset, and an indescribable apparition "among the Sylphs' faint florescent forms that hang in the edges of life's rainbows." In one passage, she is a lake spirit; in another she is a volcanic fluid, her entire being aglow with "the fire that so baffles men . . . the blood-red, heart's-blood-red of the carbuncle."[79] Again, Fuller has returned to her symbolic gem, so rich in mystery and pent-up sexual energy, but the trans-formations of Leila unfold too fast for the reader to pause over any single emblem. In yet another incarnation, Leila is a deep, explosive thought, shat-tering cities and tearing hills asunder with her madly sublime force. She is, in still another turn, "one arrow from the quiver of God"—an angel showering balms and blessings from above and converting prisons into Edens.[80] The narrator claims that, if Leila could truly be rendered in human language, the secret of moral and mental alchemy would be discovered, and all Bibles would pass "into one Apocalypse." Virtually the last image of Leila, however, shows her kneeling with her brow in the dust, borne down by "the full weight of accident and time."[81] The manic, giddy shape shifter comes to rest as a figure of degraded exhaustion.

Fuller scholars and biographers, conscious of the strange self-indulgences and metaphysical excesses of Fuller's *Dial* fiction, too often either pass over it entirely or praise its "experimental" daring before politely moving on. But stories like "Leila" and "The Magnolia of Lake Pontchartrain" merit more serious review, if only as a means of understanding Fuller's own fantasti-cally ambitious and pitiably troubled spirit. In her most idealistic moments, Fuller saw herself as the rightful inheritor of the All, as a spirit for whom the limitations of flesh and duty functioned as a thwarting prison. Her thoughts and feelings continually beat their wings against the cage of the physical world—a world that, while it was a place in which to experience beauty and exercise kindness, was also a constant impediment to achieving the perfect, disembodied state of being that Fuller imagined as her true element. Both "Leila" and "Magnolia" proclaim the aspirations of a disinherited child of God, as well as the frustration of knowing that this inheritance may never be restored.

It was during this period, too, that Fuller wrote her "autobiographical romance," the fictionalized memoir in which she remembered both the excitement and the trauma of her early education and concluded that she had had "no natural childhood." From this document come the truisms of Fuller's childhood that casual students of the era tend to receive as gospel truth: Timothy's severity, Margarett's passivity, and, above all, the "glooms and terrors" visited on a hapless child, virtually buried alive in a library before she had fairly begun to live. While the literal truth of Fuller's "romance" is questionable on many points, it is a potent statement of Fuller's state of mind in 1840. In her relationships and in her perception of herself, the adult Fuller retained some of the habits of the troubled, misunderstood child she had once been. Decades later, she was still seeking the unreserved affection of a highly intelligent but emotionally distant man—and still trying to win that affection primarily through her intellectual performances. She wrote of her father in the "romance," "He had no conception of the subtle and indirect motions of imagination and feeling. His influence on me was great, and opposed to the natural unfolding of my character," and, as a result, Margaret's own world "sank deep within, away from the surface of my life."[82] Now, in 1840, all of this must have seemed a prelude for her relations with Emerson.

Many writers turn to the written word as a means of asserting authority and control over experiences they yearn to edit and revise. Fuller at this time was certainly engaging in this kind of assertion, but only to a degree. At the same time that her writing was enabling her to rationalize the past, it was also enabling her to see her life through a prism of unreason and fantasy. The discontents that were so painful to observe objectively were easier to express in an imaginative space where magnolias spoke and women dissolved into molten gold and gleaming rainbows. Even her descriptions of trampling horses and blood-dripping trees that populate the nightmares recounted in the "autobiographical romance" had their therapeutic side, for from a nightmare one may at least wake up. Fuller's fanciful writings from this period are the work of a brilliant mind under almost intolerable stress. Though she had managed to continue her work for *The Dial*, she was doing so with a nervous energy that she later compared to "the great bodily strength of the insane."[83] The visions that her stories brought to life were part of Fuller's effort to find a more bearable mental space in which to live.

Worldly issues were pressing her as well. Beginning in April 1841, when the lease expired on Willow Brook, the home she had been sharing with her mother in Jamaica Plain, Margaret had no fixed residence for a year and a half. During that time, she shuttled among the Farrars' home in Cambridge, the Emersons' house in Concord, and a few other domiciles besides. One of these, George Ripley's experimental commune, Brook Farm, in West Roxbury, was to assume ever greater meaning for her as time went by. Fuller also paid extended visits to Caroline Sturgis at a rented farmhouse in Newport and to the Sturgis family's vacation home in Newburyport. Fuller's miscellaneous stopovers in this period have been referred to as "working vacations."[84] The description may conceal a harsher truth: Fuller was evidently in no financial condition to maintain a place of her own. At first, she must have hoped that a share of *The Dial*'s profits would enable her to put an end to her wanderings. But the profits did not come.

Indeed, as Fuller moved about in search of answers—and housing—the future of *The Dial* had begun to darken. It was suffering from what an economist might call a "free-rider" problem. Its subscribers tended to share their copies broadly with non-subscribing friends. In New York, Horace Greeley, who deeply admired *The Dial*, reprinted many of its offerings in his newspaper, the *Daily Tribune*. While these practices disseminated *The Dial*'s cultural visions to incalculably more people than were reflected in the magazine's subscription list, they brought in no revenue, and it was revenue that *The Dial* desperately needed. In April 1841, just as the magazine's fourth issue was being sent out to subscribers and as Fuller was packing her bags in Jamaica Plain, *The Dial*'s publisher, Weeks and Jordan, declared bankruptcy. Although the ever-dependable Elizabeth Palmer Peabody promptly agreed to step in as the new publisher, Weeks and Jordan initially blocked the switchover with a piece of literary hostage taking: they refused to let Fuller and Emerson have the journal's subscription list until they had received a sizable payment. Although some inspired maneuvering by Emerson soon removed this hurdle, the magazine was in for a much ruder shock. Though the details were initially unclear, it was evident that Weeks and Jordan had been painting an overly optimistic picture of the magazine's finances. Fuller admitted to her brother Richard that *The Dial* was "likely to fall through entirely."[85] Fuller was, as everyone who knew her realized, anything but a quitter. Despite the journal's murky future, she soldiered on as editor, now sometimes writing more than half an issue by herself.

Since their falling-out the previous fall, Emerson had been at pains to convince Fuller that all could again be well between them. He was also concerned about the stress to which she was subjecting herself. From spring to autumn, he was continually inviting her to come to Bush "& make the bright days brighter or the grey ones tolerable."[86] She was welcome to stay as long or as short as she wished.[87] Hoping, perhaps to relieve some of her financial woes, he eventually broadened the invitation to a bolder proposal; she might, if she wished, escape "our national hurry" by coming to live with him and Lidian.[88] She accepted his hospitality on a more modest basis. In May, she stayed with them a fortnight, enjoying the quiet country life and keeping Emerson company as he worked in his garden.[89] She also took pleasure in the company of Thoreau, who had accepted an invitation to move in with the Emersons as their hired man. On days redolent with the smell of apple blossoms, he rowed her over the still surface of Walden Pond. On a soft night, when the moon was almost gone, Fuller listened to the song of a whippoorwill and dreamed of a time "when the duties [would be] done."[90] Just a few weeks after her visit, she felt herself sinking into a depression she would not have wished on an enemy. The "perfumed and leafy June" brought no pleasure. To Caroline Sturgis, she wondered "how much of this sort of pain I must look forward to in the future."[91]

Then, gradually her letters became less agitated. In July, she recalled some stories of medieval friendship, and the sacrifices of the noble knights reminded her how mean it was to give in to one's own sorrows when others were struggling too. To Channing, she wrote that, had she lived in a heroic age, "I could not die while there was yet life in my brother's breast. I would return from the shades and nerve him for the fight."[92] Channing had expressed compassion for her troubled state of mind. She asked him not to "wish to exile me from the dark hour." She explained that, whereas a man might feel most like himself in times of triumph, a woman needed sorrow to bring her character to the fore. She "could no more stay from the foot of the cross, than from the Transfiguration."[93] Her sadness, she seemed to be suggesting, was merely the price a woman paid to experience a new season of clarity and renewal. At the end of July, Fuller went to Newport to see the Sturgises. The family's white farmhouse and its apple orchard looked down a gentle slope to the open sea. In the evenings, after the last rosy light had faded, Fuller stood "beneath the moon [and] beyond the glistening cornfields

... heard the endless surge" of the Atlantic. It was "a most melting mood."[94] The riot in her brain seemed slowly to be running its course.

Then, during the night of August 2, while she was still with the Sturgises, the tumult returned in full force, and she suddenly experienced an "intimate communion far more full" than she had previously felt. She both wanted to wake up and feared to stir. "It made me shudder," she wrote, "for I seemed no more mine own. And yet it seemed some heavenly state that once let go might ne'er again return." It seemed to her that she had been offered an invisible cup, but whether it contained knowledge, salvation, or a lethal poison she could not tell. She remembered thinking, "O let this cup pass from me, yet not so[.] Wait but a moment I will drink it all and then come death." The clock struck two. Fuller rose and looked from her window at the fading moonlight on the ocean. Although she sat there until dawn, she could not compose herself enough to know what she was feeling. She knew only that a crisis in her life had taken place.[95] Thereafter, her condition decisively changed. After almost a year of visionary upheavals, she found her mind had become "calm and sweet." There seemed to be no fire left in her either "to resist or to consume."[96]

Physically, she was exhausted; emotionally, she had finally been purged. Looking back on her crisis, Fuller maintained that everything that had befallen her had been no illusion. Seven years later, she wrote to Emerson with a hint of nostalgia, "Those were glorious hours, and angels certainly visited me." Trying to explain why the taste of what had then seemed to be "the true elixir" had failed to transform her into a creature wholly beyond the reach of pain and want, she could only murmur, "There must have been too much of earth,—too much taint of weakness and folly, so that baptism did not suffice."[97] Fuller did not make it quite clear to Emerson whether she had expected to enter a living state on the other side of desire or whether she had meant simply to die.

To Elizabeth Hoar, Fuller was more explicit. The year after her crisis, she admitted to Hoar that, throughout her long period of "illumination," she had "constantly looked forward to death," which she supposed to be the logical outcome of her great spiritual ascent.[98] The emotional crisis that reached its climax that August night was, therefore, among the most significant episodes in her spiritual journey. Since childhood, Fuller had always taken it as an article of faith that a person of strong abilities and conscience would and must always aspire to a purer, more perfect conception of herself. This idea of progress always tacitly assumed a gradual rejection of the physical world and of the body as the soul aspired toward higher knowledge and goodness. But her aspiration toward perfection bore within it a latent element of the suicidal. Though Fuller might have scoffed at the comparison, the destiny she had assumed for herself had much in common with classically self-immolating Victorian heroines who, like Dickens's Little Nell and Stowe's Eva St. Clare, become too perfect for the earth to contain them and must therefore die. This anticipation of an early death was the dark side of her quasi-religious faith in eternal spiritual progress. In early August 1841, she retreated from this logic. She realized at last that the pinnacle to which she had been striving was actually an abyss.

From this time forward, Fuller's assumptions about the meaning of life began to change. She was at the outset of a period of searching, a trying out of other possibilities whose ending points were neither quite so ethereal nor so self-destructive. She still believed in the necessity of radical self-improvement and the seeking of transcendence. However, this belief was now tempered by her having seen the dangers of pursuing it to excess. Now that this life principle had been challenged, Fuller was no longer sure what the guiding star of her life should be. Time would have to pass before she would find a satisfactory answer.

Meanwhile, familial concerns beset her. In September, she received word that her sister Ellen, who had gone west to Cincinnati to teach school, had there met up and fallen in love with one of the lesser Emersonians, the poet Ellery Channing. The news came as such a shock to Fuller that she found herself almost unable to write. Not to be confused with his brilliant uncle William Ellery Channing or with Fuller's cherished friend William Henry Channing, Ellery was, to put it gently, a breed apart. Although the transcendentalists as a group hardly deserved their reputation for lack of industry, Ellery seemed bent on raising idleness to an art form. Sometime later, when Margaret sent him a volume of Shakespeare's sonnets, Ellery wrote back cavalierly, "I do not read. I am chiefly engaged with doing nothing. I own I have a large penchant for this species of occupation."[99] Apart from writing second-rate poetry, Ellery's only known form of exercise was skirt chasing, and it seemed unlikely that marriage would do much to alter his choice of hobbies. Fuller weighed the idea of traveling at once to Cincinnati to try to restore Ellen to her senses, but she had little money and, as it turned out, no time. Before the month was over, the two were married, and Ellen was plunged into chronic indebtedness.

To make matters worse, her brothers remained mostly impecunious. William Henry, who had tried to establish himself as a businessman, had failed, in a manner that had lowered his reputation "for prudence if for nothing else." Eugene, continuing gamely to make a go of things in New Orleans, sent high-spirited letters but, as Margaret grumbled, "with no great cause to be sure."[100] The Fuller family's principal ray of light now came from Richard, who had spent a year as a store clerk in Boston and had grown into a fine, manly youth, eager to take on higher pursuits.[101] With Margaret's encouragement and help, he planned to settle in Concord in November, where he would prepare to enter Harvard. By the following summer, Richard and Thoreau were fast friends, going on hikes that lasted several days and reading Virgil's *Eclogues* together. Unfortunately Richard had absorbed some of Thoreau's contempt for moneymaking, an attitude that Margaret hastened to correct. In a letter in which she enclosed five dollars, she reminded him that "the circulating medium" he so despised had bought him his books of Horace and Virgil and that it remained essential to a civilized existence.[102]

In early October, Margaret was back at Bush, where her friendship with Emerson continued its awkward dance of attraction and repulsion. Although her guest room was just across the hall from where he slept, she sometimes avoided seeing him, resorting instead to sending him notes, dutifully carried by little Waldo, who was soon to turn five. Emerson reciprocated in this curious practice. Fuller could only have smiled to see her favorite child, looking "so lovely as if he were the living word," bearing the letters to and fro, but the necessity of even so charming a go-between underscored the lack of ease between the correspondents.[103] One evening, as she looked for a book in Emerson's stately first-floor library, Fuller had a sense that the room so full of its owner's soul that she needed no book after all. At the same time, though, she realized to her bemusement that she liked the library better when he was not in it. When he was with her, he could not give himself, and she could not receive him. Only in his absence could "the beauty and permanence" of his life break in upon her.[104] She realized that her deepest desire was an impossible one: to live with him but somehow not disturb him. She had no solution to the riddles of her feelings.

Richard fretted that overwork was killing his sister by degrees. By early November, she was down to her last five hundred dollars. Her conversation audience was smaller than ever. More than a year after *The Dial*'s first issue, she still had not seen the first dollar of her salary. Fuller often concealed her problems from her mother in hopes of sparing her from worry. However, near the end of 1841, she did not hesitate to tell her that she had fallen into "a state of extreme fatigue," brought on by the necessity of writing "in every gap of time." She had barely scrambled through another issue, she said, and now was "quite unfit to hold a pen."[105] She drove herself onward partially in loyalty to Emerson, and partly, too, because her belief in *The Dial*, though shaken, remained strong. But the most essential reason was a matter of character. She simply could not devote less than a full measure of energy and passion to the work that mattered to her. Buoyed by assurances from Elizabeth Peabody that compensation was on the way, she stayed on through the winter, "ill much of the time" and continually distracted by the wants of others whenever she seemed to be on the point of satisfying her own.[106] When William Henry Channing pleaded with her to expend herself with less abandon, she rebuffed him curtly. "If I economized," she wrote, "I should be naught."[107]

But neither economy of purse nor lavishness of effort could fend off the inevitable crisis. Finally, on Saint Patrick's Day in 1842, the last reason to hold on gave way. Until a short time earlier, the moribund Weeks and Jordan had succeeded in withholding documents that contained a devastating secret. Upon reviewing them, Peabody learned the truth: the firm had grossly overstated *The Dial*'s subscriptions. Whereas Fuller and Emerson had blithely believed that they had attracted between five and six hundred subscribers, the true figure did not top three hundred. The journal's meager revenues sufficed to cover only operating expenses. There would be nothing left from which to pay Fuller's promised salary, now or ever. For Fuller, nearing thirty-two, it was a bitter discovery, not only because it affected her personal fortunes, but also because it showed how far her country was from accepting the ideas that were life itself to her and her friends. First at the Temple School and now at *The Dial*, the living waters of transcendentalism had proved to be, from an economic standpoint, a completely dry well.

As soon as the news had sunk in, Fuller took up a sheet of paper and wrote to Emerson. She told him that she had at first hoped to ask only for a suspension of her duties at *The Dial*. Now it was impossible for her to continue on any basis. She had suffered "a perceptible diminution" of strength, and the winter's labor had been so severe that she did not expect to recover fully for two or three months.[108] Indeed, since the onset of winter, she had been too worn out to write anything other than letters. Looking back, she felt she had never done what she might have for the magazine, though she could have if she had received her promised pay. She thus resigned her editorship.

Fuller suggested Theodore Parker to replace her. However, Emerson chose to take up the reins himself, rather than have the journal pass "into hands that know not Joseph."[109] He thought he was a poor replacement, for, as he told her, "Nobody is braver & faithful & self sufficing but you." With deep embarrassment, he apologized for the "bankrupt's return" she had received on her investment of time, health, and labor, and he forlornly added, "We are all your debtors & must always be."[110] Emerson was to remain editor until the journal finally expired in April 1844. However, when he wrote to Hedge the week after Margaret's resignation, he sounded as if the magazine were already dead. "Poor Dial!" he exclaimed, "It has not pleased any mortal. No man cried, God save it!"[111]

The depressed tone of Emerson's comments on the demise of *The Dial* makes it easy to assume that the magazine was a failure. A more thoughtful judgment is required. *The Dial*'s four-year run was actually double the life expectancy of journals of the time and, thanks to Greeley's *Tribune*, it reached many more readers than the paltry subscription rolls reflected. *The Dial*'s significance can best be measured by what was lost when it ceased to exist. For the transcendental movement, the death of *The Dial* meant both the loss of its public voice and the demise of the one forum that could accommodate its diversity and its passionate love of freedom. The eminent historian Henry Steele Commager called the magazine "a place for religion without the Church, for education without the University, for law without the State."[112] Unable to agree on much of anything, the progressive writers of New England found in *The Dial* a place where Christian essays, pantheistic short fiction, and pagan poetry were equally welcome and where difference was an occasion for celebration instead of rancor. The passing of *The Dial* was also a huge step backward for experimental writing in America. For the remainder of the century, the country's foremost literary magazines—*The Atlantic Monthly* and *Harper's Magazine*, for instance—would serve and cultivate a much tamer, more centrist taste in poetry and fiction. Not until the little magazines of the modernist era would American avant-gardists again have a periodical to which to turn. The fact that *The Dial* had no successors for more than half a century gave the country a long time in which to deepen the culturally timid habits from which it has never completely emerged. For a few brave years, *The Dial* stood as the most creative, artistically diverse journal in America. In any age, such a stand has merit. But such merits could not save *The Dial*. Among Fuller's last words on the subject was a terse assessment: "It cannot be helped. It has been a sad business."[113]

Seven weeks before Fuller's resignation, however, both she and Emerson had had a much sadder business on their minds. During her many visits to Bush, Margaret had developed a singular fondness for blue-eyed Waldo, who had been born the same year she had met his father and who was every bit as charming as her younger brothers had once been—and a good deal smarter. Fuller loved the boy's "fair and noble" nature.[114] She felt that he brought her as near as she could come to the goodness of the "new creation" without becoming a parent herself.[115] But the days before penicillin were unkind to new creatures. On January 24, 1842, Waldo had come down with scarlet fever. Three days later, the brightest light in his father's life, "the world's wonderful child," was dead.[116] In a poem written in Waldo's memory, Emerson wrote, "I never called [him] mine."[117] But in the letters he wrote just after Waldo's death, the possessive pronoun is everywhere: "my little Waldo"; "my darling"; "my angel."[118] Announcing the death to Fuller, Emerson wondered if he would ever dare love anything again.[119]

Fuller shared Emerson's devastation, though hers was tinged with anger. As she walked the busy streets of Boston, they seemed filled with lives of no consequence. She inwardly asked why it had been Waldo, "who 'bore within himself the golden future,'" who had been stolen from the world.[120] Fuller's anguish over Waldo's death was visited on at least one other person in the form of thoughtless cruelty. Waldo's younger sister Ellen, three years old at the time, had caught the disease at the same time but survived it. Years later, she would recall that Fuller had made no effort to conceal her disappointment that it was Waldo, not Ellen, who had died.[121]

In the decades before the Civil War, few families were spared the loss of at least one child. It was a time when even the most devastating shocks seldom led to divorce. Yet then as now, the death of a child could shatter a marriage.

In August, as Fuller prepared to pay her first visit to Concord after young Waldo's death, she sensed that she might be "encamping on [the Emersons'] territories," and she asked pointedly whether her presence would disturb Lidian.[122] Despite this clear display of sensitivity, however, it would have been scarcely possible for her to anticipate the complex hive of emotions that she was about to stir. Emerson, his litany of losses lengthened by one, had put his initial burst of lamentations behind him, but what had replaced it was arguably worse. He had resolved, it seems, to express no feelings at all. Two years later, in his great essay "Experience," he was to claim that Waldo's death had left him "as it found me,—neither better nor worse." The boy, he would insist, was like a caducous branch that, in falling away, had left no scar.[123] His assertion lacked any grain of truthfulness; it was simply the wall he chose to erect around himself. To compensate for the appalling new emptiness in her life, Lidian turned, as always, to God. It was clear, however, that she needed human consolations too, and of these she had too few. There were dreadful silences at Bush.

Lidian had always deferred to her husband's pleasure in younger intellectual female friends. Even now, she consented to Margaret's visit. "I have consulted with the Queen," Waldo wrote Margaret, "& she can muster no objection to the plot."[124] But it was not long before Fuller's presence felt like the invasion she had feared it would be. Her face swollen and misshapen from a recent dental operation, Lidian was not feeling wonderful when Margaret arrived. The laudanum she was taking for the pain could hardly have improved the state of her nerves. She was also having to endure the presence of the barely tolerable Ellery Channing, who had left Margaret's sister behind in Cincinnati and was using Bush as a home base while he looked for a boardinghouse in Concord where he and Ellen could settle. Pleading ill health, Lidian had retreated to her room and was barely visible during the first two weeks of Margaret's visit.

With no evident consideration of how Lidian might feel about his behavior, Emerson began taking long walks with Margaret in the evenings, enjoying the "fairy effect" of the moonlight on the Concord River one night and the breezes that rippled the waters of Walden Pond the next.[125] Emerson had taken to waxing theoretical on the subject of marriage in ways that were hard not to take personally. On one "golden afternoon" during Fuller's visit, the two made their way to a grove of hemlocks, where they stayed almost until sunset. There, he proclaimed to her that love was never eternal and that "the soul knows nothing of marriage, in the sense of a permanent union between two existences." A man and a woman, he thought, were bound by no firmer tie than the "marriage" that takes place between a soul and every new thought that entered it. He added, "Ask any woman whether her aim . . . is to further the genius of her husband; and she will say yes, but her conduct will always be to claim a devotion day by day that will be injurious to him, if he yields."[126]

Emerson's capacity for abstraction was so tremendous that he could say something completely barbarous and still call it philosophy. How much of these conversations found their way back to Lidian cannot be known, but she was almost surely aware that his belief in uniting for better or worse was now functionally nil. Earlier that same day over the midday meal, Lidian had asked Fuller if she might walk with her after dinner was over. Fuller declined, saying that she had already agreed to a walk with Waldo. Lidian burst into tears, and the whole family stared at their plates as she sobbed. Belatedly, Fuller tried to placate her distraught hostess; she would be glad to walk with her. No, Lidian insisted, she did not want to be the cause of any "sacrifice," though, "perfectly desolate and forlorn" as she was, she had only hoped for a bit of fresh air. Fuller eventually persuaded Lidian to accept her offer. It somehow seemed impossible that all three might walk together. All through the embarrassing scene, the man at the third point of the unhappy triangle had betrayed no emotion. "Waldo said not a word," Fuller remembered. "He retained his sweetness of look, but never offered to do the least thing." Oddly, Fuller was not disturbed by his remoteness. To the contrary, she wrote, "I can never admire him enough at such times; he is so true to himself."[127] A little nobility toward others might have been a pleasant complement to his self-honesty.

During their walk, Lidian confessed her envy. Instead of Mrs. Emerson, she would rather be Margaret Fuller the vestal priestess or even Elizabeth Hoar, who had been engaged to Emerson's brother Charles when the latter had died. The death of her fiancé had left Elizabeth free to love an untarnished, ideal husband who, in the quiet of his grave, could never betray her. Fuller felt duped; she had actually believed that Lidian had been happy to have her in the house "solely for Waldo's sake." She was almost insulted by Lidian's suggestion that she, Fuller, who had never received an offer of marriage, was "the most privileged of women." Of women generally, Fuller wrote, "They have so much that I have not, I can't conceive of their wishing for what I have." She concluded that the Emersons would never rise above their impasse. Lidian could not set aside her vain, "lurking hope that Waldo's character [would] alter" and that he would someday be capable of more tenderness. Waldo, for his part, was sorely troubled by the imperfections in their union but could not believe in anything better. Yet, Margaret complained, neither of them could "see the whole truth about one like me; if they did, they would understand why the brow of [the] Muse . . . must wear a shade of sadness."[128]

The next day, after Emerson had expressed to her his disregard for marriage, Fuller went up to Lidian's room to pay her respects. Lidian again lost her composure and began to sob. Trying to spare Fuller from embarrassment, she initially blamed the opium, but moments later she stopped dissembling. She said she supposed that Fuller and Emerson had been spending the evenings talking. The words, simple and true though they were, struck Fuller with the force of a criminal accusation. "A painful feeling" flashed across her.[129] In an instant, the pleasantries she had meant for Lidian transformed into a torrent of alibis. No, she replied, she had been with Thoreau and Channing, and Emerson had been writing in his study. But in the atmosphere of Lidian's room, the most innocent explanation sounded like the most damning confession. After managing a ragged retreat, Fuller turned to her journal. "What does it signify whether he is with me or at his writing?" she asked. She thought Lidian must know perfectly well "that he has no regard for me." Yet Fuller must also have been surprised by her own defensiveness as she wrote:

> As to my being more his companion that cannot be helped; his life is in the intellect, not the affections. He has affection for me, but it is because I quicken his intellect.—I dismissed it all, as a mere sick moment of L's.[130]

But, of course, she had not dismissed it. Neither could Lidian.

Late summer rain blew into Concord. As the river swelled and the streets turned to quagmires, the mood inside Bush did not improve. In Fuller's phrase, they were all living "at swords' points."[131] Ellery found the atmosphere intolerable. Though his wife was due to arrive in Concord in a few days, he asked Fuller if he might leave town to visit Caroline Sturgis, with whom he had once had a romance. The visit was Caroline's idea, he pleaded, and he meant to see her just this one last time. He also promised to return the next Tuesday, the day before Ellen was expected. Fuller had no great reason to trust her brother-in-law with an old flame, but she was probably happy to get rid of him. She said yes. The rains proved more constant than Ellery. Tuesday passed without word from him. Luckily, Ellen, too, was delayed, so the scandal was forestalled for a moment. Torn between fear lest Ellery had suffered an accident and outrage lest he had found Caroline's favors too delightful to tear himself away, Fuller sent a flurry of letters to everyone who might have seen the wayward poet. All was in vain. On Friday night, in a driving storm, Ellen alighted from her stagecoach at Emerson's door, only to find her husband absent. Fearing that the probable truth would deal "a death blow" to the couple's tranquility, Fuller dodged her sister's questions.[132] Ellery returned the next morning; he had, indeed, found his time with Miss Sturgis too delicious to bring to a timely end. And yet, amazingly, there was no explosion. Ellen ventured no quarrel with her husband's faithlessness but "took it just as she ought." As Fuller described it, "Waldo looked radiant, and H[enry] T[horeau] as if his tribe had won a victory." More surprisingly, Margaret was of no different mind. She wrote, "If I were Waldo's wife, or Ellery's wife, I should acquiesce in all these relations, since they needed them. I should expect the same feeling from my husband, & I should think it little in him not to have it."[133] It did not seem to trouble her that the freedom of conscience espoused by the transcendentalists sometimes included a freedom from conscience.

There was one other romantic couple of note that season in Concord: Nathaniel Hawthorne and his wife Sophia, whom he had married in July, had settled at the spacious minister's home near the Old North Bridge called the Old Manse. The two held different views of Fuller. Sophia called her "a priestess of the Temple not made with hands" and wrote her a sonnet that lauded her "golden-cadenced intuitions."[134] Privately, Hawthorne was repelled by Fuller; his own fastidiousness suited poorly with what he called her "strong and coarse nature," a nature that, he conceded, she had done her utmost to refine, though without, as far as he could tell, very much effect.[135] Nevertheless, with a cheerfulness that some would call tact and others hypocrisy, he now gave her "a gleaming welcome."[136] He and Sophia showed her to the softest chair and, seeing that she was pale and tired, prevailed on her to stay for tea. Later, the writer escorted her back to Emerson's under a clouded moon. With an odd morbidity, he confided that "he should be much more willing to die than two months ago, for he had some real pos-

Fuller found Nathaniel Hawthorne gracious and beguiling. In private, he expressed deep reservations about her "strong and coarse nature."
(COURTESY OF BRIDGEMAN ART LIBRARY INTERNATIONAL)

session in life, but still he never wished to leave this earth; it was beautiful enough." Fuller delighted in his "many fine perceptions" and enjoyed hearing "the lightest thing he says."[137] Two days later, on a cloudless Sunday, the two chanced to meet in the woods near what is now the Sleepy Hollow Cemetery, where both Hawthorne and Emerson were later to be buried. Fuller was reclining on the grass with a book. Hawthorne sat down beside her. They spoke of crows and mountains and memories of childhood, she losing track of time and he forgetting his aversion to her until a gentleman happened by. It was none other than Emerson, who, though he had once been a minister, now "found no better way of spending the Sabbath than to ramble among the woods." In a voice tinged with deep pleasure, Emerson remarked that there were Muses in the woods that day, and whispers to be heard in the breezes.[138] In her journal, Fuller summarized it all as "a happy, happy day."[139]

Shortly after leaving Concord, Fuller had another intimate episode that mingled her highest notions of happiness with her sense of the forbidden. She traveled to Boston to stay with the Wards at the handsome apartment on Louisburg Square that Sam's father had given them. She went in October, a time of bittersweet remembrance. Her father had now been dead seven years. Since his passing, Fuller had lived what seemed like "a generation, unspotted by regrets, and rich in thought and experience, though its gifts were bathed in tears oftentimes." On the third came Sam and Anna's second anniversary, and Fuller reflected sadly that their marriage had not been as perfect and poetical a union as she had expected.[140] On the thirtieth, Sam being temporarily away, Margaret spent a dream-filled night in Anna's bed. Here is what Fuller told her diary about that encounter:

> I slept with Anna the first time in two years. It was exquisitely painful to feel that I loved her less than when we before were thus together in confiding sleep, and she too is now so graceful and lovely; but the secret of my life is sealed to her forever. I never speak of the inmost experience, but listen to her inmost talk. I took pleasure in sleeping on Sam's pillow and before closing my eyes solicited that visions like his might come to me.[141]

But she did not dream of Sam or of his cryptically mentioned visions. It seems that the excitement and perhaps the guilt of temporarily usurping his place in Anna's marriage bed turned Margaret's unconscious mind in a much more turbulent direction. As she lay beside the graceful woman who would never know her "secret," Margaret "had a frightful dream of being imprisoned in a ship at sea," a nightmare both revealing and eerily prophetic. She recalled:

> [T]he waves all dashing round, and knowing that the crew had resolved to throw me in. While in horrible suspense, many persons that I knew came on board. At first they seemed delighted to see me & wished to talk but when I let them know my danger, [and] intimated

a hope that they might save me, with cold courtliness glided away. Oh it was horrible [to see] these averted faces and well dressed figures turning from me, from captive, with the cold wave rushing up into which I was to be thrown.[142]

It was by no means the first time that Fuller had been haunted by visions of drowning. At no other time, however, did her imagination so powerfully connect drowning with the metaphors of ostracism and punishment. The "cold courtliness" of her many acquaintances is every bit as frightening as the ocean itself. Fuller seemed to fear that, if she were revealed to her friends in the true light of her fierce but hidden desires, they would abandon her without a word.

The dream may have had another self-accusatory significance. Since quitting *The Dial*, Fuller had been indulging in a series of gratifying but finally superficial and distracting social pleasures. Her time at Bush, in both its turmoil and its satisfactions, followed by her night of dreams and ambiguities with Anna, might have been the stuff of a fine romantic novel, but Fuller knew she was not made for romantic novels—not to write them and certainly not to live one. In some sense, her time in Concord had been more disturbing than her night with Anna, for it had given her troubling evidence of the degree to which, even among the equality-loving transcendentalists, the needs and feelings of women were simply ignored. The marriages of Emerson and Channing functioned only because Lidian and Ellen were willing to cast their emotions into a bonfire. Abba Alcott, also living in Concord, was the happiest she had been in years, but only because her struggling husband Bronson was away in England. While Fuller was under Emerson's roof, all the sacrifices demanded of the women seemed meet and proper, but after she left, she began to wonder. Just how ideal was the concept of life her friends had embraced? Might it not be ever so much more so, for both the men and the women, if the women had the chance to develop their own talents and live as they wished?

Fuller had heretofore regarded the problem of personal growth and development as principally an inward one; she had thought first of the necessity of overcoming one's own innate limitations as one strove toward a more perfect state of mind and spirit. So long as she remained under the tutelage of Emerson, Fuller was prone to adopt his habit of regarding the self as the most crucial subject of reform. Like him, she had been suspicious of social solutions to what appeared to be the discontents of individual consciousness. "I do not believe in Society," she had told William Henry Channing. "I feel that every man must struggle with these enormous ills in some way, in every age."[143] Lonely, personal battles with the universe had given the world Moses, Plato, and Michelangelo; she doubted that a mutual aid association could do the same. But Emerson's exaltation of the self took no cognizance of the prejudices and social conventions that can handicap the bravest spirit. To Fuller, however, it was starting to appear ever more clearly that the most fatal constraints on a woman's progress were imposed from without. Her awareness of the social causes of human failure did not evolve overnight. However, when she left Emerson's house in October 1842, she was finished with writing otherworldly, introspective stories about protean spirits and talking trees. She would not only seek perfection in herself, but also to cultivate the tiny, hopeful traces of it in the world.

CHAPTER SEVEN

SEEKER OF UTOPIA

The aim is perfection; patience the road.
The present object is to give
ourselves and others a tolerable chance.

—MARGARET FULLER,
in *Memoirs of Margaret Fuller Ossoli*

*T*HE PAIN.

The headaches had begun while she was a child in Cambridgeport. They became chronic after the death of her father. They came upon her with an intensity that rendered her helpless and made it hard to recall when they had ever been absent. The "constant irritation in [her] head" caused innumerable interruptions in her creative work, leaving her at the end of each task "quite exhausted, feel[ing] as if I could not go a step further."[1] Nothing she ever wrote, nothing she ever accomplished, should be considered without remembering that it came from someone seldom free from suffering. Emerson knew about these headaches, and he was well aware of the way in which they interrupted and conditioned Fuller's life. He saw her begin the day "in jubilant spirits," only to end it with an onset of pain that, according to Lidian, "produced total prostration."[2] All her life, Emerson observed, Fuller was "the victim of disease and pain." Yet he marveled at her ability, not only to work around her suffering but also, in her own view, to extract some benefit from it. Unable at times to remain at a desk, she read and wrote in bed. She confided to Emerson that, when she felt ill, her comprehension actually improved. He speculated that pain was a kind of stiffening agent to her thought—"girdle" was the image he used—adding a discipline or "tension to her powers." Emerson once spoke with one of Fuller's female friends who had attended to Fuller during an especially terrible attack. To the woman's surprise, "Margaret was yet in the finest of humor, and kept those who were assisting her in a strange, painful excitement, between laughing and crying, by perpetually brilliant sallies."[3] It was one of many brave performances.

Fuller traced her headaches to Timothy's early instruction, and she continued to regret deeply that the educational reforms she had seen at the Temple School and Greene Street, dedicated to improving the child's physical being as well as the mind, had come a generation too late for her. Her life was a contest between the ideal and the real, a struggle between a mind forever striving toward more ethereal space and an ailing physical form that continually pulled her back toward confinement and limitation. "My day is poor of thought and deed," she wrote. "My body is a burden, not an instrument."[4] This inner opposition made her all the more inclined to see the greater world in similar terms. Her personal desire to escape from pain found a ready parallel in her skeptical but sincere interest in those who sought to flee the discontents of society and to discover Utopia. Human beings, in Fuller's sense of things, were creatures formed for self-improvement. Yet, as they naturally sought their own perfectibility, their carnal wants and infirmities routinely thwarted them. It was a tale, as Herman Melville later put it, of "the running battle of the star and clod."[5] In 1843, Margaret Fuller was losing patience with the clod. She wanted to believe that some new principle could be discovered that would, to some degree, free mankind from its baser nature and bring the stars into closer reach. Her desire to help move humankind to its apotheosis was the great motive behind the most significant article she ever wrote for *The Dial*: "The Great Lawsuit: Man *versus* Men, Woman *versus* Women."

Fuller wrote "The Great Lawsuit" in the spring of 1843, shortly after concluding another series of her conversations. As she was drafting it, it seemed as if both outward and inward nature were doing all in their power to block her progress. On May 9, she wrote to Emerson, "I am trying to write as hard as these odious east winds will let me. I rise in the morning and feel as happy as the birds and then about eleven comes one of these tormentors, and makes my head ache and spoils the day."[6] In the end, though, neither mistral nor migraine could prevent her from pushing forward; the essay appeared in the July 1843 issue of *The Dial*. Though no one knew it at the time, the essay was essentially the rough draft of a book-length treatment of the same subject, which Fuller was to publish as *Woman in the Nineteenth Century* in February 1845.

Despite its litigious-sounding title, "The Great Lawsuit" has very little to do either with legal proceedings or with the fiercely adversarial attitudes that one associates with a courtroom drama. As Fuller later explained, she meant for her title to affirm "the destiny of Man . . . to ascertain and fulfil the law of his being, so that his life shall be seen, as a whole, to be that of an angel or messenger." On the other hand, she meant also to expose and condemn "the action of prejudices and passions, which attend, in the day, the growth of the individual, [which] is continually obstructing the holy work that is to make the earth a part of heaven."[7]

Although it is one of the most important early manifestos of American feminism, "The Great Lawsuit" is not, in its philosophical underpinnings, a partisan statement solely on behalf of women. Fuller intended her argument to be more comprehensive, and she meant her work to foster a greater good for Man and Woman alike, whom she regarded as "the two halves of one thought."[8] To the extent that it describes a "lawsuit," the essay concerns a struggle over a metaphorical inheritance: shall humankind be allowed to claim the birthright of its divine destiny? Fuller's legal metaphor fades from the essay after a few pages, and the supposed litigation is, somewhat surprisingly, not between men and women at all. The contest arises between an ideal concept of the two sexes, expressed by the singular nouns "Man" and "Woman," and a stunted, degraded vision of humanity, unconscious of its own divinity and cut off from its rightful spiritual inheritance by habits of jealousy, skepticism, and myopic self-interest. Fuller's plural "men" and "women" might as easily have shuffled through an Alcott conversation or an Emerson essay; they are one with the petty, somnolent dwarfs to whom Emerson's Orphic poet refers in the closing pages of *Nature*. But whereas Emerson and Alcott showed no inclination to connect the spiritual poverty of modern human beings with their sexual politics, Fuller seized on the association.

Like most of her transcendental friends, Fuller found it difficult to believe that positive social change could come from groups and institutions. Though her opinions were later to change, she now distrusted solutions that required people to depend too much on one another. On this point, she was staunchly Emersonian. Anyone who lived "too much in relations," she wrote, was destined to become a stranger to the resources of his own nature and, thus, to fall "into a distraction or imbecility," for which isolation offered the only cure.[9] Fuller implicitly saw the condition of women as having been worsened by the insistence of men on defining them solely by their relations: to their sewing circles, to their children, to their husbands. Society had not created sufficient spaces and opportunities to develop the strengths that emerge only in solitude. Moreover, by preparing girls only for their prescribed position in the family, the world was forever bringing forth new generations of limited, dependent souls. Fuller had been aghast one day to overhear a father, proudly convinced of his own wisdom and benevolence, proclaim, "I shall not have Maria brought too forward. If she knows too much, she will never find a husband. . . . I want her to have a sphere and a home, and someone to protect her when I am gone." The idea of a girl being raised specifically to inhabit a limiting "sphere," to be permanently a powerless child in a bubble of masculine protection, struck Fuller as the fantasy of an "unprepared and perverted mind."[10]

To redress such "perversions," Fuller referred to recent history. Her key premises were adapted from Jean-Jacques Rousseau—himself no supporter of women's rights—and the opening line of his *Social Contract*: "Man is born free but is everywhere in chains."[11] Fuller believed that, as a result of the American and French Revolutions, those chains had been somewhat loosened. However, she thought it absurd and, in the long run, impossible to seek freedom for only half the species. If it were conceded, Fuller wrote, that few men had ever had a true chance to enjoy liberty, it should be clear that "no women have had a fair chance" at freedom.[12] Already, Fuller argued, the promises of the Declaration of Independence had been broken regarding America's native peoples and African slaves, whose treatment had become "the scoff of the world." Too often, she said, the free American had felt himself free "only to pamper his appetites . . . through the misery of his fellow beings."[13] Knowing that, in the minds of too many men, there was "a tone of feeling towards women as towards slaves," Fuller insisted that the only way to keep the subjection of women from becoming permanent was to elevate them from their voiceless position and to permit them to vote, to advocate, and to legislate for themselves.[14]

Yet Fuller also maintained that legal freedoms were only a means toward a more essential end. The transcendent goal was, as always in her thinking, self-discovery and development. "What woman needs," she charged, "is not as a woman to act or rule, but as a nature to grow, as an intellect to discern, as a soul to live freely and unimpeded, to unfold such powers as were given her when we left our common home." Making explicit not only the analogy between racial injustice and gender inequality, but also the ultimately spiritual objectives of her argument, Fuller wrote, "If the negro be a soul, if the woman be a soul, apparelled in flesh, to one Master only are they accountable. There is but one law for all souls, and if there is to be an interpreter of it, he must come not as man, or son of man, but as son of God."[15] In other words, Woman must be situated, not in a domestic chain of command, but in a cosmic chain of being:

> We would have every path laid open to woman as freely as to man. Were this done, and a slight temporary fermentation allowed to subside, we believe that the Divine would ascend into nature to a height unknown in the history of past ages, and nature, thus instructed, would regulate the spheres not only so as to avoid collision, but to bring forth ravishing harmony.[16]

Inherent in Fuller's argument is the conviction that people should aim toward the perfection of their minds and talents. It is not at all surprising, then, that the ghost of Timothy Fuller walks through the pages of "The Great Lawsuit." It is in this essay that Fuller first presented a supposed acquaintance named Miranda, who is obviously Margaret herself. The key to Miranda's brilliant attainments has been the efforts of her personal Prospero, a father who has "cherished no sentimental reverence for woman, but a firm belief in the equality of the sexes." Miranda, his eldest child, "came to him at an age when he needed a companion. From the time she could speak and go alone, he addressed her not as a plaything, but as a living mind." Miranda, as a result, has grown up knowing herself to be a child of the spirit and taking her place with assurance, "not only in the world of organized being, but in the world of mind."[17] Fuller offered Miranda as living proof that the limits imposed on women remain real only for those who allow them to be.

Though just three years separate Fuller's two fictionalized portraits of

her father, the idealized Timothy of "The Great Lawsuit" is barely recogniz-
able as the imperious pedant of Fuller's "autobiographical romance." Gone
is the brusque, controlling martinet. In his place stands a wise and respectful, though still exacting, mentor who has invested his daughter with skill
and confidence. Some of the difference, of course, may be ascribed to the
different purposes of the two pieces of writing. Fuller's "romance," intended
as a private document, was an attempt at self-examination. In it, she tried to
seize control of her anxieties by writing a narrative that explained her frustrations and pain. "The Great Lawsuit," to the contrary, focuses on opportunities, not the price one pays for them. Furthermore, the time between the
two writings seems to have fostered a change in perspective. Fuller in 1843,
relieved of the strain of editing *The Dial* and almost two years removed from
the turning point of her long spiritual crisis, was more settled and serene
than the Fuller of 1840. Her anger regarding her upbringing had ebbed, an
easing of tensions in which the very writing of her "romance" may have
played a part. Like her mildly fictionalized Miranda, Fuller could now "speak
without heat or bitterness of the position of her sex."[18] One instinctively feels
the urge to choose between the Timothy who intellectually enabled his
daughter and the one who emotionally scarred her. However, Fuller herself
never really chose between them. For her, he remained forever both a blessing and a curse, both her making and her unmaking.

Fuller's readers, even some of the erudite subscribers to *The Dial*, are
likely to have stumbled over the sheer density of the literary and historical
allusions of "The Great Lawsuit." The essay quotes Ovid in Latin, Schiller
and Goethe in German, and Manzoni in Italian, deigning to translate only
the last of the four. In trying to keep pace with Fuller, the gasping reader
must absorb references to Genesis, the Gospels, the *Odyssey*, the *Rāmāyana*,
and Egyptian mythology. Alcibiades, Petrarch, Dante, and Michelangelo
crowd onto Fuller's stage, as do Queens Elizabeth and Isabella; Lady Jane
Grey; Madames Pompadour, du Barry, and de Staël; and the illustrious com-
moners Mary Wollstonecraft, Harriet Martineau, and George Sand. Somehow, these players also make room for Swedenborg, Spinoza, Wordsworth,
Shelley, Byron, and Southey. The allusions to Shakespeare alone include
*Hamlet, King Lear, Othello, Cymbeline, As You Like It, The Merchant of Venice,
Measure for Measure,* and *Julius Caesar.*

As daunting—and, for some, as off-putting—as the essay's barrage of culture assuredly was, it had a point. Rather than trying to present women's rights as a wholly new and therefore possibly frightening idea, Fuller placed her seemingly modern notions in a time-honored context. She used her host of references to show that the force of women in civilization had always been strong and that women had played an essential role in the life of society and the creative imagination for as long as writing had existed. Women had stood at the core of the world's most powerful legends and most enduring stories. Women had driven events that had shaped history. At the same time that she was making the most radical statement on behalf of sexual equality since the founding of her nation, Fuller implicitly questioned why her views should be considered radical at all. If women had been associated with wisdom and holiness since Minerva and Mary, if they had been heroes since well before Shakespeare created Cordelia, Portia, and Imogen, one might well wonder why their fitness for a larger role in modern life was still subject to question. The adroitness with which Fuller deployed her sweeping knowledge of culture was, of course, a further argument in itself. When seeking to prove that a woman could be the equal or superior of a male scholar, Fuller offered herself as her own best evidence.

"The Great Lawsuit" ends, not with a judgment, but on a note of unfulfilled prophecy. "And will she not soon appear?" Fuller seeks to know, "The woman who shall vindicate their birthright for all women; who shall teach them what to claim, and how to use what they obtain?"[19] The name of this new feminine avatar remained unclear. Perhaps, Fuller suggests, she would be a modern Nike, triumphing with unprecedented force over the pinched and ancient bigotries and bearing the name of Victoria; or perhaps she would be a reincarnated Mary, winning worship with her humble charity and chastity and bearing the name Virginia. Fuller could not say for certain; like everyone else, she would wait for the messianic maiden to come and announce her fitting name.

Though it presented itself as an outgrowth of a tradition of female influence that had grown up over millennia, "The Great Lawsuit" was unquestionably new. It gave the American debate over women's rights both a heart and a history that it had previously lacked. Thoreau hailed it as "a noble piece." Emerson called it "an important fact in the history of Woman: good for its wit, excellent for its character. . . . It will teach us to revise our habits."[20]

In 1843, Fuller was not the only one who felt a restless expectancy. It was a year unusually rife with questing spirits. In the late spring, Bronson Alcott led a motley band on an ill-starred quest for the true life at a commune he called Fruitlands. A group of German Americans known as the Inspirationists established an agrarian colony near Buffalo, New York, called Ebenezer, where all goods were held in common. The year 1843 also saw Shaker communities on the rise, and it found Joseph Smith at the height of his power, preaching to his Mormon followers at Nauvoo, Illinois. It was also the year when William Miller, leader of the Millerites, first predicted that the world would end sometime on or before April 18, 1844. Countless adherents were then disappointed when the sun continued to rise and set as usual. Few of these idealist movements achieved lasting influence, and historian Daniel Walker Howe has rightly stated that the curiosity stimulated by these groups was quite out of proportion with the negligible numbers that most of them attracted.[21] Nevertheless, the fact that so many utopian factions emerged almost simultaneously remains one of the striking features of the period.

One of the most ambitious utopians was practically at Fuller's elbow. At the same time that Fuller, Emerson, and their fellow wordsmiths were striving to articulate a paradise of the mind in the pages of *The Dial*, one of their number was seeking to build an Eden on earth. George Ripley had been the minister at Boston's Purchase Street Unitarian Church since 1826. In all those years, however, he had achieved only a middling reputation as a preacher, a failing that he ascribed to having "never been on his true ground." There was much he had longed to say to his flock, and he remained sure that, given "suitable relations," he would one day bring forth all the hope and inspiration that he felt to be living inside him. Fuller, who thought the minister capable of being a "fine, genial, manly person," sympathized with his frustrations but felt that he still had "many steps to take" before he could arrive at his "proper position."[22] Ripley blamed his personal stagnation on the very premises of American society, which he called "vicious in its foundations" and considered too polluted a stream for wholesome fish to swim in.[23] He proposed to create an alternative.

On March 28, 1841, eight days after Emerson published his first series of *Essays*, Ripley delivered his last sermon. He had devised a plan for a separatist community that would be a haven from the "great danger of our country," namely, "the inordinate pursuit, the extravagant worship of wealth."[24]

In his more anxious moments, Ripley foresaw a violent civil conflict in America, not necessarily over slavery, but between the interests of moneyed privilege and the champions of liberty and social equality. His answer to the anticipated cataclysm lay in a 170-acre dairy farm in West Roxbury, Massachusetts. At a time when, according to Emerson, there existed "not a reading man [in America] but has the draft of a new community in his waistcoat pocket," Ripley was singularly determined to make his ideal vision succeed.[25] He began to solicit investors in a joint-stock commune to be established on the site, where he hoped to place books in the hands of the worker and tools in the hands of the thinker, thereby both creating better-rounded human beings and destroying the distinctions of class and privilege that he thought were poisoning America. The farm would produce both pigs and poems, but its signature product would be "a society of liberal, intelligent, and cultivated persons."[26] By late September, as James Freeman Clarke put it, Ripley's idea had him "fermenting and effervescing to a high degree."[27]

Fuller saw Ripley shortly after he announced his decision to leave the pulpit and pronounced him "newborn."[28] On October 16, 1840, she was present at an extraordinary meeting at Emerson's house, where Ripley unfurled his plan to her, his host, and Bronson Alcott. His community would be a gathering "of the friends of the new order."[29] It would cover as much as five hundred acres and would include newly constructed cottages for the families of the faithful and halls for lectures and conversations. Armed with facts and figures galore, Ripley proved, if anything, too practical for his audience. Alcott, who had not yet caught the communalist fever, was unmoved. Emerson also felt himself inwardly retreating. Though he wished "to be convinced . . . to be made nobly mad" by Ripley's vision, all he could see in it was "arithmetic & comfort"; at no point did he find himself "inflamed."[30] Fuller was more receptive. Two days later, she wrote to Caroline Sturgis that "the Phalanx talk was useless, I should think, to all present except myself." The discussion had "brought out [our] different ways of thinking in strong relief, and helped me to a judgment."[31] Fuller did not tell Caroline the precise nature of her judgment. However, in a letter dated only 1840, she laid out her doubts to William Henry Channing. "Utopia . . . is impossible to build up," she told him. "At least, my hopes for our race on this one planet are more limited than those of most of my friends. I accept the limitations of human nature, and believe a wise acknowledgment of them one of the best conditions of progress."[32] She thought it was important to encourage people to hope for better results than the facts might warrant, lest they stop trying altogether. Nevertheless, she resisted the invitation to join Brook Farm.

As Ripley's community began to take shape, Fuller remained on the fence, positioned somewhere between Emerson, who, she wrote, "knows deepest what he wants, but not well how to get it," and Ripley, who, in her estimation, "has a better perception of means, less insight as to principles."[33] Ripley, she felt, was too impetuous for her to follow. She observed, "He is too sanguine, and does not take time to let things ripen in his mind." Though she admired his courage and clarity of mind, she protested that she could do nothing more than look on and watch "the coral insects at work" in constructing the community.[34] In point of fact, she did give two gestures of support almost immediately after the utopia was founded: she purchased a cow that was maintained on the premises, and arranged to have her mentally challenged brother, Lloyd, enrolled in the community's school.

Ripley and a handful of followers set up residence on the farm at the end of March 1841. The "coral insect" whose fame was destined to far outshine that of all the others was Nathaniel Hawthorne, not yet married to Sophia Peabody and still almost a decade away from publishing *The Scarlet Letter*. Hawthorne was still further away from writing the novel in which he was to satirize the Brook Farm experiment, *The Blithedale Romance*.[35] Expecting that feeding livestock and mucking out stables would leave him ample time for writing, Hawthorne was among the first to join the community. He was also among the first to leave, having discovered that work was, after all, work. He wrote to Sophia, "Oh! belovedest, labor is the curse of this world, and nobody can meddle with it without becoming proportionately brutified." Packing his bags in August, he mourned the loss of "five golden months."[36]

Before his departure, however, he found leisure enough for some jabs at Fuller, with whom he had not yet shared their radiant afternoon beside the path at Sleepy Hollow. Fuller visited Brook Farm at least every month or so, and Hawthorne found her exquisitely irritating. He turned his wit, not directly against Fuller herself, but against her cow, a "transcendental heifer," that he found "very fractious . . . and apt to kick over the milk pail." Hawthorne observed that Fuller's cow had made herself ruler of the herd and behaved in a very tyrannical fashion. A few days later, he noted with pleasure that the other cows had rebelled and driven the usurper to seek the farmers' protection. "She is not an amiable cow," he remarked, "but she has a very intelligent face, and seems to be of a reflective cast of character." Hawthorne left Sophia to determine "whether, in these traits of character, she resembles her mistress."[37]

Beyond doubt, Fuller's imagination and idealism were greatly engaged by Brook Farm. Though her first days spent visiting the community were desolate, and she seemed "to belong to nobody—to have a right to speak to nobody," she soon overcame her initial alienation and thereafter found the freedom of the place "delightful."[38] Eventually, she spent enough time there

Fuller never joined the Utopian colony at Brook Farm. Still, she visited
regularly and considered it "a fine studio" for the sculpting of the soul.
(COURTESY OF BRIDGEMAN ART LIBRARY INTERNATIONAL)

that the simple house on the property where she slept became known in later times as the "Margaret Fuller Cottage." The dedication of the Brook Farmers to self-culture—they once went without butter for three months to help pay for a new, communally owned piano—could only have filled her with admiration.[39] It surely pleased her, too, that her dear friend Caroline Sturgis had found satisfaction there. Sturgis, who related to her family in a spirit of "affectionate strife," had found in the colony what a number of young women had discovered there: an escape from the strictures that respectable New England households imposed on their female members.[40]

For a time, despite their thorough inexperience in farming and business, the Ripleys succeeded remarkably well in creating a microcosm of rural tranquility. Although the work of maintaining the farm sometimes threatened to crowd out the artistic and intellectual pursuits of its laborers, there was still time for picnics, dances, and contemplative walks to the property's handsome pine grove. Even looking up at the stars could feel like a delicious luxury; one member in her mid-teens recalled how one of Ripley's friends "showed us the constellations, quietly talking of all this beauty in a way that inspired love and reverence in us."[41] The Brook Farmers studied music and languages. The milking of cows and feeding of horses were interspersed with glee club recitals and presentations of dramatic tableaux. The Christmas season was celebrated with a masquerade ball, and the commune's children were regaled with presents, sugar plums, and cornucopias filled with candy.[42] It was very likely Fuller's exposure to Brook Farm that led Emerson to write optimistically of her, "I see with joy a certain progress out of her complex into a simpler life & some of the gorgeous palaces in which she has dwelt are losing their luster for her. Let us behold with love & hope."[43] Curiously, the idealism of the farm seemed to be bringing her happily down to earth.

Nevertheless, Fuller remained firm in her decision not to join the society. Between giving her conversations and editing *The Dial*, she was already at the center of two communities that demanded the greatest part of her energies. She would have had little left over to contribute to the farm. Moreover, Fuller's energies pushed her ceaselessly outward, leading her toward larger and more influential spheres of activity. She would have had trouble regarding the pastoral idyll of Brook Farm as something other than a diminution and a retreat.[44]

In addition, there was apparently a fatal disjuncture between her own inclinations and those of the community. Seeking above all to learn the mysteries of her own spirit, Fuller was subtly out of phase with an association that cared more about finding "harmony with the common mind."[45] Although the high-mindedness of the communal experiment was beyond question, Fuller's level of intellectual complexity was a bit beyond that of the average Brook Farmer. One alumnus of the commune quipped that the transcendentalists "read Dante in the original Italian, Hegel in the original German . . . and perhaps the hardest task of all, Margaret Fuller in the original English."[46] When Fuller tried at Brook Farm to replicate the successes of her Boston conversations, she found her audiences less than riveted. On one Saturday, as she spoke on the subject of education, she was considerably irked to discover that "the people showed a great deal of the sans-culotte tendency in their manners,—throwing themselves on the floor, yawning, and going out when they had heard enough."[47]

Though Fuller continued to offer the community "the cheer of her encouragement and the light of her counsel," she was not prepared for equality as Brook Farm defined it.[48] She was, she admitted, "accustomed to deference," and when the democratic spirit of the colony expressed itself in poor manners, the rejection stung deeply. Moreover, as she knew, Brook Farmers were expected to do their share of the manual labor, and her curved spine and frequent blinding headaches meant that she could never work as the others did. To Margaret's fears that she could not earn her keep in such a place, a female member, perhaps Mrs. Ripley, objected that the commune's members "would all like to work for a person of genius" and that Fuller's intellectual contributions alone would suffice.[49] She had something of a point; one of the girls in particular had eagerly made herself Fuller's servant, making sure that she ate her breakfast from the community's best china and trying to save her "some little fatigue or annoyance, during each day."[50] Nonetheless, Fuller demurred. "'Yes,' I told her," she wrote, "'but where would be my repose, when they were always to be judging whether I was worth it or not. It would be the same position the clergyman is in, or the wandering beggar with his harp. Each day you must prove yourself anew.'"[51]

She also noted a philosophic difference. Brook Farm had been built on what Fuller called "the hope of excluding evil." Although Fuller believed in continual progress toward the good and true, she maintained that evil was a growth of nature, incapable of being destroyed by instantaneous measures. Still more to the point, she regarded evil as "one condition of the development of good."[52] Evil, she argued, provides the means and the motivation for improvement; our transgressions both teach us lessons and make us yearn for something better. Take evil out of the human equation, and one would be left, not with pure virtue, but with static complacency. Yet the chief reason why Fuller finally distanced herself from Brook Farm may have been this: she feared, as William Henry Channing put it, "the danger of merging the individual in the mass to such degree as to paralyze energy, heroism, and genius." She thought it unlikely "that an organization by 'Groups and Series' would yield due incentive for personal development."[53] When she came to the farm, Fuller found herself in the amusing position of a conservative. She preferred being a liberal in the larger, rough-and-tumble society to being a reactionary in a smaller, sweeter one.

As Fuller paid further visits to the Ripleys' utopia, it seemed to her that the community was growing in gentleness, tolerance, and sincerity. Whereas its members had formerly engaged in unspecified "grotesque freaks of liberty," there was now a deeper respect for law and proper conduct. The farm seemed to her "a fine studio for the soul-sculptor."[54] However, she never overcame her distrust of the idea that one could construct the perfect society by fiat. Fuller still had faith that America could provide the scene for a glorious revision of the human condition. However, experiments like Brook Farm were too urbane and rule-bound to achieve the transformation. In her search, she soon turned from the eastern, hyperintellectual notions of the Ripleys to a very different environment for soul-building: the midwestern frontier.

For some time now, fearful of slipping into debt, Fuller had taken on all the paying work she could manage, conversing, tutoring, and generally persisting in her industriousness. While she congratulated herself on her discipline, she admitted that the effort had hurt her.[55] Toward the end of January 1843, her work had come to a gratifying lull. The household in Cambridge that she had set up for her mother was running smoothly, and it was a pleasure for Margaret to see the elder Margarett enjoying her tranquil home. There was some rest for Fuller as well, and she was grateful for the leisure that was hers when she retired to her "sunshiny room, undisturbed by fears of pain to others."[56] In such a place, even foul weather could be delightful, and she observed that the warm seclusion of her room was sweetened all the more when the howling wind drove snowflakes "thickly against the windows."[57] It was a pleasure simply to sit quietly and think.

Her season of rest and reflection did not last. With the spring came new worries about *The Dial* and a series of fretful letters from Emerson regarding the journal's imperiled future. His conscience had been especially pricked

by a comment by Elizabeth Hoar, who had pointed out that the chief contributors could write just as well out of *The Dial* as in it, and earn more
money besides. Emerson knew that Hoar was alluding particularly to Fuller,
who, although she had long since ceased to edit the magazine, had continued to contribute generously to it. Emerson told Margaret, "If by keeping
The Dial, I could make it valuable to you, at the end of a year, I would keep it:
but that seems no wise probable. On the contrary you are too valuable to it.
Ungrateful Dial, thou must be dashed in pieces."[58] Emerson realized that
there scarcely could or ought to be a *Dial* without Fuller. He told her in
April, "A great part of the reason why [*The Dial*] should continue comes
from you. You like that it should go on, & you offer so liberally after your
liberal nature."[59]

But even the most liberal nature extends only so far, and Fuller's goodwill
could not free her from the limits of her endurance. By May she found herself
possessed by an irresistible urge to flee. She felt "constantly unwell, dull,"
with headaches thwarting her whenever she tried to tackle a new piece of
work.[60] She wrote Emerson, "I am now tired of books and pens and thought
no less, and shall be glad when I take wing for an idle outdoors life, mere
sight and emotion."[61] The outdoor life was already beckoning. Sometime
that spring, James Freeman Clarke had announced his intention to take his
mother Rebecca and sister Sarah to visit his brother William in Chicago.
Sarah extended an invitation to Fuller, and she gladly accepted. They would
travel first to New York City and travel up the Hudson Valley by train. After
an almost obligatory sightseeing stop at Niagara Falls, they would proceed by
boat to their destination. When Caroline Sturgis agreed to come along as far
as the falls, the prospect must have become irresistible. On May 25, armed
with a parasol that Elizabeth Hoar rushed to the station to give her, Fuller set
forth in search of America.

As Fuller prepared to strike out toward the middle of the continent, her
frame of mind had some points in common with those of the utopians. She
shared with them a vague belief that human beings could be redeemed by
landscape. It occurred to her that the challenges of life on the frontier might
compel a person, as a matter of survival, to develop to the utmost his physical
and mental faculties, while the beauty of the place summoned forth one's
inclinations toward artistry and poetry. "I wish my lot had been cast," she had
told her brother Richard the previous year, "amid the sources of the streams,

where the voice of the hidden torrent is heard by night, where the eagle soars, and the thunder resounds."[62] She went west in hopes of seeing what prodigies might be spawned by contact with the new land.

Settling into a couch on the train from New York, Fuller almost immediately found the rest she craved. When night fell, the gentle patter of the rain outside, mingled with the patter of conversation within, supplied the perfect accompaniment for dreams and reflections on all that she was about to see. Two weeks before her departure, Emerson had written her a letter blessing her journey. Fuller must have taken pleasure from his exultant benediction: "May the sun & moon & stars be on your side when you leave the East winds behind, and [ride to] Niagara famed through the world for one thing,—that it never disappoints."[63]

And yet, in Fuller's case, it partially did. When she ventured into the outdoors, Fuller was naturally drawn to the sublime. She once remarked that she was happiest when "reading [the] bolder lines in the manuscript of nature."[64] Of all American places, Niagara would have seemed to suit her needs. Nevertheless, face-to-face with their roar and tumult, she felt something less than elation. She did not blame the falls themselves—not precisely. Their spectacle, she conceded, was "great enough to fill the whole life, and supersede thought, giving us only its own presence."[65] The problem was that the fame of the falls had too much preceded them. Fuller had read and heard so much and had seen so many paintings of them that they seemed disappointingly familiar. Instead of marveling at them, she caught herself merely comparing them with their reputation. The truly climactic feeling she experienced came when she saw some rapids that no one had described to her. Even then, she felt stupid for feeling "most moved in the wrong place."[66]

Other contingencies conspired to further diminish the moment. The skies were sullen, and the winds were bitterly cold. There was also the dreary necessity of sharing the scene with spectators not of one's choosing. Having ventured out to Table Rock, on the Canadian side, Fuller had just begun to descend into an aesthetic reverie when a man sauntered up next to her. She recalled with contempt, "He walked close up to the fall, and, after looking at it a moment, with an air as if thinking how he could best appropriate it to his own use, he spat into it."[67]

Fuller's own subjective feelings also stood between her and contentment.

The sight was, in one sense, all too overpowering. It caught hold of her long-standing fear of water and raised it to a nameless terror:

> After a while [the scene] so drew me into itself as to inspire an unde-
> fined dread, such as I never knew before, such as may be felt when
> death is about to usher us into a new existence. The perpetual tram-
> pling of the waters seized my senses. I felt that no other sound, how-
> ever near, could be heard, and would start and look behind me for
> a foe.[68]

In her overly stimulated imagination, the pouring water became strangely personified. She recalled, "[C]ontinually upon my mind came, unsought and unwelcome, images, such as never haunted it before, of naked savages steal-ing behind me with uplifted tomahawks."[69] Even after she told herself it was not real, this illusion arose again and again, making her startle and look behind herself. It was a complex anxiety in which many fears entwined. It may partly have been the sexual terror of a well-protected virgin gazing from civility into wildness. It was, as well, the guilt of a cultural trespasser, who felt in her bones that she was in a place that did not welcome her and that her invasion called out for punishment. Above all, perhaps, it was a conditioned response to the unknown, an involuntary presumption that, when Indians and whites collided, they were fated to do so on terms of subterfuge and deadly violence.

The falls did, though, appeal to her scientific mind. In its sublime violence and constant change, the cataract seemed to confirm the evolutionary ideas she had absorbed from reading Sir Charles Lyell; she could not look at it and suppose that, after the six days of Genesis, the earth had been a finished thing. To the contrary, Niagara bore witness to a world in process, affording "no escape from the weight of a *perpetual creation*; all other forms and motions come and go, the tide rises and recedes, the wind, at its mightiest, moves in gales and gusts, but here is really an incessant, an indefatigable motion."[70] In this sense, at least, the falls were as she had hoped.

After a sojourn of seven days, Fuller's party bade farewell to Caroline Sturgis, who went back home to Boston, and pressed on by steamer through Lake Erie. After touching at Cleveland and Detroit, their boat chugged up Lake Huron and around the northern coast of Michigan before pushing south again toward Chicago. The cold rains that had dampened their stay at Niagara did not end until Fuller and her friends reached Cleveland. During their passage up the Saint Clair River, which joins Lake Erie to Lake Huron, Fuller had her first glimpse of Native Americans. They were camped on the riverbank at twilight and wore blankets about their shoulders. Just as she had seen Niagara only through the earlier perceptions of others, Fuller saw these Indians somewhat as her culture influenced her to. Their movements struck Fuller as alternately listless and stealthy, and she thought their peculiar "lounge and . . . stride" differed visibly in its wildness from the ruder gait of the white settlers.[71] For the first time, she felt as if she were truly approaching the West.

But their boat could not go west without bringing the East along with it. It was filled with New Englanders, seeking their fortunes—a "cautious," calculating crowd who spoke not of what they hoped to achieve, but of what they wanted to get.[72] The sight of these unlovely travelers, bent on enlarging their purses instead of their hearts and minds, left Fuller desolate. The richness of the land, she feared, was likely to be squandered on people who would "outrage the law of love in every way."[73] For the time being, however, that richness was still extant, and it was all around her. The shore of Lake Michigan was, if not precisely primeval, still relatively untouched by European influence.[74] A traveler on a steamboat stopping for fuel at Green Bay in the early 1840s could still encounter "tall, stately, dignified warriors in . . . paint and feathers," as yet uncorrupted by contact with the new insurgent culture.[75] Fuller found the beauty of the lake both grand and desolate. Yet travelers had already scarred it. When their boat touched at the Manitou Islands for fuel, Fuller and her friends ventured into the woods and were saddened to find that "almost all the old monarch trees" had already been felled to glut the appetites of the passing steamers. Fuller's journal seethed with denunciations of the "vulgar barbarians" who seemed incapable of leaving any beauty untouched. She was witnessing a violation for which she thought the descendants of these people could never atone.[76]

Whether or not one was attracted to Chicago in the early 1840s depended largely on how one imagined what was not yet there. Oakes Shaw, the son of Massachusetts Chief Justice Lemuel Shaw, came to the settlement in the same year as Fuller and was unimpressed. He saw "a dull, uninteresting place built on a dead level prairie, built chiefly of wood, & very . . . unsubstantial at that."[77] The only point that truly impressed him was the one that astonished so many: the furious growth of the place. Shaw reported that, whereas Chicago had consisted of two log cabins in 1832, it now claimed eight thousand residents. Fuller was pleased to see that, thus far, the town exhibited no "starving want among the poor," nor was there yet a moneyed class affected by "that selfish luxury which wounds our thoughts in older and more refined societies."[78] Otherwise, however, she formed no great opinion of Chicago and its "tobacco-chewing, sharp, yet sensual-looking crowd."[79] She saw it almost exclusively as a "thoroughfare," and as a giant valve whose function was to "open and shut all the time, as the life-blood rushes from east to west and back again."[80] Yet for all the commerce and human vitality that coursed through it daily, the city struck her as oddly lacking in character. The people were active, resourceful, and genial, but they seemed to live only for their work, serving the prodigious valve that seemed so much like a beating heart and so little like a thinking brain.

To see Chicago in 1843 was to realize abruptly that "ambition" and "hope" are not synonyms. The first surged forward; the latter languished. Fuller wrote woefully to Emerson that "[t]he men are all at work for money and . . . the women belong to the men." Although the energy with which they pursued their goals was authentic enough, she found that "its objects are not invested with a poetic dignity."[81] While still at Niagara, awaiting her plunge into the heartland, she had written optimistically to Emerson: "Democracy is the way to the new aristocracy, as irreligion to religion."[82] Viewed from up close, however, the enticing, democratic West appeared to have opened the way to little more than a universal grab.

Perhaps worst of all, Fuller felt that intellectual spirits like her own were irrelevant in the boisterous boomtown. The hearty poet-pioneers she expected to find were absent. "What I had," she noted despondently, "nobody wanted."[83] Ten weeks after she first set foot in Chicago, the night before she was to quit the town on her way back to the East, she would write to Emerson, observing that "Chicago" was an Indian word for the place of onions. She added, "I can attest there is some quality here fitted to draw tears."[84]

Amid all the bustle and pulse, Fuller found that she could absorb almost nothing of the city through her senses. The physical facts were too overwhelming. Instead, she wrote, "I read all the books I could find about the new region, which now began to become real to me." This line says something about the way Fuller's education had shaped her habits of seeing. Trained from childhood to gather information from texts, she could now experience a place in person and still not feel she had seen it until she had read about it. Sitting in the heart of Chicago, she needed a stack of books to make it blossom into reality. The same was true of her initial perceptions of the Native Americans, although she eventually responded to them in a less bookish manner. In Chicago and its environs, she was close enough to native people to touch and talk with them. Nevertheless, she relied on the works of artist George Catlin and adventurer Charles A. Murray, who had lived with the Pawnee, to add tone and spirit to what she saw. She wrote paradoxically, "We believe the Indian cannot be looked at truly except by a poetic eye."[85] Fact became dependable only when reordered by the artifice of language.

If getting and spending had sapped the poetry from Chicago, Fuller felt the presence of a strong, silent companion in Lake Michigan. From her rooms at night, as she turned the pages of a romantic drama she was preparing to review, she could hear its "deep sound" as its heave and roll accompanied her reading.[86] One evening, putting aside her book and opening the blind, she looked out at the moon's reflection on the face of the water. The calm breeze, the pure light, and the somnolent voice of the lake united into an almost human presence. The drama Fuller had been reading dealt with the life of Philip van Artevelde, a medieval Flemish patriot who had died gallantly in a rebellion against Louis II of Flanders. In Fuller's mind, the abiding strength of the lake joined with her reflections on the Flemish hero. The fulfilling emotion that this impression caused her, however, gave way almost at once to a mood of emptiness, as the heroic ideal reminded her of how short her own times were falling. She wondered where she might find a modern-day Artevelde, and she realized that she did not know:

When will this country have such a man? It is what she needs; no thin Idealist, no coarse Realist, but a man whose eye reads the heavens while his feet step firmly on the ground, and his hands are strong and dexterous . . . a man of universal sympathies, but self-possessed; a man who knows the region of emotion, though he is not its slave.[87]

Fuller sensed that, until there was such an American, there could not be a true America.

Thankfully, the lake was not all that charmed her. Granted, her first impression of the prairies to the west left her dejected. However, after she had actually ridden out to see the flowers and to watch the sun set with a calmness she had never seen anywhere else, she began to feel something for the landscape that seemed like love. Not long before her first extended excursion inland, she learned the surprising pleasure of climbing up on a roof to watch the sun go down. The sunsets over the prairie affected her in a way far different from sunsets over water. But for the waving of the grasses, the earth was motionless. As distant cattle trod toward their rest, Fuller felt as if there were "no home on earth, & no need of one, for there is room enough to wander on forever."[88] She would wait until the town had turned out all its lights. Then, with nothing to distract her but the moon and stars, she gazed out upon "this lovely, still reception on the earth; no towering mountains, no deep tree-shadows, nothing but plain earth and water bathed in light."[89]

Two weeks or so after they arrived in Chicago, James Clarke headed home to Boston, and Fuller embarked with Sarah and William Clarke and their mother into the great expanse to the west of town. They traveled in a horse-drawn lumber wagon, covered with a cotton awning and laden with every kind of possession that might prove needful, since, as Fuller observed, "buying and selling were no longer to be counted on." Finally, she felt that she had found the real country. Her pleasure was greatly enhanced by the company of William, of whom she wrote, "He knows his path as a man and follows it with the spirit of a boy. We do not see such people at the East."[90] As William shared with her every detail of the natural and political history of the land, Fuller felt her impressions of the territory's dullness giving way to a sense of sweetness at the brightness and promise of it all. They rode beneath slow-moving clouds through woods bedecked with moccasin flowers and lupines, arriving in the town of Geneva on the Fox River, just in advance of a drenching thunderstorm. Here, too, New England had arrived ahead of Fuller, in the form of a host of settlers from the Northeast. However, in this town, at least, they were "of an excellent stamp, generous, intelligent, discreet, and seeking to win from life its true values."[91] She may have been attracted most by the woods that fringed the river, where she spent some happy hours as William went fishing.

Mrs. Clarke, being too fatigued to continue the trip, remained behind in Geneva as the younger members of the party continued their exploration.

Not far from town, Fuller came upon a spot that seemed to realize her ideal of frontier life. It was the unusually handsome dwelling of an Englishman and his family. Their bookcase was filled with volumes about the region, and their well-kept farmyard was full of cattle and poultry. Seen in the first light of day, the barns and farmhouse seemed to harmonize perfectly with the natural setting. The women of the family spoke excellent French and seemed equally adept at making music and killing rattlesnakes. It was a place of beautiful children, tall wild roses, and splendid blue spiderwort. There was, Fuller wrote, "that mixture of culture and rudeness in the aspect of things as gives a feeling of freedom, not of confusion."[92]

For much of the way, it was a charmed excursion. The beauty of the streams and groves by which they passed put Margaret into virtually invincible good spirits, so that even when the party spent the night at a miserable tavern with "bedchambers for twelve, a milk dish for universal handbasin, and expectations that you would use and lend your 'hankercher' for a towel," she was not greatly out of sorts. Told that the only place for her to sleep was the supper table in the barroom, from which a boisterous band of drunkards had just been forcibly ejected, Fuller accepted her fate with good cheer. She seems not even to have been bothered when the keeper of the establishment confessed that there was no fastening on the door to prevent the recently ousted revelers from returning. Trusting to the keeper's promise that, having conquered the miscreants once, he could do so again, Fuller took grateful possession of the table and "slept as sweetly as . . . in the 'bigly bower' of any baroness."[93]

As they traveled on, Fuller was compelled to admit that the general state of civilization in the region lay closer to the seedy tavern than to the Englishman's cultured retreat. In places where a modicum of care would have redeemed the scene, the tendency still ran to slovenliness and neglect. Fuller's repulsion deepened when she considered that the Indians, driven from the land just five years earlier, had occupied it with infinitely greater taste and consideration. In their refusal to profane and deface the land as the whites had already done, the tribesmen of the Sac and Fox nations had proved themselves the rightful lords of its beauty. To the ears and eyes of the great majority of the new arrivals, the natural glory seemed to be mute and invisible. Progress here, Fuller lamented, was "Gothic, not Roman," and she predicted that the natural charm of the country could survive no more than a decade or two. Ironically, Fuller took comfort while in this mood by looking up at the afternoon sky and seeing tremendous flocks of passenger pigeons, "positively in clouds, and with a swiftness and softness of winged motion. More beautiful than anything of the kind I ever knew."[94] Not even in her saddest moments did Fuller dare predict that these, too, would quickly disappear.

The knowledge that the land's purity was fleeting made its beauty all the more priceless. On the morning of the Fourth of July, on a bluff near Oregon, Illinois, called the Eagle's Nest, she stood amid scarlet flowers that resembled cut coral. Bathed in sunlight, the bluff touched the heavens with a sharp, fair line. On this pinnacle between land and sky, Margaret was certain that she had never felt so glad to be an American. The land, she thought, surely surpassed even the idealized Italy she had never seen. "I do believe," she wrote, "Rome and Florence are suburbs compared to this capital of nature's art." As the sun descended, Fuller returned to the home where she was staying for an evening of music, ice cream, and fireworks. At dinner, proud ejaculations of "Hail, Columbia" substituted for the usual saying of grace. A few weeks later, in a letter to her brother Richard, she called the hours she spent at the Eagle's Nest some of the happiest of her life.

Full of western vigor, Margaret feared that the "artificial and mechanical disciplines" of the East were depriving Richard of his "natural temper of body and mind," much as she believed they had done to her. As if to prove that even New England bluestockings can dream impractical dreams, she made him a wild proposal. "If we two could live [here] and you have a farm . . . and have our books and our pens, and a little boat on the river, how happy we might be for four or five years." It was only a pretty fantasy, one that seemed to forget how dissatisfied she had been during her father's far less drastic retreat to Groton, but it did show how highly she esteemed her younger brother. In the same letter, she told him, "We, I think, Richard, are really congenial, and if I could hope permanent peace on earth, I might hope it with you."[95]

Knowing as well as anyone that the land was already limited, Fuller still could not wholly put the illusion of boundlessness behind her. It was a truly transcendental failing, this denial of the truth of limits, as became clear when, in reaffirming the infinitude of the frontier, Fuller added, "I say, that what is limitless is alone divine, that there was neither wall nor road in

Eden."[96] She chose not to remember that the refusal to accept a divinely ordered limit was the cause of Adam's fall.

Returning to Chicago after more than a fortnight on the prairie, Fuller resolved to see the settlement with fresh and interested eyes. She failed. The July heat had descended with full force, and the sweltering days brought Fuller and Sarah Clarke "no enjoyment of life."[97] Sarah decamped for Milwaukee. After a fruitless week in Chicago, Fuller left with Sarah's mother to join her, feeling that she had failed to experience Illinois as she should have done. She accused herself of paying too much attention to the natural artistry of the region, and not nearly enough to social conditions, particularly education. She was still seeing the world more as an aesthete than as a reformer. Curiously, in *Summer on the Lakes*, the book she was to write about her western travels, Fuller concluded her remarks on Illinois with an anecdote concerning the early midwestern philanthropist Morris Birkbeck. While fording a stream with his teenage son, Birkbeck became caught in the current. His son, having crossed to the other side in safety, plunged back in to save his father but, upon reaching him, discovered that he was too weighed down by his father and his own clothes to bring the two of them back to shore. Grasping the situation, the father gave up his hold on his son, and, smiling, motioned him away. The son survived; when the father's body was found, the face still wore a serene smile.[98] Fuller was captivated by this tale of simple heroism, particularly because the thought of drowning seems to have impressed her as uniquely dreadful. She had had nightmares of drowning since childhood, and then, too, there had been her drowning dream the night she had slept with Anna Ward the previous year. Fuller wrote that she often had a vision of Birkbeck's face, peacefully smiling as the current carried him away.

After Fuller pushed on to Wisconsin, and for the remainder of her trip, her most memorable observations concerned the embattled Native Americans, whom she saw still trying to make a life for themselves on the borders of the expanding white domain. Perhaps her greatest challenge in writing about them was to set aside the preconceptions she had absorbed from the fictions of Lydia Maria Child and James Fenimore Cooper. It had become almost a reflex among American writers to poeticize Indian life beyond recognition, and Fuller herself admitted wishing that Sir Walter Scott were at her side to add the proper romantic glow to the scenes she witnessed. But, in truth, where Fuller was, she saw little to romanticize. Fuller had arrived too late to see these Indians in a proud state of freedom; most had already been driven to a condition of dispirited dependency. Though she had heard that the natives on the distant shores of Lake Superior retained "a remnant of the noble blood," the men she saw had had more contact with the new settlers.[99] Already, she found them "subjugated . . . accustomed to drunkenness and every way degraded.[100]

Very likely the greatest number of Indians she saw in one place was a gathering of people from the Ottawa and Chippewa tribes who had come to

Chippewa Indians, several years after Fuller visited the Great Lakes.
Though she initially regarded the Indians as "shrieking savages,"
Fuller soon after observed, "Their decorum and delicacy are striking."
(COURTESY OF BILDAGENTUR-ONLINE/ALAMY)

Mackinac Island in Lake Huron to receive their annual payments from the U.S. government. Arriving by the thousands, they had camped on the beach and fed themselves by fishing the lake. As Fuller's steamer approached after dark, the captain ordered the crew to set off rockets. The flash and sound "greatly excited the Indians, and their yells and wild cries resounded along the shore."[101] Their shrieks had not died down as Fuller walked to her hotel, reflecting dismally on the clash between modern and ancient ways. She was not the least bit intimidated by the campers on the shore; at dawn the next day, she was out among them, observing the children, "wild as little goblins," venturing forth from their hastily erected lodges, the women pounding corn, and the young men playing pipes with the sweetness of songbirds.[102]

Fuller was especially attracted to the women, even though they seemed least of all to provide fodder for her romantic imagination. To approach them, she had to brave the disapproval of the white women who traveled with her, who could not fathom how she endured the unwashed condition of the natives. At first, Fuller herself was only somewhat less inclined toward pejorative judgments. She perceived the women as "almost invariably coarse and ugly, with the exception of their eyes . . . and forms bent by burthens."[103] Their stride, it seemed to her, was strangely awkward, and its difference from the steady, strong step of the men plainly indicated their status as social inferiors. When she approached them, however, she was charmed by the delicacy of their manners. Although Fuller and the "little things" she had to show them filled the women with curiosity, they never pressed uncomfortably close to her, and everything she gave them to inspect was held with care and handed back with "ladylike precision."[104] Their shy, sweet expressions and their mischievous laughter as she showed them how to operate an umbrella quickly found a lasting place in her memory.

As Fuller lingered among the Ottawa and Chippewa through the day, her eye was occasionally caught by the poignant sight of "a young girl, with a baby at her back, whose bright eyes glanced, as if born into a world of courage and joy, instead of ignominious servitude and slow decay."[105] Fuller thought she could rather accurately foretell what those eyes were likely to see. When recollecting her travels in *Summer on the Lakes*, Fuller continually veers away from prolonged discourse on her personal encounters with the Indians. Just when the reader expects her to fill the page with her own observations, she resorts instead to lengthy excerpts from other authors' accounts of Indian life. It is as though Fuller required an insulating barrier of authority and scholarship between herself and her subject to buffer the sadness of what she saw.

Fuller wrote little about her journey home, but her trip did not end without a significant encounter. For a brief time, she stopped in New York, where she chanced to cross paths with both Thoreau, who had been tutoring Emerson's brother's children on Staten Island, and Bronson Alcott, who, with the help of his fellow utopian Charles Lane, was trying desperately to recruit new members and financial backing for their floundering community at Fruitlands. More important for Fuller, she was introduced to the editor of the *New-York Tribune*, Horace Greeley. Greeley was already acquainted with Fuller through her writings in *The Dial* and, as has been mentioned, the reports of his wife from the Boston conversations she had attended. About her first meeting with Greeley, Fuller had nothing to report, little guessing, it seems, the professional interest that the editor had taken in her work. As Fuller returned home, she felt that her health had very nearly been restored, "if not to its native tone," then at least to one that enabled her "to walk forward with some energy."[106] Moreover, despite the troubled tone of her journal, she found her recollections of her trip were mostly optimistic. The incidents of meanness and grasping she had witnessed were far outweighed by the possibilities of western grandeur that she had intuited and in which she still believed.

Back in Massachusetts, Fuller paid a brief visit to Concord, where she saw a sure sign that the country was growing up; while she had been away, Boston capital and Irish immigrant labor had combined to complete the first railroad link between Concord and the city. Appearing to give no thought to the hard lives of the people who occupied them, Fuller wrote to Thoreau that she found the workers' shanties "pretty" but thought the railroad looked "foreign."[107] It seems not to have occurred to her that she and Henry, with their cultured intellects, their love of nature, and their fondness for human antiquities, might be the real foreigners now, living in a country where force, technology, and newness were destined to rule.

Fuller rented a house in Cambridge, where she planned to stay for a year. She resumed her schedule of conversations as usual. Otherwise, for a time, she was content to "go on in [her] even way, woods, and fields, and books,— books and fields and woods" through the soft lustres of autumn.[108] New England, which had seemed poor and little to her when she had roamed the western wilderness, now seemed as good a place as any in the world.[109] This period of relative quiet was good for her physical health, but her mind quickly grew restless. She began looking for some intellectual means of connecting her experiences into a coherent whole. To Channing, she described what she was looking for as "the third thought"—the idea "which is to link together each conflicting two [and] is of course the secret of the universe. . . . The Philosopher exacts [it], the poet expects it, the child believes it is already here.

It is the beloved Son in whom both God and Man will be well pleased." The metaphor was obviously Christian. The concept was not. Fuller was not seeking salvation in the body of Christ. She hoped to find a unity of self and other, of spirit and matter, that no earthly church had ever preached. She wanted an idea in which faith, hope, and knowledge would become one. Lacking any other word, she called her wished-for idea "divine." Whatever it was, she thought that no mere human effort or association could bring it about. She told Channing, "It is a constellation, not a phalanx, to which I belong."[110]

More than ever, Fuller's simultaneous desires for development and synthesis were complicated by a persistent worry that no resolving third idea might truly exist. As she admitted to Albert Tracy, who had served with her father in Congress, she had thus far been more occupied with her own ideal visions than with the actual world around her.[111] Her trip to the West had jarred her nearer to reality. The chaotic growth she had seen there, as well as the uncertain progress of her own life, had suggested to her that the world of things was not governed by ideal principles. Slowly, she was becoming more of a believer in "those sharp turns of fate or character" and the unforeseen contingencies by which "an unexpected plant springs up and shadows all the remaining scene."[112] The image of a plant, seemingly not native to its soil, bursting forth from underground is recurrent in Fuller's letters in the fall of 1843, and it possessed strong meaning for her. She herself was hoping soon to germinate into a new and unanticipated life, one seldom seen in the gardens of New England. She hoped the means of that new life would lie in the writing of *Summer on the Lakes*.

Though she was in a fever to write her book, she cautioned Emerson not to expect much from it. She had grown all too accustomed to her pattern of promising him that she would write something substantial, be it a fictional romance or a biography of Goethe, and then failing to deliver it. She could not bear to keep disappointing him. She could converse and give lessons while there were minutes in the day. However, she complained, "I cannot think a thought or write a line except under certain conditions."[113] This time, however, she was determined to make her conditions. Finding to her distress that her journals and memories of her trip were too fragmented to support a complete narrative on their own, she added the poems and letters of friends who had also visited the West, with the idea of turning her book into "a kind of letter box" of impressions and reminiscences.[114] Still finding this framework insufficient, she made one of the boldest moves of her career thus far: she sought, and somewhat remarkably obtained, access to the reading room and book collection of the Harvard College Library—a permission that no other woman had ever secured. It was with some lingering astonishment that, years later, her biographer Thomas Wentworth Higginson, then a degree candidate in the Divinity School, remembered seeing his future subject "sitting, day after day, under the covert gaze of the undergraduates who had never before looked upon a woman reading within those sacred precincts."[115]

Fuller immersed herself in everything Harvard had to offer regarding western travel and, in particular, American Indians. Although the result was that her manuscript ending up feeling, in places, more like a product of study than of travel, her time in the library gave her the material she required to turn *Summer on the Lakes* from a fragmented memoir into a unique reflection on the American Midwest—a book not only about the present but also about what the region had been and was likely to become. When it came time to transform her research and recollections into writing, she went after the project in style, surrounding her desk at home with freshly cut flowers and engravings from classical Rome and the Renaissance.

Fuller's physical circumstances continued to work against her. Her improved health had proved fleeting, and her headaches constantly disrupted her work. Only months after returning from her excursion to the West, Fuller told Anna Ward that her "many years of forced exertions and complex cares under almost constant bodily suffering" had deprived her of almost all of her once prodigious vital energy, adding, "[M]y mind refuses to sustain me at times." As a result, she found it "inevitable that I should suffer a good deal of sadness."[116] Fuller confided to Emerson that she went through periods of days at a stretch when she could not write a word without pain.[117] Again, the limitless thinker struggled against the constraining body.

Fuller held herself to a writing schedule of six hours per day, ending in a walk before sundown. Emerson secured her a publishing contract with his Boston publisher, Little and Brown, that promised ten cents a copy, a generous share at the time.[118] By May 1844, she was correcting proofs and going through quiet agonies as she found the later chapters, especially her chapter on the Indians, "desultory and ineffectual."[119] On her thirty-fourth birthday, shortly after one in the afternoon, she put the last touch on the final proof sheet. She then went to Mount Auburn Cemetery and "walked gently among the graves."[120] The scene, she told herself, "was of heavenly beauty, but Oh, I am very, very sad." But along with the predictable depression that often comes with finishing a huge project also came a glorious feeling of profundity. She wrote, "The state of my mind is so deep. I think this must be an important era in my life."[121]

Of all literary genres, few would seem to have a more inherent arc and pace than travel narratives. The inescapable trajectory of departure, journey, arrival, and return would seem to provide a foolproof structure for even the most wayward of stylists. And yet *Summer on the Lakes* stands as a monument to the nonlinear and the anti-cohesive. Multitudes of genres— epistolary narrative, gothic tale, lyric poetry, book review, and informal dialogue, to give only a partial list—crowd against one another. The evident *raison d'être* of Fuller's book, the description of sights seen while traveling to and through the midwestern frontier, is continually pushed aside to make room for snippets of conversation, fictionalized personal recollections, and speculations on the spirit world. The patchwork nature of Fuller's narrative is due in part to her wanting to infuse her book with some of the spirit of the German Romantics, who were generally less concerned with telling logically connected stories than they were with revealing philosophical and psychological truth. As Fuller's friend Hedge had once observed in an essay on Schiller, the reader of German Romantic literature "is placed in a labyrinth of striking thoughts and beautiful illustrations, having no necessary connexion or dependence, through which he is left to find his way as he can."[122]

In *Summer on the Lakes*, Fuller, too, pointedly shunned the appearance of connectedness and linearity, and her book is thus, stylistically speaking, more German than American. This aesthetic choice, however, is a bit surprising, given that Fuller was, on another level, trying very hard to write an American book. She was trying to discover and demarcate a new realm for American poetic discourse—not the polite versifications of Boston studies and Cambridge libraries, but a lusty, broad-shouldered genre, informed not by classical models but by toil and sinew. On the docks of Chicago and in the fields of Illinois, she intuited the possibility of a new creative language, inclusive enough to encompass the crass but energetic man of business, the dispirited but striving frontier wife, and the noble but ill-fated Native American. Her desire to tell as many stories as her volume could contain and incorporate as many genres as taste would allow had both a literary and a political purpose. She was seeking both an untried pan-textual poetics and a virgin physical space for the development of the American mind and spirit. Fuller's aspirations were vaguely Whitmanesque, at a time when Whitman himself was still trying to acquit himself as a journalist. Among the works of Whitman's contemporaries, perhaps only Melville's *Mardi* and *Moby-Dick* surpass the effort of *Summer on the Lakes* to "contain multitudes."

But Fuller was daunted by the ambition of her own task. She worried that she had not truly Americanized herself. To Tracy, she complained of a strange sense of her own foreignness, "both from constitution and a premature and excessive culture in the thoughts of Europe, which I have had slowly to undo or transmute to live in my own place and with my own people."[123] One could not easily become the bard of a land in which one felt so peculiarly Other, and one suspects that Fuller traveled west to look not only for some idealized American landscape, but also for something that would help her to better discover the American in her own heart. She seems not to have quite succeeded; her letter to Tracy dates from a few months *after* her return from the West.

Summer on the Lakes begins with two prefatory poems. One, titled "To a Friend," discloses some of Fuller's worries about her book. Its central image is a forlorn collection of souvenirs she brought back from her journey: some tufts of dried prairie grass; a "muscle-shell"; a rack of discarded antlers; and, most poignantly, "an eagle's feather which adorned a Brave, / Well-nigh the last of his despairing band."[124] One fully appreciates the pathos of these apparently random mementos when one considers the attitude of transcendentalism toward fragments in general. As espousers of Kantian reason and as believers in a superior reality beyond the realm of physical substance, the transcendentalists did not trust the assumption, so comforting to their Enlightenment forefathers, that the patient accumulation of facts and specimens would lead to an ever more certain knowledge of the world. Fuller's generation wanted large unities and encompassing truths, and the observation of the world's fragments suggested the unpleasant possibility that those fragments might not add up to a rounded totality. The objects that Fuller mentions in her poem are conspicuous in their incompleteness. The grass is without its roots; the animal that inhabited the shell has decomposed; and both the antlers and the feather are the lifeless castoffs of larger organisms.

Even Fuller's alternate spelling of mussel-shell as "muscle-shell" points to a loss of strength and energy. In contrast to the tremendous vitality of the natural scenes she beheld on her trip, the nature she presents in her poem is broken, spent, skeletal. At the outset of her narrative, Fuller configures herself as the traveler who returns from places of astonishing sights and sounds bearing only paltry trinkets as the evidence of her journey. The shell, antlers, grass, and feather are analogous to what she fears will be her inadequate descriptions—the "slight gifts" of one who proposes to "give you what I can, not what I would."[125]

Fittingly for an author struggling to find her proper element, *Summer on the Lakes* takes as one of its early keynotes a conversation about the four ancient elements. As their boat makes its way westward across Lake Erie, Fuller, James Clarke, and his sister pass the time by discussing which of the elements best embodies the character of each. Fuller surprises her companions by identifying herself, not with air, fire, or water, but with earth. She likens herself to a gnome, laboring secretly in the subterranean dark. Such creatures of the earth, Fuller notes, "do not spend their energies on their own growth, or their own play, but to feed the veins of mother earth with permanent splendors, very different from what she shows on the surface."[126] Coming from Fuller, who had spent boundless energies on her own growth, such a sudden renunciation of upward yearnings comes as a shock. Her ecstatic declarations of a few years earlier had given way to an authorial mood that was self-consciously grotesque—not in the popular sense of ugliness or monstrosity, but in the more literal meaning concerning grottoes and caves.

One of the earliest reviews of *Summer on the Lakes* had a similar sense of the work. Writing for the *Christian Examiner*, critic Caleb Stetson detected in Fuller's writing "things connected by no apparent link of association with the objects which seem to fill her eye and mind . . . except for the fact that they occurred in the course of her reading or were called up from the depths by some mysterious association." Stetson also referred to Fuller's "underground associations, unintelligible to those who are not in the secret of her thoughts."[127] *Summer on the Lakes* is, indeed, a subterranean text—the upward emanation of a consciousness that could remain beneath the surface for only so long. For Fuller, gnomes have become "the most important of all the elemental tribes." Still, the aptness of the analogy eludes James Clarke, especially when Fuller points out that it is the gnomes "who make the money." He is swift to remind her that he had produced from his own pocket some of the funds for Fuller's passage. Accustomed to imagining gnomes as "dark, mean, [and] scoffing," he is unable or unwilling to absorb his companion's richer meaning. Fuller then tries to set him right, adding, "My people work in the secret, and their works praise them in the open light; they remain in the dark because only there such marvels could be bred." In *Summer on the Lakes*, Fuller seeks to venture below, into the darker precincts of human motivation and the grottoes of her own consciousness, hoping to bring into view "the hidden light of the earth," which, Fuller knows, is "very different from what she shows on the surface."[128] As compared to her days with *The Dial*, Fuller had, in more ways than one, come back down to earth.

Proceeding with a sense that consciousness is both underground and fragmentary, Fuller structured *Summer on the Lakes* as a forum for a multiplicity of competing genres, as if to emphasize that the processes of the mind are themselves nonlinear and multilateral. She did not wish for either her subject matter or her spirit to be hemmed in by a single mode of storytelling. In chapter 5, speaking through the persona of Free Hope, she writes:

> Subject to the sudden revelations, the breaks in habitual existence caused by the aspect of death, the touch of love, the flood of music, I [have] never lived, that I remember, what you call a common natural day. All my days are touched by the supernatural, for I feel the pressure of hidden causes, and the presence, sometimes the communion, of unseen powers.[129]

Having never experienced the common, Fuller could write nothing other than an uncommon text. She wrote the preceding passage three-quarters of a century before another woman described the "whirring of wings in her brain." Virginia Woolf wrote the following lines on the subject of modern fiction: "Examine for a moment an ordinary mind on an ordinary day. Is it not the task of the novelist to convey this varying, this unknown and uncircumscribed spirit, whatever aberration or complexity it may display . . . ?"[130] One might justly argue that, with her awareness that thought was a polyphony rather than a solo performance and with her knowledge that the continual "breaks in habitual existence" were forever transmuting the ordinary into the astonishing, Fuller had an impressive head start on the modernists.

Though Fuller was never to be a novelist, she knew that, every bit as much as a novel, *Summer on the Lakes* ought to represent life, and that life could be a travelogue, a poem, a dialogue, and a romance all at the same time. Fuller writes, "The language we habitually use is so broken and so hackneyed by ages of conventional use, that, in all deep states of being, we crave one more or less simple and primitive in its stead."[131] Nevertheless, Fuller's actual inclination is in the contrary direction; she is forever seeking out brokenness and complexity, knowing that this is the real state of our being. Fuller also regarded her own mind as a confluence of countless influences, an active and ever-changing mediator among all the impressions she had ever received from reading, seeing, hearing, and being:

> I would beat with the living heart of the world, and understand all the moods, even the fancies or fantasies, of nature. I dare trust to the interpreting spirit to bring me out all right at last—to establish truth through error. . . . Let me stand in my age with all its waters flowing round me. If they sometimes subdue, they must finally upbear me, for I seek the universal—and that must be the best.[132]

In her desire to understand all of nature's moods and to place herself amid the flow of all the currents of her time, Fuller embraces a spectrum of possibilities that could not possibly be subsumed within a unitary perspective. At the beginning of *Summer on the Lakes*, fragmentation leads only to a dejected sense of brokenness. Later in the text, it supplies the stylistic freedom that enables Fuller, at least intermittently, to escape the limits of a single subjectivity. The disjunctions that make her narrative such an exasperating text also contribute forcefully to making it a living one.

Summer on the Lakes interrupts itself so continually that its repeated fissures eventually create, in paradoxical fashion, a structure for the work. Invoking a leitmotif of recurrent disruption, Fuller continually raises buried things to the surface and brings them to life through a kind of prismatic presentation. Her practice is nowhere clearer than in her treatment of women. Constrained by law and social convention, nineteenth-century women were, as Fuller well knew, forced to conceal their natural selves beneath a surface of orderliness and conformity. Throughout *Summer on the Lakes*, this surface is prone to give way, and episodes of female freedom and individuality surprise and challenge the reader. The supreme example of these eruptions is a triptych of intercalated stories of three convention-defying women: a captain's wife named Mrs. P.; a boarding-school student called Mariana; and an ethereal mystic known as the Seeress of Prevorst.[133] All three tales hinge on the clash between feminine nature and male-ordered civilization; each concerns a figure whose natural impulses and inclinations civilization is at a loss to comprehend or govern. In each, the ordering principles of society are challenged and subverted by a woman who does not conform to ordinary codes of behavior. But the three stories, taken together, do more than reiterate this theme. The fact that these stories, which continually restate the motif of the woman who resists societal convention, appear at such odd and unanticipated moments is perhaps the most compelling instance of the subterranean quality of *Summer on the Lakes*. In a world that circumscribed both the political and the aesthetic expression of women, repression was a given condition of female existence. However, that repression functioned imperfectly. The three tales convey, in appropriately staccato fashion, the omnipresent possibility of female rebellion. Moreover, the ordering of the tales establishes an intriguing crescendo. Not only is each of the stories longer than the last, but their progression illustrates a steady spiritual evolution. They are an *Inferno*, *Purgatorio*, and *Paradiso* of female identity and resistance. Taken together, they present a spectrum of the soul that ranges from carnal sensation to spiritual vision.

Mrs. P., a creature of brutish, ungoverned appetites and publicly scandalous behavior, approximates a Freudian id before the letter. Her rebellion takes place in a series of drunken outbursts against social decorum. In her depravity, her only moral value is as a scourge to her long-suffering husband, who remains by her side as penance for an undisclosed sin. The Seeress stands at the opposite end of the moral spectrum. Clairvoyant, given to extrasensory perceptions, she lives "an almost disembodied life," weirdly angelic in her spiritual discernments.[134] The orthodoxy that most oppresses her is a medical consensus that insists on regarding her as a physical body; it is only when her spiritual nature is acknowledged and affirmed that she can move closer to being cured.

Mariana is the central figure of Fuller's triptych, both as regards the chronology of the narrative and in terms of her moral status. Mariana is the fictionalized vehicle that Fuller uses to revisit her unhappy days at Miss

Prescott's. She is the most conventionally human of the three women and also the one whose spiritual destiny is most in doubt. If Mrs. P. embodies an abyss of feminine nature and the Seeress represents a kind of gothic paradise, then Mariana inhabits the unstable middle realm, oscillating indecisively between love and hate and indulging in bizarre "freaks of passion and wit" that reflect her failure to find tranquility, both in her surroundings and in her mind.[135] Mariana is, like Fuller, a "provoking nonconformist," one who is conscious of secret riches within herself and struggles to find the proper field for their development.

Fuller arranges the three stories in an order that moves from the lowest spiritual development to the highest, as though to confirm her own belief in an ever-improving cosmic order. This concept of the evolutionary soul is made explicit in her description of the Seeress, who "receives this life as one link in a long chain; and thinks that immediately after death, the meaning of the past life will appear to us as one word."[136] However, the upward movement of each of these women taken individually, is far from assured. Mrs. P., we are told, degenerates from bad to worse. Mariana wastes away and dies as the result of an ill-considered marriage. The Seeress, even while alive, belongs more properly "to the state after death."[137] For neither Mariana nor the Seeress does Fuller imagine the reward of a Christian heaven. If Mariana has "entered into a larger freedom," it is not paradise, but "knowledge."[138] Although Fuller finds meaning and beauty in the tale of the Seeress, she finds no coherent purpose in her psychic meanderings, and she notes with regret, that the Seeress "was not transformed into a philosophic or poetic organization."[139]

The stories of all three women represent failures of instruction. Mrs. P., we are briefly told, suffers from "low habits of . . . education."[140] Mariana's boarding school is a scene of continual emotional torment; the failure of the faculty to recognize and properly guide the girl's eccentric genius all but destroys her before a kindly matron finally shows her the proper path. The education of the young Seeress is entrusted to her grandfather, who, upon discovering her psychic propensities, does all he can to repress them. These deficiencies of education lead to calamitous consequences, as, Fuller implies, must occur when the world fails to grasp and foster the positive aspects of a young woman's uniqueness.

More notably, marriage marks a decisive point in the catastrophe of each story. It is the means by which Captain P. is forever bonded to his lifelong punishment. Mariana's marriage to the thoughtless Sylvain fatally isolates her from the life of the mind, and she is lost because she has failed to "meet some man of sufficiently great soul to prize" her.[141] The depression that results in the Seeress's invalidism begins on the day of her betrothal to a husband who cannot appreciate her magnetic powers. As with Mariana, the Seeress's married life obliges her "hourly to forsake her inner home, to provide for an outer, which did not correspond with it." Like Mariana as well, the Seeress eventually finds it impossible "to conceal the inward verity by an outward action"; the disparity between performed and authentic self becomes too great.[142] In both instances, Fuller arraigns society for its incapacity to embrace women at their true value. Concerned more with matching her up to a superficially suitable man, the social world fails either to foster a woman's intelligence or, if need be, to treat her pathologies. Unable to successfully resist the confining, contorting influences of society, the women of Fuller's tales fall back into depravity, mysticism, or death.

But Fuller's tales are not merely vehicles for social critique. Taken together, they also meditate deeply on the inner human condition. Toward the end of the last panel of her triptych of female consciousness and displacement, Fuller returns to her perennial theme of cosmic progress. She writes, "The fashioning spirit, working upwards from the clod to man, proffers as its last, highest essay, the brain of man. In the lowest zoöphyte it aimed at this . . . but only in man has it perfected that immense galvanic battery that can be loaded from above, below, and around." Fuller avers that the gradual upward motion toward divinity is "the beautiful secret of nature." However, her own nearly disastrous spiritual ascension of 1840–41 had shown her the perils of trying to leave the physical world entirely behind. The creative spirit, she continues, "did not mean to destroy [man's] sympathies with the mineral, vegetable, and animal realms . . . which were the preface to his being."[143] Rather, the physical and the spiritual must work in balance. When they do not, the result is either a debased animal like Mrs. P., a tragically etherealized ghost like the Seeress, or, perhaps most poignantly, a suffering being like Mariana, within whom bodily passion and aspiring intellect are at constant and destructive war.

No critical gloss can induce Fuller's three tales to fit comfortably within the larger frame of *Summer on the Lakes*. They are intended to unsettle and disturb. Their presence reaffirms that Fuller's worries about the pitfalls of women's lives and the myriad potential downfalls of the spirit followed her everywhere, even to the Great Plains. For her questing, critically restless mind, there could never really be a summer vacation.

Only on one subject did *Summer on the Lakes* fail to bring its hidden ore satisfactorily to the surface, but it was a telling failure. Fuller saw the midwestern Indians simultaneously as subjects for philosophic and anthropological inquiry, and as objects of her sincere but helpless sympathy. Her heart, surely, was at or near the proper place. Concerned, as always, with fitting her observations into a theory of cosmic progress, Fuller sought to learn something by comparing European and Indian civilizations. In the native people she met, she saw boldness, resourcefulness, and fortitude, tarnished, however, by narrowness and ferocity. She contrasted these traits with those she considered typical of the white Americans she knew: refined sentiment and thoughtfulness, corrupted by rapaciousness and cunning. From this comparison, she reached a conclusion that Schelling would have no doubt approved: "As man has two natures—one, like that of the plants and animals, adapted to the uses and enjoyments of this planet, [and] another, which presages and demands a higher sphere—he is constantly breaking bounds, in proportion as the mental gets the better of the mere instinctive existence." Yet if Fuller expressly stated that Caucasian peoples, with their supposedly greater tendency toward more abstract and metaphysical reasoning, represented an advance beyond the native mentality, she resisted the common impulse to fix Native Americans within a rigid hierarchy of being; she declined "either [to] exalt the Red Man into a Demigod or degrade him into a beast." She continued, "As yet, [the European thinker] loses in harmony of being what he gains in height and extension; the civilized man is a larger mind, but a more imperfect nature than the savage."[144] Fuller's ethnological thinking was essentially an adaptation of her reflections on the Seeress of Prevorst; just as one's spiritual development could lure one fatally far from the physical world, so, too, could the human species err in carrying itself too far from the "savage."

Fuller earnestly lamented the loss of harmony, both with the natural world and within oneself, that comes with what is called civilization. Nevertheless, the shortness of the time she spent among the Indians and her ingrained preference for the literary over the living stood in the way of her saying all that she could have said regarding Indian culture. By far the bulk of her discourse on the Indians in *Summer on the Lakes* is a mere repetition of what had already been written by authors like James Adair, George Catlin, and Henry Rowe Schoolcraft. Fuller's learnedness could, when she chose, supply a ready buffer between her and a harsh situation. It was never truer than here. At the very moment when her narrative needed most urgently to convey Fuller's own experiences and impressions, she became most scholarly.

Fuller's thinking about the Indians was at its most troubled and hardest to understand when she contemplated the likely future of the native tribes. The downcast, defeated demeanor of the Indians she encountered, coupled with the still-powerful animosity she perceived among the frontier whites toward the remnants of a people already shorn of the means of mounting a successful resistance, persuaded her that the Indians were bound for extinction. The crucial and condemning failure, she was sure, had not lain in the inability of the natives to receive the blessings of European justice and mercy. Rather, it was the Europeans themselves who had failed to be converted to their own supposed ideals. She wrote:

> [T]he Europeans who took possession of this country felt themselves justified by their superior civilization and religious ideas. Had they been truly civilized or Christianized, the conflicts which sprang from the collision of the two races, might have been avoided; but this cannot be expected in movements made by masses of men. The mass has never yet been humanized.[145]

One can hardly deny that Fuller read the situation correctly. What is hard to accept is not the pathetic outcome that she foresaw, but the strange detachment and sense of utter inevitability with which she expressed it. *Summer on the Lakes* speaks, not of preserving the Indians as living peoples, but, with strikingly calm resignation, of keeping them present as a mere historic memory. Having related a series of stories of Native American virtue, she adds, with the dryness of an archivist, that these tales, "with what we know of Philip, Pontiac, Tecumseh and Red Jacket, would suffice to give the ages a glimpse as what was great in Indian life and Indian character." The easy use of the past tense is heavy with significance. So, too, is Fuller's next comment: "We hope, too, there will be a national institute, containing all the remains of the Indians—all that has been preserved by official intercourse at Washington, Catlin's collection, and a picture gallery as complete as can be made, with a collection of skulls from all parts of the country. To this should be joined the scanty library that exists on the subject."[146]

From such a sensitive and well-educated woman, bearing direct witness to a gradual genocide, one wishes for substantially more than the grisly hope that the bones of the victims will be kept on proper display. Perhaps she meant to be ironic; however, the context of her remark gives no clear sign of satirical intent. More likely, grasping as she did the evident hopelessness of the situation, Fuller simply believed there was little better that one could reasonably hope for. Her knowledge of history gave her to assume that, when two radically different peoples came together, the result would always be catastrophic for the one less adept at defending itself. The experience of the Indians seemed to prove that cultural clashes were governed by a law of mutual butchery, and that humane intentions were powerless to create exceptions. Their fate mattered to her; she simply felt that it was beyond changing.

It would have been wonderful if Fuller had done more to humanize the mass of white Americans in their attitudes toward the people who had come here first. She would have performed a greater task—and she would have written a better book—if she had appealed more stubbornly and more eloquently to the nobler natures of her countrymen and insisted that the Indians were not merely a historic curiosity to be preserved in memory, but equal members of the human family to be respected and preserved in fact. The resignation with which she accepted their destruction forms the saddest aspect of what is, on the whole, a melancholy book. Fuller's search for an American Arcadia had carried her from Brook Farm to the Great Plains. Ironically, she never came closer to her goal than when, almost too late, she glimpsed the faces of tribes and nations who had never sought to build the perfect society and now would never find it.

Fuller ended *Summer on the Lakes* as she began it, with poetry. Whereas her introductory poems were concerned with dead fragments and the fear of her own authorial inadequacy, her closing verses present an optimistic contrast. The controlling metaphor of the verse is a prospective blackberry hunt, whose would-be participants are warned that the thorny vines will tear at their dresses and hands as they try to pluck the well-guarded fruit. Still, we are told, the hard-won berries, "gathered in the open field," are superior to a housewife's tame, domesticated blackberry jam, sweetened with "foreign sugar." The poem is Fuller's unapologetic assertion that she has written a tangled, prickly, but earnestly American narrative, capable of drawing blood and, perhaps, better approached in rough gloves and overalls than in fashionable finery. Her poem, though, is not so much an apology for having written a difficult book, but a challenge to readers to make themselves as deliberately unrefined as Fuller has made herself, to venture as boldly into the traps and wonders of her text as Fuller has explored the environs of Lake Michigan. The poem is addressed specifically to American readers, who, Fuller claims, are wont to open their books at the end. In this way (and by cutting off her narrative before her return home), Fuller manages to write a book with no real conclusion, but rather two beginnings. Instead of the dead relics of her introductory poems, we are left with the image of a living, fruitful vine and the idea of a story without end. In the last stanza of her closing poem, Fuller returns to the mineral metaphors that bedecked her dialogue with James Clarke at the beginning of her second chapter. She invites her readers to "Take fact with fiction, silver with the lead, / And, at the mint, you can get gold instead."[147] In *Summer on the Lakes*, Fuller's gnome had brought up from the darkness of the grotto both base and precious metal. As she promised Clarke, she had finally paid for her passage, "and in gold, not in shells or pebbles."[148]

CHAPTER EIGHT

ADVOCATE

*I felt a delightful glow as if I had put
a good deal of my true life in it, as if,
suppose I went away now, the measure of
my foot-print would be left on the earth.*

—MARGARET FULLER TO
WILLIAM HENRY CHANNING,
UPON FINISHING *Woman in the
Nineteenth Century*, November 17, 1844

THE SAME MONTH THAT FULLER PUBLISHED *SUMMER ON THE LAKES*, regular rail service began between Concord and Charlestown, just across the river from Boston. The trip, which one could take for fifty cents, took about an hour, and the cars were said to be roomy and extremely handsome. A new phase of modernity had come to Concord, and the refuge that Fuller and others had always found there would never be the same.[1]

The change came only months before Margaret Fuller, the lifelong New Englander, also embarked on a new phase, leaving Massachusetts for the wider world of New York City. More than anything else, it was *Summer on the Lakes* that opened the door, though not because of its overall popularity. The book's scattered passages of incandescent perception were not, in the public view, enough to atone for its overall haphazardness. Emerson, relieved to find that Fuller's own criticisms of *Summer on the Lakes* had been exaggerated, called it "very good & entertaining" and hoped it would become as popular in the South and West as it deserved to be.[2] It didn't. The book enjoyed an initial flurry of interest as New England intellectuals, eager to learn more about the Boston prophetess of *The Dial*, rushed to secure a copy. It also earned its share of admiring reviews and impressed literary opinion makers like New York's Evert A. Duyckinck, editor of the influential *United States Magazine and Democratic Review*, who praised it to his journal as "the only genuine American book" of the season.[3] However, the book was too eccentric in form and esoteric in thought to garner a large audience, and in its first six months on the market, it found somewhat fewer than seven hundred purchasers—a respectable number for the time, but far from overwhelming. A perceptive response to Fuller's volume came from her friend Lydia Maria Child, who found that the book had stumbled slightly over its own erudition. While praising "the vigor and acuteness of intellect" that filled Fuller's pages, Child also clicked her tongue: "I might say your house is too full; there is too much furniture in your rooms. This is the result of a higher education than popular writers usually have; but it stands much in the way of extensive popularity."[4]

As it turned out, the most important reader of *Summer on the Lakes* had first read the book when it was still in manuscript. He was Horace Greeley, who well remembered his first meeting with Fuller the previous September when she passed through New York on her way home from Chicago. Greeley is now best remembered for four words spoken by someone else. The spirited advice, "Go West, young man!" was first proffered by an Indiana newspaperman named John Soule. Greeley, however, did more than give directions. The son of a poor New Hampshire farmer, he had moved to New York in 1831 with ten dollars and a small sack of belongings, hoping to make his way as a printer. In 1840, it was Greeley who refashioned the public image of presidential candidate William Henry Harrison, helping to carry the election by deftly linking the Virginia-born aristocrat to images of log cabins, hard cider, and Indian fighting. Ten years after his arrival in the city and three years before he picked up *Summer on the Lakes*, Greeley had presided over the merger of several smaller papers into the *New-York Tribune*.

First published in April 1841, the *Tribune* had risen rapidly. By decade's end, it would surpass the *New-York Herald* as the city's newspaper of choice. But Greeley had more on his mind than sales. In contrast to the lurid tales of crime and scandal that were the lifeblood of other dailies, he wanted an editorial content that spoke to the best of his readers' natures. Greeley believed his audience could be moved by good writing about charity and social jus-

tice. He sensed a need for discerning critiques of fine poetry and knowledge-
able reviews of violin concerts. He wanted a columnist who, by writing on
these subjects, could help bring more New Yorkers into the ranks of culture
and compassion. Fuller seemed right for the job.

It appears likely that Fuller's initial impressions of Greeley came to her in
an 1842 letter from Emerson, who described Greeley as "a young man with
white soft hair . . . of sanguine temper & liberal mind, no scholar but such a
one as journals & newspapers make." Emerson also caught a certain femi-

Profoundly
impressed with her
essay on women's
rights, "The Great
Lawsuit," Horace
Greeley made Fuller
his first female
employee at the
New-York Tribune.
(COURTESY OF THE
NATIONAL PORTRAIT
GALLERY)

nine, nurturing aspect in Greeley's demeanor that led him to call the editor a
"mother of men."[5] Greeley was a passionate supporter of social reform. He
had declared himself to be a transcendentalist and a defender of miracles,
and he had shown keen interest in Brook Farm. However, there was a trifle
too much material practicality in Greeley's idealism for him to see eye to eye
with the Sage of Concord. As Emerson confessed to his wife Lidian, "I am, in
all my theory, ethics, & politics a poet and of no more use in their New York

than a rainbow or a firefly."[6] Very likely, the practical leavening in Greeley's idealism, so off-putting to Emerson, was exactly what drew Fuller into his orbit in 1844. After several years of transcendental moonlight, a good dose of definite, pragmatic sunshine must have sounded irresistible. For William Henry Channing, Fuller's reason for weighing a move to New York was evident; she required, in his words, "freer fields of action." Her life in New England had given her almost all it could; only New York would allow her the "expansion" that had become the rule of her existence.[7]

Greeley had begun to take an interest in Fuller when he read her work in *The Dial*. That interest had deepened when he read *Summer on the Lakes*, which had struck him as "one of the clearest and most graphic delineations ever given . . . of the receding barbarism and the rapidly advancing but rude, repulsive semi-civilization, which were contending . . . for the possession of those rich lands."[8] Conscious as Greeley was of Fuller's literary merits, he might not have brought her to New York as promptly as he did without the intervention of his wife. Mary Greeley, as a result of her attendance at Fuller's Boston conversations, stood convinced—and convinced her husband—that Fuller was just the person to voice the literary opinions of the *Tribune*. Sometime during the spring of 1844, Greeley suggested to Fuller that she might consider moving to New York and becoming the *Tribune*'s first literary editor.

The terms of Greeley's initial offer were indefinite, and Fuller deferred her decision until the editor worked out the details. To her surprise, it took months for him to come back with a firm offer. As the spring turned to summer, Fuller found herself becoming less sociable. Some of her aloofness may have been due to the knowledge that she might soon be leaving her New England friends; the break was likely to be easier if it felt more gradual. She also realized that she often felt more toward others than she could expect to be reciprocated, and she was trying to moderate her demonstrations of feeling. She wrote, "I remain fixed to be without churlishness or coldness as much alone as possible. It is best for me—I am not fitted to be loved & it pains me to have close dealings with those who do not love, to whom my feelings are 'strange.'" She was happy to show and receive kindness and esteem, but these courtesies by themselves were not, she thought, "worth feelings such as mine."[9]

The one person exempt from Fuller's distancing was Cary Sturgis, toward whom, as she had so long done for Anna Ward, Fuller now flirted with stronger feelings. The two women stayed together in mid-June and routinely shared a bed. For Fuller, these nights were "a time of deep life" that left her "soothed and still." Her profoundest layers of emotion were beyond her ability or desire to describe. "I cannot speak of it," she wrote. "It could not be spoken of unless in verse."[10]

Margaret's greatest occasion for openness came in the journal that she kept during her last New England summer. In its pages, she often turned to poetry to express her feelings about herself and her country, both of which she was trying as hard as ever to comprehend. When she looked inward, she saw more clearly than ever that her essence lay in changefulness. She now suspected that the great aesthetic gifts of her character were its capacity for shape shifting and its ability always to conceive and strive for something higher. She began this journal with the following, self-referential lines:

> Many colored Protean changing
> Rudely shaping, widely ranging,
> Clasped to Nature's secret heart
> Distant hoping highest art[11]

Her many transformations, she conceded, were often rough and imperfect; however, she hoped they would be redeemed by their very spirit of inventiveness and their sincere obedience to "Nature's secret heart," the unseen imperative that she knew she must always follow.

It perplexed her that so few of her countrymen seemed to share her drive toward the exceptional. As the sun went down on Independence Day, precisely a year since she had stood on the Eagle's Nest in Illinois, she mulled over her great grumble against America. On that day, she had seemed to stand on a pinnacle of possibility. America had seemed physically and spiritually limitless, its great promises all irresistibly inviting. Now, however, it seemed equally clear to her that, paradoxically, the very American ideals that seemed to open an upward path for its citizens had reinforced their mediocrity. In all its deference to the common man, America had produced too many incentives for people to remain common. In a hastily scribbled, coarsely metered poem, marred by an ethnic swipe at the immigrant workers who were streaming into Massachusetts, Fuller complained that her country seemed to be a breeding ground, not for noble conquerors, but for self-satisfied day laborers:

> Good night, Fourth July
> I have kept you duly
> Setting myself free
> Even from thee, Amerikey.
> Just so, I trow that wight,
> Julius Cesar hight,
> Who gave this month his name
> Gold letters in a rich frame,
> Would have soared high above the[e],
> Leveling Amerikey,
> And built above a dome
> Such as crowned old Rome
> Fuller of conquered riches
> And adorned with hero niches
> Too high to be reached by Irishmen in ditches.
>
> Yet think not, Ameriky,
> I don't love humanity,
> Nor value independence,
> If it be fact and not pretence
> That you have such a thing:
> I know you have no king,
> But have you noblemen?
> Or have you gentlemen?
> Far more, have you men?
> No! why then, Ameriky,
> I pray you tell me
> Why make you such a noise
> With rockets, guns, and boys!—
> All the use of earth
> Is to god-men to give birth
> And if you cannot say,
> that you've done this, for shame, be still, I pray.[12]

Fuller used the variants "Amerikey" and "Ameriky" not just to produce easier rhymes. The spellings were a mildly derisive nod to the slack, untutored dialect of the working class. Fuller might have said that she was expressing frustration with the failure of ordinary people to embrace the American birthright of freedom and possibility. A more critical observer might simply have called her a snob. Either way, Fuller had concluded that the best way to use the freedoms of "leveling Amerikey" was to free oneself, if only in one's heart and mind, from America; the true task of the free person in a democratic land was to become an aristocrat in the greatness of one's thoughts and actions.

Margaret's urge to greatness, so ordinarily restless, had never been less in keeping with the outward conditions of her life. She was still wrestling with her Uncle Abraham, trying to secure something more than the bare necessities for herself and her siblings. A much-needed distribution was made from Timothy's estate in March 1844, but it totaled only $252.88 per child. Margaret was later to write regarding Abraham, "[H]e, far from aiding, wished to see me fall, because I acted against his opinion in giving my family advantages he thought, with his narrow views, useless, and defended my mother against his cruel tyranny."[13] As the summer heat came on, she passed a series of languorous days in which "[t]here was no flow in the mind, yet matters seemed settling themselves."[14] Quite out of her usual character, she "felt happy that nothing called imperatively to be done—that I was indolent enough to enjoy doing nothing."[15] The season seemed made for nothing better than sitting in the moonlight with friends and talking of dreams.

But restlessness could still burst in on her unawares. On the night of July 5, she was awakened by a howling wind. All at once, her heart was sad, and the world seemed hollow, "but not," she wrote enigmatically, "clear as glass." Her next sentence was still more ambiguous; she wrote, "I will go to bed *for good*." The primary meaning of this statement was not ominous; the context shows that Fuller meant, above all, that she was "usually in a better world when asleep." Yet the suggestion that she might like to sleep forever peered in around the edges. "Life," Fuller had written earlier that day, "begins to press with her iron glove." The next day the sky looked "heavy with sadness." Running errands in the heat made her ill, and the forebodings of the previous night intensified: "There seemed nothing in life worthy [of] the pain & weariness we bear."[16]

She sought out unnerving experiences. Others seemed to find her. She visited the graves of her father and of the sister and brother who had died in infancy, and she reflected on how these were the only persons "with whom I have seen death." One morning beneath her window, she found a dead bird with no visible wound. She kept the little feathered corpse near her for two or three days. "I shall keep its wings," she wrote.[17] Some days later, while taking a morning walk, she came upon an omnibus horse lying exhausted on the road while still in its harness. Although a bystander protested that the creature could not get up by itself, the driver rained blows on the helpless animal, which shuddered at each new assault but could only lay its head low and sigh.[18] Something in the horse's broken spirit called out to Fuller's own state of mind. It was time for flight.

A partial escape came on July 9, when Fuller retreated to the green embrace of Concord. Her sister Ellen, who had settled there with Ellery, had a six-week-old baby, formally named Margaret Fuller Channing but known to all as "Greta." Margaret took greater delight in the Hawthornes' infant red-haired daughter Una, "a most beautiful child . . . as strong as sweet." Fuller's more tender feelings were touched by Ellen Emerson's younger sister Edith. Less robust than the other children Fuller saw during this visit, Edith was a three-year-old "seraph" with a white nightgown and pretty bare feet who seemed "too frail a beauty for this world." The day after Fuller's arrival in town, Lidian Emerson gave Edith a new brother, Edward, and the joy of the birth was clouded only by the inevitable recollections it raised of little Waldo. Fuller feared that Edward would never have a self entirely his own, for he would always be pushed "into the place of our lost darling."[19]

About a week into her visit, Fuller was stirred from sleep before sunrise by the hoarse voice of Thoreau, who stood beneath her window and proposed a boat ride on the river. They drifted for two lazy hours under the early morning sun. Margaret was even more delighted to spend ten days at the Old Manse with Nathaniel and Sophia Hawthorne. Nathaniel had wisely kept his less kindly opinions of Fuller to himself, and relations between them had remained cordial. Still, Fuller's comfort under his roof likely depended on her tiptoeing around certain political subjects. Although Nathaniel was not precisely a friend of slavery, it did not appall him as it did the other Concord writers. As talk began to circulate concerning the annexation of Texas, into which southern politicians planned to extend the reach of slavery, Hawthorne told intimates that he regarded the proposed expansion as "not . . . so much a calamity as others do."[20] Clever and artistically gifted, Sophia never-theless had not a moment's patience with women's rights. Even though she had once delighted in attending Margaret's conversations (which Nathaniel had scorned as "a Babel of talkers"), Sophia had kept politely silent when Margaret turned her spoken sentiments into print in "The Great Lawsuit."[21] In a letter that Margaret thankfully never saw, Sophia referred to her friend as "Queen Margaret" and opined that "if she were married truly, she would no longer be puzzled about the rights of woman."[22]

Luckily, no quarrels seem to have erupted during Margaret's stay. There was no question that Nathaniel and Sophia, who openly adored each other, enjoyed the happiest union among the Concord literati—although the Emer-sons, Alcotts, and Channings offered poor competition. Though the Haw-thornes' bliss struck some as exaggerated and ostentatious, Fuller found only kind words for what she called their "holy and equal marriage."[23] If any-thing pleased her during these days more than seeing the Hawthornes together, it was seeing Nathaniel separately. Fuller loved being charmed by Hawthorne, and Hawthorne loved to be charming. A man of stunning good looks and a studied demeanor of shy sensitivity, he soon drew forth the gush-ing response that Fuller could seldom suppress when she befriended any handsome, intelligent man. After the two had taken a boating excursion of their own, she told her journal:

> I love him much, & love to be with him in this sweet tender homely scene. But I should like too, to be with him on the bold ocean shore. . . . I feel more like a sister to H. or rather more that he might be a brother to me than ever with any man before.[24]

Fuller would have loved Hawthorne less if she had known the opinion he had formed of her. Both in his life and in his writing, Hawthorne displayed a deep knowledge of the artifice by which one creates a character. He sensed an unnatural quality in Fuller, as though she had become the person she was by conscious design, rather than by unaffected means. His later reflections on her were scathing:

> It was such an awful joke, that she should have resolved—in all sin-cerity, no doubt—to make herself the greatest, wisest, best woman of

the age; and, to that end, she set to work on her strong, heavy, unpli-
able, and in many respects, defective and evil nature, and adorned it
with a mosaic of admirable qualities, such as she chose to possess;
putting in here a splendid talent, and there a moral excellence, and
polishing each separate piece, and the whole together, till it seemed to
shine afar and dazzle all who saw it. She took credit to herself for having been her own Redeemer, if not her own Creator; and indeed, she
was far more a work of art than any . . . statue.[25]

Hawthorne's accusation of "evil" was cruel and savagely hyperbolic.
Still, he was very near the truth when he observed the constructed quality of
Fuller's character: her capacity to choose the features she hoped to acquire
and then deliberately, methodically attain them on the way to the crafting of
a reimagined life. Hawthorne failed to appreciate that many of Fuller's reinventions were forced on her; he did not grasp that, as a woman in a masculine era, she was frequently compelled to remake herself in order to fit into
the limited opportunities that were afforded her. One might more readily call
Fuller's will to self-transformation resourceful and heroic. Hawthorne found
it morally unsettling. Say what one might of this reaction, it was at least
consistent with the values expressed in his fiction. Hawthorne's tales warn
repeatedly against the dangers of artifice. The characters who most brazenly
defy the limits and decrees of nature are among his most memorable villains.
They are his Aylmers, his Giacomo Rappaccinis, his Ethan Brands. In Fuller's
belief in her own perfectibility, Hawthorne thought he saw a blasphemous
pride. In what Fuller saw as her defining virtue, Hawthorne discerned the
outlines of unpardonable sin.

Margaret's time at the Old Manse was followed by a week at her sister's
house. Then Fuller went to stay once more with the Emersons. She had seen
Waldo every day during her Concord sojourn. He had all but completed the
set of essays he was preparing to publish as his *Second Series*, and, eager to
hear her judgments, he read extensively to her from his manuscripts. Written under the lingering cloud of his son's death, the essays of the *Second
Series* lacked the ebullient zeal of Emerson's earlier work. It was no accident
that he chose to call the best piece of this sadder and wiser collection
"Experience."

Fuller could only have been pleased that Emerson's work was now moving cautiously but steadily toward an advocacy of equality for women. "A certain awkward consciousness of inferiority in the men," he wrote in his essay on manners, "may give rise to the new chivalry in behalf of Woman's Rights. Certainly, let her be as much better placed in the laws and in social forms, as the most zealous reformer can ask."[26] These were bold, hearty words. One may say with some confidence that, had he never met Fuller, he would never have written them.

At the same time, however, Fuller was troubled to find that Waldo had been driven still further into diffidence by his accumulated sorrows. "How beautiful, and full and grand," she told her journal after he had read her the draft of "Experience," "But oh, how cold."[27] "Experience" is a noble essay, acknowledging life's cruel uncertainties but refusing to bow to them. Yet the essay's very stoicism at last persuaded Fuller, if any persuasion were still required, that the great gap in her mentor's emotional being was beyond repair.

For Fuller, hearing Emerson's new essays felt like "walking in the portico of a temple"—elegant, exquisitely tasteful, but hard and cool as marble. In a letter to him, she set forth the difference that divided them. "You are intellect," she stated, "I am life." She still believed what Emerson could not admit: "Whatever is truly *felt* has some precious meaning." Their friendship had gone as far as it could as an affiliation of mind; as an affinity of two hearts, it had never really begun. In her letter, Fuller noted that nearly eight years had passed since she had first stepped into Emerson's library. Since then, his influence on her had been both immeasurable and "benignant." But she had also asked for an attachment that he was powerless to give. Of such futile demands, she promised there would be "little . . . if any, in future."[28]

As the summer wore on, Fuller became impatient with Concord in general. "Life here," she wrote "slumbers and steals on like the river. A very good place for a sage, but not for the lyrist or the orator." Concord, she punned, was sadly lacking in "the animating influences of Discord."[29] Her tone was that of someone who knows a break is coming and who seeks to prepare herself by disparaging the thing soon to be lost. She was likely imagining herself as a denizen of abundantly discordant Manhattan.

Her last glimpses of the Emersons on this trip prompted mixed emotions. On August 1, she watched as Waldo gave "An Address . . . on . . . the Emancipation of the Negroes in the British West Indies." In his first significant public statement on the slavery question, he told his audience that he was certain that slavery was doomed, that its "coldness and blindness" would pass away, and that a "single noble wind of sentiment" would scatter its tyrannies forever.[30] Margaret thought he had never spoken better; he seemed to have achieved, before her eyes, a "new life and a nobler emulation."[31] When Fuller took her leave on the third, a drizzling rain fell on Concord. Lidian further darkened the scene with her own ideas on slavery, focusing the talk on "stories of Negro suffering" rather than, as Fuller preferred, on "the high and deep thoughts which excused the anguish incident to the history of man." Unable to see Lidian's side, Fuller accused her in her journal of "managing to extract poison from the most healthful plants." To the Goethean Fuller, much blood and pain might be pardoned if they contributed to a nobler idea in the advance of humankind. To the Christian Lidian, no philosophic revelation could compensate for the tears of the helpless. Between the two moral creeds lay every possible difference. When Fuller got up to leave, Waldo remained seated, his eyes cast down. As Fuller pressed his hand to her heart, he looked to her like "the youngest child."[32] Her last extended visit to Concord was over.

Back in Cambridge, Fuller settled in with her mother and Richard. Around the end of August, she received Greeley's formal offer: he would be delighted to engage her as the literary critic of the *Tribune*. With his wife's blessing, Greeley added a further stipulation: if Fuller accepted the offer, she would have to live with them.[33] Despite the editor's manifest generosity, Fuller still held back. One reason for delay was her health. Fuller, who had been revising "The Great Lawsuit" into book form, thought she was only three days from finishing the task when early September brought a blinding headache that did not subside for a fortnight. She called the first week of that month "one of the most suffering" weeks she had ever spent, and she did not dare write further "for fear of exasperating [her] head by thought."[34] She was also in no mood to make a momentous decision. But the pain was not the sole obstacle. On the tenth she awoke "much depressed," not seeing clearly which course to take.[35] In her journal, she noted having written a long letter to Greeley, now lost, but she failed to mention whether that letter contained an acceptance or a refusal. All she wrote regarding her choice was, "I fear it is not the right one."[36]

She tried to forget her anxieties on a four-day visit to Cary Sturgis, who had rented rooms for the summer at Nantasket Beach. But if dreams and maladies offer any clue, the escape did little to soothe her. On the night of the twelfth, she had nightmares of slipping from the rocks and huge spiders running over her, and every time she woke, her head hurt worse. On the fourteenth, feeling well again at last, she returned to Cambridge, only to discover that her letter to Greeley had not been mailed.[37] She did not send it. Her indecision resumed.

Margaret had not fretted so long over a decision since she decided against going to Europe after her father's death. Her agitation was understandable. Greeley's offer was a serious test for her Romantic credo of growth. Thus far she had always been able to pursue her continuing metamorphosis without permanently putting aside the associations that had defined her: her family; the moral and physical landscape of New England; the intellectual company of men like Clarke, Hawthorne, and Emerson. Her growth had always meant acquiring new influences, but seldom had it required walking away from old ones. In 1844, New York was already so different from Boston as to constitute a separate world: less contemplative and emotionally reserved; more fanatical in its pursuit of gain; more chaotic, raw, and tough. The distance was great enough that visits would be few. Then, too, Fuller's journey to New York would be a truly bold step away from traditional female identity. Her conversations, certainly, had always brought her back into a feminine sphere of thought and feeling, and through them she had created a sphere of female intellectualism that had, as yet, no counterpart in New York. Furthermore, no woman had ever before gone to work at the *Tribune*'s offices; until Greeley had sent his offer to her, American newspaper work had been almost exclusively male. Traversing the barrier would call for courage.

Fuller also weighed her decision with the knowledge that she would be leaving behind her a duty that her family had every reason to expect her to fulfill. Among New England families of the time, it was usual for an unmarried daughter to take care of her aging parents. Ellen Tucker Emerson later fulfilled this duty for Waldo and Lidian; Louisa May Alcott was to do so for Bronson and Abba. Fuller was the only member of her family in a position to perform this office for her mother. In this respect as well, Fuller's contemplated move to New York would carry her away from what was expected of her as a woman.

Fuller's revisions of "The Great Lawsuit" were already causing her to think deeply about the arbitrariness of the line that divided masculine and feminine. There was a difference, to be sure, but she could not name the essence in which that distinction lay. As she debated Greeley's offer, Fuller wrote in her journal of a boy baby she saw, who, "in every act and attitude," was thoroughly dissimilar from Una Hawthorne and Greta Channing. "And yet," she queried, "where lies this difference betwixt male and female? I cannot trace it. . . . How all but infinite the mystery by which sex is stamped in the germ. By what modification of thought is this caused? Impossible to trace: here am I the child of masculine energy & [my brother] Eugene of feminine loveliness, & so in many other families."[38] Yes, the difference was there, and impossible to reason or legislate away. But what did it mean? More to the point, what should it be permitted to mean? Perhaps all she could say with certainty was that it must not be allowed to mean limitation. And yet the things that clearly limited a woman's life, particularly her duties to family, had their own satisfactions. In New York there would be no such limits for her, but no such contentments either. Growth was sure to come, but at a cost.

Margaret consulted Eliza Farrar, who had long ago coached Margaret on how to become a lady, and she was perhaps surprised to learn that her old teacher was thrilled with the New York plan. Fuller's brother Richard concurred; he thought the offer was "a leading of Providence."[39] The issue was not decided, though, until, as Fuller was in the midst of helping her mother move to a smaller house, Greeley himself arrived to plead his case. Before he had gone, Margaret had agreed to start work in December "& at least try it."[40] Only after she had made her promise did Fuller go for a weekend to Concord to take the temperature of Emerson and Hawthorne regarding the matter.

Privately, Emerson had his doubts. He later told Sam Ward that, after the lofty aesthetics of the now-defunct *Dial*, the quotidian grind of newspaper work could only strike Fuller as "unworthy." He wrote to Ward, "The muses have feet, to be sure, but it is an odd arrangement that selects them for the treadmill."[41] The idea of New York particularly frightened him. Although he admitted his conviction that the city was destined for "an imperial prosperity," he found that "the air of Wall Street, the expression of the male & female crowd of Broadway, the endless rustle of newspapers" all taught him to cling more tightly than ever to his worship of the wild and sacred muse.[42] Nevertheless, when Fuller put the question to him, he laid aside his cavils and, it appears, offered no opposition to her leaving. Indeed, to his credit, he joined with Hawthorne in telling her that her New York venture was one of "great promise" and that she ought to go.[43] Surprised but grateful for their encouragement, Fuller said another farewell to Concord and wrote a heartfelt quatrain for Emerson in her journal:

> *Winding hence afar,*
> *O mild and steady star,*
> *The oft deserted stream*
> *Will ne'er forget thy silver beam.*[44]

Even after she had begun making arrangements for her journey, though, her nightmares did not cease. In one, her feet seemed rooted to the ground as Caroline, at the seashore, drowned before her eyes. In another came a vision that had haunted her before; she dreamed of her mother's death and burial. Half awake but strangely unable to bring herself into full consciousness, Margaret lay sobbing.[45] Perhaps Fuller merely felt guilty about leaving her mother behind. Yet one might also suppose that, in these dreams that killed those nearest to her, Fuller was laying her old life to rest. One might even argue that, when Margaret's dream-self gazed upon the coffin of Margarett Crane Fuller, it was not truly her mother she was committing to the graveyard, but rather her mother's passive, dependent, flowery ideal of womanhood. More obliquely, this dream recalled as well her earliest memory of all, the funeral of her little sister Julia Adelaide—the first time that Margaret had ever felt small and separate from the world around her.

The days that followed these terrible dreams were filled with touching farewells. The last words written in her journal before her journey south were not in her hand but in her mother's, written for the "dear daughter" whom she still called "Sarah." Mrs. Fuller inscribed her blessing "on this last page of this journal as if it were [her] last" and prayed that God would restore her daughter to her "in his own good time."[46]

On October 4, 1844, Fuller bade farewell to Massachusetts. Although her first stop was the Greeleys' home, she did not stay long. Along with Caroline Sturgis, she took up temporary lodgings on the Hudson River about sixty miles north of the city, in a hamlet then known as Fishkill Landing. She came there both to rest and to perform a necessary task—one that may be seen either as the last act of her old New England life or as the first one performed by her emergent, more independent self. She finished transforming "The

Great Lawsuit" into the book she had chosen to call *Woman in the Nineteenth Century*.[47] The setting in which she made the revisions was everything she hoped for: a place of mountain paths, lonely glens, and rushing streams. From her first walk along the river, Fuller was delighted by the light that played on the water and the surrounding hills. She relished her escape "from hacknied human thoughts and petty cares."[48]

Nevertheless, the work took considerably longer than the anticipated three days. Fuller redacted virtually none of the material that had gone into

Fuller finished *Woman in the Nineteenth Century* while staying with the impulsive, idealistic Caroline Sturgis. Of their times together, Fuller wrote, "[P]leasant is our independent life."

(COURTESY OF THE INTERNATIONAL MUSEUM OF PHOTOG-RAPHY AT THE GEORGE EASTMAN HOUSE, ROCHESTER, N.Y.)

"The Great Lawsuit." She meant not to refashion her arguments, but to supplement them. If "The Great Lawsuit" had been the most audacious statement on behalf of women's rights ever written in America, *Woman in the Nineteenth Century* would be the most comprehensive. Fuller advised Greeley that she could not join the *Tribune* until December. Visions continued to haunt her. She copied into her journal an item from a Poughkeepsie newspaper titled "The Changed," which, she said, "expresses so exactly my thought."

It began: "It not infrequently happens that people, whether it arises from physical or moral causes, become wonderfully unlike themselves. Irritability, violence, indiscretion and unkindness suddenly reveal themselves in a hitherto gentle and amiable character, and, as if by a magic stroke, a beautiful form has been transformed into a witch."[49] Whether the Margaret-to-be was demon or angel, she knew she would not remain the same.

One of the reasons it took her longer than expected to complete her work was that her new environs gave her an unlikely source of new material. Fishkill Landing was not too far distant from Mount Pleasant, the women's division of Sing Sing Prison in Ossining, New York. One general dissatisfaction with "The Great Lawsuit" was that it had focused too exclusively on the intellectual life of Woman. Before she could offer a more comprehensive statement on the nature of Woman, Fuller needed to know more about the forces of passion that drew women away from the fulfillment of their divine destinies. For this reason, she was fascinated with the female inmates of Mount Pleasant, particularly those who had been jailed for prostitution. She had heard about them from her friend Georgiana Bruce, a late resident of Brook Farm who, at Fuller's prompting, had signed on as an assistant to Eliza Farnham, the prison's new matron. Farnham, a liberal reformer, had taken immediate steps to better the moral condition of the prisoners, but prior to her arrival, the more boisterous of the inmates had routinely "made [the] night hideous by singing blasphemous and obscene songs" and had eventually attacked the former matron and ripped her clothes off.[50] Fuller peppered Bruce with questions, mainly in hopes of correcting the images of prostitutes she had absorbed from romantic fiction. She specifically wanted to know what the prisoners thought about chastity. She inquired of Bruce:

> You say few of these women have any feeling about chastity. Do you know how they regard that part of the sex, who are reputed chaste? Do they see any reality in it; or look on it merely as a circumstance of condition, like the possession of fine clothes? You know novelists are fond of representing them as if they looked up to their more protected sisters as saints and angels![51]

Bruce replied in part by sharing some of the inmates' journals. Fuller was particularly impressed with the account given by an African-American woman named Satira, whose "idealizing of herself in the face of cruelest facts" belonged, according to Fuller's estimate, "to the fairest, most abused part of feminine Nature."[52] That Satira could retain a favorable view of herself despite her erstwhile profession and the penal price she had paid for it astonished Fuller. She wanted to know whether the ex-prostitute's self-idealization arose from a moral possibility that Fuller herself had failed to consider. Perhaps chastity was merely an appurtenance of social standing, imbued with only that degree of value which one's fellows were inclined to acknowledge.

Bruce also questioned some of the inmates, though she was skeptical of receiving any honest answers. She was astonished when one of the more intelligent women spoke her mind. Of course, the prisoner explained, "everybody in the world knew that promiscuity was wicked." However, "if no one knew," it was as if the sin did not exist; rather, "you did not seem a bit different from anybody else. In fact, you did not stop to think of yourself at all." It was very curious, the woman reflected, "that your being ashamed was caused by people knowing your life, not by the life itself." The woman added that she and her fellow inmates recognized Mrs. Farnham and Miss Bruce as "good," but only because they were refined, sincere, and unselfish, not for their reputations as "chaste." These observations were far from comfortable for Bruce to contemplate, and she concludes her account of the episode in her memoirs with the peremptory statement, "It is not best to dwell on this subject."[53]

Fuller, however, wished to dwell on the subject as long as she had more to learn, and her education continued when she visited Mount Pleasant less than a month after arriving in New York. She told a group of inmates that she was writing about Woman, and, since her path had been a favored one, she hoped "to ask some information of those who had been tempted to pollution and sorrow." Fuller's record of the women's specific responses, if any, has been lost. However, she observed that her listeners "were among the so called worst, but nothing could be more decorous than their conduct, and frank too." To her evident pleasure, the time passed "much as in one of my Boston Classes."[54] Fuller had suspected that there was much more that united different classes of women than there was to divide them. Before her visit, she had written, "[T]hese women in their degradation express most powerfully the present wants of the sex at large. What blasphemes in them must fret and murmur in the perfumed boudoir, for a society beats with one great heart."[55] Meeting the women face-to-face confirmed her opinion. But the women's indifference to chastity troubled her. She reached for her pen.

As Fuller concluded her work on *Woman in the Nineteenth Century*, the experience she acquired at Mount Pleasant came just in time. Although the focus of her work remained the spirits and intellects of women, she was newly agitated by society's mistreatment of women's bodies. Inspired by what she had seen at the prison, Fuller added a discourse of thirty-seven pages—almost a quarter of the book's total length, not counting its appendices—on the modern world's contempt for chastity. When "The Great Lawsuit" addresses the social disadvantages of women, it most often imagines the typical woman as a middle-class housewife, confined and frustrated by her lot in life but at least not immediately financially threatened. In that essay, the stereotypic man who resists the movement toward equality is an "irritated trader" who fears that women's rights will break up his family.[56] In *Woman in the Nine-teenth Century*, the trader remains, but he has been joined by a more dissolute cousin: a systematic flatterer and breaker of promises, to the likes of whom Fuller attributes the fall of "nine thousand out of the ten [thousand]" mis-guided, maltreated women.[57] Although Fuller had written "The Great Law-suit" with passionate conviction, nothing in that essay had approached the anger with which she now denounced those she held accountable for "the degradation of a large portion of women into the sold and polluted slaves of men."[58] These she berated with the fury of an inflamed prophet:

> Your forms degraded and your eyes clouded by secret sin; natural harmony broken and fineness of perception destroyed in your mental and bodily organization; God and love shut out from your hearts by the foul visitants you have permitted there; incapable of pure mar-riage; incapable of pure parentage; incapable of worship; oh wretched men, your sin is its own punishment![59]

Fuller suspected that such men were beyond her power to influence. Somewhat surprisingly, she directed the great majority of her comments on sexual continence toward other women. She made her appeal, not to the prostitutes themselves, but to those in easier circumstances who had cor-rupted the lower orders by their subtly meretricious examples. In a devastating juxtaposition, Fuller set a description of a fashionable resort for ladies alongside a recollection of her experiences at Ossining. At the former place, she had seen women dressed, "without regard to the season or the demands of the place," in mindless imitation of what was taken to be European fashion. In this parade of folly, jealousy, and vanity, Fuller thought she had witnessed a kind of crime that was not written in any statute book, a crime made all the worse because it was perpetrated by "American *ladies* . . . of that class who have wealth and leisure to make full use of the day, and confer benefits on others."[60] It mattered not to Fuller whether these women might have no lovers other than their husbands. Call them whatever else you might, they were not chaste. She exhorted them to put aside their superficial finery and to "seek out these degraded women, give them tender sympathy, counsel, employment. Take the place of mothers, such as might have saved them originally."[61] Otherwise, the stories of degradation that filled the newspapers would continue to "outshame antiquity, and vie with the horrors of war."[62]

Fuller knew that her defense of chastity would call forth accusations of prudery, especially from "the heart that has once chosen the evil path." She considered such criticisms unfair, for she felt her views on sexual conduct were the very opposite of repression. To her mind, the social machinery that had produced the Satiras of the world had spawned no freedom; it had literally sent them to prison. Moreover, it had engineered "the moral death, the damnation, so far as the action of society can insure it, of thousands of women for each splendid metropolis."[63] But Fuller also looked higher. Her task was the liberation of the human spirit, and she believed that promiscuity was a form of enslavement, chaining both men and women to an inferior concept of themselves. So long as women were treated principally as sexual bodies rather than as genderless souls, Fuller argued, their spiritual destinies could never be fulfilled. "The power of continence," she insisted, "must establish the legitimacy of freedom."[64]

Between the publication of "The Great Lawsuit" and her drafting of *Woman in the Nineteenth Century*, not all of Fuller's thoughts had concerned the sexual abasement of women. She had also thought about little girls she had known whose great delight was to use the carpenter's tools that had been intended for their brothers. "Where these tastes are indulged, cheerfulness and good humor are promoted," she observed. "Where they are forbidden, because 'such things are not proper for girls,' they grow sullen and mischievous." Fuller had seen "the immediate glow and serenity" that came over a woman, previously restless and fretful, who had found even a modest means of expression through building, gardening, and art. Such work, she felt, "draws forth life toward the infinite."[65]

It was a plea that women should be allowed to be useful according to their own terms and talents, that they should be encouraged to find the work they could do best and to do it. With clarity and with confidence that her logic was beyond dispute, Fuller brought *Woman in the Nineteenth Century* toward its close. If only men would remove the arbitrary barriers, Fuller was sure that women would show themselves in all their "native dignity" and in all the variety of their undiscovered skills. Fuller insisted that her appeal was only incidentally on behalf of women.[66] She stood for "the law of right, the law of growth, that speaks in us, and demands the perfection of each being in its kind, apple as apple, woman as woman."[67] What concerned her was simply "that my life be a beautiful, powerful, in a word, a complete life in its kind. Had I but one more moment to live, I must wish the same."[68] She desired this completeness for everyone. Fuller saved for her closing pages the lines that were to become the signature statement of her book: "But if you ask me what offices they [women] may fill; I reply—any. I do not care what case you put; let them be sea-captains, if you will."[69]

The writing of *Woman in the Nineteenth Century* and the experiences that had inspired it marked a turning point in Fuller's thinking. As a younger woman, she had never been political by nature. Indeed, her lack of interest in public affairs had elicited some of her father's most scalding criticism. Her preferred solutions had always been cerebral; the key to life had always lain in the evolution and reform of one's inner consciousness. Fuller still believed in the primacy of one's inner world. However, as her revisions of "The Great Lawsuit" made clear, she was more conscious than before of the ways in which the real world could thwart one's yearnings for perfection. Toward the end of *Woman in the Nineteenth Century*, using the masculine noun but clearly speaking of all humankind, Fuller observed, "To address man wisely, you must not forget that his life is partly animal, subject to the same laws with nature. But you cannot address him wisely unless you consider him still more as soul, and appreciate the conditions and destiny of soul."[70] Fuller's meditations on the imprisonment of the human soul had led her to realize that the spirit could not be separated from the life of the body or from life in society. Her visits to Sing Sing had reminded her that poverty and physical abuse and neglect can destroy a soul as efficiently as any more metaphysical devil. The ends that she now proposed were to be attained not solely through scholarship or Concord-style philosophizing, but also by society's reform. In *Woman in the Nineteenth Century* she evinces the understanding that the spiritual is the social and, as many more in later times would realize, the personal is the political. Her thought was more balanced, practical, and holistic than ever before.

Woman in the Nineteenth Century also signaled a more generally significant broadening, one that affected the cause of women's rights as a whole. To the very limited extent that the condition of women had entered the national discussion before Fuller published her book, the controversy had turned principally on questions of law: the right of married women to own property; the right to divorce and to have custody of children; and, in extremely radical circles, the right to vote. In their very framing, legal questions tended to emphasize the differences between the sexes. Fuller's argument looked beyond these categories. To a wide audience, *Woman in the Nineteenth Century* expressed the conviction that the legal issues, though critical to the advancement of women, were only ancillary to a higher objective: the self-realization of human beings, both male and female. Fuller's book made its greatest contribution to women's rights by setting the terms of this self-realization: it called on its audience to recognize that masculine and feminine are fluid classifications and that talent must be respected and developed without regard to the type of body in which it resides. Fuller had taken the great lesson of her conversations to a more visible place; she had invited the women of her nation to seek their highest worth, and she had challenged men to respect them for it. The later, more widely acknowledged founders of the American women's rights movement, Susan B. Anthony and Elizabeth Cady Stanton, acknowledged Fuller's inspiration, and *Woman in the Nineteenth Century* led them to aver that Fuller had "possessed more influence on the thought of American women than any woman previous to her time."[71]

Carried to the finish line by a final rush of inspiration, Fuller completed the draft of *Woman in the Nineteenth Century* on November 17, 1844. After a long walk on an "exhilarating" morning, she sat down to write and marveled as the words "kept spinning out beneath [her] hand" until, just before nine in the evening, she was done. At last, she felt she had done something worthy of a small slice of immortality. She wrote to William Henry Channing, "I felt a delightful glow as if I had put a good deal of my true life in it, as if, suppose I went away now, the measure of my foot-print would be left on the earth."[72] Her only concern, though it did not much deter her, was her sense that her writing demanded "too much culture in the reader to be quickly or extensively diffused."[73] Yet it probably occurred to her that it had to be so; to claim that women were entitled to civil and economic rights, it was helpful to demonstrate that one woman, at least, was more than the intellectual equal of the sex that already enjoyed them.

She hoped that the book, which was somewhat longer than an issue of *The Dial*, might be out by Christmas. However, although she signed a contract with Greeley's own publishing imprint, Greeley and McElrath, in late November, *Woman in the Nineteenth Century* did not appear until February 16, 1845. The reception was beyond anything Fuller had dared to imagine. She had told Channing that she hoped it might sell a thousand copies in a few years' time. The first edition of fifteen hundred was sold within a week. Though denying that money had been her object, Fuller cheerfully pocketed the eighty-five dollars that came her way and took her popular success as "the most speaking fact" about the book, as well as the one that most pleased her.[74] Meanwhile, although conservative reviewers were quick to chastise her perceived radicalism, more moderate voices praised her as a "thinking, right-judging person" and ranked her achievement with that of the great English rights advocate Mary Wollstonecraft.[75] "The book is . . . the theme of all the newspapers and many of the journals," Fuller reported to her brother Eugene. Sweeter still, she was able to add, "Respect [is] expressed for me personally."[76] In a letter to Cary Sturgis, with a mixture of pride and surprise, Fuller reported seeing placards around New York hailing *Woman in the Nineteenth Century* as the "Great Book of the Age."[77] She was, at last, a literary celebrity.

Though seldom in perfect lockstep and sometimes even seen to be in competition with each other, the struggles for rights for American blacks and American women have frequently taken almost simultaneous steps forward. In 1845, booksellers in the United States were able to offer not one but two groundbreaking polemics on behalf of equality: *Woman in the Nineteenth Century* and the more elaborately titled *Narrative of the Life of Frederick Douglass, an American Slave, Written by Himself.* Fuller reviewed the latter for the

Tribune. At once, she fastened onto the image of Douglass as a representative man and hailed his work "as a specimen of the powers of the Black Race."[78] In this, her own recent work had an affinity with Douglass's; just as Douglass offered himself as the best evidence for proving the humanity of America's slaves, Fuller was her own leading argument for the intellectual power of women. Yet Douglass's work, although it proudly displays its author's highly unusual gifts, at least partially succeeds in representing him as a dark-skinned everyman. Rooted in vividly reconstructed experience, the *Narrative* elevates Douglass's personal sufferings into a synecdoche for the miseries of an enslaved nation. By contrast, Fuller's striking intellectual performance in *Woman in the Nineteenth Century* only widened the perceived gap between the author and the other women of her time.

In the piece on Fuller that he included in *The Literati of New York City*, no less an observer than Edgar Allan Poe crystallized the issue. Acknowledging Fuller for her "high genius," he wrote, "*Woman in the Nineteenth Century* is a book which few women in the country could have written, and no woman in the country could have published, with the exception of Miss Fuller." Removed from its context, his statement sounds like high praise, yet in it Poe framed what he saw as the besetting problem of the work. He added, "Miss Fuller has erred . . . through her own excessive objectiveness. She judges *woman* by the heart and intellect of Miss Fuller, but there are not more than one or two Miss Fullers on the whole face of the earth."[79] Instead of seeing Fuller as an example of what women, with education and encouragement, might become, Poe could only regard her as an anomaly.

Another crucial difference between Douglass's work and Fuller's lay in their respective emotional impacts. Both Douglass and Fuller were riveting speakers, but only Douglass was consistently adept in transmuting his verbal panache into passionate writing. As Fuller noted in her review of his *Narrative*, Douglass's "feelings and . . . adventures that have been so affecting through the living voice . . . are [no] less so from the printed page."[80] Cary Sturgis, who knew Fuller as well as anyone, felt the lack of a similar impassioned force in her friend's volume. She lamented, "There seems to be a want of vital powers, as if you had gathered flowers and planted them in a garden but had left the roots in their own soil. [Your pamphlet] is full of suggestions . . . but one living child is worth a whole series of tableaux. It is not a book to take to heart, and that is what a book upon woman should be."[81] Fuller might reasonably have replied that "a book to take to heart" was precisely what *Woman in the Nineteenth Century* could not afford to be—that a more emotional treatment of her subject would have called forth damning accusations of womanish sentimentality. Instead, she humbly conceded that what Sturgis had said of her book was "very true, mostly."[82] Still, Fuller was able to bear her friend's critique with grace, in large part because her spirits had been lifted "by the ardent interest it excites in those who have never known me." She added, "Those, you know, are the persons to whom it is addressed, and they do feel their wounds probed, and healing promised by it."[83] Fuller knew that she had given both genuine comfort and a necessary voice to women who craved the freedom to explore their talents and live as their divine natures directed them. Not surprisingly, after she finished *Woman in the Nineteenth Century*, her headaches diminished and she felt "most unusually well."[84] Her cup was full.

CHAPTER NINE

LOVER AND CRITIC

*It is great sin even to dream of wishing
for less thought, less feeling than one has.*

—MARGARET FULLER TO JAMES NATHAN,
February 22, 1845

*[W]hen . . . over intellectual beings do swerve
aside, it is to fall down a precipice, for their narrow
path lies over such.*

—MARGARET FULLER, *Summer on the Lakes*

*A*S FULLER READIED *WOMAN IN THE NINETEENTH CENTURY* FOR publication—and as she prepared herself for her new career as a New York newspaperwoman—she read with deep interest Emerson's newly published *Essays, Second Series*. The book, indeed, was the very first that she was to review for Greeley's *Tribune*. Initially, Emerson's essays seemed somehow out of place in the world. They seemed to have so little natural feeling that Fuller could not read them outdoors, but they "did not chime with in-door life either."[1] Eventually, though, she softened. She wrote Emerson that she found in his new book "more glow, more fusion" than in the first series and declared her expectation that these new essays would be "a companion through [her] life."[2] Yet not all the companionship Fuller found there was perfectly congenial. Among the collection was one piece, an essay called "Character," that she could hardly have helped but find pertinent to her own situation. The essay begins with a litany of personages whose achievements, in Emerson's view, fell short of their acknowledged genius; there was something greater in them as spirits and people than what they had been able to express in words and actions. Emerson did not believe that the disparity between reputation and deeds could be explained merely by observing that "the reverberation is longer than the thunder-clap."[3] Rather, there was something in them that produced expectations that outran their best performances. Therefore, the largest part of their power remained latent. This unexercised power was what Emerson defined as character, a kind of reserved, undemonstrable force "by whose impulses the man is guided, but whose counsels he cannot impart."[4]

When Fuller first read her friend's words, the publication of *Woman in the Nineteenth Century* was still months away. As she was uncomfortably aware, her friend might well have added her own name to his list of underachievers. As no one knew better than she, Fuller had thus far succeeded more at being than at doing. In 1842, she had confessed feeling that "the darkest hue on my own lot is that I have neither children, nor yet am the parent of beautiful works by which the thought of my life might be represented to another generation." With something approaching anger—and with a hint of exaggeration—she reflected, "I have not lived my own life, neither loved my own love; my strength, my sympathies have been given to others; their lives are my aims."[5]

Some of her incentive for pursuing a new life in New York certainly had to do with changing that pattern. Her desire to live for herself had never been stronger. Yet she also knew that her work for an important newspaper would allow her to add to the general quality of American intellectual life as she had never done before. She rightly perceived that newspapers were remaking the country, giving its citizens something unprecedented: a shared, continually self-renewing culture of print. Near the end of her time in New York, Fuller reflected on the minor revolution that newspapers had been propelling:

> The life of intellect is becoming more and more determined to the weekly and daily papers, whose light leaves fly so rapidly and profusely over the land. . . . This mode of communication is susceptible of great excellence in the way of [the] condensed essay, narrative, criti-

cism, and is the natural receptacle for the lyrics of the day. . . . The means which this organ affords of diffusing knowledge and sowing the seeds of thought where they may hardly fail of an infinite harvest, cannot be too highly prized.[6]

Fuller saw in the rise of print journalism nothing less than the chance to serve "the grand purposes of Destiny."[7] She believed not only that newspaper writing was similar to conversation, her preferred way to communicate, but also that it made conversation possible on a far grander scale. Through her

Horace Greeley's house, where Fuller lived for most of her time in New York, looked out on the idyllic vistas of Turtle Bay. She observed, "I have never been so well situated."
(COURTESY OF THE GREATER ASTORIA HISTORICAL SOCIETY)

columns, Fuller could "address, not our neighbor, who forces us to remember his limitations and prejudices, but the ideal presence of human nature. . . . We address America rather than Americans."[8] As she had done at *The Dial*, Fuller was taking a place in the vanguard of the nation's thought.

The New York to which Margaret Fuller came in late November 1844 was, as it has been throughout much of its existence, both irresistibly enticing and faintly horrifying. It has been estimated that, in the year of Fuller's arrival, one percent of the city's population controlled half its wealth. In the stately homes around Washington Square Park, the parlors resounded with music and laughter. Not too far away, in Five Points, the shadows concealed drunkards and thieves. Blaming immigration instead of class stratification for the city's hard times, nativists railed against Catholicism and the thousands of Irish who had recently come to build new lives. Street gangs routinely set upon each other with brickbats and clubs. Less than a year before Fuller arrived, the state government had reorganized the city's police into a semi-military force that some referred to as a civic army. Its effect on the perceived upsurge in lawlessness was hard to judge.[9]

This was the Manhattan that Walt Whitman, then a poor boarding-house denizen and sometime newspaper editor, hailed rhapsodically as "the great place of the Western Continent, the heart, the brain, the focus, the main spring, the pinnacle, the extremity, the no more beyond of the new world."[10] Less impressed, Herman Melville saw a city enslaved to capital, populated by drudges "tied to counters, nailed to benches, clinched to desks."[11] Still more wretched were those unable to find a bench or counter, the destitute, "diseased-looking men and women" who seemed to have emerged from "some unmentionable cellar."[12] New York was, in the words of Fuller's friend and fellow reformer Lydia Maria Child, a "great Babylon" where crushing poverty and sybaritic wealth stood virtually side by side. Child observed a blind African-American beggar, crouching in tatters and holding out a calloused hand only minutes from Wall Street, where Mammon "coolly calculate[d] his chance of extracting a penny from war, pestilence, and famine." Child could bring the two worlds together only through alliteration; she framed the city as a strange, immense canvas of "magnificence and mud, finery and filth, diamonds and dirt."[13]

As she moved around the city, Fuller saw "victims of vice" literally lying in the gutters. She was more deeply saddened by the ones who fought to rise out of abjection but lost, falling back beneath the indifference of the restless city.[14] Nevertheless, Fuller enjoyed living there. She was glad to have found a place where the currents of life flowed freely, and, if there was "wickedness and wretchedness" in New York, she considered it no worse than Boston's "pettiness and coldness."[15] She also took comfort in the fact that all the hub-bub gave her no time to think about being alone. New York, then as now, can either intimidate or invigorate. It invigorated Fuller. Although a bout of flu in early January temporarily weakened her body and spirits, her health remained "most unusually good."[16]

According to Caroline Sturgis, Fuller had embarked on a new era.[17] If those who populated her new life were less moral and less poetical than those who had previously helped to form her character, they were also more varied and more forceful. If at times they shocked her with their energy and lack of reserve, it pleased her that they lacked the Puritanism that drained some of the vigor from the New England soul. All in all, she felt she had never been so well situated.[18]

Fuller especially relished her situation in Greeley's house, which he jokingly called "the Farm," in the Turtle Bay neighborhood of Manhattan. In later decades, the area was fated to become decidedly less picturesque. After the Civil War it would become best known for its railroad piers and slaughterhouses. In the 1840s, however, it remained, in the words of Lydia Maria Child, "as rural as you can imagine." As she put it, the Greeleys had "a very old house, with a very old porch, and very old vines, and a very old garden."[19] Child used the phrase "very old" three more times before ending her sentence.

The lane that led to the Greeleys' home extended for almost a quarter mile, and callers passed a small brook and pond before they came into view of the spacious house, framed amid shrubs and vines.[20] The mellow-tinted wooden structure, situated on approximately eight acres of land amid tall, sheltering trees, had only lately become the Greeleys' home. The editor had been tired out by the just-concluded presidential campaign, in which he had toiled without success for the election of Henry Clay, and he wanted a place of rustic quiet in which to regain his strength.[21] About two miles from the settled part of the city but readily accessible by omnibus, the Farm was a handsome, if slightly broken-down retreat.

Fuller herself found the house dilapidated and noted that the Greeleys' theory of housekeeping was patterned on "a Castle Rackrent style."[22] In addition, Greeley's wife, Mary, was no easy housemate. Possessed of a violent temper, Mrs. Greeley was given both to hypochondria and to outbursts of eccentric self-righteousness. One day, for example, she touched the leather glove on Margaret's hand and said, condemningly, "Skin of a beast! Skin of a beast!" Not to be outdone, Margaret touched her accuser's silken glove and cried out, "Entrails of a worm!"[23] Mary and Horace fought savagely at times, and it surprised no one that Mr. Greeley preferred keeping long hours at the *Tribune* office to submitting to Mary's "wild nature."[24]

Nevertheless, the Greeleys expressed sincere affection for Fuller and were eager to make her feel at home, and this generous spirit excused their sins against tidiness and decorum. The general shabbiness and chaos of the house were also offset by the beauty of its surroundings. The Greeleys' piazza nearly touched the East River, and they had a fine view of Blackwell's Island. Fuller's room looked out on a little woody knoll that ran down into the water, and a steady stream of ships and boats passed beneath her view. She had a particular fondness for a great willow tree outside her window, which shook its "long graceful locks" with what sounded like "deep sighs." Fuller liked to imagine that the tree could somehow know what it meant to her human heart.[25]

As time went by, she found her friendship with Greeley himself every bit as rewarding. Both as a friend and as an employer, he shared with her a wealth of goodwill and respect. In addition, more than anyone she had previously known, he was capable of opening her mind to new ideas. She considered him, apart from her mother, "the most disinterestedly generous person" she had ever known.[26] Greeley, for his part, was slower to warm to Fuller. One reason was simply that it took him several months after her arrival to get to know her. One might think that, sharing both a roof and a workplace, the editor and his literary critic would have suffered from too much contact, rather than too little. However, as he reminisced about Fuller after her death, Greeley recalled that, for quite some time, they barely had breakfast together.

When they did, the conversations could be frosty. A devotee of dietary reformer Sylvester Graham, Greeley was appalled by Fuller's eating habits, which he blamed for her chronic ill health. He especially deplored her apparent addiction to strong tea and coffee. One morning when Fuller came to breakfast complaining of an intense headache, Greeley accused her of having overindulged in tea the night before. Fuller snapped back that she "declined being lectured on the food or beverage she saw fit to take."[27] Greeley stayed off the subject thereafter, though their dispute continued long afterward by way of "looks and involuntary gestures."[28] It was perhaps well that, alternately immersed in her editorial work and in the novel sights and sounds of the city, Fuller had little time for small talk with her famous landlord.

Almost from the moment of her arrival, the city did much to satisfy Fuller's incessant craving for stimulation and growth. Yet this period of excitement and discovery came at a price that she had never before been forced to pay. While in New England, she could pursue her editorial and scholarly work and enjoy the company of the best minds of Cambridge and Concord, all the while taking pleasure in her wider circle of friends and seeing to the needs of her mother. Fuller's relocation to New York shattered this configuration. She was never to piece it together again. While she welcomed the challenges and opportunities of her new life, she also realized that she could no longer be the same person to many of those for whom she deeply cared. She was fully conscious that, once she was settled at the *Tribune*, "a noble career" at last lay open to her, and she wanted every opportunity to seize it.[29] She had been in New York for less than two months when she confessed to her brother Richard:

> I am very busy, and I receive, now I am separated from all my friends, letters in great number, which I do not attempt to answer, except in urgent cases. Nor do they expect it. . . . They know that, if I had the time and strength which I have not, I must not fritter away my attention on incessant letter writing. I must bend it on what is before me, if I wish to learn or do.[30]

When the first delivery of this message failed to strike home with her brother, she put it to him with even greater bluntness two months later:

> I want to be unimpeded by cares which I cannot, at this distance, attend to properly. I want that my friends should *wish* me now to act in my public career rather than towards them personally. I have given almost all my young energies to personal relations. I no longer feel inclined to do this, and wish to share and impel the general stream of thought.[31]

Fuller had reached a critical moment at which further learning and doing required, not a return to the foundations of her earlier life, but a conscious rejection of them. Ambition and the urge to discover pressed her forward.

Only occasionally, Fuller wrote, did she even have time to miss anyone.[32] During 1845, her first year in New York, she sent only one known letter each to the Hawthornes and Anna Ward, and only three to Caroline Sturgis. It seems evident, too, that Margaret's departure from New England widened the emotional distance between her and Emerson. After settling into work for Greeley at the beginning of December, Fuller sent Emerson a single, terse letter over the next nineteen months; if he sent her any letters at all over the same period, she did not keep them.

Sparse and aloof as her correspondence with New England became, however, there was a private side of Margaret that found separation more difficult. She decorated her room in Greeley's house with pictures of her parents that she had carried with her ever since Timothy's death. As a fire blazed in her bedroom's hearth, she would look at these pictures in the evening light, feeling "the want of the soft mother's arms, and father's sheltering breast, and the music of love's heartbeat tuned to perfect melody."[33] Though she tried to look principally forward, the old Margaret stubbornly remained, and her oldest affections pulled her into the past.

Yet, she insisted, her new circles satisfied her wants.[34] Indeed, it was these wants themselves that had been transformed. Fuller's great but realizable ambition was to use her position at the *Tribune* to help foster a new American literary culture. She could not have chosen a better time. The age of the Knickerbocker author—the genteel, conservative Anglophile who considered it gauche to write for money—was gradually coming to an end. For the first time in its existence, New York in the 1840s played host to a generation of young intellectuals whose livelihood was founded on literature.[35] Fuller met many of them on Saturday evenings, when the slender, dark-haired poet Anne Charlotte Lynch opened her doors at 116 Waverly Place to receive the rising literary lions of the city. The daughter of an Irish patriot who had died when she was not yet five, Lynch was not fabulously wealthy. However, she possessed magnetic charm and a refined intellect that drew others toward her. Fuller professed not to like Lynch's parties, where she claimed to encounter "too much second hand literary gossip," yet she found her way to Waverly Place again and again, and with good reason.[36] Although Lynch, who called friendship her "mental sustenance," invited only the most select company to her soirées, no one ever seems to have accused her of social climbing or pretension. Apart from tea and cookies, she offered her guests "no entertainment except what they find in each other."[37] What they found was extraordinary. Greeley was often there. One was also likely to catch a glimpse of the poet William Cullen Bryant, the novelist Catharine Maria Sedgwick, *Evening Mirror* editor Nathaniel Parker Willis, and the Kentucky abolitionist Cassius M. Clay. When there was enough room, the guests danced quadrilles and polkas. When there was not, they sat on the crowded stairs and sated one another with talk. On a given evening, one might be treated to a violin performance by the renowned Ole Bull, whom Fuller praised in her journals, or hear frequent attendee Edgar Allan Poe, in his soft, gentlemanly voice, recite his new, wildly popular poem, "The Raven."

Fuller was obviously intrigued by Poe, though she was never able to penetrate much beyond his courtly façade. To her, he seemed always to be "shrouded in an assumed character," and though Fuller conceded that women were often attracted by the illusions he built up around himself, she suspected that, in truth, he had no friends.[38] Certainly, she did not become one; indeed, she had a nasty tangle with him over his disrespectful treatment of a woman.[39] Poe, a married man, had been attracted to the popular poet Frances Sargent Osgood, a married woman who had separated from her husband. Not only did Poe publish a somewhat scandalous valentine poem for Osgood, praising her "luminous eyes, / Brightly expressive as the twins of Lœda," but also he refused to return a packet of ill-advised letters that Osgood had sent him and now feared would compromise her.[40] Without Osgood's sanction, Fuller, accompanied by Lynch and another friend, Elizabeth Ellet, presented themselves unannounced at Poe's cottage in the Bronx and demanded the packet. Poe refused, but the incident was not over. Ellet's brother later turned up at the cottage as well and threatened the poet with a pistol, and Osgood's estranged husband threatened legal action. Cooler temperaments finally prevailed. Incensed at Fuller's effrontery, Poe thereafter pronounced her a "busybody."[41] She also became an irresistible target for his satirically descriptive pen. The description of her that he included in his *Literati of New York City* is one of the deftest and most subtly damning sketches of her ever written:

> She is of the medium height; nothing remarkable about the figure; a profusion of lustrous light hair; eyes a bluish gray, full of fire; capacious forehead; the mouth when in repose indicates profound sensibility, capacity for affection, for love—when moved by a slight smile, it becomes even beautiful in the intensity of this expression; but the

upper lip, as if impelled by the action of involuntary muscles, habitually uplifts itself, conveying the impression of a sneer. Imagine, now, a
person of this description looking you at one moment earnestly in the
face, at the next seeming to look only within her own spirit or at the
wall; moving nervously every now and then in her chair; speaking in
a high key, but musically, deliberately, (not hurriedly or loudly) with a
delicious distinctness of enunciation—speaking . . . words . . . not by
impulsion of breath . . . but by drawing them out as long as possible,
nearly closing her eyes the while—imagine all this, and we have both
the woman and the authoress before us.[42]

Fuller came to Lynch's salons less to see Poe than to spend time among
the adherents of Young America, a literary circle that Evert Duyckinck had
cofounded with Cornelius Mathews in 1839. The group patterned itself
after Young Italy, the democratic movement led by Giuseppe Mazzini, and it
was likely through the Young Americans that Fuller first became interested
in Mazzini's efforts to revolutionize Italian society. The Young Americans
quarreled among themselves on the question of slavery and for the most
part were unimpressed by New England transcendentalism. They were
united, however, by their desire to create a national literature that would
break once and for all with European tradition. They sought to write works
that would, in the words of *Democratic Review* editor John L. O'Sullivan,
"breathe the spirit of our republican institutions [and] be imbued with the
God-like aspiration of intellectual freedom—the elevating principle of
equality."[43]

Just as Fuller was getting to know Young America, it was beginning to
undergo a wrenching schism. A political wing of the movement had started
down an imperialist path; committed to aggressive westward expansion and
supportive of the looming war with Mexico, it espoused much of what Fuller
found most heinous in American politics. However, the more artistic faction
of Young America, led by Duyckinck, stood strongly committed to literature
as an engine for spreading democracy and equal rights. Duyckinck himself,
who had admired *Summer on the Lakes*, followed her work at the *Tribune*. He
eventually declared his faith in her by publishing her *Papers on Literature and
Art* in his landmark series, The Library of American Books.[44]

Either at a Valentine's Day party thrown by Lynch in 1845 or at a Fourierist convention some time earlier, Fuller made the acquaintance of Marcus and Rebecca Buffum Spring, a wealthy Quaker couple devoted to social reform.[45] They had much to talk about; the Springs were good friends of the Greeleys and had contributed considerably to the financial support of Brook Farm. A

Originally appearing in *Le Diable à Paris: Paris et les Parisiens*, this caricature was not meant by its creator, Paul Gavarni, to represent Fuller. However, it was published in the *Broadway Journal* of March 8, 1845, along with a negative review of *Woman in the Nineteenth Century*. Edgar Allen Poe wrote a caption linking the image to Fuller and declared, "The portrait will be recognized the world over."
(COURTESY OF THE NEW YORK PUBLIC LIBRARY)

frequent guest at the Springs' impressively appointed home in Brooklyn, Fuller became a favorite of the couple, who not only encouraged her to examine social causes that she later endorsed in her *Tribune* columns, but also offered welcome financial relief when her expenditures outran her paycheck.

Given the tremendous amount of writing that Fuller completed during her time in New York, it seems marvelous that she had any time at all to engage with the city's literary lions. Between December 1844 and early August 1846, she published approximately 250 pieces in the *Tribune*. While some were only a paragraph or so in length, the more typical essay ran to several pages. When one considers as well the tremendous amount of reading Fuller had to do in order to write her literary reviews, one can only conclude that her workload was truly staggering. At the outset of her tenure at the *Tribune*, matters were made worse by Fuller's decidedly non-journalistic writing habits. Editing a quarterly review in no way prepared her for the slam-bang deadlines of a daily paper, and Greeley was initially exasperated by the tardiness of Fuller's muse. "She could write only when in the vein," he later bemoaned, "and this often needed to be waited for through several days, while the occasion sometimes required an immediate utterance." Greeley himself had learned "to write at any time, on any subject," his speed limited only by his physical ability to form letters with his rapidly moving pen. In Fuller's preference to wait for better health, "a brighter day, or a happier frame of mind," Greeley feared the makings of disaster.[46]

Fuller did eventually adapt to the discipline of the newsroom. Although, on occasion, tortuous Germanic sentences continued to plague her style, she began to exert a strong influence on popular opinion, both in New York and, thanks to the paper's innovative, nationally distributed weekly edition, across New England, the Great Lakes, and the Ohio Valley. She had a great deal to say, much of it aimed at encouraging an authentically American literary culture. For despite the steady stream of books for her to review, the cultural atmosphere in which she was forced to labor remained lamentably thin. When, for example, she wrote a critique of Robert Browning's poetry, she could not even obtain a copy of his "Paracelsus" and was forced to base her observations on distant memories. His "Sordello" she had never seen at all, though she boldly hazarded a critique founded on reports that others had given her.

As to her audience, she did not veil her condescension toward the typical American reader, whom she described in her column as "not generally prepared by early training for the enjoyment of books that require attention and reflection." She was still less charitable toward the great majority of her country's writers and speakers, whom she accused of having lent "all their efforts to flatter corrupt tastes and mental indolence, instead of feeling it their duty to admonish the community of the danger and arouse it to nobler energy."[47]

As a first step toward redeeming the country from its artistic and literary deficiencies, Fuller began her work at the *Tribune* as she had done at *The Dial*: by publishing a miniature manifesto on the duties of an educated person in a comparatively unlettered society. The person of genius or talent, she urged, should take upon himself "a sacred commission. He is the natural priest, the shepherd of the people. He must raise his mind as high as he can toward the heaven of truth, and try to draw up with him those less gifted by nature with ethereal lightness."[48] Whoever used his superior abilities instead to further confirm others in their mental poverty, Fuller maintained, was false to God and man. Fuller, as a literary critic, aspired to be true to both. In a letter to James Freeman Clarke, she spoke of her desire to use her position to bring people together into a community of cultural discourse and understanding; she said that she "never regarded literature merely as a collection of exquisite products, but rather as a means of mutual interpretation." Granted, Fuller had traded her voice for a pen in her task of "aid[ing] in the great work of popular education," but she was still intent on leading the conversation.[49] Desiring that readers should know more about her opinions than her identity, she "signed" her columns not with her name, but with a small black star. The star kept its secret on only a superficial level; anyone who asked to whom it belonged was freely told. Indeed, the star became a part of Fuller's journalistic persona, both teasingly concealing her and calling attention to her uniqueness. Though it befuddled some—one reader wrote to laud her "bold and manly independence"—Fuller's star also proclaimed her forthright ambition.[50] Quite literally, she meant to be and soon became the "star" of Greeley's *Tribune*.

In her search for truth and beauty, Fuller reviewed writing of all genres. She also ranged further, commenting with equal confidence on violin recitals, symphonic and operatic performances, paintings, and museum exhibits. When she approved of a work, she could be ecstatic, as when she ranked the English poet Elizabeth Barrett Browning "above any female writer the world has yet known," or when she hailed a new edition of Shelley's poems as the work of "an incarnation of what was sought in the sympathies and desires of instinctive life, a light of dawn."[51] In the main, however, her evaluations were more balanced. She never bowed down before an established reputation, and even close personal ties did not shield an author from her frankness. Her notice regarding Hawthorne's brilliant volume of short stories, *Mosses from an Old Manse*, admired the author's "gentle and sincere companionship with Nature" and "delicate but fearless scrutiny of the secrets of the heart." In almost the same breath, however, she arraigned her friend for a lack of definiteness. "Hawthorne intimates and suggests," she complained, "but he does not lay bare the mysteries of our being."[52] Emerson, too, felt the lash of her exacting critique. Though her review of his new volume of essays was mostly favorable, she also opined that Emerson had "never written one good work, if such a work be one where the whole commands more attention than the parts."[53]

Other budding icons of the American literary scene, especially the so-called Fireside Poets, fared far worse. It made no difference to Fuller that young James Russell Lowell had been "extravagantly lauded" in New England literary circles or that the intensely popular Henry Wadsworth Longfellow had "receive[d] honors which should be reserved for the highest."[54] If she honestly found that the former was "absolutely wanting in the true spirit and tone of poesy" or that the latter was essentially an imitative genius, "the greater part of [whose] mental stores were derived from the works of others," she did not hesitate to say so.[55]

Perhaps Fuller was not fully conscious of the pain she could inflict with an overly blunt remark; more likely, she was too principled in her role as critic to greatly care. In either case, her refusal to soften her rhetoric made her some durable enemies. Emerson, well familiar with his friend's acid tongue and pen, did not react. Longfellow's skin was thinner; he wrote bitterly in his journal of Fuller's "bilious attack" and called her "a dreary woman."[56] Lowell was considerably less restrained. In 1848, after Fuller had gone to Europe and could no longer easily return fire, he published a book-length poem called *A Fable for Critics*, in which he satirized all the leading American writers of the moment. For the most part, Lowell's jibes were lighthearted, but when he came to Fuller he could not suppress his spleen. He made clear that she was, in his view, a monument to vanity and condescension, "the whole of whose being's a capital I." She exhausted everyone but herself in "asking if [they] don't observe a / Particular likeness 'twixt her and Minerva." Her prose, Lowell quipped, was quite apt at sounding the depths, "for 'tis one of the functions of lead." Lowell concluded his skewering of Fuller by mocking her "I-turn-the-crank-of-the-Universe air / And a tone which, at least to my fancy, appears / Not so much to be entering as boxing your ears."[57]

Unlike the self-avenging Lowell, however, Fuller never intended a personal affront in her reviews. She meant only to reserve her praise for the most deserving work and to chide those who, though blessed with talent, made more trifling use of it than they might. Apart from their consistent aspiration to seek and praise the highest aims and qualities of art, no particular critical agenda immediately announced itself in Fuller's columns. With time, however, a devoted reader might have observed a handful of abiding principles. Like Emerson, she was pained by the failure of America to create its own distinct artistic forms. Despite flashes of artistic promise, the country had failed to accurately comprehend its own potential. Fuller's indictment of America as a home for artists ran thus:

> She is vain. Her pothooks and trammels are of giant size, Cyclopean promise, but she insists that they are also of as refined beauty as Raphael's drawings. The more she does so the more she is laughed at, of course. Beside [sic], she is often servile. She copies Europe and tries to hide it. She is afraid of Europe, and puts on airs of "independence." *Then* she is sneered at of course.[58]

Fuller hoped for, but did not dare to expect, a great American poet who would not succumb either to slavish imitation or to infantile rebellion. She had a few ideas as to what this poet might look like.

Her own occasional excesses as a writer notwithstanding, Fuller respected clean, simple style. When a master writes, she asserted, "there is no self-indulgence, no slovenliness, the thing is clearly said and fully said."[59] Still, she was seldom satisfied with a mere display of talent; she favored work that came not merely from "the man of ideas," but also from "the ideal man"; the "heart and genius of human life" should be visible on the page.[60] A poet earned her favor by being "at home in the Universe," observing its laws and sympathizing with its motions.[61] Fuller looked imaginatively forward to a time when men's lives would be all poetry, when every act would reveal beauty and all speech would be music. Until then, she wrote, poets were necessary—not merely people who understood the rules of versification, but people who had souls "from which metres grow as acorns from the oak."[62]

To a degree almost unfathomable to a modern critic, Fuller was deeply concerned with the moral tendencies of a writer's work. For instance, while she marveled at Balzac for his "quickness and fidelity of eye" and his perfect diagnoses of "the symptoms of human passions," she was appalled by his refusal to make ethical judgments. "He has no hatred for what is loathsome," she wrote with astonishment, "no contempt for what is base, no love for what is lovely, no faith in what is noble. To him there is no virtue and no vice." Such technical skill wedded to such amorality seemed almost satanic to Fuller; she finally thrust his work aside as "suicidal."[63]

For a woman who had spent much of her life striving to break down barriers, Fuller's moral conservatism can seem surprising. However, it was actually integral to her particular vision of social reform. Eager as she was to sweep away the features of existing institutions that held women in their place, she also believed that codes of manners and morals needed to exist if society were to retain any structure at all. Over meals at his home in Turtle Bay, Greeley habitually sparred with Fuller over what he saw as a glaring inconsistency in her politics: although he agreed with her that women should have the freest access to all stations and professions, he bristled at her insistence that they should also be entitled to special deference and courtesy as women. Greeley thought that, as long as ladies needed the arms of gentlemen to lead them out of a dining room, equal opportunities in the workplace and the legislature would remain a mirage.[64] Fuller, to the contrary, feared a world in which competition would become too free and equal. She saw no true liberty in a no-holds-barred state of nature. Here, indeed, was what troubled her most about Balzac: she saw in him the character of a dispassionate scientist, to whom "noble and tender conduct is more agreeable than the reverse, because it argues better health; that is all."[65] More than a decade before Darwin published *On the Origin of Species*, Fuller was anticipating the social applications of natural selection with slowly mounting worry.

Sensing the need to resist the brutal implications of a freely competitive society, Fuller used her *Tribune* columns to observe social ills and their attempted remedies. At Greeley's suggestion, Fuller continued the practice she had begun at Sing Sing, visiting and reporting on the institutions that had been built to save New York from itself: the madhouses, poorhouses, and penitentiaries of the growing Gotham. Under "leaden and lowering" skies in the last days of winter, 1845, Fuller braved piercing winds to judge for herself how the city cared for its most miserable. The almshouse at Bellevue was surprisingly clean and comfortable, though Fuller worried over the state of forced idleness to which the inmates were consigned. With no other work than raising vegetables for the establishment and making and mending their own clothes, the men especially had acquired "the most vagrant, degraded air," and Fuller suspected that they had become easy prey to "every bad habit."[66] An open boat then carried Fuller to the Farm School, an orphanage located, as the name suggests, on a small farm where the children were given a basic education before being bound out, at the age of twelve, to various types of work. Again, Fuller was put off by the general climate of idleness. She could see no reason why on a farm, where there were always chores to be done, the staff had found no useful labor for the children's bodies as well as their minds. Worse, the unformed features and mechanical movements of the children testified that they were being treated "wholesale," with no consideration given to their individual talents and needs.[67]

From the Farm School, Fuller moved on to the Asylum for the Insane, an institution for the indigent whose unimaginative name fit too well with the thoughtless treatment its inmates received. Here, she descended deeper into the pit. Not only did she find the same disregard for individuals, but also terrible cases of illness and neglect. "Stupid, wild, or despairing," madmen crouched in corners and failed to return her well-intentioned gaze. They had "no heart for hope, no . . . expectation of light." Attendants stood by "with faces brutal and stolid." A gray-haired woman who had gone mad while preparing to be a nun sat on the floor, endlessly chanting the Catholic service.[68]

Lowest of all stood the penitentiary on Blackwell's Island, which she called "one of the gloomiest scenes that deforms this great metropolis." She believed that the seven hundred women she saw there could not possibly be so bad as to deserve so much disdain, or that society itself was so good that it could thus condemn them. Lover of Dante that she was, Fuller argued that a prison should not be an Inferno. Rather, it ought to be a purgatory: a place for keeping its inmates temporarily away from the corrupt-ing conditions in the outside world that had produced them, as well as a place where the lost might still find their souls again. She saw many pris-oners in whom the feelings of innocent childhood were still alive and who, she thought, needed "only good influences and steady aid to raise them from the pit of infamy."[69]

In the twenty-seven-hundred-word essay about her tour that she wrote for the *Tribune*, Fuller enumerated three reforms she thought would imme-diately improve the lives of the paupers, orphans, and felons she had seen and sorrowed over. First, the redeemable ought to be separated from the truly hopeless, "that the bad may not impede those who wish to do well."[70] Second, she called for education to bring new light to minds that had not been corrupted, but merely darkened. Finally, she appealed for better sani-tation, to promote pure and healthy bodies, as well as minds. She did not directly mention a fourth criterion for change, but it was evident through-out her essay. The sight of old women in the almshouse enjoying gossip and tea while mothers cared for their little children touched her deeply. At the Farm School, one of her few pleasures came in seeing the nurses feed the babies "like a nest full of little birds."[71] At the prison, she bemoaned the absence of "proper matrons, or any matrons," to care for the mental and physical improvement of the prisoners,[72] Wherever she had gone, in short, Fuller had found the most hope in scenes that reminded her of family. For her, successful social reform did not emerge solely from the discovery of the proper system of governance. It depended also on the feelings of the home: "intelligent sympathy—[and] love."[73] Charity demanded "great nobleness and faith in human nature"; above all, it must never be dis-pensed in a way that "assail[ed the receiver's] self-respect," for to break one's feeling of personal honor was to hurt a man "as a wound to its bark does a tree."[74]

In her newly found concern for charitable institutions, Fuller found rea-sons to reconsider her own nature. She spent her first New York Valentine's Day, a date that had "always had great charm" for her, at the privately man-aged Bloomingdale Asylum for the Insane, whose governors were putting on a dance for their charges. Fuller, to her gratified surprise, reported that the occasion was marked by "care and taste" and that the dancing was actually better than was usual among the sane. Her judgment of the inmates she saw there was deeply generous; she merely thought of them as "too deeply wounded or disturbed . . . to keep up that semblance . . . of sanity which the conduct of affairs in the world at large demands." To those who would scoff at such a party, she warned, "let no one dare to call another mad who is not himself willing to rank in the same class for every perversion and fault of judgment. Let no one dare aid in punishing another as criminal who is not willing to suffer the penalty due to his own offenses." She added, "We are all mad, all criminal."[75]

Fuller had come to New York as part of her quest to fashion a higher, more perfected self. However, what she was finding, even as she reached higher, were more reasons to consider her imperfections. Her visits to the prostitutes of Sing Sing had reminded her of how short a distance lay between her appetites and theirs. Her more recent meetings with mad-women and felons had also shown her the moral nearness of people who might once have seemed impossibly distant. Her statements in the *Tribune* that sanity is partly a matter of mere semblance and that all people are potentially mad and criminal show more than an unusual willingness to sympathize and understand. They reveal as well a woman who, despite all her confidence in her own perfectibility, felt that she might be nearing the limits of her own self-improvement. She could read her Goethe and write her books and travel to intellectual heights that few had ever seen, but, perhaps like all of us, she could never extinguish the hint of madness, the whiff of lust, the little child of the devil, always on the verge of breaking out and spoiling everything.

Fuller's interest in prisons and almshouses was also drawing her away from her previous, transcendentally based assumptions about society. Apart from Ripley, and, to a lesser extent, Alcott, the transcendentalists distrusted institutions and argued tirelessly that true reform must begin with the solitary person, not an organization. However, when Fuller exposed the short-comings of the charitable institutions of New York, it was not to question their usefulness, but to suggest ways to make them better. Emerson had inclined to regard the choice between soul and society as an either-or proposition. Fuller, to the contrary, was coming to see a higher wisdom in uniting the two; she wanted to infuse the reforming mechanism of the institution with the redemptive warmth of the human heart.

In her reformist writings for the *Tribune*, Fuller took on topics both small and large. One day on the Brooklyn ferry, she saw a fashionably dressed woman savagely berating a boy in a patched jacket who, at his father's behest, had taken a sickly younger sibling out for fresh air on a chilly day. The woman insinuated that the boy was willfully harming the infant and angrily accused him of lying to her. The woman's insolence so offended Fuller that she published an entire column decrying the familiarity and presumption with which the rich felt entitled to address the poor. Charity, she insisted, was not simply a matter of an open purse, but also of "an open eye and open heart, ready to cheer the downcast, and enlighten the dull by words of comfort and looks of love."[76]

But Fuller had always been compassionate in small matters. The greater change lay in how she observed the world of public affairs. Previously, she had taken almost no visible interest in politics. Now, however, her exposure to Greeley's newsroom caused the affairs of the larger world to burst in on her awareness. When freedom movements in Poland and Italy faltered, her columns mourned them. As the conservative governments of France and Austria encroached ever more arrogantly on the liberties of their subjects, Fuller wished publicly that Louis-Philippe and Metternich would quickly leave the scene. With impressive clairvoyance, she predicted the further rise of Russia, an empire that, she foresaw, might one day, "animated by despotic will . . . stride over Europe and face us across the water. Then would be opposed to one another the two extremes of Autocracy and Democracy, and a trial of strength would ensue between the two principles more grand and full than any ever seen on this planet."[77]

However, if Fuller accurately foretold the conflict between authoritarian East and republican West, she was not as ready to award clear moral superiority to either side. Nor could she. If Tsar Nicholas and his nobles held serfs, Fuller's president and her southern countrymen still owned slaves, and the power of those slaveholders had never been greater. When Fuller made her prediction regarding Russia, the United States had only recently annexed Texas, throwing open a vast new region to the expansion of slavery. In this imperial action, Fuller found positive proof that "the lust of gain" had become the ruling passion of America.[78] In a column written at the end of 1845, she surveyed the political and moral wreckage:

What a year it has been with us! Texas annexed, and more annexa-
tions in store; slavery perpetuates, as the most striking feature of
these movements. Such are the fruits of American love of liberty!
Mormons murdered and driven out, as an expression of American
freedom of conscience. [Abolitionist] Cassius Clay's paper expelled
from Kentucky; that is American freedom of the press. And all these
deeds defended on the true Russian grounds: "We (the stronger)
know what you (the weaker) ought to do and be, and it shall be so."[79]

The American eagle, Fuller feared, had taken on the features of a vulture.
She hoped that it would soon more closely imitate a reborn Phoenix, "even
if," she added ominously, "the bird need first be purified by fire."[80]

Fuller the columnist was writing with reason and discernment. The logic
of her private life was becoming less certain. As she solidified her reputation
as a leading cultural critic, she was forming a liaison founded on anything
but reasonableness. In such moments, it is perhaps not so much that the
logic of the life vanishes but rather that it inwardly changes. Without warning, the principles one has previously followed no longer seem to govern and,
abruptly, a new truth holds sway. While many of Fuller's past choices had
been bold and unconventional, none had been especially inconsistent with
the growth and development of a rising intellectual. More than once, she
had been diverted for a time by the urgings of her heart, but she had always
been able to quickly regain her balance. However, no mathematician of the
emotions has ever worked out the equation by which Margaret Fuller fell in
love with James Nathan.

At a time when Fuller was overtly distancing herself from emotional
attachments in the names of career and culture, Nathan stood as the single
great exception. He was, at first glance, many things that a New England
congressman's daughter and a veteran of transcendental pursuits might
predictably have rejected out of hand. Unlike so many of the men in Fuller's
acquaintance, whose social station or moral fastidiousness had held them
aloof from commerce, Nathan was a product of the hard, hot struggles of
the marketplace. An immigrant from Hamburg who, in 1830, had come to
America while still in his teens, Nathan had begun his search for success at
a time of life when young men, whatever their disadvantages, believe in their
expectations. He had seized his hopes and made the most of them. Nathan

did not shrink from reminiscing about his penniless origins and, presumably, relished the looks on his listeners' faces as they considered the huge distance he had come. He had earned his first success as a broker in the clothing business. From there he had made a daring jump to Wall Street, where his financial savvy had firmly established him as a banker. Whereas men like Emerson, Clarke, and Greeley were contemplative and idealistic, the energetic Nathan dealt in facts and dollars. With his thick, black beard and his reddish complexion, he exuded a forcefulness that was finely counterbalanced by impec-

This is the only known photograph of James Nathan. Fuller wrote to him, "You attract beings so much that after a while it is too much for their good."

cable manners. He attracted some and repelled others. Few regarded him with neutrality.

Whatever tussles had detained him on his way to wealth, Nathan in no way lacked feeling for the finer things. He played guitar, sang German art songs, and expressed some indistinct literary aspirations. He was sufficiently sensitive to the power of the word that Fuller felt no discomfort in sharing favorite books and poems with him. He despised cruelty and, remembering his own threadbare beginnings in America, sympathized with the deserving poor. When bothered by the "uncongenial" aspects of life, he had a habit of knitting his brows in a way that made Fuller wish to smooth away the trouble with her hand.[81] Such were some of the details of Nathan's character that one could see by looking closely enough. Inevitably, however, in a nation where the non-Christian population was quite small, one of Nathan's features aroused particular curiosity and attention: he was a Jew.

The degree of prejudice that informed other people's opinions of James Nathan is hard to determine, yet it seems likely that many of his New York acquaintances consciously or unconsciously adapted their ideas of him to previously formed conceptions. By one account, Greeley took an interest in Nathan "as a decent and rather intelligent sort of a Jew." Fuller's friend Rachel Spring reacted to him less generously, calling him "selfish and self-seeking" and claiming that he was attracted to Margaret primarily because he thought he could gain from their friendship.[82] In Greeley's and Spring's perceptions there can be seen a battle of stereotypes—the sensitive intellectual striving against the cunning, self-promoting arriviste. Or perhaps Nathan really possessed all these qualities. When, as is the case with Nathan, one sees a person almost exclusively through the reports of people who regarded him as a cultural alien, the lens darkens. When Margaret Fuller saw James Nathan, however, the lens through which she saw him was decidedly rose colored. In *Summer on the Lakes*, she had acknowledged the pains and perils that awaited a woman who loved more ardently or impulsively than the man whose attentions she craved.[83] Now she rapidly put aside her own advice.

Nathan began to win Fuller's sympathies almost from the moment they met on the last day of 1844. The first time he saw her, he regaled her with the story of his arrival in America—of how he had once confessed to a New York landlord that he had no money for a room. As he spoke to Fuller, "the tears ran down [his] boyish cheeks." There was probably no swifter way to Fuller's sympathies. Nathan was only a few months younger than Fuller, but she now imagined him as the rejected boy he had been fourteen years earlier. She later recalled, "My heart sprang towards you and across the interval of years and I stood beside you and wiped away those tears and told you they were pearls consecrated to Truth."[84] Almost from the moment of that first meeting, Fuller felt toward Nathan "the attraction of a wandering spirit toward a breast broad enough and strong enough" to give it rest.[85] She thought she heard an inborn poetry in his soul—bold and fervid, yet reassuringly simple.[86] In her second letter to him, she already called him "my dear friend" and protested that she could not bring herself to use a more distant form of address.[87] Before long, she was claiming that his thoughts had enfolded her mind "as a branch with flame."[88] Well before the springtime was half over, she called him her "sunshine and green woods."[89] She felt uneasy when he was away too long, and, as she candidly told him, she wanted him more and more. Nathan did not discourage her; she was, he said, "the sister of [his] soul."[90]

As with many other subjects, Fuller's ideas of Judaism had been shaped more by her reading than by interaction; it is even possible that Nathan was the first Jew she ever met. In any event, it is plain that she had imagined something different. Since, unfortunately, Nathan's replies to Fuller's early letters apparently do not survive, one can only guess his feelings when she first wrote him to register her surprise:

> I have long had a presentiment that I should meet, nearly, one of your race, who would show me how the sun of today shines upon the ancient Temple,—but I did not expect so gentle and civilized an apparition and with blue eyes![91]

Nathan could hardly have been flattered by the insinuation that his relatives and ancestors were, as a rule, rougher and less civilized than he, and the expectation that he would personify "the ancient Temple" probably struck him as a trifle odd. Indeed, Nathan's Jewishness continued for some time to kindle Fuller's curiosity in ways he might well have found uncomfortable. In one letter to him, she regretted not knowing Hebrew and thus being unable to express a sentiment "in that ancient noble speech of the chosen people."[92] In another, she wondered aloud whether he had chosen to live on Cedar Street because it reminded him of Lebanon.[93] She did not, perhaps, display the deepest tact in quoting the Lord's Prayer to him and inviting him to attend Handel's *Messiah*.[94]

Fuller's awkwardness was not just a matter of ethnic insensitivity. Around the time that Fuller met Nathan, Sam Ward bluntly told her that her "way of viewing things" was unnatural, and suggested that her ideas of life would alter considerably once she had "had the experience of passionate life."[95] Fuller, so intellectually powerful, so finely attuned to the demands of ordinary friendship, remained a painfully awkward stranger in the realm of romance. Her utter frankness and her love of vivid expression had served her well when she conversed on gender and natural forces in Elizabeth Palmer Peabody's bookshop, and they continued to be assets as she built her reputation as a literary critic. However, these same qualities continually deserted or disserved her when she tried to present herself as a lover. As she herself admitted, "I know little about the mystery of life, and far less in myself than in others."[96]

When Ward claimed that Fuller had no experience of passionate life, he was referring only to exteriors. In her reading, thoughts, and feelings, no one could feel more passion than Margaret Fuller. But the passions that she felt were idealized. Because of the very strength of her feelings, she could not conceive of a world where love is always imperfect. When she released her passionate thoughts into the world, it was almost certain that they would come back bruised or broken. As Fuller, who often thought in terms of myths and archetypes, would have agreed, the ancients, with their systems of many gods, observed a practical truth. There are different forces in our lives, and we worship them, not with sacrifices at their literal temples, but by the choices we make. The gods whom we honor with our conduct, though fickle, tend to reward us. Fuller's long years of study had been, in their way, a chaste and noble worship of Minerva. Fuller had sacrificed for knowledge, and knowledge had given her much in return. Yet in serving her chosen goddess, Fuller had neglected the other gods of the Pantheon, and they had scorned her. Plutus, the god of wealth, had paid her no mind, and, after her long disregard of love, she had few reasons to expect kinder treatment from Venus. But something about Nathan gave her hope. Women, Fuller once wrote to Nathan, "love what is pure."[97] In the recollected tears of James Nathan, Fuller thought she saw purity, and she rushed toward it headlong.

There was music and moonlight in their friendship. Fuller's work for the *Tribune* gave her free passes to her choice of performances, and Nathan seems to have accompanied her often. For a time, they met at Greeley's house, walking and talking beside the craggy rocks on the shore of the East River. When Mary Greeley's delicate sensibilities began to be offended by the presence of a gentleman caller, Fuller and Nathan found more citified meeting places, including Lydia Child's rooms in the East Village and the home of minor transcendentalist Christopher Cranch.[98] She never mentioned Nathan in letters to her friends, and even to Nathan himself she wrote few specifics about their meetings, happy for the most part to live these moments instead of recording them. Fuller once told Nathan that she liked best to see him in sunshine.[99] Still, it was the hours after sunset that made her think of him most poetically. One twilit evening, she wrote to him of a spot where they had often been where "the young moon lent her pure crescent above the rocks [and] the waves stole in, vibrating the silence with insidious murmurs." In the same letter, she wrote, "You shall upbear me to the stars, when your energies overflow."[100]

Nathan emboldened Fuller in a way that not even Emerson had done. He became, not surprisingly, another vehicle in her quest for self-improvement; she felt that she "could be so much to [him] to refine, expand, and exalt."[101] Under Nathan's influence, she became ever more grandiose and self-confident, believing herself to be the vessel of some great destiny. "There are," she wrote him in a spirit of ecstasy that drowned every vestige of her modesty, "in every age *a few* in whose lot the meaning of that age is concentrated. I feel that I am one of those persons in my age and sex. I feel *chosen among women*. I have deep mystic feelings in myself and intimations from elsewhere."[102] Yet again, Fuller was falling prey to her need to find the epic possibilities in every new experience. She needed to press her relationship with Nathan, at first based on a shared appreciation of culture, into a romance. The romance, in turn, speedily drove her to a conviction of divine mission and appointment. When one entrusts one's heart to another, one always gambles something precious. In this game, Fuller's only stratagem was continually to raise the stakes.

If Nathan fueled Fuller's euphoric ambitions, he also drew out of her a kind of infantile vulnerability. One expects sugarcoated banalities in love letters, and Fuller's steady stream of notes to Nathan certainly meet that expectation. However, they also express something more disconcerting— an all-too-ready willingness to shed her mature womanhood and to become a little girl. In her public life, Fuller was a respected and influential cultural commissar, dispensing her judgments with regal authority. In her private life, however, she remained Sarah Margaret, seeking affection in the way she had once been surest to find it: as a bright child on a strong man's lap. Fuller's yearning to be a child in Nathan's arms is an unceasing motif in her letters to him. She writes of having glimpsed the possibility of "a truly happy intercourse, simple as between little children"; and of experiencing a feeling with Nathan that "was so delightful . . . a feeling of childhood."[103] When she walked beside him, it was as "a child with its brave playmate."[104] Even when Nathan offended her, she became a child whose "nurse has . . . given it a blow" but seeks consolation from the hand that struck her, "for it only the more feels the nearness of the relation."[105] In an effort to explain these regressions, Fuller wrote to him, "Perhaps it is, that I was not enough a child at the right time, and now am too childish; but will you not have patience for that?"[106] A man trying to maintain a romantic mood with a woman who continually presents herself as a little girl requires patience indeed, to say nothing of a certain tolerance for creepiness. During most of the relationship, however, the greater need for patience was to be on Margaret's side.

Early in their friendship, in a way that only sharpened her curiosity, Nathan told Fuller that he had both a higher and a lower self than she realized. Given Fuller's prodigious ability to idealize, she may have imagined James's higher state very well. The lower was soon on display. Although the details cannot be fully pieced together, it is clear that a scandalous report of some kind reached Fuller's ears through the landlady of Nathan's lodging house. Though Fuller's letter about the matter is far from definite, the most probable interpretation is that Nathan had, at some point, lived with a woman under some false pretense, perhaps that she was his ward or relative. Seeking to disprove the gossip, Fuller sent a query to Nathan. To her astonishment, his return letter confirmed that all was true. However, he had an explanation. He told her that the lady in question was, as Fuller later called her, "an injured woman."[107] Evidently, Nathan's story was that he had rescued the woman from the gutters and could think of no way to save her that did not involve cohabitation and deception.

Nathan's alibi notwithstanding, Fuller felt a "cold faintness" come upon her.[108] She removed the flowers she had cheerfully put on an hour before and gave them to a blind girl. After thinking it over, she decided she believed him, and, after she regained her inner balance, he was her deepest concern. Might others hear the story and be less forgiving than she? There is no sign to suggest that this possibility troubled him. In any event, Margaret pledged her loyalty and asked that his revelation make no difference in their relationship.

As a token of her understanding, she wrote a handful of lines that stand among her most tantalizing. "There have been circumstances in my life," she confided, "which if made known to the world [and] judged by conventional rules, [would] subject me as probably to general blame, as these could you. They will, probably, never be made known, but I am well prepared for the chance. Blame could not hurt me for I have not done wrong, and have too much real weight of character to be sunk."[109] Later records establish almost certainly that, at this time, Margaret was still a virgin. So what, then, could her "circumstances" have been? A dalliance with Anna Ward or Cary Sturgis that went too far? An undisclosed episode with a male suitor that stopped short of intercourse? We can only speculate, for no witness to Margaret's secret sin ever made it known.

To her sorrow, Margaret had more to learn about Nathan. On the evening of April 9, a few days after the existence of Nathan's ambiguous other woman had been revealed, Fuller wrote him a letter, filled with references to little birds and white, fragrant lilies, in which she seemed to put aside all of her defenses. "I am with you as never with any other one," she told him. "Sweetly you answer to my thoughts, and even in the same images in which I myself had clothed them. I will trust you deeply."[110] This expression of trust was, it appears, received by Nathan as Margaret's carte blanche. He was mistaken. Fuller's letters are too discreet to reveal exactly what happened next, though it is clear that, on Sunday, April 13, Nathan made some kind of openly sexual move toward her. Revolted by his presumption, Fuller responded with a mixture of hurt and outrage. The next day, both invoking a standard anti-Semitic trope and figuratively accusing Nathan of pedophilia, she wrote him, "[T]he sweet little garden with which my mind had surrounded your image lies all desecrated and trampled by the hoofs of the demon who conducted this revolution, pelting with his cruel hail-stones me, poor child."[111] After upbraiding him for several pages for his abuse of her innocent trust, Fuller at last put aside her girlish pose and assumed a mantle of regal dignity. "Think of me with love and honor," she said simply. "I deserve them." She could speak so frankly, she told him, because she had "been in her way a queen and received her guests as also of royal blood."[112] In her next letter, she likened herself to a sacred lute and cautioned him, if he took it up again, to "do it with religious care; on it have been played hymns to the gods, and songs of love for men, and strains of heroic courage."[113]

Confronted and, by his own admission, "embarrassed" by such fierce self-regard, Nathan could have chosen either to walk away or to amend his manners.[114] He did not walk away, and neither, though she might well have, did Fuller. To the contrary, by the end of the week she was apologizing to him for her pride and suspicion. Having settled their misunderstandings, she wrote, "We have now been embraced in the eternal goodness and truth. . . . The world may be wicked, but it is impossible on such a day not to rejoice that we have been born into it."[115]

For a time thereafter, the turbulence in their relationship subsided, and it did seem to Fuller as if they had truly found the goodness and truth of which she had written. She passed into what she called a "pure soul communion" with Nathan that seemed almost too powerful for her to bear.[116] She took to addressing him as "mein liebster"—my beloved. Still, however, she sensed a difference between them, and she recalled Ward's observation that, until she had known physical passion, her way of viewing life would remain incomplete and "unnatural."[117] She had pursued perfection since childhood, but only now did it begin to occur to her that perfection might not demand that she transcend and forsake ordinary human desires. It might be possible to discover a kind of perfection within the earthly condition, one that could be achieved by embracing the world and its pleasures with a sense of their goodness and fitness. Instead of yearning toward a pure angelic state, as her feelings toward Anna Barker had caused her to do, she now wrote to Nathan, "I wish, I long to be human, but divinely human."[118] She thought that perhaps he would be, at last, the "guardian" who would "domesticate [her] in the body, and attach it more firmly to the earth."[119] However, Fuller had been so long immersed in the belief that true improvement meant spiritualization, that accepting her humanness remained difficult for her. She could only hope that she and Nathan might somehow eventually entwine the physical with the spiritual.

Fuller's verbal efforts to unite the two realms likely confused Nathan. Though she had rebuffed his sexual advances in horror, her letters were drenched in sensual metaphors, as when she likened him to a crimson tulip with "rich and mystical" stamens.[120] In another letter, she wrote to him of a "deep wound" that might "seem to be a mine which opened . . . precious treasures."[121] In truth, however, each of her letters was itself another subtle barricade of words. Sometimes gushy and at others merely tedious, her letters kept their relationship on a level of artful language, moving it no closer to a physical bond.

There can be no doubt that Fuller's verve and intelligence attracted Nathan; if they did not, he would not have stood for all the bewildering and operatic emotionalism of her letters. Still, it must have been with a sense of relief that, at the beginning of June 1845, carrying a copy of Shelley's poems that Fuller had given him, he boarded a ship bound for England, on the pretense of returning the "poor maiden" in his care to her parents. He left Margaret to look after his Newfoundland dog Josey and assured her that he would soon return.

Fuller would surely have given his promise far less credence if she had known what a more objective person might readily have guessed: Nathan's "poor maiden" was actually his mistress. Oblivious to the ongoing betrayal, Fuller arranged for her most influential friends to write letters of introduction for Nathan. Once he had sailed, she sent long letters of her own after him. When she reminded him that the early weeks of June were "the bridal days of the year," he could hardly have missed the hint. However, Nathan's letters back were few; he could best be depended on to write when he needed another letter of introduction. Only days after his departure, Fuller felt "alone among the multitude of men."[122]

Deprived of the company of the man she loved, Fuller redoubled her efforts at the *Tribune*.[123] More than happy to give her all that she could handle, Greeley kept her desk piled with new works to read and review.[124] The happiest moments of her summer were supplied by a much older visitor and a much younger housemate. From mid-June to the Fourth of July, she enjoyed the company of her mother, who came down to New York and stayed with her at the Greeleys'. Fuller had only one regret about their time together: the elder Margarett refused to believe that her daughter could possibly be happy at the house on Turtle Bay. She was not able to appreciate the "goodness and honor" that her daughter perceived so clearly in Horace and Mary, nor did the natural beauty of the spot persuade her to excuse "the want of order, comfort, and . . . mental harmony" in the Greeleys' housekeeping arrangements.[125] Margaret took her mother's thoughts off these deficiencies by showing her the town. The two spent the day of the elder Margarett's departure reading on the rocks beside the river.[126] As Fuller gazed at her mother, her mind ran to comparisons. Her mother was much taller than she, as well as "larger and prettier and kinder."[127] With much less conscious effort, it seemed, Margarett the elder had made herself into a person who in many ways excelled her daughter. Though she did not expressly say so, the younger Margaret likely wondered at the secret of people who, instead of struggling ceaselessly to become, were able simply to be. While her mother had been with her, New York felt "almost like home."[128]

Fuller's other summer companion was the Greeleys' one-year-old son, Arthur, known to everyone as "Pickie." Though his temper could be tyrannical, even for his age, Pickie was, in Fuller's judgment, "one of the finest [children] imaginable," and he too shared with Margaret the joy of plain existence. In a hammock slung on the Greeleys' piazza, Fuller liked to lie and swing to and fro with Pickie, who loved to be talked to even if the words meant nothing to him. When she carried him around, talking with him, he would cling to her neck, stare deep into her eyes, and offer "little assenting sounds" to her poetic remarks. In his frankly adoring presence, Fuller felt the sensation of "unbroken love."[129] At night, after Pickie was in bed, Fuller would sometimes return to the hammock and rock gently as the moon shone through the stately trees. One evening, she ventured out to bathe in the river. As the ships glided past under full sail, casting a dreamy white over the silver waters, it seemed to her "almost too beautiful to bear and live."[130]

The idyllic perfection of the summer days and nights did not last. During the autumn, Horace and Mary Greeley became increasingly quarrelsome, and, by December, Fuller thought it best to leave. She moved first to a quiet, efficiently run establishment on Warren Street near the southern tip of Manhattan, which she liked well enough except for having to dine alongside "men of business who seem like perfect machines."[131] She stayed only two months before resettling in Greenwich Village at 4 Amity Place, where she set up residence in "the prettiest little room imaginable."[132] With handsomer quarters came more expenses, though, and by March 12, 1846, she was back with the Greeleys. She might have stayed with them for the rest of her time in New York, but for their decision to rent out their house at the end of April. Margaret then crossed the East River to live out the rest of her New York sojourn with Richard and Mary Manning, a Fourierist couple who, like Greeley and Marcus and Rebecca Spring, had furnished some of the financial backing for Brook Farm. All the while, she pined for Nathan and sent him letters imploring him for news. During the last three months of the year, he did not send a single letter in reply.

When she had first come to New York, Fuller had expected to remain at the *Tribune* for eighteen months. Her presence in Greeley's offices might have been considerably longer if she had so chosen, but Fuller had not been fashioned for sitting still. In September 1845, she had received a tempting offer. The Springs announced their intentions to travel to Europe the following year. They initially planned to sail to England and to continue on through Germany, France, and Italy.[133] The Springs told Margaret they would be pleased if she were to go with them as a tutor for their son, Eddie, and that they would compensate her by paying a portion of her expenses. Fuller wept for joy when she received the invitation.[134] In February 1846, as the plan was beginning to look definite, Nathan, who had been traveling in Italy, broke his silence with a letter from Rome. In it, he enclosed a rose from Shelley's grave, belatedly but artfully reciprocating Fuller's farewell gift. Battling one of her migraines, Fuller wrote back; perhaps she and Nathan could reunite in Europe.

Financial questions stood in her way. Even with the Springs' subsidy, there was no prospect of her being even close to affording the trip unless she took on additional work. Fortunately, Greeley heroically intervened. Fuller could continue in the *Tribune*'s employ during her travels, provided that she send back regular columns regarding the political, social, and artistic life of Europe. Fuller accepted his offer. In so doing, she became the first full-time foreign correspondent, male or female, to work for an American newspaper.

The news that she was at last to see Europe was deeply welcome to Fuller. Nonetheless, her joy was largely offset when she recalled how she had missed going there a decade earlier and when she thought of everything the lost opportunity had cost her. "At every step," she told Sam and Anna Ward in an openly self-pitying letter, "I have missed the culture I sought in going. . . . It was what I wanted after my painful youth, and what I was ready to use and be nourished by. It would have given my genius wings and I should have been . . . far superior to what I can be now."[135] Nevertheless, she felt that the trip was almost essential to her future in journalism. Even though she regarded newspaper work as something inferior to what destiny had once offered her, she felt she could still achieve importance as a journalist by exploring the "new field of observation" that awaited her in Europe. As for her personal development, however, seeing Europe no longer seemed "so very important"; she believed that her mind and character were now too fully formed for travel to have a decisive influence. All she could hope for at this late date, she wrote sadly, was to add to her stores of knowledge.[136]

For the first time in her life, Fuller underestimated her capacity to grow and change. Whether she realized it or not, she was still seeking a forum large enough for her spiritual and intellectual ambitions. She had first grown beyond New England; now New York, as well, offered insufficient scope. It was time to measure herself against the centers of western culture and see whether these could finally offer the life she had imagined.

Fuller wrote to the Wards with a more important purpose than airing her feelings. She also asked them for a credit line of five hundred dollars to help with her traveling expenses. The terms she offered were reasonable— she promised to repay them with interest—but they were also strangely lugubrious. She wrote of her intention to repay the Wards "in case I live and return," as though her survival was hardly to be counted on. She went on to assure them that, if she died, the debt could be taken from her share of her mother's estate. The elder Margarett, she told them, was "likely to be driven prematurely" to the grave, although, Margaret added, "truly I wish I might go first."[137]

As she looked forward to leaving America, Fuller found more than ever that, in order to embrace the future, she had to free herself from the attachments of the past—even those dearest to her. An epiphany of sorts came in the late winter of 1846. Margaret's brother-in-law, Ellery, never a good husband to her sister, was sinking to new depths of selfishness. With Ellen expecting the couple's second child in April, he had concluded that March would be the perfect time for him to travel unaccompanied to Europe. He wrote to Margaret explaining that he had been "only a bugbear in the house" during the birth and first year of his daughter, Greta, so it was really better for him to go off and look at works of art.[138] With astounding presumption, Ellery asked not only that Margaret take up a collection among her friends to fatten his travel budget, but also that she ask Greeley to make him the paper's foreign correspondent. Evidently, he took it as given that Fuller would again sacrifice for a family member.

Enraged, Fuller refused his requests, though he went on his trip anyway.

Spineless even in rebellion, however, Ellery was to return from Rome after only sixteen days, "full of distaste for all things foreign."[139] What most outraged Fuller was that, in Ellery's absence, Ellen had no place to turn except to their "poor frail Mother." In a letter to Cary Sturgis, Margaret fumed as she recalled how long she had striven to give her mother some measure of repose and freedom from worry, only to see her efforts dashed by the problems of her incessantly needy siblings. At long last, she had had enough; they must all shift for themselves. "I am going to let every thing go in this world," she announced, "and scud where the wind drives. I shall have no chance to think of any body but myself, as I have to exert myself laboriously and unremittingly, or give up going to Europe."[140]

Through the first half of the summer, defying her headaches and the searing heat, Fuller kept up her steady flow of pieces for the *Tribune*, while simultaneously publishing a two-volume collection of her critical essays that she called *Papers on Literature and Art*. In her last few days in the city, she dashed off a half-dozen reviews for Greeley. Before shutting up her New York desk, she also penned a brace of heartfelt farewells. In the first, she bade adieu to the offices of the *Tribune*. Her agreement with its editorial positions, she conceded, had been by no means perfect. Nevertheless, she believed that, "in sincerity and generosity of purpose, [the *Tribune*] has never been surpassed, perhaps never equaled, by any journal of France, Germany, England or America."[141] Fuller's other valedictory, a paean to Manhattan, remains as current today as the hour she wrote it: "The place is large enough: there is room enough, and occupation enough, for men to have no need or excuse for small cavils or scrutinies. A person who is independent, and knows what he wants, may lead his proper life here, unimpeded by others. . . . New York is the focus, the point where American and European interests converge. There is no topic of general interest to men, that will not betimes be brought before the thinker by the quick turning of the wheel."[142] She concluded with an exhortation to the country at large. Whatever wonders she expected to see in Europe, she felt that none of them would rise "beyond what my country is capable of producing in myriad variety, if she has but the soul to will it."[143]

On July 28, Fuller corrected the final proof pages of her *Papers on Literature and Art*. Early on the thirtieth, she took a train to Boston. The next day, her last in America, was spent at her mother's rented house in Cambridgeport, only a short walk from the house where Margaret had been born. Throughout the day, well-wishers filed through the halls, though some of them had to wait their turn as Fuller spent just one more hour with Emerson. In a sentimental gesture, her brother Richard gave her the thirty dollars he had saved as a child from the "bridge fares" given him by their father.[144] On August 1, the subscribers of the *Tribune* read that New York had given Fuller "a richer and more varied exercise for thought and life, than twenty years could in any other part of these United States."[145] Now, as she felt for the first time the winds of the open Atlantic, Fuller was about to learn about thought and life in ways she could scarcely have imagined.

CHAPTER TEN

INTERNATIONALIST

*Could and would America but take from other lands
more of the talent, as well as the bone and sinew,
she would be rich.*

—MARGARET FULLER, February 2, 1847

*A*UGUST 1, 1846, THE DAY THAT SHE AND THE SPRINGS BOARDED THE British Cunard steamer *Cambria*, bound for Liverpool, marked one of the brightest lines of demarcation in the life of Margaret Fuller. She had striven since childhood to internationalize her mind—to absorb as much of western European culture as her circumstances allowed her. Yet always, even in New York, she had felt that her life had been provincial. She believed that, as long as she remained rooted in American soil, she would be less than her ambitions and abilities might otherwise enable her to become. When the *Cambria* chugged forth into open waters, Fuller left behind, not only America, but the constrictive aspects of her Americanness.

Had she thought of it, Fuller might have seen the *Cambria* as a metaphor for her own spirit. The *Cambria* was a new, modern vessel. Unlike the sailing ships that still dominated the Atlantic sea lanes, she had no need to take an indirect line when the wind was against her. Fuller was proud to sail on a ship commanded by Charles H. E. Judkins, who had captained the ship that had taken Frederick Douglass to England. Judkins, to the dismay of the ship's southern passengers, had given Douglass "equal rights upon his deck."[1] The *Cambria* set a new record on Fuller's voyage, arriving in Liverpool in eleven days. Although she enjoyed spacious, well-ventilated quarters, the voyage was long enough for Fuller, who found the smell and clank of the ship's machinery a high price to pay for speed. She wrote her mother from the British port that she had "enjoyed nothing on the sea" and "could hardly have borne another day."[2] She was delighted at the sight of land, with its tall crags and circling seabirds, and she decided that, if she needed to look at the foaming sea, she would rather do so from a firm, green shore.[3]

From the moment Fuller set foot on British soil, her curiosity was engaged. Above all, she wanted to know two things: how did England differ from the United States, and how was the country moving forward? The first difference she noted was on the docks. The English way of doing things, though no less active, was slower and solider. Traveling, she observed, was not afflicted with "that rushing, tearing and swearing, that snatching of baggage, that prodigality of shoe-leather and lungs" that plagued travelers in America.[4] Yet, despite the lack of frenzy, she found that people still caught their carriages and that meals arrived on time. She quickly warmed to the new—or, actually, very old—spirit of gentility. Still, it seemed to her that, in Britain, too, the pace of life went on too fast.

To take the measure of Britain's progress, she was eager to inspect the Mechanics' Institutes that had been created in Liverpool and Manchester to promote adult education among the working classes. She was pleased to see instruction available not only in vocational fields, but also in such less utilitarian subjects as French, German, and the theory and practice of the fine arts. She found well-furnished libraries and met students as interested in landscape as in architectural drawing. Especially gratifying was a quite recent innovation: in the last two years, the doors of the institutes had been opened to women, a step that Fuller expected "wherever true civilization is making its way."[5]

It was not all wonderful. The hotels where her traveling party stayed in Liverpool and Manchester offered no bathing facilities. When Fuller asked her chambermaid in Chester where she might find a bath, the woman suggested that she might try the infirmary. Fuller came within a trice of advising her *Tribune* readers, "None but the sick ever bathe in England," but fortunately found herself proven wrong by the more modern facilities at her next hotel.[6]

In the middle of the decade still remembered as "the hungry forties," there was poverty as well as progress to be observed in the streets of Britain.

Fuller remained especially concerned with women whose want of means had endangered their morals, and she took time for "talking by night in the streets of Manchester to the girls from the Mills, who were strolling bare-headed, with [a] coarse, rude and reckless air through the streets." Through

Looking prematurely weary at thirty-six, Fuller sat for her daguerreotype in New York less than a month before sailing for Europe.

the windows of the city's taverns, she saw women filling their glasses with gin, "too dull to carouse." It seemed to her that the reputed sweetness of English homes was fading into fable, as liquor beguiled their female guardians from their place of duty. She had strangely less to say about "the squalid and shameful beggars of Liverpool," noting only that she felt "compelled to turn a deaf ear" in their direction.[7]

Nevertheless, though Fuller's first dispatch for the *Tribune* acknowledged the grit and swill of England, it seemed at pains to stress the happier aspects of the place. It was as if, having waited so long for a glimpse of life beyond America, Fuller was initially determined not to find it dissatisfying. Nevertheless, British poverty had shocked her as the American version never had. The question of how the wealthiest kingdom on earth could have so many poor was both strange and unavoidable. Though she had moved on from Liverpool, she found herself unable to drive its beggars from her mind. Days later, as their voices came back to her, she realized that she had heard "the cry of men in the jaws of destruction."[8]

Fuller sent Greeley about one dispatch each week. There was one pursuit, however, that she did not share with the *Tribune*'s readers: she wanted very much to track down James Nathan. Soon after her arrival, she wrote to Thomas Delf, a London bookseller who was now their go-between, inviting Nathan to join her traveling party on a tour of Scotland. Failing that, she at least hoped that Delf would forward to her any letters Nathan had left for her. Receiving no prompt response, Fuller and the Springs left the smoky cities behind and ventured to the countryside.

The ordinary people of England captured her imagination. In her dispatches to the *Tribune*, without particular rhyme or reason, Fuller included sketches of a thirteen-year-old boy who proudly displayed a wooden model he had crafted of his town's cathedral, complete with a ringing bell; a handsome young Bengali who had come to Britain for his education, resplendent in an embroidered broadcloth robe and black satin cap; and an elderly Scottish woman of sonorous voice and dignified manner, "such as Walter Scott and Burns knew how to prize."[9]

These outlines were but a prelude to her description of the man whom she traveled to the Lake District to meet. At seventy-six, poet laureate William Wordsworth was the last great survivor of the Romantic era. Though some might have expected to meet a god, Fuller was surprised—and rather pleased—to find in Wordsworth "no Apollo, flaming with youthful glory," but merely "a reverend old man clothed in black . . . walking with cautious step along the level garden path."[10] As he showed Fuller and her party around his gardens, Wordsworth seemed less proud of his poetry than of his hollyhocks and fuchsias. Secluded in his quiet bower, he knew little of the troubles that afflicted the less fortunate of his country, and Fuller's efforts to draw him into political conversation brought few results. The poet seemed to take more interest in another pilgrim who had arrived that same day, a boy who rode horses in the circus and who had slipped away from the troupe to spend a few hours with the great man whose work, by some miracle of education, he had gratefully discovered. To her credit, Fuller was evidently happy to yield center stage to the extraordinary young equestrian.

Fuller accompanied the Springs on to Scotland, mildly annoyed that she could not both write and experience at the same time; exciting moments slipped from her memory if she took too long to set them down, yet every hour spent with pen and paper was an hour less in which to see and feel and hear. As she traveled north, she was, as she had been at Trenton Falls and Niagara, entranced by a vista of falling water. At Dungeon Ghyll Force, a waterfall that had inspired one of Wordsworth's poems, she made her way through a deep chasm, bridged by a slender arch of rock, as the water pounded down at the far end of the ravine. Looking up, she could see the sky only through a narrow fissure, seeming "very pure and distant." It was a grand scene—one of many in the region that carried her back to Words-worth's poetry. The landscapes made her especially mindful of his long poem *The Excursion*, a work she had discovered during "a feverish period" in her life, and which had acted on her spirit, "bringing a sense of eternity that gave an aspect of composure to the rudest volcanic wrecks of time."[11] Fuller had come to meet Wordsworth in hopes that their interview would bring her in closer touch with the poet's spirit. She found much more of that spirit in the land that inspired him.

As Fuller and her friends crossed into Scotland and observed its ruined towers and castles, the very absence of modernity reminded her of its inces-sant press. It seemed to her that, when populations and mechanical improve-ments were scant, human strength and virtue had achieved their highest form, now lost amid a mass of machinery and no more to be recovered.

Fuller offered her view that ten of the rebel Scots who resisted the army of James V in the 1520s probably had "more intelligence, resource and genuine manly power" than ten regiments of modern redcoats, whose only talent was to fire cannons whose operation scarcely needed men at all.[12] The fact that force, not character, now ruled the world haunted her reflections. Her personal creed had always exhorted her to change, improve, and move forward. Yet the same urge toward progress, when applied to society, had led to steam, dirt, hunger, and monstrous engines of war. Fuller would have ceased to be Fuller had she failed to march ahead, yet the world of which she dreamed was already behind her.

She came to Edinburgh out of season. The university and schools were not in session, and, although the great, moonlit castle still impressed her with its majesty, the city had a deserted feel. The high point of her stay was an interview with the charmingly eloquent Thomas De Quincey, the author of *Confessions of an English Opium-Eater*. De Quincey's quaint and outdated observations impressed her less than how he spoke them. Though he was a native of Manchester, De Quincey's slow, urbane speech seemed much in keeping with the stately atmosphere of Edinburgh. Like Wordsworth, he was a remnant of a more richly mannered era. His words, falling "gently . . . as the evening dew," made Fuller nostalgic for the days of De Quincey's youth, when "men had time to do things better and more gracefully than now."[13] Fuller's days in Edinburgh were more a time for reflection than for action, and she wrote that it would take her a week to retell half of what she saw or thought there. But she never retold it.

Just before she had reached Edinburgh, she had at last received word from Nathan. His letter, forwarded by Delf, disclosed that he was now in Hamburg and announced that he was soon to marry a young German woman. Fuller had, of course, known disappointment before, but Nathan's declaration broke upon her as a consummate betrayal. She destroyed the letter and promptly developed a merciless headache.

After that, her behavior became erratic. Though she hardly ever stooped to racial insinuations, Fuller became briefly anti-Semitic in her assessment of Nathan. "I understand more and more," she told her journal, "the character of the *tribes*."[14] Then, for her journey with the Springs to Perth, Fuller refused to make the trip by rail, testily informing her *Tribune* readers that she found railroad travel "the most stupid process on earth."[15] Instead, she and the Springs bundled their belongings onto a stagecoach, and, despite a drenching September rain, Fuller sat, fully exposed, on the top of the carriage. She told her *Tribune* readers she enjoyed the soaking. It seems as likely as not that she meant to make herself ill.

Though the weather had cleared by the time the party came to Perth and the sun shone as Fuller toured the tasteful mansion of Lord Grey, her spirits were again brought low as she looked upon the "swarms of dirty women and dirtier children" at the doors of the nearby cottages.[16] In contrast to her first days in England, she was no longer willing to downplay such scenes. She wrote for the *Tribune*:

> To the horrors and sorrows of the streets in such places as Liverpool, Glasgow, and, above all, London, one has to grow insensible or die daily; but here in the sweet, fresh, green country, where there seems to be room for everybody, it is impossible to forget the frightful inequalities between the lot of man and man, or believe that God can smile upon a state of things such as we find existent here.[17]

Her party's travels soon took them to a country inn in Rowardennan, a tiny hamlet on the eastern shore of Loch Lomond. As they crossed the lake, a young, athletic ferryman regaled them with Gaelic songs. Inadvertently, he rubbed some salt in Fuller's invisible wounds by starting with "a very wild and plaintive air" sung in the persona of a girl whose lover has left her and married another, and is now too ashamed to look at her when they meet on the road.[18] Fuller supposed that the boatman was too kind ever to willfully torment a poor woman in love, though she confessed that what was true elsewhere also held in the Highlands: "Maidens lend an ear too oft / To the careless wooer; / Maidens' hearts are *always soft! / Would that men's were truer*."[19]

The next day, finding that a larger group of travelers had hired all the available horses, Fuller and Mr. Spring decided to climb the neighboring mountain, the thirty-two-hundred-foot-high Ben Lomond, on foot. They took no guide. The upward journey passed without incident, and Fuller delighted in the beauty of the view from the summit, which presented groups of lower hills on every side, blanketed with the soft purple of the heather. Shimmering lakes gleamed forth from among the hillocks, making Margaret think of "eyes that tell the secrets of the earth and drink in those of the heavens." She wrote later to the *Tribune* that, "had that been . . . the last act of my life, there could not have been a finer decoration painted on the curtain which was to drop upon it."[20]

That curtain nearly did fall. Soon after starting their descent, she and Spring lost the path. Leaving Fuller to catch her breath, Spring went to seek out the elusive trail. He soon called back to her that he had found it, and Fuller followed the direction of his voice. However, she overshot the place and, in her melancholy words, "saw him no more."[21] After ten minutes of anxious waiting, she became truly alarmed and called out for him many times. There was no reply. Fuller decided that her best chance was to try to make her way down on her own, but this proved no easy matter. Her descent brought her into cold, boggy areas where, without warning, she would sink up to her knees. Repeatedly, she was forced back to higher ground in search of a better place to ford. As twilight fell, she caught a glimpse of the inn in the distance. Sunlight was almost gone as she found herself on a high, heathery hill, surrounded on three sides by a watercourse, which she would somehow have to cross.

With great difficulty, she made her way down the steep incline to the water's edge. The inn, it seemed to her, must lie on the other side, but it was impossible to judge whether the water was shallow enough for her to ford. Cautiously, she threw in a stone. The splash sounded ominously hollow, and she was too frightened to jump in. She sank down exhausted. Before she could stir again, the darkness around her was complete, except for the pinprick of light shining from the unattainable inn. There was no hope of moving on until daybreak.

Fuller's feet and dress were soaked through, and she had only a little shawl to throw around herself. Convinced that, if she stopped moving, she would die of the cold before morning, she paced back and forth all through the night. After two hours or so, the stars, whose light had cheered her, vanished in the fog. Queer, visionary shapes appeared to her tortured fancy. Slow and graceful, as their white robes unfolded from the ghostly mist that bore them, they came upon her with a kiss as cold as death. Fuller fell prey to "thoughts beyond what the common sunlight will ever call to being."[22] From time to time, she cried out with all her might. Though at least twenty shepherds and their dogs were patrolling the hills in search of her, no human or canine sound ever came to her. Her universe contracted to the rush of the water, the sighing of the wind, the rustlings of a startled grouse, and the looming phantoms that circled her. She wrote later to Richard, "I should have feared my bodily strength and mental patience alike unequal" to the task of remaining alive, "*if* I had not tried."[23]

But she did try. Both her recent exposure atop the stagecoach and her decision to attempt the long hike up Ben Lomond without a guide, coming so soon after Nathan's letter, suggest that, in her despondency, she felt a blank indifference to her well-being. Though not suicidal, she had carelessly flirted with catastrophe. If, in these days, she had pictured herself suffering the demise of a scorned romantic heroine, such morbid reveries would not have been entirely out of character. However, when the actual prospect of death reared itself, she resisted. She found that even a broken heart desires to keep beating.

At last daylight returned. Little flies rose up from the heather and bit her, and she was glad of the sensation. But the fog persisted, and she could only guess the right direction. She climbed back up some distance and followed the sound of water until she came to a waterfall. After slaking her thirst, she crossed the falls and, as she put it, "kept on scrambling."[24] Luck finally favored her; a party of shepherds came into view. At the sight of them, her strength vanished, and they carried her back to the inn, where the distraught Springs rejoiced at her return. Fuller lay ill for some days afterward. When she was well enough, she asked to be led back to the place where she had spent her night of ghostly visitations. Seen by daylight in the company of friends, it looked majestic and alluring. The shepherds confirmed that, if she had jumped into the water as she had considered doing, she would almost certainly have been crushed against the sharp stones of the torrent's bed and drowned.

Fuller wrote to her brother Richard that she was "glad of the experience for it was quite a deep one," and, indeed, the night on the mountain had subtly changed her.[25] She had never regarded herself as a passive person. However, in the weeks before her mountainside adventure, she had been all too willing to submit—to Nathan, to the possibility of a morbid destiny, to an acceptance of the way things were. When she fought for her life on Ben Lomond, the importance of fighting, which she had long understood but sometimes forgotten, came back to her. One sign of her renewed spirit was the letter she wrote to Nathan. Since lost, its contents can be deduced only from the letter that Nathan wrote back to her—ironically the second of only three of his letters to her that have survived. Given its sputtering tone, it is evident that Fuller had given him a ferocious dressing-down. It is also apparent that she accused him of merely pretending to admire what, in response, he called her "great, superior and well-stored mind." She also apparently claimed that a "fancifull present" he had given her when they last parted had led her to assume that he had meant for their connection to be deeper and more permanent. Fuller now demanded nothing more from him, apart from the return of her letters.[26]

Fuller's rebuke threw "a cold shower of uncertainty and distrust" over Nathan, whose version of events had little in common with her recollection. He protested that his regard for her character, sentiments, and womanly virtues had been sincere. However, the hopelessness of their situation had been clear to him virtually from the beginning. He told her that, throughout their friendship, he had never once been able to forget his "entire deficiency and inferiority of education," as well as their "moral and social inequality." Worse yet, it had seemed to him that Fuller had not let him forget these differences; Nathan recalled that Fuller's remarks regarding the gap between them had been "*very clearly made*." Indeed, her comments had been so blunt that they had "settled the point long since" as far as he was concerned. Furthermore, Fuller had made him mindful of his Jewishness in unwelcome ways. With ironic self-mockery, Nathan remarked that "the native mysticism of my being, perhaps race . . . was . . . enough cause not to let me hope to dare join so clear, broad and disciplined an understanding as yours." On one point above all others, he remained firm; he would not return her letters now. Although he intended to do so at the proper time, he could not yet bring himself to part with "this spiritual offspring of our friendship."[27]

Still intent on recovering her letters, Fuller wrote back, apparently with an even more caustic tone, dismantling Nathan's protestations with what he termed "the skill of a Philadelphia lawyer." Though this letter, too, is lost, Nathan later quoted a few of her phrases back to her: "Mr. N. you know you have deceived me," "Mr. N how can you thus play with truth and appeal to God in heaven the while?" and "How can you talk of holiness and add sin to sin the while?" Nathan replied in torment, decrying the "weak and inexperienced Eye" with which she had conjured up her "ghastly visions [of] falsehood, desperation, malice and treachery." If he were not certain of his innocence, he said, she would have destroyed him. Nonetheless, he assured her, he might as well bid his heart to cease beating as to stop feeling for her "a true and tender regard." He closed with a forlorn benediction, "the prayer of one, of whom you say he was your friend."[28] With that, the correspondence broke off, never to resume.

One reads Nathan's final letters with a pang of sympathy for both parties. One marvels both at Fuller's capacity for romantic suffering and, if one finds in Nathan a shred of credibility, her persistent capacity to misread the intentions of the men who moved her feelings. As had previously been the case with George Davis and Sam Ward, however, Fuller was determined not to be degraded by the loss of a lover. Her dismissal of Nathan was harsh, but it purchased a precious thing for her: she had defended her self-respect.

Another sign of Margaret's restored ginger came when she and the Springs arrived in Glasgow. Up to this point in her travels, Fuller's responses to poverty had always been sympathetic. In Glasgow, however, flashes of anger at what she saw entered her writing for the first time. More than in any place she had ever seen before, she felt that she had descended into an inferno. Recalling ancient times when dangerous animals had been imported for the entertainment of Scottish courtiers, Fuller railed, "Still lords and ladies dance above, unknowing or uncaring that the laborers who minister to their luxuries . . . are turned into wild beasts—below."[29] The dirt, the tatters, and the listless woe of the lowest classes impressed her as truly desperate. So long convinced that the benevolent energies of hearts and minds could rescue and redeem the poor, Fuller still expressed her hope that "the devoutest application of intellect and love" might cure the social pestilence, but now she acknowledged a new possibility: that the dispossessed "*must* ere very long seek help by other means than words."[30] A year and a half earlier, when Fuller scribbled out her rebuke to the imperious woman who had harangued the poor boy on the Brooklyn ferry, she had prescribed no remedy for society's disease beyond a dose of loving kindness. Now, for the first time, it occurred to her that the cure might call for gunpowder.

After Glasgow, Fuller and the Springs took a circuitous route to London. After a brief return to Edinburgh, they crossed the moorlands in a heavy rain and came in the dark of night to Newcastle. Fuller saw her share of man-made darkness the following day when, at her request, she was lowered into a coal mine. She was fascinated to see that horses, too, had been taken into the mine to drag the cars along the subterranean rails. Once brought there, they never saw the sun again. Fuller never saw the miners at work. They were a mile and a half away at the other end of the damp and dirty tunnel. After walking a third of the distance, Fuller chose to turn back, her face and hands blackened by the dust. Later in her journey, though, she observed soot-covered workers in Sheffield, tending their steel furnaces by day and, on a Saturday night, slouching off with colorless faces to accept their meager wages. It seemed to her that the vital force that should have gone toward strengthening their manhood had gone for steel instead.

Arriving in London and lacking money for better quarters, Fuller settled into humble lodgings in a narrow street where she had more than a few opportunities to witness the struggles of the urban poor "beneath that perpetual fall of soot" of the industrial city.[31] The pleasure of her evenings in polite society was repeatedly punctured by her journey back to her room, during which she always encountered "the misery, squalid, agonizing, ruffianly, which stares one in the face in every street . . . and hoots at the gates of her palaces more ominous a note than ever was that of owl or raven." It seemed to her that, to a person of decent sympathies, every day in London must be a purgatory of the conscience. And yet no conscience seemed moved to say, "No more!" There was no romance to this poverty. Her word for it was "terror."[32]

Seeking perhaps to dilute her political anxieties with further infusions of art and beauty, Fuller continued to seek out the British writers whom she most admired. She was often disappointed. Alfred, Lord Tennyson, the future poet laureate, was out of town, and Elizabeth Barrett, having just eloped with Robert Browning, had gone to Italy with her new husband. To her surprise, the most radiant person she encountered in London, and in all of the British Isles for that matter, was an Italian: Giuseppe Mazzini. Exiled from Italy in his mid-twenties for his revolutionary activities with the Carbonari, Mazzini had lived in Marseilles and Switzerland before settling in London in 1837. There he had lived a hand-to-mouth existence for several years, spending long days reading at the British Museum and keeping his creditors at bay.

In November 1841, his financial position having improved, Mazzini founded a school for Italian peasant boys who had been illegally transported in large numbers to London. Beaten and half-starved, the boys had been thrust into working conditions little better than slavery. While instigating the prosecution of the worst of the slave drivers, Mazzini had joined with a group of friends to rescue many of the poor children from the streets and had undertaken, in his words, to give "both moral and intellectual instruction to several hundred youths and children who were in a state of semi-barbarism."[33] The actual enrollment was closer to sixty, but it was said that the boys Mazzini had managed to enroll revered him as a god and loved him as a father.[34] He repaid them with the best thing he could give: "the most patient and constant devotion of time and effort."[35]

The man whom the children adored was five feet, eight inches tall and "slightly made" but drew admiring looks with his delicately chiseled features.[36] If his once jet-black hair had now receded somewhat, exposing a high and imposing forehead, his years of struggle and privation had not compromised the sweetness and openness of his expression. The Russian radical expatriate Alexander Herzen marveled at the noble shape of Mazzini's head, "so severely classical, so elegant in its gravity." He observed "an infinity of persistence" in the Italian's melancholy eyes and in the lines of his brow, etched by years of anxiety and sleepless nights.[37] Fuller, who had learned about Mazzini while in New York, first met him on October 24, 1846, when she was introduced to him by the German poet Harro Harring. Like Fuller, Mazzini deplored the inhumanity and gloom of the capital, whose perpetual reddish haze recalled to him the phosphorescent light of Dante's *Inferno* and whose citizens looked to him "like ghosts," making him feel almost like a ghost himself.[38] Impressed with the acuteness of his conscience, Fuller invited Mazzini to tea with the Springs two weeks later. On that occasion, her sympathies were again stirred toward him, perhaps primarily because of the verbal going-over he received from another of her guests, Thomas Carlyle.

A man of brusque manners, razor-sharp insights, and terrible indigestion, Carlyle had been a friend of Emerson's since the latter had visited him in his native Scotland in 1833. The otherworldly musings of his *Sartor Resartus*, as well as the essays that Fuller had devoured in the early thirties, qualified Carlyle as a father of transcendental thought, though lately he had acquired the habit of turning against his philosophical children. An enthusiastic destroyer of old icons and humbugs, Carlyle was less gifted at building new things in their place. He was, as Fuller quickly saw, guilty of "fearing new shams worse than the old, unable to trust a general action of a thought."[39] Carlyle scanned the modern world for heroes, and he found them only in the past.

Carlyle enjoyed feasting on idealists. He had verbally demolished Bronson Alcott when the defrocked schoolmaster had come to London to see him in 1842. Having read much of *The Dial*, he had dismissed it as idealistic moonshine—"[v]ery high flights about Art, Self-sacrifice, Progress, etc., etc. . . . all of a very ghostly (not ghastly) character" had been his rude assess-

Fuller first knew Giuseppe Mazzini as a rescuer of exploited children. She later knew him as the leader of a nation.

(COURTESY OF MARKA/ ALAMY)

ment.[40] Carlyle's most memorable jibe at Fuller had already been delivered a year or two earlier when Henry James Sr. had come to call. Carlyle asked him who was this "Margaret Fooler," about whom he had been hearing. After speaking well of Fuller, James added, "When I last saw Margaret Fuller she told me she had got to this conclusion to accept the universe." Carlyle replied with a laugh, "God, accept the universe, Margaret Fooler accept the universe! . . . [W]hy perhaps upon the whole it is the best thing she could do—it is very kind of Margaret Fooler!"[41] However, if, as one imagines, Carlyle looked forward to sharpening his claws on Fuller when they finally met, it did not work out that way. While she came away from their first meeting admiring Carlyle's "very sweet humor, full of wit and pathos" and "the hearty noble earnestness of his personal being,"[42] Carlyle found her "a *strange* lilting lean old-maid, not nearly such a bore as I expected."[43] The sweetness of Carlyle's humor failed him, however, when Fuller and the Springs asked him to tea with Mazzini.

As a conversationalist, Carlyle was at the mercy of his very changeable moods. On a good night, he was swift and sparking, "singing his great full sentences, so that each one was like the stanza of a narrative ballad." At such times, he was not ashamed to laugh when amused, a trait that, Fuller bluntly told Emerson, made the Scotsman "worth a thousand of you."[44] But Carlyle had more talent for monologue than conversation. "You cannot interrupt him," Fuller complained. "You are a perfect prisoner when he has once got hold of you."[45] When Carlyle perceived a weakness in another's position, he could attack ruthlessly. Mazzini and Carlyle had known each other for years, and they had spent many evenings over their tobacco—Mazzini with his cigar and Carlyle with a clay pipe—arguing about politics and seldom agreeing.[46] On the day they came to see Fuller, however, the Scotsman was especially testy. His humor was not improved when Mazzini steered the conversation toward social reform. Carlyle disliked nothing more than what he took to be unexamined optimism. He proceeded to carve Mazzini up, waxing fluent in his condemnation of the Italian's hopes for a better world and dismissing them as "rose-water imbecilities."[47] For a while, Mazzini tried to resist, but Carlyle's momentum was unbreakable. Fuller watched as Mazzini's sadness deepened. Carlyle's wife, Jane, took no pleasure in his performance. After the flogging had ended, she took Fuller aside to privately deplore her husband's lack of grace. "These are but opinions to [him]," said Jane, "but to Mazzini, who has given his all, and helped bring his friends to the scaffold, in pursuit of such subjects, it is a matter of life and death."[48]

After the regrettable party, Fuller observed, "All Carlyle's talk, that evening, was a defence of mere force,—success the test of right;—if people would not behave well, put collars round their necks;—find a hero, and let them be his slaves."[49] On this point, Mazzini was Carlyle's opposite; he once observed, "Carlyle worships force; I combat it with all my might."[50] Mazzini wanted to believe there was a beauty and poetry and decency to life that was stronger than strength itself. After his mistreatment by Carlyle, Mazzini rose still higher in her regard. She now called him "pure music" and wrote that she enjoyed his company "more than any." Ten or fifteen years earlier, Fuller might well have sided with Carlyle. In younger days, she, too, had worshipped force, at least in the form of individual genius. Now, she was ever more attracted to those who did not live for personal greatness, but who sought to establish the dignity of all.

Fuller was plainly delighted when Mazzini invited her to his school's fifth-anniversary dinner. Funded principally by the donations of Italians, many of whom had little to spare, Mazzini's school consisted of two rather forlorn-looking rooms with a few chairs for distinguished visitors and hard, backless benches for the boys. Beyond a few maps on the walls, its only noteworthy adornment was a bust of Dante above the fireplace. What distinguished the school was its curriculum, which would have warmed the hearts of Alcott and Hiram Fuller: the course of study included not only the three Rs and elementary science, but also investigations of such matters as the nature of duty and the social values of the Sermon on the Mount. From her own experience, Fuller knew how unusual it was for "minds capable of great thoughts, large plans and rapid progress" to express the love and sincerity that a school like Mazzini's demanded.[51] The idea of such an exceptional man giving so freely of his time and energy to a band of exploited children moved her profoundly.

While attending a ceremony where prizes were given to some of the boys, Fuller was, to her surprise, asked to say a few words. Luckily, words were easy to find. After praising the pupils for their work, she offered her vision of a world of "international moral exchange," in which the people of each nation might absorb the "peculiar excellence" of all the others. The Germans might teach the world about their capacity for hard work and their extensive mental culture. The English might share their mechanical genius and sense of honor, and the Italians would add to the common good with their artistic brilliance, refining the human soul with their portrayals of beauty, grace, and goodness. Fuller also stated her belief that charity of the purse was not as precious as the work of those who gave their time and effort. Whereas those who gave money could seldom be sure if their gifts were well spent, those who gave directly of themselves "could [not] possibly do wrong." Fuller then concluded, "I do not know that I have anything more to say, except, 'Heaven bless you.'" She took her seat amid a burst of applause.[52]

Fuller had moved decisively toward a belief in personal involvement in the solving of problems. Still a person of searching thought, she was becoming more than ever an advocate of action. Just as important, she articulated an ideal that had begun to germinate during her time in New York. Now that she had met Mazzini, that ideal began to quicken. It was to form the very core of her growing perception of herself as an internationalist. Though her observations of national characteristics in her speech to Mazzini's pupils may have sounded simple and stereotypic, she chose this approach not merely because of her immature audience. She was positing such categories in order to think beyond them, toward a more rounded and integrated vision of a superior human being.

In the dispatch that introduced the *Tribune*'s readers to Mazzini, Fuller voiced more strongly than ever her maturing belief in an international brotherhood and sisterhood, as well as her conviction that sympathy with the entire world was a necessary part of a fully human soul. Mazzini, she wrote, was already famous among those

> who take an interest in the cause of human freedom, who, not content with the peace and ease bought for themselves by the devotion and sacrifices of their fathers, look with anxious interest on the suffering nations who are preparing for a similar struggle. Those who are not, like the brutes that perish, content with the enjoyment of mere national advantages, indifferent to the idea they represent, cannot forget that the human family is one, "and beats with one great heart." They know that there can be no genuine happiness, no salvation for any, unless the same can be secured for all.[53]

As she declared "this universal interest in all nations and places," it seemed to Fuller that America, with its free institutions, could be a natural gathering ground for the world's best energies. Thus far, she thought, America had principally imported Europe's muscle; eventually, she hoped, it would attract its brains. She wrote, "Could and would America but take from other lands more of the talent, as well as the bone and sinew, she would be rich."[54]

She also imagined a more broadly felt enrichment. She had been convinced that the urge to be governed by one's own conscience and intelligence and to speak the truth as it arises in one's own mind was no mere American anomaly. It was an ambition for the world, and it burned nowhere brighter than in Italy. Long before she had ever seen Mazzini's country, her friendship with him confirmed her vision of Italy as "the mother of our language and our laws, our greatest benefactress in the gifts of genius, the garden of the world." In the words "coraggio" and "speranza," as she heard them spoken by the expatriated Italian nationalists of London, she found a message of courage and hope that would ring true in any language.[55]

Fuller felt nearer than ever to her goal of ideal self-realization. She wrote to Caroline Sturgis that her instinct had been correct in telling her that "I might here [in Europe] find an atmosphere needed to develope [sic] me in ways I need." Still, this exultation came with a tinge of regret. The fear she had expressed to Sam and Anna Ward had come true, for it seemed to her that her escape to Europe had come too late. "Had I only come ten years earlier;" she lamented, "now my life must ever be a failure, so much strength has been wasted . . . because I was not in the soil most fitted to my nature." She could never again think of herself as merely a New Englander or an American, and the years when circumstances had compelled her to do so now seemed tragically misspent. As she usually did when the regrets of the past threatened to overtake her, though, Fuller looked to the future for redemption: "Heaven has room enough and good chances enough in store, no doubt, and I can live a great deal in the years that remain."[56]

Arriving with the Springs in Paris on November 13, Fuller was not sorry to have left Britain. To Emerson, she criticized England as "that mountain of shams" and implied that its self-deceptions were well deserving of Carlyle's splenetic assaults.[57] While she conceded to Caroline Sturgis that the men of England offered "a greater range of interesting character" than their American counterparts, she also wrote that her three months there, and especially her six weeks in London "were months of the most crowded life," of which she had grown "almost sick."[58] Although she recognized that going to Paris was a strange method of getting away from hubbub and disorder, she went there "resolved to rest."[59] Knowing that she would be socially invisible until she presented her letters of introduction, she held on to them for a few days, using the interval to catch her breath. Fuller's first days in Paris were plagued by sodden weather, giving her all the more incentive to recover her strength beside a bright wood fire, charmingly welcome after the incessant coal smoke of London.

When she did feel like venturing outdoors, distraction awaited her in the Parisian theater, which she found far more "living" and less bombastic than England's. She was especially taken with an actress born with the name Elisabeth Félix, who had since become one of those rare performers needing only one name to identify her: Rachel. Her story would later inspire Henry James to write his novel *The Tragic Muse*. George Eliot's lover George Henry Lewes called her "the panther of the stage."[60] She was, in Fuller's eyes, "a true genius," on whose lips the French language transformed into "a divine dialect . . . the pure music of the heart and soul." As sincerely as Fuller admired Rachel's artistry, there were perhaps other dimensions to her adulation. To begin with, Rachel's style of performance spurned the assumption that women should be frilly and submissive. She was not at all pretty. Furthermore, as Fuller noted, she excelled at "the darker passions, and grief in its most desolate aspects." Severe to the point of austerity, she was majestic when her part called for hatred and revenge. Fuller had always found the sublime more alluring than the beautiful, and it particularly pleased her to see it expressed in a female form. Fuller noted ruefully that there was no male tragedian in Paris who came up to her standard. Thus, Fuller wrote, "beside the tragedy intended by the author, you see also that common tragedy, a woman of genius who throws away her precious heart, lives and dies for one unworthy of her." Fuller found this spectacle "productive of too much pain."[61] One need hardly explain why it affected her so strongly.

Fuller was also intrigued by Rachel's offstage persona; the actress enjoyed "a really bad reputation as a woman." Whereas the gender-bending novelist George Sand had committed what could be politely regarded as "errors," the stories of Rachel's private life caused Parisians to fret about the condition of her soul.[62] Fuller felt once more the fascination with which she had regarded the prostitutes of Sing Sing—the excitement of the erstwhile "Margaret Goodchild" brought up close to the kind of experience that both shocked and seduced her. Fuller could hardly get enough of Rachel, going to see her perform seven or eight times before a particular viewing finally broke the spell. One evening, Rachel's lover was played by her real-life brother, whom Fuller decried as "a wretched automaton," bearing "the most unhappy family likeness to herself."[63] The vision of female excellence conjoined by blood with male mediocrity may have been a touch too familiar to Fuller. From that time on, she hardly cared to see Rachel anymore.

To Fuller's distaste, Paris too often denied its real women the freedom that it applauded its actresses for acting out on stage. In January, she went to the Sorbonne, expecting to hear a lecture by an eminent astronomer. A guard with an impertinently barking little dog barred her at the gate. Hoping to mollify the indignant Fuller, the guard named a number of nearby colleges and museums where women were admitted. "What, sir?" Fuller retorted. "Is it your institution alone that remains in a state of barbarism?" The guard could respond only with a hapless "Que voulez-vous, Madame? C'est la règle." In the *Tribune*, Fuller remarked that his sputtering reply made her laugh "even now."[64]

Fuller's sex was not the only attribute that made her feel like an outsider during her time in Paris. Although her reading knowledge of French was impeccable and she had taught the language more than once, her verbal fluency was far from perfect. While she could make herself understood, she struggled when she tried to infuse some of her natural spirit into her discourse. For Fuller, who had always depended on the brilliance of her conversation to open doors and win friends, the loss of her ability to dazzle others with her speech was a substantial handicap. She found that she needed an interpreter—someone who could, in a large sense, explain the city to her and her to the city. But no such friend appeared, and she grew anxious as her time in Paris grew short and too many of its sights and sounds remained veiled in mystery.

She understood enough, however, to realize that the French people were suffering greatly under the repressive rule of Louis-Philippe, who had done virtually nothing to alleviate the hunger that was sweeping the countryside that winter. Moving in advance of the government censors, she was able to procure a copy of a pamphlet, called "The Voice of Famine," whose stark facts appalled her. Overestimating the power of the reactionary king, Fuller did not expect the gases "compressed by his strong grasp" to burst into light during his lifetime.[65] She looked forward to leaving France, which, echoing her judgment of Britain, she later decried as "the empire of sham."[66]

Curiously, Fuller chose not to write in her dispatches to the *Tribune* of her meeting and subsequent friendship with George Sand. She had stoutly

defended Sand in the past. Still, she knew that Sand's libertine image continued to make her a volatile topic for an American newspaper, and she may
have chosen, just this once, to avoid controversy. Then again, her meeting
with Sand was delicious enough that she may simply have wished to keep it
to herself.[67] Her first Parisian impressions of Sand came indirectly, through
the reports of mutual acquaintances. From these, Fuller concluded that the
choices that had made Sand's life a subject of scandal were more properly a
matter for applause, not condemnation. She learned that Sand had left her
husband because of his brutality. True, she had had a series of lovers, but
Fuller evidently admired the fact that Sand and her current lover, the com-
poser Frédéric Chopin, lived on a footing that Fuller described as "combined
means [and] independent friendship."[68] It is hard to know what impressed
Fuller more: the fact that Sand had scorned the strictures of womanhood
and had achieved a position in society "like a man, for the weight of her
thoughts," or that she had donated twenty thousand francs for the relief of
the poor who lived near her country chateau.[69]

With tremendous excitement, Fuller tried to arrange a face-to-face meeting, though she had few hopes of success. A subject of intense interest
among the rudely curious, Sand guarded her privacy carefully. Fuller had
discovered that polite deference was usually a failing strategy. Rather, the
Parisian custom among those who carried letters of introduction was simply
to turn up at the addressees' quarters "and push yourself upon their notice,"
with no assurance of being admitted.[70] Thus, on the appointed day, Fuller
thrust herself forward and hoped for the best.

By now she was used to having French servants massacre her name. For
some reason, the non-English speakers she encountered had great trouble
with it and often fell back on calling her "la dame Américaine." Sand's servant, who was also her god-daughter, was bolder than that, but still the best
she could manage was "Madame Salère." Little wonder, then, that, upon
hearing the name, Sand claimed not to recognize it. Luckily, as Fuller was
protesting, Sand made the right connection. As she stood in the opened door,
the eyes of the two women met. Fuller swore she would never forget the
famous novelist's look at that moment. Indeed, given that Fuller only rarely
took detailed notice of physical appearances, the precision of her memory of
Sand is remarkable. Large and well formed, France's most notorious woman
wore a robe of dark violet silk and a black mantle across her shoulders.

Above a fine, expressive face that struck Fuller as more Spanish than French, her dark hair was dressed with the utmost taste. She was, in sum, an impressive contrast to the vulgar caricatures by which she was typically known.[71] All the portraits, Fuller thought, showed her as too earthy or tragic, whereas, in person, she possessed "a noble face, and not tragic at all."[72]

Although they talked for hours that day, Fuller recorded next to nothing of what they said. Obviously more important to her was the sheer presence of a woman who, in her physical person, seemed so much greater than her writings or her reputation. Fuller observed that Sand was "never coarse, never gross," and had, incredibly, a kind of "purity in her soul."[73] What transfixed Fuller above all else was "the expression of *goodness*, nobleness, and power, that pervaded the whole,—the truly human heart and nature that shone in the eyes."[74] Fuller's italicization of the word "goodness" reflects the astonishment with which the proper Bostonian discovered that this libertine Parisian, who had shared her bed with Liszt, de Musset, Chopin, and countless others, could, in fact, be good—that it just might be possible for someone of great character, guided by a love of beauty and superior intentions, to dismiss the moralizing quibbles of smaller souls and to live and love precisely as her spirit moved her. It occurred to Fuller that Sand had loved so variously because a woman of her tremendous range of thought and feeling could not possibly find a single man to "interest and command her." Nothing in Fuller's life could have completely prepared her for this interview. She may have surprised herself with her confession: "I liked the woman in her . . . very much; I never liked a woman better."[75]

Fuller had lived most of her life as the loyal servant of Apollo. She was now hearing the whispers of Dionysus. Her New England upbringing had impressed upon her the importance of controlling one's passions. It had always been somewhat troubling to her philosophy that two of her greatest European literary idols, Goethe and Sand, had not only achieved monumental creativity while flouting the demands of monogamy, but also evidently drew artistic vitality from their sexual indulgences. Something, it seemed, had spoken to them. Might that same messenger deign to speak to a Massachusetts bluestocking with squinting eyes and a curved spine? Sand had now appeared to Fuller as a bacchante, a lover "of night and storm, and free raptures," a modern priestess of "Cybele, the great goddess, the great mother"—an earth-deity of midnight rites and howling, moonlit orgies.

While editing *The Dial*, Fuller had flirted, at least in her mind, with a spirit of bacchic abandon, but had eventually retreated from it as a kind of madness. Sand's example suggested that such a life could actually be lived. It was an astonishing revelation.

In *Summer on the Lakes*, Fuller had characterized herself as a subterranean being, fated to deliver up her gold in darkness. In her private papers, one finds the line, "It is only when Persephone returns from lower earth that she weds Dyonysos, and passes from central sadness into glowing joy."[76] Her European travels had been, indeed, a kind of surfacing. Perhaps the bacchic wedding might finally transpire. The farther Fuller traveled, the more she doubted the authorities of her youth, and the enticements of the unknown grew greater.

Fuller left Paris not long after meeting Sand, but not before seeing her again "in her circle," and, thankfully, not before hearing Chopin perform.[77] One of his students, Jane Wilhelmina Stirling, brought her as a guest on Valentine's Day, 1847, to his rooms for a private recital. Fuller seems not to have noted which of his pieces Chopin played that day; her impressions were of a more general nature. She saw at once that he was "as frail as a snowdrop, but an exquisite genius."[78] She told her *Tribune* readers, "Only a person as exquisitely organized as he can adequately express those subtle secrets of the creative spirit."[79] Fuller very possibly sensed that relatively few people would have the pleasure of hearing Chopin's music from his own hands. A year later, he would give his last Parisian concert. In just over two and a half years, he would be dead from tuberculosis.

As her days in Paris neared their end, Fuller sought out the company of an expatriated Polish poet, then famous enough that she referred to him in her dispatches only by his surname. The reputation of Adam Mickiewicz rivaled that of Alexander Pushkin. He was the author of *Pan Tadeusz*, the national epic of Poland that remains compulsory reading there today. Poverty, an unhappy marriage, and despair over the political situation in his oppressed homeland had eroded Mickiewicz's sense of well-being, and he had turned progressively to religious mysticism. Poles came to meet him as if on a pilgrimage, and they approached him "as monks approach an abbot."[80] Fuller felt encouraged to meet Mickiewicz when she learned that it was he who had first introduced Emerson's essays to a Parisian readership. She sent him a copy of Emerson's poems, along with an invitation to visit her.

Fuller immediately regretted that she had not contacted him sooner. They seemed to meet on some unreal plane. With no one she had met in Paris—not Chopin, not Sand—did she feel "a deeper-founded mental connection."[81] She impressed him just as greatly, though his response to her was less conventional. Having somehow gotten it into his head that she was a kind of sibyl who had come to Europe to find a messianic "messenger of God," he sent her a cryptic, quasi-prophetic message, in which he tried to define her psychic nature. Proclaiming that Fuller was the only woman who had been empowered both "to touch what is decisive in the present world" and to have "presentiments of the future," the poet's augury read in part:

> Your spirit is linked with the history of Poland, of France and is
>   beginning to link itself with the history of America.
> You belong to the second generation of spirits.
>   Your mission is to contribute to the deliverance of Polish, French
>   and American womanhood.
> You have acquired the right to know and the exigencies of virginity.
> For you the first step of your deliverance and of the deliverance of
>   your sex . . . is to know, whether you are permitted to remain a
>   virgin.
> Thou shouldst bring to the new world fruit matured by centuries,
>   exciting fruits.[82]

Fuller was more intrigued than repelled by Mickiewicz's strange assertions. She wrote to him continually during the rest of her stay in Europe and, in letters now lost, made him her special confidant.

In departing Paris, Fuller felt she was leaving behind a great school, the only one she had known where so many of the teachers "could bear being examined by the pupil in their special branches." Still, she felt she had not yet learned enough of its lessons, and she promised herself she would return before her time in Europe was through. In America, she had sometimes gone for years carrying around some trifling question that no one could answer. In Paris, answers were everywhere. Yet Fuller knew that "really deep questions we must all answer for ourselves," and the knowledge she found in Paris was, by comparison, only "a crowd of details." Greater issues besieged her. She had seen much poverty and desperation in her travels, and she was to see more. She was becoming less content merely to narrate the woes of the unfortunate; she wished more and more to know what she could do about them. Then, too, the questions she had asked herself so many years ago on her father's staircase—"How is it that I seem to be this Margaret Fuller? What does it mean? What shall I do about it?"—were now demanding different answers. On the twenty-fifth of February, under "a large share of magnificent moonlight," Fuller and the Springs rode south by diligence from the capital.[83] At the end of their itinerary lay Italy.

CHAPTER ELEVEN

INAMORATA

The Gods themselves walk on earth,
here in the Italian spring.

—MARGARET FULLER TO
JANE TUCKERMAN KING, April 1848

*F*ULLER'S EXPERIENCE OF FRANCE WAS NOT YET COMPLETE. IN LYONS, a young girl in wooden sabots led her and the Springs to a tall building on a hill overlooking the Rhône, where they discovered that each chamber was tenanted by a family of poor weavers, in which every hand over the age of nine was busied with turning out fabric. Fuller was surprised to learn that their guide, whom she had taken for a mere child, had been a wife for at least six years and was the mother of two sickly looking children. The girl had considered following her community's usual practice of sending her children out to be wet-nursed. However, after seeing the children of her friends "brought back so little, so miserable," she had resolved to nurse them herself.[1] It had been a Hobson's choice, for the girl plainly had little nourishment to spare. The girl struck Fuller as one "on whom the Graces have smiled in their cradle," blessed with a natural loveliness of character, a vivacious, bird-like voice, and the simple love of those around her.[2] Yet Fuller was quick to perceive that these blessings of nature, when bestowed on a poor girl, were little better than a curse. If she had been a merchant's daughter in Boston, the girl would be just entering a life of parties and laughter. As it was, she knew the price of every article of food and clothing that she fought to give her family, and only a weaver's precarious income stood between her and prostitution. Fuller railed at the evil that could turn such beauty into a potential source of shame. "And there are those," she seethed, "who dare to say that such a state of things is well enough, and what Providence intended for man—who call those who have hearts to suffer at the sight, [and] energy and zeal to seek its remedy, visionaries and fanatics!"[3] Fuller was now quite ready to entertain such visions and fanaticisms.

Fuller made two literary pilgrimages before quitting the country. At Avignon, she waded through melting snow to stand at the tomb of Laura, the beloved inspiration of the Italian Renaissance poet Petrarch. At Arles, the snows and blasting winds continued, but they did not deter her from visiting the town's ancient amphitheater, where she saw her first reminder of Caesar's empire—"the great hand-writing of the Romans in its proper medium of stone." She beheld with contentment a remnant of days when, as it seemed to her, "life . . . was thought worth the having, the enjoying, and the using."[4] For her remaining time on the continent, she was never to lose this feeling of romance, this book-learned supposition that everything Roman or Italian was nobler and worthier for the very fact of being Roman or Italian. As her politics carried her forward to an ideal future, her academic nostalgia carried her back with equal force toward a mythic and unattainable past.

They went by steamer from Marseilles to Genoa. In the squally weather, the ship that normally took sixteen hours to cover the distance took thirty, and, as it traversed the bay, Fuller had to brave a cold, cutting wind to catch her first glimpse of Genoa's luxuriant gardens and marble palazzi. The electricity she expected to feel when she first touched Italian soil was absent. She had imagined that, in the instant, "the heart would expand, and the whole of nature be turned to delight." Instead, she came ashore at a busy port on a gloomy day. She could see the beauty, she told her readers back home, but not feel it. Brief visits to Pisa and Livorno brought her no closer to an ideal state of feeling. It was not until they arrived in Naples on March 8 that Fuller could report, "I *have* at last found *my* Italy."[5]

She almost never got there. The boat that brought her from Livorno, an English vessel called the *Tiger*, slammed into a French mail steamer, which was going at full speed in the opposite direction. Fuller reacted with admirable calm, and her joking about the crash immediately afterward helped avert a panic in the ladies' cabin. Nonetheless, she knew she had survived a close call. She told the readers of the *Tribune* that the captain's carelessness had narrowly missed sending the entire ship's company to the bottom.[6] Water remained for her a singularly threatening element. Fuller's stay in Naples, however, more than rewarded her for the scare. She found the people refined, courteous, and, unlike most Americans, possessed of an apparent capacity for "pure, exalting passion." She passed through the Grotto of Pausilippo, toured the ruins at Cumae, gazed on the Mediterranean from the hillsides of Capri, and climbed Mount Vesuvius. As with so many of the other places she had visited, her reading had made it all familiar to her beforehand. This time, however, the impressions had not been spoiled, for the one thing that felt new to her was the most important: "the sense of enchantment, of sweet exhilaration" that the scenes conveyed. Baia held for her a hidden goddess; Vesuvius was a fresh baptism of fire. Sorrento was beyond both picture and poetry. The entire region was, in Fuller's enraptured eyes, "a thing apart in the journey of life." For once, there was no dissatisfaction, none of her perennial sense of exclusion. She had seen, as she put it, "the fulfillment of a hope."[7]

Yet Fuller also took the natural beauty of Naples as a symbol of hopes yet unfulfilled. When Nature had formed this bay for the pleasure and use of humankind, Fuller thought, she must have regarded her offspring as "a princely child, angelic in virtue, genius and beauty, and not as a begging, vermin-haunted, image-kissing Lazzarone."[8] On the Italian peninsula in 1847, the exalted natural state of human beings and their actual political and economic condition were grossly out of phase. Fuller could see at once the hunger and the simmering unrest. For her to understand the politics behind them required a bit more time.

The Italy to which Margaret Fuller came was weak and fragmented. In 1815, as part of its reaction to the nationalist emotions that Napoléon had aroused in various parts of Europe, the Congress of Vienna had attempted to divide Italy so thoroughly that unification would be impossible. As a result of the Congress, led by the Austrian archconservative and über-diplomat Prince von Metternich, the Italian peninsula in 1847 was not one state but nine. Thirty-two years after redrawing the map of Europe, Metternich remained the power behind the Austrian throne, and Austria remained firmly in control of northern Italy. Indeed, almost half of the Italian states were politically irrelevant, either too small to influence events or controlled by foreign powers, or both. The ruler of Lucca was literally insane. The adjacent duchies of Parma and Modena, to the northwest of Rome, were ruled by puppets of the Austrian Empire and were, as Fuller put it, "obliged to hold their breath, while their poor, ignorant sovereigns skulk in corners, hoping to hide from the coming storm."[9] San Marino, aloof, independent, and barely larger than the island of Manhattan, entered into no one's political calculations. Only the five remaining states mattered politically.

Life was hardest in the impoverished south. There, the Kingdom of the Two Sicilies was ruled with dictatorial harshness by the craven Spanish Bourbon Ferdinand II, who little realized that his despotism did more to advertise his cowardice than to conceal it. To the north, the Kingdom of Piedmont-Sardinia was governed by the House of Savoy, in the person of King Charles Albert, who had earned Fuller's eternal contempt by condemning Mazzini to death in absentia for treason. She denounced him in the *Tribune* as "a worthless man, in whom nobody puts any trust so far as regards his heart or honor." Seeking always to expand his boundaries, Charles Albert maintained the strongest army on the peninsula. In Fuller's opinion, only "the stress of things" had thus far contained his bloodthirsty ambitions.[10] Across the rest of the northern third of the peninsula lay Lombardy-Venetia, where the Austrians also held sway. The political future looked only somewhat brighter in the Grand Duchy of Tuscany, ruled by Leopold II, whom Fuller considered "a well-intentioned, though dull man."[11] Left to his own devices, Leopold inclined toward tolerance and a cautious brand of liberalism. He had been known on occasion to express sympathy for unification and republican reforms. However, if the presence of surrounding powers made Charles Albert a somewhat better monarch by keeping his expansionist urges in check, it made Leopold a worse one. Though Leopold was regarded as one of the most powerful men in Italy, Fuller perceived correctly that he was walking a tightrope between the still larger powers of Austria and the pope. Desperate to offend neither, Leopold kept imploring his people to voice no republican sentiments, and an uneasy quiet reigned over Tuscany.

Everyone knew, however, that the essential piece in the puzzle of prospective unification was the domain known as the Papal States. Ruled, obviously enough, by the Catholic Church, they extended in a broad swath across the center of Italy from Ferrara to the north to Terracina on the Tyrrhenian Sea. The Papal States cut Italy in two. At that time, the pope not only wielded tremendous religious authority but also was a political force to be reckoned with. As a matter of both spiritual and geographical fact, it would be impossible to unite Italy without either securing the pope's support or destroying his secular power.

This truth was well known to the leaders of the reunification movement. Since the 1830s, when it had been known as Young Italy, that movement had captured an enthusiastic following among the peninsula's artists, professionals, and intellectuals. Although the various reform factions differed as to the means by which they hoped to unite the country, they all vibrated in sympathy with a single word: "Risorgimento," the resurgence of nationalism and democratic freedoms. Preeminent among the most radical and popular leaders of the Risorgimento was Fuller's friend Mazzini, who had founded Young Italy and who, many believed, had a destiny greater than that of a London schoolmaster.

Committed and energetic as Mazzini and his fellow insurgents were, the prospects for change in Italy depended far more crucially on the choices of those already in power, and none more so than the pope himself. Until the current moment, no hope from this quarter had even been imaginable. Certainly no reform had been possible under Pope Gregory XVI, who had ruled in Rome since 1831. Reflexively conservative, Gregory had allied himself closely with Europe's Catholic monarchies and had bristled at any threat to the established order. Under Gregory, Carlyle complained, the Church of Rome had been reduced to a creaking spectacle of stage machinery, all pageantry and no policy. Speaking of the pope himself, Carlyle concluded bitterly, "The Quack has become God."[12]

However, less than a year before Fuller and the Springs arrived in Italy, Gregory had died. He had been succeeded by the fifty-four-year-old Cardinal Giovanni Maria Mastai-Ferretti, who had taken the papal name of Pius IX, or, in Italian, Pio Nono. Determined from the outset that his papacy should be one of justice and mercy, Pio began his reign by granting amnesty to large numbers of political prisoners. He appeared open to giving the Papal States a constitution. The perceived likelihood that he would continue to move the papacy in a progressive direction inspired young Italians to inscribe the word "speranza," or hope, on their political banners. Rome in March 1847 was a buoyantly optimistic place, electrified by Pio's early reforms and eagerly expectant of further change. Fuller observed soon after arriving that the Italians had "deliver[ed] themselves, with all the vivacity of their temperament, to perpetual hurra, vivas, rockets, and torch-light processions," all in honor of their new and visionary pontiff.[13] It was with intense curiosity about these hopes and the man of God who had inspired them that Fuller made her way to Rome.

"[O]nly *in* Rome," her idol Goethe had once written, "can one prepare oneself for Rome."[14] The city that Fuller entered on March 27, 1847, had not yet learned to primp for tourists. Its paintings were uncleaned, its churches unrestored, its ruins largely unexcavated.[15] For Fuller, arriving there was the culmination of a lifelong desire. All of her studies and aspirations had pointed her toward this place—the city of Minerva and of Staël's Corinne. If one can have a homecoming to a city where one has never been, such were Fuller's feelings now. Nevertheless, despite all her preparation, Rome did not open up to her as readily or as magically as she might have wished. She was grateful upon arriving to form friendships with Americans in residence like Christopher Cranch, who had also opened his doors to her in New York, and ex–Brook Farmer George William Curtis. However, she was displeased to find herself in a position that she naturally despised: the role of the sightseer. Not expecting at the time that she would ever become a resident of the city, she arose each morning with the dreadful sense that there lay in the city around her a host of marvelous objects she must see that day or never hope to see again. Bustling from church to church and gallery to gallery, she had almost no moment of peace in which to let the beauty of any single painting or building breathe its life into her soul.

Though she knew she ought to feel elated at every new discovery, Fuller lacked the stamina that such interminable viewing and marveling required. The tremendous influx of aesthetic glories left her "wearied, body and mind, confused, dissipated, [and] sad."[16] It also pained her to be caught up in the tide of tourists, whose philistine intrusions she compared to a foreign invasion.[17] She had contempt for those who thought they could visit the city for a few days and claim to have seen it. She thought that one might as readily "appreciate the Venus by throwing a stone at it."[18]

Fuller's own appreciation of the love goddess was surely enhanced by her being in Rome, for surely nowhere else on earth do the sacred and the sensual so freely and improbably mingle. The American sculptor William Wetmore Story, who, along with his wife, Emelyn, became fast friends with Fuller when they settled in Rome later in 1847, deftly summarized the casual physicality of the city: "All things are easy and careless in the out-of-doors life of the common people—all poses unsought, all groupings accidental, all actions unaffected and unconscious. One meets Nature at every turn—not braced up in prim forms, not conscious in manners, not made up into the fashionable or the proper, but impulsive, free and simple."[19]

Impulse, freedom, and simplicity were soon to occupy an unaccustomed place in Fuller's life. While she was in Italy, her public thought was immersed in politics. Most of the journals she presumably kept there do not survive, and, in her letters, she carefully edited the discussion of her private life. She did not chronicle her changing ideas on chastity and the body, nor did she comment on how living in Italy helped to change them. The following lines from Fuller biographer Joseph Deiss are admittedly speculative, though one suspects they are not too far from the mark:

> Babies were suckled openly at uncovered breasts, and were constantly hugged and petted. Children urinated at will in the streets, and men made little effort to conceal themselves in the public urinals. Boys and men strolled arm in arm, and lovers caressed and kissed on public benches. . . . Margaret was immediately aware of what she saw. Here was an expansion of human warmth and feeling in accord with her most secret dreams.[20]

Given the formidable strength of her character, there was no feature of Fuller's personality more remarkable than her ability to internalize and adapt to new surroundings. While a Bostonian, she assumed enthusiastically the mental habits of a New England transcendentalist. While under the roof of a progressive New York editor, she promptly became a soldier in the armies of reform. Now, in Rome, her mind resonated to the frankness of body and spirit that was on view all around her. It was not just that she was preternaturally perceptive and impressionable. It was also that there lay within her soul a host of teeming potentialities—mystical, intellectual, moral, and, indeed, sexual—each needing only its proper milieu to burst forth with bold intensity. In a city like Rome, with all its polymorphous influences and limitless energies, what might Margaret Fuller not become?

A few moments stood out from the voluptuous blur. Titian's *Sacred and Profane Love* raised her powers of gazing to a height she had never known before, and she called Michelangelo's *Moses* the only thing in Europe that had entirely surpassed her hopes. She felt the urge to leave a sacrifice at the sculpture's feet but could think of no offering that might be worthy. She beheld the pomp and show of Holy Week at Saint Peter's. She heard the hoots of the owls in the moonlit Colosseum. She saw the pines and fountains of the city by sunlight and the marbles tombs of its popes by torchlight.[21] She spent nine weeks in Rome instead of nine days, but it was still not nearly enough. She departed feeling that she had gained no real knowledge, had absorbed no authentic spirit or substance.

The three deepest impressions she had received were produced not by art or architecture, but by three very different men. The first was a twenty-three-year-old painter of portraits and landscapes, an American named Thomas Hicks who had come to Europe in 1845. Fuller visited his studio and reported glowingly to the *Tribune*, "His pictures are full of life, and give the promise of some real achievement in Art."[22] She also conceived for him another of those desperate, one-sided attractions that had become a motif in her private life. With a forwardness that was striking even for her, she sent him a letter, headed by the salutation "Dear Youth," that hailed him as "the only one I have seen here" whom she recognized as a kindred soul. She continued, "I want to know and to love you and to have you love me. . . . How can you let me pass you by, without full and free communication[?]" She pleaded with him not to let her leave Rome "without giving me some of your life."[23] Hicks's response, if a trifle melodramatic, was at least more mercifully candid than some of the other objects of Margaret's crushes. He wrote back, "I would like to tell you all about myself; you would then see that there is but little fire in the hut. . . . You speak of my youth. . . . Do you not perceive that my heart has grown grey?"[24] With that, the world-weary twenty-three-year-old doused the fire of the ever-hopeful thirty-six-year-old, and neither was further wounded by the other's folly.

The second man who captivated Fuller did so in a far different way, though her fascination with him was no less powerful. He was, not surprisingly, Pio Nono. Moving in obviously different circles, the pundit and the pontiff never exchanged a single word. However, Fuller seldom missed an opportunity to see him from afar or to sketch him for the readers of the *Tribune*. Fuller's overall impressions of the Catholic Church had been formed by her Protestant upbringing and her temporary immersion in transcendentalism. Those impressions were essentially hostile, and they never entirely changed. She regarded the Jesuit order as a "cancer," its objectives wholly contrary to "the free progress of humanity."²⁵ The sight of municipal officers kissing the foot of the pontiff struck her as "disgustingly abject," and she protested to her *Tribune* readers that a truly heavenly God would not want his children at his feet, "but in his arms, on a level with his heart."²⁶

In one dispatch to the *Tribune*, Fuller wrote bitterly of a young man she had met whose beloved uncle had contracted a deadly strain of malaria, a disease so common in the city that it was called Roman fever. As the elder man lay dying, his nephew, who was nearly penniless, had offered the priests a dollar to say six masses for the sick man's soul, only to be told that they would say just five—and that after receiving another seven baiocchi, or pennies.²⁷ In another dispatch, she described the great feast at the church of Santa Maria d'Aracoeli, in honor of the Bambino, a wooden effigy of the infant Christ whom Fuller sardonically called "the most venerated doll of Rome."²⁸ Highly reputed as a miracle worker among the sick, the Bambino toured the streets of Rome throughout the year in a carriage, attended by two priests and two footmen and much besieged with requests for blessings. On the day of the feast, Fuller found the church overflowing with peasant farmers and the urban poor. She watched in dismay as the priests, in their finest vestments, held "the ugly little doll" aloft and carried him twice around the church as the song "Sons of Rome Awake!" played ironically in the background. "Awake, indeed, Romans!" she later foamed in the *Tribune*, "and you will see that the Christ who is to save men is no wooden dingy effigy of bygone superstitions, but . . . a Man . . . loving Man, with sympathy and faith death cannot quench." Fuller was at a loss to understand how anyone who had seen Catholicism as it existed in Italy could "remain a Catholic."²⁹ The anti-Catholic bent of her columns became so evident that Greeley himself published a mild apology to his Catholic readers.

And yet Fuller was enraptured by Pio Nono. He was, she said, "a man of noble and good aspect," with his heart plainly set on the betterment of humankind.³⁰ After her return to Rome, Margaret encountered the pope while she was in the company of a sick friend who, though he was not Catholic, knelt to receive a benediction. As the pontiff turned toward him, Margaret saw in Pio's face a magnetic sweetness, "that expression of melting love, the true, the only charity, which assures all who look on him that, were his power equal to his will, no living thing would ever suffer more."³¹ By the time she left Rome for the first time, Fuller already knew enough about the political complexities of Italy to realize that the good intentions and tremendous popularity of Pio Nono were not in themselves enough to dramatically change the social landscape. Nevertheless, her faith in the goodness of his heart was absolute. As a metaphorical father to the Italian people—and in some smaller way to Fuller herself—Pio Nono seemed ideal.

Fuller later complained to her brother Richard that her first sojourn in Rome was "all outside . . . just finding out where objects were."[32] She did not feel as yet as if her inquisitive gaze had penetrated the hearts and minds of the city's people. Yet there was at least one Roman who felt that her spirit had pierced him deeply. Interested as she was in the reverence the Italians paid to female saints like Teresa of Avila, who possessed "intellect as well as piety," Fuller could hardly have avoided walking up the hill from the Piazza Barberini to the church of Santa Maria della Vittoria, which houses Bernini's renowned sculpture *Ecstasy of Saint Teresa*.[33] The sculpture depicts the saint in an impassioned state as an angel prepares to penetrate her heart with a golden arrow. Some see the angel as beatific; others regard him as cheerfully cruel. Although it has become popular to regard the scene as one of erotic passion, the sculpture might as easily be seen as an allegory of youth and lost youth. Bernini's angel is slightly muscled and childlike. The saint's face is more angular and worn, her nose a trifle sharp, the eyes a trifle sunken. She is, indeed, ecstatic, but she also seems more than a little tired. Fuller, too, was tired and conscious of her advancing age. She, too, was about to meet an ambiguous angel in the form of her third indispensable denizen of Rome: a polite, slender man almost eleven years her junior named Giovanni Angelo Ossoli.

It began with a chance meeting. On April first, Holy Thursday, 1847, Fuller went to Saint Peter's with the Springs. She had gone there in a spirit of ennui, and the crowd of several thousands did not improve her outlook; though she had long adored the art of Michelangelo, she now felt barely inclined to lift her head to take in the ceiling of the Sistine Chapel. She stayed with her friends to hear vespers and, when the prayers were finished, wandered off to inspect the various chapels housed within the great cathedral. When she saw the crowd dispersing, she went to the place where she thought she had agreed to meet the Springs, only to find them not there. As she looked around, trying to find them, her agitation evidently attracted some unwanted attention; Evert Duyckinck received a letter describing the scene, which he wryly summarized in his diary. Within "the precincts of the sanctuary," he wrote, "it is said she received very singular suggestions from the young men of Rome which may afford instructive notes to a future edition of Woman in the Nineteenth Century."[34] As she began to feel alarmed, a young, tall, slender, black-haired man came to her aid.

The Marchese Giovanni Ossoli had his likeness captured in only one known photograph. He had large, dark, deep-set eyes, and his rather prominent nose gave his face an air of strength and nobility. Although he sported a jaunty mustache, his cheeks and jaw were smooth. If anything, he looked younger than his twenty-six years. With smooth courtesy, Ossoli offered to help Fuller find her friends. She took his arm.

After this point, accounts of their first meeting diverge. George Palmer Putnam, who had published Fuller's *Papers on Literature and Art* and whose path intersected more than once with Fuller's during her European travels, claimed that she and Ossoli walked up to him as he emerged from the Sistine Chapel. Putnam recalled that, although Ossoli had offered either to find her a cab or to escort her home, Fuller promptly and rather ungraciously took leave of the young man as soon as she joined Putnam's party. The publisher believed that Ossoli had left knowing neither who she was nor where she lived. Putnam had no knowledge of when or how they met again.[35]

Emelyn Story told a more romantic tale, which she claimed to have heard from Fuller herself. According to Story, after Ossoli approached her, the two of them searched the entire church together for Fuller's friends. By the time they finished their search, the hour was late, and they could find no carriage for hire. Ossoli responded to Fuller's plight with a fine piece of gallantry; though his own rooms lay in a different direction, he offered to escort her home.[36]

No one can be sure of the precise route the two new acquaintances followed on their way to the Via del Corso. It is at least probable that, in hopes of impressing her with his artistic taste and flair for romance, Ossoli guided Margaret to the ancient Ponte Sant'Angelo, whose stately span is lined with immense, beatific marble angels. To travel on foot from the Vatican to the Corso at a pace congenial to conversation takes about forty-five minutes—more than long enough for a significant dialogue, even between two people not well skilled in each other's languages. Neither Fuller nor Ossoli set down their conversation in any form that survives, but it is clear they impressed each other favorably. Ossoli may have spoken of his elder brothers Alessandro and Ottavio and their respected positions in the pope's Noble Guard. He may even have explained the slight scar on his face, placed there by a jealous dog when, as a boy, he had nestled in his mother's arms. He may have mentioned, too, that that tenderest of mothers had passed away when he was only six. As she and Giovanni grew closer, Fuller could not have failed to notice that Ossoli was as desperate to fill the void left by his mother as she had been to replace her lamented father. The two parted at Fuller's door on the

Giovanni Angelo Ossoli posed for only one known likeness. Of her love for him, Fuller wrote, "[S]omething of the violet has been breathed into my life, and will never pass away."
(COURTESY OF HOUGHTON LIBRARY, HARVARD UNIVERSITY)

Corso. As Ossoli made his way back to his apartment in his family's palazzo on the Via Santa Eufemia, a shadowy street a few paces from Trajan's ancient marketplace, it was with strong hopes for a second meeting.

A few days after she met Ossoli, Fuller turned her thoughts toward love, though only in a general sense. She told the Springs, "I have never sought love as a passion; it has always come to me as an angel bearing some good tidings. I have wished to welcome the messenger noble, but never to detain it, or cling with a weak personality to a tie which had ceased to bind the soul."

She predicted that she would always behave thus, no matter what the pain of parting might cost her. She added that she did not know if she had ever loved "in the sense of oneness" and that she had "never yet loved any human being so well as the music of Beethoven."[37] Evidently, Ossoli had not immediately swept her off her feet.

This was far from surprising. For more than two years, Fuller kept all knowledge of Ossoli away from her family and friends in America. When she finally did make his existence known, in letters where she had every motive to paint as glowing a portrait of him as possible, Fuller made no secret of his almost total lack of culture and formal education. To someone accustomed to fastening her romantic attentions on the likes of James Clarke, Sam Ward, and even James Nathan, Ossoli must have seemed at first to be little more than an earnest but callow and ignorant youth.

But the marchese had only begun his campaign. The day after they met, Fuller spied him from her window, pacing to and fro in the street, trying to summon the courage to have himself announced to her. Only the barest record exists of what took place between them from the time of that sighting and Fuller's departure from Rome near the end of May. Evidently, she stimulated his political awareness; that spring, Giovanni enlisted in the leftist Civic Guard and, by mid-November, was to be promoted to sergeant. Moreover, something obviously happened that jostled him out of his initial shyness. Before Margaret left town, he surprised her with a proposal of marriage. As she later admitted, Margaret had developed feelings for the deep-eyed marchese. At the same time, though, the proposed connection was, to her practical mind, in "every way unfit."[38] Without any hesitation, she turned him down. Still, he did not despair; something told him that this American woman, so different from him, would return to him.

There is nothing in the tone of Fuller's writings about her first sojourn in Rome to suggest that her romance with Ossoli began in earnest that spring. Her romance with the Eternal City, however, was fully fledged. A friend would later write that Fuller's heart was too deeply rooted in Rome for her ever to bear a lifelong separation, and, indeed, Fuller would spend the rest of her life either residing in Rome or contemplating the means of returning to it.[39]

In late May, just after turning thirty-seven, Fuller set out with the Springs for an ambitious tour of northern Italy. For the next four and a half months, she traveled—time enough for the grapes in the vineyards that she passed in

Tuscany to ripen from "little clusters" into mature fruit, "full of light and life." Assisi, her first destination, she found charming and serene, as though all the world's noise and ramble had been hushed by the presiding spirit of Saint Francis, a soul "sincere in its service of Truth."[40] Almost the sole reminder that the saint's era was long past was the graffito "Viva Pio Nono," which seemed to have been written on every wall. Next came Perugia, perched on a "noble" hill and overflowing with treasures of early art, which Fuller was forced to view so briefly that she had only trancelike recollections of them afterward.[41]

In Florence, the Tuscan capital, Fuller had more leisure, almost too much. During the month she spent there, she grew disaffected with the city's atmosphere. Always, she craved an ambience more "purely Italian," an idea she rather stereotypically connected with carefree vivacity. The political moment in Florence was far from lighthearted. As Grand Duke Leopold II, desperate to offend neither the pope nor Austria, struggled to prevent tensions from erupting, virtually all discussion of republican reform had been driven underground. Fuller found the outward demeanor of the region "glum as death."[42]

One place where the gloom did not penetrate was the house of the Marchioness Costanza Arconati Visconti, to whom Fuller had been introduced while in Rome. Well read, gracious, and aristocratic, Arconati maintained her principal residence in Milan, though she was known in all the cities of northern Italy. A strong supporter of democracy and Italian unification, she cultivated friendships with progressive American women, including the future lyricist of the "Battle Hymn of the Republic," Julia Ward Howe. Arconati not only received Fuller in Florence but also gave her letters of introduction to use in Bologna and Ravenna. Both women looked forward to their next meeting in Milan.

Fuller was, in the main, strangely harsh in her judgment of Florence, the home of the spectacular Duomo, the galleries of the Uffizi, and Michelangelo's *David*. At first, she could not bear the change from Rome.[43] Even though she conceded that Florence was the better place for studying fine art, the city's cultural treasures rather oppressed than amazed her. She wrote, "There is too much that is really admirable in art—the nature of its growth lies before you too clear to be evaded."[44] She greatly preferred her next stopping place, Bologna, not only for the glories of its ancient university, but also for the way the Bolognese had long respected and cherished the intellect of women. Having previously regarded the status of Italian women as "so depressed," she was both relieved and delighted to see that, in Bologna at least, there were busts and monuments to female professors of anatomy and Greek, and that female artists stood among the highest places of honor.[45]

All the while, Fuller distilled the essence of her travels into dispatches for the *Tribune*. As a travel writer, she was capable of lyrical moments. Too often, though, what she saw was too rich and beautiful for her to describe in a way she thought adequate. At such times, she made almost no attempt. She promised her readers that, one day, she would take the time to send along her awed impressions of Ravenna and Padua. She never did. Of Venice and its enchanted life, Fuller wrote that she was unable to speak; her perceptions, she said, could be rendered only in music.[46] The galleries and churches of the city made her the happiest she had been thus far in Europe, but she confided this elation only in a letter to her brother Richard.[47] Again, she promised to write of them when "time, place and mode agree to make it fit."[48] This promise, too, went largely unfulfilled.

Still, the few Venetian images to which she treated her readers were tantalizing. Too briefly, she wrote of a grand soirée given by the Duchess Caroline de Berri at her palace on the Grand Canal. Fuller compared the evening to "a scene of fairy land; the palace full of light," and even her deeply democratic heart fluttered at the sight of brilliantly dressed aristocrats who "seemed to rise from the water," gliding up the magnificent staircase and rustling their plumes as they welcomed one another. Fuller thought that the social life of the Venetian palazzi might make a pretty perpetual holiday for the unjust rulers of Europe. After being exiled from their suffering countries, Fuller imagined, the deposed princes, "more rich in blood than brains," might find in Venice all the elegance their vanities required, without having to rob their subjects to obtain it.[49]

It was amid such splendors that Fuller said farewell to the Springs, who proceeded on to Austria and Germany. It was a measure of Fuller's infatuation with Italy that she did not join them. Compared with Italy, the homelands of Mozart, Beethoven, and her beloved Goethe no longer tempted her. Moreover, though she remained fond of them, Fuller had grown tired of the Springs, who "never knew what I was feeling, and always brought forward what I wanted to leave behind."[50] Also arguing for a separation was the independence that the Springs' departure gave her. Though she was being placed in the unorthodox and slightly shocking position of an unchaperoned woman traveling through Europe, it also felt good to see her last, most tangible human tie to America being loosened. She was on her own.

Fuller's remaining time in Venice passed like a languid dream, in which "there was no disappointment" and art and life embraced each other in "one glow of joy."[51] Once her two weeks there were finished, however, the destinations flew past almost in a blur: Vicenze, Verona, Mantua, Brescia, Milan. Traveling alone excited her, and, to her great pleasure, it forced her to rapidly improve her Italian. Her perception of beauty was acquiring a new, exhilarating keenness, and she thought she was learning more than in any comparable period in her life.[52] It all would have been nearly perfect if ill health had not begun to dog her once again. She had continual feverish attacks of what she thought was cholera—a dire word for her ever since her father's death. Once she fell so ill that she feared she would die on the road, with only her obsequious swindler of a courier to take notice of her passing.[53]

As she traveled, word intermittently reached her of the political clouds that were gathering over much of the peninsula. An Austrian spy had been assassinated in Ferrara, and Austria's Field Marshal Radetzky had promptly seized the city. From Rome came word of a supposed conspiracy, which the authorities had used as a pretext for several arrests. A National Guard was being formed. Fragmentary and imperfectly reliable, the news seemed to announce that change was coming. Fuller hoped the vague portents were pointing toward unification, a republican government in Rome, and a more egalitarian social order. Nothing seemed too remote to imagine.

As the revolutionary rumblings reached her, Fuller moved on to Milan, where the two most interesting attractions in her judgment were neither scenery nor statuary. With the first, the Marchioness Arconati, Fuller's rendezvous was sad and brief. The marchioness had just lost a nephew. Distressed and overcome with fatigue, Arconati spent only a few minutes with Fuller, though they agreed to meet again.[54] Fuller had a happier meeting with a man of tender expression and engaging manners: the elderly poet Alessandro Manzoni. Fuller was greatly impressed with Manzoni's consummate poetic taste, and she enjoyed his company. However, she grouped him with earlier acquaintances like Wordsworth and De Quincey as a representative of "the last epoch in thought."[55] Despite their depth of spirit and beauty of form, Fuller saw clearly that Manzoni's verses embodied a kind of genteel passivity that the times no longer wanted. In its new, hopeful fervor, Young Italy demanded a poetics not of urbane eloquence, but of revolutionary fire. In Fuller's view, Young Italy was right.

After a brief sortie into Switzerland, Fuller slowly made her way south, visiting Lake Como and Lake Lugano. As if to underscore her growing disdain for the prejudices of her own country, she told the *Tribune* that any American who claimed that the Italian lakes were no finer than their New World counterparts "must be exceedingly obtuse in organization—a defect not uncommon among Americans."[56] As she took in the sights of Lake Como, Fuller also felt prompted to compare the Italian and American people. Here, too, she favored her hosts. Even though it seemed to her that the Italians swindled her at every opportunity, she found in the lower classes "a winning sweetness, a ready and discriminating love of the beautiful, and a delicacy in the sympathies, the absence of which always made me sick in our own country."[57] Fuller's time there was further brightened by the arrival of Arconati, with whom she discussed German, American, and Italian literature and who helped acquaint Fuller "with some of the high society, duchesses, marquises and the like."[58] Their friendship was now fast. Though Arconati distrusted the politics of Fuller's more radical admirers, Mazzini and Mickiewicz, she called Fuller herself a woman "of true merit and veritable greatness."[59]

On a return visit to Milan, Fuller took her measure of the region's hated Austrian occupiers, who, she believed, had no faculties for understanding the Italian character. All their efforts, she wrote, had been to placate the ruling families instead of serving the people. The Austrians had preserved a tenuous outward peace, but the inner lives of the Milanese had languished. The Austrian policy regarding the lower orders had been to allow them a modest material well-being, while using a rigorous press censorship and a ban on public meetings to keep them in a mentally torpid state. Among the middle classes, however, Fuller observed a fermentation of political unrest that, Fuller predicted, would soon "produce a wine that shall set the Lombard veins on fire." Fuller had only scorn for traveling Americans she met who argued that the Milanese, full-stomached but empty-headed, were "*happy enough*." Bitterly, she denounced the American perspective that mistook porcine complacency for happiness. Such blindness, she argued, was the ugly consequence of America's own glutted prosperity; its lust for gain and love of show had robbed its upper classes of any concept of true freedom.[60]

Fuller herself was unable to grasp a possibility that her despised traveling Americans considered obvious. They assumed that a person without political freedom might still find a satisfactory happiness in the firm authority of the church, a full kettle of soup, and the blessings of a family—that these pleasures might actually mean more to some people than constitutional liberties. These countrymen of Fuller's saw her as a reckless troublemaker, willing to jeopardize the satisfactions of people she scarcely knew in furtherance of a revolution whose success no one could guarantee. Fuller stood convinced that "happy enough" was not enough for her. She could not accept that it might possibly suffice for others.

Passing again through Florence, Fuller again fell ill and could not press on toward Rome according to schedule. Thankfully, she had arranged to stay with the American sculptor Joseph Mozier and his wife, Isabella, who generously provided the rest, nourishment, and gentle exercise that she needed to recover.[61] As Fuller slowly regained her strength, she heard working-class laborers singing patriotic anthems as they walked home in the moonlight. She went to the theater, where plays with liberal political themes could now be staged.[62] The joyous enthusiasm of the audience assured her that, with slow and prudent steps, Tuscany, too, was on the move.

Fuller returned to Rome around October 10, 1847, having seen what she considered the most important features of Italy's past. She came back hoping to witness the beginnings of a greater future. By now, her long abstinence from speaking English had made her fluent in Italian. But it was not just facility with the language that made her feel at home. The Italians, she told her mother in a long, ecstatic letter, "sympathize with my character . . . as no other people ever did; they admire the ready eloquence of my nature, and highly prize my intelligent sympathy (such as they do not find often in foreigners) with their sufferings . . . and hopes."[63] Only three or four rainy days disturbed the sunlit autumn, and every day grapes and fresh roses graced her table. No longer a tourist, she lived as much like a Roman as an American could live. The city ceased to be a place of taverns, lodging houses, and cheating chambermaids and began to confide to her some of its actual life. "Now," she wrote to the *Tribune*, "I begin to see and feel the real Rome."[64]

She only wondered why she had not been born there. Although she still complained about her want of money, she found it within her budget to rent a charming suite of rooms on the narrow but vibrant Corso, within easy distance of the places that, for many visitors, define the essence of Rome: the Piazza del Popolo, the Borghese gardens, the Spanish Steps. She exulted to her mother, "to live here, alone and independent . . . Oh! What joy!"[65]

She had every reason to rejoice. At home in the city she adored, her long mental and cultural growth essentially complete, she felt as if she had reached a high point of her life, one where she might reasonably hope to remain for some time. One of the few people who knew her in both America and Rome, Emelyn Story, observed a profound difference in Fuller. She was more generous, more relaxed. The "person on intellectual stilts with a large share of arrogance & little sweetness of temper" was now gentle, confiding, and affectionate. Story admitted to Fuller that she had misjudged her; Fuller confessed the change: "I am not the same person but in many respects another. My life has new channels now & how thankful I am that I have been able to come out into larger interests."[66] Of Fuller's many metamorphoses, none had given her more immediate satisfaction.

Fuller continued in her admiration of Pio Nono, whom she continued to go out of her way to observe on public occasions. One of these took place on November 4, just down the street from her rooms, at the baroque church of San Carlo. In another place, the façade of San Carlo would be exceptional. In Rome, it is merely one of many. Once inside, however, one is likely to feel transported. Above the altar, the structure's alabaster columns, crowned by golden capitals, rise toward a high, spectacular dome. To those inclined to believe, the church's interior can feel like physical proof of the triumph of Christ. It is a place where a person of significance, for instance, the foreign correspondent of the *New-York Tribune*, might feel dwarfed and humbled.

Pio entered, carried on a chair of state and grandly imposing in his white and gold robes. The pontiff's vestments, however, did not impress Fuller as deeply as the expression on his face, which again transfixed her. It was a face, she wrote, "to shame the selfish [and] redeem the skeptic." His gestures of blessing seemed not at all rehearsed, but rather "the spontaneous act of a soul which felt [at] that moment more than usual its relation with things above it, and sure of support from a higher Power." Fuller called him "the beloved Father." She wrote earlier in the same dispatch, "It makes me very happy to be for once in a place ruled by a father's love."[67] The choice of word was no mere formality. Pio was, for Fuller, an embodiment of paternal love—as cheerful, patient, and understanding as she had always imagined it.

Happy as she was, and even though she told her mother she was settling into "six months of quiet occupation," Fuller did not take naturally to peaceful satisfaction.[68] Feeling less of a need to revolutionize herself, Fuller turned her reformist impulses outward. She immersed herself in the debates and forces that were driving Rome and all of Italy toward political upheaval. She filled her dispatches from Rome in the fall of 1847 with bold exhortations, urging Americans to realize that the cause of Italian nationalism belonged to the United States as well. She called on her countrymen not to wait for their government to act, but to act as individuals for the good of humankind—in her words, to "take a good chance and do something."[69]

Beyond the level of the purely symbolic—she wanted Americans to buy the Romans a cannon emblazoned with the name of the explorer John Cabot to be used by the National Guard on festive occasions—Fuller had no clear idea as to what that "something" might be. Still, her larger objectives were clear. The pure-hearted but penniless champions of Italian freedom stood in need of America's wealth and power. Conversely, America, whose acceptance of slavery had made it into "a robber and a jailer" and whose power and wealth had led it to forget its own republican ideals, stood in equally desperate need of inspiration and reform.[70] Fuller hoped that, by encouraging an alliance between Italy and America, she could help the former to win its unity and the latter to recover its soul. If Fuller actually doubted that publicizing Italy's noble striving might induce her own country to throw off the curse of slavery, to renounce the lust for conquest that had led to war with Mexico, and to turn its gaze away from plunder and toward the stars, she nonetheless considered it worth a try.

To her greatest source of satisfaction, Fuller made no allusion in either her public or her private writings. To Emerson, she wrote, "I live alone, eat alone, walk alone, and enjoy unspeakably the stillness."[71] She misled him. Her meals, walks, and other enjoyments were now regularly being taken in the company of the Marchese Ossoli, whose confident hope that she would come back to him had been rewarded. They did not advertise their relationship, and Fuller rather enjoyed the insularity of their secret. "With Ossoli," she recalled more than two years later, "I liked when no one knew of our relation, and we passed our days together in the mountains, or walked beautiful nights amid the ruins of Rome."[72]

If Fuller needed a helpful nudge as she stood on the brink of romance, she had it in the form of a letter from Mickiewicz, which he had sent her the previous spring, shortly after she had first met Ossoli. "Prolong your good moments!" the poet had urged her. "Don't leave lightly those who would remain close to you. In this I refer to that young Italian whom you met in the church."[73] A few months later, he had written her:

> You have pleaded the liberty of woman in masculine and frank style. Live and act as you write! . . . You have persuaded yourself that all you need is to express your ideas and feelings in books. . . . Do not forget that even in your private life as a woman you have rights to maintain. Emerson says rightly: give all for love, but this love must not be that of the shepherds of Florian nor that of schoolboys. . . . The relationships which suit you are those which develop and free your spirit, responding to the legitimate needs of your organism and leaving you free at all times.[74]

Now, she heeded his advice, but it was her own impulse, not Mickiewicz's counsel or anyone else's, that guided her. As to all that happened next, she later wrote, "I could not analyze at all what passed in my mind. I neither rejoice nor grieve, for bad or for good I acted out my character."[75]

As the days shortened and the leaves of Rome clung to their trees against the breezes of the late autumn, Fuller spent days and evenings with Ossoli. The particular notes they heard at concerts, the slant of light they saw as they walked through trees and gardens, the tastes of pastries and coffees and wines they savored in cafes—all these are lost to history. We know for certain only one fact of these days and nights of Margaret and Giovanni: that at least one of them ended in bed.

It was more likely hers than his. That way they would have evaded the suspicious, disapproving Ossolis. It was probably then, above the teeming bustle of the Corso, on an early December evening, that Margaret Fuller changed once again. Perhaps she felt as if she had risen to a marvelous height. Yet, simultaneously, something also crumbled. No one can say whether she realized in full that, after this moment, the answer to her old, persistent question, "Who is this Margaret Fuller?" would never be the same. Never again would there be the free ascension, the unfettered striving for oneness with her prophetic, Platonic god. Her life's struggle to become a self-perfecting being had always run counter to the inconvenient human wants of her body—to be free from loneliness, to know the shocks and enfoldings of passion, to be loved. One night in Rome, Giovanni Ossoli gave her these long-awaited gifts, but they came at a price. Never again could Margaret Fuller hope to stand alone atop her immaculate mountain. The pure spirit submitted freely to its human chains.

The beautiful but intimate church of San Luigi dei Francesi, a short walk from the Pantheon, receives pleasant natural light on sunny days. However, when Fuller came to mass there on Christmas Day, 1847, the skies were dark and the rain fell steadily. In the church's celebrated Contarelli Chapel, adorned by three majestic chiaroscuro paintings by Caravaggio on the theme of Saint Matthew, all was more dark than light. A darkness was within her too. And the tone of her dispatches darkened as well. During the early winter of 1848, the rainy season shrouded Rome in sultry, damp, and brooding atmosphere. The city that had greeted Fuller with sunlight now appalled her with its gloomy aspect and the reek of its "malignant vapors." Even a rendez-vous with her old friend Henry Hedge, who was passing through the city, did little to dispel the melancholy. Abruptly, she changed her eating habits, adopting what she called "the Greeley diet." She swore off meat, wine, and tea—even her beloved strong coffee—and resolved to subsist "on a little rice cooked with milk and such vegetables as Rome supplies."[76] In winter, the available vegetables were few, except for a "horrible cabbage," in which the Romans delighted but she heartily deplored. The rice was a good deal better, especially since it reminded her of her time in Lombardy. Still, she found that even this gentle regime annoyed her stomach. At the same time, her writings grew ominously morose. Remembering the rice fields of Lombardy in a *Tribune* dispatch, she also recalled the region's "tall plantations of hemp." Death by hanging was in her thoughts as she added darkly, "[I]t is dangerous just at present to think of what is made from hemp."[77]

It is a peculiar practice for a journalist to use her column to hint at sui-cide. Fuller's private writings were just as troubled. On New Year's Day, 1848, she wrote a letter to her brother Richard that was a study in gloom. In it, she imagined him married, traveling to Italy and "perhaps visiting [her] grave."[78] The letter's images are of blighted flowers and of trees stripped of their leaves and bearing no harvest. She added enigmatically, "God knows I have not myself been wise in life."[79] On January 11, she sent Caroline Sturgis, recently married to William Tappan, a letter that she could "hardly write for tears." She confessed, "I feel as if I had received a great injury. I am tired and woe-worn; often, in the bed, I wish I could weep my life away." Her view of the future gave her no hope, and she bared her soul in some of the most despondent lines she had ever written:

> [W]ith this year, I enter upon a sphere of my destiny so difficult, that I, at present, see no way out, except through the gate of death. It is useless to write of it; you are at a distance and cannot help me;— whether accident or angel will, I have no intimation. I have no reason to hope I shall not reap what I have sown, and do not. Yet how I shall endure it I cannot guess, it is all a dark, sad enigma. The beautiful form of art charms no more, and a love, in which there is all fondness, but no help, flatters in vain.[80]

Beneath these evasive hints and vague forebodings lay a shameful feeling, a sense that she had brought an unhappy fate upon herself and that a reckoning was soon to come. "I am all alone," she continued, "nobody around me sees any of this."[81] But she knew that they soon would see and that the nature of her "great injury" would be evident to all. At thirty-seven, in a foreign land, Margaret Fuller was pregnant.

CHAPTER TWELVE

REVOLUTIONARY

Bodies rotten and trembling cannot long
contend with swelling life. Tongue and hand
cannot be permanently employed to keep
down hearts. . . . Joy to those born in this day.

—MARGARET FULLER, "ITALY,"
New-York Daily Tribune, February 13, 1850

*T*HE WINTER WORE ON, A SEASON OF CONTINUAL BLACK RAIN AND
impassable mud. Everything Fuller saw seemed to mirror back to her the
guilt and desolation she felt as she brooded on her irremediable error. In the
first *Tribune* dispatch that she wrote after discovering her pregnancy, Fuller
noted going to a church to watch a young woman from a good family become
a nun. There was no romance in what she saw, and she deduced from the
woman's "quite worldly air" that her taking the veil "was one of those
arrangements made because no suitable arrangement could otherwise be
given her."[1] Fuller found the ceremony painful to watch; she could not toler-
ate the idea of embracing seclusion once and for all—the deathly concept of
wedding oneself forever to a given fate or purpose. The very notion of such
permanency clashed with her theory of life. And yet, like the young nun,
Fuller, too, had crossed into a place where she could never again reinvent
herself at will. Mickiewicz had represented sexual experience to her as liberation; in fact, it had stolen her freedom. Where a condition "is enforced or
repented of," Fuller wrote, "no hell could be worse."[2] She never wrote with
greater personal conviction. Her emotional woes were only part of her mal-

aise; she was going through severe first-trimester nausea, and everything she ate made her ill. She could not escape believing that her identity as a woman, which had always restricted her, had viciously betrayed her yet again. She wrote to Cary Sturgis, newly married to William Tappan, "There is, undoubtedly, foundation for the story of a curse laid on Eve."[3] She had one shining consolation. Ossoli, whatever else might be said of him, was no coward. There is no hint that he ever dreamed of abandoning Fuller.

There was no question that Margaret and Giovanni cared greatly for each other. Had no need for a deeper commitment arisen, they would likely have continued as lovers for quite some time. "But for the child," Fuller observed later, "I should have wished to remain as we were, and feared we should lose much by entering on the jog-trot of domestic life."[4] In an age that could impose crushing disadvantages on children born out of wedlock, however, going on as before was out of the question. Just what the couple did do, however, remains uncertain to this day. As a social proposition, it was impossible for the two to openly marry. Though Margaret and Giovanni may well have wondered what the Fullers and Margaret's friends, not to mention Greeley's readership, would have thought of such a marriage, the principal reasons for caution came from the couple's fear of how Giovanni's family would respond.

The Ossolis lived in a traditional world in which children married to forge and strengthen alliances, not to affirm love or legitimize bastards. Moreover, Giovanni's ancestors had served the papacy closely and loyally for centuries, a tradition they meant to preserve. Giovanni's father, Filippo, now in his seventies, was a regional administrator in the papal government. Giovanni's three older brothers were also in the service of Pio Nono: eldest brother Giuseppe was a secretary in the pope's Privy Chamber, and middle brothers Alessandro and Ottavio wore colonels' uniforms in Pio's Noble Guard. Giovanni's leftist politics were already an uncomfortable subject for his family. It did not matter how warmly Fuller may have praised the pope in her columns for the *Tribune*; the idea of Giovanni's being married to an American Protestant, and a radical republican at that, would have been at best a grave embarrassment to the Ossolis, and surely of no help in winning further favors from the papal court.

The crowning reasons for Fuller and Ossoli to conceal both their attachment and her pregnancy were economic. Though Fuller had been living tolerably well in Rome, much of her comfort had been purchased on credit. She was earning only ten dollars a column from the *Tribune*, and the transatlantic mail made payments unreliable. Apart from his service in the Civil Guard, Ossoli had no profession. Largely dependent on the generosity of his family, he could ill afford to share with them the news of Margaret's condition. Indeed, Giovanni's position in the family was soon to worsen for another reason. When Fuller discovered she was pregnant, Filippo Ossoli was already in failing health. He was to die in February. His estate was to be administered by Giovanni's brother Giuseppe. By all accounts a grasping, manipulative man, Giuseppe had made no secret of his intention to seize every available scudo of his father's estate. He would surely have used his younger brother's indiscretion as a means of keeping him from his inheritance. Fuller disliked evasiveness, and she remembered Goethe's observation that, as she paraphrased it, "[t]here is nothing men pardon so little as singular conduct for which no reason is given."[5] But honesty at this point seemed a risky course. Whatever the two lovers chose to do, it was evident that they must do it quietly.

No researcher has ever been able to unearth a marriage certificate with the names Margaret Fuller and Giovanni Ossoli. Nevertheless, the existing evidence makes it more likely than not that they were married, though the time and place remain uncertain. The proof begins with Margaret's friend in Rome, Emelyn Story, who writes of having received in May 1849, from Fuller's own hands, a parchment document, which Story was to hold for safekeeping. The document, prepared by the priest who, according to Fuller, had performed her marriage, stated that the couple's son was the legal heir to his father's estate. Story also attested to receiving a book from Fuller, in which the latter had inscribed "the history of her acquaintance and marriage with Ossoli, and of the birth of her child."[6] Fuller took these documents back again when Story and her husband, William, made ready to leave Rome for Switzerland a few weeks later.

Second, Lewis Cass Jr., the American ambassador to the Papal States, wrote of going to see Fuller just before the fall of Rome in late June 1849. Fuller handed him a packet that, she said, contained the certificates of her marriage and of the birth and baptism of her son. Still more persuasive is the recently discovered certificate of the boy's baptism, which expressly refers to "the married Mr. Giovanni Angelo of Marquis Ossoli from Rome and Mrs.

Margaret Fuller heterodox from America."[7] Unless Fuller and Ossoli were carrying on a sustained campaign of outright deception, lying to family friends, a representative of the American government, and the church itself, it is clear that, sooner or later, they had become husband and wife.

Some shreds of evidence argue that their nuptials took place on April 4, 1848, when Fuller was approximately five months pregnant. In a letter dated April 3 the following year, when Ossoli was in Rome and Fuller was in the town of Rieti, he wrote to her, "Dear, how much I wish to spend tomorrow with you, since I well believe you will remember that it is the 4th April."[8] On the fourth itself, Margaret wrote to Ossoli, "How very strange it is we cannot spend this day together. We must pray to be happier another year."[9] The date, clearly of strong significance to both of them, was evidently an anniversary. It takes an effort to argue that that anniversary commemorated something other than their wedding.[10]

If the surviving documents offer only probable evidence as to the date of the Ossolis' wedding, they offer none at all as to the ceremony's details. Since the couple managed to keep the fact of their marriage almost perfectly dark for more than a year, it may be assumed that the wedding involved only the necessary parties and as little ceremony as possible. Even to imagine the thoughts that passed through Fuller's mind as the priest recited the liturgy is to descend into guesswork. Yet she could hardly have avoided reflecting on the absence of her family, particularly of her mother, who had yet to witness any of her children's weddings. Almost certainly, too, she must have wondered about her future with the man beside her, who shared none of her passion for ideas and whom she might never have taken as a husband if it were not for the child in her womb. In a letter to William Henry Channing, one of the first that disclosed her relationship with Ossoli, she was to write, "If earthly union be meant for the beginning of one permanent and full, we ought not to be united."[11] In *Woman in the Nineteenth Century*, Fuller had described the ideal marriage as "an intellectual communion" and "a pilgrimage towards a common shrine."[12] Ossoli, she knew, was hardly capable of such a communion or journey. He was loving and loyal. In the coming months, he was also to prove himself both patriotic and brave. These qualities might more than suffice in an ordinary marriage, but could such a man suffice for a woman who had always searched for the extraordinary? No matter; it was a time not for asking questions but for exchanging vows. Henceforth, Ossoli was, in her letters, not merely "mio caro" or "mio amore," but also "Cmo Consorte"—Dear husband.[13]

Meanwhile, the wider world had been driving on. It was 1848, that remarkable fissure in time still known as the Year of Revolutions. In Rome, as the year began, the people were restive and apt to react to the slightest provocation. On New Year's Day, a crowd requested permission to go to the papal residence at the Palazzo del Quirinale to receive Pio's blessing. The governor, knowing that Pio was ill, refused, saying only, "He is tired of these things; he is afraid of disturbance." In response to this brusque communiqué, the people grew agitated. The governor doubled the pope's guard. Tensions had reached a volatile point by the time Pio was informed of the situation. The next day, declaring that, if the people might not come to him, he would go to them, he defied his illness and passed through the principal parts of the city. People fell to their knees, imploring him not to desert them. Weeping, Pio reassured the public, "Fear nothing; my heart is yours."[14]

Fuller took the incident as proof that not only the future of reform but also public order itself might well depend on the goodwill and generosity of one mortal man. She almost dared to believe what she had been told in Bologna: "If Pius IX be spared to us five years, it will be impossible for his successors ever to take a backward course."[15] Fuller still could not be wholly optimistic. It appeared to her, quite rightly, that Pio Nono would need more than brave and good intentions to reform his church and unite Italy. He would require political genius as well, and Fuller had never suspected the pope of being a great thinker. She had been especially disappointed by a speech he had given to the consistory, in which he had reaffirmed the doctrine that only members of his church could be saved from eternal damnation. In Pio's adherence to long-established dogma, Fuller saw the fetters of a bigoted education and the outlines of a man "terribly afraid to seem or be less the Pope of Rome, in becoming a Reform Prince, and father to the fatherless."[16] She seemed not to recognize the strangeness of her own position; she was essentially denouncing the pope for failing to be Protestant.

In a dispatch published in the *Tribune* on February 19, 1848, Fuller included the full text of an open letter from Mazzini to the pontiff, exhorting him to openly endorse the unification of Italy. All would be well, Mazzini insisted, if only the pope were to rise above the squabbles of politics and "embrace in your love the twenty four millions of Italians, your brothers;

[and show them] that you believe them called by God to unite in family unity under one and the same compact."[17] Though Fuller praised Mazzini's letter for its simple nobility and fervent truth, neither she nor her exiled friend could be sure that the pope had even read it.

Nevertheless, as the winter of 1847–48 unfolded, it was easy to believe that an extraordinary new era was dawning across Europe. Surprisingly, the first of the revolts had come in one of the corners of the continent where authority seemed least subject to challenge: King Ferdinand's staunchly repressive Kingdom of the Two Sicilies. On January 12, the people of Palermo took up arms, and the unrest soon spread to the mainland portion of the kingdom. In a gesture that thrilled the radicals in Rome, Pio Nono refused to permit Austrian troops to cross his territory to quell the rebellion. Before the month was out, a humiliated King Ferdinand had issued an edict forming the basis for a constitutional government. A far larger domino fell on February 24, when, the day after a bloody clash between a civilian crowd and the municipal guard in the streets of Paris, King Louis-Philippe abruptly abdicated. Two days later, the poet-statesman Alphonse de Lamartine proclaimed a new republican government, which promptly instituted universal male suffrage and created National Workshops to assist unemployed workers in finding jobs. Less than three weeks later, an armed insurrection broke out in Vienna. Within days, the Austrian emperor was forced to dismiss Metternich from his position as chancellor. His career suddenly over, Metternich emigrated to England. When news of the Viennese revolt reached Rome, Austrian arms were dragged through the streets and thrown onto a bonfire in the Piazza del Popolo as members of a jubilant crowd embraced and cried, "Miracolo! Providenza!"[18]

Almost at once, the center stage of insurgency returned to Italy. Heartened by the uprising in Vienna, the people of Milan rose up against the Austrian occupying force and, after five days of heavy fighting, drove their oppressors from the city. Simultaneously, Venice threw off her Austrian rulers and declared herself a republic. If Rome remained relatively calm, it was only because of the people's tremendous faith in Pio Nono and their confidence that, when the time was right, the pope would embrace constitutional reform without needing a rebellion to persuade him.

Throughout a rainy February and almost all of March, Fuller did not write a word for the *Tribune*. Some small part of her silence may have derived

John Hicks painted Fuller in Rome during her pregnancy. Pale and tired,
she was showing the strain of her personal and political worries.

(COURTESY OF CONSTANCE THREINEN AND THE NATIONAL PORTRAIT GALLERY)

from her innate skepticism; she may have wanted more time to digest the rapid succession of events before reacting. For the most part, though, the cause of her silence was physical; her pregnancy had, for a time, made her too ill to write. Thoughts of her family depressed her too; in a letter to Richard, she went over the fortunes of their siblings in a sobering litany. Eugene had, "after all his tribulation," found some satisfaction as a New Orleans newspaperman, but Margaret feared that either his health or his finances might give way. William Henry, limping along as a businessman in Cincinnati, seemed likely to achieve nothing memorable. Ellen could be freed from want and woe only if Ellery were to die. Of one-eyed Arthur, she wrote, "His calamity hangs on him like a cloud." Her own courage, she told Richard, had given way. In her letter, she revisited the old pipedream of living with Richard on a farm. It sounded preferable to her work for the *Tribune*, "where the excitements of the hour use up my strength and prevent my doing any thing of permanent value."[19]

Not daring to disclose the chief reason for her weakness and dejection, she blamed the dirt, gloom, and desolation of the Roman winter, calling the three months from December to March "the most idling and suffering season of [her] life." On March 29, however, when she finally wrote a dispatch for Greeley, her tone was buoyant. All at once, almost in unison with the coming of the equinox, both the pounding winter rains and her sickness subsided. The sun shone gloriously, and hundreds of larks sang above her cherished city. She mentioned with approval the uprisings in Milan and crowed over the downfall of "the serpent" Metternich.[20] She greeted with thankful disbelief the political demise of Louis-Philippe and his "empire of sham," confessing that she had never dreamed that France, with its soul "held fast as in an iron vice [sic] . . . would burst its chains so soon."[21]

Nearer to home, on March 14, Pio Nono added to the revolutionary momentum by declaring a constitution for the Papal States, modeled on the French constitution of 1830. As a statement of human rights, the pope's constitution was tepid at best; it granted full civil rights only to Catholics and expressly denied citizenship to Jews. Yet it was a start. A few days later, Fuller narrated with tender joy the Romans' belated celebration of Carnival. It was customary for the people who lived along the Corso to conclude the festival by lighting countless little wax candles, or "moccoletti," and holding them out from windows and balconies above the street. The candles' flames would dance and flutter like swarms of fireflies, illuminating the brown façades of the buildings and suffusing the smiling faces of the crowd with a soft yellow glow. Usually, the festival concluded with the people blowing out one another's candles. In 1848, however, the lighting of the moccoletti was initially renounced, in sympathy, it was said, with the struggles of the resisters in Milan. Near the end of the third week in March, however, as republican flags flew over Milan, Venice, and Paris, the moccoletti appeared in a demonstration of solidarity and hope. Fuller watched as the cheerful little lights appeared by the thousands up and down the Corso, as a surge of triumphant noise arose from the dancing crowds that filled the avenue. Some rattled chains to symbolize the casting off of tyranny. On this night, too, the people did not extinguish one another's lights. Instead, the candles were allowed to burn until they naturally expired, symbolizing the flickering light of freedom that it was every Roman's duty to keep alive. The evening ended around nine when, after singing hymns for Pio Nono, the crowd peaceably dispersed. The people then retired to their homes and, as Fuller put it, lay down "to dream of hopes they yet scarce understand."[22]

Every day, young men in Rome were taking up arms—not to be used against their own government but to carry with them as they marched off to the western border of the Papal States. It was generally supposed that they would soon be ordered into battle against the Austrians. On March 24, news was sent from Piedmont-Sardinia: Charles Albert, quick to spot a weakness in his adversary, had declared war on Austria. That day and the next, some sixteen thousand troops marched from Rome to support the cause. The pope blessed their banners. While choosing not to state his precise military intentions, the pope proclaimed on March 31, "The events which these two months past have seen rush after one another in so rapid succession, are no human work. Woe to him who in this wind, which shakes and tears up alike the lofty cedars and humble shrubs, hears not the voice of God!"[23]

Fuller spent the thirty-first, just four days before she likely became the Marchesa d'Ossoli, at the mouth of the Tiber on the Mediterranean. "A million birds sang," she wrote, "and the woods teemed with blossoms." Still pale from the rainy winter, Fuller left her face exposed too long. However, the sea breezes that she accused of burning her face also revived her heart. "I felt the calm of thought, the sublime hopes of the Future," she told her *Tribune* readers, "Nature, Man—so great, though so little—so dear, though incomplete."[24]

When she returned to the city, not only to the news of the pope's procla-
mation but also to word that the Austrian viceroy charged with governing
Lombardy and Venetia had surrendered to the insurgency, Fuller was
ecstatic. She wrote excitedly to Channing, "It is a time such as I always
dreamed of, and for long secretly hoped to see. . . . A glorious flame burns
higher and higher in the hearts of the nations."[25] To the *Tribune*, she sent a
resounding, though highly premature report: "Italy is free, independent, and
One."[26] It seemed to Fuller that Europe had awakened to a new, aspiring
truth. She dared to predict that the continent was soon to teach the rest of
the world—and especially slave-holding, imperialist America—the real
meaning of fraternity and equality. She predicted that America might even
learn in time to revere and protect what she boldly called "the true aristocracy of a nation, the only really noble—the LABORING CLASSES."[27] Long
ago, Fuller had left behind the self-reliant individualism of Emerson and Thoreau. Now, her political transformation was complete: for the rest of her life,
Margaret Fuller would identify herself as a socialist.

As revolution swept Europe, Fuller was learning a lesson that it would
take scientists a few more generations to translate into physics: that every
reality, no matter how outwardly solid, is a form of energy. Up to this time,
Fuller's writings and thinking had been slow translations of potential energy
into action. She was now to discover that the world was seldom moved solely
by the slow releases that came through words—even words as passionate
and incendiary as hers. She was to see with her own eyes the terrible power
of violence to cut the cords of restraint and to drive history forward. The
controlled, measured burn of her life was erupting into consuming fire.
Schelling, it now seemed clear, had been right: the logic of the universe was
indeed progress, and before her eyes that progress was happening.

But there was another physical law already known, which was also applicable to states and human beings. For every action, there is a reaction, and
the political reaction in Europe came so swiftly that it surprised Fuller even
more than the initial leftward movement. On some level of transcendental
abstraction, the logic of the universe might be progress, but the logic of
churches and governments called for stasis, and they were not slow now to
impose that law. In the early days of April, the Risorgimento continued to
look like a juggernaut. Constitutions had been adopted in Piedmont and Tuscany. The Piedmontese army defeated the Austrians at the battle of Goito. On

the seventh, Mazzini arrived in Milan, ending seventeen years of exile. On April 19, when Fuller began to write her next dispatch, she was pleased to report that, while there had still been no decisive victory for freedom and unification, everything had thus far turned in the republicans' favor. In the last lines she wrote that day, Fuller expressed a more radical hope than Mazzini's vision of a Christian democracy. She claimed to foresee a truly radical reordering of society "of which the cry of Communism, the systems of Fourier, &c, are but forerunners."[28]

Fuller then set aside her unfinished essay. When she took it up again only eighteen days later, everything had changed. In this crucial interim, Pio Nono had become more conscious of the bind in which his dual identities as leader of the Catholic Church and as a secular Italian prince had placed him. A bracing dose of reality came on Saint Mark's Day. The pope's army on the western border was under the command of Giacomo Durando, a politically ambitious general eager to make a name for himself. On April 25, despite having been ordered by the pope only to secure the border, Durando commanded his force across the frontier to join Charles Albert in his fight with the Austrians. The pope was aghast. Usurping and imperialist though it might be, Austria was a Catholic nation, and its soldiers were as much Pio's spiritual children as the citizens of Rome. As an Italian prince, he might or might not support unification and reform. As pope, however, he clearly could not wage a war of aggression against a Catholic power. Four days after Durando began his march, Pio published an allocution in which he declared that joining in the war with Austria was "altogether alien from our counsels" and that, as vice regent of Christ, "the Author of Peace and lover of Charity," he meant to approach all peoples and nations "with equal solicitude of paternal affection." The pope also repudiated in the clearest terms the hope, held by countless Italians, that he might willingly serve as the ruler of a new republic of the whole Italian people. Rather, Pio urged the Italians "to abide in close attachment to their respective sovereigns, of whose good will they have already had experience."[29] In the space of a few paragraphs, the most powerful spiritual leader in the western world had, in the name of peace and charity, withdrawn his support from the causes of Italian unity and European democracy. The revolutionary tide of 1848 had reached its high watermark.

When the pope's words were posted on the walls of Rome, a wail went up

around the city. After a moment's stupefaction, the people rose up in indignation. Lips that had blessed the holy name of Pio only days before now
formed the words "imbecile" and "traitor." Amid the turbulence, mass meetings were called. The pope's ministers resigned en masse. For a few anxious
days, the city teetered on the brink of open revolt. Yet the city did not erupt.
Fuller credited the maintenance of order to the gentleness and good sense of
the people. But she, like them, was plainly devastated. Now that the pope had
denounced the cause, no one could say how many Italians would still resist
the Austrians. Furthermore, there was no one who could restore the moral
momentum that Pio had just depleted. Fuller thought the damage to the
papal throne was permanent. "There will never more be really a Pope," she
declared, "but only the effigy or simulacrum of one." Recalling the good that
he had done, she did not join with those who called him a traitor; in her eyes,
he was merely "weak," "blind," and traduced by his advisors.[30] She could not
appreciate the moral imperative that prevented the pope from raising a sword
against a Catholic nation. His allocution was, in her words, a "final derelic-
tion."[31] In her letters, Pio was "a modern Lot's wife and no more a living soul,
but cold pillar of the Past."[32]

Fearing for her safety, Fuller's American friends, Emerson among them,
urged her to come home.[33] From the pages of the Tribune, she vowed to see
the crisis through, with a severity of rhetoric that made her criticisms of the
pope seem mild. America had become to her a land "spoiled by prosperity,
stupid with the lust of gain, soiled by crime in its willful perpetuation of slavery, shamed by an unjust war [with Mexico] . . . the aims of [its] politicians
selfish or petty, the literature frivolous and venal."[34] The values that had
made her America—its earnest words of pure faith and love, its noble deeds
of brotherhood—she had found in much greater profusion in Italy. One day,
she was sure, America would rise out of its gluttony and falsehood and would
fulfill its promise. For the time being, though, the nobler spirit was in Europe.
"Everything," she wrote to Costanza Arconati, "confirms me in my radicalism."[35] If she could do nothing of substance to advance the Risorgimento,
she was glad at least to be its historian.

Then, without a word of explanation to her readers, Fuller fell silent.
After finishing her May 13 dispatch on the defection of the pope, she wrote
no more columns for six and a half months. For the early part of that time,
she was almost too dejected to write. Three weeks after the pope's allocution,

she wrote to Thomas Hicks with all the gaiety of a suicide note: "I have suffered in life far more than I enjoyed, and I think quite out of proportion with the use my living here is of to others. I have wished to be natural and true, but the world was not in harmony with me—nothing came right for me." She was, she said, "willing to die."[36] Her spirits recovered, but for most of her long journalistic silence, she was not in Rome at all. In late May, she moved to the countryside, telling her brother Richard that she was going in search of a healthier climate and cheaper living.[37] This was true enough, especially the part about her finances. Fuller's rich Uncle Abraham had died the previous year of heart disease.[38] Despite their long wranglings over Timothy's estate, Margaret had dared to hope that, in death, her uncle would be more generous than in life and would leave her a substantial legacy. She was disappointed; her share of his estate came to less than a thousand dollars, at a time when she owed about four hundred. She was saddened to think how easily her uncle might have brushed aside her chronic need, and she imagined that he remained flinty and vindictive even in death. If his ghost should ever discover that he had somehow helped her, Fuller wrote, it would sigh at the thought.[39]

Real as her financial need may have been, though, the true reason for her departure was more delicate. The Ossolis' child was due in early September. If they hoped to conceal for much longer the fact of the baby's illegitimate conception, Margaret had to leave Rome. For her long sequestration, she and Ossoli chose the town of L'Aquila, a town some sixty miles to the northeast, situated near the highest of the Apennines and sheltered by medieval walls in the broad valley of the Aterno River. Politically, the circumstances of the town were not ideal; it lay within the Kingdom of the Two Sicilies and, therefore, under the intolerant rule of Ferdinand. It would clearly be best for Fuller to keep her political opinions to herself. On the other hand, as Fuller herself observed, it was a place "where no foreigner goes," and no old acquaintances were likely to turn up out of the blue, asking unwelcome questions about her interesting condition.[40] She left Rome half suspecting that she would never again write for the *Tribune*. Now she had a book in mind: a memoir of her experiences in Europe, culminating in a personal history of the Italian revolutions.

Ossoli was unable to join her. His duties as a sergeant in the Civic Guard kept him in Rome. It was common at that time to refer to a pregnancy as a confinement. For Fuller, in her self-imposed exile in L'Aquila, the term had a literal resonance. Divided from her friends, cut off from the surge of events, able to see Ossoli only when he obtained leave, she had suddenly passed from one of the most exciting episodes of her life to one of the most stultifying. To Costanza Arconati, she described her new abode as "a lonely mountain home."[41] She found some relief from the maddening isolation by going on daily excursions of three to four hours, sometimes on foot and sometimes astride a donkey. The trails she followed, fringed with olive trees, almond groves, and vineyards, were almost handsome enough to take her mind off her loneliness. However, when she discovered that two of the paths out of town led to monasteries, she could hardly have failed to see the similarity between the solitude of the draped, red-cheeked monks and her own. When she passed by clusters of country people, they would say, "'Povera, sola, soletta [poor one, alone, all alone]! The saints keep her."[42] Yet her solitude was also an advantage. Seeing "no one but Italian Contadines," she had little to distract her from her writing. Her book was advancing rapidly.[43]

In one sense, L'Aquila supplied a balm to her ego. The people there, knowing almost nothing of the larger world, regarded Fuller as "a divine visitant . . . telling them wonderful tales of foreign customs and even legends of their own saints."[44] Regarding current events, however, Fuller's ignorance was almost as complete as theirs. Beyond the encircling mountains that now defined her existence, the fate of a continent was being determined, but she could have no part in it. She was connected to events only by newspapers and Ossoli's letters. But Ossoli was not a man of verbal gifts, and, although she pleaded in her letters to him for more details of his life and days, he had little inclination or ability to oblige. Every so often, he did manage some specific word about the fight for independence, as when he wrote excitedly of a victory by Charles Albert's army. Even then, however, he could be exasperatingly unreliable; the "victory" was only a successful rear-guard action covering the king's retreat. As for the newspaper accounts, she knew she should be writing them, not reading them. "I know nothing about the things I am interested in," she complained to Ossoli, and her lament was very nearly true.[45]

Her letters to him grew peevish: L'Aquila was too hot; she had terrible headaches; when her head felt better, her teeth were a torment; she would die if he did not visit.[46] His visits, when they happened, calmed her nerves and relaxed her, but they were too infrequent. Endless and numbing, the long wait for the birth continued. Her one dependable solace came from writing the narrative of her European experience, on which she worked all day except when taking food or exercise.[47] On June 22, she speculated that it would take her three months to finish. She said of the project, "It grows upon me." If she was right, then both her baby and her finished manuscript would see the light of day in September. As she wrote, her experiences sometimes did not seem "worth making such a fuss about," but, knowing that "one must persist to get anything done in this dissipated world," she continued to fill up her pages.[48]

Although, in her letters, she was modest and dismissive of her writing, she must have sensed that this might be the book for which she had been preparing her entire life. So often, her most memorable writing had come from righteous anger: despair in *Summer on the Lakes* over the degradation of the prairies; fury at the routine subjection of women in *Woman in the Nineteenth Century*. Again she had another topic worthy of her most regal wrath: the needs, the hopes, and the betrayals of the European working classes. Quite literally, there was no American living whom education, experiences, and political disposition had rendered more fit to relay the strivings of Europe to the readers of America. Though she complained that her sequestration and her want of money made it impossible for her "to procure reference books which would have been most precious to me," her lack of access to a library was also probably working in her favor.[49] Always in the past, her tendency to interpose a wall of books between herself and the world of experience had stolen some of the pulse and the immediacy from her writing. Now, of sheer necessity, her only materials were her memories and her passion. If it were ever published, her narrative had the potential to turn heads as none of her previous work had done. And so, day by day, both the child of her flesh and the child of her mind acquired life. And the calendar drew closer to September.

L'Aquila at last became too oppressive to bear. Toward the end of July, Fuller packed up her belongings and moved twenty-five miles west to Rieti, whose landscape, she thought, could busy the thoughts of a painter for years. At sunset, the mountains put on the same rosy hue as the Alps, and the downward rush of the ice-cold streams delighted her.[50] Rieti, too, was situated within the borders of the Papal States, a far friendlier regime to political dissidents like herself. Still better, it was only forty-two miles from

Rome and Ossoli. Perhaps most important, though, Rieti was a change. Fuller arrived there only to discover that the inn where she had hoped to reside while looking for an apartment had been destroyed. Thankfully, she had little trouble finding accommodations, in the form of a large, brick-floored room in the home of the local bishop's chancellor. Overlooking the Velino River and an attractive vineyard, she could see the contadini working a little and singing and playing more. She had never had a room that she liked so well.[51] Cool and quiet, it was an easy place in which to pass the languid days of August.

However, Fuller's peaceful detachment promptly fled whenever she picked up a newspaper. On the sixth, Radetzky's Austrians retook Milan. When Fuller learned that Charles Albert, who had vowed to defend the city "to the last drop of his blood," had withdrawn his troops without a fight, her longtime scorn for the Sardinian king redoubled. "Had the people slain him in their rage," she later fulminated, "he well deserved it at their hands."[52] Two days after the fall of Milan, a detachment of Radetzky's army invaded the Papal States and attacked Bologna. The city held, however, and it was widely supposed that this latest Austrian outrage would finally startle Pio out of his passivity and goad him into issuing a declaration of war.

This possibility mattered greatly to Ossoli, for it was also rumored that the pope would soon dispatch the Civic Guard, to which Ossoli belonged, to the battlefield. When Pio summoned the Guard to the Quirinal hill for a public statement, the mobilization seemed a fait accompli. With his wife more than eight months pregnant, Ossoli mentally prepared himself for war. Again, however, the pope chose forbearance, though others had a less kind word for it. When he addressed the guards, Pio did nothing more than bestow a renewed benediction on them. There was no rallying rhetoric, no stirring call in the name of Italy and God. Ossoli and his fellow guardsmen went home sad and angry. The forced idleness inflamed Ossoli's sense of honor. He seriously considered going to the front anyway. In agitation, he wrote to Margaret, "My state of mind is deplorable. My inner struggle is continual. But for your condition, I could decide more easily, but in the present moment I cannot leave you. I cannot go so far from you, my dear love; ah! how cruel is my destiny in this emergency."[53] Fuller at first could only advise Ossoli to do what was best for him. If a higher duty called him away from her, she would try to take care of herself. A few days later, however, she was not as resolute. Now, unless duty and honor compelled it, she thought it a bad moment to be joining the army; she could not imagine any campaign under the papal government's direction ending well. She advised Giovanni to postpone his decision for two or three weeks—that is, until after the baby was born.[54]

The waiting continued, and, as it did, Margaret's greatest enemies were boredom and dread of the unknown. She thought it entirely possible that she would die alone in childbirth "without touching a dear hand."[55] Her peace of mind was hardly helped by the family with whom she stayed, who presumed her to be rich and, as she later discovered, charged her twenty-five percent more for wine than anyone else in town.[56] As a whole, Fuller came to regard the population of Rieti as "the worst people whom I have ever seen."[57] As her pregnancy neared its end, her nights became more and more disturbed. Unable to come promptly to her side, Ossoli sent her a little portrait of himself, which Margaret looked at often. Everything, she told him, was going badly, but she could not imagine that it would always be thus.[58]

The irrevocable alteration, for good or ill, came on September 5, 1848, when Angelo Eugenio Filippo Ossoli made his squalling entry into a world concerned with larger matters. Giovanni, having secured leave from his post in the Civic Guard, had come to Rieti a week earlier and was there when his son was born. There may have been an incongruity in the Ossolis' heaping their infant with so many syllables, but they wanted to pay honor to a number of people. "Angelo" was for Ossoli himself; Fuller chose "Eugenio" in honor of her femininely handsome eldest brother, no doubt hoping that her boy would be as comely; "Filippo" was added in memory of Ossoli's late father.

Giovanni could not remain long at Margaret's bedside. The next day, he was back in Rome, where he promptly resumed the steady flow of newspapers and pamphlets to Rieti. Fuller wrote back with news about the baby. For more than two months, she wrote to no one else. Though he cried a great deal at first, little Angelo pleased her greatly. She enjoyed looking at him, and everyone said he was beautiful. Fuller's reports on his developing temperament were hopelessly contradictory. On the one hand, he was, at twelve days old, "very naughty [and] very obstinate to have his will." In the same letter, though, Fuller noted that people who did not know his name called him "Angiolino because he is so nice." Margaret and Giovanni soon shortened this pet name to "Nino." Despite the pleasure of exchanging gazes with her prepossessing bundle, however, Fuller could not help being generally uneasy about their situation. "It is a great anxiety," she told her husband, "to be alone and so ignorant with a baby in these first days of his life."[59]

Almost immediately, a more specific cloud came over the new mother and child. Fuller developed what was then known as a "nursing fever," and her milk proved insufficient to the baby's needs. The local girl to whom she had hoped to turn in such a case proved either unwilling or unable to stand in, and Fuller immediately started blaming the girl for her fever as well.[60] She sent the girl packing, telling her not to look for Ossoli in Rome, as she wanted nothing further to do with her. The drama of Nino's nourishment went on for some days. Fuller found a wet nurse whom she liked, a beautiful young mother named Chiara Fiordeponte, to supplement her own feedings. But Chiara's availability made Nino even less interested in Margaret's breast. Then the nurse's own baby became ill, and Margaret feared she would have to make another change. To her relief, though, Chiara's baby recovered, and relative calm settled over the house in Rieti.

It could not last. Fuller was willing to abide by the conventional wisdom of the time, which held that a new mother should convalesce for forty days. However, she was itching to return to Rome, where she could resume writing for Greeley and again feel a part of the great events of the moment. This desire, however, raised another problem: what to do with little Angelo? Chiara said she would be happy to come to Rome and keep Angelino with her, but her husband did not wish to leave Rieti. As an alternative to bringing Chiara with her, Margaret asked Giovanni to find out about procuring a nurse in Rome. However, he found fault with both options. Foremost in his mind was keeping Angelo's existence a secret, and bringing his son to Rome seemed risky. He wrote, "This matter ought to be treated with the greatest imaginable caution, since my thought would be, to keep the baby out of Rome, for the sake of greater secrecy, if we can find a good nurse who will take care of him like a mother."[61]

Ossoli had spoken like a true nineteenth-century European aristocrat, wholly and unthinkingly accustomed to the idea that the rearing of his child could be, and perhaps ought to be, someone else's business. While Fuller admitted the need for caution, however, her own instincts and social conditioning were impossible to ignore. "He is always so nice, how could it be possible for me to leave him? I wake up in the night, look at him, and I think, ah, it is impossible to leave him."[62] Moreover, as she had written Ossoli earlier, she knew "very well that no one else can take care of him as well as I."[63] Her apprehensions about leaving Nino in Rieti were further aroused when she arranged for Angelino to be inoculated against smallpox, of which, she wrote, "all around here are dying." For obscure reasons, possibly because he wanted more money, the doctor dragged his feet, leading Fuller to call him "detestable, untrustworthy like the others."[64] The prospect of returning to Rome, once so irresistible, now filled her with misgivings. She lamented, "I do not know how to leave my dear ones."[65]

The world contains quite a few parents, both male and female, who would never dream of leaving their infant child for anything but the strictest necessity, much less with a family who had cheated them, in the care of a "detestable" doctor, and in a town populated by the people they considered "the worst people" they had "ever seen."[66] Such people—as well as others— would likely wish that Margaret had replied to Giovanni that there were things that mattered more in life than reputation. They would wish she had further told him that, even if Giovanni's family used his indiscretion to undermine his inheritance, many men his age had found ways of supporting an intact family in Rome, and that not all of them had wives who could bring in additional income as well. Fuller had not shrunken from giving men much harsher dressings-down in the past. Now, however, her fighting spirit failed her. Instead of braving the world's judgment and returning to Rome with her head held high and Angelino in her arms, she struck a compromise: Giovanni would find her an apartment in Rome on a short-term lease, so that she could come to the city to do her writing and be close to her husband, but would be free to return to Rieti and her baby "if I am too anxious and grieved about him."[67]

Giovanni's apartment search came up empty. He and Margaret agreed that she would take a hotel room while they continued to look together. One or two matters needed to be resolved before she departed. The last of these was Angelino's baptism, which was delayed by a frustrating search for a godfather. Fuller wanted Mickiewicz, but the poet was then in Paris. After much ado, the couple settled on Giovanni's discreet and obliging nephew Pietro. On the night of November 4, Giovanni rode through a driving rain to Rieti. He and Margaret stood by the next day as Angelo Eugenio Filippo Ossoli was received into the life of the church. The next day, having entrusted him to

Chiara and her family, the baby's parents boarded a stagecoach to return to the city that had brought them together and that still spoke eloquently to their hopes for the future.

Fuller settled into a single sunlit room on an upper floor of a building that overlooked the Piazza Barberini, a pleasing location whose charms were accentuated by Bernini's dramatic Triton Fountain. From her window, she could see the grand Palazzo Barberini and, at a greater distance, the papal residence and gardens at the Palazzo del Quirinale. She could not have asked for more inspirational surroundings in which to resume both her book and her work for Greeley, and it was not long before she had more to write about.

About a week after her return, on November 15, the pope's able but unpopular conservative minister, Pellegrino Rossi, rode to the Palazzo della Cancelleria for the opening session of the Chamber of Deputies. As he descended from his carriage and made his way through a hostile crowd, an assassin stabbed him in the neck. The minister sank into the arms of a cardinal and died almost instantly. On cue, a host of men in the crowd near the spot where Rossi fell all held daggers aloft; it was impossible to know who had struck the blow. The deputies inside the chamber received the news of Rossi's death with cold silence. Fuller wrote to her mother, "I never thought to have heard of a violent death with satisfaction, but this act affected me as one of terrible justice."[68]

The next day, the tide of violence turned toward Pio Nono himself. Fuller began the day by visiting a pair of churches. At the first, a funeral mass had been scheduled to honor the citizens of Vienna who had been killed during the recent uprisings, but then it was cancelled. Rome was thinking of its own victims now. At the church of San Luigi dei Francesi, the tricolor republican flag was on display. Fuller tarried to gaze at an image of Saint Cecilia, stretching out her arms above a suffering multitude, and to wonder whether the time for such merciful gestures was now past. Walking north to the Piazza del Popolo, she found a horde of civilians and Civic Guards, gathering for a march to the Palazzo del Quirinale with a list of reforms.[69] Their mood was peaceful but determined. As the crowd departed for the palace, Fuller made her way back to her apartment to observe, from a safe distance, what would happen next.

The marchers were met, not by the pope, who refused to show himself, but by the Swiss Guard. From her apartment, Fuller heard gunfire. Her landlady ran up and down, crying, "Jesu Maria, they are killing the Pope!"[70] In fact, the Swiss Guard had fired first. Fuller briefly thought of rushing to the scene, but the sight of a man being carried past, grievously wounded, changed her mind. Inside the palazzo, the pope's confessor fell dead, struck by a bullet that passed through a window. A member of the crowd set fire to one of the palace doors. Revolution had come at last to Rome.

Though little more blood was shed, Fuller had no doubt that the skirmish had sent the pope into a panic. He now protested that all his earlier promises to liberalize had been extorted by violence. She surmised, quite correctly as it turned out, that Pio now associated the ideas of unification and republicanism with anarchy and the guillotine. After the events of the sixteenth, it was apparent that the pope could no longer govern. He had squandered his goodwill in spectacular fashion. Barely a week after the assault on the Palazzo del Quirinale, disguised as a common priest, he fled the realm, seeking asylum at Gaeta. Pio's choice to find sanctuary in the Kingdom of the Two Sicilies angered Fuller. King Ferdinand of that country had quickly reneged on the constitution he had given his people earlier in the year and, in September, had responded to an uprising in Messina by ordering a naval squadron to bombard his own people, earning himself the scornful nickname of "King Bomba." Fuller flayed her former hero in the *Tribune*: "To fly to Naples to throw himself in the arms of the bombarding monarch, blessing him and thanking his soldiery for preserving that part of Italy from anarchy—to protest that all his promises at Rome were null and void . . . these are the acts either of a fool or a foe." Fuller had finally run out of excuses for the pope. "No more of him!" she wrote, "His day is over."[71]

Her political thoughts were already turning to the possibility of a new day. "It is a time such as I always dreamed of: and that fire burns in the hearts of men around me which can keep me warm." The great question was how to speed the arrival of the new dawn. Her evident function—"to cheer on the warriors, and after write the history of their deeds"—seemed paltry to her.[72] She fantasized about taking some grand, official role; when, in the *Tribune*, she called on America to send a wise, experienced ambassador to Rome, she wrote, "Another century, and I might ask to be made Ambassador myself . . . but woman's day has not yet come."[73]

That day, to her regret, seemed far more distant in most of Italy. True, she had two female Italian friends whom she highly respected: the Mar-

chioness Arconati and the gallant, celebrated Princess Cristina di Belgioioso, a respected scholar and staunch republican activist who, Fuller
speculated, had had several lovers and whose public life had been a model
of energy and charity. But these two were of the upper classes, and they
hardly represented the common women of Italy. For the women of the
lower orders, she confessed, she had no regard. "They are too low for me,"
she privately noted. "It will be centuries before they emerge from a merely
animal life."[74] Fuller was quick to observe, however, that the degraded condition of women, both in Italy and elsewhere, could not be called their
fault. In Rieti, she had heard repeatedly the cries of women being beaten by
drunken sons and husbands. She had spoken too often with women who
excused their lies by saying, "I *dare not* tell my husband, he would be ready
to kill me."[75] She wished for more power to advertise and cure these wrongs
than she knew she had.

For Italy as a whole and Rome in particular, however, Fuller was far more
optimistic. Though she had feared that law and order would soon vanish in
the wake of the pope's desertion, Fuller observed that the city was perfectly
tranquil. The only things missing were the rich carriages and liveries of the
ecclesiastic elite. New leaders would surely be needed, but she had strong
hopes that the city would settle upon her dear friend Mazzini, whom she now
regarded as "the only great Italian."[76] To Marcus Spring, she wrote that
Mazzini "stood on a sunny height, far above the stature of other men. He has
fought a great fight against folly, compromise, and treason; steadfast in his
convictions, and of almost miraculous energy to sustain them, is he."[77]
When she heard him suggested as the next to govern Rome, she felt that she
was hearing the true spirit of the people.

On December 21, Fuller went alone to Rieti for Nino's first Christmas. As
to the baby himself, she was pleased by what she saw. He enjoyed seeing all
the local people who came to play with him and who seemed to love him.
Though he had not grown much, he looked very plump and was "very gracious." She even wrote that the child was doing "better than with me; he
sleeps well at night, cries rarely and then not loudly."[78] However, his physical
surroundings could have inspired some of Dickens's starker pages: "The
house is terrible; the wind comes in from all sides. . . . He had small pox very
badly. His head and body were all covered with spots. It is only thanks to
heaven that it all went away so well. Doctor Mogliani never came to see him;

his family say[s] that I am stingy. I suppose he thought it wasn't worth saving our child. . . . During the day it doesn't go so well; there is hunger, cold."[79]

Fortunately, Angelino's illness turned out only to be chicken pox, and Fuller later opined that, swaddled and robed in wool, he did not suffer from the cold.[80] Nevertheless, many parents would have conveyed these facts with alarm. Fuller, except for her harsh words about the doctor, was almost shockingly blithe. As for the freezing conditions in the house, she merely observed, "He doesn't seem to have a cold; surely he will be stronger for having be[en] so exposed in his first few months."[81] Regarding the pox, she noted that his face had not been scarred, and then shifted to another topic. When she first took Nino in her arms, guilt overcame her; as the child leaned his head against her bosom, he seemed to say to her, "How could you abandon me[?]"[82]

But she did not change course. A few days later, as she prepared to leave Rieti, she wrote to Giovanni that she was "very sorry to leave our dear child." However, she added that, even if she wanted to, she "could not stay any longer in this house. I have a terrible cold and my head hurts me."[83] All the day of her departure, she later learned, Nino could not be comforted. He refused his nurse's breast and looked continually toward the door. So it was. So, she thought, it had to be. Only a week or so after she had come, Fuller returned to Rome, leaving her "dear child" behind to continue his regimen of strengthening.

As 1848 came to a close and a new, uncertain year began, Fuller's emotions were in tremendous conflict, and she passed the winter, which was much sunnier than the previous one, "beset by cares and perplexities in strange combination."[84] Her greatest pleasure came from political developments. She commenced her diary for the year with the excited words, "This year cannot fail to be rich in events most important for Italy, Europe, [and] the world. Rome has at last become the focus of the Italian revolution and I am here."[85] In late December, the Provisional Government that had been instituted in Pio's absence called for elections for a Constituent Assembly. As the New Year dawned, a democratic government ruled Venice. Grand Duke Leopold was soon to withdraw hastily from Florence and add another displaced monarch to the population of Gaeta. By February, Tuscany, too, would have a democratic assembly. It seemed possible that the new Tuscan government would merge with the territory that had comprised the Papal

States and form a Republic of Central Italy—a key first step toward unifying the peninsula. The church, Fuller knew, would throw obstacles in the path to unification, and she believed that the priestly power would have to be "utterly overthrown" before a new age could truly begin in Italy. Marvelously, however, such an occurrence no longer seemed implausible. Of the clergy, Fuller wrote, "Everything tends to destroy their authority."[86]

From his exile in Gaeta, Pio was sounding desperate. On New Year's Day, he issued an encyclical threatening excommunication to anyone who voted to create a Constituent Assembly or dared to impugn the secular power of the papacy. Far from having the desired effect, his attempts at menace provoked only derision. When copies of the papal communiqué were distributed, the people carried them up the Corso in a mock procession before dumping them into a privy. Speakers in the capital were soon competing to outdo one another in their appeals for liberal measures and their ridicule of Pio. Fuller felt sure that she had witnessed "the finale of St. Peterdom."[87]

Papal threats and denunciations notwithstanding, elections for the new Assembly, in which all adult men were eligible to vote, took place on the twentieth and twenty-first of January. A quarter-million voters defied the papal injunction, and the Constituent Assembly ceased to be merely a dream. On February 5, Fuller watched from a balcony of the Piazza di Venezia as Roman regiments paraded into view to the strains of "La Marseillaise" and the Assembly's newly chosen deputies strode by in honor, wearing no badges of distinction other than the red, white, and green scarf of the republic.[88] On February 8, the Assembly declared the pope's temporal power to be officially at an end. The Roman Republic was proclaimed, and bells rang forth across the city. Though Fuller heard some Englishmen mutter the next day that "they hoped to see all those fellows shot yet," the atmosphere was otherwise ecstatic, and the imposing grandeur of the spectacle swelled Fuller's heart.[89] On the eleventh, Fuller was at Saint Peter's listening to the unimaginable sound of a Te Deum being sung in thanks for the republic. The following day, the Assembly made Mazzini a Roman citizen in absentia, and, about two weeks later, by "a great vote," he was elected as a member of the Assembly. In recording his election in her journal, Fuller was so excited that she marked the date as February thirtieth.[90] The great man arrived in the city on March 5, and the next evening gave a simple speech to a crowd that had gathered below his window, promising he would stay with them to the last. "Now he is here," Fuller wrote, "I hope matters will be governed with new energy and less egotism."[91]

It was a sign of Mazzini's deep regard for Fuller that, only four days later, in the midst of all the excitement of his return, he came unbidden to her apartment and spoke with her for two hours. Though he looked too tired for a man of forty-two, he seemed more divine to Fuller than ever. His recent cares had etched a new distinction into his features. He had a soft, radiant look that, as Fuller later wrote, produced a brooding music in her soul. They talked about everything. He said he would like to visit her often, though a full resumption of their friendship would have to wait until the current crisis had been resolved. Both of them realized how much of that burden would fall on him. Mazzini admitted to Fuller that he doubted it would come out well. The enemies of Italy, he thought, were too many, too strong, too subtle. "Yet," he added, "Heaven helps sometimes."[92]

Fuller went to see her hero speak at the Assembly. His voice was still fine and commanding. But when he finished, an exhausted, melancholy expression came over him. It seemed to Fuller that the battles he had already fought had drained him of the strength to fight the ones that still awaited, and that he was being kept alive only by the fire in his soul. And yet he remained Mazzini, utterly devoted and loyal to his vision of Italy. She had met only two other men, Emerson and William Channing, who possessed the same essential nature, the same purity, the same celestial fire.[93] When Mazzini told the Assembly, "We will conquer," Fuller could not wholly disbelieve him.[94]

The farther Fuller looked across Europe, however, the less cheerful the prospects seemed. To the north, after an uneasy truce, Charles Albert had resumed his war with Austria, but victory seemed unlikely. To the south, the brutal Ferdinand stood staunchly with the pope. The Austrian government had survived the tremor of the previous year and would be delighted to see the infant Roman Republic smothered in its cradle. Most daunting of all, however, had been the course of events in France. Following the removal of Louis-Philippe, the government of the Second Republic had succeeded neither in stabilizing the economy nor in maintaining public order. In December 1848, desperate for a firm hand, the French people had elected as its new president the highly conservative Prince Louis-Napoléon Bonaparte, the nephew of the famous emperor. Eager to shore up his new regime, Louis-Napoléon courted Catholic support by allying himself with the exiled pope.

Fuller predicted, quite accurately, that Pio would appeal to France to help crush the Roman Republic and restore him to power. All would depend on whether France would remain true to her revolutionary principles, or whether Bonaparte would seek his own political interest. "Will France suffer herself again to be hoodwinked and enslaved?"[95] Fuller asked her *Tribune* readers. She was afraid of the answer. It seemed probable now that Mazzini would soon be called on to lead the government in Rome. How terrible, she thought, if he were to come to power only to preside over the republic's early demise.

The continual excitement of political events contrasted with the barrenness of Fuller's social sphere. As she explained to her brother Richard, she was living with the severest economy that her health would allow. Her room was too small for her to receive many of the people whose friendships would be valuable to her, and, lacking the money "to dress or to ride," she could visit others very little.[96] Moreover, most of her American friends had departed for less turbulent places. Good English society, she complained to her old friend Sarah Clarke, was closed to Americans, while bad English society was all too easy to encounter.[97] Furthermore, the mail was maddeningly unreliable. Because of letters lost between New Orleans and Europe, she had heard nothing until after the fact of her brother Eugene's courtship and marriage. Eugene had construed Fuller's silence as icy disapproval. Though the rift was later patched, the bond of intimacy between them was temporarily broken.[98] Fuller's small but brilliantly situated apartment was an apt metaphor for the huge difference between her political life and her private one—long and unobstructed vistas of the world without, and a cramped emptiness within.

She commented on her loneliness to Emerson, to Emelyn Story, to her sister.[99] Certainly some of her feelings of isolation were also due to her forced separation from Nino, though there were few to whom she dared to write about that. One of the very few she took into her confidence was Caroline Tappan, now a new mother herself and one of the few friends free-spirited enough not to be aghast at Margaret's indiscretion. To her, Fuller admitted that Nino's situation was far from ideal. Not only did she tell of the cold winds that had blown through Rieti at Christmas, but she also expressed a new fear. Fuller had not yet come to trust the man who would one day save Italy, Giuseppe Garibaldi, and she regarded his legion as a band of desperadoes. She anxiously told Caroline that Garibaldi's men were now stationed in

Rieti. Worse than that, the soldiers of King Ferdinand were only six miles from Nino's door. She hoped to go to Nino and stay with him in Rieti or, if that proved impossible, "at all risks, remove him." Every day, she confided, was a day of "mental doubt and conflict."[100]

She worried, too, about the state of her inner being. It was in Fuller's nature to examine her inner life in comparison with its earlier phases. Since her becoming pregnant, these comparisons were seldom comfortable. Some indefinable, sacred spark seemed to have been put out. Though she had always fretted over what she thought to be her limitations, she had almost always believed that she would overcome her funks and flaws. Now, a sense of inevitable defeat darkened her pages. While expecting Nino, she had written to Emerson saying, "I do not prize myself, or expect others to prize me." She recalled that, when she had been editing *The Dial*, she believed that she had tasted some eternally redemptive "true elixir, and that the want of daily bread, or the pangs of imprisonment, would never make me a complaining beggar." Now, it was clear to her that the cup of her seemingly magical communion had contained "too much earth,—too much taint of weakness and folly, so that baptism did not suffice. I know now those same things, but at present they are words, not living spells."[101] In the incongruously sunny winter of 1848–49, the spells had refused to return. "I have no genius at all," she wrote Tappan.[102] To William Channing, she lamented, "I am not what I should be on this earth. I could not be." Having been denied the nourishment of "profound and steadfast sentiment," her nature had achieved "no steadfast greatness, no creative power." In her soul, she confessed, "faith soars and sings no more."[103] In every bud, she now perceived the strange, destroying worm. To Anna Ward, she concluded, "There is nothing quite untouched and wholesome in this world."[104]

Feelings of impurity clung to her. Once, she had freely likened herself to Minerva, the virginal goddess of wisdom. Now the ancient figure to which she most often referred was Mary Magdalene. In one of the many instances when she almost dared a correspondent to guess that she had been sexually indiscreet, she had written to her mother the previous November, "In earlier days, I dreamed of doing and being much, but now am content with the Magdalen to rest my plea hereon, '*She has loved much.*'"[105] She repeated the phrase, "She loves much," to Channing the following March, and she also wrote to Tappan regarding Mazzini, "His soft, radiant look . . . consecrates my present life that, like the Magdalen, I may at the important hour shed all the consecrated ointment on his head."[106] Fuller's image of herself as a penitent whore is striking in its harshness; her hope that she might redeem herself through humility and love is far indeed from her former Goethean belief that her striving for excellence would save her. She was now much more Gretchen than Faust. Not to be overlooked in her letter to Tappan is another inference: if Fuller was Magdalene in her allegory, then Mazzini was the Christ. Mary Magdalene had borne witness to the crucifixion. Fuller's metaphors held a grim portent for Mazzini and the revolution.

On March 27, Fuller returned to Rieti. Now aged almost seven months, Nino still had no hair, but he was very plump and in excellent health. Fuller, however, felt dreadful, and the pain in her ears, head, and teeth made it difficult even to write a short letter to Ossoli. Three nights later, while she sat upstairs watching Nino sleep, a tremendous row erupted downstairs. Fuller descended in time to see Chiara's husband, Pietro, in the throes of a roaring fight with his older brother Niccola. The two men seemed intent on killing each other. The women had taken hold of Niccola's arm so that he could not throw the knife he had drawn. Pietro defended himself by throwing pieces of wood; a large brickbat almost struck Fuller in the head. A horde of neighbors promptly arrived, and order was restored. Fuller left the scene convinced that Niccola was an alcoholic and that, had Nino been downstairs, he would likely have been killed.[107]

Fuller's reaction to the melee was oddly mixed. On the one hand, she reported to Ossoli, "I feel calm" and advised him, "Do not feel anxious about our child for a moment." On the other, she wrote, "If it is necessary for him, we will tell our secret," apparently paving the way to bring the baby to live with them in Rome. "Who knows," she continued, "if [admitting Nino's existence] will not be the best thing in the end?" Yet, in the next sentence, she retreated from the idea of disclosure: "But it is necessary to think of everything, because our whole future lives depend upon the discretion of this moment."[108] Though Ossoli was "very much disquieted" to receive Fuller's letter, he did not act, and, in the end, no new arrangements ensued.[109] Nor were any changes made after Fuller's letter of April 4, which advised Ossoli that Niccola had just come out of a mad delirium of more than forty hours and that Garibaldi's desperadoes were suspected of killing a friar and two other citizens of the town.[110]

The Ossolis' conduct regarding Nino is perplexing in the extreme. Fuller's descriptions of him are warm and doting. And yet, it is evident that virtually nothing—neither cold nor disease, neither the presence of a violent drunkard nor the near proximity of an army of brigands—could persuade the Ossolis to remove their child from a manifestly dangerous situation. One hesitates to charge the couple, and especially Fuller, with willful neglect. Although she had seldom been shy with her opinions, and although Ossoli would, during the rest of their marriage, prove quite deferential to her desires, Fuller seems to have been unable to confront him directly during this period. She may have believed that, if she simply presented her husband with the evidence that their son was in jeopardy, Ossoli would soon conclude on his own that Nino must be brought to Rome. If so, she misjudged her husband.

Perhaps more than anything else, the chain of incidents reveals how thoroughly convinced Giovanni and Margaret were that disclosing their marriage and the existence of their child would ruin them. However, their failure to correct the situation may also suggest something about their psychology. Both Margaret and Giovanni had grown accustomed to behaving toward others as if Nino did not exist. One wonders whether the habit of outward denial somehow made its way into their inner thoughts as well— whether the unacknowledged Nino and their obligations to him did not seem quite real even to them. Whatever the motivations of the parties, the circumstance was sad indeed—sad for the mother in her speechless regrets; sad for the father who could not put aside his stubbornness or his passivity; but saddest of all for the infant whose only offense was in being born.[111]

Fuller stayed three weeks in Rieti. On her way back to Rome, she stopped at a small inn for food and rest. She had taken a seat when the owner burst in, in great distress. Garibaldi's men, he said, had arrived, and he expected them either to take everything he and his patrons owned or to shoot them all dead. Fuller, however, kept calm. When the blue-coated soldiers arrived, she commanded the proprietor, in a voice for all to hear, to give them bread and wine on her account, for they must be in need of refreshment. The men proved undeserving of their gruesome reputation. They bowed respectfully to Fuller and, as they ate, regaled her with stories of their adventures in the field. When all was done, they escorted her to her coach and left her with a much revised opinion of Garibaldi's dreaded legion.[112]

In Fuller's absence, Rome's experiment with democracy had begun to teeter. Days before Fuller had gone to Rieti, the Austrians had again defeated Charles Albert, this time in a rout at the Battle of Novara. The Sardinian king abdicated in favor of his son, Victor Emmanuel II, and sought asylum in Spain. Rome's hope for support from Tuscany also turned out to be misplaced. Fuller grimly told her diary that the republican party there had proved to be only a small minority, and a reactionary party now held sway in Florence.[113] If, as was widely expected, a foreign power were to try to restore the papal government by force, Rome would be on its own.

The city received some thirteen thousand refugees from adjacent states, "striplings & blanched heads; wild, visionary enthusiasts [&] grave, heroic men," all determined to make Rome their last rallying point.[114] On March 29 the Assembly had turned over control of the city to a triumvirate, headed by Mazzini and invested with the authority to wage the anticipated war. In the brief time before the crisis came, the triumvirate acted in keeping with its highest liberal aspirations. It abolished the death penalty and reaffirmed the freedom of the press. It reformed the tax structure and granted civil rights to Jews and other non-Catholics. Yet, like many post-revolutionary governments built on the ruins of states with great power but little justice, Mazzini's government dispensed great justice but wielded little power. It had, by and large, the confidence of the Roman people, but there its credit began and ended. Foreign governments declined to recognize the republic, and most sent their ambassadors to Gaeta, not to Rome. With no international confidence behind it, the currency could not be stabilized. On all fronts, the outlook was dismal.

It then grew worse. On April 24, less than a month after the installation of the triumvirate and barely a week after Fuller's return from Rieti, a French expeditionary force of some ten thousand men, commanded by General Nicolas Oudinot, landed at Civitavecchia, thirty-five miles northwest of Rome. This act of aggression stunned Rome; many there, Mazzini included, could not believe that one republic would raise its swords against another. And yet, when Fuller began her next dispatch for the *Tribune*, dated May 6, it was with the shocked and sobering lines, "I write you from barricaded Rome. The Mother of Nations is now at bay against them all."[115]

Oudinot had first hoped to conquer the city with words instead of cannon fire. He had advised the people of Rome that his government would "respect the wishes of the majority of the Roman people." Despite this overture, as Fuller was proud to tell her readers, "no one declared for the Pope."[116] The day after the French landing, an emissary sent by Oudinot told the Constituent Assembly that his army had been deployed to protect Rome from the aggression of Austria and the Kingdom of the Two Sicilies. All the Assembly would have to do, he said, was to return temporal power to the pope, and all would be well. If not, of course, then the French would have no choice but to move against the city.

The Assembly replied with indignation. To a man, and supported by the triumvirate, they voted to fight. Promptly thereafter, the Civic Guard, on whom the defense of Rome would rest, was marching in review and displaying, in Fuller's opinion, "great order." Giovanni, of course, was with them. As the French moved toward the city, placards appeared, urging those loyal to the pope to rise up against Mazzini's government. Again, Fuller proudly proclaimed, "Not a soul stirred."[117] Against daunting odds, the city was at least united. From her window, she watched as men carried boards to high ground to fashion supports for cannon. Women, as well as men, hastily trained with firearms. There was a strange festivity in the air as the blockades began to fill the streets. "It seems to be such play," Fuller wrote in her diary, "for men and boys alike."[118]

Those words, written on April 28, were the last that Fuller wrote in her Roman diary. From then on, there was little time to write. The next day, Oudinot advanced, establishing headquarters at the Castel di Guido just west of the city. On the morning of the thirtieth, Fuller received a notice from her friend Princess Belgioioso, who was preparing the city's hospitals for the expected battle. The princess had appointed Fuller as "regolatrice," or director, of the Ospedale Fatebenefratelli, where she was to report at noon to organize the nurses. Later that same day—whether before or after her first visit to the hospital is unclear—a man Fuller did not know appeared at her door. He was Lewis Cass Jr., son of the Democratic candidate who had lately lost the American presidential election to Zachary Taylor. The younger Cass was the American chargé d'affaires and one of the few foreign diplomats in communication with the generally unrecognized Assembly. Though personally sympathetic with the republicans, Cass was under orders from a cautious American government to deliver his credentials neither to the papal representatives nor to the revolutionary government until the political situation became clearer. On April 21, Cass had written to the secretary of state in favor of the republicans. In those days before transatlantic telegraphy, however, his message had virtually no chance of affecting American policy before the impending hostilities began. Cass had come to Fuller with a somber message. If she remained at the Piazza Barberini, he could do nothing to guarantee her safety. She must move nearer to the Spanish Steps, to the Casa Dies on the Via Gregoriana, where Americans would be under the protection of the State Department. Fuller complied within a few days.

Cass had delivered his warning in the nick of time. That same day, two of Oudinot's columns marched toward Saint Peter's, where they encountered Roman infantry and artillery fire. Bullets fired by Catholic soldiers in the name of papal power struck the Vatican itself. In the great cathedral's gardens, Roman blood stained the walls. Then Garibaldi, who had arrived from Rieti three days earlier, launched a ferocious two-pronged counterattack, striking an infantry unit a mile to the south and a detachment of French regulars near the stately Villa Pamphili. Their confidence rudely shattered, the French fell back in disarray, leaving more than 850 men either dead or in enemy hands. The republic had carried the first day.

The Tiber flows fast and white under the bridge to the tiny island where the Ospedale Fatebenefratelli still receives patients. Greatly expanded during the time of Mussolini, the hospital in Fuller's time was a modest three-story structure, not terribly far from the ruins of the Forum but a considerable distance from Margaret's lodgings at the Casa Dies. If she walked to the hospital, she arrived with sore feet. The weather was intensely hot, and Cass observed that she looked feeble and delicate.[119] But Fuller felt "but little about [her] self."[120] With no time to lose, she organized her staff and put them to work. That first night, she attended personally to approximately seventy soldiers from both sides of the battle. Thereafter, she made the trip to the island almost every day, and each day was an education in suffering and compassion. About a different war, Herman Melville was to write, "What like a bullet can undeceive!"[121] Fuller quickly learned what her books had never shown her.

To the west of the city, a stalemate had followed the initial bloodletting. Newly respectful of their enemy, the French marched back to Civitavecchia, but they did not leave the coast. In the ensuing lull, one of Fuller's greatest fears was for the physical city itself. The thought that the beauties and treasures of Rome might soon be burned and broken sickened her. And yet, as the battle loomed, she held herself firm. She told the *Tribune* that even if "mankind [should] be forever despoiled of the most beautiful inheritance," she would still vote to defend Rome to the last.[122] Fuller had seen the higher hope that had dawned in the city. She had watched as the people had begun the slow, hard rise from servility and corruption. She could not bear to think they would fall back again.

In the meantime, Ossoli, at his post in the Civic Guard, was also confronting the demons that come with warfare. If being raised in a noble family had prepared him for anything useful, it was military action, and on the first day of the fighting he had held to his position and done his duty. But a brave man, too, knows horror when he sees it. When Fuller went up to the line to see him the next day, Giovanni looked pale and haggard. A man within a few feet of Ossoli had been shot dead, and the dried blood from his wound was still on the wall for Margaret to see. Fuller knew the ensuing days would pass more easily if she could see Giovanni regularly. She pleaded with him to come and see her whenever he could, but leaving his unit was often impossible. Though he was never far away, she went days at a stretch with no news of him.

Her worries about Nino were still more distracting. She was well aware that, during Charles Albert's campaigns in the north, babies had not been exempt from the atrocities of war. Now that Rome was under siege, however, there was no way to visit her son. The news she did receive from Rieti was cruel: Chiara sent word that she would abandon the boy if she received no more money. Fuller managed to send what amounted to a ransom, and the woman was placated. Still, it must have stunned her to know that her family had other enemies as treacherous as the French.

Sadnesses both great and small were on Fuller's mind as she wrote to her brother Richard on May 22. Having had only letters to unite them for the better part of three years, the two had slowly heaped one petty misunderstanding on another until, as they had both come to realize, they had "los[t] the clues to each other's minds." Time and distance were gradually making strangers of the people she knew best and needed most, and she doubted whether she would see any of them again. She was not deceived for a moment by the French diplomats who seemed to be "amusing us with a pretence of treaties" as a prelude to another attack. Even as she wrote, an Austrian force stood no more than three days away. Margaret did not fully expect to live through the coming conflict, though she told Richard only that she feared she might suffer an "accident." She added that, if such a mishap should occur, the family should have no regrets. "There must be better worlds than this," she wrote, "where innocent blood is not ruthlessly shed, where treason does not as easily triumph, where the greatest and best are not crucified."[123]

Before the decisive assault, there were diplomatic maneuverings on both sides, more suitably addressed in a history of statecraft than in the story of a single life. To the very last, Mazzini and the Assembly hoped to persuade the

Fuller watched the desperate struggle for the Janiculum Hill from across the Tiber. She found the sight of battle both terrible and majestic.

French that their republic and the government in Paris had no real quarrel; the French hoped mainly to give Oudinot extra time to receive reinforcements. On May 31, the talking ended, with a compromise agreement that the French never intended to observe and that General Oudinot refused to sign. The city prepared itself for more bloodshed.

The prize that the French undertook to win and that the Romans had resolved to defend at any cost was the Janiculum Hill, which rises more than two hundred feet above the floodplain of the Tiber, although, as one stands on its summit, it feels much higher. Known as part of the "balcony of Rome," the Janiculum has a broad, flat top, and its eastward view of the city is unobstructed and commanding. It is a site profoundly appealing to an artist—or to a captain of the artillery. Everyone knew that, if the French could take and hold this hill, ordnance would rain down on all quarters of Rome, and further resistance would be futile. Lose the Janiculum, and the republic would perish. Yet the same features that made the hill so desirable to the French also made it highly defensible. If Garibaldi's men, fortified by an unknown number of college students and other volunteers, could keep Oudinot's force from mounting the steep slopes, then freedom might endure a little longer in Rome. The key to it all was the gate of San Pancrazio, at the base of the road that led up the southern slope to the top of the Janiculum. The general in charge of the city's defense, Pietro Roselli, stationed much of his force at the stately villas that overlooked the gate. On Saturday, June 2, he toured the positions and then retired in satisfaction. When the French came, he thought, his soldiers would be ready.

As it turned out, the Italians never had a chance. Though he had rejected the truce, Oudinot had promised he would not attack until Monday, June 4, so as to allow foreign nationals time to leave the city. He therefore attacked on June 3. At four in the morning on the Christian Sabbath, less than two miles from Saint Peter's, the shooting resumed. Roselli had taken Oudinot's word as "a strict Catholic and a very religious man" that the French would hold their fire until Monday.[124] Thus, only a few sentries were even awake when brigades from Oudinot's force, thirty-five thousand strong and supported by seventy-five siege guns, stormed the villas near the all-important gate. Before dawn, most of them were under French control. Garibaldi rushed to the front, and his legion managed to retake one of the villas. The city awoke to gunfire. The streets were soon filled with cries of shock and anger and shouts of "Roma o Morte!"—Rome or Death![125] Three times, the Italians, outnumbered and outgunned, retook the Villa Corsini, only to be driven back each time. The approaches to the French positions were narrow and uphill. For many of the young Romans who boldly charged the French-held villas, the rush forward was the equivalent of suicide. Over the reports of the guns could sometimes be heard an Italian military band, playing "La Marseillaise." It was an ironic serenade to the French army, whose every salvo showed that, on this day, liberty, equality, and fraternity were no more than words.

The fighting did not end until after sundown. Though the Italians obstinately clung to two small positions near the gate, the day had been a thor-

ough defeat. The battle had been clearly visible from the loggia of the Casa
Dies on the other side of the river. Fuller, now the only American left at the
Casa except for Cass and the American consul, looked on, fascinated by the
"terrible" but strangely "majestic" struggle.[126] She saw the smoke of the
rifles and the flash of bayonets. Using an eyeglass, she could see individual
men. The Italians, she said, "fought like lions," but the French were just as
obstinate in their valor.[127]

The fighting during the succeeding days was continual and deadly. Fuller
was now at the hospital almost constantly, working shifts of eight to ten
hours, and she cared for her soldiers to the sounds of cannonade and mus-
ketry. "I had no idea before," she wrote to Emerson, who knew no better than
she, "how terrible gunshot wounds and wound-fever are."[128] She suppressed
her revulsion and carried on. Cass later recalled, "Her heart & soul were in
the Cause for which these men had fought, & all was done that woman could
do, to comfort them in their sufferings. I have seen the eyes of the dying, as
she moved among them, extended on opposite beds, meet in commendation
of her unwearied kindness."[129] In sympathy with the injured men, Fuller
also suffered, but she also wrote of feeling a solemn pleasure in being among
the wounded, for she found among them "scarcely one who is not moved
with a noble spirit."[130] She was especially touched by young men from Lombardy, who, having survived the republican downfall in the north, had joined
the second front in the shadow of the Vatican. These men, pierced and damaged though they were, Fuller called "the flower of Italian youth."[131] As
these metaphorical flowers mended, she brought them real flowers and
books as well. In reading and in talk, they shared some private comfort in the
midst of the catastrophe. When she was among them, they eagerly asked,
"[H]ow long will the Signora stay?" and "When will the Signora come
again?"[132] In heartbreaking fashion, Fuller's chance to do more than write
for the cause of liberty had finally come.

In her letter to Emerson, Fuller catalogued the places of sacred beauty
that had been consumed by the war: "the villa of Raphael, the villa of Albani,
the home of Winckelmann."[133] As the French lobbed shells haphazardly into
the city, even the sanctuary of Fatebenefratelli was prone to violation. On
June 5, a missile exploded in the courtyard of the hospital just as Fuller was
arriving. Fuller did not record her reaction, but the patients responded with
understandable agitation; they had no desire to be killed like mice in a trap.[134]

When the wounded were not afraid for their lives, they were indignant. During the long cease-fire, some of them had exchanged visits across the lines and had spoken with the French soldiers of brotherhood and solidarity. They could not understand how descendants of the French Revolution could fight with such fury for so infamous a cause.

The island hospital was not the only one that Fuller visited as the fighting raged. The Palazzo del Quirinale, home to his papal majesty only a few months before, was farther from the fighting, and it had been converted to a haven for convalescents. Fuller walked with them in Pio's still-resplendent gardens, this one with his sling, that one with his crutch. Bright-eyed boys came to the pope's pavilion to sit at the feet of the injured heroes and hear their stories, even as cannon fire rumbled in the distance. On one such evening, Fuller wrote, the light of the setting sun, shining on the ivory tents of the French cavalry on the opposite side of the Tiber, was a vision of contrasting loveliness. The tales the soldiers told seemed to her a nobler version of Boccaccio's *Decameron*. In the midst of sorrow and ruin, beauty and reverence had found a fleeting space.[135]

Though the cannonades and skirmishes continued, sniper fire from the Italians made it impossible for the French to advance quickly. Instead they adopted a tactic that they plainly considered prudent, but which Mazzini could not distinguish from the basest cowardice. They took, he said, "some inch of ground every day; and as soon as they had conquered it, fortifying it: advancing like moles, never showing themselves."[136] Fuller took enough time from her hospital work to write, with many interruptions, a dispatch that she herself called "confused" and "incomplete."[137] In it, she lengthened the litany of destruction that she had sent to Emerson. As she grieved over the fallen oaks, the blasted gardens, and the scarred and wasted villas, she marveled at the courage of her wounded, who were anxious to be discharged only so they could go back up to the line.[138] Some, whom she described in her next dispatch, could not possibly return to duty. One, a young university student, raised his amputated arm to his lips. Another kept the pieces of bone extracted from his wound as mementos of "the best days of his life."[139] With astonished pride, Fuller wrote of women, armed with pans of wet clay, rushing to extinguish unexploded bombs before they could burst. She heard them say, "Madonna protects us against the bombs; she wills not for Rome to be destroyed."[140]

The June heat intensified. Provisions grew short in the city, and the casualties mounted. In France, some recoiled in horror at their government's brutality. On June 12, invoking a clause in the French constitution that forbade the use of force against the liberties of other peoples, the left wing of the French Assembly introduced a resolution to impeach Louis-Napoléon, though it was easily defeated. The next day, a large pro-Italian demonstration in Paris was violently suppressed, and any hope of a change in French policy evaporated.

The reasonable course for Rome at this point was surrender. However, Mazzini, in Fuller's words, stood "firm as a rock." The reason she gave for his steadfastness was simple: "He believes in a God bound to protect men who do what they deem their duty."[141] Perhaps this was true, but Mazzini also believed in the power of martyrdom. His eye turned coolly to the future, he felt confident that the causes of republicanism and unification would rise again. When they did, he wanted the people to take courage from the blood-stained memories of the heroes of 1849, and he wanted it to be remembered that they had never given up. "We are only initiators," he wrote to George Sand as the bombs fell, "and therefore we must die."[142] All he could promise was that she would never see his name on a document of capitulation. The triumvirate and the Assembly both rejected Oudinot's June 12 demand for surrender, and the bombardment continued with redoubled fury.

On the sixteenth, Ossoli was made a captain and assumed command of the Second Company of the First Mobile Battalion, a unit stationed on the Pincian Hill on the fringes of the Villa Borghese gardens. Though both the river and a walk of well over an hour separated the Pincian from the heaviest fighting around the Janiculum, Ossoli's battalion, which possessed some of the few functioning cannon in his sector of the line, was a prime target for French artillery fire. Fuller thought it likely that Ossoli would not survive. In the closing days of June, the nighttime artillery attacks became truly fearful. On the twenty-eighth, as many as thirty projectiles struck the luxurious Hôtel de Russie, the site of Ambassador Cass's temporary quarters and barely a stone's throw from the Pincian. As Fuller sat alone in her exposed apartment in the Casa Dies, she thought, "If one strikes me, I only hope it will kill me at once."[143] The assault continued the next night, though Ossoli and Fuller remained unharmed.

On the thirtieth, Fuller summoned Cass to her apartment. He discovered her on the sofa, pale, trembling, and exhausted. Disclosing to him for the first time that she and Ossoli were married, she gave him a packet of documents, which she said contained proof of their marriage, as well as Nino's birth and baptismal certificates. She told Cass that Ossoli was with his men on the Pincian, "the highest & most exposed position in Rome, & directly in the line of the bombs from the French Camp." She could hardly imagine his surviving a third night of shelling, and she meant "to remain with him and share his fate."[144] At the Ave Maria, he would come for her, and they would proceed together to his post. After a few more words, Cass respectfully departed, leaving Fuller to make what she expected to be her final preparations. Some time later, as the sun declined over one of the longest evenings of the year, Cass saw Fuller and Ossoli together. Not knowing what portion of the world still lay before them, the tired woman and the faithful marchese took their slow and solitary way toward the Pincian.

Fuller wrote nothing that survives about the hours of waiting that followed. By a stroke of mercy, however, the French did not renew the bombing that night. Only later did Fuller learn that, on the afternoon of the thirtieth, Garibaldi had gone to the Assembly to tell its members that further resistance was futile. He had been persuasive. As Mazzini and his fellow triumvirs, dogged to the end, resigned in protest, the Assembly agreed to give up the defense of the city. On July 2, Garibaldi left the city with four thousand volunteers to continue the war as guerillas. On the third, Mazzini wrote a brief note to Fuller. It began, "Dear Friend. It is all over."[145] The same day, the French entered the city. After lingering several days in Rome, giving the French every chance to capture him, Mazzini left on a circuitous journey that took him to Switzerland. Armed with bayonets, the French barred the doors of the Assembly and shut down every newspaper in the city. The Roman Republic was no more.

In Gaeta, Pio received the news without a sign of gratitude. To the contrary, he was annoyed that neither Mazzini nor Garibaldi had been taken prisoner. In Rome, some of the republicans who had not escaped were publicly flogged. Ironically, though Mazzini's allegedly "Jacobin" republic had not executed a single person, the French occupiers promptly instituted death by guillotine as a common punishment. Fuller's outspoken support of the defeated republic was, by now, well known to the French, and they resented her powerfully. Fearing for her safety, the American vice-consul personally raised an American flag on the balcony of Fuller's apartment as a sign to the occupying army that she was to be left alone.[146] On July fifth, Fuller went to visit the recent battlefield in the western part of the city, where once proud homes had been reduced to shattered hulks. A peasant farmer showed her a place where French cannon fire had caused a wall to collapse, crushing thirty-seven defenders of the city who had been standing beneath it. She then walked to where the French line had been and saw a dog that had just unearthed a uniformed corpse, staring at his strange discovery in "stupid amazement."[147] On the eighth, she wrote her brother Richard that her private hopes had fallen with the hopes of Italy.[148] On March 10, long before Oudinot and his legions had given the deathblow to the revolution, Fuller had written a letter to William Henry Channing that reads like a psalm of woe: "I am tired of seeing men err and bleed. I am tired of thinking, tired of hoping. . . . [B]ut man will still blunder and weep, as he has done for so many thousand years. Coward and footsore, gladly would I creep into some green recess, apart from so much meddling and so much knowing, where I might see a few not unfriendly faces, where not more wretches would come than I could relieve. Yes! I am weary."[149] Now the words were truer than ever. She felt to the core her fatigue, her sorrow over man's fate and folly, her desolate awareness that the hope and faith of a city had risen in vain.

Throughout Rome, the French were applying muscle and steel to the problem of restoring what they regarded as order. Assaulting a French soldier was declared punishable by death. Three families were carted off to prison because a boy, standing at the window of the house where they were staying, had crowed like a rooster at some occupying troops. At the Palazzo del Quirinale, many of the wounded had been "driven well nigh mad, and their burning wounds exasperated [sic]" by the trumpets and drums of French soldiers who had set up quarters in the courtyard.[150] The French forces, who desired the palace for themselves, decreed that the wounded must depart within eight days, even though no other place had been prepared for them.[151] The chaplains who had been tending to Fuller's former patients were summarily dismissed. To Fuller's anguish, they had been replaced by reactionary monks, who threatened their charges with death from thirst and starvation if they did not confess to crimes against the papal regime. On July 10, the French army commanded all foreigners who had served the republican government to leave the city within twenty-four hours. Though she hated to abandon Rome, even in its shattered state, Fuller packed her bags. She consoled herself that she would no longer have to breathe the same air as the invaders.[152]

Fuller never lived more intensely than during the twenty-one months that had begun with her reunion with Ossoli and ended with the collapse of the revolution. She was to look back on her life in Rome as "that great tide of life in which my heart had gone forward with as much force as was left it."[153] Now the tide was rolling back again, leaving a woman both strengthened and scarred by experience, one whose store of life was unbelievably rich, but whose future prospects were anything but clear. A supremely adaptable soul, she knew that she would have to adapt once more. But only time would reveal what new lives and transformations were still possible for Margaret Fuller Ossoli.

CHAPTER THIRTEEN

VICTIM

*Often it has seemed that I have come
near enough to the limits to see what
they are. . . . Then, as I would draw near,
my little bark is shattered on the rock,
and I am left on the cold wave. Yet with
my island in sight I do not sink.*

—MARGARET FULLER, in *Memoirs of
Margaret Fuller Ossoli*, II, 83

$\mathcal{F}$ULLER'S "FAREWELL" COLUMN FOR THE *TRIBUNE*, DATED "ROME, AUG. 31, 1849," was erroneous in two respects. She actually wrote two more dispatches. And, at the end of August, having been driven out by Oudinot's order the previous month, she was no longer in Rome. In mid-July, before they could think of the more extended future, Margaret and Giovanni had traveled to Rieti to reunite with Nino. Though Fuller was more than eager to see her son, now more than ten months old, she still could not bring herself to tell her family of his existence. When she wrote to her brother Richard that she was about to travel into the mountains, she said that it was the bracing air and the restorative stillness that she was going off to find, not a needy infant.

Looking back was no easier than looking forward. In a matter of weeks, she and Ossoli had seen "our dearest friends laid low, our fortunes finally ruined, and every hope for which we struggled, blighted."[1] Fuller's most rueful moments came when she thought about the wounded men she had tended, whom she half-accused herself of abandoning. For some of them, she had no doubt, falling into the hands of the French was a death sentence. Others, horribly maimed, would have no recourse but to beg. With no money of her own to spare, Fuller wished she could persuade a rich friend among the American expatriates to buy some comfort for the wounded, but all of them were long departed. Before leaving the city, she had thought of selling her hair and blood to provide a small sum for one of the wounded, but there was no one who would buy.[2] She had done all she could.

Although most of those who had seen Fuller at the hospital lauded her courage and dedication, her own assessment of her work there was far more critical. When William Henry Channing, reviewing her efforts from a comfortable distance, suggested to Margaret that the revolution had been a "great opportunity" for her to put her principles into action, she was quick to contradict him. "Would it were so!" she exclaimed. "I found myself inferior in courage and fortitude to the occasion. I knew not how to bear the havoc and anguish incident to the struggle for these principles." Even her love of beauty and history now seemed to her like weaknesses, preventing her from feeling the single-minded ruthlessness necessary to the cause. During the siege, she would have been tempted to set aside her political principles to save a historic villa or a stand of ancient trees. She would have given them up still sooner to avert the sacrifice of "far nobler growths, the beautiful young men mowed down in their stately prime." Fuller even doubted whether she had been much comfort to the wounded and the brokenhearted at the hospital. Channing supposed that she had sustained them; it seemed to Margaret that, to the contrary, they had bolstered her. "God is good; God knows," they had often told her, but she had not always found a word of cheer with which to respond.[3] She had seen heroes, she told Channing, and she now knew that she was "not of that mould."[4]

Witnessing the revolution had acquainted Fuller with the price in blood and pain so often paid when an ideal struggles to become fact. Until 1849, she had believed that struggling for an ideal raised people toward a state of truth and beauty. Then, the most idealistic battle in which she had ever taken part had dissipated into horror, leaving an aftermath of blank ugliness. She had had a sobering preview of the disillusion that awaited millions of Americans with the coming of the Civil War. In her heart, Fuller remained steadfast in her ardor for reform, but she now held her views with a sadness and a gravity that she had never attached to them before. With Channing she shared her hope that, when she returned to America, God would make her "entirely humble." She added, "In future, while more than ever deeply penetrated with principles, and the need of the martyr spirit to sustain them, I will ever own that there are few worthy, and that I am one of the least."[5]

When the Ossolis came to Rieti, it seemed that they had traveled to a different world, not so much a town as a "little red-brown nest," lying quietly among the vineyards.[6] The closer view was less enchanting. The dirt piled high in the streets, disturbed only by the pigs and children that wallowed there. People counted themselves lucky to earn five cents a day. The dandies of the town squandered their time in barbershops and cafes, having nothing of greater value to exchange than gossip. After the excitement of Rome and revolution, Rieti was an idle, dejected slough.

The situation was made far worse by the condition in which they found Nino. The Ossolis discovered that his nurse, who had "seemed so lovely and innocent," had been pocketing the money they had sent for his maintenance and, instead of breastfeeding the baby as agreed, had given all her nourishment to her own child.[7] Nino had been kept alive on a diet of wine-soaked bread, and, by the time his parents reached him, he was "wasted to a skeleton" and could barely lift the pale hand that Margaret pressed to her lips.[8] He seemed to be hovering between life and death, and it appeared to Fuller that he was leaning more toward "the abyss." No one could say with certainty whether his mother had come too late to save him. In a letter to Cass, Fuller railed against the faithless nurse, whom she accused of withholding her milk from Nino "for fear of spoiling the shape of her bosom."[9] Margaret feared that, even if her baby lived, malnutrition had permanently broken his health; if so, she told Cass, she would rather see him die. Life was hard enough for the strong; for the feeble it was intolerable. If Nino were to die, she prayed that she might die as well. Already fatigued by all her disappointments, she felt that "this last shipwreck of ho[pes]" would be more than she could stand.[10]

Anxious weeks passed. Toward the end of August, though Margaret wrote that his hold on life was still "a frail tenure," Nino had rallied. In a sad irony, death came instead to another child far away. A letter from Greeley arrived in Rieti, announcing that the editor's son Pickie had died of cholera. Margaret commiserated in her reply, mourning Pickie's "heart of natural poetry." It seemed a good opportunity to disclose to Greeley the existence of Nino, now eleven months old and still unmentioned to most of her American correspondents. Fuller no sooner mentioned him than she confessed that she half expected to lose her son too. It seemed to her that the world was no longer deserving of her faith. Her brave Italians had been crushed, and the two children whom she had most loved other than her own, Waldo and Pickie, had been taken before they had truly begun to live. The universe of growth and goodness in which she had placed her confidence was nowhere to be seen. She lamented, "Oh, it is all over; and indeed this life is over for me. The conditions of this planet are not propitious to the lovely, the just, the pure; it is these that go away; it is the unjust that triumph."[11]

It was over, and yet it was not over. Fuller's cherished idea of life as a tale of steady progress toward perfection did, indeed, seem dead. But the life of solemn duty, of patient toiling for freedom and fairness, and of ordinary satisfactions still remained. In her August 31 dispatch, she was already reevaluating the Roman debacle, seeing it not as an end but as a beginning. "All the more for what has happened in these sad days," she predicted, "will entire Europe, at the end of this century, be under [a] Republican form of Government."[12] It was only as to time frame, not result, that she was mistaken. In her less public thoughts, Fuller left off searching for transcendent meanings. She now resolved simply to "labor in the good spirit here [in the material world], but leave all thoughts of results to Eternity."[13]

After dealing so many blows to Fuller, Eternity now offered a kindness: Nino recovered. The knowledge that he would survive compelled Fuller to face a less dire but still delicate problem. It was time to acknowledge his existence to her family. On August 31, the same day she dated her "farewell" column for the *Tribune* and just five days before Nino's first birthday, she ended a long, guilt-ridden silence. The letter to her mother took six paragraphs of preamble to come to the point. Having mentioned in earlier paragraphs the deaths of Waldo, Pickie, and James Freeman Clarke's young son Hermann, thus subtly reminding her mother of what blessings living children are, Fuller finally wrote, "The first moment, it may cause you a pang to know that your eldest child might long ago have been addressed by another name than yours, and has a little son one year old."[14] She omitted the eyebrow-raising chronology. One might read her letter and assume, as her mother no doubt did, that Nino's conception had followed his mother's marriage.

Fuller's letter to her mother also downplayed the more distressing facts concerning Nino's health. In words chosen to spare her mother's nerves (and, perhaps to some extent, to shield Margaret from suspicions of neglectful parenting), Nino was "a fair child, with blue eyes and light hair; very affectionate, graceful, and sportive." The only hint of worry came in a single phrase: "Thinking of those other sweet ones fled, I must look upon him as a treasure only lent."[15] Instead of discussing Nino's coughs and moans, as she had done with Greeley and Channing, Fuller gave her mother the much more cheering tidbit that her grandson had inherited the title of marchese. The woman who had once asserted, "Nothing but truth will do," was now wise enough to know that a bit less than the truth is sometimes preferred.[16]

Margaret did not try as hard to put the best face on her marriage to Giovanni. If Mrs. Fuller was pleased to learn that Ossoli was from a noble house, Margaret immediately dampened her pleasure by stating that her husband's family was "impoverished."[17] Not only was his family's property encumbered by debts, but he could make no claim on it so long as Rome remained in the hands of the papal government. Her candor continued. "He is not in any respect such a person as people in general would expect to find with me. He has had no instructor except an old priest, who entirely neglected his education; and of all that is contained in books he is absolutely ignorant, and he has no enthusiasm of character."[18] Then, mercifully, the tenor of her description changed. Ossoli, she assured her mother, had a kind temperament, excellent practical sense, and an exacting code of honor. His devotion to her was unsurpassed, and she had never suffered a pain if he had been able to relieve it. Fuller was to offer similar portraits of Ossoli to many of her friends. Consistently in her letters, he comes across as both remarkably loving and almost impossibly brainless—almost more plausible as a Newfoundland puppy than as a man.

Fuller seems to have had only two great fears regarding him. The first of these, that the Roman authorities would eventually track him down and avenge his offenses against the papal government, was real enough. Barely three weeks before Fuller wrote to her mother, Ossoli had inadvertently strayed across the border into the Kingdom of the Two Sicilies. Promptly detained on suspicion of being a soldier in Garibaldi's resistance force, he had been spared only because he happened to have on his person a letter addressed to him as the Marchese Ossoli.[19] The chaplain of the regiment that arrested him recalled that the Ossoli name had long been connected with loyal service to the pope. To this happenstance, Giovanni owed his freedom.

Margaret's other worry about her husband was more speculative but also potentially quite real: she could not quite let herself believe that a handsome man more than ten years her junior could be trusted to remain in love with her. "I am the elder," she told her mother, "and the difference will become, in a few years, more perceptible than now." She was, of course, aware that European men of a certain social stature were all but assumed to have mistresses. Giovanni was faithful now; she could not depend on him to remain so. She did her best, however, to banish the thought. "Life is so uncertain," she observed regarding Ossoli's continued fidelity, "and it is so necessary to take good things with their limitations, that I have not thought it worth while to calculate too curiously."[20] But the curiosity was there.

On August 31, the same day Fuller wrote to her mother, the Ossolis set off toward Florence, where they planned to stay the winter. Florence had never been one of Fuller's favorite places. She had always regarded it as a place for study and business, where the pleasures of daily life were "not . . . so great."[21] In a tone that complimented neither city, she had once called it the Italian counterpart of Boston.[22] Fuller also looked down on the Florentines for being slow to rally as revolution swept through other parts of Italy; even after living there for nearly half a year, she was to persist in calling the city "cowardly."[23] Now, however, the city's moderation meant that the post-revolutionary reaction was less fierce there than elsewhere. A radical refugee might live there for months practically unmolested. Florence also offered quiet surroundings for Nino; a small but welcoming community of American and English expatriates; and, most important, a modest cost of living.

The family stopped in Perugia for a few idyllic weeks, attending church every morning, breakfasting at noon, and spending their afternoons taking drives to the countryside or sitting and reading under the trees. Fuller told Cass, who had now become a close friend, that the mountain air was a perfect elixir. Nino gained strength rapidly until he was "full of life and gaiety." Fuller dared to hope that he might "grow into a strong man yet."[24]

Approximately ninety miles of rolling countryside divide Perugia from Florence. Rounded, wooded hills look down on vineyards, sheep pastures, and baked red roofs. The Ossolis made their journey during the first days of the grape harvest, and the fruit hung heavy on the ripened vines. The women in the fields, with their pretty bare feet and their shy, soft eyes, quickly became fixed in Margaret's memory as the family rode toward Florence.

The Tuscan capital, which seemed "so cheerful and busy after ruined Rome," had undergone rapid changes of its own.[25] Grand Duke Leopold had initially shown sympathy for the liberal uprisings of 1848. However, much like Pio Nono, he had begun to panic as the demands of the pro-democracy forces became more ambitious. In February 1849, Leopold had fled the capital and eventually joined the pope in exile in Gaeta. A Tuscan republic was proclaimed in Florence, but, like Mazzini's government, it had almost no chance of surviving. On May 25, as the wave of antidemocratic reaction swept through Europe, Austrian troops, with Leopold's secret authorization, seized control of Florence. By the time the Ossolis arrived at the end of September, Leopold had returned with the Austrians' blessing, the republican assembly had been dissolved, and the city was effectively under military rule.

Shortly after the family's arrival, Ossoli was arrested and briefly interrogated. Only after Fuller appealed through a friend to the grand duke's minister of foreign affairs was Ossoli issued a pass that entitled him to remain in Tuscany until the following summer. Throughout the remainder of their stay, Margaret and Giovanni were under government surveillance. Thankfully, though, the Austrian occupiers conducted themselves with restraint. "One would not think," Fuller commented, "that men installed where they are not wanted and ought not to be could seem so gentlemanly."[26]

The Ossolis chose to live on the Piazza di Santa Maria Novella because Margaret wanted to be near the imposing Gothic church that gives the square its name. With its fresco-lined chapels that seem like "eremitic caves swarming with importunate visions," the church of Santa Maria Novella could not have failed to call to Margaret's tired, peace-seeking soul.[27] To this day, the broad, open piazza feels like a world apart from the rest of the city, and it was wonderfully suited to a couple in need of rest and a toddler in need of space to try out his legs. Fuller found the air there "delightfully pure and animating."[28] Despite its secluded atmosphere, the piazza is only a few minutes' walk from the Duomo, the enormous domed cathedral that stands at the physical and spiritual center of the city. Though not nearly as rich in artwork and ornament as the churches Fuller had known in Rome, the interior of the Duomo possesses, in the largeness of its dimensions, a kind of naked majesty. In it, one breathes a different atmosphere. Fuller called the experience of walking through the Duomo when no one else was there, when only the altars were lit and the chanting priests could be heard but not seen, "the finest thing."[29] She was also relieved to find that the members of Florence's small American community, none of whom had heard about either Fuller's marriage or Nino, were happy to receive them and, almost as important, disinclined to ask embarrassing questions. All in all, Florence received the Ossolis in just the form they needed: as an enfolding sanctuary.

Ensconced in a small, square bedroom with a view of the campanile that stands next to the Duomo, Fuller gave her mornings to writing. The space was sparingly yet adequately furnished, and it had the virtues of a polished floor and a frescoed ceiling. Fuller worked at an oval table, lighted by a monk- ish lamp of brass as a cheerful fire blazed in the grate. Giovanni was usually close beside her, reading about politics and often nostalgically dressed in the dark brown, red-corded uniform coat hc had worn when defending Rome— a garment that he wisely chose to put on only when at home.

From Florence, Fuller wrote just two more dispatches for the *Tribune*, one in November and the other in January 1850. Though both communiqués still reflected Fuller's dejection over the failed revolution, each also showed signs of resurgent optimism. In November, when the political situation still seemed to be worsening daily, Fuller wrote of her long walks in the country- side around Florence. The beauty of nature had reassured her that the God who had created such harmony "will not suffer his highest, ardent, aspiring, loving men to live and die in vain; . . . phoenix births rise from each noble sacrifice."[30] With perfect assurance, Fuller predicted that socialism would soon hold sway in Europe. Vast changes in politics, education, and daily liv- ing were but a short time away, if only because "the world can no longer stand without them."[31]

In January, as Florence lay shrouded in snow, Fuller's tone turned still more boldly prophetic, and her words linked social revolution with celestial vengeance. Every inch of Roman ground, she declared, had been seeded with hatred, and the growth from those seeds would be stopped only when "Heaven shall waft a fire that will burn down all, root and branch, and pre- pare the earth for an entirely new culture." Greatly underestimating the human need for spiritual authority, Fuller took it as given that "the Roman Catholic religion must go." She also foretold an "uncompromising," Pan- European revolution that France could not betray, that Germany could not bungle, and that Russia could not stamp down. After that searing, purifying ordeal, a new life would irresistibly spring up: "The New Era is no longer an embryo; it is born; it begins to walk—this very year sees its first giant steps, and can no longer mistake its features."[32] The time was at hand when "men shall . . . be represented as souls, not hands and feet, and governed accordingly. A congress of great, pure, loving minds, and not a congress of selfish ambitions, shall preside." Rose-colored and impetuous, Fuller's was a still-born manifesto; the spirit of European radicalism had been much more battered than she guessed. In her mind, however, sorrow had already yielded to hope. The last words she wrote for the *Tribune* were these: "Glory to God in the highest, for peace and love from man to man is become the bond of life."[33]

With her newspaper work behind her, Fuller directed the greater part of her creative energies to the narrative of her travels she had started writing in L'Aquila while expecting Nino. She now planned to dispense with her travels in Britain and France and to focus on the revolution in Rome. By this time, Fuller was no longer the diffident aesthete who had infuriated Greeley by waiting patiently for her muse. Her creative impulse was so natural and strong that, as she told William Henry Channing, she could "let the Genius lead."[34] She had every reason to want to pile up the pages. It was not only that she hoped for pecuniary profit, though she did hope the sales might prove strong. She also hoped to write "a worthy chapter in the history of the world," a work of such spirit and energy that it might become "a possession forever for man."[35]

In the evenings, after Margaret's work was done, the Ossolis appear to have had visitors more often than not. If the conversation was in Italian, Ossoli would remain, though even then he was far from vivacious. If the guests spoke in English, he would slip out to the Caffe d'Italia, not wishing to discomfit his wife's friends with his uncomprehending silence. Little Nino had evidently not inherited his father's love of quiet. During his second autumn, his mother wrote, "He laughs, he crows, he dances in the nurse's arms . . . he blows like the bellows . . . and then having shown off all his accomplishments, calls for his playthings." The toddler took special pleasure in mimicking the bands that played in the piazza, trying to sing and drum in soldierly fashion. Fuller had never felt so happy as when she came back from a walk or visit to see his glad eyes as he welcomed her home.[36]

Unlike her father, however, Fuller had no impulse to regard her firstborn child as a nascent prodigy. She wrote enigmatically to the Springs that she thought his faculties were "not in very good balance" and that she did not "cherish sanguine visions about him."[37] Indeed, his maltreatment in Rieti seems to have made Nino something of a slow developer; at seventeen months, he still could not walk.[38] To one correspondent, she admitted that she did not expect Nino to be brilliant, and to another she wrote bluntly, "My little one seems nothing remarkable."[39] As Nino grew up, there were sure to

While in Florence, Fuller posed for the American sculptor Horatio Greenough. His sketch of her is now published for the first time.

(COURTESY OF GEORGE R.
RINHART AND THE
NATIONAL PORTRAIT
GALLERY)

be no late-night readings of Virgil, no unreasoning pressure always to be the best. It was enough for Margaret that he was giving her "the first unalloyed quiet joy" she had ever known. She knew, of course, that like all mortal creatures "he must grow up in sorrow and to strive and have less and less [of] the sweet music that seems to flow around him now." If he were like his mother, he would learn to find himself "full of faults and much unreasonable." Margaret was too wise to hope her son would always be happy. She merely asked instead that "there will be in him a conquering, purifying energy" that might finally lead him to redemption.[40] Her great hope for herself was simply stated: to know that she had "not . . . learned and suffered quite in vain for the next generation."[41]

Though the Ossolis were in no position to spend lavishly, some comforts lay within their reach. Their building employed a porter, whose wife assisted them with sundry chores, and they maintained a nursemaid for Nino. Yet the presence of these domestics did not make life on the piazza a perfect idyll. The porter, who inhabited "a dark, cavernous hole" on the first floor, was dying of tuberculosis. The Ossolis' maid quarreled constantly with the tenant upstairs and once even mounted the stairs with a knife in hand, intent on avenging some especially malicious insult. Only Margaret's calm intervention appears to have averted bloodshed.[42] Moreover, the Tuscan winter of 1849–50 was unusually harsh. Although it was beautiful to watch from their windows as the piazza filled up with snow, the couple's fireplace proved an inadequate defense against the plunging temperatures, which Fuller described as "quite as cold as Boston."[43] Her bedroom, where she had been doing her writing, became uninhabitable, and she was forced to put aside her manuscript for six or seven weeks. Both she and Ossoli fell ill around New Year's Day and did not fully recover for a month. Prevented by the cold and damp from going out regularly, Nino grew bored and fitful, and Margaret briefly worried that the lack of exercise and fresh air might further retard his growth. Nevertheless, even this forced repose felt like a balm after all of Fuller's former agitation and struggles. She summed up their life succinctly when she wrote to her mother, "We . . . now live comfortably . . . tormented by no one, helping ourselves."[44] A small hint of boredom, however, crept into her tone when she wrote in February, "Nothing special has happened to me."[45]

Yet there were special people all around her. Fuller's experiences of cities had always been shaped by the friends she found there. Among the Italians in Florence, by far the greatest of these was Costanza Arconati, who had taken residence there for the winter. Fuller initially feared the reaction of Arconati, a model of social correctness, to the strange circumstances of Fuller's marriage and motherhood. However, understanding that a true gentlewoman overlooks such awkwardnesses, Arconati looked on the bright side. Fuller's having become a mother, Arconati assured her, had simply given them another spot of common ground. As for Ossoli, the anti-radical Arconati merely gave lighthearted thanks that Fuller had not gone and married Mazzini himself. Relieved by her friend's leniency, Fuller became a frequent guest at Arconati's villa and a regular companion on walks and rides in the countryside. With her willingness always to listen and never to judge, Arconati became Fuller's most cherished confidante.

Fuller was surprised to find in Florence a reminder of a now distant chapter of her life. One evening, she and Ossoli were accosted by a man in his midtwenties who announced himself as Horace Sumner. Horace, who shared the idealism but not the ambition of his older brother, the future senator Charles, had met Fuller while living on the commune at Brook Farm. Fuller had begun to weigh the merits of leaving Italy and returning to America, and she was pleased to come across a living "echo of the old pastoral masquerade."[46] Horace soon took up the habit of coming to read with Ossoli every evening, and the two attempted to teach each other something of their native languages.[47] On Ossoli's side, the learning proceeded with no particular success. After months of effort, it remained a great exercise for him to pronounce the word "mother," and Fuller could not boast that he said it very well.[48]

Fuller also added yet another pair to her long list of famous companions. She had yearned to meet the poet Elizabeth Barrett ever since narrowly missing her in London. Now, almost exactly three years later, Madame Ossoli was quick to pay her respects at the home that Barrett shared with her husband, Robert Browning, almost adjacent to the Palazzo Pitti on the other side of the river. Margaret was delighted with Mr. Browning, who was destined for lasting fame as the author of poems like "My Last Duchess," "Fra Lippo Lippi," and *The Ring and the Book*. "[He] enriches every hour I pass with him," she wrote, and she called him "a most cordial, true, and noble man."[49]

With Elizabeth she found a still deeper affinity. Mrs. Browning was at first mildly taken aback by the strange pairing of the talkative, intellectual American wife and her polite but thoroughly taciturn Italian husband, and she suspected that, if the two ever did remove to America, the "Yankees" would more or less ignore Giovanni. To Margaret, however, Elizabeth warmed more than she had expected to. They had much to discuss. Both had grown up with demanding fathers. Both had been born into comfortable circumstances, only to see their families' fortunes erode. Elizabeth had a son about six months younger than Nino, as well as a keen interest in the endless anecdotes about American literati that Margaret was pleased to tell. When Elizabeth put aside her writing to receive Madame Ossoli on a rainy afternoon, the visit could easily last through both the midday meal and afternoon tea. "I like her much," was Elizabeth's judgment of the singular American.[50]

She might have liked her even better if the two had managed to avoid politics. Elizabeth Browning, whose poem "The Cry of the Children" had helped to galvanize British public opinion against child labor, was a woman of generous sentiments. However, if her patrician upbringing had led her to sympathize with the lower classes from a safe distance, it had not taught her to trust them. With all her talk of revolution and overthrow, Fuller alarmed the genteel Mrs. Browning, who saw such views as a desecration of the class distinctions and proprieties that had given structure to her world. Fuller, she anxiously declared, was "one of the out & out Reds, & scorners of grades of society."[51] Yet it is a proof of their friendship that their disagreements barely scratched the sympathy between them. When the Ossolis at last prepared to leave Florence, Elizabeth, who had been an invalid since her twenties, had her husband carry her up six flights of stairs to the couple's apartment so that she could attend their farewell party.

None of Margaret's trials had ever made an invalid out of her, though neither she nor Ossoli had quite the same vitality as when they had met. Fuller observed that the strife of the revolution had "plowed furrows" in her husband's spirit. But at least Giovanni had come through their recent trials looking outwardly youthful and fit. He had, Fuller noted, "a simple child-like piety" that made ill fortune easier for him to bear.[52] The toll on Margaret had been visible. There were now enough lines and wrinkles on her face for a woman of sixty. Her old friend Frederic Henry Hedge, who had seen her in Rome, brought back the report that she had developed a disease of the spine and could no longer carry herself upright.[53] Frederick Gale, an American living in Florence, found her looking sad and depressed, bent in body and an old woman before her time. Yet, remarkably, Gale detected neither scorn nor contempt in her conversation.[54]

She was not embittered. Yet she was unmistakably tired, and she could not afford to be. For reasons not entirely clear—he may have been blackballed for his political associations, passed over because he could not stay long in Florence, or simply thwarted by his aristocratic lack of practical skills—Ossoli seems to have been incapable of finding employment. George William Curtis, a young American journalist who knew the family in Florence, thought that the happy little household on the sixth floor of the Casa Libre would have made a very pretty picture but for the knowledge that its future depended chiefly "upon that brave and steady but not strong woman."[55]

It is little wonder, then, that in the spring of 1850, Fuller found her domestic comfort marred by a host of fears, many of which chiefly concerned Nino. Worried that any new stimulus might bring disease, she feared heat and cold and mosquitoes. Perhaps most of all, she feared poverty.[56] She could hardly bear to spend a cent for fear that Nino might later need it. "I have great service offered," she observed, " and can't do enough to merit my salt, to say nothing of bread."[57] Her great hope remained her history of the revolution, the materials for which she had purchased "by . . . many hours of bitter care."[58] According to Elizabeth Barrett Browning, the manuscript was still a long way from completion; she later wrote that, when Fuller left for America, she had amassed only "the raw material. . . . [N]othing was finished."[59] Undeterred by the long work ahead, Fuller labored on over her notes and drafts. If she could not make something great and, yes, profitable out of that rich and poignant substance, she conceded, "My future is dark indeed."[60]

Fuller very likely did not pass a single day in Florence without contemplating her return home. The fact that Ossoli's official welcome in Tuscany would end during the coming summer was only one reason. Although she and her husband had been able to carve out a small slice of personal happiness, Italy as a whole was passing through a "time of incubus," and an atmosphere of defeat was all around her.[61] Fuller never regarded Florence as anything more than "an oasis," a place for refreshing herself and replenishing her courage before setting forth again "on the difficult way."[62] She felt certain that her book on the Roman revolution would fare better in America if she were on hand to see it through press.[63] Her American friends began to "look very lovely . . . in the distance."[64] Above all else, she felt the need to reunite with her mother. "I want to talk with you," Margaret wrote to her in February, "and know for myself how you are and have you see the baby."[65]

Fuller envisioned her return to America as only temporary; she had little zeal for living forever in the country that she now called the land of "'eighteen millions of bores,' with their rail-roads, electric telegraphs, mass movements and ridiculous dilettant phobias, but with ever successful rush and bang."[66] She hoped only "to make some arrangements by which we may pass together at least three or four years of our lives" in the States, and then to resettle in Italy once the political crisis had passed.[67] When, as they confidently assumed, the republican forces regrouped and drove the pope from power, they might return to Rome. It was not too much to hope that, in recognition of Giovanni's erstwhile service in defense of the city, a new liberal government would support a claim to transfer the Ossoli family property into his hands. If so, then he, Margaret, and Nino might thereafter live a life of modestly privileged comfort amid the most extraordinary man-made beauties on earth.

Fuller must have been somewhat surprised when, after she had already arranged for passage to America, a letter came from Emerson, telling her that he considered it best for her to stay where she was for the time being; he thought her book would have more credibility if it came from a resident of Italy than from a repatriated American.[68] Soon after, another letter came, this one from her former traveling companion Rebecca Spring, who expressed an unexpected consensus: all of Margaret's friends in America with whom she and her husband had spoken—a group that included Lydia Maria Child, Greeley, and Greeley's fellow liberal journalist Parke Godwin— felt that, as much as they would love to see her, it would be undesirable for her to come home at present. Rebecca's reasons had some force to them. Fuller's continued writings about Italy, she urged, would be better received than anything she could write from a domestic vantage point. Moreover, it seemed probable to Mrs. Spring that, if Margaret came home, she would "lose the power to write as well, for you will not be so happy and your husband . . . would not and could not be so happy here as in his own beautiful Italy." Adding that she thought Margaret's stateside acquaintances paled in comparison with the Brownings and others, Rebecca added an emotional appeal: "It is because we love you we say stay!—It is because we believe it best for you."[69]

Three days later, emphasizing more practical arguments, Marcus Spring added his concurrence. He reminded her that it cost far less to live in Florence; burdened with a child and an unemployable husband, she would find it hard "to make anything like a living" in the States. Knowing, too, how deeply she cherished the dream of Italian liberty, Spring declared that she could much better serve "that noble & aspiring people" by staying where she was and, through her writings, further quickening American sympathies for the ongoing patriotic struggle. Spring said that he had consulted William

Henry Channing, and that he, too, agreed: "Your truest welfare might be best promoted by one or two years longer sojourn where you are."[70]

These letters were too polite to touch on another argument against Fuller's coming home, but she knew quite enough about it from other sources. As word of Fuller's marriage had circulated stateside, it had generated a swirl of gossip and innuendo. Some guessed correctly that Fuller's pregnancy had been premarital; one especially virulent story had it that she had purchased Nino from baby traffickers.[71] If she were to return to America, Fuller and her husband would inevitably face both prejudice and persiflage. In response to a letter from Cary Tappan that had alluded to "the meddling curiosity of people," Fuller bristled; she had encountered no one in Italy who "asked or implied questions," and it clearly pained her to think that American manners were so inferior.[72]

Fuller's American friends were not alone in their objections. Companions in Florence came daily to dissuade her. They said that she could not imagine the fatigue and suffering that a two-month voyage would inflict on her, to say nothing of the risks of taking a twenty-month-old child across the ocean with neither a female servant nor any medical care if he fell ill. The cabin, being on deck, would be horribly exposed if a gale should strike. The supply of wholesome water would be uncertain. Furthermore, a merchantman of the kind they thought of taking would provide neither the she-goat for Nino's milk nor the stocks of poultry, citrus fruit, hard bread, and medicine essential to the voyage, and the cost to the Ossolis of supplying these themselves would be tremendous. Fuller largely discounted the advice, knowing "the proneness of volunteer counsellors to frighten and excite one all they can."[73] But not all the voices that warned her were human. "Various little omens," she wrote, had come together to give her "a dark feeling," and it seemed entirely possible to her that "I should perish with my husband and child, perhaps to be transferred to some happier state."[74] She told William Henry Channing that she "fear[ed] terribly the voyage home."[75] Yet these forebodings, the cost of the journey, and the earnest advice of friends did not change her mind. She remembered the practicality of her reasons and resolved to move forward.

To assume that Fuller's decision to return to America was grounded solely in reason is to ignore some essential parts of the picture. Choices have their own curious momentum. Fuller had written and talked for so long about coming to America in the summer of 1850 that backing away from the plan would have felt almost cowardly. She had to contend as well with the fact that the narrative of her life that she had been telling herself since childhood—a story of ever upward motion and advancement toward personal perfection—had been all but shattered by the twin crises of unplanned motherhood and the collapse of the Roman revolution. If the upward trajectory had in fact been broken, however, her belief in it had not. She needed to believe that she would rise again. She needed to recover the inner force that had always driven her forward. What better place to do it than in the land where her life had begun?

A final reason seems least rational of all, but it was almost surely there: Fuller's premonitions of disaster on her trip home served, not as a deterrent, but as an incentive to her sailing. Fuller's theory of life had always been teleological; there had always been a greater power behind her actions than either impulse or chance. Fuller told Channing that her life was going forward with a regularity greater "than the fates of a Greek tragedy."[76] If the omens were true, then they supported Fuller's sense that she was acting out the will of destiny. If, on the other hand, her premonitions were no more than superstition, she needed, as a brave woman, to face down her fears and prove their emptiness. By representing to herself that her journey was filled with peril, Fuller perversely obliged herself to make it. She wrote to Channing that she was ready to "shuffle the cards, till Fate is ready to deal them out anew."[77]

The Ossolis booked passage to New York on the *Elizabeth*, a Philadelphia merchantman preparing to sail from Livorno. Fuller's decision to take a cargo vessel instead of one of the packet ships now sailing regularly from the ports of northern France was motivated primarily by thrift; to make the journey from Le Havre, for example, would have cost the Ossolis about four hundred dollars. The fare on the merchantman would be only half as much. Weighed down by debts of more than fifteen hundred dollars—the price of a decent house in those days—Fuller was loath to add more red ink to the family's accounts. However, when people sailed on packet ships, they got what they paid for. The navigational equipment, particularly the ship's chronometer, which enabled the captain to pinpoint the ship's longitude, was far superior to what was used on a cargo ship like the *Elizabeth*. To sail in a merchantman was to save money, but potentially to pay it back in the form of heightened risk.

Though still "suffering as never before from the horrors of indecision," Fuller set about giving herself reasons for booking the passage. The ship, she was told, was "an uncommonly good vessel for the merchant service, nearly new, and well kept."[78] To convince herself further, she had an interview in mid-April with the ship's captain, a native of Maine named Seth Libby Hasty. Hasty was only thirty-eight, but he seemed to Fuller "among the best and most highminded of our American men."[79] The kind interest that he showed in Fuller reassured her. On April 16, Fuller wrote that it was "likely" that her family would sail on the *Elizabeth*.[80] By May 2, the plan was definite. Some months earlier, Fuller had written a letter to Sam and Anna Ward, asking them to prepare her an old, worn easy chair beside their nursery fire.[81] Now that place might be prepared in earnest. She was coming home.

The Ossolis spent their last evening in Florence at the Brownings'. The sadness of departing appears to have outweighed the excitement of the coming voyage. Five months earlier, Margaret had written to the Springs that she had "never pretended to be [a Christian] except in dabs and sparkles here and there."[82] Nevertheless, as a good-bye present from Nino, she surprised the Brownings by giving their son a Bible. Stranger and more surprising still was the inscription she wrote inside: "In Memory of Angelo Eugene Ossoli."[83]

On May 17, the *Elizabeth* lay at anchor two miles off the coast of Livorno. A smaller boat took the three Ossolis aboard. Fuller brought along her precious manuscript of the revolution, knowing that one of her first tasks at the end of the journey would be to find a publisher. Also on board the merchantman was Horace Sumner, Ossoli's companion in his fumbling study of English. So were Captain Hasty's wife, Catherine, and a young Roman girl, Celesta Pardena, whom the Ossolis, stretching their budget, had been able to engage as Nino's nursemaid. According to Fuller, the ship was laden "with marble and rags," but she also carried hats, silk, and olive oil.[84] Fuller's bland description of the marble hardly did it justice: she was talking about 150 tons of fine Carrara, along with a significant finished piece of art: a statue of the recently deceased Senator John C. Calhoun on its way to Charleston, South Carolina.

A constant rain and dampness had hung over Livorno as the *Elizabeth* lay at anchor, and the captain had suffered more than usual fatigue in getting the vessel loaded, but as the ship began its progress toward Gibraltar, the weather was "not unpleasant."[85] Fuller passed the time by giving Italian lessons to

Captain and Mrs. Hasty, which they repaid by trying to help Ossoli with his still-sputtering English. Mrs. Hasty remembered the first days of the voyage fondly. "We studied in the morning," she wrote, "walked or sat on deck in the afternoon and sang and played in the evening."[86] Finally ambulatory, Nino darted about the deck, amusing the deckhands with his bilingual chatter, and Captain Hasty, despite a cough and persistent fatigue, seemed cheerful. Fuller's initial seasickness subsided after a fairly brief interval, and she looked forward to a voyage that would afford her a "respite from care and pain."[87]

Care and pain, however, soon descended on the *Elizabeth* with a determination that, as Margaret put it, began to feel like "the stern assaults of Destiny."[88] One evening, the captain complained of violent pain in his head and back. The next day, he was racked with fever, and reddish pustules gradually formed over his entire body. Before long, his weakness and suffering were extreme. His coughing became convulsive, and his throat swelled so greatly that he could not swallow.[89] There being no doctor aboard, the *Elizabeth* moved with all possible speed to Gibraltar, where the crew hoped to enlist the aid of a surgeon. Fuller cared for Hasty whenever his wife was too physically or emotionally exhausted to do so. She wrote to Marcus Spring from aboard the ship that nothing she had seen in the hospital in Rome compared with the captain's agony.[90] At the captain's request and in a moment of highly questionable parental judgment, Fuller twice brought Nino to see Hasty in his sickroom. Nino laughed and pointed, oblivious to the tragedy he was observing.[91] The *Elizabeth* made port in Gibraltar, but in vain; the ship was immediately quarantined, and no one, not even a doctor, was permitted to board her. On June 2, the morning after the ship arrived, Captain Hasty died. Judging his body to be too dangerous a contaminant to be brought ashore, the port authorities would not allow him to be buried on land. The somber rites took place in the harbor. On June 8, with former first mate Henry P. Bangs at the helm, the *Elizabeth* sailed into the Atlantic. Bangs had captained only one or two ships in his life.

The horror of Hasty's passing increased when a posthumous diagnosis was rendered: confluent smallpox. Ossoli, who had had the disease, was safe. However, Margaret and the carelessly exposed Nino had no such immunity. Margaret sent a letter to Marcus Spring acknowledging the dangers that now awaited her son, but she tried to dismiss them, saying that it was "vain by prudence to seek to evade" what had been decreed by fate.[92] Two days after the *Elizabeth* left Gibraltar, Nino began to manifest the same symptoms as the captain. He, too, was soon covered with pustules from head to toe. His face was so swollen that it seemed to have lost its shape, and he could no longer open his eyes. For a week, no one could say whether the boy would live or die. As Nino languished, the Ossolis' tempers frayed. Mrs. Hasty recalled that, when Margaret repeatedly asked Giovanni in English to bring her a book and he failed to understand, she snapped, "Ossoli, if you don't understand me now, it is of no use to tell you." The barb hit home, but the marchese checked himself a moment before responding. "I know I am stupid," he finally said, with supreme forbearance and perhaps a touch of passive aggression, "but I want you to have everything exactly as you wish—and cannot unless I am sure what you want."[93]

Finally, however, Giovanni lost patience with Margaret and her willingness to confuse the hand of destiny with her own recklessness. She had already left their child in the care of peasants who had nearly killed him with neglect. The fact that she had done so with his acquiescence probably mattered little to him as he recollected the episode. How many more times would she place his son in harm's way? When a quarrel, its precise subject unrecorded, arose between them as to the proper course of Nino's care, Giovanni abruptly recollected that he possessed a spine. He threw his arm around Margaret's neck and exclaimed, "I wish we could always think the same thing—& I never could differ from you, if it were not that the baby's life depends on it."[94] Thankfully, Nino, to his mother's boundless joy, recovered. As his strength returned, she spent hours by his side, singing to him. In an added blessing, the boy's pockmarks faded almost completely away—a relief to Margaret, who had fretted over the prospect of presenting her mother with a scarred grandchild. The Ossolis made up so sweetly that Captain Hasty's widow thought she had never seen two people more devoted to each other and their child.[95] How much of this marital devotion depended on the submission and forbearance of Marchese Ossoli, and what would have become of it if Nino had died, can only be speculated.

As the ship continued to sail against the wind, Margaret learned to take delight in the beautiful nights on the ocean; the moonlight affected her in a way for which her best word was "holy."[96] After weeks of slow progress and interminable tacking, the wind shifted, and as the *Elizabeth*'s sails filled with the southeastern air, her passengers sent up a hurrah. Captain Bangs had chosen a course that took the ship to the vicinity of Bermuda. He then made a sweeping right turn and guided the *Elizabeth* northward along the eastern seaboard toward New York. They passed Bermuda on July 14. The wind behind them was so strong that the passengers were told to start packing their belongings; the end of the journey was but a few days distant. But they sailed on in ignorance. No one realized that the *Elizabeth* was being pursued by a hurricane. On July 18, the storm struck Wilmington and Elizabeth City, North Carolina, with tremendous force, causing widespread damage before swirling north toward Long Island, where it was to demolish the bathhouses at Coney Island.[97] The Ossolis could not have known how spectacularly dreadful their luck was. On the New York coast, hurricanes in July are exceptionally rare phenomena. During Margaret's and Giovanni's lifetimes, only one storm comparable to the one now trailing them had hit New York so early in the season. Another of similar force would not strike the state so early in the year until 1972.[98]

It was not only the elements that were conspiring against the *Elizabeth.* An experienced captain like Seth Hasty, familiar with the coast and sure of his bearings, would have been able to guide the ship into New York Harbor comfortably in advance of the approaching storm. But Henry Bangs was not Seth Hasty. Finding it too hard a task to calculate the ship's longitude, Bangs and Charles Davis, an Englishman newly promoted to first mate, took only her latitude. Consequently, after sundown on July 18, Bangs put his location some twenty-five to thirty miles west of where he actually stood. Around two thirty in the morning, Bangs and Davis recorded a sounding of twenty-one fathoms, easily deep enough for the ship's passage. Not realizing that the *Elizabeth*'s surging tailwind was now carrying her far faster than he supposed, the novice captain went to bed, thinking only of the safe haven that he imagined lay ahead.[99] His vessel drove forward into the darkness.

IN ITS PHYSICAL DIMENSIONS, Fire Island, a barrier island along the southern edge of New York's Long Island, is an unusual place. It extends more than thirty miles from east to west, but to traverse it from the bay side to the surf requires a leisurely stroll of less than five minutes. In good weather, it is blissful. Gulls angle and wheel through the ocean wind. Swift-footed plovers and the rolling surf play their ancient game of tag. Smith Oakes, a beachcomber who kept a shanty in 1850 at a site now known as Point O'Woods, had seen the island in other moods.

To call Oakes a ne'er-do-well was perhaps the kindest thing one could say about him. The shack he and his wife maintained near the island's shore was, by all reports, little more than a storehouse for the stolen goods the two had amassed over an untold period. A goodly part of their living came from other people's woe, in the form of the items they scavenged from boats that had broken up near the shore. When Oakes awoke on the morning of July 19, 1850, to the news that a ship had run aground within sight of his part of the shoreline, he literally jumped out of bed.[100] He must have been taking some delight in his great good fortune. Other local inhabitants assembled with Oakes on the beach to keep a predatory vigil. It would be only a matter of time before the ship broke apart. For the moment, however, the tides were low. There was good reason to believe that, if the men and women on shore had acted promptly, rescue boats might have been launched. One of the onlookers later told William Henry Channing, much to the latter's disgust, that, had they known anyone of importance was aboard the vessel, they would surely have made the attempt.[101] Of course he said so. It is impossible to know whether any sort of knowledge could have instantly transformed a group of rogues like Smith Oakes from reprobates to rescuers. Meanwhile, events that Oakes and his fellow bystanders neither knew nor greatly cared to know about were rapidly unfolding aboard the *Elizabeth*, barely two hundred yards from the beach on which they stood.

When Bangs retired to his cabin, he had guessed that his ship was nearing the mouth of New York Harbor from the southwest. However, a lighthouse that Bangs presumed to be shining its beacon from the New Jersey shore was actually on Fire Island. He was more than fifty miles east of his supposed location. Instead of sailing along the shore, the *Elizabeth* was heading directly toward it. Over the next hour or so, the winds intensified. At three fifty, the mate heard a low, scraping sound. Then the *Elizabeth* was shivered by a jolt that awakened the passengers and brought them to their feet, wondering what had caused it. The truth was soon known. The ship had struck a submerged sandbar. An unstoppable flow of water was already surging in.

The crew realized at once that the battered ship would hold together longer if the masts were cut, and the work of felling the main mast and the mizzen was soon done, though the foremast was left standing.[102] The hulk, however, soon shifted awkwardly. With the grounded bow acting as a pivot, the stern swung around, exposing the broad side of the ship to the impact of the waves. In the first few minutes, the breakers slammed through the skylight of the cabin and put out all the lamps. Ripped from its hinges, the cabin door was borne away, and the waves rolled freely in and out. In his or her own way, each of the passengers felt the gravity of the situation. Sumner clasped hands with Mrs. Hasty and said simply, "We must die." Mrs. Hasty, whose firmness of nerve was to prove extraordinary in the coming hours, replied, "Let us die calmly, then."[103] Nino, shivering in the wet, sent up a steady wail until Fuller was able to wrap him in some clothing, hold him to her bosom, and, amazingly, sing him back to sleep. The Ossolis' servant Celesta was the hardest to calm; she was in hysterics until Giovanni managed to soothe her with a fervent prayer.[104]

The ship had come to rest at a pronounced angle, making it hard to remain standing. Furniture and trunks floated to and fro. The most sheltered place was beside the cabin walls to windward, and here the six passengers, still in their nightclothes, took refuge, seated side by side, their feet propped against a long table. There was much they could not know. They did not know that, down in the hold, moments after impact, the tremendous, inadequately secured load of marble had slammed against the hull and broken through, producing a gaping hole. They did not know that the lifeboats had been swamped or washed away, or that the carpenter's tools had also been lost. More immediately distressingly, they did not know the whereabouts of the crew. Hearing nothing from the deck, they assumed that the officers and seamen had abandoned ship. For three hours they waited in the dark, not daring to move.[105]

Around sunrise, the cabin seemed close to breaking up. Mrs. Hasty seized the initiative. With difficulty, she made her way to the doorway, looked out on the deck, and shouted for help. No one could hear her over the shriek of the storm. However, Davis, the mate, who had been in the more strongly built forecastle with the rest of the crew, glimpsed her through the rain and called to the other men to commence a rescue of the passengers. When no one else dared to risk the attempt, Davis himself, holding onto the bulwarks, moved carefully toward the cabin. Two other men, encouraged by his example, followed, and the three prepared to pull the passengers up to the forecastle. Mrs.

Hasty volunteered to go first. Though the waves once came close to snatching her away, Davis kept his hold on her, even seizing her long hair in his teeth to prevent her from being dragged off. In turn, with the help of the sailors, each of the other passengers made the perilous trip to the forecastle, including Nino, whom a sailor thrust into a canvas bag, which he then carried around his neck.[106]

Once in the forecastle, wrapped in the sailors' overcoats, the passengers revived a little. The fearless Davis made three additional trips to the cabin to salvage important belongings. Accounts differ as to whether he retrieved Margaret's portable desk, which contained her history of the revolution. In one version of what happened, he gallantly brought it to her. In another, although she told Mrs. Hasty, "There still remains [in the cabin] what, if I live, will be of more value to me than anything," Fuller declined to risk a man's life to save her work.[107]

Despite the driving rain, there was now ample sunlight by which to see the shore, a stark waste of sand hills, dotted here and there with people who appeared to be steadily watching the *Elizabeth*. Hopes rose. The ship was so close to land. With so many onlookers aware of their plight, it seemed only a matter of time until the rescue of the twenty-two persons aboard the *Elizabeth* would commence. Yet, inexplicably, the people on the shore were making no move to send a boat out to the wreck. Indeed, the only mode of transportation that appeared on the beach was not a boat, but a wagon. Evidently, no one on board imagined that their observers were intent on retrieving, not the living people, but the salable cargo.

A general rule of survival at sea holds that, all other things being equal, it is wiser to stay with a distressed ship than to leave it. Perhaps adherence to this rule helps to explain why the huddled group on the *Elizabeth* waited another two hours before taking further action. Finally, around nine, it was decided that someone should try to swim to shore and get help. One of the sailors put on a life preserver and dived into the waves. A few minutes later, he was seen again, safe on shore. A second sailor, taking hold of a spar, also jumped and made it to land. Now Horace Sumner decided to try his luck. It failed him. Some thought that a piece of the wreck struck him as he jumped. Others thought the surf was simply too powerful for him. In either case, Sumner slid beneath the ocean's surface and was never seen again.[108] Around this time, despite the entreaties of the sailors on shore, the scavengers of Point O'Woods could be seen gathering flotsam from the wreck, still indifferent to the lives less than a quarter mile away. If more of the crew and passengers of the *Elizabeth* were to survive, they would have to help themselves.

With Captain Bangs apparently in a funk, the coolheaded Davis continued to take charge. He devised a makeshift evacuation method that, while hardly ideal, seemed to present the best chance of survival. They would pull planks from the wreckage and fit them with rope handles. The passengers would each sit atop a plank, grasping the handles, while a sailor swam behind to keep them upright. Mrs. Hasty was the first to try, and, after making Captain Bangs promise that he would stay to the last, Davis leapt in behind her. At least twice, the plank capsized, but Davis righted it again. Within minutes, around eleven o'clock, Davis, with the help of a bystander, pulled Mrs. Hasty onto the sand, half-drowned but still alive.[109]

Perhaps it had made sense for the two bravest people on the ship to try Davis's plan first. However, their departure left no one on board with the same amount of pluck, and the evacuation effort promptly broke down. Celesta was likely too terrified to try. Among the passengers, that left only the three Ossolis. Here courage, prudence, and fear so mingled that they are impossible to separate. Had they made the plunge individually, with sailors to assist them as Davis had directed, Margaret and Giovanni would have had a reasonable chance of making it to shore. However, even with a sailor to support him, Nino's prospects were much less certain. Perhaps Fuller remembered what she had written to Lewis Cass just four months earlier: "I feel the tie between him and me so real, so deep-rooted, even death shall not part us. I shall not be alone in other worlds, whenever Eternity may call me."[110] Certainly she still felt what she had written to Emelyn Story in April, prompted by the loss of the child of a mutual friend: "[T]hese things make me tremble with selfish sympathy. I could not, I think, survive the loss of *my* child. I wonder daily how it can be done."[111] Neglectful as she might have been toward Angelino in the past, Fuller now redeemed herself as a steadfast mother. She was determined not to leave Nino now, and Giovanni would not leave her. The Ossolis bravely determined that, if they should perish, they would perish together. Moreover, even as the situation on the *Elizabeth* grew more desperate, another argument arose for staying aboard. Around midday, the men from the area's lighthouse brought a lifeboat down to the

beach, and aboard the ship the hope of rescue flickered up again. It was easier, and perhaps wiser, to stay where they were, and so Margaret and
Giovanni refused to move.

Yet it is also unimaginable that Fuller was not horribly afraid. From childhood, she had been haunted by dreams of floods and drownings. The metaphor of shipwreck had turned up in her writings countless times. The mere
sight of Niagara Falls had filled her with terror. Caroline Tappan was later to
recall that, on their various trips to rivers, lakes, and beaches, Fuller had
been easily frightened by turbulent water, the nearness of which had driven
her to seek shelter. True, she had behaved with unusual courage when her
steamer nearly went down on the way to Naples, but, if her writings could be
trusted, death by water had always been one of her most devastating fears.
Now that fear was closing in with paralyzing reality. The cold was not helping either. Soaked through to the skin, everyone on the ship was prey to
hypothermia. Severe loss of body heat impairs judgment. As the situation
worsened, it cannot be known whether Fuller was completely rational. Captain Bangs remonstrated with Fuller and Ossoli. The ship would break up
soon; to stay where they were was suicide. At last, in desperation, Bangs
declared that he himself would carry Angelino. Still Fuller demurred.[112] The
moment of no return ticked closer.

Meanwhile, on the shore, Davis was in agonies. He had seen whaleboats
lower in rougher seas, and he was sure that the lifeboat that had finally been
brought from the lighthouse could make the trip to and from the stricken
ship in perfect safety. But the lighthouse men would not launch her. The
other sailors who had made it to shore were in no shape to man the oars, and
the scavengers, now more than thirty in number, were useless. Oakes, as if to
show he was not a thorough knave, offered his shanty as temporary shelter
for the survivors. But this was not the help that was needed. In a moment of
British chauvinism, Davis later told Thoreau, "If it had been the coast of
England, they could all have been saved."[113] But the ragtag Americans
remained unmovable.

Back on the *Elizabeth*, Captain Bangs made a final appeal to the Ossolis.
Then, having received Fuller's final refusal and declaring that, as a married
man, he saw no sense in throwing *his* life away, Bangs ordered the crew to
save themselves as they might, and, with all but four of the sailors, he dived
into the sea. When Bangs reached shore, bruised and unconscious but alive,

Davis was tempted to tear him to pieces for having deserted Fuller and the others.[114] Now only the Ossolis, Celesta, the cook, the steward, the carpenter, and an old retired deckhand remained onboard.

It was more than ten hours since the ship had run aground. She now began to break apart. As the forecastle filled with water, the group was driven to the area on deck near the foremast. The steward, who loved Nino, took the child in his arms and declared that he would save the boy or die trying. Before he could leap, a wave caught him. He and Nino were thrown overboard and vanished under the tide. Twenty minutes later, their bodies washed ashore, so near to having survived that they were still warm.[115] Pitifully, Celesta and Ossoli became caught in the rigging and were swallowed by the next wave.[116] Celesta's naked body was recovered the next day. Ossoli's was never found. Of the passengers, Fuller was the last to go.[117] Just before the cook and the carpenter swam to safety, they saw her by the felled foremast with her hands on her knees and her long hair hanging loose about her shoulders. Her white nightgown, shroud-like, clung to her exhausted form. Just before the final surge, the last words the cook heard her say were, "I see nothing but death before me—I shall never reach the shore."[118]

Margaret Fuller always explained and justified her life by its next step. With her ever unfolding discoveries and ambitions, she gave a coherency to what had gone before and an anticipation to what was to come. The logic of her life was supplied by her insatiable desire to change, to progress, to keep moving. It is both fitting and chilling that almost the last words she was ever heard to say were "I see nothing but death before me." If any idea would have been intolerable to Fuller, it was the absence of a future, for, without a future, nothing about her made a particle of sense. Her lifelong belief that, through adversity, she would always grow, progress, and prevail died moments before she did.

The news did not reach Concord for three days. Emerson refused to believe that the body was lost. His entire thought depended on life and change. He could hardly bear to leave an idea alone and settled on a page, lest it harden into the inert deadness of fact. And yet it had been his lot continually to deal with death: his first wife Ellen, his brothers Edward and Charles, little Waldo. Now Margaret. He dispatched Thoreau to the scene, charging him with the mission of combing the area in search of any trace of her. Amid all the emotions of a shocked and grieving friend, however, Emerson retained the instincts of a scholar. Aware that Fuller's unpublished book on the Roman revolution had been swept into the waves along with its author, he was especially anxious that Thoreau should be on the lookout for "any fragments of manuscript or other property."[119] Reaching Point O'Woods on the morning of the twenty-fourth, some five days after the catastrophe, Thoreau was too late to discover much more than a frustrating blank of sand, surf, and sky. The beach, he wrote, was "completely smooth and bare." Initially, debris from the *Elizabeth* had strewn the beach for a distance of three to four miles. However, the scavengers had worked faster than Thoreau could travel. The silk, the hats, the almonds, and other cargo that had drifted to shore had been carried off at once. There was no manuscript, no body. Thoreau tracked down Oakes at his shanty—"a perfect pirate's house" of ill-gotten miscellany. Oakes had taken possession of two of the Ossolis' trunks that had washed ashore. One of them, in which the first mate had seen Fuller deposit her gold watch, stood suspiciously empty. Oakes told Thoreau about his role in the affair without embarrassment, seemingly oblivious of the rising contempt he was kindling in his guest.

Thoreau did make a pair of haunting discoveries. At some distance from the scene of the wreck, he found some bones that had been picked clean by fish. Beyond recognizing them as human, he could not identify them further. He also happened onto a jacket that had belonged to Ossoli. Thoreau ripped a button from the garment and put it in his pocket. When his search was done, the small souvenir made him think about the strangeness of a world in which inanimate objects survive and the living can vanish overnight. To his friend H. G. O. Blake, Thoreau wrote that Ossoli's button was "an actual button so called—And yet all the life it is connected with is less substantial to me than my faintest dreams." With acute melancholy, he added, "Our thoughts are the epochs in our lives: all else is but as a journal of the winds that blew while we were here."[120] It was absurd to think how quickly the evidence of the wreck had already begun to vanish and how swiftly nature had returned to her usual quiet business.

MARGARET-GHOST

All biographies . . . make me sick at heart and
make it hard to realize that there is a Heaven.

—MARGARET FULLER
TO JAMES FREEMAN CLARKE,
August 30, 1833

Though many have suffered shipwreck,
still beat noble hearts.

—MARGARET FULLER,
Woman in the Nineteenth Century

HE FIRST TIME THE GREAT NOVELIST HENRY JAMES RECALLED HEARING Margaret Fuller's name was on the day after she died. The seven-year-old boy and his father, Henry Sr., were on a steam-powered ferry from Manhattan to Fort Hamilton when they were approached by a man in his late sixties: Washington Irving, the famous creator of Rip van Winkle and Ichabod Crane. Irving gravely announced to Henry's father that Fuller had drowned.[1] In retrospect, it was an extraordinary moment: the man who had helped to invent American literature stood unawares next to the boy who would one day revolutionize it. They had been brought together by news of one of the greatest members of the generation that both connected and divided them. That middle generation was now in mourning.

Emerson considered the fact that Fuller died within 220 yards of the American shore a sadly fitting emblem of her country's inhospitable reaction to her entire life.[2] In his journal, he preserved a comment by their mutual friend Elizabeth Hoar, who observed that Fuller "was the largest woman; & not a woman who wished to be a man."[3] It was a fair tribute. Every bit as significant was Emerson's own lament: "I have lost in her my audience."[4] In the months that followed Fuller's death, Emerson returned to her in his journals again and again. He was defenseless against this almost laughable wrong in which the indifference of the cosmos had been advertised.[5]

Despite Fuller's religious ambivalence, her death was quickly enshrined in the visual vocabulary of religious martyrdom. In this contemporary illustration, Fuller awaits her demise in a prayerful pose.
(COURTESY OF THE NEW YORK PUBLIC LIBRARY)

Emerson's sense of loss was further inflamed by those who tried to reassure themselves that Fuller's death had actually been for the best. Elizabeth Barrett Browning thought that Fuller had lost little in leaving the world and that the change could not be a loss to her.[6] Fuller's longtime friend Almira Penniman Barlow had "the superiority to say" that the wreck was "a fit & good conclusion" to her life.[7] Even Emerson's own wife was trying to put a pious, consoling face on things. "I am very glad for her," Lidian told Emerson's Aunt Mary. "How happy to be taken with Husband and child—to know no pang of separation to be, after a short struggle with the waters, 'alive forever more.' The difficulties of life, the conflict with bodily infirmities— with poverty—and perplexities of various kinds; the *prose* of life and the decays of age all escaped."[8] For a brief interval, hoping to console himself, Waldo agreed with Lidian. At the very least, the tragedy had silenced the scandalmongers: "It sets the seal on her marriage," he wrote, "[and] avoids all questions of Society."[9] But Emerson bristled when he learned that others were at a loss to imagine how, with the infant Nino and the commercially useless Ossoli to burden her, Fuller could have done anything further of consequence. Emerson was infuriated at the assumption that "the best use to put a fine woman to, is, to drown her to save her board."[10] He believed that she had been snatched away just on the verge of new and greater victories. "She had only to open her mouth," he wrote, "& a triumphant success awaited her. She would fast enough have disposed of the circumstances & the bystanders. For she had the impulse, & they wanted it."[11] At least once, Emerson forgot himself and used the present tense to discuss her in his journal.[12] It was too early for her to belong solely to history.

The souls of the dead are so easy to tyrannize over: to bend to an agenda, to imprison in a litany of dates and occupations, or to let sink entirely into the forgetfulness of time. In dying young, Fuller had lost something more than life. She had lost the power to shape her story. Emerson could not save Fuller from the sins and blunders of biographers to come. But he could get in the first word. At the suggestion of Greeley and William Henry Channing, Emerson began to make plans for a memorial volume. He began committing to paper his observations on Fuller's life and work. In short order, most of the other living men who had played prominent roles in her life—Davis, Hedge, Clarke, Ward, Alcott, Greeley, even James Nathan—were asked to contribute to the project. A select number of women were also apprised of the project, including Caroline Tappan, Eliza Farrar, and Ossoli's sister, Angela de Andreis.[13] At Emerson's request, Carlyle wrote to Mazzini and the Brownings and promised Emerson that letters from them could be expected.[14]

With typical enthusiasm, Greeley wanted the book out "by the middle of September or at farthest the first of October."[15] Channing and Emerson had a better feel for the project's magnitude. They knew the book would require patience, as well as the work of many hands. They also realized that, for people as literary as Fuller's friends, the writing out of their memories could be of tremendous help in coping with the shock of losing her. Most important, though, Channing and Emerson grasped that no single portrait of Fuller, perhaps not even a half dozen, could do justice to all the facets of a woman who had meant so much to so many. They understood the half-despairing feeling that prompted Sam Ward to ask Emerson, "How can you describe a Force? How can you write a life of Margaret?"[16] Emerson answered that Ward's question itself was some description of her, but he knew that the difficulties of the project could not be so easily dismissed. The work, he feared, might be "above our courage."[17]

The gap between the initial enthusiasm for the project and the actual participation of the solicited contributors was almost a replay of what had transpired with *The Dial.* Davis and Ward offered letters and scattered reminiscences, but they wrote nothing substantial. Alcott proffered a paragraph from his journals. Nathan clung to his sheaf of letters and refused all assistance. The Brownings were silent. Mazzini, busy with weightier matters, also failed to respond. Hedge and Greeley did substantially better. The rusticated clergyman and the cosmopolitan editor each submitted warm and detailed reminiscences that would rank among the best portions of the completed memoir. In the end, though, the real work was done by a triumvirate of editors. After letting Fuller's own reminiscences tell her story from her birth to her departure from Miss Prescott's school, Clarke, Emerson, and Channing each took responsibility for unequal thirds of Fuller's life story: Clarke managed the span from Fuller's teen years in Cambridge through her teaching sojourn in Providence; Emerson took charge of *The Dial* period; and Channing oversaw the years from Fuller's departure from New England to her death. The resulting volume was thus dominated by the perspectives of these three men, and their views have in turn dominated perspectives on Fuller ever since.

Some materials never reached them. Untold sources had been lost in the wreck. Some of the manuscripts in Margaret's family's possession had already been "much mutilated by the knife."[18] Before sailing from Italy, Fuller had evidently mailed a packet of documents, including some of her journals, to Caroline Tappan, who then exercised her own control over "what is for the fire, & what for the eyes."[19] Nevertheless, with the help of Fuller's friends, Clarke, Emerson, and Channing amassed the greatest collection of Fuller documents that will ever be assembled. They then proceeded to edit them in ways that were accepted practice at the time but which now seem like vandalism. They literally cut the passages they liked out of larger documents and pasted them into their own work without bothering to record the dates or sources of their snippets. To protect the feelings and reputations of Fuller's acquaintances, they often elided names and then kept no private notes of the identities they had omitted. Primary documents that do survive illustrate that the editors—Clarke and Channing, in particular—sometimes altered quotations to fit their arguments. To this day, the study of Fuller's life begins with the *Memoirs of Margaret Fuller Ossoli.* However, thanks to the editors' destruction of so much primary material, no Fuller scholar will ever have the means necessary to reach conclusions entirely independent of those of her earliest editors. In their efforts to restore Fuller to life, her friends also permanently disfigured her.

Clarke began his section of the memoir by observing, "[T]he difficulty which we all feel in describing our past intercourse friendship with Margaret Fuller, is, that the intercourse was so intimate, and the friendship so personal, that it is like making a confession to the public of our most interior selves."[20] He was right. Each section not only expresses its editor's personality to a tremendous degree, but also treats Fuller according to the particular part of each editor's character with which Fuller's influence had especially resonated.

Clarke had been most affected by Fuller when he was a shy and tentative young man in desperate need of the encouragement she had abundantly given him. Thus, he quite naturally emphasized Fuller's role as an inspiring, transformative companion. The changes she had wrought upon his intellect and sense of self were, for him, the foremost fact of her existence. Clarke was also likely influenced by the widely held perception of Fuller as a real-life version of Staël's heroine Corinne. In Staël's novel, one of Corinne's admirers observes, "Corinne is the bond that unites her friends; she is the motive, the force, that animates our lives; we count on her kindness; we are proud of her genius."[21] Had these words been transplanted verbatim into Clarke's memoir, no one would have thought them out of place. When Clarke recalls how Fuller "discerned elements of worth and beauty where others could only have seen what was common-place and poor," when he observes that she "saw all her friends . . . idealized. She was a balloon of sufficient power to take us all up with her into the serene depth of heaven," he seems to suggest that Fuller's greatness lay not in herself, but in what she was able to call forth from others.[22] Through most of his account, Clarke gives Fuller to the reader as a kind of magic looking-glass, mirroring the observer back to himself in an improving light, but allowing only limited insight beneath its shining surface.

Clarke's portrait of Fuller was also deeply colored by his mental habits as a minister. Unable to rescue Margaret's body, he wished not only to present her as a remarkable human being but also to assure skeptical readers—and himself—as to the likely salvation of her soul. This latter goal led to difficulties. Clarke knew that, both in her fascination with pagan thought from Virgil to Goethe and in her lack of humble piety, Fuller did not fit the ordinary idea of a Christian. He had perhaps even read the December 1849 letter to the Springs in which she had admitted, "I never pretended to be [a Christian] except in dabs and sparkles here and there."[23] Still, Clarke felt compelled to argue the case for Fuller's redemption, even if his reasoning took him rather far from the typical salvation narrative.

Clarke asserts that Fuller's goal in life was self-culture. No surprises there, but Clarke's framing of this ambition told more. He asserted, not once but twice, that Fuller's urge toward earthly self-perfection was "wholly religious, almost Christian."[24] He returned to the second half of the phrase yet a third time.[25] In doing so, Clarke hoped to answer those who criticized Fuller's evident lack of religion and to claim her as one of the faithful. Prominent in his discussion is the reminiscence of Eliza Farrar, who had told Fuller the story of her religious awakening—of how, after a long period of spiritual darkness, "His great mercy came in an infinite peace to my soul."[26] Thereafter, Fuller frequently asked her about this state of bliss and had said, "I would gladly give all my talents and knowledge for such an experience as this."[27] Through the poignancy of this vignette, Clarke revealed the Fuller whom his perspective as a minister counseled him to see: the reluctant pagan, quietly and painfully yearning for a conversion that the independence of her mind and the strangeness of her circumstances had never allowed her. Clarke added that, during her time in Cambridge, Fuller had "felt how empty and worthless were all the attainments and triumphs of the mere intellect" and had sunk very near despair.[28]

But Clarke could not leave Fuller spiritually adrift. He maintained that, thereafter, Fuller had "passed on and up, leaving one by one these dark ravines and mist-shrouded valleys, and ascending to where a perpetual sunshine lay."[29] Clarke concluded his chapter by quoting in full the passage from Fuller's journal on Thanksgiving 1831, the day when she sat by the dark, silent pool and asked herself, "How is it that I seem to be this Margaret Fuller?" and felt herself "taken up into God."[30]

That passage answered Clarke's need to end his story of Fuller's spiritual bewilderment with what seemed to be a saving conversion experience. By emphasizing the "almost Christian" quality of her dedication to the highest and best, Clarke moved toward the possibility that a high ideal, served with selfless passion, might serve as a substitute for divine grace. If Fuller was not technically Christian, she could still be claimed as religious in that her devotion to perfectibility "recognized something divine, infinite, imperishable in the human soul,—something divine in outward nature and providence, by which the soul is led along its appointed way."[31] In the name of self-culture, Fuller had, like the most earnest Christian, set aside earthly joys and lower pleasures. The only thing missing had been literal faith.

Loving both Margaret and the Christian God, Clarke wished devoutly for a way to reconcile the two. He felt the appeal of being able to declare, like Goethe, that the angels may also save the unbelieving person who strives for excellence. Yet Clarke realized that, according to everything he had come to believe, "almost Christian" was not enough. As he was forced to confess, Fuller's dedication to self-culture, although it was the noblest form of selfishness, was self-centered all the same. Fuller's later repudiations of Christianity reveal that her conversion, if it was one to begin with, did not stick. Clarke was forced to concede that, in her "idolatrous" worship of strength and genius, Fuller had not accepted the Heaven that existed for the tired and broken, as well as the gifted and brilliant.[32]

While Clarke would have preferred to give Fuller's tale a more unambiguously Christian finish, there is a darker message beneath the surface of his narration: Fuller's absence of Christian faith left her with a daunting suspicion that life, unless one acted with supreme courage and energy to make it otherwise, would prove at last to have had neither meaning nor value. By gorging herself on the world's knowledge and by exhorting her friends to discover and use all the talents they possessed, Fuller beat back against the frightening void, all in the uncertain hope that, through pure, furious striving, she might leave some inscription on the blank wall of the cosmos. Her strivings were aimed, not at proclaiming the glory of God, but at compensating for His perceived insufficiency.

Of the three editors, Emerson was the least worshipful. Still only recently removed from writing his great essay on Montaigne for *Representative Men*, he was taken with the observation that lived experience was like a coin, one side representing the apparent or the finite and the other the real or the infinite, and that "life is a pitching of this penny."[33] In this dualistic frame of mind, Emerson had no wish to present only the idealized side of Margaret; indeed, he may well have seen the need to counterbalance the adulations of Clarke and Channing. For the Fuller of Emerson's pages, humility is "always an afterthought."[34] She squints. She talks through her nose. She satirizes those she disdains as a "pastime and necessity of her talent."[35] Emerson dismisses her pen as "a non-conductor," and he broadly implies that, as a lover of beauty and society, Fuller resented her own plainness and lack of position "among the fairest and highest" of social circles.[36] Moreover, it is hard to tell whether he is indicting or reaffirming the biases of his time when he refers to her being female as a "negative."[37] At the same time, however, Emerson's admiration remains clear; he is pleased to praise her "strength of mind" and "her good heart."[38] He pronounces her, in sum, "a right brave and heroic woman."[39]

Paradoxically, Emerson's section, which strove hardest toward realism, struck the Fuller family as the least accurate. Surely, they expected a more grateful commentary from the man for whom their departed daughter and sister had worked so hard and selflessly. Understandably, too, they wanted an aura of light to encircle her memory, and they did not care to see it dimmed by the shades of Emersonian dualism. Margarett Crane Fuller complained to Richard, "Mr. E. never understood Margaret—that is evident enough."[40] Mrs. Fuller seems not to have appreciated that, precisely because he had declined to sanctify her, Emerson had made Margaret more approachable and humanly appealing.

Whereas Emerson renders Fuller sympathetic through realism, Channing's portion of *Memoirs* alternates between reverence and condescending pity. At times he sensibly suggests that Fuller's discontentment arose from being too exalted for the world around her. "Contrasted with her radiant visions," Channing writes, "how dreary looked actual existence; how galling was the friction of petty hindrances; how heavy the yoke of drudging care!"[41]

He is less plausible and more annoying when he suggests that Fuller's emotional essence was that of a disappointed lover for whom the life of the scholar was only a substitute for more personal fulfillments. In his rendering, Fuller appears as a figure "the very restlessness of [whose] intellect was the confession that her heart had found no home."[42] Her superiority, he argues, was really "virgin pride, and her absorption in study the natural vent of emotions, which had met no object worthy of life-long attachment."[43] It seems astonishing that one who knew Fuller so well could so unthinkingly diminish her.

To be sure, the writings of Fuller that came into Channing's hands gave him ample material for a sentimentalized reading. When, for example, he quotes her as writing, "Shall I never be able to act and live with persons of views high as my own?" and "No fellow-being will receive me. I cannot pause; they will not detain me by their love," and, again, "I feel as, when a suffering child, I would go and lie with my face to the ground, to sob away my little life," it is hard not to give credence to his image of Fuller as the abandoned sibyl, the child who had sharpened her intellect in hopes of approval and had risen to distinction only to find that it was another name for solitude.[44]

One suspects that Fuller would have disliked being so patronized. In rhapsodizing on Fuller's self-doubt and isolation, Channing fails to explain the strength and courage that offset her frailty and, despite the complaints of loneliness that he so powerfully emphasizes, won her a host of loyal friends. One-sided though it may be, Channing's rendering of Fuller is strikingly memorable. For those who prefer to regard her as a creature of pain and disappointed hopes, no source could be more satisfying. Channing's Fuller is perhaps best summarized by a line that he excerpted from her writings with neither citation nor date, a remarkably chilling meditation on existence: "I have no belief in beautiful lives; we are born to be mutilated; and the blood must flow till in every vein its place is supplied by the Divine ichor."[45] Like the heroes of Aeschylus, Channing's Fuller suffered into truth.

As a whole, *Memoirs* portrays its subject in a highly indulgent light. The prickly arrogance that many perceived in her receives only occasional notice. Those whom Fuller slighted or ignored are made to bear the blame for not having been interesting or smart enough to have deserved her good opinion. More noticeably sanitized is Fuller's romantic and sexual life: James Nathan is wholly absent, and the memoir asserts as settled fact that Fuller and Ossoli were married before Nino was conceived.[46] Perhaps the most subtly distorting feature of the Fuller memoir, however, was that it was assembled by three transcendentalists. Both overtly and implicitly, Clarke, Emerson, and Channing used their work to claim Fuller for the transcendentalist movement. To this day, when students of the period think of Fuller, they tend to associate her first with her time in Boston and Concord, even though her full development as a thinker, writer, and social activist took her well beyond her transcendental phase.

Another related deficiency of *Memoirs* demands notice: the last years of Fuller's life were known to the editors chiefly through a few letters and her *Tribune* dispatches. They had not witnessed her reactions as she met the victims of poverty in Britain and the politically oppressed in Italy. They were not there to observe how the secret shame of her pregnancy had acquainted her with humility, or how Ossoli's affections had broadened her thinking about the forms of human goodness. They were not privileged to know her in the final phase of her personal odyssey, in which the values of kindness, compassion, and social transformation displaced her credo of striving and self-improvement. The Fuller of *Memoirs* was not the Fuller who died in the wreck of the *Elizabeth*.*

One feature of the work was profoundly troubling to the Fuller family, especially her brothers Arthur and Richard. The first volume begins with the thirty-two-page "autobiographical romance" that Margaret wrote during a period of despondency in 1840. As a unique commentary on her emotional hardships of her childhood, the romance could hardly have been dispensed with. However, Arthur Fuller saw its inclusion as "a most unintentional injustice to my father's memory," and he claimed that his sister would never have permitted such a public airing of her dissatisfactions with Timothy Fuller.[47] In his *Recollections*, not published until the 1930s, Richard also took his own private turn at redeeming his father's reputation, calling him "the strong pillar of all our security" and remembering his love "with much satisfaction."[48]

---

* One should keep in mind that even a biography of Fuller that assigns due weight to her final years is, in a sense, incomplete, for Fuller's life was itself an unfinished work. At her death, Fuller was on the verge of further change, and she likely would have kept changing for as long as she lived. The "final" Margaret Fuller of 1850 was an arbitrary and ephemeral creature of a given moment, just as much as the Fuller who had left America four years earlier.

Whatever its editors' sins against objectivity, good scholarly practice, or the memory of Timothy, the *Memoirs of Margaret Fuller Ossoli* in no way disappointed the public. A thousand copies sold on the day the book was published in 1852. Until *Memoirs* was pushed out of the limelight by the publication of *Uncle Tom's Cabin,* it was briefly the most popular book in America. It remained the best-selling biography in the country for approximately four years.

After Fuller's death, surviving members of her family came together to be photographed. Clockwise from the left are Arthur Fuller, Eugene Fuller, Margarett Crane Fuller, Richard Fuller and Ellen Fuller Channing.

(COURTESY OF FRAN SOTO)

The popularity of Fuller's life story was more than vaguely troubling to some conservative observers. In a culture in which Christian worship was widely considered essential to a good moral character, Fuller's refusal to embrace religious orthodoxy rendered her legacy suspect. A representative judgment was offered by the highly influential Sarah Josepha Hale. Though Hale's authorship of the nursery rhyme "Mary Had a Little Lamb" itself ensures her a sliver of cultural immortality, it was as the editor of the tre-

mendously popular women's magazine *Godey's Lady's Book* that Hale helped
to define American popular taste for forty years. Like Fuller, Hale advocated
education for women. However, she could endorse that cause only within a
larger context of Christian humility and self-denial. The year after *Memoirs*
was published, Hale published the ambitious volume *Woman's Record*, which
purported to offer a sketch of every prominent woman in the history "from
'the beginning' till A. D. 1850." In her sketch of Fuller, Hale alleged that she
had "abandoned the only safe guide in her search for truth. Whatever be the
genius or intellectual vigor possessed by a woman, these avail her nothing
without that moral strength which is nowhere to be obtained, save from the
aid God has given us in His revealed Word." Once a woman strayed from the
rock of salvation, Hale averred, she was destined for error. The greater her
intellectual force, the more fatal her errors would inevitably become. Defi-
cient in "true moral life," Fuller's works were not "destined to hold a high
place in female literature."[49]

Hale and women like her advised women who desired social reform to
pursue strategies of gentle persuasion rather than bold self-assertion. For
decades to follow, this meeker ethic exerted a far greater influence over
American women than did Fuller's legacy. No other American woman rose
up to replace Fuller as an intellectual standard bearer, and the life of the
American mind, both male and female, became a somewhat barer landscape. Attuned to the values of mainstream religion, popular feminine sentimentality, and middle-class love of fashion, *Godey's Lady's Book*, not *Woman
in the Nineteenth Century*, was the more likely place for female America to
turn for its models and inspirations. In her conversations and writings, Fuller
had returned often to examples from scripture and myth, seeking to foster an
image of women that restored them to a classical grandeur. Yet, fifty years
after her death, Henry Adams was to observe that Woman as a force was
"unknown in America" and that "the monthly-magazine-made American
female had not a feature that would have been recognized by Adam."[50] The
cultural climate that emerged was one in which Fuller's works would indeed
be denied "a high place in female literature" for well over a hundred years.

Fuller was to be missed in another quarter. The event that, in the view of
most historians, inaugurated the women's rights movement in America, the
Seneca Falls Convention of 1848, took place while Fuller was in Italy, two
years to the day before the wreck of the *Elizabeth*. No one can say with cer-

tainty how Fuller might have helped to advance that movement if she had returned safely from Europe. It is reasonable to suppose, however, that she would have continued to provide the cause of women's rights with a scholarly center, reminding the nation that the rise of women was not a mere fad of the moment, but a force of history. Furthermore, it is inconceivable that Fuller would not have continued to emphasize self-culture as an essential part of women's progress. With her continued involvement, the women's movement of her time would have retained an even more intense awareness of womankind, not only as a subject in need of political and economic freedom, but also as a collective mind and soul to be enlightened and ennobled. The loss of Fuller changed the face of America's incipient feminism.

As copies of *Memoirs* gradually disappeared from bookstore shelves, interest in Fuller slowly and predictably subsided. Toward the end of the 1850s, Greeley and Arthur Fuller tried earnestly to fan the flames. With Greeley as his publisher, Arthur issued a series of collections of his sister's works, including a new edition of *Woman in the Nineteenth Century.* Arthur, though unquestionably earnest, had no surpassing skills as an editor. Sometimes with a view to brevity, sometimes with an overactive sense of delicacy or fear of controversy, he redacted long passages of his sister's writing, often expunging the very portions in which her distinctive passion and incisive thought were most vividly displayed.

Arthur's efforts were not enough to keep Fuller's memory present in the public mind. The strongest, most vital memories of Margaret were, of course, in the minds of those who had known her, and as time silenced one by one these repositories of her legacy, further portions of her died as well. Within ten years of Fuller's death, three more members of her immediate family passed away. Her sister, stricken with tuberculosis, was the first to die. Having finally left her incurably faithless and self-centered husband in 1852, Ellen reunited with Ellery long enough to give birth to Edward, the last of their five children, in 1856. Seventy years later, Edward Channing was awarded a Pulitzer Prize for a six-volume history of the United States. Ellen came to her quiet end the same year Edward was born. Though she left a record of few accomplishments, it was said after her passing, "[S]he was herself a poem."[51]

Eugene, Margaret's oldest brother, made a successful go of his newspaper work in New Orleans, where he became known for his "industry, reliability, and intelligence" as well as the mild and affable demeanor he had possessed since childhood.[52] In the end, he, like Margaret, was overtaken by tragedy at sea. In the mid-1850s, Eugene reportedly suffered a severe sunstroke, which resulted in what was nebulously termed "a softening of the brain."[53] In June 1859, after local doctors had failed to improve his shattered condition, his friends placed him on a ship bound for New York, in hopes that physicians there might effect a cure. On the second day of the voyage, his attendant, being overcome with seasickness, momentarily left Eugene alone. Before he could return, Eugene fell overboard and drowned.[54]

Margarett Crane Fuller, the seventy-year-old *materfamilias*, outlived her eldest son by a little more than a month. During her last decade, Margarett honored her eldest daughter's memory by taking an interest in poor Italian immigrants. She made a habit of paying visits to "suffering Italian women," and giving them modest gifts of charity.[55] Otherwise, the aging Mrs. Fuller mostly occupied herself, as she had long done, with tending her radiant garden. Under her nearsighted gaze, her son Richard remembered, "Families and generations of plants adhered to her . . . like the tenantry of a feudal lord."[56] Suffering from a slow and painful disease that the sources choose not to name, she moved in with Richard in September 1858 to await her death. Even in her weakened state, her son observed, "[E]very day she pursued the even tenor of her Christian life."[57] As her life ebbed, she told Arthur, who had also come to be with her, that she was done with earth and wanted "to go home now."[58] With him, she sang, "We are passing away, passing away! / Let us hail the glad day."[59] She died, as she might have wished, on a Sunday, July 31, 1859.

Arthur Fuller's life was changed by the loss of his eye at Groton. Indulged and protected because of his injury, he faced the challenge of proving that he, to the same extent as his fully sighted brothers, was manly and independent. He graduated from Harvard Divinity School, became a Unitarian minister, and served, at different times, as the chaplain of both houses of the Massachusetts legislature. After the outbreak of the Civil War, Arthur enlisted in the Union Army as a chaplain. Honorably discharged on the eve of the Battle of Fredericksburg, he insisted on going into battle with the army before returning home to his family. Before the heavy fighting had even begun, he was shot and killed.[60] He, like Margaret, was dead at forty. Arthur's most notable contribution to the world came long after his death. In 1895, his second son, Richard Buckminster Fuller, fathered a son of the same name who grew up to become one of the great architects and visionaries of the twentieth century. R. Buckminster Fuller's awareness of his great-aunt's legacy inspired him to seek, on a more scientific level, the universal harmonies that Margaret had sought to discover and expose through language. When the younger Fuller's Dymaxion House was displayed in 1930, an architecture critic observed, "Margaret Fuller . . . who attacked the moral and social problems of a new world, [is] alive in him."[61]

Richard, after graduating near the top of his class at Harvard, maintained a close friendship with Thoreau and joined him on many of his woodland rambles. Inspired by the memory of his father's example, Richard took easily to the practice of law and forged a successful career while living in the town of Wayland, Massachusetts. Twice married, he named a son after his brother Eugene. Richard published an adoring biography of his slain brother Arthur, as well as a book of theological poetry, titled *Visions in Verse,* in which he attempted to explain why God had chosen to place humankind in a world of sin and suffering and to show that "there may be some very good reason for our probationary state."[62] In it, Richard echoes some of his sister's conviction that life's tendency was meant to be forever upward: "I sometimes think, the human stature / Not the apex of our nature. / Its watch seems set to look before, / Toward powers reserved for us in store."[63] His own time of earthly probation having ended at the age of forty-five, Richard Fuller moved onward to another mystery on May 30, 1869.

William Henry Fuller, the sibling whose relationship with Margaret was weakest, pursued an undistinguished business career in Cincinnati. He eventually made his way first back to Cambridge and thence to New York City, where he died in 1878. The youngest and, in many ways, the saddest of the Fullers lived the longest. The disturbed, half-witted Lloyd, the final, stunted remnant of Timothy and Margarett's proud family, never acquired the ability to live independently. Neither of Richard's family memoirs mentions him. He passed away in 1891 at sixty-five, having survived his famous sister by just less than forty-one years.

A host of Fuller's friends and colleagues lived into the 1880s. By the end of the century, though, their ranks had greatly thinned. Emerson's lament that, with the death of Fuller, he had lost his audience contained some truth. He still had much of importance to write, including *English Traits, The Con-*

duct of Life, and *Society and Solitude.* However, having published his brilliant collection of essays *Representative Men* earlier, in 1850, he now had only one work left in him that is universally accounted great: an essay appropriately called "Fate." As the Civil War approached, he lectured vigorously against slavery. His exile from Harvard, which had begun after the uproar over his Divinity School address in 1838, finally ended in 1867, when he was asked to deliver the school's Phi Beta Kappa oration. Emerson's memory started to fail in the early 1870s, and the shock of a fire that severely damaged Bush in 1872 appears to have accelerated his mental decline. His powers steadily weakened thereafter, and he died at seventy-eight in 1882.

All three Unitarian ministers whose youthful inspirations so freely intermingled with Fuller's lived well past seventy. James Freeman Clarke purchased Brook Farm in 1855, in hopes of reviving the utopian experiment, but failed. Appointed a professor at Harvard Divinity School in 1867, he persuaded his colleagues to give more attention to non-Christian faiths and lobbied without success to make the school coeducational. He continued to preach until a month before his death in 1888. Frederic Henry Hedge eventually left Bangor for a home in Brookline, Massachusetts, nearer to the intellectual center of New England. He edited the *Christian Examiner* for four years and became, in later times, a professor of German at Harvard, where an imposing portrait of him still glowers down on visitors to the Faculty Club. Having never written the great works that his early career had seemed to promise, Hedge died in Cambridge in 1890. William Henry Channing, after a time in the Unitarian pulpit in Rochester, New York, accepted an appointment to a church in England. He returned to America on the eve of the Civil War, during which he served as the chaplain to the House of Representatives. He returned to England after the war and died there in 1884.

Caroline Sturgis enjoyed a long marriage to William Tappan. In the early 1850s, she and her husband lent their home in Lenox, Massachusetts, to the Hawthornes, and, while availing himself of their kindness, Nathaniel wrote both *The House of the Seven Gables* and a psychological novel inspired by Brook Farm, *The Blithedale Romance.* The Tappans spent the late 1850s in Europe, where Caroline's free spirits made a mixed impression on Henry James, who praised her "admirable intelligence" but categorized her in the "incurable ironic or mocking order."[64] Perpetually carefree, "with a fortune inherited . . . and a genial gravity of expression confirmed," Caroline led a life whose length, comfort, and casual irreverence contrasted deeply with that of her friend Margaret.[65] She died in 1888.

Fortune also smiled on Sam and Anna Ward. After years of living on a farm in the Berkshires, they settled in Boston not long after Fuller's death so that Sam could assume control of his father's banking firm. As the American agent for the London banking house of Baring Brothers, Sam added to his family's fortune. While traveling in Europe for her health in 1858, Anna Ward converted to Catholicism. Her decision prompted Emerson, in a letter he wisely never sent, to accuse her of having made a "foreigner" of herself.[66] Rather more understandingly, Sam had a chapel built for her near their country home in Lenox. After the Civil War, the Wards relocated to New York, where Sam became a founder of the Metropolitan Museum of Art. He also supplied the funding for the scientific expedition that sent the young William James up the Amazon with Louis Agassiz, thus making his own unintended imprint on a new generation of American philosophy. The Wards were two of the last survivors of Fuller's transcendental circle; Anna passed away with the coming of the new century in 1900, and Sam followed her in 1907.

James Nathan, who eventually tired of anti-Semitic prejudice and changed his surname to the more Christian-sounding Gotendorf, never parted with Fuller's love letters. After a long career in banking, he died in Hamburg in 1888. His family eventually sold the letters for publication, over the protests of the Fuller family and to the fascination of Fuller's more gossipy followers.

A more supportive soul, Horace Greeley maintained his stature as a voice for radical reform. In 1872, Greeley ran for president as the nominee of the Democratic and Liberal Republican Parties, campaigning for an early end to Reconstruction. Routed by the inept but popular incumbent Ulysses S. Grant and bereaved by the death of his wife, Greeley collapsed shortly after the election and died before the electoral votes could be counted.

Mazzini continued his efforts to found an Italian republic, though a series of failed uprisings finally reduced him to a minor role in the Risorgimento, which found new and, eventually, more effective leadership in the persons of King Charles Albert's son, Victor Emmanuel II, and his able prime minister, Cavour. In 1870, at sixty-five, Mazzini witnessed the unification of Italy of which he had dreamed for decades. His funeral, two years later, attracted a hundred thousand mourners. After returning to power, Pio Nono never again lived in the Palazzo del Quirinale from which he had been driven in 1848. Thenceforth, he and all subsequent pontiffs made their home in the Vatican. The French conquest of Rome won only a temporary reprieve for Pio's secular power; the reunification of 1870 effectively marked the end of the papacy as a political power. Ironically, it was later during Pio's papacy that the Catholic Church adopted the doctrine of papal infallibility. Although this doctrine applies only to matters of church dogma, it was strange indeed to consider the idea of infallibility attached to Pio, a man whose political foibles had caused such woe to so many.

As the century lengthened, the task of writing about Fuller passed more and more into the hands of those who had not known her. In short order, her memory became, as the novelist Henry James put it, "a sort of legend, so that the people who had known her well grew at last to be envied by later comers."[67] In the hands of these later comers, however, the legend faded and suffered. Direct recollections of her personal charisma and the incandescent glories of her conversation became sparser, and she fared less well with those who came to know her through her most durable remnant: her notoriously challenging prose. The surviving band of those who did remember her routinely mounted the defense that she had spoken brilliantly. However, set against the visible deficiencies of her writing, this protest inevitably sounded like faint praise—so much so that a recent scholar has perhaps somewhat hastily concluded that all of the honors paid to Fuller's speech were actually a form of sexist denigration; she has suggested that describing Fuller "chiefly as a talker . . . accesses enduring stereotypes of the woman as chatterbox, who cannot exercise restraint or listen, who unthinkingly repeats and passes on information."[68]

Into the twentieth century, there also lingered the perception that Fuller had been victimized rather than benefited by her education and that Timothy Fuller, by insisting on giving a man's education to a talented girl, had created an "intellectual monstrosity."[69] "Perhaps," a critic condescendingly observed in the 1920s, "it was a mistake to force her into the rigid groove of classical learning when she should have been playing with her dolls."[70] Some even blamed Fuller's "premature development" for her unconventional romantic life and, by a remarkable flight of illogic, for her terrible demise. "If she had married early, as Harriet Beecher did," clucked Vernon Parrington, "and her excessive energy had been turned into domestic channels, her life might have been less tragic, whatever the effect might have been on her intellectual development."[71] Critical opinion seemed unable to accept that Fuller had died because of a novice sea captain and a freak hurricane; for those who regarded Fuller's lifelong defiance of social conventions as a presumptuous revolt against nature and propriety, cosmic retribution for her refusal to be ordinary was a much more satisfying explanation.

Fuller's works went out of print. After abusing her memory during the early decades of the twentieth century, the male-dominated academy proceeded to largely ignore her for generations. Even within the women's suffrage movement, the name of Margaret Fuller never achieved the same reverence as those of Elizabeth Cady Stanton and Susan B. Anthony. If Fuller's reputation had continued to languish forever in the shadows to which it had been consigned by the 1920s, the most perceptive postscript to her story might well have been the one written in 1903 by Henry James. By that time, of course, James had only distant memories of the day when, at the age of seven, he had heard Washington Irving repeat the news of Fuller's death. In his biography of Fuller's friend from her Roman days, William Wetmore Story, James meditated on the persistence of "the unquestionably haunting Margaret-ghost, looking out from her quiet little upper chamber at her lamentable doom."[72]

For James, Fuller had become not so much a memory as a cultural riddle. The question "*why* she may, to any such degree, be felt as haunting" filled him with perplexity.[73] He wondered all the more whether, in the luminous world of the recently started twentieth century, she could have laid any claim whatever to what he called "the cosmopolite crown," and whether, indeed, she would have garnered any notice at all.[74] At best, he supposed, she might have been a "possibly picturesque New England Corinne"; at worst, "a somewhat formidable bore . . . a culture-seeker without a sense of proportion."[75] In either case, James marveled that, more than a half century after her drowning, Fuller's sharp identity, her plentiful life, and her active courage somehow remained durable enough for people still to be talking about her. Nevertheless, because James regarded her writings as "naught" and because he thought her greatest influence was in "the beautiful moral complexion" that she had encouraged among her friends and admirers, Fuller struck him as a strange kind of absence in the midst of astonishing presence, the central space that gives shape to the circle and the sphere.[76] There is always irony when individual will collides with impassive fate, and life, James wrote, had dealt with "the somewhat angular Boston sibyl on its own free lines."[77] Fuller, at last, had failed to bend the world to her desires, and this, in part, was why the Margaret-ghost "still unmistakably walks the old passages."[78] The elder Oliver Wendell Holmes had a similar sense of her evanescence. He concluded that "none know her aspect who have not seen her living."[79] Add to these assessments the statement of Ednah Dow Cheney, "You may say many things of Margaret, but the personal magnetism is incommunicable, and died with her," and one might well wonder whether James was finally right: that there is no true way of ever recovering "the Margaret-ghost."[80]

Thankfully, however, a good deal of life has now returned to the spirit who, according to James, Holmes, and Cheney, seemed lost beyond recovery. The resurrection began in earnest in the 1970s, when a handful of dedicated scholars, including Bell Gale Chevigny, Robert Hudspeth, Meg McGavran Murray, and Joel Myerson, embarked on groundbreaking efforts to restore Fuller to a pivotal place in literary studies of the American Renaissance. Hudspeth collected and published an admirable edition of Fuller's letters. Myerson compiled meticulous bibliographies and wrote and edited a rich compendium of articles about her. Chevigny and Murray have added sage and essential biographical work. More recently, Mary Kelley and Jeffrey Steele both edited fine anthologies of Fuller's most significant writings, and Joan von Mehren and Charles Capper have written superb university press biographies. Thanks to Myerson and Judith Mattson Bean, Fuller's New York columns for the *Tribune* are in print, and Larry Reynolds and Susan Belasco Smith have added Fuller's dispatches from Europe to the published Fuller legacy. There is a thriving Margaret Fuller Society, and *Woman in the Nineteenth Century* is now an indispensable text for students of the American Renaissance. In academic circles, the rehabilitation of Margaret Fuller is substantially complete.

But Fuller's rebirth has remained largely an academic revival, and this is not enough. One of the hardest early lessons that Fuller herself was compelled to learn is that intellectual attainment, no matter how spectacular, does not make either a complete or greatly appealing person. More than 160 years after her death, we may benefit from learning an analogous lesson. Fuller lived most richly when she was able to combine her extraordinary mental abilities with the warmth of spirit and love of humankind that took her much longer to develop. Though always formidable as a thinker, she became great only as she came to sympathize with the hopelessness of imprisoned prostitutes, the hunger of exploited children, and the pain of wounded soldiers who had offered everything they had for freedom. Timothy Fuller knew that his daughter possessed an extraordinary mind. He little dreamed that she would grow into a woman whose passion for social justice would eventually equal her intelligence. If we try to know her only as an intellect, we repeat Timothy's error. It is only when we discover her as a misfit, as an apostle, as a seeker of Utopia, and in all the other identities through which she passed that she ceases to be the Margaret-ghost and lives for us once more.

Margaret Fuller lives, as well, as an unacknowledged influence, in the way that she called on both men and women to become more than they had ever been. Her urging was felt by the youthful Elizabeth Cady Stanton, who attended Fuller's conversations in 1842 and 1843, five years before she wrote the "Declaration of Sentiments," now considered the founding document of women's rights in America. It was felt as well by Julia Ward Howe, another patron of Fuller's conversations and the lyricist of the "Battle Hymn of the Republic," who firmly believed that the Coming of the Lord was not only for abolition, but for women's freedom as well. Fuller was also no ghost to the countless progressive women across the Middle and Far West who formed literary and political Margaret Fuller Clubs, dedicated to "the value of personality through intellectual and social development on a high level of responsibility."[81] At the first National Woman's Rights Convention in Worcester, Massachusetts, on October 1850, the delegates fell silent for a moment in Fuller's memory.[82] That silence was the prelude to a great refusal to remain silent that remains with us today.

In her final years, amid the chaos of war, Fuller achieved a new and highly innovative revolutionary consciousness. When, in the page of the *Tribune,* she decried the selfish propensities of capitalism and deplored the frequent indifference of the wealthy to the struggles of the poor, Fuller wrote with sincerity and zeal. Yet, her frustrations, unlike those of some of her contemporaries, never hardened into hatred, and her ideals never ossified into dogma. Unlike another famous radical who wrote for Greeley's *Tribune*—Karl Marx—Fuller did not accept that the deliverance of the working classes would come only with the sacrifice of the individual and the devaluation of the human soul. Harvard Divinity School lecturer Dan McKanan has suggested that, now that Marxist attempts to rewrite the social contract have been repudiated across the globe, the next hope for radical reform might benefit from a strong infusion of Fuller's ideals. The next upsurge toward reform and human redemption might carry at its heart some of Fuller's dearest principles: a sincere antipathy to violence and cruelty; a belief in the power of art and literature to assist in social change; and, above all, a confidence that the best, most durable revolution begins with the liberal education of every human being. It remains possible that the author of *Woman in the Nineteenth Century* may yet become the woman of the twenty-first century.[83]

As James Freeman Clarke observed, much of Margaret Fuller's greatest work was in showing other people the unique power and genius in themselves and, once they had discovered that uniqueness, giving them the urging, the cajoling, and the love that they required to bring their own greatness into the world. In the minds of people who continue to discover Fuller, that work goes on. This book began with the assertion that Margaret Fuller's life was her most remarkable creation. It is just possible, however, that her most wonderful creations may still lie in the future. Fuller's most precious gift to us may reside in the ideas and the works, still yet to be imagined, of women and men who follow her example. We may decide that, despite all that Margaret Fuller endured and suffered in order to become exceptional, her life, or rather her lives, well deserve imitating.

Think last of beginnings.

ACKNOWLEDGMENTS

This book began over a burger and fries on the last day of a Modern Language Association conference in Philadelphia, the first day I was prompted to consider Margaret Fuller as a subject for a biography. Since then, my road has been strewn with discoveries and blessings, the greatest of which have arisen from getting to know the endlessly sharing and thoughtful people for whom Margaret Fuller has been a glorious obsession for a very long time. I thank Joel Myerson, Robert N. Hudspeth, Meg McGavran Murray, and Robert Ferguson for reading my manuscript and bringing to it their astute and transformative suggestions. Writing on Fuller would be immeasurably more arduous without the marvelous, dedicated research of Professors Myerson and Hudspeth, Susan Belasco, Larry Reynolds, Judith Mattson Bean, and Jeffrey Steele. I doubt that I can ever repay the debt that I owe to a trio of great biographers of Fuller whose work has preceded mine: Professor Murray, Joan von Mehren, and Bell Gale Chevigny. Their books have helped to light my path, and their personal encouragement has made the journey easy and delightful. A very special thanks is due to Charles Capper, whose masterful, tremendous work is the place where any modern study of Fuller must begin and without whose sturdy and erudite foundations this book would have taken years longer to complete.

The consummate professionals at Houghton Library, the Boston Public Library, and the Fruitlands Museum made researching a pleasure. Jack Putnam of the South Street Seaport supplied important guidance in the early stages. The visual images graciously shared by Kent Bicknell, Professor von Mehren, George R. Rinhart, Fran Soto, and Constance Threinen have made this book beautiful.

I thank the Leon Levy Center for Biography, whose generous fellowship support in 2009–10 was indispensable to this project. I am deeply grateful to the moving forces behind the Levy Center—Brenda Wineapple, David Nasaw, and Nancy Milford—for all their fine suggestions and grand inspiration. Thanks go as well to the other fellows with whom I shared a marvelous year of inquiry and friendship: Mary Lisa Gavenas, Wendy Lesser, Helen Decker, Lars Kokkonen, and my dear friend Vanda Krefft. Daniel McKanan and Claudia Stokes supplied indispensable inspirations for the epilogue. The support, recognition, and professional example of Stacy Schiff have changed my life.

I continue to reap the benefits of serving on the outstanding faculty of John Jay College of Criminal Justice, where President Jeremy Travis, Provost Jane Bowers, and my department chair, Marny Tabb, along with a host of others, are giving new and significant meanings to the mission of educating for justice. Litna McNickle and Mady Swimm are the heart and soul of the undergraduate honors program that it is my pride and pleasure to lead.

My agent, Peter Steinberg, has been the sine qua non of my career. At W. W. Norton, my editor, Amy Cherry, and her assistant, Laura Romain, have done everything right. The copyediting of Mary Babcock has been superb.

My wife Michelle, daughter Rebecca, and sister Ann Shumard have given help and inspiration beyond description or recompense. My parents, Tom and Rosemary Matteson, can no longer read these words, but my deepest debt will forever be to them.

NOTES

ABBREVIATIONS

Letters: *The Letters of Margaret Fuller,* edited by Robert N. Hudspeth. 6 vol. (Ithaca: Cornell University Press, 1983–94.

  LJFC: *The Letters of James Freeman Clarke to Margaret Fuller.* Edited by John Wesley Thomas. Hamburg: Cram, de Gruyter, 1957.

LRWE: *The Letters of Ralph Waldo Emerson,* vol. I–VI, edited by Ralph L. Rusk; vol. VII–X, edited by Eleanor M. Tilton. 10 vol. (New York: Columbia University Press, 1939; 1990–95).

  MFFP: Margaret Fuller Family Papers, MS Am 1086, Houghton Library, Harvard University, Cambridge, Massachusetts.

MoMFO (1859 ed.):   *Memoirs of Margaret Fuller Ossoli.* Edited by Ralph Waldo Emerson, William Henry Channing, and James Freeman Clarke. New York: Tribune Association, 1859.

  SMF: Sarah Margaret Fuller, Margaret Fuller Ossoli.

PROLOGUE

1. Javier Marias has explored this phenomenon to striking effect in his novel *Poison, Shadow, and Farewell* (New York: New Directions, 2009).
2. SMF to Caroline Sturgis, 27 January 1839, in *Letters,* II, 41.
3. SMF to William H. Channing, June 1844, in *Letters,* III, 199.
4. Johann Wolfgang von Goethe, *The Collected Works,* vol. II: *Faust I & II,* edited and translated by Stuart Atkins (Princeton, N.J.: Princeton University Press, 1984), 301.
5. R.W. Emerson to Margaret Fuller, 25 September 1840, in *LRWE,* II, 336.
6. Bell Gale Chevigny's excellent anthology of Fuller documents, *The Woman and the Myth: Margaret Fuller's Life and Writings* (Boston: Northeastern University Press, 1994), also categorizes Fuller's life according to a series of named identities, although it does not follow that approach throughout. My work uses the conceit of successive identities for, I believe, a somewhat different range of purposes, and I arrived at my construct independently of Chevigny's work. However, when one has an opportunity to acknowledge so great and generous a scholar, one is foolish not to do so.

CHAPTER ONE: PRODIGY

1. Charles Capper, *Margaret Fuller: An American Romantic Life*, vol. I: *The Private Years* (Oxford: Oxford University Press, 1992), 5.
2. MFFP, I, 11.
3. Ibid., 1.
4. Ibid., 20.
5. "Genealogy of the Family Fuller," MFFP, I, 126.
6. Thomas Wentworth Higginson, *Margaret Fuller Ossoli* (Boston: Houghton, Mifflin, 1890), 10.
7. MFFP, I, 72.
8. Richard F. Fuller, *Recollections of Richard F. Fuller* (Boston: n.p., 1936), 21.
9. SMF, "Autobiographical Romance," in *MoMFO*, I, 12.
10. T. Fuller, "Diary," 13 December 1799, MFFP, II, 1. Emphasis in original.
11. T. Fuller, "Diary," 6 March 1800, MFFP, II, 1.
12. T. Fuller, "Diary," 13 March 1800, MFFP, II, 1.
13. T. Fuller, "Diary," 4 March 1800, MFFP, II, 1. Emphasis in original.
14. T. Fuller, "Whether Familiarity with Females Be Beneficial to Students," MFFP, Box B.
15. T. Fuller, "Diary," 19 February 1802, MFFP, II, 3.
16. T. Fuller, "Diary," 15 February 1802, MFFP, II, 3. Emphasis in original.
17. T. Fuller, "Diary," 15 March 1800, MFFP, II, 1.
18. Benjamin Peirce to Timothy Fuller, 6 February 1799, MFFP, I, 49.
19. Benjamin Peirce to Timothy Fuller, 8 August 1798, MFFP, I, 44.
20. Robert Ferguson offers a superb overview of this cultural sea change in *Law and Letters in American Culture* (Cambridge, Mass.: Harvard University Press, 1984), 11–33.
21. Higginson, *Margaret Fuller Ossoli*, 11.
22. Ibid., 11.
23. SMF, "Autobiographical Romance," in *MoMFO*, I, 12.
24. Nathaniel Hawthorne, *The House of the Seven Gables, A Romance* (Boston: Ticknor, Reed, and Fields, 1851), iii.
25. R. F. Fuller, *Recollections*, 10.
26. T. Fuller, "Diary," 26 January 1813, MFFP, II, 8.
27. T. Fuller, "Diary," 28 February 1813, MFFP, II, 8.
28. SMF, "Autobiographical Romance," in *MoMFO*, I, 12.
29. R. F. Fuller, "Memorial of Mrs. Margaret [*sic*] Fuller," in *MoMFO* (1859 ed.), I, 377.
30. SMF to James Freeman Clarke, 14 August 1845, in *Letters*, VI, 360.
31. M. C. Fuller to Timothy Fuller, 16 March 1824, MFFP, VII, 118.
32. Higginson, 23.
33. Ibid., 11.
34. M. C. Fuller to Timothy Fuller, 23 December 1818, MFFP, VI, 41.
35. M. C. Fuller to Timothy Fuller, 26 December 1818, MFFP, VI, 43.
36. T. Fuller, "Diary," 23 January 1813, MFFP, II, 8.
37. Oliver Wendell Holmes, "Cinders from the Ashes," *Atlantic Monthly* 23 (January 1869), 115.
38. SMF to Timothy Fuller, 16 January 1820, in *Letters*, 95.
39. SMF to Richard F. Fuller, 5 August 1842, in *Letters*, III, 81. To avoid confusion between Fuller and her mother, I will henceforth dispense with the second "t" in Sarah Margarett's name.

40. SMF, *Woman in the Nineteenth Century* (New York: Greeley and McElrath, 1845),146.
41. SMF, "Autobiographical Romance," in *MoMFO*, I, 13.
42. Ibid., I, 14.
43. Ibid.
44. M. C. Fuller, "Attempt by Margarett (Crane) Fuller to Recall Margaret Fuller's Childhood," MFFP, VIII, 183.
45. Ibid.
46. SMF, "Autobiographical Romance," in *MoMFO*, I, 24.
47. M. C. Fuller, "Attempt by Margarett (Crane) Fuller to Recall Margaret Fuller's Childhood," MFFP, VIII, 183.
48. SMF, in *MoMFO*, I, 139–41.
49. T. Fuller, "Diary," 16 January 1814, MFFP, II, 8; Meg McGavran Murray, *Margaret Fuller, Wandering Pilgrim* (Athens: University of Georgia Press, 2008), 13.
50. SMF, "Autobiographical Romance," in *MoMFO*, I, 14.
51. T. Fuller to Margarett C. Fuller, 26 April 1814, MFFP, III, 7. Emphasis added.
52. T. Fuller, "Diary," 1 January 1815, MFFP, II, 8.
53. M. C. Fuller, "Attempt by Margarett (Crane) Fuller to Recall Margaret Fuller's Childhood," MFFP, VIII, 183.
54. J. F. Clarke, in *MoMFO*, I, 62n.
55. R. F. Fuller, *Recollections*, 10.
56. M. C. Fuller, "Attempt by Margarett (Crane) Fuller to Recall Margaret Fuller's Childhood," MFFP, VIII, 183.
57. SMF, "Autobiographical Romance," in *MoMFO*, I, 17.
58. M. C. Fuller, "Attempt by Margarett (Crane) Fuller to Recall Margaret Fuller's Childhood," MFFP, VIII, 183.
59. SMF, *Woman in the Nineteenth Century*, 28.
60. T. Fuller, "Diary," 14 May 1815, MFFP, II, 8.
61. Capper, *Margaret Fuller*, I, 31.
62. SMF, *Woman in the Nineteenth Century*, 27–28.
63. SMF, "Autobiographical Romance," in *MoMFO*, I, 14.
64. SMF to Timothy Fuller, 16 January 1820, in *Letters*, I, 94.
65. SMF, "Autobiographical Romance," in *MoMFO*, I, 17–18.
66. Ibid., 28.
67. SMF to Marcus and Rebecca Spring, 10 April 1847, in *Letters*, IV, 263.
68. SMF, "Autobiographical Romance," in *MoMFO*, I, 18.
69. Capper, *Margaret Fuller*, I, 31.
70. SMF, "Autobiographical Romance," in *MoMFO*, I, 15.
71. Higginson, *Margaret Fuller Ossoli*, 17, 22.
72. SMF, "Autobiographical Romance," in *MoMFO*, I, 15.
73. Ibid., 16.
74. Ibid.
75. Ibid., 15.
76. A. B. Fuller, "Preface," in *MoMFO* (1859 ed.), I, 5.
77. Frederick Augustus Braun, *Margaret Fuller and Goethe* (New York: Henry Holt, 1910), 24n.
78. A. B. Fuller, "Preface," in *MoMFO* (1859 ed.), I, 5.
79. T. Fuller, "Diary," 15 May 1814, MFFP, II, 8.
80. T. Fuller, "Diary," 14 March 1813, MFFP, II, 8.
81. T. Fuller to Margarett Crane Fuller, 24 January 1818, MFFP, III, 24.
82. SMF, "[Penmanship Exercise]," MFFP, IX, 9.

83. See M. C. Fuller to Timothy Fuller, 28 January 1818, MFFP, VI, 10, for a detailed discussion of Margaret's dental woes. It is one small measure of Margaret's desire to please her father that, during the tooth's painful extraction, she "tried to exert her fortitude" only after her mother told her that Timothy would be "grieved and disappointed to know that she had no more courage." Ibid.

84. T. Fuller to Margarett C. Fuller, 20 January 1818, MFFP, III, 22.

85. T. Fuller to Margarett C. Fuller, 15 December 1819, MFFP, III, 62.

86. M. C. Fuller to Timothy Fuller, 26 January 1818, MFFP, VI, 9.

87. M. C. Fuller to Timothy Fuller, 12 January 1818, MFFP, VI, 5.

88. T. Fuller to Margarett C. Fuller, 29 January 1818, MFFP, III, 27.

89. Ann Douglas, *The Feminization of American Culture* (New York: Alfred A. Knopf, 1977), 264.

90. T. Fuller to S. M. Fuller, 13 April 1820, MFFP, V, 6.

91. SMF to Timothy Fuller, 13 March 1822, in *Letters*, I, 119.

92. Ellen Kilshaw to M. C. Fuller, 20 July 1818, MFFP, II, 25.

93. Martha L. Berg and Alice de V. Perry, "'The Impulses of Human Nature': Margaret Fuller's Journal from June through October 1844," *Proceedings of the Massachusetts Historical Society*, 3rd series, 102 (1990), 115.

94. Ibid., 114.

95. M. C. Fuller, "Attempt by Margarett (Crane) Fuller to Recall Margaret Fuller's Childhood," MFFP, VIII, 183.

96. M. C. Fuller to Timothy Fuller, 12 January 1818, MFFP, VI, 5.

97. Ibid. First emphasis added.

98. M. C. Fuller to Timothy Fuller, 20 January 1818, MFFP, VI, 7.

99. M. C. Fuller to Timothy Fuller, 12 January 1818, MFFP, VI, 13.

100. Higginson, *Margaret Fuller Ossoli*, 23. Emphasis in original.

101. M. C. Fuller to Timothy Fuller, 26 December 1818, MFFP, VI, 43.

102. Capper, *Margaret Fuller*, I, 43.

103. SMF to Richard F. Fuller, 5 August 1842, in *Letters*, III, 81.

104. SMF, "Autobiographical Romance," in *MoMFO*, I, 16.

105. SMF to James Nathan, 22 July 1845, in *Letters*, IV, 137.

106. SMF, "Autobiographical Romance," in *MoMFO*, I, 18.

107. Ibid., 22.

108. M. C. Fuller to Timothy Fuller, 8 December 1822, MFFP, VII, 46.

109. SMF, "Autobiographical Romance," in *MoMFO*, I, 32.

110. SMF to James Freeman Clarke, 1 February 1835, in *Letters*, VI, 251.

111. Matthew Arnold, *Culture and Anarchy: An Essay in Political and Social Criticism* (London: Smith, Elder, 1869), 162.

112. SMF to Sarah W. Fuller, 1 November 1820, in *Letters*, I, 103.

113. SMF to Timothy Fuller, 8 January 1819, in *Letters*, I, 86.

114. R. W. Emerson, in *MoMFO*, I, 202.

CHAPTER TWO: MISFIT

1. SMF to Sarah W. Fuller, 1 November 1820, in *Letters*, I, 103.

2. SMF, "Autobiographical Romance," in *MoMFO*, I, 17.

3. SMF, *"These Sad But Glorious Days" Dispatches from Europe, 1846–1850*, edited by Larry J. Reynolds and Susan Belasco Smith (New Haven, Conn.: Yale University Press, 1991), 167.

4. SMF, "Autobiographical Romance," in *MoMFO*, I, 24.

5. Ibid., 25.
6. Ibid., 29.
7. Ibid., 26–27.
8. Ibid., 27.
9. Ibid., 28.
10. Ibid., 28.
11. Ibid., 30.
12. SMF to Albert H. Tracy, 6 November 1843, in *Letters*, III, 156.
13. SMF, "Autobiographical Romance," in *MoMFO*, I, 16.
14. Ibid., 33.
15. Baptismal records of the Church of Saint Peter in Liverpool state that Ellen Kilshaw was born to John and Elizabeth Kilshaw of Bold Street on November 18, 1794. See http://www.lan-opc.org.uk/Liverpool/Liverpool-Central/stpeter/baptisms_1795-1796.html (accessed 3 May 2011).
16. SMF, "Autobiographical Romance," in *MoMFO*, I, 35.
17. Ibid., 34.
18. Ibid., 33–38.
19. Ibid., 34.
20. Ibid., 36.
21. Sir Sidney Lee, ed., *Dictionary of National Biography*, 2nd suppl., vol. III, Neil–Young (New York: Macmillan, 1912), 193.
22. SMF to Ellen Kilshaw, 20 November 1819, in *Letters*, I, 88.
23. Ibid., 89.
24. R. W. Emerson, in *MoMFO*, I, 235.
25. SMF, "Autobiographical Romance," in *MoMFO*, I, 40–41.
26. T. Fuller to Sarah Margaret Fuller, 13 April 1820, MFFP, V, 6.
27. SMF, "Autobiographical Romance," in *MoMFO*, I, 41.
28. Holmes, "Cinders," 116–17.
29. M. C. Fuller to Timothy Fuller, 20 January 1821, MFFP, VI, 117.
30. SMF to Timothy Fuller, 15 January 1821, in *Letters*, I, 109; SMF to Timothy Fuller, 5 January 1821, in *Letters*, I, 108.
31. SMF to Timothy Fuller, 5 January 1821, in *Letters*, I, 107.
32. SMF to Timothy Fuller, 3 February 1820, in *Letters*, I, 96.
33. Capper, *Margaret Fuller*, I, 57.
34. SMF to Timothy Fuller, 5 January 1821, in *Letters*, I, 107.
35. SMF to Timothy Fuller, 25 January 1821, in *Letters*, I, 110.
36. SMF, *Summer on the Lakes, in 1843* (Boston: Charles C. Little and James Brown, 1844), 8–9.
37. M. C. Fuller to Timothy Fuller, 11 March 1822, MFFP, VII, 21.
38. Ibid.
39. SMF to Margarett C. Fuller, 2 December 1821, in *Letters*, I, 113.
40. SMF to Timothy Fuller, 13 March 1822, in *Letters*, I, 119.
41. SMF to Timothy Fuller, 22 March 1822, in *Letters*, I, 120.
42. Caroline Healey Dall, "[Journal Comments on Fuller in 1851 and 1852]," in Joel Myerson, ed. *Fuller in Her Own Time: A Biographical Chronicle of Her Life, Drawn from Recollections, Interviews, and Memoirs by Family, Friends, and Associates* (Iowa City: University of Iowa Press, 2008), 115.
43. Holmes, "Cinders," 116.
44. Caroline Healey Dall, "[Reminiscences of Margaret Fuller]," in Myerson, ed., *Fuller in Her Own Time*, 202.

45. Holmes, "Cinders," 116.

46. SMF, "Journal," March 1839, MFFP, Box A.

47. Ralph Waldo Emerson, *The Journals and Miscellaneous Notebooks of Ralph Waldo Emerson*, 16 vol. (Cambridge, Mass.: Belknap Press of Harvard University Press, 1960–82), XI, 482. The stigmatizing force of this last attribute can hardly be overstated. In the 1820s and for a long time thereafter, Christian piety stood firmly at the center of America's ideal of female virtue, and religion was thought to be the sine qua non of a woman's identity. Even after her death, Fuller's irreligiosity was sometimes held before the public as a cautionary example. In 1853, Sarah Josepha Hale excoriated Fuller for rejecting the revealed word of God and thus dispensing with the "only safe guide in her search for truth." Hale observed, "[T]he greater the intellectual force, the greater and more fatal the errors into which women fall who wander from the Rock of Salvation, Christ the Saviour." Sarah Josepha Buell Hale, *Woman's Record, or, Sketches of All Distinguished Women, from "The Beginning," Till A.D. 1850* (New York: Harper and Brothers, 1853), 666.

48. W. H. Channing, in *MoMFO*, II, 5.

49. SMF to Margarett C. Fuller, 23 December 1821, in *Letters*, I, 117.

50. Russel Blaine Nye, *George Bancroft, Brahmin Rebel* (New York: Alfred A. Knopf, 1945), 49.

51. F. H. Hedge, in *MoMFO*, I, 92–93.

52. Ibid., 93.

53. SMF to Timothy Fuller, 22 December 1822, in *Letters*, I, 121–22.

54. SMF to Timothy Fuller, 2 February 1823, in *Letters*, I, 129.

55. Higginson, *Margaret Fuller Ossoli*, 23.

56. SMF to Timothy Fuller 30 January 1823, in *Letters*, I, 127.

57. SMF to Timothy Fuller, 2 February 1823, in *Letters*, I, 128–29.

58. SMF to Timothy Fuller, 12 January 1823, in *Letters*, I, 126.

59. SMF to Timothy Fuller, 30 December 1822, in *Letters*, I, 124.

60. SMF to Margarett C. Fuller, 6 February 1850, in *Letters*, VI. 59.

61. T. Fuller to Sarah Margaret Fuller, 15 December 1822, MFFP, V, 11.

62. SMF, "Journal," March 1839, MFFP, Box A.

63. Oliver Wendell Holmes, "Of Cambridge and Female Society," in William Bentinck Smith, *The Harvard Book* (Cambridge, Mass.: Harvard University Press, 1953), 151.

64. John Quincy Adams, *Memoirs of John Quincy Adams*, vol. V: *Comprising Portions of His Diary from 1795 to 1848* (Philadelphia: J. B. Lippincott, 1875), 90.

65. T. Fuller, "Diary," 25 April 1824, MFFP, II, 13.

66. F. H. Hedge, in *MoMFO*, I, 92.

67. Ibid.

68. T. Fuller to Margarett C. Fuller, 14 December 1823, MFFP, IV, 93.

69. T. Fuller to Margarett C. Fuller, 10 January 1821, MFFP, IV, 5.

70. SMF to George T. Davis, 23 January 1830, in *Letters*, VI, 163.

71. F. H. Hedge, in *MoMFO*, I, 91–92. Fuller's hair evidently darkened over time. In her two photographs, her hair appears quite dark. Frederick L. H. Willis, who met her in 1837, recalled her hair as reddish brown. Frederick L. H. Willis, *Alcott Memoirs* (Boston: Richard G. Badger, 1915), 95. In 1848 Fuller herself wrote, "[M]y hair . . . is still brown and the admiration of the Italians." SMF to Richard F. Fuller, 7 December 1848, in *Letters*, V, 160.

72. F. H. Hedge, in *MoMFO*, I, 91. Emphasis added.

73. Ibid.

74. Braun, *Margaret Fuller and Goethe*, 45.
75. Joan von Mehren, *Minerva and the Muse: A Life of Margaret Fuller* (Amherst: University of Massachusetts Press, 1994), 26.
76. M. C. Fuller to Timothy Fuller, 29 December 1823, MFFP, VII, 89.
77. Fuller scholar Robert N. Hudspeth, who once identified this school as being led by Ralph Waldo Emerson's brother William (*Letters*, I, 33), now thinks it probable that this school was run by George B. Emerson.
78. M. C. Fuller to Timothy Fuller, 16 March 1824, MFFP, VII, 118. Emphasis in original.
79. T. Fuller to Margarett C. Fuller, 2 March 1824, MFFP, IV, 134.
80. T. Fuller to Sarah Margaret Fuller, 24 December 1823, MFFP, V, 13.
81. SMF to Timothy Fuller, 25 January 1824, in *Letters*, I, 132.
82. T. Fuller to Sarah Margaret Fuller, 3 April 1824, MFFP, V, 15.
83. SMF to Timothy Fuller, 19 April 1824, in *Letters*, I, 137.
84. T. Fuller to Sarah Margaret Fuller, 24 April 1824, MFFP, V, 16.
85. S. M Fuller to Timothy Fuller, 21 May 1824, in *Letters*, I, 139.
86. Ibid.
87. Ibid.; SMF to Abraham W. Fuller, 29 September 1824, in *Letters*, I, 143.
88. T. Fuller to Sarah Margaret Fuller, 15 May 1824, MFFP, V, 17.
89. SMF, in *MoMFO*, I, 132.
90. SMF to Timothy Fuller, 21 May 1824, in *Letters*, I, 139.
91. Ibid., 138.
92. T. Fuller to Sarah Margaret Fuller, 7 June 1824, MFFP, V, 20.
93. SMF to Timothy Fuller, 14 February 1825, in *Letters*, I, 149.
94. SMF to William H. Channing, June 1844 [?], in *Letters*, III, 198–99.
95. SMF, *Summer on the Lakes*, 82.
96. Ibid., 83.
97. Ibid., 84.
98. Ibid., 87.
99. Ibid., 89.
100. Ibid., 91.
101. Ibid., 93.
102. Ibid., 82.
103. Ibid., 86.
104. SMF to Susan Prescott, January 1830, in *Letters*, I, 160.
105. SMF, in *MoMFO*, II, 101.
106. SMF, in *MoMFO*, I, 98–99.
107. SMF to Elizabeth P. Peabody, 26 December 1844, in *Letters*, III, 253.

CHAPTER THREE: "MARGARET GOODCHILD"

1. SMF to George T. Davis, 23 January 1830, in *Letters*, VI, 162.
2. SMF, in *MoMFO*, II, 11.
3. SMF to William H. Channing [?], 3 December 1840, in *Letters*, II, 187.
4. Ibid.
5. SMF to James F. Clarke, 11 October 1831, in *Letters*, VI, 182.
6. J. F. Clarke, in *MoMFO*, I, 112.
7. SMF, "American Literature: Its Position in the Present Time, and Prospects for the Future," in *Papers on Literature and Art [in Two Parts]* (New York: John Wiley, 1848), 122.
8. The most comprehensive statement regarding Fuller's reading as a late adoles-

cent is given in Capper, *Margaret Fuller*, I, 89–92. It is important not only to know what Fuller was reading during this formative time, but also to understand what the act of reading meant to her. In the year Fuller turned eighteen, Thomas Carlyle, of whom more will be said later, published an essay that was eventually to have a strong effect on Fuller. In "Goethe's Helena," published in the *Foreign Review*, Carlyle articulated the goals of reading in a way that Fuller surely found appealing. "Everywhere in life," he wrote, "the true question is, not what we *gain*, but what we *do*: so also in intellectual matters, in conversation, in reading, which is more precise and careful conversation, it is not what we *receive*, but what we are made to *give*, that chiefly contents and profits us. . . . [W]ere there an artist of a right spirit; a man of wisdom, conscious of his high vocation, [whose writings embodied] the creations of a deep and noble soul,—should we not draw near to him reverently, as disciples to a master and . . . study him even to his minutest meanings. For were not this to think as he had thought, to see with his gifted eyes, to make the very mood and feeling of his great and rich mind the mood also of our poor and little one?" Thomas Carlyle, *Complete Works of Thomas Carlyle* (New York: P. F. Collier and Son, 1901), XIII, 146. It was something like this spirit of reverence and desire to participate in the thoughts of outstanding minds that made Fuller's reading so transformative.

9. SMF to [?], n.d., in *Letters*, VI, 138.
10. SMF to Almira P. Barlow, 6 October 1834, in *Letters*, I, 210.
11. Joel Myerson has suggested that the two women may have been brought together by Lydia's brother Convers Francis, a Harvard-educated minister who later joined the Transcendental Club. Letter to the author, 19 December 2010.
12. Madame de Staël, *Corinne, or Italy*, translated by Sylvia Raphael (Oxford, UK: Oxford University Press, 2008), 47.
13. SMF to Susan Prescott, 10 January 1827, in *Letters*, I, 154.
14. SMF to Susan Prescott, 11 July 1825, in *Letters*, I, 151.
15. Ibid., 152.
16. Bernard Bailyn, *The Ideological Origins of the American Revolution*, enlarged ed., (Cambridge, Mass.: Belknap Press of Harvard University Press, 1992), 27.
17. Edward Taylor, *The Poems of Edward Taylor*, edited by Donald E. Stanford (Chapel Hill: University of North Carolina Press, 1989), 129.
18. The Unitarian belief in one God and the subordinate nature of Jesus is essentially an updating of the Arian heresy, propounded by the Christian priest Arius of Alexandria, Egypt, around the year 300.
19. William E. Channing, "Unitarian Christianity," in William Ellery Channing, *The Works of William E. Channing, D.D.*, 5 vol. (Boston: James Munroe, 1841), III, 83.
20. Channing, "Likeness to God," in Channing, *Works of William E. Channing*, III, 228.
21. Douglas, *Feminization of American Culture*,123–24.
22. Emerson, *Journals and Miscellaneous Notebooks*, IX, 381.
23. James Freeman Clarke, *Autobiography, Diary and Correspondence*, edited by Edward Everett Hale (Boston: Houghton, Mifflin, 1891), 39.
24. Van Wyck Brooks, *The Flowering of New England* (New York: E. P. Dutton, 1952), 37.
25. Clarke, *Autobiography*, 38–39.

26.   S. T. Coleridge to Thomas Poole, 16 October 1797, in *Letters*, I, 210. Emphasis in original.

27.   Kant, *Critique of Practical Reason*, quoted in Paul Guyer, ed., *The Cambridge Companion to Kant and Modern Philosophy* (Cambridge, U.K.: Cambridge University Press, 2006), 1.

28.   Samuel Taylor Coleridge, *Aids to Reflection* (Eugene, Ore.: Wipf and Stock, 2006), 143–44.

29.   Frederic Henry Hedge, "Coleridge's Literary Character," *Christian Examiner* (March 1833), 120.

30.   R. W. Emerson to Edward Bliss Emerson, 22 December 1833, in *LRWE*, I, 402.

31.   R. F. Fuller, *Recollections*, 26.

32.   Timothy Fuller's diary tells of how Adams came to his law office to discuss electoral issues as late as August 1832. T. Fuller, "Diary," 23 August 1832, MFFP, II, 15.

33.   Higginson, *Margaret Fuller Ossoli*, 29.

34.   Murray, *Margaret Fuller, Wandering Pilgrim*, 60.

35.   Clarke, *Autobiography*, 37.

36.   Higginson, *Margaret Fuller Ossoli*, 36.

37.   [Eliza W. Farrar], *The Young Lady's Friend: A Manual of Practical Advice and Instruction to Young Females, on Entering upon the Duties of Life, after Quitting School, by a Lady* (London: John Parker, 1837), 76.

38.   Ibid., 246.

39.   W. H. Channing, in *MoMFO*, II, 8.

40.   E. P. Peabody, quoted in Capper, *Margaret Fuller*, I, 99.

41.   J. F. Clarke, in *MoMFO*, I, 107.

42.   Ibid., 96–97.

43.   Berg and Perry, "'Impulses of Human Nature,'" 87.

44.   Joel Myerson, "Caroline Dall's Reminiscences of Margaret Fuller," *Harvard Library Bulletin* 22 (October 1974), 414–28, 416.

45.   J. F. Clarke, in *MoMFO*, I, 64.

46.   Capper, *Margaret Fuller*, I, 97; J. F. Clarke to Margaret Fuller, 14 June 1835, in *LJFC*, 97.

47.   J. F. Clarke, in *MoMFO*, I, 65.

48.   SMF to James F. Clarke, 27 March 1830, in *Letters*, VI, 164.

49.   SMF, in *MoMFO*, II, 10.

50.   Ibid., 10–11. Emphasis in original.

51.   Ibid., 10.

52.   SMF to James F. Clarke, 27 March 1830, in *Letters*, VI, 164.

53.   J. F. Clarke, in *MoMFO*, I, 139, 138.

54.   J. F. Clarke, in *MoMFO*, I, 104.

55.   SMF to George T. Davis, 29 December 1829, in *Letters*, VI, 160.

56.   SMF to George T. Davis, 19 December 1829, in *Letters*, VI, 155.

57.   Sarah F. Clarke, "Letters of a Sister," 26 January 1834, Additional Papers of James Freeman Clarke, Houghton Library, Harvard University, MS Am 1569.3, III, 12.

58.   SMF to James F. Clarke, 6 December 1835, in *Letters*, VI, 272.

59.   SMF to George T. Davis, 19 December 1829, in *Letters*, VI, 155.

60.   SMF to George T. Davis, 23 January 1830, in *Letters*, VI, 161–62.

61.   SMF to George T. Davis, 2 February 1831, in *Letters*, I, 174.

62.   SMF to George T. Davis, ca. winter 1829–30, in *Letters*, I, 158–159.

63. Ibid., 159. It is not possible to know whether or to what extent, at this time, Fuller was acquainted with the philosophical writings of Friedrich Wilhelm Joseph von Schelling, though by the time she was editing *The Dial*, she considered him important enough to print a translation of one of his lectures. In his *System of Transcendental Idealism* (1800), Schelling had suggested that all of nature was not only evolving in physical form, but also rising toward an ever higher state of spiritual consciousness. This idea of nature's ascension toward the Absolute has quite a bit in common with Fuller's sense of Eternal Progression.

64. SMF to George T. Davis, 23 January 1830, in *Letters*, VI, 163.

65. Ibid.

66. SMF to James F. Clarke, 26 January 1832, in *Letters*, VI, 185.

67. Ibid.

68. SMF, "[Fragments of Margaret Fuller's Journal]," Fruitlands Library, Harvard, Mass., 34–35.

69. Ibid.

70. J. F. Clarke, in *MoMFO*, I, 107.

71. J. F. Clarke to Margaret Fuller, 11 April 1830, in *LJFC*, 13.

72. J. F. Clarke to Margaret Fuller, [?] October 1830, in *LJFC*, 28.

73. J. F. Clarke to Margaret Fuller, 16 December 1830, in *LJFC*, 28; J. F. Clarke to Margaret Fuller, November [?] 1830, in *LJFC*, 26.

74. J. F. Clarke to Margaret Fuller, 11 April 1830, in *LJFC*, 13–14.

75. J. F. Clarke to Margaret Fuller, 16 December 1830, in *LJFC*, 29.

76. J. F. Clarke to Margaret Fuller, 11 April 1830, in *LJFC*, 15.

77. Caroline Healey Dall, "Studies towards the Life of a Business Woman," James Freeman Clarke Additional Papers, Houghton Library, MS Am 1569.3 (24), I, 22–23.

78. J. F. Clarke to Sarah M. Fuller, [?] October 1830, in *LJFC*, 28.

79. SMF to James F. Clarke, 28 October 1830, in *Letters*, VI, 172.

80. Ibid.; SMF to James F. Clarke, 2 November 1830, in *Letters*, VI, 175.

81. SMF to James F. Clarke, 29 October 1830, in *Letters*, VI, 174.

82. SMF to Jane F. Tuckerman, 21 October 1838, in *Letters*, I, 347.

83. SMF, in *MoMFO*, I, 140.

84. Thanksgiving Day had not yet been fixed as the fourth Thursday in November. In 1831, it was observed on December 1.

85. SMF, in MoMFO, I, 139–140.

86. Ibid., 140.

87. Ibid.

88. Ibid.

89. Ibid., 140–41.

90. Ibid., 141.

91. Ibid. Emphasis in original.

92. Ibid.

93. SMF to Jane F. Tuckerman, 21 October 1838, in *Letters*, I, 347–48.

94. R. W. Emerson, *Nature*, in *Essays and Lectures* (New York: Library of America, 1983), 10.

95. SMF to Ralph Waldo Emerson, 12 April 1840, in *Letters*, II, 128.

96. Carlyle, "Signs of the Times," in *Complete Works of Thomas Carlyle*, I, 468, 475.

97. Carlyle, "Goethe," in *Complete Works of Thomas Carlyle*, I, 203. Emphasis in original.

98.   R. W. Emerson, in *MoMFO*, I, 242.
99.   SMF to James F. Clarke, 7 August 1832, in *Letters*, VI, 187.
100.   R. W. Emerson, in *MoMFO*, I, 242.
101.   SMF, "Goethe," *Dial* 2, no. 1 (July 1841) 1, 2–3.
102.   Ibid., 5.
103.   Walter Kaufmann, "Goethe's Faith and Faust's Redemption," in *From Shakespeare to Existentialism: An Original Study* (Princeton, N.J.: Princeton University Press, 1959), 72.
104.   Johann Wolfgang von Goethe, *Iphigenia in Tauris*, II, 1892–7, in *The Collected Works*, vol. VIII: *Verse Plays and Epic*, edited by Cyrus Hamlin and Frank Ryder (Princeton N.J.: Princeton University Press, 1994), 46–47.
105.   Goethe, *Torquato Tasso*, II, 1018–21, in *Collected Works*, vol. VIII: *Verse Plays and Epic*, 80.
106.   Emerson, in *Memoirs*, I, 243.
107.   SMF to James F. Clarke, 17 August 1833, in *Letters*, VI, 212.
108.   R. F. Fuller, *Recollections*, 19.
109.   Ibid., 14.
110.   A. B. Fuller, "Preface," in *MoMFO* (1859 ed.), I, 5.
111.   Ibid., 13–14.
112.   SMF to Richard F. Fuller, 17 March 1848, in *Letters*, V, 56.
113.   R. F. Fuller, *Recollections*, 12.
114.   Charles Phillips Huse, *The Financial History of Boston, From May 1, 1822, to January 31, 1909* (Cambridge, Mass.: Harvard University Press, 1916), 14. I have extrapolated Timothy Fuller's probable income from Richard's statement that his father earned twenty dollars a day. R. F. Fuller, *Recollections*, 12.
115.   Samuel Abbott Green, *Facts Relating to the History of Groton, Massachusetts*, 2 vol. (Groton: n.p., 1914), II, 36.
116.   Von Mehren, *Minerva and the Muse*, 54.
117.   Murray, *Margaret Fuller, Wandering Pilgrim*, 76.
118.   SMF to Abraham Fuller, 17 November 1835, in *Letters*, I, 239.
119.   W. H. Channing, in *MoMFO*, II, 7.
120.   SMF to Eliza R. Farrar, 25 April 1833, in *Letters*, I, 180.
121.   M. C. Fuller to Timothy Fuller, 18 April 1833, MFFP, VII, 176.
122.   R. F. Fuller, *Recollections*, 15.
123.   SMF to James Freeman Clarke, 17 August 1833, in *Letters*, VI, 212
124.   SMF to Richard F. Fuller, 11 August 1842, in *Letters*, III, 85.
125.   Von Mehren, *Minerva and the Muse*, 54.
126.   SMF to James Freeman Clarke, 17 [?] June 1833, in *Letters*, VI, 206.
127.   SMF to James Freeman Clarke, 30 August 1833, in *Letters*, VI, 216.
128.   SMF, in *MoMFO*, I, 145.
129.   SMF to Richard F. Fuller, 11 August 1842, in *Letters*, III, 85.
130.   SMF to [?], 1833, in *Letters*, I, 180.
131.   Ibid.
132.   SMF to Timothy and Margarett C. Fuller, 2 June 1835, in *Letters*, I, 230. Eugene tutored the children of Stephen and Louisa Higginson (including Margaret's future biographer, Thomas Wentworth Higginson) and Colonel Samuel Storrow. William Henry worked in Boston for his uncle Henry Holton Fuller.
133.   SMF to James F. Clarke, 26 November 1833, in *Letters*, VI, 230.
134.   R. F. Fuller, *Recollections*, 17.
135.   Ibid., 19.

136. Ibid.
137. Ibid., 17.
138. Richard F. Fuller, *Chaplain Fuller: Being a Life Sketch of a New England Clergyman and Army Chaplain* (Boston: Walker, Wise, 1863), 45.
139. R. F. Fuller, *Recollections*, 21.
140. SMF to Richard F. Fuller, 11 August 1842, in *Letters*, III, 85.
141. SMF, "[Journal]," MFFP, Works, III, 385
142. SMF to James Freeman Clarke, 3 May 1833, in *Letters*, VI, 200.
143. SMF. "To James Freeman Clarke, 27 July 1833, in *Letters*, VI, 210.
144. SMF to James Freeman Clarke, 24 December 1833, in *Letters*, VI, 232.
145. SMF to [?], in *Letters*, VI, 130.
146. SMF to James Freeman Clarke, 17 August 1833, in *Letters*, VI, 212.
147. R. F. Fuller, *Recollections*, 30.
148. Ibid.
149. *MoMFO*, II, 124.
150. SMF to [?], ca. February 1835, in *Letters*, I, 218.
151. Goethe, "The Drama of Torquato Tasso," translated by SMF, in Margaret Fuller Ossoli, *Art, Literature, and the Drama*, edited by Arthur B. Fuller (New York: Tribune Association, 1869), 384–85.
152. Ibid., 439.
153. SMF to James Freeman Clarke, 13 November 1834, in *Letters*, VI, 246.
154. SMF to James Freeman Clarke, 27 July 1833, in *Letters*, VI, 209–10.
155. SMF to Timothy and Margarett C. Fuller, 2 June 1835, in *Letters*, I, 230.
156. SMF to Timothy and Margarett C. Fuller, 13 August 1835, in *Letters*, I, 232.
157. SMF to Samuel Gray Ward, 20 April 1836, in *Letters*, I, 249.
158. SMF to Timothy and Margarett C. Fuller, 13 August 1835, in *Letters*, I, 232.
159. Von Mehren, *Minerva and the Muse*, 68.
160. R. W. Emerson [to Samuel G. Ward], 26 November 1839, in *Letters from Ralph Waldo Emerson to a Friend, 1838–1853* (Boston: Houghton, Mifflin, 1899), 15.
161. R. W. Emerson to Samuel G. Ward, 25 January 1840, in *LRWE*, VII, 368.
162. SMF to Timothy and Margarett C. Fuller, 13 August 1835, in *Letters*, I, 233.
163. Von Mehren, *Minerva and the Muse*, 69.
164. SMF. "To Samuel Gray Ward, 20 April 1836, in *Letters*, I, 249–50.
165. SMF to Samuel Gray Ward, 24 February 1850, in *Letters*, VI, 67.
166. Harriet Martineau, *Harriet Martineau's Autobiography*, 2 vol. (Boston: James B. Osgood, 1877), I, 382.
167. SMF to Samuel Gray Ward, 24 February 1850, in *Letters*, VI, 67.
168. R. F. Fuller, *Recollections*, 25.
169. SMF, MFFP, Works, III, 379.
170. SMF to Almira Barlow, 1 February 1836, in *Letters*, I, 243.
171. R. F. Fuller, *Recollections*, 25.
172. SMF, "[Journal]," MFFP, Works, III, 377–79.
173. R. F. Fuller, *Chaplain Fuller*, 32–34.
174. SMF to James Nathan, 29 September 1845, in *Letters*, IV, 163.

CHAPTER FOUR: APOSTLE

1. SMF to James Nathan, 29 September 1845, in *Letters*, IV, 163.
2. Higginson, *Margaret Fuller Ossoli*, 54.

3. SMF to [?], 3 November 1835, in *Letters*, I, 237.
4. M. C. Fuller to Abraham Fuller, 7 December 1835, MFFP, VIII, 2.
5. M. C. Fuller to Abraham Fuller, 14 January 1836, MFFP, VIII, 3.
6. Ibid.
7. M. C. Fuller to Abraham Fuller, 15 May 1836, MFFP, VIII, 6.
8. SMF to Eugene Fuller, 13 December 1835, in *Letters*, I, 240.
9. M. C. Fuller to Abraham Fuller, 15 May 1836, MFFP, VIII, 6.
10. M. C. Fuller to Abraham Fuller, 3 September 1837, MFFP, VIII, 9.
11. Margaret Fuller to [?], 3 November 1835, in *Letters*, I, 237.
12. M. C. Fuller to Abraham Fuller, 15 April 1838, MFFP, VIII, 10.
13. R. F. Fuller, *Recollections*, 27.
14. SMF, in *MoMFO*, I, 155–56.
15. SMF to [?], 3 November 1835, in *Letters*, I, 237.
16. SMF to Abraham W. Fuller, 6 November 1835, in *Letters*, I, 237.
17. SMF to Georgiana Bruce, 27 [?] July 1845, in *Letters*, IV, 143.
18. SMF to [?], 1836 [?], in *Letters*, I, 241.
19. SMF to Samuel G. and Anna B. Ward, 3 March 1846, in *Letters*, IV, 192.
20. R. F. Fuller, *Recollections*, 26.
21. SMF to James F. Clarke, 29 January 1836, in *Letters*, VI, 275–76.
22. SMF to Eugene Fuller, 30 January 1836, in *Letters*, I, 243.
23. SMF, "Lines written in Mar. 1836, by Margaret," MFFP, Works, I, 79.
24. SMF to Eliza R. Farrar, 17 April 1836, in *Letters*, I, 247.
25. SMF to [?], 23 May 1836, in *Letters*, I, 254.
26. SMF to Ellen K. Fuller, 21 April 1836, in *Letters*, I, 251.
27. SMF to Arthur B. Fuller, 31 December 1837, in *Letters*, I, 319.
28. SMF to Caroline Sturgis, 22 October 1840, in *Letters*, II, 168–69.
29. SMF to James F. Clarke, 19 April 1836, in *Letters*, I, 248. Emphasis in original.
30. SMF to Samuel G. Ward, 20 April 1836, in *Letters*, I, 249.
31. SMF to Frederic H. Hedge, 1 February 1835, in *Letters*, I, 224.
32. SMF to Almira P. Barlow, 6 October 1834, in *Letters*, I, 210.
33. SMF to Frederic H. Hedge, 30 November 1834, in *Letters*, I, 213.
34. SMF to Frederic H. Hedge, 1 February 1835, in *Letters*, I, 224.
35. R. W. Emerson, *Journals and Miscellaneous Notebooks*, III, 149.
36. Robert D. Richardson Jr., *Emerson: The Mind on Fire* (Berkeley: University of California Press, 1995), 3.
37. R. W. Emerson, "Experience," in *Essays and Lectures*, 472.
38. Ellen Tucker Emerson, *The Life of Lidian Jackson Emerson* (Boston: Twayne, 1980), 47.
39. R. W. Emerson to Lidian Jackson, 24 January 1835, in *LRWE*, VII, 232.
40. SMF to Frederic H. Hedge, 6 March 1835, in *Letters*, I, 225.
41. Richardson, *Emerson*, 84.
42. Ibid.
43. R. W. Emerson, in *MoMFO*, I, 201.
44. D. C. French, "A Sculptor's Reminiscence of Emerson," in Ronald A. Bosco and Joel Myerson, eds., *Emerson in His Own Time: A Biographical Chronicle of His Life, Drawn from Recollections, Interviews, and Memoirs by Family, Friends, and Associates* (Iowa City: Iowa University Press, 2003), 234; Julian Hawthorne, "Personal Glimpses of Emerson," in ibid., 227.
45. French, "Sculptor's Reminiscence of Emerson," in Bosco and Myerson, eds., *Emerson in His Own Time*, 235.

46. R. F. Fuller, "The Younger Generation in 1840 from the Diary of a New-England Boy," in Bosco and Myerson, eds., *Emerson in His Own Time*, 17.

47. R. W. Emerson, in *MoMFO*, I, 202.

48. Ibid.

49. J. Hawthorne, "Personal Glimpses of Emerson," in Bosco and Myerson, eds., *Emerson in His Own Time*, 227.

50. George William Curtis to [Daniel Ricketson], 23 April 1856, George William Curtis Papers, Houghton Library, Harvard University, bMS Am 1124 (110).

51. W. H. Channing, in *MoMFO*, II, 36.

52. R. W. Emerson, in *MoMFO*, I, 202, 203.

53. Ibid., 202–3.

54. R. W. Emerson, *Journals and Miscellaneous Notebooks*, V, 187.

55. L. J. Emerson to Elizabeth Palmer Peabody, [late July 1836], in *The Selected Letters of Lidian Jackson Emerson*, edited by Delores Bird Carpenter (Columbia: University of Missouri Press, 1987), 49.

56. R. W. Emerson to William Emerson, 8 August 1836, in *LRWE*, II, 32.

57. R. W. Emerson, *Journals and Miscellaneous Notebooks*, V, 190.

58. John Matteson, *Eden's Outcasts: The Story of Louisa May Alcott and Her Father* (New York: W. W. Norton, 2007), 71.

59. S. F. Clarke to James Freeman Clarke, 27 February 1835, "Letters of a Sister," James Freeman Clarke Additional Papers, Houghton Library, III, 12.

60. SMF to A. Bronson Alcott, 25 August 1836, in *Letters*, I, 256.

61. Matteson, *Eden's Outcasts*, 56.

62. SMF to A. Bronson Alcott, 25 August 1836, in *Letters*, I, 256.

63. SMF, [Advertisement], MFFP, IX, 41.

64. Von Mehren, *Minerva and the Muse*, 81.

65. Matteson, *Eden's Outcasts*, 58.

66. A. Bronson Alcott, "Journal for 1837," in Larry A. Carlson, "Bronson Alcott's 'Journal for 1837' (Part One)," *Studies in the American Renaissance* (1981), 27–132, 93.

67. Ibid.

68. SMF to James F. Clarke, 13 May 1837, in *Letters*, VI, 294.

69. SMF, "Memoranda," MFFP, Box 3.

70. In a letter to Clarke, Fuller acknowledged in retrospect that her labor at the Temple School had been "quite exhausting." SMF [to James F. Clarke], in *Letters*, I, 279.

71. SMF to [?], 23 April 1837, in *Letters*, VI, 292.

72. SMF, in *MoMFO*, I, 172.

73. A. B. Alcott, "Scripture for 1840," Amos Bronson Alcott Papers, Houghton Library, Harvard University, MS Am1130.10 (10).

74. SMF to Frederic H. Hedge, 6 April 1837, in *Letters*, I, 265.

75. SMF to Harriet Martineau, ca. November 1837, in *Letters*, I, 309.

76. SMF to Frederic H. Hedge, 6 April 1837, in *Letters*, I, 266.

77. SMF to R. W. Emerson, 11 April 1837, in *Letters*, I, 268–69.

78. SMF to Jane F. Tuckerman, 2 May 1837, in *Letters*, I, 272.

79. SMF to Caroline Sturgis, 14 May 1837, in *Letters*, I, 273.

80. SMF to Jane F. Tuckerman, 2 May 1837, in *Letters*, I, 272. Emphasis in original.

81. SMF to Caroline Sturgis, 14 May 1837, in *Letters*, I, 273. Emphasis in original.

82. R. W. Emerson, "An Address Delivered at Providence, Rhode Island, on the Occasion of the Opening of the Greene Street School, 10 June 1837," in *The*

Selected Lectures of Ralph Waldo Emerson (Athens: University of Georgia Press, 2005), 47.

83. SMF to James F. Clarke, 13 May 1837, in *Letters*, VI, 293.

84. SMF to John S. Dwight, 31 May 1837, in *Letters*, I, 281.

85. SMF to James F. Clarke, 13 May 1837, in *Letters*, VI, 293; SMF to John S. Dwight, 31 May 1837, in *Letters*, I, 281.

86. SMF to John S. Dwight, 31 May 1837, in *Letters*, I, 281.

87. SMF to Frederic H. Hedge, 6 April 1837, in *Letters*, I, 266.

88. SMF to James F. Clarke, 13 May 1837, in *Letters*, VI, 293, 295.

89. SMF to Elizabeth Palmer Peabody, 8 July 1837, in *Letters*, I, 291.

90. Richardson, *Emerson*, 195.

91. SMF to Jane F. Tuckerman, 16 June 1837, in *Letters*, I, 284.

92. R. W. Emerson, "Address Delivered at Providence," in *Selected Lectures*, 46.

93. Ibid., 48.

94. Emerson, "Address Delivered at Providence," in *Selected Lectures*, 50.

95. SMF to Jane F. Tuckerman, 16 June 1837, in *Letters*, I, 284; SMF to Caroline Sturgis, 18 June 1837, in *Letters*, I, 285.

96. SMF to Arthur Fuller, 5 July 1837, in *Letters*, I, 289, 291.

97. SMF to Arthur Fuller, 5 July 1837, in *Letters*, I, 290.

98. SMF to A. Bronson Alcott, 27 June 1837, in *Letters*, I, 286–287. Emphasis in original.

99. M. W. Allen, "[Fuller as a Teacher in 1837–1838]," in Myerson, ed., *Fuller in Her Own Time*, 13.

100. Ibid., 14. The signatures on a round robin are written in the form of the spokes of a wheel, such that it is impossible to determine which of the signatories signed first.

101. Ibid., 15. Emphasis in original.

102. Quoted in von Mehren, *Minerva and the Muse*, 102.

103. SMF to Jane F. Tuckerman, 16 June 1837, in *Letters*, I, 284.

104. SMF to Caroline Sturgis, 14 October 1837, in *Letters*, I, 303.

105. SMF to Margarett C. Fuller, 18 November 1837, in *Letters*, I, 315.

106. SMF to Ralph Waldo Emerson, 14 August 1837, in *Letters*, I, 295.

107. M. C. Fuller to Abraham Fuller, 3 September 1837, MFFP, VIII, 9.

108. SMF to Margarett C. Fuller, 5 September 1837, in *Letters*, I, 301.

109. SMF to Margarett C. Fuller, 18 November 1837, in *Letters*, I, 315.

110. Capper, *Margaret Fuller*, I, 218.

111. R. W. Emerson to Margaret Fuller, 18 July 1837, in *Letters*, II, 88.

112. SMF to Lidian J. Emerson, 19 August 1838, in *Letters*, I, 341.

113. Eleanor M. Tilton, "The True Romance of Anna Hazard Barker and Samuel Gray Ward," *Studies in the American Renaissance* (1987), 56.

114. Ibid., 58.

115. R. W. Emerson, *Journals and Miscellaneous Notebooks*, V, 425–26.

116. E. T. Emerson, *Life of Lidian Jackson Emerson*, 81–83.

117. SMF to Ralph Waldo Emerson, 1 March 1838, in *Letters*, I, 328.

118. Richardson, *Emerson*, 245. The two other ministers were George Ripley and George Putnam.

119. R. W. Emerson, "The American Scholar," in *Essays and Lectures*, 58.

120. SMF to Margarett C. Fuller, 18 November 1837, in *Letters*, I, 315.

121. R. W. Emerson, "The American Scholar," in *Essays and Lectures*, 70.

122. R. W. Emerson, *Journals and Miscellaneous Notebooks*, V, 407.

123. SMF to Caroline Sturgis, 16 November 1837, in *Letters*, I, 314–15.
124. R. W. Emerson, "Address," in *Essays and Lectures*, 80, 81, 88.
125. "Emerson's Address," *Christian Examiner*, in Perry Miller, ed., *The Transcendentalists: An Anthology* (Cambridge, Mass.: Harvard University Press, 1950), 197; Andrews Norton, "The New School in Literature and Religion," in ibid., 195.
126. SMF to Jane F. Tuckerman, 21 September 1838, in *Letters*, I, 341.
127. A. D. Gale, "[Fuller as a Teacher in 1838–1839]," in Myerson, ed., *Fuller in Her Own Time*, 28.
128. J. Graves, quoted in M. W. Allen, "[Fuller as a Teacher in 1837–1838]," in Myerson, ed., *Fuller in Her Own Time*, 16–17.
129. M. W. Allen, quoted in Capper, *Margaret Fuller*, I, 236.
130. SMF to Caroline Sturgis, 24 [?] July 1838, in *Letters*, I, 338.
131. SMF to Lidian J. Emerson, 19 August 1838, in *Letters*, I, 341.
132. SMF to Lidian J. Emerson, 19 August 1838, in *Letters*, I, 340.
133. Tilton, "True Romance," 61.
134. R. W. Emerson, in *MoMFO*, I, 208–9.
135. SMF, to Jane F. Tuckerman, 21 September 1838, in *Letters*, I, 341.
136. SMF to Almira P. Barlow, October 1838, in *Letters*, I, 343.
137. SMF to Jane F. Tuckerman, 21 October 1838, in *Letters*, I, 347.
138. SMF to James F. Clarke, 7 January 1839, in *Letters*, VI, 309. Emphasis in original.
139. SMF to William H. Channing, 9 December 1838, in *Letters*, I, 353–54.
140. SMF, TO Almira P. Barlow, 8 November 1838, in *Letters*, I, 351.
141. SMF to Richard F. Fuller, 30 October 1838, in *Letters*, I, 349–50.
142. SMF to William H. Channing, 9 December 1838, in *Letters*, I, 354.
143. Ann Brown, "[Fuller as a Teacher in 1838]," in Myerson, ed., *Fuller in Her Own Time*, 24.
144. M. W. Allen, "[Fuller as a Teacher in 1837–1838]," in Myerson, ed., *Fuller in Her Own Time*, 19.

CHAPTER FIVE: CONVERSATIONALIST

1. SMF to James F. Clarke, 7 January 1839, in *Letters*, I, 309.
2. SMF to Caroline Sturgis, 4 March 1839, in *Letters*, II, 58–59.
3. Andrew P. Peabody, *Memoir of James Freeman Clarke* (Cambridge, Mass.: John Wilson, 1889), 8.
4. SMF to James F. Clarke, 26 June 1839, in *Letters*, VI. 314.
5. SMF to James F. Clarke, 7 January 1839, in *Letters*, VI, 309–10.
6. SMF to Caroline Sturgis, 10 January 1839, in *Letters*, II, 35.
7. SMF to Charles K. Newcomb, 4 March 1839, in *Letters*, II, 56; SMF to Caroline Sturgis, 4 March 1839, in *Letters*, II, 58–59.
8. SMF to Caroline Sturgis, 4 March 1839, in *Letters*, II, 57.
9. Ibid., 56.
10. SMF to James Freeman Clarke, 8 January 1839, in *Letters*, II, 33–34.
11. SMF, transl., *Conversations with Goethe in the Last Years of His Life, Translated from the German of Eckermann* (Boston: Hilliard, Gray, 1839), 95, 32.
12. Ibid., 50.
13. SMF, "Translator's Preface," in *Conversations with Goethe*, x.
14. Ibid., xii.

15. Ibid., xiii.
16. Ibid., xv.
17. Ibid.
18. SMF, transl., *Conversations with Goethe*, 351, 279, 264–65, 370–71, 108, 361.
19. SMF to George Ripley, 21 February 1838, in *Letters*, II, 52.
20. SMF, "Translator's Preface," in *Conversations with Goethe*, xxiii.
21. SMF, transl., *Conversations with Goethe*, 41.
22. John Oxenford, transl., *Conversations of Goethe with Johann Peter Eckermann* (1930; Cambridge, Mass.: Da Capo Press, 1998), xxv.
23. R. W. Emerson to Margaret Fuller, 7 June 1839, in *LRWE*, II, 201–3.
24. J. F. Clarke to Margaret Fuller, 8 October 1839, in *LJFC*, 137.
25. Von Mehren, *Minerva and the Muse*, 107.
26. SMF to Eugene Fuller, 8 June 1839, in *Letters*, II, 73.
27. Madeleine B. Stern, *The Life of Margaret Fuller* (New York: E. P. Dutton, 1942), 224.
28. R. W. Emerson to Margaret Fuller, 7 June 1839, in *LRWE*, II, 203.
29. SMF to James F. Clarke, ca. 14 February 1836, in *Letters*, I, 244.
30. R. W. Emerson to Margaret Fuller, 1 and 2 May 1839, in *LRWE*, II, 197. It was a common practice with Fuller, Emerson, and their friends to share their journals.
31. SMF to Ralph Waldo Emerson, 3 June 1839, in *Letters*, II, 69.
32. SMF to Charles K. Newcomb, 18 April 1839, in *Letters*, II, 64. Emphasis in original.
33. SMF to Charles K. Newcomb, 29 May 1839, in *Letters*, II, 68.
34. SMF to Elizabeth Hoar, 15 May 1839, in *Letters*, II, 66.
35. SMF to Caroline Sturgis, 10 January 1839, in *Letters*, II, 35.
36. SMF to Caroline Sturgis, 27 January 1839, in *Letters*, II, 40, 41.
37. SMF to Jane F. Tuckerman, ca. 21 June 1839, in *Letters*, II, 77.
38. SMF to Caroline Sturgis, 7 October 1839, in *Letters*, II, 93.
39. Caroline Sturgis, marginalia in SMF to Caroline Sturgis, 7 October 1839, in *Letters*, II, 94n.
40. SMF to Caroline Sturgis, 7 October 1839, in *Letters*, II, 93. Meg McGavran Murray's chapter on Fuller's interlude with Sturgis at Nahant is worthy of special attention. Murray, *Margaret Fuller, Wandering Pilgrim*, 150–58.
41. SMF to Samuel G. Ward, July 1839, in *Letters*, II, 81.
42. SMF to Samuel G. Ward, [early September] 1839, in *Letters*, II, 90.
43. SMF, in *MoMFO*, I, 234.
44. SMF to Samuel G. Ward, [early September] 1839, in *Letters*, II, 91.
45. Ibid., 90.
46. SMF to Samuel G. Ward, July 1839, in *Letters*, II, 80–81.
47. SMF to Jane F. Tuckerman, August 1839, in *Letters*, II, 82.
48. SMF to Samuel G. Ward, [early September] 1839, in *Letters*, II, 91.
49. SMF to Samuel G. Ward, July 1839, in *Letters*, II, 81; SMF to Samuel G. Ward, [early September] 1839, in *Letters*, II, 91.
50. SMF, *Summer on the Lakes*, 94.
51. SMF to Caroline Sturgis, 7 October 1839, in *Letters*, II, 93.
52. R. W. Emerson to Margaret Fuller, 16 October 1839, in *LRWE*, II, 228.
53. SMF to Caroline Sturgis, 7 October 1839, in *Letters*, II, 93.
54. SMF to Samuel Gray Ward, 15 October 1839, in *Letters*, II, 96. The phrase

quoted appears in the letter inside quotation marks. My conclusion that Fuller is quoting Ward back to himself is an unproven, but I believe justifiable, inference.

55. SMF to Samuel Gray Ward, 15 October 1839, in *Letters*, II, 95–96.

56. SMF, in *MoMFO*, II, 103.

57. Robert D. Habich, "Margaret Fuller's Journal for October 1842," *Harvard Library Bulletin* 33 (summer 1985), 280–91, 283.

58. Fuller quotes Goethe's poem "Mignon." Translation: "No one asks if you are a man or a woman."

59. Habich, "Margaret Fuller's Journal for October 1842," 286–87.

60. Ibid., 287.

61. Ibid.

62. R. W. Emerson, in *MoMFO*, I, 281–82.

63. Habich, "Margaret Fuller's Journal for October 1842," 285.

64. A. Bronson Alcott to Anna Bronson Alcott, 18 March 1839, in *The Letters of A. Bronson Alcott* (Ames: Iowa State University Press, 1969), 40–41. Emphasis in original.

65. A. Bronson Alcott, quoted in von Mehren, *Minerva and the Muse*, 114.

66. SMF to [Sophia Ripley?], 27 August 1839, in *Letters*, II, 86.

67. Ibid. Though superlative throughout, Charles Capper is particularly fine in his assessment of the importance of Fuller's conversations in the nascence of American feminism. Capper, *Margaret Fuller*, I, 297–306.

68. SMF to [Sophia Ripley?], 27 August 1839, in *Letters*, II, 87.

69. Ibid.

70. Ibid.

71. Megan Marshall, *The Peabody Sisters: Three Women Who Ignited American Romanticism* (Boston: Houghton Mifflin, 2005), 384.

72. Carlos Baker, *Emerson among the Eccentrics: A Group Portrait* (New York: Viking Penguin, 1996), 134.

73. William Harley Hale, *Horace Greeley: Voice of the People* (New York: Harper Brothers, 1950), 32.

74. SMF to [?], ca. Autumn 1839 [?], in *Letters*, II, 97.

75. Anonymous, in *MoMFO*, I, 340.

76. S. F. Clarke to James Freeman Clarke, 17 November 1839, "Letters of a Sister," James Freeman Clarke Additional Papers, Houghton Library, MS Am 1569.3 (12).

77. Nancy Craig Simmons, "Margaret Fuller's Boston Conversations: The 1839–1840 Series," *Studies in the American Renaissance* (1994), 203.

78. R. W. Emerson, "Experience," in *Essays and Lectures*, 483.

79. SMF to [?], in *Letters*, I, 97.

80. Simmons, "Margaret Fuller's Boston Conversations," 204. Emphasis in original.

81. Ibid., 207.

82. Ibid., 209.

83. Ibid.

84. Ibid., 214.

85. S. F. Clarke to James Freeman Clarke, 14 December 1839, "Letters of a Sister," James Freeman Clarke Additional Papers, Houghton Library, bMS Am 1569.3 (12). Emphasis in original.

86. Simmons, "Margaret Fuller's Boston Conversations," 215.

87. Ibid., 217. Emphasis in original.
88. Ibid., 215.
89. Ibid., 219.
90. Anonymous, in *MoMFO*, I, 332; Simmons, "Margaret Fuller's Boston Conversations," 203.
91. Myerson, "Caroline Dall's Reminiscences," 422.
92. Ibid.
93. Ibid., 426.
94. Higginson, *Margaret Fuller Ossoli*, 118.
95. R. W. Emerson to Margaret Fuller, 31 July 1839, in *LRWE*, II, 211.
96. George Ripley, *"The Latest Form of Infidelity" Examined: A Letter to Mr. Andrews Norton* (Boston: James Munroe, 1839), 10.
97. R. W. Emerson to Margaret Fuller, 16 October 1839, in *LRWE*, II, 229.
98. R. W. Emerson to Margaret Fuller, 14 November 1839, in *LRWE*, II, 234.
99. R. W. Emerson to Margaret Fuller, 14 November 1839, in *LRWE*, II, 234.
100. Matteson, *Eden's Outcasts*, 92–93.

CHAPTER SIX: ECSTATIC EDITOR

1. SMF to James Freeman Clarke, 1 January 1840, in *Letters*, VI, 319.
2. Ibid.
3. SMF to William Henry Channing, 1 January 1840, in *Letters*, II, 111.
4. R. W. Emerson to Margaret Fuller, 30 March 1840, in *LRWE*, II, 271.
5. SMF to Frederic Henry Hedge, 1 January 1840, in *Letters*, II, 113.
6. SMF to James Freeman Clarke, 1 January 1840, in *Letters*, VI, 319.
7. SMF to William H. Channing, ca. 1839, in *Letters*, II, 31.
8. SMF to William H. Channing, 1 January 1840, in *Letters*, II, 111.
9. R. W. Emerson to Margaret Fuller, 12 December 1839, in *LRWE*, II, 243.
10. [Frederic Henry Hedge], "The Art of Life,—The Scholar's Calling," *Dial*, 1, no. 2 (October 1840), 175. Emphasis in original.
11. F. H. Hedge to Margaret Fuller, 24 March 1840, quoted in Joel Myerson, ed., "Frederic Henry Hedge and the Failure of Transcendentalism," *Harvard Library Bulletin* 23 (October 1975), 396–410, 403.
12. Higginson, *Margaret Fuller Ossoli*, 152.
13. SMF to William H. Channing [?], 1840, in *Letters*, II, 108–9.
14. Ibid., 109.
15. SMF to Ralph Waldo Emerson, 3 December 1844, in *Letters*, III, 251.
16. SMF to William Henry Channing, 19 April 1840, in *Letters*, II, 130.
17. Capper, *Margaret Fuller*, I, 336.
18. SMF, MFFP, Works, I, 589.
19. SMF to Elizabeth Hoar, 15 May 1839, in *Letters*, II, 66.
20. [R. W. Emerson], "The Editor to the Readers," *Dial* 1, no. 1 (July 1840), 1.
21. Ibid., 2.
22. Ibid., 3.
23. Ibid., 4.
24. [E. T. Emerson], "Lines," *Dial* 1, no. 1 (July 1840), 72.
25. [SMF], "A Short Essay on Critics," *Dial* 1, no. 1 (July 1840), 7.
26. Matteson, *Eden's Outcasts*, 94.
27. Charles Capper, *Margaret Fuller: An American Romantic Life*, vol. II: *The Public Years* (Oxford: Oxford University Press, 2007), 4.

28. R. W. Emerson to Margaret Fuller, 2 July 1840, in *LRWE*, II, 311; SMF to Ralph Waldo Emerson, 5 July 1840, in *Letters*, II, 146.

29. SMF to Ralph Waldo Emerson, 5 July 1840, in *Letters*, II, 146.

30. SMF to Ralph Waldo Emerson, 19 July 1840, in *Letters*, II, 150.

31. [R. W. Emerson], "The Editors to the Reader," *Dial* 1, no. 1 (July 1840), 4.

32. SMF to Charles K. Newcomb, 25 February 1841 [?], in *Letters*, II, 205.

33. [SMF], "A Dialogue," *Dial* 1, no. 1 (July 1840), 134.

34. SMF to Caroline Sturgis, 24 July 1840, in *Letters*, II, 154.

35. Habich, "Margaret Fuller's Journal for October 1842," 283.

36. SMF to William Henry Channing, 25 and 28 October 1840, in *Letters*, II, 174.

37. SMF to William Henry Channing, 22 March 1840, in *Letters*, II, 126.

38. SMF to Almira P. Barlow, July 1840, in *Letters*, II, 145.

39. SMF to Caroline Sturgis, 8 September 1840, in *Letters*, II, 157–58. Emphasis in original. Fuller attached great symbolic significance to carbuncles and wore one on her wrist when she wrote letters to friends. R. W. Emerson, in *MoMFO*, I, 219. As a sufferer from migraines, she is likely to have known the folk tradition of using carbuncles to assuage headaches. *The Esoteric: A Magazine of Advanced and Practical Esoteric Thought* (Esoteric Publishing, Boston) 1 (1888), 457. A carbuncle figures in Novalis's mystical work *Heinrich von Ofterdingen*, which Fuller read and praised in her early twenties. In an impressive gloss, Charles Capper has noted that the carbuncle is "a glowing, rubylike alchemic stone revered by hermetic writers of the Renaissance as a sign of . . . mysterious power" and "intensely energizing and revelatory knowledge." Capper, *Margaret Fuller*, II, 21. Although he notes that the carbuncle held some bisexual significance for Fuller, Capper stops short of identifying it, as one plausibly might, as a metaphor for female autoeroticism. Another possible significance comes from Nathaniel Hawthorne's 1837 short story "The Great Carbuncle," in which a band of travelers go in search of a fabulous gem. The character who most resembles Fuller is a poet who hopes to carry it away to his attic chamber, where, night and day, he will "gaze upon it; my soul shall drink its radiance; it shall be diffused through my intellectual powers, and gleam brightly in every line of poesy that I indite." Nathaniel Hawthorne, *Tales and Sketches* (New York: Library of America, 1982), 109–29, 440. If Fuller had Hawthorne in mind, then her "carbuncle" symbolizes some hidden source of inspiration that, once unearthed, has lighted her private world with its unearthly radiance.

40. SMF to Caroline Sturgis, 26 September 1840, in *Letters*, II, 158.

41. SMF to Caroline Sturgis, 18 October 1840, in *Letters*, II, 163.

42. SMF, "Journal," Margaret Fuller Ossoli Collection, Boston Public Library, 119. Emphasis in original.

43. SMF to Caroline Sturgis, 18 October 1840, in *Letters*, II, 163; SMF, in *MoMFO*, II, 83.

44. R. W. Emerson, in *MoMFO*, I, 308.

45. W. H. Channing, in *MoMFO*, II, 93.

46. SMF to William H. Channing, 25 and 28 October 1840, in *Letters*, II, 171.

47. SMF to Ralph Waldo Emerson, 29 September 1840, in *Letters*, II, 159.

48. R. W. Emerson to Caroline Sturgis, 16[?] August 1840, in *LRWE*, II. 325.

49. R. W. Emerson, *Journals and Miscellaneous Notebooks*, VII, 509.

50. R. W. Emerson, in *MoMFO*, I, 288.

51. R. W. Emerson to Caroline Sturgis, 16 August 1840 [?], in *LRWE*, II, 325.

52. R. W. Emerson, *Journals and Miscellaneous Notebooks*, VII, 509.
53. R. W. Emerson, in *MoMFO*, I, 288.
54. R. W. Emerson, *Journals and Miscellaneous Notebooks*, VII, 509–10.
55. R. W. Emerson to Lidian Emerson, 10 November 1840, in *LRWE*, II, 358.
56. R. W. Emerson to Margaret Fuller, 16 August 1840, in *LRWE*, II, 323.
57. R. W. Emerson to Margaret Fuller, 29 August 1840, in *LRWE*, II, 327.
58. R. W. Emerson to Caroline Sturgis, 16 August [?] 1840, in *LRWE*, II, 325.
59. R. W. Emerson to Caroline Sturgis, 13 September 1840, in *LRWE*, II, 334.
60. Caroline Sturgis to Ralph Waldo Emerson, 11 September 1840, Caroline Sturgis Tappan Papers, Houghton Library, Harvard University, MS Am 1221, I, 318.
61. R. W. Emerson to Margaret Fuller, 13 September 1840, in *LRWE*, II, 332.
62. R. W. Emerson to Margaret Fuller, 25 September 1840, in *LRWE*, II, 336–37.
63. SMF to Ralph Waldo Emerson, 29 September 1840, in *Letters*, II, 159.
64. Ibid., 159–60.
65. Ibid.
66. SMF to Ralph Waldo Emerson, ca. 4 December 1840, in *Letters*, II, 188.
67. SMF to William H. Channing [?], 3 December 1840, in *Letters*, II, 187.
68. SMF to Caroline Sturgis, 22 October 1840, in *Letters*, II, 167.
69. SMF to William H. Channing [?], 19 October 1840, in *Letters*, II, 165.
70. [SMF], "The Magnolia of Lake Pontchartrain," *Dial* 1, no. 3 (January 1841), 299, 300.
71. Ibid., 301.
72. Ibid., 302.
73. Ibid., 303.
74. Ibid., 304.
75. Ibid., 305.
76. SMF to James F. Clarke, 9 January 1845, in *Letters*, VI, 357.
77. [SMF], "Leila," *Dial* 1, no. 4 (April 1841), 462.
78. Ibid., 463.
79. Ibid., 464.
80. Ibid., 466.
81. Ibid., 467.
82. SMF, "Autobiographical Romance," in *MoMFO*, I, 17–18.
83. SMF to Elizabeth Hoar, 20 March 1842, in *Letters*, III, 55.
84. Capper, *Margaret Fuller*, II, 67.
85. SMF to Richard F. Fuller, 5 November 1841, in *Letters*, II, 249.
86. R. W. Emerson to Margaret Fuller, 6 May 1841, in *LRWE*, II, 398.
87. R. W. Emerson to Margaret Fuller, 17 September 1841, in *LRWE*, II, 450.
88. R. W. Emerson to Margaret Fuller, 6 May 1841, in *LRWE*, II, 398; SMF to Ralph Waldo Emerson, 10 May 1841, in *Letters*, II, 209.
89. SMF to Richard F. Fuller, 25 May 1841, in *Letters*, II, 210.
90. Ibid.
91. SMF to Caroline Sturgis, June 1841 [?], in *Letters*, II, 211.
92. SMF to William H. Channing, July 1841 [?], in *Letters*, II, 214.
93. Ibid., 215.
94. SMF to William H, Channing, 31 July 1841, in *Letters*, II, 220–21.
95. SMF, "[Fragments of Margaret Fuller's Journal]," Fruitlands Library, 35–36.
96. SMF to Elizabeth Hoar, 20 March 1842, in *Letters*, III, 55.
97. SMF to Ralph Waldo Emerson, 11 July 1848, in *Letters*, V, 86.

98. SMF to Elizabeth Hoar, 20 March 1842, in *Letters*, III, 55.
99. W. E. Channing to Margaret Fuller, 26 February 1842, in Francis B. Dedmond, "Selected Letters of William Ellery Channing the Younger (Part One)," *Studies in American Renaissance* (1989), 115–218, 165.
100. SMF to Richard F. Fuller, 1 December 1841, in *Letters*, II, 254.
101. SMF to Ralph Waldo Emerson, 16 September 1841, in *Letters*, II, 232.
102. SMF to Richard F. Fuller, 15 January 1842, in *Letters*, III, 40.
103. SMF to Ralph Waldo Emerson, October 1841 [?], in *Letters*, II, 236.
104. SMF to Ralph Waldo Emerson, October 1841 [?], in *Letters*, II, 234.
105. SMF to Margarett Crane Fuller, 24 December 1841, in *Letters*, II, 261.
106. SMF to Ralph Waldo Emerson, 8 March 1842, in *Letters*, III, 49; SMF to Elizabeth Hoar," 8 March 1842, in *Letters*, III, 47.
107. SMF to William Henry Channing, July 1841 [?], in *Letters*, II, 215.
108. SMF to Ralph Waldo Emerson, 17 [?] March 1842, in *Letters*, II, 53.
109. R. W. Emerson to Margaret Fuller, 18 March 1842, in *LRWE*, III, 33; R. W. Emerson to Margaret Fuller, 21 March 1842, in *LRWE*, III, 35.
110. R. W. Emerson to Margaret Fuller, 18 March 1842, in *LRWE*, III, 33–34.
111. R. W. Emerson to Frederic Henry Hedge, 23 March 1842, in *LRWE*, III, 37.
112. Henry Steele Commager, "The Significance of the *Dial*," in *The Search for a Usable Past, and Other Essays in Historiography* (New York: Alfred A. Knopf, 1967), 156.
113. SMF to Ralph Waldo Emerson, 17 March 1842, in *Letters*, III, 54.
114. SMF to William Henry Channing, February 1842, in *Letters*, III, 43.
115. SMF to Albert H. Tracy, 6 November 1843, in *Letters*, III, 157.
116. R. W. Emerson to Mary Moody Emerson, 28 January 1842, in *Letters*, III, 7.
117. Ralph Waldo Emerson, "Threnody," in *Collected Poems and Translations* (New York: Library of America, 1994), 120.
118. R. W. Emerson to William Emerson, 27 January 1842, in *Letters*, III, 6; R. W. Emerson to Mary Moody Emerson, 28 January 1842, in *Letters*, III, 7.
119. R. W. Emerson to Margaret Fuller, 28 January 1842, in *Letters*, III, 8.
120. SMF to William H. Channing, February 1842, in *Letters*, III, 43.
121. Richardson, *Emerson*, 359.
122. SMF to Ralph Waldo Emerson, 10 August 1842, in *Letters*, III, 83.
123. R. W. Emerson, "Experience," in *Essays and Lectures*, 173.
124. R. W. Emerson to Margaret Fuller, 12 August 1842, in *LRWE*, III, 80.
125. Joel Myerson, ed., "Margaret Fuller's 1842 Journal: At Concord with the Emersons," *Harvard Library Bulletin* 21 (July 1973), 320–40, 322–23.
126. Ibid., 330–31.
127. Ibid., 331.
128. Ibid., 332.
129. Ibid., 331.
130. Ibid.
131. Ibid., 327.
132. Ibid., 334.
133. Ibid., 336.
134. Sophia Hawthorne to a Priestess of the Temple," MFFP, XVI, 29.
135. Julian Hawthorne, *Nathaniel Hawthorne and His Wife: A Biography*, 2 vol. (Boston: Houghton, Mifflin, 1884), I, 260.
136. Sophia Hawthorne to Mrs. Elizabeth Palmer Peabody, 22 August 1842, quoted in Capper, *Margaret Fuller*, II, 89.

137. Myerson, "Margaret Fuller's 1842 Journal," 325.
138. Nathaniel Hawthorne, *Passages from the American Note-Books* (Boston: Houghton, Mifflin, 1868), 307–8.
139. Myerson, "Margaret Fuller's 1842 Journal," 325.
140. Habich, "Margaret Fuller's Journal for October 1842," 283.
141. Ibid., 290.
142. Ibid.
143. SMF to William H. Channing, 29 March 1841, in *Letters*, II, 205.

CHAPTER SEVEN: SEEKER OF UTOPIA

1. SMF to Elizabeth Hoar, 20 March 1842, in *Letters*, III, 55.
2. R. W. Emerson, in *MoMFO*, I, 227. Various Fuller scholars, including Bell Gale Chevigny and Margaret McGavran Murray, have identified Fuller's headaches as migraines. Chevigny, *Woman and the Myth*, 21; Murray, *Margaret Fuller, Wandering Pilgrim*, 106.
3. R. W. Emerson, in *MoMFO*, I, 227, 229.
4. Quoted in von Mehren, *Minerva and the Muse*, 124.
5. Herman Melville, *Clarel: A Poem and Pilgrimage in the Holy Land* (Evanston, Ill.: Northwestern University Press and Newberry Library, 1991), 498.
6. SMF to Ralph Waldo Emerson, 9 May [1843], in *Letters*, III, 123.
7. SMF, *Woman in the Nineteenth Century*, v–vi.
8. Ibid., vi.
9. Ibid., 106.
10. SMF, "The Great Lawsuit," *Dial* 4, no. 1 (July 1843), 45.
11. Jean-Jacques Rousseau, *The Social Contract, or, The Principles of Political Rights*, translated by Rose M. Harrington (New York: G. P. Putnam's Sons, 1893), 2.
12. SMF, "Great Lawsuit," 7.
13. Ibid., 8.
14. Ibid., 11–12.
15. Ibid., 14.
16. Ibid.
17. Ibid., 15.
18. Ibid., 14–15.
19. Ibid., 47.
20. H. D. Thoreau, quoted in R. W. Emerson to Margaret Fuller, 11 July 1843, in *LRWE*, III, 183.
21. Daniel Walker Howe, *What Hath God Wrought: The Transformation of America, 1815–1848* (Oxford, UK: Oxford University Press, 2007), 293.
22. SMF to Ralph Waldo Emerson, 31 May 1840, in *Letters*, II, 135–36.
23. Sterling Delano, *Brook Farm: The Dark Side of Utopia* (Cambridge, Mass.: Belknap Press of Harvard University Press, 2004), 25.
24. G. Ripley, quoted in ibid., 8.
25. R. W. Emerson to Thomas Carlyle, 30 October 1840, in Ralph Waldo Emerson and Thomas Carlyle, *The Correspondence of Thomas Carlyle and Ralph Waldo Emerson, 1834–1872*, 2 vol. (Boston: James R. Osgood, 1883), I, 308.
26. G. Ripley to Ralph Waldo Emerson, 9 November 1840, in Octavius Brooks Frothingham, *George Ripley* (Boston: Houghton, Mifflin, 1882), 307–8.
27. J. F. Clarke, *Autobiography, Diary and Correspondence*, 133.
28. SMF to Ralph Waldo Emerson, 31 May 1840, in *Letters*, II, 135.

29. Delano, *Brook Farm*, 32.
30. R. W. Emerson, *Journals and Miscellaneous Notebooks*, VII, 407–8.
31. SMF to Caroline Sturgis, 18 October 1840, in *Letters*, II, 163.
32. SMF to William H. Channing, 1840, in *Letters*, II, 109.
33. SMF to William H. Channing, 13 December 1840, in *Letters*, 194.
34. SMF to William H. Channing, 25 and 28 October 1840, in *Letters*, II, 174.
35. There are few literary rumors more persistent than the story that Hawthorne based Zenobia, a central character in *The Blithedale Romance*, on Fuller. Other than the evidently coincidental fact that Zenobia dies by drowning, there has never been much reason for believing this speculation. Brook Farm alumnus John Van Der Zee Sears calls the supposed connection "so far-fetched as to be near absurdity." John Van Der Zee Sears, *My Friends at Brook Farm* (New York: Desmond FitzGerald, 1912), 116. The best interpretation seems to be that, in creating Zenobia, Hawthorne drew on a variety of sources, among whom Fuller is far from predominant.
36. Nathaniel Hawthorne to Sophia Peabody, 12 August 1841, in Nathaniel Hawthorne, *The Letters, 1813–1843* (Columbus: Ohio State University Press, 1984), 558.
37. N. Hawthorne to Sophia Peabody, 13 April 1841, in *Letters, 1813–1843*, 527.
38. SMF, in *MoMFO*, II, 74.
39. Sears, *My Friends at Brook Farm*, 82.
40. Delano, *Brook Farm*, 84.
41. Oda Gannett, "A Girl of Sixteen at Brook Farm," in Joel Myerson, ed., *The Brook Farm Book: A Collection of First-Hand Accounts of the Community* (New York: Garland, 1987), 275.
42. Delano, *Brook Farm*, 105.
43. R. W. Emerson to Caroline Sturgis, 1840, in *LRWE*, II, 374.
44. There was the additional problem that, whether or not it was so intended, the greater share of the work within utopian communities of the 1840s tended to fall on the women. Brook Farm was evidently no exception in this regard. For example, Sterling Delano observes that, in the twelve-month period from May 1844 to April 1845, nine of the ten hardest-working Brook Farmers were female. Delano, *Brook Farm*, 172. Fuller, already stretched to her limit at *The Dial*, could hardly have fancied a social arrangement that might well have demanded still more from her.
45. Sears, *My Friends at Brook Farm*, 92.
46. Ibid., 25.
47. SMF, in *MoMFO*, II, 74.
48. W. H. Channing, in *MoMFO*, II, 72.
49. SMF, in *MoMFO*, II, 75.
50. Ibid., 79.
51. Ibid., 75.
52. Ibid., 75–76.
53. W. H. Channing, in *MoMFO*, II, 80.
54. SMF, in *MoMFO*, II, 78.
55. Ibid.
56. Ibid., 119.
57. SMF to Mary Rotch, 5 February 1843, in *Letters*, III, 119.
58. R. W. Emerson to Margaret Fuller, 21 March 1843, in *LRWE*, III, 160.

59. R. W. Emerson to Margaret Fuller, 20 April 1843, in *LRWE*, III, 165.
60. SMF to Sarah Ann Clarke, 8 May 1843, in *Letters*, III, 123.
61. SMF to Ralph Waldo Emerson, 9 May 1843, in *Letters*, III, 124.
62. SMF to Richard Fuller, 5 August 1842, in *Letters*, III, 81.
63. R. W. Emerson to Margaret Fuller, 11 May 1843, in *LRWE*, III, 174.
64. SMF to Richard Fuller, 5 August 1842, in *Letters*, III, 81.
65. SMF, *Summer on the Lakes*, 3.
66. Ibid., 12.
67. Ibid., 6.
68. Ibid., 5.
69. Ibid.
70. Ibid., 3–4. Emphasis added.
71. Ibid., 18.
72. Ibid.
73. Ibid., 19.
74. Hershel Parker, *Herman Melville: A Biography*, vol. I: *1819–1851* (Baltimore: Johns Hopkins University Press, 1996), 176.
75. Ibid.
76. SMF, "[Western Journal]," MFFP, bMS Am1086, Box A.
77. Oakes Shaw, quoted in Parker, *Herman Melville*, 176.
78. SMF, "[Western Journal]," MFFP, Box A.
79. SMF, *Summer on the Lakes*, 130.
80. Ibid., 30.
81. SMF to Ralph Waldo Emerson, 16 June 1843, in *Letters*, III, 129.
82. SMF to Ralph Waldo Emerson, 1 June 1843, in *Letters*, III, 128.
83. SMF, "[Western Journal]," MFFP, Box A.
84. SMF to Ralph Waldo Emerson, 17 August 1843, in *Letters*, III, 143.
85. SMF, *Summer on the Lakes*, 30–31.
86. Ibid., 103.
87. Ibid.
88. SMF, "[Western Journal]," MFFP, Box A.
89. SMF, *Summer on the Lakes*, 35.
90. SMF, "[Western Journal]," MFFP, Box A.
91. SMF, *Summer on the Lakes*, 37.
92. SMF, "[Western Journal]," MFFP, Box A.
93. SMF, *Summer on the Lakes*, 40–41.
94. Ibid., 47.
95. SMF to Richard F. Fuller, 29 July 1843, in *Letters*, III, 133.
96. SMF, *Summer on the Lakes*, 65.
97. Ibid., 70.
98. Ibid., 107–8.
99. Ibid., 182–83.
100. Ibid., 182.
101. Ibid., 169.
102. Ibid., 173.
103. Ibid., 175.
104. Ibid., 180.
105. Ibid., 173.
106. SMF to Albert H. Tracy, 26 September 1843, in *Letters*, III, 150.
107. SMF to Henry D. Thoreau, 25 September 1843, in *Letters*, III, 148.

108. SMF to Richard F. Fuller, 7 September 1843 [?], in *Letters*, III, 145–46.
109. SMF to Henry James Sr., 13 October 1843, in *Letters*, III, 151.
110. SMF to William H. Channing, 27 October 1843, in *Letters*, III, 154.
111. SMF to Albert H. Tracy, 6 November 1843, in *Letters*, III, 156.
112. Ibid.
113. SMF to Ralph Waldo Emerson, 12 November 1843, in *Letters*, III, 160.
114. Ibid., 159.
115. Higginson, *Margaret Fuller Ossoli*, 194.
116. SMF to Anna Barker Ward, 26 December 1843, in *Letters*, III, 164–65.
117. SMF to Ralph Waldo Emerson, 28 January 1844, in *Letters*, III, 179.
118. Von Mehren, *Minerva and the Muse*, 181.
119. Higginson, *Margaret Fuller Ossoli*, 195.
120. SMF to [?], [Summer] 1844, in *Letters*, III, 202.
121. SMF "[Fragments of Margaret Fuller's Journal]," Fruitlands Library, 16.
122. F. H. Hedge, "Schiller," in Miller, ed., *Transcendentalists*, 81.
123. S. M. Fuller to Albert H. Tracy, 6 November 1843, in *Letters*, III, 156.
124. SMF, *Summer on the Lakes*, 2.
125. Ibid.
126. Ibid., 15.
127. Caleb Stetson, "Notice of Recent Publications," *Christian Examiner* 37 (September 1844), 275.
128. SMF, *Summer on the Lakes*, 15.
129. Ibid., 128.
130. Virginia Woolf, "Modern Fiction," in *The Common Reader, First Series* (New York: Harcourt, 1925), 150.
131. SMF, *Summer on the Lakes*, 154.
132. Ibid., 132.
133. The Seeress was a real person. Frederica Hauffe was a young German woman, treated and made somewhat famous by the medical writer Justinus Kerner. In her early twenties, Hauffe suffered a severe fever with violent convulsions. Thereafter, she fell into a state of "mental exaltation" in which she remained for the last seven years of her life. Kerner told her story in Justinus Kerner, *The Seeress of Prevorst; Being Revelations Concerning the Inner Life of Man, and the Inter-Diffusion of a World of Spirits in the One We Inhabit* (New York: Partridge and Brittan, 1856).
134. SMF, *Summer on the Lakes*, 145.
135. Ibid., 81.
136. Ibid., 164.
137. Ibid., 151.
138. Ibid., 99.
139. Ibid., 164.
140. Ibid., 20.
141. Ibid., 102.
142. Ibid., 138–39.
143. Ibid., 159.
144. Ibid., 175.
145. Ibid., 234.
146. Ibid., 233.
147. Ibid., 256.
148. Ibid., 15.

CHAPTER EIGHT: ADVOCATE

1. R. W. Emerson to William Emerson, 17 June 1844, in *LRWE*, III, 256, n69.
2. R. W. Emerson to William Emerson, 7 June 1844, in *LRWE*, III, 255.
3. Capper, *Margaret Fuller*, II, 155.
4. L. M. Child to Margaret Fuller, 23 August 1844, in Lydia Maria Child, *Selected Letters, 1817–1880*, edited by Milton Meltzer and Patricia G. Holland (Amherst: University of Massachusetts Press, 1983), 211–12.
5. R. W. Emerson to Margaret Fuller, 1 March 1842, in *LRWE*, III, 19.
6. R. W. Emerson to Lidian Emerson, 1 March 1842, in *LRWE*, III, 18.
7. W. H. Channing, in *MoMFO*, II, 100, 110.
8. Horace Greeley, in *MoMFO*, II, 152
9. SMF, in *MoMFO*, I, 292.
10. Berg and Perry, "'Impulses of Human Nature,'" 56.
11. Ibid., 55.
12. Ibid., 75–76.
13. SMF to Mary Rotch, 29 May 1848, in *Letters*, V, 71.
14. Berg and Perry, "'Impulses of Human Nature,'" 58.
15. Ibid., 62.
16. Ibid., 78–79. Emphasis in original.
17. Ibid., 57–58.
18. Ibid., 81.
19. Ibid., 81–82.
20. Sophia Hawthorne, quoted in Brenda Wineapple, *Hawthorne: A Life* (New York: Alfred A. Knopf, 2003), 187.
21. Wineapple, *Hawthorne*, 153; Chevigny, *Woman and the Myth*, 133.
22. J. Hawthorne, *Nathaniel Hawthorne and His Wife*, I, 257.
23. Berg and Perry, "'Impulses of Human Nature,'" 89.
24. Ibid., 89, 108.
25. J. Hawthorne, *Nathaniel Hawthorne and His Wife*, I, 261.
26. R. W. Emerson, "Manners," *Essays, Second Series*, in *Essays and Lectures*, 529.
27. Berg and Perry, "'Impulses of Human Nature,'" 83.
28. SMF to Ralph Waldo Emerson, 13 July 1844, in *Letters*, III, 209. Emphasis added.
29. SMF to Ralph Waldo Emerson, 20 [?] July 1844, in *Letters*, III, 213.
30. Ralph Waldo Emerson, "An Address . . . on . . . the Emancipation of the Negroes in the British West Indies," in *Emerson's Antislavery Writings*, edited by Len Gougeon and Joel Myerson (New Haven, Conn.: Yale University Press, 2002), 32.
31. Berg and Perry, "'Impulses of Human Nature,'" 107.
32. Ibid., 109.
33. *MoMFA*, II, 127.
34. Berg and Perry, "'Impulses of Human Nature,'" 114.
35. Ibid., 115.
36. Ibid., 116.
37. Ibid., 117.
38. Ibid., 114–15.
39. R. F. Fuller, *Recollections*, 69.
40. Berg and Perry, "'Impulses of Human Nature,'" 118.
41. R. W. Emerson to Samuel Gray Ward, 2 December 1844, in *LRWE*, III, 268.
42. R. W. Emerson to Margaret Fuller, 1 March 1842, in *LRWE*, III, 20.

43. Berg and Perry, "'Impulses of Human Nature,'" 118.
44. Ibid.
45. Ibid., 119.
46. Ibid., 122.
47. The source of one of the quotations that Fuller chose as an epigraph for *Women in the Nineteenth Century*, "The Earth waits for her Queen," has long eluded scholars. I identify it now: Fuller copied the line from the Fourierist journal *The Phalanx* 1, no. 8 (April 20, 1844).
48. SMF to Christopher P. Cranch, [Autumn 1844], in *Letters*, III, 233; SMF to Richard F. Fuller, 15 October 1844, in *Letters*, III, 234.
49. Berg and Perry, "'Impulses of Human Nature,'" 122.
50. Georgiana Bruce Kirby, *Years of Experience: An Autobiographical Narrative* (New York: G. P. Putnam's Sons, 1887), 190.
51. SMF to Georgiana Bruce, 20 October 1844, in *Letters*, III, 236.
52. Ibid.
53. Kirby, *Years of Experience*, 218–19.
54. SMF to Elizabeth Hoar, 28 [?] October 1844, in *Letters*, III. 237.
55. Fuller to Georgiana Bruce, 15 August 1844, in *Letters*, III, 223.
56. Fuller, *Woman in the Nineteenth Century*, 18.
57. Ibid., 119.
58. Ibid., 118.
59. Ibid., 119.
60. Ibid., 132. Emphasis in original.
61. Ibid., 133.
62. Ibid., 134.
63. Ibid., 119.
64. Ibid., 106.
65. Ibid., 160.
66. Ibid., 158.
67. Ibid., 162.
68. Ibid., 163.
69. Ibid., 159.
70. Ibid., 154.
71. Elizabeth Cady Stanton, Susan B. Anthony et al., eds., *History of Woman Suffrage*, 3 vol. (New York: Fowler and Wells, 1881), I, 801.
72. SMF to William H. Channing, 17 November 1844, in *Letters*, III, 241.
73. Ibid., 242.
74. SMF to Eugene Fuller, 9 March 1845, in *Letters*, IV, 56.
75. Capper, *Margaret Fuller*, II, 188.
76. SMF to Eugene Fuller, 9 March 1845, in *Letters*, IV, 56.
77. SMF to Caroline Sturgis, 13 March 1845, in *Letters*, IV, 59.
78. SMF, "[Review of *Narrative of the Life of Frederick Douglass*]," in *Margaret Fuller, Critic: Writings from the* New-York Tribune, *1844–1846*, edited by Judith Mattson Bean and Joel Myerson (New York: Columbia University Press, 2000), 131.
79. Edgar Allen Poe, "Sarah Margaret Fuller," in *The Literati of New York City*, in *Essays and Reviews* (New York: Library of America, 1984), 1173. Emphasis in original.
80. SMF, "[Review of *Narrative of the Life of Frederick Douglass*]," in *Margaret Fuller, Critic*, 131.
81. Caroline Sturgis to Margaret Fuller, 4 March 1845, in Francis B. Dedmond,

"The Letters of Caroline Sturgis to Margaret Fuller, *Studies in the American Renaissance* (1988), 201–251, 239.

82.   SMF to Caroline Sturgis, 13 March 1845, in *Letters*, IV, 58.

83.   SMF to Caroline Sturgis, 13 March 1845, in *Letters*, IV, 59.

84.   SMF to Richard F. Fuller, 23 November 1844, in *Letters*, III, 248.

CHAPTER NINE: LOVER AND CRITIC

1.   SMF to William H. Channing, 3 [?] November 1844, in *Letters*, III, 240.

2.   SMF to Ralph Waldo Emerson, 17 November 1844, in *Letters*, III, 243.

3.   Ralph Waldo Emerson, "Character," in *Essays and Lectures*, 495.

4.   Ibid.

5.   SMF to George T. Davis, 17 December 1842, in *Letters*, III, 105.

6.   SMF, *Papers on Literature and Art*, II, 139.

7.   Ibid., 140.

8.   Ibid.

9.   Edwin G. Burrows and Mike Wallace, *Gotham: A History of New York City to 1898* (Oxford, U.K.: Oxford University Press, 1999), 631–38.

10.   Joseph J. Rubin, ed., *Walt Whitman of the* New York Aurora (State College, Pa.: Bald Eagle Press, 1950), 19.

11.   Herman Melville, *Moby-Dick, or, The Whale* (Evanston, Ill.: Northwestern University Press and Newberry Library, 1988), 4.

12.   Herman Melville, *Pierre, or, The Ambiguities* (Evanston, Illinois: Northwestern University Press and Newberry Library, 1971), 240–41.

13.   Lydia Maria Child, *Letters from New-York*, edited by Bruce Mills (Athens: University of Georgia Press, 1998), 9.

14.   SMF, "1st January, 1846," in *Margaret Fuller, Critic,* 325.

15.   SMF to Sarah Shaw, 25 February 1845, in *Letters*, IV, 51.

16.   SMF to Mary Rotch, 15 January 1845, in *Letters*, IV, 45.

17.   Caroline Sturgis Tappan to Ralph Waldo Emerson, 1 August 1850, quoted in *LRWE*, VIII, 256, n95.

18.   SMF to Eugene Fuller, 9 March 1845, in *Letters*, IV, 56.

19.   L. M. Child to Anna Loring, 6 February 1845, in Child, *Selected Letters*, 217–18.

20.   SMF to [?], December 1844, in *Letters*, III, 250.

21.   L. U. Reavis, *A Representative Life of Horace Greeley* (New York: G. W. Carleton, 1872), 83.

22.   SMF to Eugene Fuller, 9 March 1845, in *Letters*, IV, 56.

23.   Beman Brockway, *Fifty Years in Journalism* (Watertown, N.Y.: Daily Times Printing and Publishing House, 1891), 157.

24.   SMF to Caroline Sturgis, 22 August 1847, in *Letters*, IV, 291

25.   SMF to James Nathan, 29 September 1845, in *Letters*, IV, 163.

26.   SMF to [?], 1845, in *Letters*, IV, 40.

27.   SMF, in *MoMFO*, II, 153–54.

28.   Ibid., 154.

29.   SMF, in *MoMFO*, II, 131.

30.   SMF to Richard F. Fuller, 9 January 1845, in *Letters*, IV, 41.

31.   SMF to Richard F. Fuller, 2 March 1845, in *Letters*, IV, 53. Emphasis in original.

32.   SMF to Anna Loring, 2 April 1845, in *Letters*, IV, 66.

33.   SMF to James Nathan, 27 April 1845, in *Letters*, IV, 90.

34. SMF to [?], 1845, in *Letters*, IV, 40.

35. Burrows and Wallace, *Gotham*, 686.

36. SMF to Caroline Sturgis, 13 March 1845, in *Letters*, IV, 59–60.

37. Kenneth Silverman, *Edgar Allan Poe: Mournful and Never-Ending Remembrance* (New York: HarperCollins, 1991), 278–79; Dwight Thomas and David K. Jackson, *The Poe Log: A Documentary Life of Edgar Allan Poe, 1809–1849* (Boston: G. K. Hall, 1987), 620.

38. SMF to Elizabeth Barrett Browning, 6 December 1849, in *Letters*, V, 289.

39. The affair, which involved Frances Sargent Osgood, is addressed in rich detail in Silverman, *Edgar Allan Poe*, 280–93.

40. Edgar Allan Poe, "A Valentine to — — —," in *Poetry and Tales* (New York: Library of America, 1984), 86.

41. Von Mehren, *Minerva and the Muse*, 225.

42. Poe, *The Literati of New York City*, in *Essays and Reviews*, 1180.

43. Michael Paul Rogin, *Subversive Genealogy: The Politics and Art of Herman Melville* (New York: Alfred A. Knopf, 1983), 72.

44. Edward L. Widmer, *Young America: The Flowering of Democracy in New York City* (New York: Oxford University Press, 1999), 107.

45. Robert Hudspeth asserts that Fuller met the Springs at Lynch's party. *Letters*, IV, 49n. Charles Capper makes the case for their having met at the convention. Capper, *Margaret Fuller*, II, 218.

46. H. Greeley, in *MoMFO*, II, 154–55.

47. SMF, "Emerson's Essays," in *Margaret Fuller, Critic*, 1.

48. Ibid., 2.

49. SMF to James Freeman Clarke, 14 August 1845, in *Letters*, VI, 359.

50. Quoted in Capper, *Margaret Fuller*, II, 198.

51. SMF, "Miss Barrett's Poems," in *Margaret Fuller, Critic*, 20; SMF, "[*Review of the Poetical Works of Percy Bysshe Shelley*]," in *Margaret Fuller, Critic*, 318.

52. SMF, "[Review of Nathaniel Hawthorne, *Mosses from an Old Manse*]," in *Margaret Fuller, Critic*, 454.

53. SMF, "Emerson's Essays," in *Margaret Fuller, Critic*, 5.

54. SMF, "[Review of James Russell Lowell, *Conversations on Some of the Old Poets*]," in *Margaret Fuller, Critic*, 35; SMF, "[Review of Henry Wadsworth Longfellow, *Poems*]," in *Margaret Fuller, Critic*, 287.

55. SMF, "American Literature: Its Position in the Present Time, and Prospects for the Future," in *Papers on Literature and Art*, I, 132, 154.

56. Henry Wadsworth Longfellow, *The Letters of Henry Wadsworth Longfellow*, 6 vol. (Cambridge, Mass.: Harvard University Press, 1972), III, 93n.

57. James Russell Lowell, *A Fable for Critics*, in *The Poetical Works of James R. Lowell*, 2 vol. (Boston: Ticknor and Fields, 1858), II, 66–68.

58. SMF, "[Review of Frederick Von Raumer, *America and the American People*]," in *Margaret Fuller, Critic*, 284. Emphasis in original.

59. SMF, "Writers Little Known among Us. Milnes . . . Landor . . . Julius Hare," in *Margaret Fuller, Critic*, 109.

60. SMF, "Emerson's Essays," in *Margaret Fuller, Critic*, 5

61. SMF, "Miss Barrett's Poems," in *Margaret Fuller, Critic*, 22.

62. SMF, "[Review of Henry Wadsworth Longfellow, *Poems*]," in *Margaret Fuller, Critic*, 286.

63. SMF, "French Novelists of the Day: Balzac . . . George Sand . . . Eugene Sue," in *Margaret Fuller, Critic*, 56–57.

64. H. Greeley, in *MoMFO*, II, 155–56.

65. SMF, "French Novelists of the Day," in *Margaret Fuller, Critic*, 56.

66. SMF, "Our City Charities. Visit to Bellevue Alms House, to the Farm School, the Asylum for the Insane, and Penitentiary on Blackwell's Island," in *Margaret Fuller, Critic*, 98.

67. Ibid., 101.

68. SMF, "Our City Charities," in *Margaret Fuller, Critic*, 101–2.

69. Ibid., 102.

70. Ibid.

71. Ibid., 101.

72. Ibid., 102.

73. Ibid., 99.

74. Ibid.; SMF, "Prevalent Idea That Politeness Is Too Great a Luxury to Be Given to the Poor," in *Margaret Fuller, Critic*, 129.

75. SMF, "St. Valentine's Day—Bloomingdale Asylum for the Insane," *New-York Daily Tribune*, 22 February 1845, 2.

76. SMF, "Prevalent Idea," in *Margaret Fuller, Critic*, 130.

77. SMF, "1st January, 1846," in *Margaret Fuller, Critic*, 327.

78. Ibid., 328.

79. Ibid.

80. Ibid., 332.

81. SMF to James Nathan, 22 April 1845, in *Letters*, IV, 85.

82. Capper, *Margaret Fuller*, II, 222.

83. SMF, *Summer on the Lakes*, 94.

84. SMF to James Nathan, 6 April 1845, in *Letters*, IV, 68.

85. SMF to James Nathan, 14 April 1845, in *Letters*, IV, 74.

86. Ibid.

87. SMF to James Nathan, 22 February 1845, in *Letters*, IV, 50.

88. SMF to James Nathan, 1 March [?] 1845, in *Letters*, IV, 52.

89. SMF to James Nathan, 14 April 1845, in *Letters*, IV, 74.

90. SMF to James Nathan, 15 April 1845, in *Letters*, IV, 78.

91. SMF to James Nathan, ca. 7 February 1845, in *Letters*, IV, 47.

92. SMF to James Nathan, 19 March 1845, in *Letters*, IV, 63.

93. SMF to James Nathan, 8 April 1845, in *Letters*, IV, 71.

94. SMF to James Nathan, 19 March 1845, in *Letters*, IV, 63; SMF to James Nathan, 22 February 1845, in *Letters*, IV, 50.

95. SMF to James Nathan, 27 April 1845, in *Letters*, IV, 91.

96. SMF to James Nathan, 24 [?] April [?] 1845, in *Letters*, IV, 87.

97. SMF to James Nathan, 16 [?] April 1845, in *Letters*, IV, 79.

98. Von Mehren, *Minerva and the Muse*, 208–9.

99. SMF to James Nathan, 2 March 1845 [?], in *Letters*, IV, 53.

100. SMF to James Nathan, 9 May 1845, in *Letters*, IV, 98.

101. SMF to James Nathan, 14 April 1845, in *Letters*, IV, 74.

102. SMF to James Nathan, 4 May [?] 1845, in *Letters*, IV, 95. Emphasis in original.

103. SMF to James Nathan, 9 May 1845, in *Letters*, IV, 98; SMF to James Nathan, 31 March 1845, in *Letters*, IV, 65; SMF to James Nathan, 6 April 1845, in *Letters*, IV, 70. One may be sure that Fuller used the word "intercourse" simply to mean interaction, though the reference in a love letter to the interactions of children is sufficiently strange on its own.

104. SMF to James Nathan, 16 April 1845, in *Letters*, IV, 79.

105. SMF to James Nathan, 15 April 1845, in *Letters*, IV, 78.

106. SMF to James Nathan, 9 May 1845, in *Letters*, IV, 98.

107. SMF to James Nathan, 6 April 1845, in *Letters*, IV, 68.

108. Ibid., 69.

109. Ibid.

110. SMF to James Nathan, 9 April 1845, in *Letters*, IV, 72.

111. SMF to James Nathan, 14 April 1845, in *Letters*, IV, 73.

112. Ibid., 76.

113. SMF to James Nathan, 15 April 1845, in *Letters*, IV, 78.

114. SMF to James Nathan, 16 April 1845, in *Letters*, IV, 79.

115. SMF to James Nathan, 19 April 1845, in *Letters*, IV, 83.

116. SMF to James Nathan, 27 April 1845, in *Letters*, IV, 91.

117. Ibid., 91.

118. SMF to James Nathan, 4 May [?] 1845, in *Letters*, IV, 95.

119. SMF to James Nathan, 4 May 1845, in *Letters*, IV, 95–96.

120. SMF to James Nathan, 9 May 1845, in *Letters*, IV, 98.

121. SMF to James Nathan, 26 May 1845, in *Letters*, IV, 108.

122. SMF to James Nathan, 5 June 1845, in *Letters*, IV, 113.

123. SMF to Caroline Sturgis, 10 July 1845, in *Letters*, IV, 132.

124. SMF to James Nathan, 22 July 1845, in *Letters*, IV, 138.

125. Ibid., 137.

126. Ibid.

127. Ibid.

128. SMF to James Nathan, 24 June 1845, in *Letters*, IV, 120.

129. SMF to James Nathan, 22 July 1845, in *Letters*, IV, 138.

130. Ibid., 137.

131. SMF to James Nathan, 31 December 1845, in *Letters*, IV, 178.

132. SMF to James Nathan, ca. 28 February 1846, in *Letters*, IV, 189. Amity Place is now West Third Street.

133. Ibid.

134. Capper, *Margaret Fuller*, II, 271.

135. SMF to Samuel G. and Anna B. Ward, 3 March 1846, in *Letters*, IV, 192.

136. Ibid., 193.

137. Ibid.

138. Dedmond, "Selected Letters of William Ellery Channing the Younger (Part One)," 171.

139. R. Hudspeth, in *Letters*, IV, 216, n3.

140. SMF to Caroline Sturgis, 9 March 1846, in *Letters*, IV, 195.

141. SMF, "A Few Words in Reply to Mr. U. C. Hill," *New-York Daily Tribune*, 15 May 1846, suppl. 1.

142. SMF, "Farewell," in *Life Without and Within, or, Reviews, Narratives, Essays, and Poems* (Boston: Brown, Taggard, and Chase, 1859), 354.

143. SMF, "Farewell," in *Life Without and Within*, 355.

144. R. F. Fuller, *Recollections*, 14.

145. SMF, "Farewell," in *Life Without and Within*, 354.

CHAPTER TEN: INTERNATIONALIST

1. Fuller, *"These Sad But Glorious Days,"* 40.

2. SMF to Margarett Crane Fuller, 16 August 1846, in *Letters*, IV, 225.

3. SMF, *"These Sad But Glorious Days,"* 39.

4.   Ibid., 41.
5.   Ibid.
6.   Ibid., 49.
7.   Ibid., 47.
8.   Ibid., 57.
9.   Ibid., 49–52.
10. Ibid., 52.
11. Ibid., 59.
12. Ibid., 61.
13. Ibid., 68.
14. SMF, *Love-Letters of Margaret Fuller, 1845–1846* (New York: D. Appleton, 1903), 187. Emphasis in original.
15. Fuller, *"These Sad But Glorious Days,"* 69.
16. Ibid., 72.
17. Ibid.
18. Ibid., 73.
19. Ibid., 74. Emphasis in original.
20. Ibid., 74–75.
21. Ibid., 75.
22. Ibid., 76.
23. SMF to Richard F. Fuller, 27 September 1846, in *Letters*, IV, 228. Emphasis in original.
24. SMF, *"These Sad But Glorious Days,"* 77.
25. SMF to Richard F. Fuller, 27 September 1846, in *Letters*, IV, 228.
26. J. Nathan to Margaret Fuller, 6 November 1846, MFFP, X, 113.
27. Ibid. Emphasis in original.
28. J. Nathan to Margaret Fuller, 27 November 1846, MFFP, X, 115.
29. SMF, *"These Sad But Glorious Days,"* 80.
30. Ibid., 79. Emphasis in original.
31. Ibid., 103.
32. Ibid., 88.
33. Joseph Mazzini, *Joseph Mazzini: His Life, Writings, and Political Principles* (New York: Hurd and Houghton, 1872), 222.
34. Bolton King, *Mazzini* (London: J. M. Dent, 1903), 98.
35. SMF, *"These Sad But Glorious Days,"* 99.
36. King, *Mazzini*, 36.
37. Alexander Herzen, *My Past and Thoughts: The Memoirs of Alexander Herzen*, translated by Constance Garnett, abridged by Dwight Macdonald (Berkeley: University of California Press, 1982), 366.
38. King, *Mazzini*, 74.
39. Fuller, *"These Sad But Glorious Days,"* 101.
40. Thomas Carlyle, *The New Letters of Thomas Carlyle*, edited by Alexander Carlyle, 2 vol. (London: John Lane, The Bodley Head, London, 1904), I, 246.
41. Capper, *Margaret Fuller*, II, 298. The story is usually told in pithier, though probably less accurate form. It is more often said that, when James told Carlyle that Fuller had proclaimed, "I accept the Universe," Carlyle's chortling response was, "Gad! She'd better!"
42. SMF, To Ralph Waldo Emerson, 16 November 1846, in *Letters*, IV, 246.
43. James Anthony Froude, *Thomas Carlyle: A History of His Life in London, 1834–1881* (New York: Charles Scribner's Sons, 1884), 342. Emphasis in original.
44. SMF to Ralph Waldo Emerson, 16 November 1846, in *Letters*, IV, 246.

45. Ibid., 248.
46. King, *Mazzini*, 87.
47. SMF to Ralph Waldo Emerson, 16 November 1846, in *Letters*, IV, 248.
48. Ibid., 249.
49. Ibid.
50. King, *Mazzini*, 84.
51. SMF, *"These Sad But Glorious Days,"* 99.
52. C. S. H., "[Fuller at the Italian School, London, in 1846]," in Myerson, ed., *Fuller in Her Own Time*, 74–76.
53. SMF, *"These Sad But Glorious Days,"* 98.
54. Ibid., 93.
55. Ibid., 98.
56. SMF to Caroline Sturgis, 16 [?] November 1846, in *Letters*, IV, 239–40.
57. SMF to Ralph Waldo Emerson, 16 November 1846, in *Letters*, IV, 248.
58. SMF to Caroline Sturgis, 16 [?] November 1846, in *Letters*, IV, 239–41.
59. Ibid., 241.
60. George Henry Lewes, "Retrospects of Actors," *Pall Mall Gazette*, vol. 170, 24 August 1865, 191.
61. SMF, *"These Sad But Glorious Days,"* 104–6.
62. SMF to Caroline Sturgis, 28 November 1846, in *Letters*, IV, 250–52.
63. SMF, *"These Sad But Glorious Days,"* 106.
64. Ibid., 109.
65. Ibid., 119.
66. Ibid., 211.
67. SMF to Mary Howitt, 18 April 1847, in *Letters*, IV, 267.
68. SMF, in *MoMFO*, II, 193.
69. SMF to Elizabeth Hoar, 18 January 1847, in *Letters*, IV, 256.
70. SMF, in *MoMFO*, II, 194.
71. Ibid., 195.
72. SMF to Mary Howitt, 18 April 1847, in *Letters*, IV, 267.
73. SMF, in *MoMFO*, II, 197.
74. Ibid., 195. Italics in original.
75. Ibid., 197.
76. Ibid., 101.
77. Ibid., 196.
78. Ibid., 198.
79. SMF, *"These Sad But Glorious Days,"* 126.
80. Herzen, *My Past and Thoughts*, 343.
81. SMF to Ralph Waldo Emerson, 15 March 1847, in *Letters*, IV, 262.
82. Leopold Wellisz, *The Friendship of Margaret Fuller D'Ossoli and Adam Mickiewicz* (New York: Polish Book Importing, 1947), 12–13.
83. SMF, *"These Sad But Glorious Days,"* 126–127.

CHAPTER ELEVEN: INAMORATA

1. SMF, *"These Sad But Glorious Days,"* 128.
2. Ibid., 127.
3. Ibid., 128.
4. Ibid., 129.
5. Ibid. Emphasis in original.

6. Ibid., 130.
7. Ibid.
8. Ibid., 131.
9. Ibid., 155.
10. Ibid., 158.
11. Ibid., 157.
12. Thomas Carlyle, *Past and Present and Chartism* (New York: George P. Putnam, 1848), 142.
13. SMF, *"These Sad But Glorious Days,"* 136.
14. Johann Wolfgang von Goethe, *Italian Journey,* translated by Robert R. Heitner (Princeton, N.J.: Princeton University Press, 1994), 107. Emphasis in original.
15. Henry Adams, *The Education of Henry Adams: An Autobiography* (Boston: Houghton Mifflin, 1918), 90.
16. Ibid., 168.
17. Ibid., 132.
18. Ibid., 168.
19. William W. Story, *Roba di Roma,* 7th ed. (Philadelphia: J. B. Lippincott, n.d.), 174.
20. Joseph Jay Deiss, *The Roman Years of Margaret Fuller* (New York: Thomas Y. Crowell Company, 1969), 48.
21. SMF, *"These Sad But Glorious Days,"* 135–36.
22. Ibid., 134.
23. SMF to Thomas Hicks, 23 April 1847, in *Letters,* IV, 269.
24. T. Hicks to Margaret Fuller, 4 May 1847, quoted in *Letters,* IV, 271n.
25. SMF, *"These Sad But Glorious Days,"* 187.
26. Ibid., 184.
27. Ibid., 185–86.
28. Ibid., 203.
29. Ibid., 204–5.
30. Ibid., 136.
31. Ibid., 172.
32. SMF to Richard F. Fuller, 1 July 1847, in *Letters,* IV, 277.
33. SMF, *"These Sad But Glorious Days,"* 143.
34. Donald Yannella and Kathleen Malone Yannella, "Evert A. Duyckinck's 'Diary: May 29—November 8, 1847,'" *Studies in the American Renaissance* (1978), 207–58, 225.
35. Von Mehren, *Minerva and the Muse,* 256.
36. Emelyn Story, "The Private Marriage," quoted in Myerson, ed., *Fuller in Her Own Time,* 82.
37. SMF to Marcus and Rebecca Spring, 10 April 1847, in *Letters,* IV, 263.
38. SMF to Ellen Fuller Channing, 11 December 1849, in *Letters,* V, 292.
39. G. W. Curtis to William W. Story, 26 November 1849, Story Family Papers, University of Texas, Austin.
40. SMF, *"These Sad But Glorious Days,"* 140–41.
41. Ibid.
42. Ibid., 142.
43. SMF to Richard F. Fuller, 1 July 1847, in *Letters,* IV, 278.
44. SMF, *"These Sad But Glorious Days,"* 142.
45. Ibid., 143.
46. Ibid., 144.

47. SMF to Richard F. Fuller, late July 1847, in *Letters*, IV, 284.
48. SMF, *"These Sad But Glorious Days,"* 144.
49. Ibid., 145.
50. SMF to Caroline Sturgis Tappan, 11 January 1848, in *Letters*, V, 42.
51. SMF to Caroline Sturgis, 22 August 1847, in *Letters*, IV, 291.
52. Ibid.
53. SMF to Margarett C. Fuller, 16 October 1847, in *Letters*, IV, 300.
54. SMF to Marcus Spring, 9 August 1847, in *Letters*, IV, 286.
55. SMF, *"These Sad But Glorious Days,"* 146.
56. Ibid., 148.
57. SMF to [?], 22 [?] August 1847, in *Letters*, IV, 288.
58. SMF to Caroline Sturgis, 22 August 1847, in *Letters*, IV, 291.
59. Quoted in Capper, *Margaret Fuller*, II, 340.
60. SMF, *"These Sad But Glorious Days,"* 153–54. Emphasis in original.
61. SMF, To Richard F. Fuller, 25 September 1847, in *Letters*, IV, 295.
62. SMF, *"These Sad But Glorious Days,"* 160.
63. SMF to Margarett C. Fuller, 16 October 1847, in *Letters*, IV, 299.
64. SMF, *"These Sad But Glorious Days,"* 168.
65. SMF to Margarett C. Fuller, 16 October 1847, in *Letters*, IV, 302.
66. E. Story, "Private Marriage," quoted in Myerson, ed., *Fuller in Her Own Time*, 81.
67. SMF, *"These Sad But Glorious Days,"* 172.
68. SMF to Margarett C. Fuller, 16 October 1847, in *Letters*, IV, 301.
69. SMF, *"These Sad But Glorious Days,"* 160.
70. Ibid., 165.
71. SMF to Ralph Waldo Emerson, 28 October 1847, in *Letters*, IV, 309.
72. SMF to Arthur Hugh Clough, 16 February 1850, in *Letters*, VI, 65.
73. A. Mickiewicz to Margaret Fuller, 26 April 1847, in Wellisz, *Friendship*, 20.
74. A. Mickiewicz to Margaret Fuller, 3 August 1847, in Wellisz, *Friendship*, 23–24.
75. SMF, To Ellen Fuller Channing, 11 December 1849, in *Letters*, V, 292.
76. SMF to Marcus Spring, 1 February 1848, in *Letters*, VI, 372.
77. SMF, *"These Sad But Glorious Days,"* 206.
78. SMF to Richard F. Fuller, 1 January 1848, in *Letters*, V, 39.
79. SMF to Richard F. Fuller, 1 January 1848, in *Letters*, V, 40.
80. SMF to Caroline Sturgis Tappan, 11 January 1848, in *Letters*, V, 43.
81. SMF to Caroline Sturgis Tappan, 11 January 1848, in *Letters*, V, 43.

CHAPTER TWELVE: REVOLUTIONARY

1. SMF, *"These Sad But Glorious Days,"* 179.
2. Ibid.
3. SMF to Caroline Sturgis Tappan, 11–12 January 1848, in *Letters*, V, 44.
4. SMF to Arthur Hugh Clough, 16 February 1850, in *Letters*, VI, 65
5. SMF to Costanza Arconati Visconti, 16 October 1849, in *Letters*, V, 269.
6. E. Story, "Private Marriage, " quoted in Myerson, ed., *Fuller in Her Own Time*, 87.
7. Joan von Mehren, "Establishing the Facts on the Ossoli Family: An Experiment in E-Mail Research," *Margaret Fuller Society Newsletter* (Winter 2001). The wording of the certificate has been translated by Dr. Robert Colzi.

8.   G. A. Ossoli to Margaret Fuller Ossoli, 3 April 1849, in *Letters*, V, 224, n1.
9.   SMF to Giovanni Angelo Ossoli, 4 April 1849, in *Letters*, V, 223.
10. Joseph Jay Deiss has argued that, in their letters of April 3–4, 1849, the couple were alluding to the *two-year* anniversary of their first meeting at Saint Peter's. Deiss, *Roman Years*, 215. This supposition is very likely in error, even as to the underlying matter of fact. April 4, 1847, was Easter Sunday. Fuller wrote of going to Saint Peter's that year during "Holy Week," a curious way to phrase the matter if she had gone precisely on Easter. SMF, *"These Sad But Glorious Days,"* 135. The scrupulously reliable Charles Capper states without equivocation that Fuller's first encounter with Ossoli took place on April 1. Capper, *Margaret Fuller*, II, 331.
11. SMF to William H. Channing, late July 1849, in *Letters*, V, 248.
12. SMF, *Woman in the Nineteenth Century*, 69.
13. SMF to Giovanni Angelo Ossoli, 10 September 1848, in *Letters*, V, 112.
14. SMF, *"These Sad But Glorious Days,"* 187–88.
15. Ibid., 157.
16. Ibid., 189.
17. Ibid., 197.
18. Ibid., 212.
19. SMF to Richard F. Fuller, 17 March 1848, in *Letters*, V, 57.
20. SMF, *"These Sad But Glorious Days,"* 209.
21. Ibid., 211.
22. Ibid., 210–11.
23. Ibid., 216.
24. Ibid.
25. SMF to William H. Channing, 29 March 1848, in *Letters*, V, 58–59.
26. SMF, *"These Sad But Glorious Days,"* 216.
27. Ibid., 211.
28. Ibid., 225.
29. "Allocution of His Holiness Pope Pius IX, delivered in the Secret Consistory of April 19, 1848," in Luigi Carlo Farini, *The Roman State: From 1815 to 1850*, 4 vol. (London: John Murray, 1851), II, 110.
30. SMF, *"These Sad But Glorious Days,"* 228–29.
31. Ibid., 225.
32. SMF to Elizabeth de Windt Cranch, 14 May 1848, in *Letters*, V, 65.
33. SMF, *"These Sad But Glorious Days,"* 230; R. W. Emerson to Margaret Fuller, 25 April 1848, in *LRWE*, IV, 61.
34. SMF, *"These Sad But Glorious Days,"* 230.
35. SMF to Costanza Arconati Visconti, 27 May 1848, in *Letters*, V, 69.
36. SMF to Thomas Hicks, 17 May 1848, in *Letters*, V, 66.
37. SMF to Richard F. Fuller, 20 May 1848, in *Letters*, V, 68.
38. A. B. Fuller to Eugene Fuller, 11 April 1847, MFFP, XIII, 138.
39. SMF to Mary Rotch, 29 May 1848, in *Letters*, V, 71.
40. SMF to [?], in *Letters*, V, 101.
41. SMF to Costanza Arconati Visconti, 22 June 1848, in *Letters*, V, 73.
42. SMF to Charles King Newcomb, 22 June 1848, in *Letters*, V, 77.
43. SMF to Emelyn Story, 22 June 1848, in *Letters*, V, 74.
44. SMF to Ralph Waldo Emerson, 11 July 1848, in *Letters*, V, 86.
45. SMF to Giovanni Angelo Ossoli, 27 June 1848, in *Letters*, V, 79.
46. Ibid.; SMF to Giovanni Angelo Ossoli, 13 July 1848, in *Letters*, V, 88.

47. SMF to Costanza Arconati Visconti. 22 June 1848, in *Letters*, V, 73; SMF to Emelyn Story, 22 June 1848, in *Letters*, V, 74.

48. SMF to Emelyn Story, 22 June 1848, in *Letters*, V, 74.

49. SMF to Richard F. Fuller, 16 August 1848, in *Letters*, V, 103.

50. SMF to [?], ca. 15 August 1848, in *Letters*, V, 101.

51. SMF to Richard F. Fuller, 16 August 1848, in *Letters*, V, 104.

52. SMF, *"These Sad But Glorious Days,"* 237.

53. G. A. Ossoli to Margaret Fuller, 17 August 1848, MFFP, XVI, 118–19.

54. SMF to Giovanni Angelo Ossoli, 18 August 1848, in *Letters*, V, 107.

55. SMF to Giovanni Angelo Ossoli, 22 August 1848, in *Letters*, V, 109.

56. SMF to Giovanni Angelo Ossoli, 11 October 1848, in *Letters*, V, 128.

57. SMF to Giovanni Angelo Ossoli, 18 October 1848, in *Letters*, V, 134.

58. SMF to Giovanni Angelo Ossoli, 22 August 1848, in *Letters*, V, 109.

59. SMF to Giovanni Angelo Ossoli, 17 September 1848, in *Letters*, V, 117.

60. SMF to Caroline Sturgis Tappan, 16 March 1849, in *Letters*, V, 209.

61. G. A. Ossoli, quoted in *MoMFO*, II, 299.

62. SMF to Giovanni Angelo Ossoli, 26 September 1848, in *Letters*, V, 123.

63. SMF to Giovanni Angelo Ossoli, 19 September 1848, in *Letters*, V, 118.

64. SMF to Giovanni Angelo Ossoli, 20 October 1848, in *Letters*, V, 135.

65. SMF to Giovanni Angelo Ossoli, 15 October 1848, in *Letters*, V, 131.

66. SMF to Giovanni Angelo Ossoli, 18 October 1848, in *Letters*, V, 134.

67. SMF to Giovanni Angelo Ossoli, 15 October 1848, in *Letters*, V, 131.

68. SMF to Margarett Crane Fuller, 16 November 1848, in *Letters*, V, 109.

69. SMF, *"These Sad But Glorious Days,"* 241.

70. Ibid., 242.

71. Ibid., 244.

72. SMF to [?], 23 November 1848, in *Letters*, V, 153.

73. SMF, *"These Sad But Glorious Days,"* 245.

74. SMF to Jane Tuckerman King, January 1849, in *Letters*, V, 168.

75. SMF, *"These Sad But Glorious Days,"* 245. Emphasis in original.

76. SMF to Marcus Spring, 9 March 1849, in *Letters*, V, 201.

77. SMF to Marcus Spring, 23 November 1848, in *Letters*, V, 152.

78. SMF to Giovanni Angelo Ossoli, 22 December 1848, in *Letters*, V, 164.

79. SMF to Giovanni Angelo Ossoli, 22 December 1848, in *Letters*, V, 164–65.

80. SMF to Caroline Sturgis Tappan, 16 March 1849, in *Letters*, V, 209.

81. SMF to Giovanni Angelo Ossoli, 22 December 1848, in *Letters*, V, 164.

82. SMF to Caroline Sturgis Tappan, 16 March 1849, in *Letters*, V, 209.

83. SMF to Giovanni Angelo Ossoli, 27 December 1848, in *Letters*, V, 167.

84. SMF to Anna Barker Ward, 18 March 1849, in *Letters*, V, 217.

85. Leona Rostenberg, "Margaret Fuller's Roman Diary," *Journal of Modern History* 12, no. 2 (June 1940), 209–20, 211.

86. Ibid.

87. Ibid., 213.

88. Ibid., 216.

89. SMF, *"These Sad But Glorious Days,"* 256.

90. Rostenberg, "Margaret Fuller's Roman Diary," 217.

91. Ibid., 219.

92. SMF to Marcus Spring, 9 March 1849, in *Letters*, V, 201; SMF to Caroline Sturgis Tappan, 16 March 1849, in *Letters*, V, 210.

93. SMF to Marcus Spring, 9 March 1849, in *Letters*, V, 201.

94. SMF, *"These Sad But Glorious Days,"* 263.

95. Ibid., 259.

96. SMF to Richard F. Fuller, 17 March 1849, in *Letters,* V, 213.

97. SMF to Sarah Ann Clarke, 18 January 1849, in *Letters,* V, 171.

98. SMF to Richard F. Fuller, 19 January 1849, in *Letters,* V, 180.

99. SMF to Ralph Waldo Emerson, 21 January 1849, in *Letters,* V, 187; SMF to Emelyn Story, 7 January 1849, in *Letters,* V, 169; SMF to Ellen Fuller Channing, 13 March 1849, in *Letters,* V, 207.

100. SMF to Caroline Sturgis Tappan, 16 March 1849, in *Letters,* V, 209.

101. SMF to Ralph Waldo Emerson, 11 July 1848, in *Letters,* V, 86.

102. SMF to Caroline Sturgis Tappan, 8 March 1849, in *Letters,* V, 199.

103. SMF to William Henry Channing, 10 March 1849, in *Letters,* V, 205–6.

104. SMF to Anna Barker Ward, 18 March 1849, in *Letters,* V, 216.

105. SMF to Margarett C. Fuller, 16 November 1848, in *Letters,* V, 145. Emphasis in original.

106. SMF to William Henry Channing, 10 March 1849, in *Letters,* V, 205; SMF to Caroline Sturgis Tappan, 16 March 1849, in *Letters,* V, 210.

107. SMF to Giovanni Angelo Ossoli, 30 March 1849, in *Letters,* V, 220.

108. Ibid.

109. G. A. Ossoli to Margaret Fuller, 31 March 1849, MMFP, Works, II, 79.

110. SMF to Giovanni Angelo Ossoli, 4 April 1849, in *Letters,* V, 223.

111. Meg McGavran Murray has observed that, to some degree, Fuller was reenacting the abandonment she may have felt as a child when her father was in Washington and her mother was busied with caring for Fuller's younger siblings. Note to the author, 14 February 2011.

112. Capper, *Margaret Fuller,* II, 435.

113. Rostenberg, "Margaret Fuller's Roman Diary," 220.

114. L. Cass Jr. to Ellen Fuller Channing, 10 May 1851, MFFP, Works, I, 669–71.

115. SMF, *"These Sad But Glorious Days,"* 274.

116. Ibid., 275.

117. Ibid.

118. Rostenberg, "Margaret Fuller's Roman Diary," 220.

119. L. Cass Jr. to Ellen Fuller Channing, 10 May 1851, MFFP, Works, I, 673.

120. SMF to Richard F. Fuller, 22 May 1849, in *Letters,* V, 229.

121. Herman Melville, "Shiloh, A Requiem," in *Battle-Pieces and Aspects of the War* (New York: Harper Brothers, 1866), 63.

122. SMF, *"These Sad But Glorious Days,"* 276.

123. SMF to Richard F. Fuller, 22 May 1849, in *Letters,* V, 229–30.

124. Deiss, *Roman Years,* 254.

125. Ibid., 255.

126. SMF to Emelyn Story, 6 June 1849, in *Letters,* V, 238.

127. SMF, *"These Sad But Glorious Days,"* 292.

128. SMF to Ralph Waldo Emerson, 10 June 1849, in *Letters,* V, 239.

129. Lewis Cass Jr. to Ellen Fuller Channing, 10 May 1851, MFFP, Works, I, 673.

130. SMF to Ralph Waldo Emerson, 10 June 1849, in *Letters,* V, 239.

131. SMF, *"These Sad But Glorious Days,"* 292.

132. Emelyn Story, in *MoMFO,* II, 286.

133. SMF to Ralph Waldo Emerson, 10 June 1849, in *Letters,* V, 240.

134. SMF to Emelyn Story, 6 June 1849, in *Letters,* V, 238.

135. SMF to Ralph Waldo Emerson, 10 June 1849, in *Letters,* V, 239.

136. G. Mazzini to Emilie Hawkes, 7 July 1849, in Mazzini, *Joseph Mazzini*, 140.
137. SMF, *"These Sad But Glorious Days,"* 294.
138. Ibid., 292–94.
139. Ibid., 300.
140. Ibid., 299.
141. Ibid., 294.
142. G. Mazzini to George Sand, 28 June 1849, quoted in R. B. Mowat, *The States of Europe, 1815–1871: A Study of Their Democratic Development* (New York: Longmans, Green, 1932), 315.
143. SMF, *"These Sad But Glorious Days,"* 303.
144. Lewis Cass Jr. to Ellen Fuller Channing, 10 May 1851, MFFP, Works, I, 675–77.
145. G. Mazzini to Margaret Fuller, 3 July 1849, MFFP, XI, 108.
146. William L. Vance, *America's Rome*, 2 vol. (New Haven: Yale University Press, 1989), II, 106.
147. SMF, *"These Sad But Glorious Days,"* 310.
148. SMF to Richard F. Fuller, 8 July 1849, in *Letters*, V, 244.
149. SMF to William Henry Channing, 10 March 1849, in *Letters*, V, 206.
150. SMF, *"These Sad But Glorious Days,"* 307.
151. Ibid., 307–8.
152. Ibid., 308.
153. SMF to Samuel G. and Anna Barker Ward, 21 October 1849, in *Letters*, V, 273.

CHAPTER THIRTEEN: VICTIM

1. SMF to Horace Greeley, 25 August 1849, in *Letters*, V, 257.
2. SMF to William H. Channing, late July [?] 1849, in *Letters*, V, 247.
3. SMF to William H. Channing, 28 August 1849, in *Letters*, V, 258.
4. SMF to William H. Channing, late July [?] 1849, in *Letters*, V, 247.
5. Ibid.
6. SMF to Lewis Cass Jr., 19 July 1849, in *Letters*, V, 245.
7. SMF to Lewis Cass Jr., 30 July 1849, in *Letters*, V, 249.
8. SMF to Horace Greeley, 25 August 1849, in *Letters*, V, 257; SMF to Caroline Sturgis Tappan, 28 August 1849, in *Letters*, V, 258.
9. SMF to Lewis Cass Jr., 30 July 1849, in *Letters*, V, 249.
10. SMF, To Lewis Cass Jr., 19 July 1849, in *Letters*, V, 246.
11. SMF to Horace Greeley, 25 August 1849, in *Letters*, V, 257.
12. SMF, *"These Sad But Glorious Days,"* 313.
13. SMF to Horace Greeley, 25 August 1849, in *Letters*, V, 257.
14. SMF to Margarett Crane Fuller, 31 August 1849, in *Letters*, V, 260.
15. Ibid., 261.
16. SMF, in *MoMFO*, II, 303.
17. SMF to Margarett Crane Fuller, 31 August 1849, in *Letters*, V, 260.
18. Ibid., 261.
19. SMF to Lewis Cass Jr., 13 August 1849, in *Letters*, V, 254.
20. SMF to Margarett Crane Fuller, 31 August 1849, in *Letters*, V, 261.
21. SMF to Samuel G. and Anna Barker Ward, 21 October 1849, in *Letters*, V, 274.
22. SMF to William Wetmore Story, 9 December 1848, in *Letters*, V, 161.
23. SMF to Lewis Cass Jr., 5 March 1850, in *Letters*, VI, 70.
24. SMF to Lewis Cass Jr., 30 September 1849, in *Letters*, V, 265.
25. Ibid.; SMF to Lewis Cass Jr., 8 October 1849, in *Letters*, V, 268.

26. SMF to Arthur Hugh Clough, 16 February 1850, in *Letters*, VI, 64.

27. Henry James, *Italian Hours* (New York: Penguin Books, 1995), 269.

28. SMF to Lewis Cass Jr., 8 October 1849, in *Letters*, V, 268.

29. SMF to Caroline Sturgis Tappan, ca. 17 December 1849, in *Letters*, V, 305.

30. SMF, *"These Sad But Glorious Days,"* 317.

31. Ibid., 320.

32. Ibid., 321.

33. Ibid., 322–23.

34. SMF to William Henry Channing, 17 December 1849, in *Letters*, V, 301.

35. SMF to Richard F. Fuller, 17 March 1849, in *Letters*, V, 213.

36. SMF to [?], in *Letters*, V, 265–66; SMF to Margarett Crane Fuller, 6 February 1850, in *Letters*, VI, 58; SMF to Lewis Cass Jr., 5 March 1850, in *Letters*, VI, 69.

37. SMF to Marcus and Rebecca Spring, 5 February 1850, in *Letters*, VI, 54.

38. SMF to Margarett Crane Fuller, 6 February 1850, in *Letters*, VI, 60.

39. SMF to Costanza Arconati Visconti, 16 October 1849, in *Letters*, V, 269; SMF to [?], 29 November 1849, in *Letters*, V, 283.

40. SMF to Arthur Hugh Clough, 16 February 1850, in *Letters*, VI, 64.

41. SMF to Emelyn Story, 16 April 1850, in *Letters*, VI, 77.

42. William Henry Hurlbert, "[Fuller in Florence in 1850]", in Myerson, ed., *Fuller in Her Own Time*, 96.

43. SMF to Caroline Sturgis Tappan, ca. December 1849, in *Letters*, V, 306; SMF to Emelyn Story, 15 February 1850, in *Letters*, VI, 61.

44. SMF to Margarett Crane Fuller, 15 December [?] 1849, in *Letters*, V, 299.

45. SMF to Margarett Crane Fuller, 6 February 1850, in *Letters*, VI, 58.

46. SMF to George W. Curtis, 25 October 1849, in *Letters*, V, 277.

47. SMF to Margarett Crane Fuller, 6 February 1850, in *Letters*, VI, 58.

48. Ibid., 60.

49. SMF, in *MoMFO*, II, 311.

50. Elizabeth Barrett Browning to Arabella Barrett, 15–16 April 1850, in *The Letters of Elizabeth Barrett Browning and Her Sister Arabella*, edited by Scott Lewis, 2 vol. (Waco, Tex.: Wedgestone Press, 2002), I, 309.

51. Elizabeth Barrett Browning to Mary Russell Mitford, 1 December 1849, in *The Letters of Elizabeth Barrett Browning* (New York: Macmillan, 1899), 428.

52. SMF to William H. Channing, 17 December 1849, in *Letters*, V, 301.

53. Myerson, "Caroline Dall's Reminiscences," 427.

54. Frederick William Gale, "[Fuller in Rome [*sic*] in 1849]," in Myerson, ed., *Fuller in Her Own Time*, 93.

55. George William Curtis, "Editor's Easy Chair," *Harper's New Monthly Magazine* 68 (March 1884), 640–41, 641.

56. SMF to William H. Channing, Spring 1850, in *Letters*, VI, 70.

57. SMF to Samuel G. and Anna B. Ward, 8 January 1850, in *Letters*, VI, 47.

58. SMF to Marcus and Rebecca Spring, 5 February 1850, in *Letters*, VI, 55.

59. Elizabeth Barrett Browning to Mary Russell Mitford, 24 September 1850, in *Letters of Elizabeth Barrett Browning*, 460.

60. SMF to March and Rebecca Spring, 5 February 1850, in *Letters*, VI, 55.

61. SMF to Arthur Hugh Clough, 16 February 1850, in *Letters*, VI, 63–64.

62. SMF to Emelyn Story, 15 February 1850, in *Letters*, VI, 61.

63. SMF to [?], ca. February 1850, in *Letters*, VI, 51.

64. SMF to Samuel G. and Anna B. Ward, 8 January 1850, in *Letters*, VI, 48.

65. SMF to Margarett Crane Fuller, 6 February 1850, in *Letters*, VI, 60.

66. SMF to Arthur Hugh Clough, 16 February 1850, in *Letters*, VI, 64.

67. SMF to Margarett Crane Fuller, 6 February 1850, in *Letters*, VI, 60.

68. R. W. Emerson to Margaret Fuller Ossoli, 11 April 1850, in *LRWE*, IV, 199.

69. Rebecca Spring to Margaret Fuller, 14 April 1850, MFFP, XI, 136.

70. Marcus Spring to Margaret Fuller, 17 April 1850, MFFP, XI, 136.

71. Lydia Maria Child to Louisa Gilman Loring, 21 October 1849, in *Selected Letters*, 250.

72. SMF to Caroline Sturgis Tappan, ca. 17 December 1849, in *Letters*, 303.

73. SMF, To Costanza Arconati Visconti, 12 April 1850, in *Letters*, VI, 75.

74. SMF, To Costanza Arconati Visconti, 6 April 1850, in *Letters*, VI. 74.

75. SMF to William H. Channing, Spring 1850, in *Letters*, VI, 70.

76. SMF to William H. Channing, 6 February 1850, in *Letters*, VI, 57.

77. SMF to William H. Channing, Spring 1850, in *Letters*, VI, 70.

78. SMF to Costanza Arconati Visconti, 12 April 1850, in *Letters*, VI. 75.

79. SMF to Marcus Spring, 3 June 1850, in *Letters*, VI, 89.

80. SMF to Emelyn Story, 16 April 1850, in *Letters*, VI, 76.

81. SMF to Samuel G. and Anna B. Ward, 8 January 1850, in *Letters*, VI, 48.

82. SMF to Marcus and Rebecca Buffum Spring, 12 December 1849, in *Letters*, V, 296.

83. Murray, *Margaret Fuller, Wandering Pilgrim*, 404.

84. SMF to Lewis Cass Jr., 2 May 1850, in *Letters*, VI, 83.

85. SMF to Marcus Spring, 3 June 1850, in *Letters*, VI, 89.

86. C. F. Hasty to Margarett Crane Fuller, 2 September 1850, quoted in Capper, *Margaret Fuller*, II, 504.

87. SMF to Marcus Spring, 3 June 1850, in *Letters*, VI, 89.

88. Ibid., 90.

89. SMF to Samuel and Hannah Fogg Thompson, 3 [?] June 1850, in *Letters*, VI, 91.

90. SMF to Marcus Spring, 3 June 1850, in *Letters*, VI, 89.

91. Ibid., 90.

92. Ibid.

93. Elizabeth Hoar to Caroline Sturgis Tappan, 3 September 1850, Boston Public Library, Department of Rare Books and Manuscripts.

94. Ibid.

95. Ibid.

96. Capper, *Margaret Fuller*, II, 505.

97. David M. Ludlum, *Early American Hurricanes: 1492–1870* (Boston: American Meteorological Society, 1963).

98. Ibid.; http://en.wikipedia.org/wiki/List_of_New_York_hurricanes (accessed 3 May 2011).

99. John Rousmaniere, *After the Storm: True Stories of Disaster and Recovery at Sea* (Camden, Maine: International Marine / McGraw-Hill, 2002), 45–46.

100. H. D. Thoreau, "H. Thoreau's Notes," Boston Public Library, Department of Rare Books and Manuscripts.

101. W. H. Channing, quoted in Capper, *Margaret Fuller*, II, 507.

102. William H. Channing, in *MoMFO*, II, 342.

103. Ibid., 342–43.

104. Ibid., 343.

105. Ibid.

106. Ibid., 344–45.

107. Ibid., 345.

108. Ibid., 345–46.

109. Ibid., 346.

110. SMF to Lewis Cass Jr., 5 March 1850, in *Letters*, VI, 69.

111. SMF to Emelyn Story, 16 April 1850, in *Letters*, VI, 77. Emphasis in original.

112. William H. Channing, in *MoMFO*, II, 347.

113. H. D. Thoreau, "H. Thoreau's Notes," Boston Public Library, Department of Rare Books and Manuscripts.

114. Capper, *Margaret Fuller*, II, 510.

115. William H. Channing, in *MoMFO*, II, 348.

116. Ibid., 348–49.

117. Accounts differ as to whether the deaths of Ossoli and the maid preceded Fuller's. The carpenter, John Helstrom, was "very sure" that Fuller drowned before her husband and son. Capper, *Margaret Fuller*, II, 512.

118. Anonymous, "From the Wreck on Fire Island," *New-York Daily Tribune*, 24 July 1850, 4.

119. R. W. Emerson to Horace Greeley, 23 July 1850, in *LRWE*, IV, 219.

120. H. D. Thoreau to H. G. O. Blake, 9 August 1850, *The Writings of Henry David Thoreau*, edited by Franklin B. Sanborn, 20 vol. (New York: AMS Press, 1968), VI, 186.

EPILOGUE: MARGARET-GHOST

1. Henry James, *A Small Boy and Others* (New York: Charles Scribner's Sons, 1913), 61.

2. R. W. Emerson, *Journals and Miscellaneous Notebooks*, XI, 256.

3. Ibid., 257.

4. Ibid., 258.

5. Richardson, *Emerson*, 486.

6. Quoted in Henry James, *William Wetmore Story and His Friends from Letters, Diaries and Recollections*, 2 vol. (Boston: Houghton, Mifflin, 1904), I, 259.

7. Quoted in R. W. Emerson, *Journals and Miscellaneous Notebooks*, XI, 259.

8. L. J. Emerson to Mary Moody Emerson, 11 August 1850, in *Selected Letters of Lidian Jackson Emerson*, 173.

9. R. W. Emerson, *Journals and Miscellaneous Notebooks*, XI, 259.

10. Ibid., XIII, 139.

11. Ibid., XI, 256–57.

12. Ibid., XI, 297.

13. Von Mehren, *Minerva and the Muse*, 340–42.

14. R. W. Emerson to William Wetmore Story, 13 September 1851, in *LRWE*, IV, 258.

15. H. Greeley to Ralph Waldo Emerson, 27 July 1850, in *LRWE*, IV, 225.

16. R. W. Emerson, *Journals and Miscellaneous Notebooks*, XI, 488.

17. R. W. Emerson to Samuel Gray Ward, 23 September 1850, in *LRWE*, IV, 231.

18. R. W. Emerson to Samuel Gray Ward, 16 September 1850, in *LRWE*, IV, 229.

19. R. W. Emerson to Samuel Gray Ward, 7 September 1850, in *LRWE*, IV, 228.

20. J. F. Clarke in *MoMFO*, 61.

21. Staël, *Corinne*, 27.

22. Ibid., 61, 97.

23. S. M. Fuller to Marcus and Rebecca Buffum Spring, 12 December 1849, in *Letters*, V, 296.

24. J. F. Clarke, in *MoMFO*, I, 132, 133.

25. Ibid., 133.
26. Ibid., 138. The friend is anonymous in Clarke's recounting. Charles Capper and Meg McGavran Murray identify her as Farrar. Capper, *Margaret Fuller*, I, 112–13; Murray, *Margaret Fuller, Wandering Pilgrim*, 68.
27. J. F. Clarke in *MoMFO*, 138.
28. Ibid.
29. Ibid., 139.
30. Ibid., 139–42.
31. Ibid, 133.
32. Ibid., 134.
33. R. W. Emerson, "Montaigne; or, The Skeptic," in *Representative Men* in *Essays and Lectures*, 690.
34. R. W. Emerson in *MoMFO*, I, 237.
35. Ibid., 203.
36. Ibid., 291.
37. Ibid., 298.
38. Ibid., 299.
39. Ibid., 300.
40. M. C. Fuller to Richard F. Fuller, 19 February 1852, MFFP, VIII, 157. Still, Mrs. Fuller was grateful that *Memoirs* as a whole had brought back a portion of her past life, and she blessed God that Margaret had been given to her. Ibid.
41. W. H. Channing, in *MoMFO*, II, 100.
42. Ibid., 37.
43. Ibid.
44. SMF in ibid., 103, 39, 11.
45. Ibid., 101.
46. Ibid., 290.
47. A. B. Fuller, "Preface," in *MoMFO* (1859 ed.), I, 4.
48. R. F. Fuller, *Recollections*, 25, 18.
49. S. J. B. Hale, *Woman's Record*, 666–67.
50. H. Adams, *Education of Henry Adams*, 384.
51. "Appendix: Thomas Fuller and His Descendants," in *MoMFO* (1859 ed.), I, 368.
52. Ibid, I, 367.
53. Ibid.
54. Thomas Cushing, *Memorials of the Class of 1834 of Harvard College, Prepared for the Fiftieth Anniversary of Their Graduation* (Boston: David Clapp, 1884), 20.
55. R. F. Fuller, "Appendix: Memorial of Mrs. Margaret Fuller," in *MoMFO* (1859 ed.), I, 383.
56. Ibid.
57. Ibid., 385.
58. Ibid.
59. Ibid., 384.
60. Francis Augustin O'Reilly, *The Fredericksburg Campaign: Winter War on the Rappahannock* (Baton Rouge: Louisiana State University Press, 2003), 89.
61. Inez Cunningham, "Fuller's Dymaxion House on Display," *Chicago Evening Post Magazine of the Art World*, 16 May 1930, 10.
62. R. F. Fuller, *Visions in Verse, or, Dreams of Creation and Redemption* (Boston: Lee and Shepard, 1864), 3.
63. Ibid., 84.
64. Henry James, *Notes of a Son and Brother* (New York: Charles Scribner's Sons, 1914), 213.

65. Ibid.
66. R. W. Emerson to Anna Barker Ward, 5 May 1859, in *LRWE*, V, 143n.
67. Henry James, *Hawthorne* (New York: Harper and Brothers, 1899), 77.
68. Claudia Stokes, *Writers in Retrospect: The Rise of American Literary History, 1875–1910* (Chapel Hill: University of North Carolina Press, 2006), 131. Stokes's examination, while valuable, underestimates the significance and influence of Fuller's conversations.
69. Barrett Wendell, *A Literary History of America* (New York: Charles Scribner's Sons, 1900), 300.
70. Vernon Parrington, *The Romantic Revolution in America, 1800–1860* (New York: Harcourt Brace, 1927), 428.
71. Ibid.
72. James, *William Wetmore Story*, I, 127.
73. Ibid.
74. Ibid.
75. Ibid., 128.
76. Ibid., 128–29.
77. Ibid., 130.
78. Ibid., 131.
79. Holmes, "Cinders from Ashes," 116.
80. Ednah Dow Cheney, *Reminiscences* (Boston: Lee and Shepard, 1902), 205.
81. Barbara Ozieblo, *Susan Glaspell: A Critical Biography* (Chapel Hill: University of North Carolina Press, 2000), 23.
82. Von Mehren, *Minerva and the Muse*, 339.
83. For much of this paragraph, I gratefully acknowledge a debt to Daniel McKanan and his paper, "Margaret Fuller and 1848: Forging a United Radical Tradition," delivered at the Arlington Street Church, Boston, Mass., 7 November 2010.

ADDITIONAL SOURCES

Alcott, A. Bronson. *Concord Days.* Boston: Roberts Brothers, 1872.

Coleridge, Samuel Taylor. *The Collected Letters of Samuel Taylor Coleridge.* Edited by Earl Leslie Griggs. Oxford: Clarendon Press, 1956.

Dedmond, Francis B. "The Selected Letters of William Ellery Channing the Younger (Part Two)." *Studies in the American Renaissance* (1990), 159–241.

Kelley, Mary, ed. *The Portable Margaret Fuller.* New York : Penguin Books, 1994.

Lester, Charles Edwards. *My Consulship.* New York: Cornish, Lamport, 1853.

Nichols, Thomas Low. *Forty Years of American Life.* London: John Maxwell, 1864.

Ossoli, Margaret Fuller. *At Home and Abroad, or, Things and Thoughts in America and Europe.* Edited by Arthur B. Fuller. Boston: Crosby, Nichols, 1856.

Smith, Denis Mack. *The Making of Italy. 1796–1866.* New York: Holmes and Meier, 1988.

———. *Mazzini.* New Haven, Conn.: Yale University Press, 1994.

Steele, Jeffrey, ed. The Essential Margaret Fuller. New Brunswick, N.J.: Rutgers University Press, 1992.

Story, Emelyn. "The Private Marriage." Margaret Fuller Ossoli Collection, Boston Public Library.

Trilling, Lionel. *The Liberal Imagination: Essays on Literature and Society.* New York: NYRB Classics, 2008.

Vance, William L. *America's Rome*, vol. I: *Classical Rome.* New Haven, Conn.: Yale University Press, 1989.

———. *America's Rome*, vol. II: *Catholic and Contemporary Rome.* New Haven, Conn.: Yale University Press, 1989.

Whiting, Lilian. *The Florence of Landor.* Boston: Little, Brown, 1912.

INDEX

Page numbers in *italics* refer to illustrations.
Page numbers beginning with 449 refer to notes.